COMPARATIVE
INTERNATIONAL ACCOUNTING

PEARSON
Education

We work with leading authors to develop the strongest
educational materials in business and finance, bringing
cutting-edge thinking and best learning practice to a
global market

Under a range of well-known imprints, including
Financial Times Prentice Hall, we craft high quality print
and electronic publications which help readers to understand
and apply their content, whether studying or at work

To find out more about the complete range of our
publishing, please visit us on the World Wide Web at:
www.pearsoned.co.uk

Tenth Edition

COMPARATIVE
INTERNATIONAL
ACCOUNTING

Christopher Nobes

and

Robert Parker

FT Prentice Hall
FINANCIAL TIMES

An imprint of **Pearson Education**
Harlow, England • London • New York • Boston • San Francisco • Toronto
Sydney • Tokyo • Singapore • Hong Kong • Seoul • Taipei • New Delhi
Cape Town • Madrid • Mexico City • Amsterdam • Munich • Paris • Milan

Pearson Education Limited
Edinburgh Gate
Harlow
Essex CM20 2JE
England

and Associated Companies throughout the world

Visit us on the World Wide Web at:
www.pearsoned.co.uk

First edition published in Great Britain under the Philip Allan imprint 1981
Second edition published 1985
Third edition published under the Prentice Hall imprint 1991
Fourth edition published 1995
Fifth edition published under the Prentice Hall imprint 1998
Sixth edition published 2000
Seventh edition published 2002
Eighth edition published 2004
Ninth edition published 2006
Tenth edition published 2008

ISBN: 978-0-273-71476-7

British Library Cataloguing-in-Publication Data
A catalogue record for this book is available from the British Library

Library of Congress Cataloging-in-Publication Data
Comparative international accounting / [edited by] Christopher Nobes
and Robert Parker. – 10th ed.
    p. cm.
  Includes bibliographical references and index.
  ISBN-13: 978-0-273-71476-7 (alk. paper)   1. Comparative accounting.
I. Nobes, Christopher.   II. Parker, R. H. (Robert Henry)
  HF5625.C74 2008
  657—dc22

                                                        2008007524

10   9   8   7   6   5   4   3   2   1
12   11   10   09   08

Typeset in 9.5/12.5pt Stone Serif by 35
Printed by Ashford Colour Press Ltd., Gosport

The publisher's policy is to use paper manufactured from sustainable forests.

Brief contents

Part VI ANALYSIS AND MANAGEMENT ISSUES

Contents

9 Enforcement of Financial Reporting Standards 189

10 Political lobbying on Accounting Standards – US, UK and international experience 206

Contributors

Co-editor, author of Chapters 2, 3, 4, 5, 6, 7, 8, 12, 13, 16 and 22, and co-author of Chapter 17

Christopher Nobes   Professor of Accounting at Royal Holloway College, University of London. He has also taught in Australia, Italy, the Netherlands, New Zealand, Scotland, Spain and the United States. He is currently a visiting professor at the Norwegian School of Management. He was the 2002 'Outstanding International Accounting Educator' of the American Accounting Association. He was a member of the Accounting Standards Committee of the United Kingdom and Ireland from 1986 to 1990, and a UK representative on the Board of the International Accounting Standards Committee from 1993 to 2001. He is vice-chairman of the accounting committee of the Fédération des Experts Comptables Européens.

Co-editor, author of Chapters 1, 9, 11, 14 and 15, and co-author of Chapter 17

Robert Parker   Emeritus Professor of Accounting at the University of Exeter and former professorial fellow of the Institute of Chartered Accountants of Scotland. He has also practised or taught in Nigeria, Australia, France and Scotland and was editor or joint editor of *Accounting and Business Research* from 1975 to 1993. He was the British Accounting Association's 'Distinguished Academic of the Year' in 1997, and the 2003 'Outstanding International Accounting Educator' of the American Accounting Association.

Authors of other chapters

Jan Buisman   IFRS Senior Technical Partner for PricewaterhouseCoopers in Sweden and partner in the firm's Global Corporate Reporting Group. He was formerly the Netherlands representative on the International Auditing Practices Committee, and chairman of Royal NIVRA's Auditing Standards Board. He is now chairman of the Accounting Practices Committee of FAR in Sweden. (Co-author of Chapter 21)

John Flower   Formerly, Director of the Centre for Research in European Accounting (Brussels), and earlier with the Commission of the European Communities and Professor of Accounting at the University of Bristol. He now lives in Germany. (Chapter 18)

Graham Gilmour   Senior Manager in the Global Corporate Reporting Group of PricewaterhouseCoopers. (Co-author of Chapter 21)

Stuart McLeay   Professor of Treasury at the University of Wales, Bangor. Formerly, he worked as a chartered accountant in Germany, France and Italy, and was a financial analyst at the European Investment Bank. Co-editor of the ICAEW *European Financial Reporting* series. (Chapter 20)

Clare B. Roberts Professor of Accounting at the University of Aberdeen Business School. (Chapter 19)

Stephen Salter Associate Professor and Director of the Center for Global Competitiveness at the University of Cincinnati. Formerly, he was a partner at Ernst & Young Management Consultants. (Chapter 23)

Stephen A. Zeff Herbert S. Autrey Professor of Accounting at Rice University. (Chapter 10)

Preface

Purpose

Comparative International Accounting is intended to be a comprehensive and coherent text on international financial reporting. It is primarily designed for undergraduate and postgraduate courses in comparative and international aspects of accounting. We believe that a proper understanding requires broad overviews (as in Part I), but that these must be supported by detailed information on real countries and companies (as in Parts II to IV) and across-the-board comparisons of major topics (as in Parts V and VI).

This book was first published in 1981. This present edition (the tenth) is a complete updating of the ninth edition which constituted the most extensive revision that we had ever made. One chapter (7) has been added: an examination of the possible motivations and opportunities for different national versions of IFRS practice.

A revised manual for teachers and lecturers is available from http://www.pearsoned.co.uk/nobes. It contains several numerical questions and a selection of multiple-choice questions. Suggested answers are provided for all of these and for the questions in the text. In addition, there is now an extensive set of PowerPoint slides.

Authors

In writing and editing this book, we have tried to gain from the experience of those with local knowledge. This is reflected in the nature of those we thank below for advice and in our list of contributors. For example, the original chapter on North America was co-authored by a Briton who had been assistant research director of the US Financial Accounting Standards Board; his knowledge of US accounting was thus interpreted through and for non-US readers. The amended version is by one of the editors, who has taught in several US universities. This seems the most likely way to highlight differences and to avoid missing important points through over-familiarity. The chapter on political lobbying has been written by Stephen Zeff, an American who is widely acknowledged as having the best overview of historical and international accounting developments. Other contributors presently live or work in Germany, in Sweden and in the United States.

Structure

Part I sets the scene for a study of comparative international financial reporting. Many countries are considered simultaneously in the introductory chapter and when examining the causes of the major areas of difference (Chapter 2). It is then possible to try to put accounting systems into groups (Chapter 3) and to take the obvious next step by discussing the purposes and progress of international harmonization of accounting (Chapter 4).

All this material in Part I can act as preparation for the other parts of the book. Part I can, however, be fully understood only by those who become well-informed about the contents of the rest of the book, and readers should go back later to Part I as a summary of the whole.

Part II examines financial reporting by listed groups. In much of the world this means, at least for consolidated statements, using the rules of either the International Accounting Standards Board or the United States. In addition to an overview and chapters on these two 'systems' of accounting, Part II also contains a chapter on whether national versions of IFRS exist, one on enforcement of accounting regulations, and one on political lobbying.

Part III contains two chapters that examine the processes of harmonization and transition as applied in the EU and East Asia. Part IV concerns the financial reporting of individual companies, where large international differences remain. There are three chapters: context, regulatory styles, and accounting differences.

Part V examines, broadly and comparatively, particular major financial reporting topics: key non-consolidation issues, consolidation, foreign currency translation and segment reporting. Part VI considers four issues of international analysis and management: international financial analysis, international auditing, international aspects of corporate income taxes, and managerial accounting.

At the end of the book, there is a glossary of abbreviations relevant to international accounting, suggested answers to some chapter questions, and two indexes (by author and by subject).

Publisher's acknowledgements

We are grateful to the following for permission to reproduce copyright material:

Table 1.4: United Nations Conference on Trade and Development (UNCTAD) (2007) *World Investment Report 2007: Transnational Companies, Exractive Industries and* Development. Geneva, UNCTAD. Copyright © United Nations 2007; Table 1.8: United Nations Conference on Trade and Development (UNCTAD) (2007) *World Investment Report 2007: Transnational Companies, Exractive Industries and Development*. Geneva, UNCTAD. Copyright © United Nations 2007; Table 2.3: Source of data: Datastream. Reproduced by kind permission of Jon Tucker and David Bence of Bristol Business School; Figure 3.1: American Accounting Association (1977) *Accounting Review*, Supplement to Vol. 52, 1977, p. 99. Copyright © 1977 American Accounting Association. Reproduced with permission; Figure 3.2: Puxty, A.G., Willmott, H.C., Cooper, D.J. and Lowe, A.E. (1987) 'Modes of regulation in advanced capitalism: locating accountancy in four countries', *Accounting, Organizations and Society*, Vol. 12, No. 3, p. 283. Reproduced with permission of Elsevier; Table 3.1: Nair, R.D. and Frank, W.G. (1980) 'The impact of disclosure and measurement practices on international accounting classifications', *Accounting Review*, Vol. 55, No. 3, p. 429. Reproduced with permission of the American

Accounting Association; Table 5.3: Adapted from BASF (2005) *BASF Annual Report 2004*, pp. 92, 93, BASF SA, Ludwigshafen, Germany. Reproduced with permission; Table 5.6: Extracted from the Bayer AG (2007) *Bayer AG Annual Report 2006*, Bayer AG, Leverkusen, Germany. Reproduced with permission; Table 5.8: Adapted from the Degussa AG (2005) *Degussa AG Annual Report 2004*, Degussa AG, Düsseldorf, Germany. Reproduced with permission; Tables 7.1, 7.2 and 7.3: Nobes, C.W. (2006) 'The survival of international differences under IFRS: towards a research agenda', *Accounting and Business Research*, Vol. 36, No. 3. Reproduced with permission; Table 8.2: American Institute of Certified Public Accountants (AICPA) (2006) *Accounting Trends and Techniques* (issued annually). AICPA, Jersey City, New Jersey, p. 133. Copyright © 2006 by the American Institute of Certified Public Accountants, Inc. All rights reserved. Reprinted with permission; Table 8.3: American Institute of Certified Public Accountants (2006) *Accounting Trends and Techniques* (issued annually). AICPA, Jersey City, New Jersey, p. 295. Copyright © 2006 by the American Institute of Certified Public Accountants, Inc. All rights reserved. Reprinted with permission; Table 8.4: American Institute of Certified Public Accountants (2006) *Accounting Trends and Techniques* (issued annually). AICPA, Jersey City, New Jersey, p. 273. Copyright © 2006 by the American Institute of Certified Public Accountants, Inc. All rights reserved. Reprinted with permission; Table 8.5: American Institute of Certified Public Accountants (2006) *Accounting Trends and Techniques* (issued annually). AICPA, Jersey City, New Jersey, p. 278. Copyright © 2006 by the American Institute of Certified Public Accountants, Inc. All rights reserved. Reprinted with permission; Table 8.8: American Institute of Certified Public Accountants (2006) *Accounting Trends and Techniques* (issued annually). AICPA, Jersey City, New Jersey, p. 153. Copyright © 2006 by the American Institute of Certified Public Accountants, Inc. All rights reserved. Reprinted with permission; Table 13.1: Adapted from BASF (2005) *BASF Annual Report 2004*, pp. 92, 93, BASF SA, Ludwigshafen, Germany. Reproduced with permission; Table 13.2: Bayer AG (2005) *Bayer AG Annual Report 2004*, Bayer AG, Leverkusen, Germany, pp. 74–84. Reproduced with permission; Figure 16.2: Adapted from FEE (1995) 'A classification of non-state pension schemes' in *Survey of Pensions and Other Retirement Benefits in EU and non-EU Countries*, Routledge, London. Reproduced with permission of the Taylor & Francis Group, Ltd; Table 19.2: Honda (2007) *Honda Annual Report 2006*, Honda, Tokyo, Japan, p. 63. Reproduced with permission; Table 20.4: The Volvo Group (2005) *The Volvo Group Financial Report, 2004*, AB Volvo, Goteborg, Sweden. Reproduced with permission; Table 23.1: Landry, S., Chan, W. and Jalbert, T. (2002) Balanced scorecard for multinationals, *Journal of Corporate Accounting and Finance*, p. 38. Copyright © 2002 John Wiley & Sons. Reprinted by permission; Table 23.4: Derived from Harrison, G. and McKinnon, J. (1999) 'Cross-cultural research in management control systems design: A review of the current state', *Accounting, Organizations and Society*, Vol. 24, p. 486 where full references to cited papers are given. Reproduced with permission from Elsevier.

In some instances we have been unable to trace the owners of copyright material, and we would appreciate any information that would enable us to do so.

Other acknowledgements

In the various editions of this book, we have received great help and much useful advice from many distinguished colleagues in addition to our contributors. We especially thank Sally Aisbitt (deceased); Dr Ataur Rahman Belal, Aston Business School, Aston University; Andrew Brown of Ernst & Young; John Carchrae of the Ontario Securities Commission; Terry Cooke of the University of Exeter; John Denman and Peter Martin of the Canadian Institute of Chartered Accountants; Brigitte Eierle of Regensburg University; Maria Frosig, Niels Brock Copenhagen Business School, Denmark; Michel Glautier of ESSEC; Dr Jing Hui Liu, University of Adelaide, Australia; Horst Kaminski, formerly of the Institut der Wirtschaftsprüfer; Jan Klaassen of the Free University, Amsterdam; Yannick Lemarchand of the University of Nantes; Ken Lemke of the University of Alberta; Klaus Macharzina of the University of Hohenheim; Malcolm Miller and Richard Morris of the University of New South Wales; Geoff Mitchell, formerly of Barclays Bank; Jules Muis of the European Commission; Ng Eng Juan of Nanyang Technological University of Singapore; Graham Peirson of Monash University; Jacques Richard of the University of Paris Dauphine; Alan Richardson of York University, Toronto; Alan Roberts of the University of Rennes; Paul Rutteman, formerly of EFRAG; Etsuo Sawa, formerly of the Japanese Institute of Certified Public Accountants; Hein Schreuder, formerly of the State University of Limburg; Marek Schroeder of the University of Birmingham; Patricia Sucher, formerly of Royal Holloway, University of London; Lorena Tan, formerly of Price Waterhouse, Singapore; Ann Tarca of the University of Western Australia; Peter van der Zanden, formerly of Moret Ernst & Young and the University of Tilburg; Gerald Vergeer of Moret Ernst & Young; and Ruud Vergoossen of Royal NIVRA and the Free University of Amsterdam; Dr Yap Kim Len, HELP University College, Malaysia. We are also grateful for the help of many secretaries over the years.

Despite the efforts of all these worthies, errors and obscurities will remain, for which we are culpable jointly and severally.

Christopher Nobes
Robert Parker
*Universities of London
and Exeter*

Part I

SETTING THE SCENE

1 Introduction

Robert Parker

OBJECTIVES

After reading this chapter, you should be able to:

- explain why international differences in financial reporting persist, in spite of the adoption of international financial reporting standards (IFRS) by the member states of the European Union and some other important countries;

- illustrate the ways in which accounting has been influenced by world politics, the growth of international trade and foreign direct investment, the globalization of stock markets, varying patterns of share ownership, and the international monetary system;

- outline the nature and growth of multinational enterprises (MNEs);

- explain the historical, comparative and harmonization reasons for studying comparative international accounting.

1.1 Differences in financial reporting

Differences in financial reporting are the norm. If a number of accountants from different countries, or even one country, are given a set of transactions from which to prepare financial statements, they will not produce identical statements. There are several reasons for this. Although all accountants will follow a set of rules, whether implicit or explicit, no set of rules covers every eventuality or is prescriptive to the minutest detail. Thus there is always room for professional judgement, a judgement that will depend in part on the accountants' environments (e.g. whether or not they see the tax authorities as the main users of the statements). Moreover, the accounting rules themselves may differ not just between countries but also within countries. In particular the rules for company groups may differ from the rules for individual companies. Multinational enterprises (MNEs) which operate as company groups in more than one country may find inter-country differences particularly irksome.

Awareness of these differences has led in recent decades to impressive attempts to reduce them, in particular, by the International Accounting Standards Board (IASB), which issues International Financial Reporting Standards (IFRS), and by the European Union (EU), which has issued Directives and Regulations on accounting and financial reporting. The importance of American stock markets has meant that US generally accepted accounting principles (GAAP), the most detailed and best known of all national sets of rules, have greatly influenced rule-making worldwide. The work of all these regulatory agencies has certainly led to a lessening of international differences but, as this book will show, many still remain and some will always remain.

An example of the differences that can, and continue, to arise is provided by the record of GlaxoSmithKline (GSK) and its predecessor GlaxoWellcome (GW) since 1995. GW merged with SmithKlineBeecham. It is listed in New York as well as on the London Stock Exchange, and in accordance with requirements of the US Securities and Exchange Commission (SEC) provides a reconciliation to US GAAP of its earnings and shareholders' equity as measured under UK rules (from 2005 onwards under IFRS). The differences as disclosed in Tables 1.1 and 1.2 are startling. Data from other such reconciliations are given later in this book. Not all are as extreme as those of GSK, but it is clear that the differences can be very large and that no easy rule-of-thumb adjustment procedure can be used. One reason for this is that the differences depend not only on the differences between two or more sets of rules, but also on the choices allowed to companies within those rules. The adoption by listed companies within the EU of IFRS from 2005 onwards, and greater convergence between those standards and US GAAP, has reduced, but not removed, these differences.

Understanding why there have been differences in financial reporting in the past, why they continue in the present, and will not disappear in the future, is one of the main themes of comparative international accounting. In the next two sections of this chapter we look at the global environment of accounting and financial reporting, and in particular at the nature and growth of multinational enterprises. We then explore in more depth the reasons for studying comparative international accounting. In the last section we explain the structure of the book.

Table 1.1 **GlaxoSmithKline reconciliations of earnings to US GAAP**

	UK £m	IFRS £m	US £m	Difference (% change) %
1995	717		296	−59
1996	1,997		979	−51
1997	1,850		952	−49
1998	1,836		1,010	−45
1999	1,811		913	−50
2000	4,106		(5,228)	−227
2001	3,053		(143)	−105
2002	3,915		503	−87
2003	4,484		2,420	−46
2004	4,302		2,732	−36
2005		4,816	3,336	−31
2006		5,498	4,465	−19

Table 1.2 **GlaxoSmithKline reconciliations of shareholders' equity to US GAAP**

	UK £m	IFRS £m	US £m	Difference (% change) %
1995	91		8,168	+8,876
1996	1,225		8,153	+566
1997	1,843		7,882	+328
1998	2,702		8,007	+196
1999	3,142		7,230	+130
2000	7,517		44,995	+499
2001	7,390		40,107	+443
2002	6,581		34,992	+432
2003	5,059		34,116	+574
2004	5,925		34,042	+475
2005		7,570	34,282	+353
2006		9,648	34,653	+259

1.2   The global environment of accounting

Accounting is a technology which is practised within varying political, economic and social contexts. These have always been international as well as national, but since at least the last quarter of the twentieth century, the globalization of accounting rules and practices has become so important that narrowly national views of accounting and financial reporting can no longer be sustained.

Of particular contextual importance are:

- major political issues, such as the dominance of the United States and the expansion of the European Union;
- economic globalization, including the liberalization of, and dramatic increases in, international trade and foreign direct investment;
- the emergence of global financial markets;
- patterns of share ownership, including the influence of privatization;
- changes in the international monetary system;
- the growth of multinational enterprises (MNEs).

These developments are interrelated and all have affected financial reporting and the transfer of accounting technology from one country to another. They are now examined in turn.

1.2.1 Accounting and world politics

Important political events since the end of the Second World War in 1945 have included: the emergence of the United States and the Soviet Union as the world's two superpowers, followed by the collapse of Soviet power at the end of the 1980s; the break-up of the British and continental European overseas empires; and the creation of the European Union, which has expanded from its original core of six countries to include, among others, the UK and eventually many former communist countries. More detail on the consequences that these events have had for accounting is given in later chapters. The following illustrations may suffice for the moment:

- US ideas on accounting and financial reporting have been for many decades, and remain, the most influential in the world. The collapse of the US energy trading company, Enron, in 2001 and the demise of its auditor, Andersen, had repercussions in all major economies.
- The development of international accounting standards (at first of little interest in the US) owes more to accountants from former member countries of the British Empire than to any other source. The IASC and its successor are based in London; the driving force behind the foundation of the IASC, Lord Benson, was a British accountant born in South Africa.
- Accounting in developing countries is still strongly influenced by the former colonial powers. Former British colonies tend to have Institutes of Chartered Accountants (set up after the independence of these countries, not before), Companies Acts and private sector accounting standard-setting bodies. Former French colonies tend to have detailed governmental instructions, on everything from double entry to published financial statements, that are set out in national accounting plans and commercial codes.
- Accounting throughout Europe has been greatly influenced by the harmonization programme of the EU, especially its Directives on accounting and, more

recently, its adoption of IFRS for the consolidated financial statements of listed companies.

● The collapse of communism in Central and Eastern Europe led to a transformation of accounting and auditing in many former communist countries. The reunification of Germany put strains on the German economy such that large German companies needed to raise capital outside Germany and to change their financial reporting in order to be able to do so.

1.2.2 Economic globalization, international trade and foreign direct investment

A notable feature of the world economy since the Second World War has been the globalization of economic activity. This has meant the spreading round the world not just of goods and services but also of people, technologies and concepts. The number of professionally qualified accountants has greatly increased. Member bodies of the International Federation of Accountants (IFAC) currently have well over two million members. Accountants in all major countries have been exposed to rules, practices and ideas previously alien to them.

Much has been written about globalization and from many different and contrasting points of view. One attractive approach is the 'globalization index' published annually in the journal *Foreign Policy*. This attempts to quantify the concept by ranking countries in terms of their degree of globalization. The components of the index are: political engagement (measured, *inter alia*, by memberships of international organizations); technological connectivity (measured by internet use); personal contact (measured, *inter alia*, by travel and tourism and telephone traffic); and economic integration (measured, *inter alia*, by international trade and foreign direct investment). The compilers of the index acknowledge that not everything can be quantified; for example, they do not include cultural exchanges. The ranking of countries varies from year to year but the most globalized countries according to the index are small open economies such as Singapore, Switzerland and Ireland. Small size is not the only factor, however, and the Top 20 typically also include the US, the UK and Germany. A possible inference from the rankings is that measures of globalization are affected by national boundaries. How different would the list be if the EU were one country and/or the states of the US were treated as separate countries?

From the point of view of financial reporting, the two most important aspects of globalization are international trade and foreign direct investment (FDI) (i.e. equity interest in a foreign enterprise held with the intention of acquiring control or significant influence). Table 1.3 illustrates one measure of the liberalization and growth of international trade: merchandise exports as a percentage of gross domestic product (GDP). Worldwide, the percentage has more than trebled since the end of the Second World War. The importance of international trade to member states of the EU is particularly apparent; much of this is intra-EU trade. At the regional level, economic integration and freer trade have been encouraged through the EU and through institutions such as the North American Free Trade Area (NAFTA) (the US, Canada and Mexico). The liberalization has also been due to the dismantling of trade barriers through 'rounds' of talks under the aegis of the General Agreement on

Table 1.3 **Merchandise exports as a percentage of gross domestic product at 1990 prices (selected countries, 1950–98)**

	1950	1973	1998
France	7.7	15.2	28.7
Germany	6.2	23.8	38.9
Netherlands	12.2	40.7	61.2
United Kingdom	11.3	14.0	25.0
Spain	3.0	5.0	23.5
United States	3.0	4.9	10.1
Mexico	3.0	1.9	10.7
Brazil	3.9	2.5	5.4
China	2.6	1.5	4.9
India	2.9	2.0	2.4
Japan	2.2	7.7	13.4
World	5.5	10.5	17.2

Source: Maddison, A. (2001) *The World Economy: A Millennial Perspective*. Organisation for Economic Co-operation and Development (OECD), Paris.

Tariffs and Trade (GATT) and its successor the World Trade Organization (WTO). One area in which trade is insufficiently liberalized is agricultural products, leading to the criticism that liberalization has benefited developed rather than developing countries. For a discussion of both the positive and negative aspects of international trade, see Finn (1996).

The importance of foreign direct investment is illustrated in Table 1.4, which ranks the 10 leading MNEs by the size of their foreign assets. It also shows the

Table 1.4 **World's top ten non-financial multinationals ranked by foreign assets, 2004**

Company	Country	Industry	Foreign Assets (US $bn)	% that is foreign of			
				Assets	Sales	Employees	TNI
General Electric	US	Electrical	449	60	37	46	48
Vodaphone	UK	Telecoms	248	96	85	80	87
Ford Motor	US	Motors	180	59	42	46	49
General Motors	US	Motors	174	36	31	35	34
BP	UK	Oil	155	80	81	83	81
Exxon Mobil	US	Oil	135	69	70	50	63
Royal Dutch/Shell	NL/UK	Oil	130	67	64	84	72
Toyota Motor	Japan	Motors	123	53	60	36	49
Total	France	Oil	97	86	81	56	74
France Telecom	France	Telecoms	86	65	41	40	49

Note: TNI = transnationality index, calculated as an average of the assets, sales and employees percentages.
Source: United Nations Conference on Trade and Development (UNCTAD) (2007) *World Investment Report 2007: Transnational Companies, Extractive Industries and Development*. Geneva, UNCTAD. Copyright © United Nations 2007. Reproduced with permission.

percentages of their assets, sales and employees that are foreign, and a simple transnationality index (TNI), calculated as the average of the percentages. The home countries of these MNEs are the US (4 MNEs), France (2), the UK (2), Japan (1) and the Netherlands/UK (1). The industries represented are electrical equipment, telecommunications, motor vehicles and oil. Two UK companies, Vodafone and BP, have the highest transnationality indices.

1.2.3 Globalization of stock markets

At the same time as international trade and FDI have increased, capital markets have become increasingly globalized. This has been made possible by the deregulation of the leading national financial markets (e.g. the 'Big Bang' on the London Stock Exchange in 1986); the speed of financial innovation (involving new trading techniques and new financial instruments of sometimes bewildering complexity); dramatic advances in the electronic technology of communications; and growing links between domestic and world financial markets. Table 1.5 lists the countries where there are stock exchanges with more than 250 domestic listed companies and also a market capitalization (excluding investment funds) of more than $800 billion.

Table 1.5 **Major stock exchanges, April 2007**

Country	Exchange	Domestic listed companies	Market capitalization of domestic equities ($bn)	Market capitalization as % of United Kingdom
Europe and Africa				
–	Euronext	956	2,229	56
Germany	Deutsche Börse	658	1,022	26
South Africa	Johannesburg	345	807	20
Switzerland	Swiss exchanges	256	1,342	34
United Kingdom	London	2,603	3,961	100
The Americas				
Brazil	São Paulo	362	845	21
Canada	Toronto	3,832	1,823	46
United States	NASDAQ	2,788	4,061	102
	New York	1,795	16,112	406
Asia-Pacific				
China	Hong Kong	1,177	1,821	46
India	Bombay (Mumbai)	4,826	932	23
Japan	Tokyo	2,396	4,653	117
Korea	Korean	1,695	905	23
Australia	Australian	1,777	1,282	32

Sources: World Federation of Exchanges; Euronext.

Precise measures of the internationalization of the world's stock markets are hard to construct. Two crude measures are cross-border listings and the extent to which companies translate their annual reports into other languages for the benefit of foreign investors. For example, French companies are listed on stock exchanges in Australia, Belgium, Canada, Germany, Luxembourg, the Netherlands, Spain, Sweden, Switzerland, the UK and the US (Gélard, 2001, pages 1038–9). Table 1.6 shows the extent of listing by foreign companies on eight of the world's major stock exchanges. In absolute terms, the largest number of foreign listings is on the New York stock exchange; in percentage terms, Switzerland has the most foreign listings. The lack of foreign listings in Tokyo (the world's second largest stock exchange) and Toronto is very apparent. Davis *et al.* (2003) examine the international nature of stock markets from the nineteenth century onwards, and chart the rise in listing requirements on the London, Berlin, Paris and New York exchanges.

Some companies publish their annual reports in more than one language. The most important reason for this is the need for large MNEs to raise money and have their shares traded in the US and the UK. This explains why English is the most common secondary reporting language. Other reasons for using more than one language are that the MNE is based in a country with more than one official language, that the MNE has headquarters in more than one country or that it has substantial commercial operations in several countries. For example, the Finnish telecommunications company, Nokia, publishes its annual report and financial statements not only in Finnish and Swedish (the two official languages of Finland) but also in English. The Business Review section of the report is also available in French, German, Italian, Portuguese, Spanish, Chinese and Japanese (Parker, 2001b). The translation of annual reports is further discussed in Chapter 20. Evans (2004) discusses the problems of translating accounting terms from one language to another.

A more sophisticated measure of internationalization is the extent to which stock markets have become 'integrated', in the sense that securities are priced according to international rather than domestic factors (Wheatley, 1988). Froot and Dabora (1999) show that domestic factors are still important even for such Anglo-Dutch 'twin' stocks as Unilever NV/PLC.

Table 1.6 **Foreign company listings on eight major stock exchanges, April 2007**

	No.	As % of total listings
Euronext (France, Netherlands, Belgium, Portugal)	246	20
Germany	101	13
London	648	20
NASDAQ	326	10
New York	447	20
Switzerland	89	26
Toronto	54	1
Tokyo	26	1

Source: World Federation of Exchanges.

National stock exchange regulators not only operate in their domestic markets but are also, through the international bodies to which they belong, such as the International Organization of Securities Commissions (IOSCO) and the Committee of European Securities Regulators (CESR), playing increasingly important roles in the internationalization of accounting rules (see Chapters 4 and 11).

1.2.4 Patterns of share ownership

The globalization of stock markets does not mean uniformity of investor behaviour around the world. Patterns and trends in share ownership differ markedly from country to country. The nature of the investors in listed companies has implications for styles of financial reporting. The greater the split between the owners and managers of these companies, the greater the need for publicly available and independently audited financial statements. La Porta *et al.* (1999) distinguish companies whose shares are widely held from those that are family controlled, state controlled, controlled by a widely held financial corporation, or controlled by a widely held non-financial corporation. According to their data, which cover 27 countries (not including China, India and Eastern Europe) in the mid-1990s, 36 per cent of the companies in the world were widely held, 30 per cent were family controlled and 18 per cent were state controlled. The countries whose largest 20 companies were most (60 per cent or more) widely held were, in descending order, the UK, Japan, the US, Australia, Ireland, Canada, France and Switzerland. The countries whose largest 20 companies were most (60 per cent or more) family controlled were Mexico, Hong Kong and Argentina. The countries with companies with most (35 per cent or more) state control were Austria, Singapore, Israel, Italy, Finland and Norway. The countries with companies held 15 per cent or more by a widely-held financial corporation were Belgium, Germany, Portugal and Sweden.

More up-to-date data is available from surveys of share ownership. These show different trends in different countries. In the US the percentage of persons investing in shares directly or through mutual funds (known as unit trusts in the UK) rose from 19 per cent in 1983 to 37 per cent in 1992 to 50 per cent in 2002 (Investment Company Institute, 2002). By contrast, in the UK the equivalent percentages were 26 per cent in 1990, 20 per cent in 1998 and 16 per cent in 2002 and 2004. Continuing trends in the UK have been the growth of shareholdings by foreign investors (12 per cent in 1990, 28 per cent in 1998, 33 per cent in 2004) and by financial institutions such as pension funds and insurance companies (33 per cent in 2004, down from a peak of 52 per cent in 1991 as holdings by foreign investors increased) (National Statistics, 2005).

Privatization , i.e. the selling-off of state-owned businesses, has greatly expanded the private sector in many countries. In the UK, for example, the privatization of public utilities and other publicly owned enterprises from the 1980s onwards brought several very large organizations within the ambit of company law and accounting standards. In the short run this increased the number of shares held by persons, but many of them later sold out and some companies have deliberately tried to reduce the number of their small shareholders. Privatization has opened companies up to foreign ownership, thus stimulating the growth of FDI, and facilitating their expansion into foreign markets. Privatization has been most dramatic in the former communist countries of Central and Eastern Europe. In some cases, notably in Russia, privatization has transferred the ownership of large companies from the state to a small group of so-called 'oligarchs'.

1.2.5 International monetary system

From 1945 to 1972, the international monetary system under the Bretton Woods Agreement was based on fixed exchange rates with periodic devaluations. From 1973, major currencies have floated against each other and exchange rates have been very volatile (as illustrated in Table 18.1). Within the EU, however, most national currencies, with the notable exception of the pound sterling, were replaced by a single currency, the euro, in 1999. Accounting standard-setters have been much concerned with hedging activities and other transactions in foreign currency. There is discussion of these issues in Chapters 16 and 18.

1.3 The nature and growth of MNEs

MNEs may be broadly defined as those companies that produce a good or a service in two or more countries. 'MNE' is an economic category not a legal one. The size of most MNEs is such that they need to raise external finance and hence to be incorporated companies listed on stock exchanges. As listed companies (i.e. whose shares are publicly traded), their financial reporting is subject to special regulations that are discussed at length in Part II of this book. The existence of MNEs brought a new dimension to areas such as auditing, which already existed at the domestic level (see Chapter 21). Issues such as the translation of the financial statements of foreign subsidiaries for the preparation of consolidated statements (see Chapter 18) are peculiar to multinational companies. Most of the world's MNEs produce consolidated financial statements in accordance with either US GAAP, IFRS or approximations thereto.

The above definition of MNEs is broad enough to include early fourteenth-century enterprises such as the Gallerani company, a Sienese firm of merchants that had branches in London and elsewhere and whose surviving accounts provide one of the earliest extant examples of double entry (Nobes, 1982). From the late sixteenth century onwards, chartered land and trading companies – notably the English, Dutch and French East India Companies – were early examples of 'resource-seeking' MNEs, i.e. those whose object is to gain access to natural resources that are not available in the home country. The origins of the modern MNE are to be found in the period 1870 to 1914, when European people and European investment were exported on a large scale to the rest of the world and when the United States emerged as an industrial power. On the eve of the First World War, the stock of accumulated FDI was greatest in, by order of magnitude, the United Kingdom, the United States, Germany, France and the Netherlands. Two world wars decreased the relative economic importance of European countries and increased that of the United States. Table 1.7 shows how the rankings changed from 1914 to 2005. After the Second World War, the United States became, as it remains, the world's largest exporter of FDI. More recently, however, European-based multinationals have

Table 1.7 **Percentage shares of estimated stock of accumulated foreign direct investment by country of origin, 1914–2005** (%)

	1914	1938	1980	1990	2000	2005
United Kingdom	45	40	15	13	14	12
United States	14	28	42	24	20	19
Germany	14	1	8	8	8	9
France	11	9	5	6	7	8
Netherlands	5	10	8	6	5	6
Other Western Europe	5	3	9	16	22	17
Japan	–	–	4	11	4	4
Rest of world	6	9	9	16	20	25
	100	100	100	100	100	100

Sources: Based on Dunning (1992) and UNCTC (2006).

regained some of their relative importance and both US and European MNEs were challenged, at least for a time, by those of Japan. All these countries are major recipients of FDI as well as providers of it.

MNEs can be classified according to their major activity. Most nineteenth-century and earlier multinationals were 'resource-seeking'. In the twentieth century other types have developed. Some MNEs are 'market-seeking', i.e. they establish subsidiaries whose main function is to produce goods to supply the markets of the countries in which they are located. Other MNEs are 'efficiency-seeking', i.e. each subsidiary specializes in a small part of a much wider product range, or in discrete stages in the production of a particular product. Manufacturing MNEs have also developed subsidiaries that specialize in trade and distribution, or in providing services such as insurance, banking or finance. Some MNEs, such as the larger banks and accountancy firms, provide services on a global basis. Improvements in technology have led to the creation of overseas subsidiaries specializing in information transfer.

The extent to which the production of goods and services has been internationalized varies between countries and industries. The United States has the world's highest absolute value of FDI, but the size of its economy is such that investment overseas is relatively less important for the United States than for many European countries, although it is higher in percentage terms than that of Japan (see Table 1.8). Table 1.9 demonstrates the extent to which the headquarters of the largest MNEs are located in the US, Japan and the European Union.

Economists and others have sought to explain why MNEs exist. The most favoured explanation is Dunning's eclectic paradigm, which states that the propensity for firms of a particular country to engage in, or to increase, overseas production is determined by three interrelated conditions. These are the extent to which the enterprises possess, or can gain privileged access to, assets that provide them with a competitive advantage over local firms; the extent to which relative transactions costs make it appropriate for the enterprises to use such advantages themselves rather than to license or franchise them to other firms; and the extent to which relevant costs and government policies push enterprises towards locating

Table 1.8 Accumulated stock of outward foreign direct investment as percentage of GDP in 2005 (selected countries)

Country	%
Norway	123
Switzerland	107
Belgium	104
Netherlands	103
Sweden	57
United Kingdom	56
France	41
Canada	35
Germany	35
Italy	17
United States	16
Japan	9
World	24

Source: United Nations Conference on Trade and Development (UNCTAD) (2007) *World Investment Report 2007: Transnational Companies, Extractive Industries and Development*. Geneva, UNCTAD. Copyright © United Nations 2007. Reproduced with permission.

Table 1.9 Share of the world's top 500 MNEs by revenues, 2005

United States		170
France	38	
United Kingdom	38	
Germany	35	
Netherlands	14	
Italy	10	
Spain	9	
Sweden	6	
Belgium	4	
Finland	2	
Denmark	2	
UK/Netherlands	1	
Belgium/Netherlands	1	
Ireland	1	
Luxembourg	1	
Total EU		162
Japan		70
China		20
Canada		14
Switzerland		12
South Korea		12
Australia		8
India		6
Brazil		4
Mexico		5
Russia		5
Taiwan		3
Norway		2
Other countries (one each)		7
		500

Source: *Fortune Global 500*, 2006.

production overseas rather than towards meeting demand by exports from the home country. An important consequence of the growth of multinational enterprise is that much of the world's trade takes place within firms as well as between countries. The prices at which the transactions take place are internal transfer prices, which are often not the same as open market prices. This has important implications, for taxation, management control, and the relationships between MNEs and their host countries. These matters are considered further in Chapters 22 and 23.

The rise of the MNE is one of the main factors responsible for the internationalization of the accountancy profession. Accountancy firms have followed their clients around the world, setting up new offices overseas and/or merging with overseas firms. The audit of MNEs is considered further in Chapter 21.

1.4   Comparative and international aspects of accounting

Given the global context set out above, there are clearly strong arguments for studying international accounting. Moreover, there are at least three reasons why a comparative approach is appropriate. First, it serves as a reminder that the US and other Anglo-Saxon[1] countries are not the only contributors to accounting as it is practised today. Secondly, it demonstrates that the preparers, users and regulators of financial reports in different countries can learn from each others' ideas and experiences. Thirdly, it explains why the international harmonization of accounting has been deemed desirable but has proved difficult to achieve (Parker, 1983). These three reasons are now looked at in more detail.

Historically, a number of countries have made important contributions to the development of accounting. The Romans had forms of bookkeeping and the calculation of profit, although not double entry. In the Muslim world, while Christian Europe was in the Dark Ages, developments in arithmetic and bookkeeping paved the way for later progress. In the fourteenth and fifteenth centuries, the Italian city states were the leaders in commerce, and therefore in accounting. The 'Italian method' of bookkeeping by double entry spread first to the rest of Europe and eventually round the whole world. One lasting result of this dominance is the number of accounting and financial words in English and other languages that are of Italian origin. Some examples in English are bank, capital, cash, debit, credit, folio, imprest and journal.

In the nineteenth century, Britain took the lead in accounting matters, to be followed in the twentieth century by the United States. As a result, English has become established as the world's language of accounting (Parker, 2000 and 2001a). Table 1.10, which gives details of some members of IFAC, shows, *inter alia*, that the modern accountancy profession developed first in Scotland and England. The table also shows that some countries (e.g. Australia, Canada and the UK) have more

---

[1] This expression is used in this book with its common European meaning, i.e. the UK, the US and other mainly English-speaking countries such as Canada, Australia and New Zealand.

Table 1.10 **Age and size of some members of IFAC**

Country	Body	Founding date*	Approx. members 2006 (000s)
Australia	CPA Australia	1952 (1886)	112
	Institute of Chartered Accountants in Australia	1928 (1885)	43
Brazil	Conselho Federal de Contabilidade	1946	194
Canada	Canadian Institute of Chartered Accountants	1902 (1880)	71
	Certified General Accountants Association of Canada (CGAA-Canada)	1913	42
	Society of Management Accountants of Canada (CMA-Canada)	1919	37
China	Chinese Institute of Certified Public Accountants	1988	142+
France	Ordre des Experts Comptables	1942	18
Germany	Institut der Wirtschaftsprüfer	1932	13
India	Institute of Chartered Accountants of India	1949	131
Japan	Japanese Institute of Certified Public Accountants	1948 (1927)	17**
Netherlands	Koninklijk Nederlands Instituut van Registeraccountants	1967 (1895)	13
New Zealand	Institute of Chartered Accountants of New Zealand	1909 (1894)	29
United Kingdom and Ireland	Institute of Chartered Accountants in England and Wales	1880 (1870)	128
	Institute of Chartered Accountants of Scotland	1951 (1854)	17
	Association of Chartered Certified Accountants	1939 (1891)	115
	Chartered Institute of Management Accountants	1919	70
	Institute of Chartered Accountants in Ireland	1888	13
United States	American Institute of Certified Public Accountants	1887	330

Notes: *Dates of earliest predecessor bodies in brackets. The names of some of the bodies have changed from time to time.
**Excluding junior CPAs.

than one important accountancy body. A multiplicity of bodies has been the norm in Anglo-Saxon countries. The largest body is the American Institute of Certified Public Accountants.

Table 1.10 does not show rates of growth; the Chinese Institute of Certified Public Accountants has grown in recent years to become the third largest in the world. The table also does not show the extent to which bodies have worldwide and not just national membership. Two UK-based bodies, the ACCA and the CIMA, have been notably active and successful in this regard. A look at the table also suggests that some countries have far more accountants per head of population than others: compare, for example, France (population 60 million; accountants 18,000) and New Zealand (population 4 million; accountants 29,000). Of course, comparisons such as these depend in part on how the term 'accountant' is defined in each country. There is further discussion of the accountancy profession in Chapter 2.

Table 1.11 demonstrates the overwhelmingly British and American origins of the largest international accountancy firms. Accounting techniques, institutions and concepts have been imported and exported around the world. Britain, for example, has not only imported double entry from Italy and exported professional accountancy to the rest of the world, but has also exported the concept of a true and fair view, first to the other countries of the British Commonwealth and, more recently, to the other member states of the European Union (Parker, 1989; Nobes, 1993). The concepts and practices of management accounting throughout the industrialized world owe much to American initiatives. In the second half of the twentieth century, Japan contributed to management accounting and control. Carnegie and Napier (2002) make a persuasive case for the study of comparative international accounting *history*.

The second reason for taking a comparative approach is that it allows one to learn from both the achievements and failures of others and to avoid the perils of accounting ethnocentrism. It is possible for a country to improve its own accounting by observing how other countries react to problems that, especially in industrialized nations, may not differ markedly from those of the observer's home country. It is also possible to examine whether, where accounting methods differ, the differences are justified by differences in the economic, legal and social environment and are not merely the accidents of history. Such accidents may not impede harmonization (see Section 2.6), whereas more fundamental differences are likely to be much more difficult to deal with.

Table 1.11 Leading international accountancy firms, 2008

	Main countries of origin
Deloitte	UK, USA, Canada, Japan
Ernst & Young	USA, UK
KPMG	Netherlands, UK, USA, Germany
PricewaterhouseCoopers	UK, USA

Note: The names given above are those of the international firms. National firms may have different names.

A feature of recent decades has been the extent to which countries have been willing to adopt and adapt accounting methods and institutions from other countries. Examples will be found in many of the chapters of this book. The UK accepted continental European ideas about greater uniformity in the layout of financial statements. France and Germany accepted US and UK approaches to consolidated statements. The Netherlands accepted a much greater degree of regulation of company accounting and auditing than previously. France and Australia set up their own versions of the US Securities and Exchange Commission (SEC). Germany, where enforcement of accounting standards had been weak, is trying a compromise between the SEC and the UK Financial Reporting Review Panel. Even the US, shaken by accounting scandals from 2001 onwards, is showing itself willing to consider the virtues of the principles approach to accounting standard-setting espoused in the UK and by the IASB.

The third reason for taking a comparative approach is better to understand harmonization, a process that has grown steadily in importance since the 1970s. The arguments for and against are considered in Chapter 4. At this point it may be noted that, as is demonstrated in Part V of this book, major problems such as lease accounting, consolidation accounting and foreign currency translation have been tackled in different countries in significantly different ways, although a pattern may sometimes be discerned. Solutions devised by the Financial Accounting Standards Board (FASB) in the US – the world's most powerful national accounting standard-setting body – have been very influential but have not always been accepted. Indeed, one reason for the acceptance by many countries and companies of international standards is that they are not US GAAP. On the other hand they are sufficiently close to US GAAP to be acceptable to most stock-exchange regulators.

The growing strength of the IASB and the adoption of its standards by the EU (in part in order to prevent EU-based MNEs adopting US GAAP) can be seen as a process of regulatory competition (Esty and Geradin, 2001), with the IASB and the FASB competing in a 'race to the top'. The process of harmonization within the EU meant that all the major countries had their own regulatory solutions challenged and had to accept compromises of both a technical and a political nature. It is clear that any attempt to harmonize financial reporting touches on wider issues than accounting. In Chapter 2 we look at some of the underlying reasons for the differences that exist. Before that, we explain the structure of this book.

1.5 Structure of this book

1.5.1 An outline

The book is divided into six parts. Part I sets the context, covering the causes and nature of differences in financial reporting, classification of accounting systems, and an introduction to international harmonization. Part II deals with financial reporting by listed groups, which is dominated worldwide by IFRS and US GAAP and the competition between them. Part III looks at the problems of harmonization and transition in Europe (both West and East) and in East Asia, with particular reference to Japan and China. Part IV covers the financial reporting (particularly that by individual legal enterprises) that continues to be governed by sets of national rules, some of which differ considerably from IFRS and US GAAP. Part V examines some major technical accounting issues faced by MNEs. Part VI examines some analysis and management issues.

The chapters in the six parts of the book are described in more detail below.

1.5.2 Setting the scene (Part I)

The adoption of IFRS by the 27 member states of the European Union and the convergence of IFRS and US GAAP, both formally agreed in 2002, have not removed the differences in financial reporting among countries. This is partly because IFRS is used in many countries only for consolidated statements, and partly because different national versions of IFRS practice exist. The causes and nature of these differences are discussed in Chapter 2. Several writers on international accounting have attempted classifications of financial reporting. These are discussed and evaluated in Chapter 3. Most classifications have been of countries, which are explicitly or implicitly assumed to have homogeneous financial reporting. More recently the emphasis has shifted to 'accounting systems', in recognition of the fact that countries (and even companies) can use more than one type of accounting. In this book we discuss differences between countries, between systems and between companies. This examination of international differences and patterns in them leads to Chapter 4, which discusses international harmonization, explaining why and how the need for this has grown in recent decades. We particularly look at the extent to which it has been met by the establishment of an International Accounting Standards Committee (IASC) and its successor the International Accounting Standards Board (IASB).

1.5.3 Financial reporting by listed groups (Part II)

Chapter 5 follows on from the material of Chapter 4 by exploring the relationship between international and national standards, including 'competition' and 'convergence' between IFRS and the most influential set of national standards, US GAAP. The requirements of IFRS are summarized in Chapter 6, first in terms of topics (conceptual framework, assets, liabilities, group accounting, disclosures) and secondly in the numerical order of extant standards. Chapter 7 examines the possible motives and opportunities for different national versions of IFRS practice. Chapter 8 describes and analyzes corporate financial reporting and its environment in the US, including a comparison of US rules with international rules. Chapter 9 discusses how the application of IFRS and US GAAP to the financial statements of listed groups is governed and enforced in the US, in leading member states of the EU (UK, France and Germany), and in other important countries such as Australia. The setting and enforcement of accounting rules is in part a political issue, and Chapter 10 therefore examines the politicization of accounting and particularly political lobbying by preparers of financial statements.

1.5.4 Harmonization and transition in Europe and East Asia (Part III)

Chapter 11 looks at the attempts that have been made to harmonize the great variety of financial reporting that exists within the EU, as part of a more general aim of eliminating economic barriers. The chapter explains the initial difficulties of reconciling Continental European and Anglo-Saxon approaches, and the more recent problems of the accession to the EU of many economies which have had to make a transition from communist to market-based accounting. Chapter 12 compares and contrasts financial reporting in the two major economies of East Asia: Japan and China. Both have been and still are subjected to a variety of outside influences, but both retain their own special national characteristics.

1.5.5 Financial reporting by individual companies (Part IV)

Financial reporting by individual business enterprises is much more diverse than that of listed company groups. Chapter 13 explains why this is the case, with special emphasis on the information needs of tax authorities and the determination of distributable profit. Chapter 14 analyzes the different ways of rule-making that have evolved (accounting plans, legal codes, statutes, standards) and assesses their usefulness. Chapter 15 explains how the accounting rules applicable to individual business enterprises may differ from IFRS or US GAAP, with particular reference to France, Germany and the UK.

1.5.6 Major issues in financial reporting by MNEs (Part V)

Accounting standards are always in a state of change and those contained within IFRS and US GAAP are no exception. It is never sufficient merely to learn the detailed content of standards at a particular date. All standards are compromises and this is especially so when they have to be agreed at an international level. Chapter 16 examines eight key financial reporting topics: recognition of intangible assets, asset measurement, financial instruments, provisions, employee benefits, deferred tax revenue recognition and comprehensive income. The chapter shows how the valuation rules in the standards do not fit into a consistent conceptual framework and discusses the differences between IFRS and US GAAP from a conceptual perspective. Chapters 17 to 19 examine three problems which relate especially to MNEs: consolidated financial statements, foreign currency translation and segment reporting, with comparisons of the solutions arrived at in IFRS and US GAAP.

1.5.7 Analysis and management issues (Part VI)

Chapter 20 examines the problems faced by non-domestic readers and analysts of financial reports, problems that for listed groups have been lessened but not removed by the increasing use of IFRS and US GAAP. Chapter 21 explains how auditing has been internationalized, with particular reference to the role of MNEs, international capital markets, international accounting firms and IFRS. It looks at international standards on auditing (ISAs), the international audit process in practice, and the audit expectations gap in an international context. Chapter 22 discusses international aspects of corporate income taxes, including the relationship between taxable income and accounting income, international tax planning, tax systems, and the harmonization of taxation. Chapter 23 concludes the book by examining managerial accounting within MNEs, with particular reference to the problems of operating with different currencies and coping with differences in national cultures.

SUMMARY

- The scale of international differences in corporate financial reporting remains large, despite the adoption of IFRS for listed companies within the EU and elsewhere.

- Financial reporting since the Second World War has taken place within a global context which has been characterized by: vast changes in world politics; dramatic growth in international trade and foreign direct investment (FDI); the globalization of stock markets; varying patterns of share ownership; an unstable international monetary system; and the rise of MNEs, which are the main exporters and importers of FDI and a major factor in the internationalization of the accountancy profession.

- Historically several countries have made important contributions to the development of accounting and financial reporting.

- The comparison of accounting rules and practices between countries is a strong antidote to accounting ethnocentrism. Successful innovations in one country are being copied in others.

- Harmonization is taking place at both regional and international levels.

- This book is arranged into six parts: setting the scene; financial reporting by listed groups; harmonization and transition; financial reporting by individual companies; major issues for MNEs; and analysis and management.

References

Carnegie, G.D. and Napier, C.J. (2002) 'Exploring comparative international accounting history', *Accounting, Auditing & Accountability Journal*, Vol. 15, No. 5.

Davis, L., Neal, L. and White, E.N. (2003) 'How it all began: the rise of listing requirements on the London, Berlin, Paris, and New York Stock Exchanges', *International Journal of Accounting*, Vol. 38, No. 2.

Dunning, J.H. (1992) *Multinational Enterprises and the Global Economy*, Addison-Wesley, Wokingham.

Esty, D.C. and Geradin, D. (eds) (2001) *Regulatory Competition and Economic Integration*, Oxford University Press, Oxford.

Evans, L. (2004) 'Language, translation and the problem of international accounting communication', *Accounting, Auditing & Accountability Journal*, Vol. 17, No. 2.

Finn, D. (1996) *Just Trading. On the Ethics and Economics of International Trade*, Abingdon Press, Nashville.

Froot, K.A. and Dabora, E.M. (1999) 'How are stock prices affected by the location of trade?' *Journal of Financial Economics*, August.

Gélard, G. (2001) 'France – Individual Accounts', in D. Ordelheide, and KPMG, *Transnational Accounting*, Vol. 2, Palgrave Publishers, Basingstoke.

Investment Company Institute and the Securities Industry Association (2002) *Equity Ownership in America. 2002*. Available at www.ici.org/stats.

La Porta, R., Lopez-de-Silanes, F. and Shleifer, A. (1999) 'Corporate ownership around the world', *Journal of Finance*, April.

Maddison, A. (2001) *The World Economy. A Millenial Perspective*, OECD.

National Statistics (2005) *Share Ownership. A Report on Ownership of Shares as at 31ˢᵗ December 2004*. Available at www.statistics.gov.uk/StatBase.

Nobes, C.W. (1982) 'The Gallerani account book of 1305–8', *Accounting Review*, April.

Nobes, C.W. (1993) 'The true and fair view requirement: impact on and of the Fourth Directive', *Accounting and Business Research*, Winter.

Parker, R.H. (1983) 'Some international aspects of accounting', in S.J. Gray (ed.), *International Accounting and Transnational Decision*, Butterworths, London.

Parker, R.H. (1989) 'Importing and exporting accounting: the British experience', in A.G. Hopwood (ed.), *International Pressures for Accounting Change*, Prentice Hall, London.

Parker, R.H. (2000) 'Why English?' *Accountancy*, August.

Parker, R.H. (2001a) 'European languages of account', *European Accounting Review*, Vol. 10, No. 1.

Parker, R.H. (2001b) 'Read with care', *Accountancy*, June.

United Nations Center on Transnational Corporations (UNCTC) (2006) *World Investment Report*.

Wheatley, S. (1988) 'Some tests of international equity integration', *Journal of Financial Economics*, Vol. 21, No. 2.

Useful websites

Accounting Education	www.accountingeducation.com
British Accounting Association	www.baa.group.shef.ac.uk
European Accounting Association	www.eaa-online.org
International Accounting Standards Board	www.iasb.org
International Federation of Accountants	www.ifac.org
United Nations Conference on Trade and Development	www.unctad.org
World Bank	www.worldbank.org
World Federation of Exchanges	www.world-exchanges.org
World Trade Organization	www.wto.org

QUESTIONS

Suggested answers to the asterisked questions are given at the end of the book.

1.1∗ What effects have the major political events in the world since the end of the Second World War had on accounting and financial reporting?

1.2∗ Why have the major accounting firms become 'international'? From what countries have they mainly originated? Why?

1.3 What major contributions to accounting and its terminology have been made historically by the following countries: Italy, the United Kingdom, the United States, Japan?

1.4   Which are the top three developed countries in respect of each of:

    (a)   share of the world's top 500 companies;
    (b)   number of qualified accountants;
    (c)   market capitalization of stock exchange?

Why is the answer not the same for all three questions?

1.5   What factors have made possible the 'internationalization' of the world's stock markets?

1.6   What factors have led to the establishment of multinational enterprises?

1.7   Which countries historically have been the home countries of MNEs? Are they the same countries from which international accounting firms have originated?

1.8   Why are there more accountants per head of population in New Zealand than in France?

1.9   Why are some EU companies listed on non-European (especially North American) stock exchanges?

1.10 Why is English the leading language of international corporate financial reporting?

1.11 Access the website of GlaxoSmithKline (www.gsk.com) to explain the differences disclosed in its annual reports between US GAAP and IFRS and UK GAAP from 2004 onwards. Could these differences (summarized in Tables 1.1 and 1.2) have been smaller if the company had made other choices of options available within IFRS and UK GAAP? Are the size of the differences influenced by the fact that GSK is a pharmaceutical company?

2 Causes and examples of international differences

Christopher Nobes

OBJECTIVES

After reading this chapter, you should be able to:

- discuss the degree to which international cultural differences might explain accounting differences;
- outline the two main types of legal system to be found in the Western world and how these are related to accounting differences;
- explain how the predominant methods of financing of companies can differ internationally and how this may affect the purpose and nature of accounting;
- illustrate the linkages between taxation and financial reporting, and show how these are stronger in some countries than in others;
- outline the relationships between international accounting variations and differences in the accountancy profession;
- synthesize all the above relationships to begin to explain international differences in financial reporting;
- outline various ways in which accounting under German national rules is more conservative than that under UK rules;
- explain the difference between a provision and a reserve, and show how the definition of provision is wider in some countries than in others;
- outline the main valuation bases used for assets in major countries;
- summarize the international differences in formats of financial statements.

2.1   Introduction

That there are major international differences in accounting practices is not obvious to all accountants, let alone to non-accountants. The latter may see accounting as synonymous with double entry, which is indeed similar universally. Much of this book investigates the major differences in accounting. Some examples are given in Section 2.9. As a prelude to this, we try to identify the likely causes of the differences. It is not possible to be *sure* that the factors discussed below cause them, but a relationship can be established and reasonable deductions made.

A large list of possible causes of international differences can be found in the writings of previous researchers (e.g. Choi and Meek, 2005, Chapter 2; Radebaugh, Gray and Black, 2006, Chapter 3). Some researchers have used their estimates of such causes as a means of classifying countries by their accounting systems (see Chapter 3). Other researchers have studied whether perceived differences in accounting practices correlate with perceived causal factors (e.g. Frank, 1979; Doupnik and Salter, 1995).

Before going further, it is also important to define 'accounting'. In this context, we mean published annual financial reporting by companies. To the extent that it is useful to use a term such as 'accounting system', we mean the set of financial reporting practices used by a particular company for an annual report. Different companies in a country may use different accounting systems. The same applies to different purposes. For example, in many EU countries, consolidated statements are prepared using IFRS whereas unconsolidated statements use national rules. This chapter investigates why and how national systems differ. However, the ideas here can be used to explain why different countries might exhibit different styles of IFRS practice, as explained further in Chapter 7.

Several factors that seem linked to the differences in accounting systems are now examined. These are not necessarily *causes* of the differences; they might be results, as will be discussed later.

2.2   Culture

Clearly, accounting is affected by its environment, including the culture of the country in which it operates. Hofstede (1980) develops a model of culture as the collective programming of the mind that distinguishes the members of one human group from another. Hofstede argues that, much as a computer operating system contains a set of rules that acts as a reference point and a set of constraints to higher-level programs, so culture includes a set of societal values that drives institutional form and practice. As Gray (1988, page 5) notes:

> societal values are determined by ecological influences and modified by external factors . . . In turn, societal values have institutional consequences in the form of the legal system, political system, nature of capital markets, patterns of corporate ownership and so on.

Culture in any country contains the most basic values that an individual may hold. It affects the way that individuals would like their society to be structured and how they interact with its substructure. Accounting may be seen as one of those substructures. As Gray (1988, page 5) explains:

> the value systems or attitudes of accountants may be expected to be related to and derived from societal values with special reference to work related values. Accounting 'values' will in turn impact on accounting systems.

To get some idea of the basic cultural patterns of various countries, we turn again to Hofstede. Based on a study of over 100,000 IBM employees in 39 countries, Hofstede (1984, pages 83, 84) defined and scored the following four basic dimensions of culture, which can be summarized as follows:

1 *Individualism versus collectivism.* Individualism stands for a preference for a loosely knit social framework in society wherein individuals are supposed to take care of themselves and their immediate families only. The fundamental issue addressed by this dimension is the degree of interdependence that a society maintains among individuals.

2 *Large versus small power distance.* Power distance is the extent to which the members of a society accept that power in institutions and organizations is distributed unequally. People in societies that have large power distance accept a hierarchical order in which everybody has a place which needs no further justification. The fundamental issue addressed by this dimension is how society handles inequalities among people when they occur.

3 *Strong versus weak uncertainty avoidance.* Uncertainty avoidance is the degree to which the members of a society feel uncomfortable with uncertainty and ambiguity. This feeling leads them to beliefs promising certainty and to maintain institutions protecting conformity. Strong uncertainty avoidance societies maintain rigid codes of belief and behaviour and are intolerant towards deviant persons and ideas. Weak uncertainty avoidance societies maintain a more relaxed atmosphere in which practice counts more than principles and deviance is more easily tolerated. A fundamental issue addressed by this dimension is how a society reacts to the fact that time runs only one way and that the future is unknown: whether it tries to control the future or lets it happen.

4 *Masculinity versus femininity.* Masculinity stands for a preference in society for achievement, heroism, assertiveness and material success. Its opposite, femininity, stands for a preference for relationships, modesty, caring for the weak, and the quality of life.

Gray (1988) applies these cultural differences to explain international differences in the behaviour of accountants and therefore in the nature of accounting practices. For example, Gray suggests that a country with high uncertainty avoidance and low individualism will be more likely to exhibit conservative measurement of income and a preference to limit disclosure to those closely involved in the business. Conservatism is examined as an example of international differences later in this chapter.

Gray developed the following pairs of contrasting 'accounting values':

- professionalism versus statutory control;
- uniformity versus flexibility;

- conservatism versus optimism;
- secrecy versus transparency.

The first two relate to authority and enforcement. Here Gray sees a clear contrast between the 'Anglo' culture area on the one hand and Asian areas on the other. The second two relate to measurement and disclosure. Gray contrasts the 'Anglo' and the Latin and Germanic cultures.

This approach may well be particularly useful for examining such issues as international differences in the behaviour of auditors (e.g. Soeters and Schreuder, 1988). However, for financial reporting, the measures of cultural attributes seem vague and indirect, compared with the measurement of directly relevant elements of the external environment of accounting, such as legal systems or equity markets (see below). Also, the cultural data may not be reliable in an accounting context. For example, Hofstede classifies West African countries together, but they have very different legal and accounting systems. Another problem arises from the fact that, for good reasons, Hofstede looked at employees in a large multinational company. When measuring cultural attributes, how does one cope with the fact that many employees of multinationals in Abu Dhabi, Singapore, etc. come from other countries or from particular minority populations? Baskerville (2003) suggests that it is dangerous to equate nation with culture and that there are difficulties in trying to understand a culture by means of numerical indices. However, Hofstede (2003) replies to the criticisms.

Salter and Niswander (1995) tried to test Gray's hypothesis for 29 countries but met considerable difficulty in measuring several of Gray's 'accounting values', so that indirect measures were generally used. For example, the degree of uniformity was partly measured by whether a country has common law or code law, but this is not really a test of differences in accounting practices but a test of a possible cause of them. For a more direct measure of uniformity, Gray's hypothesis did not hold. For conservatism, some hypothesized relationships held and others did not. The most convincing support for an element of Gray's hypothesis was that transparency increased as uncertainty avoidance decreased, but the other predictions related to secrecy did not hold. Chanchani and Willett (2004) sampled the accounting values of preparers and users of financial statements in India and New Zealand. They found some support for Gray's constructs of professionalism and uniformity.

Another way of looking at the environment of accounting is to identify more direct potential influences such as legal systems, corporate financing, tax systems and so on. These interact with culture in a complex way, and they seem to affect the style of financial reporting and accountancy profession that a country has. We look at some of these external environmental factors in the rest of this chapter.

When studying possible causes of accounting differences, it will also be useful to note that the environment of accounting may include the effects of imperialism. Many countries are heavily influenced by others, particularly former colonial powers whose culture may be overwhelming. Consequently, when predicting or explaining the accounting requirements of many African or Asian countries, it may be more efficient to look at the colonial history rather than at other possible causes. These issues are taken up again when classification is discussed in Chapter 3, and they are referred to in some later chapters for particular countries.

Chanchani and MacGregor (1999) provide a summary of papers on accounting and culture. Doupnik and Tsakumis (2004) update this.

2.3 Legal systems

Some countries have a legal system that relies upon a limited amount of statute law, which is then interpreted by courts, which build up large amounts of case law to supplement the statutes. Such a 'common law' system was formed in England, primarily after the Norman Conquest, by judges acting on the king's behalf (van Caenegem, 1988). It is less abstract than codified law (see below); a common law rule seeks to provide an answer to a specific case rather than to formulate a general rule for the future. Although this common law system emanates from England, it may be found in similar forms in many countries influenced by England. Thus, the federal law of the United States, the laws of Ireland, India, Australia, and so on, are to a greater or lesser extent modelled on English common law. This naturally influences commercial law, which traditionally does not prescribe rules to cover the behaviour of companies and how they should prepare their financial statements. To a large extent accounting within such a context is not specified in detail in law. Instead, accountants themselves establish rules for accounting practice, which may come to be written down as recommendations or standards.

Other countries have a system of law that is based on the Roman *ius civile* as compiled by Justinian in the sixth century and developed by European universities from the twelfth century. Here, rules are linked to ideas of justice and morality; they become doctrine. The word 'codified' may be associated with such a system. This difference has the important effect that company law or commercial codes need to establish rules for accounting and financial reporting. For example, in Germany, company accounting under domestic rules is to a large extent a branch of law.

Table 2.1 illustrates the way in which some developed countries' legal systems fall into these two categories. In some Roman law countries, *dirigisme* (centraliza-

Table 2.1 **Western legal systems**

Common law	Codified Roman law
England and Wales	France
Ireland	Italy
United States	Germany
Canada	Spain
Australia	Netherlands
New Zealand	Portugal
	Japan (commercial)

Note: The laws of Scotland, Israel, South Africa, Quebec, Louisiana and the Philippines embody elements of both systems.

tion and a desire to control the economy) results in the existence of an 'accounting plan' (see Chapter 14). Classification of legal systems is discussed by David and Brierley (1985).

It is clear that the nature of accounting *regulation* in a country (as opposed to the content of the accounting rules) is affected by its general system of laws. This is the subject of Chapters 9 and 14. There also seems to be some association of common law countries and large equity markets (see Section 2.4). Further, there seems to be an association of common law countries with particular types of accounting practices, but causation is unclear (see Section 2.8). Jaggi and Low (2000) find, for example, that companies in common law countries have higher levels of disclosures. Bushman and Piotroski (2006) examine the greater incentives to report losses quickly in common law countries.

Even if a country's regulatory system for accounting is affected by the nature of its legal system, the accounting rules and practices might be more affected by other issues. At the extreme, a country might adopt International Financial Reporting Standards (IFRS) for some or all purposes, irrespective of its legal system.

2.4 Providers of finance

The prevalent types of business organization and ownership also differ. In Germany, France and Italy, capital provided by banks is very significant, as are small family-owned businesses. By contrast, in the United States and the United Kingdom there are large numbers of companies that rely on millions of private shareholders for finance. Evidence that this characterization is reasonable may be found by looking at the number of listed companies in various countries. Table 1.5 in the previous chapter shows the numbers of domestic listed companies on Stock Exchanges where there are over 250 such companies with a market capitalization of $800 billion or more in 2007. Table 2.2 takes such data for four countries for 2005 and puts them into context by deflating them for the size of the economy or population.

The comparison between the United States or United Kingdom and Germany or Italy is instructive. A two-group categorization of these countries is almost as obvious as that for legal systems in Table 2.1. La Porta *et al.* (1997) find a statistical connection between common law countries and strong equity markets. La Porta *et al.*

Table 2.2 **The strength of equity markets**

	Domestic listed companies/ million of population	Equity market capitalization/GDP
Italy	4.7	0.60
Germany	7.9	0.56
United States	18.0	1.57
United Kingdom	44.4	1.75

Sources: As Table 1.5 and 'Pocket World in Figures, 2005', *The Economist*.

Table 2.3 **Gearing ratios of selected countries**

Rank	Country	Gearing*
1	Spain	240.26
2	Germany	236.35
3	Ireland	223.20
4	Greece	194.15
5	Denmark	186.32
6	Italy	177.99
7	Japan	175.33
8	Australia	146.82
9	Belgium	129.95
10	Sweden	129.15
11	Austria	121.61
12	France	120.64
13	Norway	112.15
14	Poland	108.72
15	UK	107.07
16	Switzerland	100.55
17	US	98.03
18	Canada	87.10
19	New Zealand	72.68

Note: *Debt as percentage of common equity.
Source: Data from Datastream. By kind permission of Jon Tucker and David Bence of Bristol Business School.

(1998) note that common law countries have stronger legal protection of investors than Roman law countries do. Roe (2003) argues that the differences between corporate structures in the developed West are caused by political differences. These political differences not only directly affect corporate structures, they also influence the technical institutions (e.g. legal arrangements) that affect corporate structures.

Incidentally, the country with the longest history of 'public' companies is the Netherlands. Although it has a fairly small stock exchange, many multinationals (such as Unilever, Philips, Royal Dutch) are listed on it. It seems reasonable, then, to place the Netherlands with the English-speaking world in an 'outside shareholder' group as opposed to a 'bank/family' group. Also, Table 2.3 shows average gearing ratios of companies in various countries. On the whole these fit the hypothesis, because less reliance on equity suggests more reliance on debt. The United States has low gearing, like the United Kingdom.

A proposed grouping of countries into types by financial system has been formalized by Zysman (1983) as follows:

- capital market systems (e.g. United Kingdom, United States);
- credit-based governmental systems (e.g. France, Japan);
- credit-based financial institution systems (e.g. Germany).

Parker (1994) applies this analysis to 10 countries of the western Pacific and suggests its explanatory power for financial reporting practices.

Zysman's three types could be simplified further to 'equity' and 'credit'. A further point of comparison is that, in 'credit' countries, even the relatively few listed companies may be dominated by shareholders who are bankers, governments or founding families. For example, in Germany, the banks in particular are important owners of companies as well as providers of debt finance. A majority of shares in many public companies are owned or controlled as proxies by banks, for example, by the Deutsche Bank. In such countries as Germany, France or Italy, the banks or the state will, in many cases, nominate directors and thus be able to obtain information and affect decisions. If it is the case that even listed companies in continental European countries are dominated by banks, governments or families, the need for published information is less clear. This also applies to audit, because this is designed to check up on the managers in cases where the owners are 'outsiders'. Franks and Mayer (2001) discuss the ownership and control of German companies.

Although it is increasingly the case that shares in countries such as the United Kingdom and the United States are held by institutional investors rather than by individual shareholders (see Chapter 1), this still contrasts with state, bank or family holdings. Indeed, the increased importance of institutional investors is perhaps a reinforcement for the following hypothesis: in countries with a widespread ownership of companies by shareholders who do not have access to internal information, there will be a pressure for disclosure, audit and 'fair' information. Institutional investors hold larger blocks of shares and may be better organized than private shareholders. So, they should increase this pressure, although they may also be able successfully to press for more detailed information than is generally available to the public.

'Fair' needs to be defined. It is a concept related to that large number of outside owners who require unbiased information about the success of a business and its state of affairs (Flint, 1982; Parker and Nobes, 1994). Although reasonable prudence will be expected, these shareholders are interested in comparing one year with another and one company with another; thus some degree of realism will be required. This entails judgement, which entails experts. This expertise is also required for the checking of the financial statements by auditors. In countries such as the United Kingdom, the United States and the Netherlands, this can, over many decades, result in a tendency for accountants to work out their own technical rules, as suggested earlier. This is acceptable to governments because of the influence and expertise of the accounting profession, which is usually running ahead of the interest of the government (in its capacity as shareholder, protector of the public interest or collector of taxation). Thus 'generally accepted accounting principles' control accounting and these are set by committees dominated by accountants and in the private sector. To the extent that governments intervene, they impose disclosure, filing or presentation requirements and these tend to follow best practice rather than to create it.

In most continental European countries and in Japan, the traditional paucity of 'outsider' shareholders has meant that external financial reporting has been largely invented for the purposes of protecting creditors and for governments, as tax collectors or controllers of the economy. This has not encouraged the development of flexibility, judgement, fairness or experimentation. However, it does lead to precision, uniformity and stability. It also seems likely that the greater importance of creditors in these countries leads to more careful (prudent, conservative) accounting. This is because creditors are interested in whether, in the worst case, they are likely to get their money back, whereas shareholders may be interested in an unbiased estimate of future prospects.

Nevertheless, even in such countries as Germany, France or Italy, where there are comparatively few listed companies, governments have recognized the responsibility to require public or listed companies to publish detailed, audited financial statements. There are laws to this effect in the majority of such countries, and governments have also set up bodies specifically to control the securities markets: in France in the 1960s the *Commission des Opérations de Bourse* and its successor the *Autorité des Marchés Financiers*, and in Italy in the 1970s the *Commissione Nazionale per le Società e la Borsa* (CONSOB). More recently, the *Bundesanstalt für Finanzdienstleistungsaufsicht* (BaFin) was set up in Germany. These bodies are to some extent modelled on the Securities and Exchange Commission (SEC) of the United States (see Chapter 8). They have been associated with important developments in financial reporting, generally in the direction of Anglo-American practice. This is not surprising, as these stock exchange bodies are taking the part otherwise played by private and institutional shareholders who have, over a much longer period, helped to shape Anglo-American accounting systems.

To some extent, this clear picture has been changing. For example, institutional and private investors have been increasing in importance in France and Germany. Also, as explained in Chapter 14, private sector standard-setters were set up in those two countries in the late 1990s. Nevertheless, the two-way contrast seems intact.

In conclusion, we suggest that this differentiation between credit/insiders and equity/outsiders is the key cause of international differences in financial reporting. An initial classification of some countries on this basis is suggested in Table 2.4.

Several important results flow from this two-way split. First, in credit/insider countries, there is no great market demand for audited and published financial reporting. The demand for annual accounting is therefore strongly associated with the government's need for a calculation of taxable income. Consequently, tax considerations will dominate accounting rules. By contrast, in equity/outsider

Table 2.4 **Initial classification based on corporate financing**

A	B
Features	
Strong equity market	Weaker equity market
Many outside shareholders	Core, insider shareholders
Large auditing profession	Small auditing profession
Separate accounting and tax rules	Tax dominates accounting rules
Examples of countries	
Australia	France
United Kingdom	Germany
United States	Italy

countries, accounting performs a market function, and so the rules need to be separated from taxation. The result is two sets of accounting rules: one for financial reporting and one for the calculation of taxable income. This is examined in the next section.

If a significant equity market does develop, one approach to satisfying its demand for a different type of information is to impose a different set of rules (e.g. IFRS) for the consolidated statements of listed companies. This can be done without affecting domestic accounting rules or the calculation of taxable income or distributable income.

A second effect of the split of countries based on financing systems is that credit/insider countries will need far fewer auditors than equity/outsider countries. This will affect the age, size and status of the accountancy profession, as examined in Section 2.7.

2.5 Taxation

Although it is possible to make groupings of tax systems in a number of ways, only some of them are of relevance to financial reporting. For example, it is easy to divide countries into those using 'classical' and those using 'imputation' systems of corporation tax (see Chapter 22). However, this distinction does not have a major effect on financial reporting. What is much more relevant is the degree to which taxation regulations determine accounting measurements, for reasons discussed in the previous section. To some extent this is seen by studying deferred taxation, which is caused by differences between tax and accounting treatments. In the United Kingdom and the United States, for example, the problem of deferred tax has caused much controversy and a considerable amount of accounting standard documentation. Turning to national accounting rules in France or Germany, it is found that the problem is minor; for in these countries it is largely the case that the tax rules *are* the accounting rules. In Germany, the tax accounts (*Steuerbilanz*) should be the same as the commercial accounts (*Handelsbilanz*). There is even a word for this idea: the *Massgeblichkeitsprinzip* (Haller, 1992).

One obvious example of the areas affected by this difference is depreciation. In the United Kingdom the amount of depreciation charged in the published financial statements is determined according to custom established over the last century and influenced by the accounting standard FRS 15, which requires (paragraph 77) that:

> The depreciable amount of a tangible fixed asset should be allocated on a systematic basis over its useful economic life. The depreciation method used should reflect as fairly as possible the pattern in which the asset's economic benefits are consumed by the entity.

The injunctions contained in the standard are of a fairly general nature (rather like those in the similar International Financial Reporting Standard, IAS 16), and their spirit is quite frequently ignored. Convention and pragmatism, rather than exact rules or even the spirit of the standard, determine the method chosen (usually straight-line, because it is easier), the size of the scrap value (usually zero, because it is easier) and the expected length of life.

The amount of depreciation allowed for *tax* purposes in the United Kingdom is quite independent of these accounting figures. It is determined by capital allowances, which are a formalized scheme of tax depreciation allowances designed to stand-ardize the amounts allowed and to act as investment incentives (see Chapter 22). Because of the separation of the two schemes, there can be a complete lack of sub-jectivity in tax allowances, but full room for judgement in financial depreciation charges.

At the opposite extreme, in countries such as Germany, the tax regulations lay down maximum depreciation rates to be used for particular assets. These are gener-ally based on the expected useful lives of assets. However, in some cases, accelerated depreciation allowances are available: for example, for industries producing energy-saving or anti-pollution products or for those operating in parts of eastern Germany. If these allowances are to be claimed for tax purposes (which would normally be sensible), they must be charged in the financial statements. Thus, the charge against profit would be said by a UK accountant not to be 'fair', even though it could certainly be 'correct' or 'legal'. This influence is felt even in the details of the choice of method of depreciation in Germany, as shown by BASF's explanation: 'Movable fixed assets . . . are mostly depreciated by the declining balance method, with a change to straight-line depreciation when this results in higher depreciation amounts' (2004 Annual Report, page 87). BASF was still using German accounting rules for its consolidated statements of 2004, unlike many large German companies (see Chapter 5).

Further examples are easy to find: bad debt provisions (determined by tax laws in Italy or Spain) or government-induced revaluations of assets (e.g. in France in 1978, Spain in 1986 and Italy in 2000).

The effects of all this are to reduce the room for operation of the accruals con-vention (which is the driving force behind such practices as depreciation) and to reduce 'fairness'. With some variations, this *Massgeblichkeitsprinzip* operates in Germany, France, Belgium, Japan and many other countries. It is perhaps due partly to the pervasive influence of codification in law, and partly to the predominance of tax authorities as users of accounting. A major exception to this point, concerning consolidated statements, became especially important in the 1990s. Since taxation generally relates to the taxable income of individual companies rather than that of groups, national tax authorities are able to take a relaxed view of consolidated statements. This has facilitated international harmonization of accounting at the group level.

The alternative approach, exemplified by the United Kingdom, the United States, Australia and the Netherlands, is found in countries where published financial statements are designed mainly as performance indicators for investment decisions, where commercial rules operate separately from tax rules in a number of account-ing areas. The countries on the left in Table 2.1 are, in varying degrees, like this. In most cases, there is not the degree of separation between tax and financial reporting that is found in the United Kingdom in the shape of capital allowances. However, in all such countries the taxation authorities have to make many adjust-ments to the commercial accounts for their own purposes, after exerting only minor influence directly on them. There is a major exception to this in the use of LIFO inventory valuation in the United States, largely for tax reasons (see Chapter 8).

Attempts have been made to put countries into groups by the degree of connection between tax and financial reporting. For example, Hoogendoorn (1996) classifies 13 countries. However, there are problems with this because seven groups are necessary for the classification, and two matters are being considered at the same time: the tax/reporting connection, and the treatment of deferred tax. Lamb *et al.* (1998) try to separate out the first issue. They conclude that it is possible to distinguish between UK/US separation of tax and accounting and a German close connection. Nobes and Schwencke (2006) study the development of tax and reporting links over time. They take Norway as a case study, and chart its move from close connection to separation over a century.

2.6 Other external influences

Cultural influences on accounting development have already been discussed. Also, it has been suggested that colonial influence may overwhelm everything else. Many other influences have also been at work in shaping accounting practices. An example is the framing of a law in response to economic or political events. For example, the economic crisis in the United States in the late 1920s and early 1930s produced the Securities Exchange Acts that diverted US accounting from its previous course by introducing extensive disclosure requirements and state control (usually by threat only) of accounting standards. Other examples include the introduction into Italy of Anglo-American accounting principles by choice of the government, and the introduction into Luxembourg of consolidation and detailed disclosure as a result of EU Directives – both against all previous trends there. In Spain, the adoption of the accounting plan from France followed French adoption of it after influence by the occupying Germans in the early 1940s. Perhaps most obvious and least natural is the adaptation of various British Companies Acts or of international standards by developing countries with a negligible number of the sort of public companies or private shareholders that have given rise to the financial reporting practices contained in these laws or standards. In its turn, the United Kingdom in 1981 adopted uniform formats derived from the 1965 *Aktiengesetz* of Germany because of EU requirements. For their part, Roman law countries now have to grapple with the 'true and fair view' (see Chapter 11).

A major example of external influence is the adoption of, or convergence with, the standards of the International Accounting Standards Board (IASB). For example, the EU has made these standards compulsory for the consolidated statements of listed companies. This was done for political and economic reasons (see Chapter 5) and it overrides the other factors in this chapter. More subtly, the remaining national standards of the EU and elsewhere are gradually converging with the international standards.

Another factor which affects accounting practices is the level of inflation. Although accountants in the English-speaking world have proved remarkably immune to inflation when it comes to decisive action, there are some countries where inflation has been overwhelming. In several South American countries, the most obvious feature of accounting practices has been the use of methods of general price-level adjustment (Tweedie and Whittington, 1984). The use of this comparatively simple method is probably due to the reasonable correlation of inflation with any particular specific price changes when the former is in hundreds of per cent per year; to the objective nature of government-published indices; to the connection of accounting and tax; and to the paucity of well-trained accountants. Without reference to inflation, it would not be possible to explain accounting differences in several countries severely affected by it.

In continental Europe, the fact that it was *governments* that responded to inflation in France, Spain and Italy from the 1970s is symptomatic of the regulation of accounting in these countries. By contrast, in the United States, the United Kingdom and Australia, it was mainly committees of accountants that developed responses to inflation in the 1970s. One might conclude that, although any country will respond to massive inflation, the more interesting point is that the reaction of a country's accounting system to inflation is an illustration of the basic nature of the system.

In a few cases, theory has strongly influenced accounting practice, perhaps most obviously in the case of microeconomics in the Netherlands. Accounting theorists there (notably Theodore Limperg, Jr) had advanced the case that the users of financial statements would be given the fairest view of the performance and state of affairs of an individual company by allowing accountants to use judgement, in the context of that particular company, to select and present accounting figures. In particular, it was suggested that replacement cost information might give the best picture. The looseness of Dutch law and tax requirements, and the receptiveness of the profession to microeconomic ideas (partly due, no doubt, to their training by the academic theorists), have led to the present diversity of practice, the emphasis on 'fairness' through judgement, and the experimentation with replacement cost accounting.

In other countries, theory is less noticeable. In most of continental Europe and Japan, accounting has been the servant of the state (e.g. for tax collection). In the Anglo-Saxon world, theory was traditionally of little importance in accounting practice, although the development of conceptual frameworks since the mid-1970s has changed this (see Chapters 6 and 8).

2.7 The profession

Other issues are closely related to financial reporting, and have been thought by some researchers to cause international differences. One of these is the accountancy profession. However, this may be a dependent variable, not an explanatory one.

The strength, size and competence of the accountancy profession in a country may follow to a large extent from the various factors outlined above and from the type of financial reporting they have helped to produce. For example, the lack of a substantial body of private shareholders and public companies in some countries means that the need for auditors is much smaller than it is in the United Kingdom or the United States. However, the nature of the profession also feeds back into the type of accounting that is practised and could be practised. For example, a 1975

Decree in Italy (not brought into effect until the 1980s), requiring listed companies to have extended audits similar to those operated in the United Kingdom and the United States, could only be brought into effect initially because of the substantial presence of international accounting firms. This factor constitutes a considerable obstacle to any attempts at significant and deep harmonization of accounting between some countries. The need for extra auditors was a controversial issue in Germany's implementation of the EU's Fourth Directive (Chapter 11).

The scale of the difference is illustrated in Table 1.10 in Chapter 1, which lists some accountancy bodies whose members act as auditors of the financial statements of companies. These remarkable figures need some interpretation. For example, let us more carefully compare the German and the British figures in that table. First, in Germany there is a separate, though overlapping, profession of tax experts (*Steuerberater*), which is larger than the accountancy body. By contrast, in the United Kingdom the 'accountants' figure is inflated by the inclusion of many who specialize in or occasionally practise in tax. Second, a German accountant may only be a member of the *Institut* if in practice, whereas at least half of the British figure represents members in commerce, industry, government, education, and so on. Third, the training period is much longer in Germany than it is in the United Kingdom. It normally involves a four-year relevant degree course, six years' practical experience (four of them in the profession) and a professional examination consisting of oral and written tests plus a thesis. This tends to last until the aspiring accountant is 30 to 35 years old. Thus, many of the German 'students' would be counted as part of the qualified figure if they were in the British system. Fourth, in the late 1980s, a second-tier auditing body (of *vereidigte Buchprüfer*) was established in Germany for auditors who may only audit private companies.

These four factors help to explain the differences. However, there is still a very substantial residual difference which results from the much larger number of companies to be audited in the UK and the different process of forming a judgement on the 'fair' view. The differences have diminished as auditing has been extended to many private companies in EU countries and withdrawn from many private companies in the UK, and as German auditors grapple with IFRS consolidated statements.

2.8   Conclusion on the causes of international differences

International differences in financial reporting are many and various, as is examined in detail throughout this book. Cultural differences are clearly of relevance here, at least as causes of factors that influence financial reporting. Doupnik and Salter (1995) suggest a model in which accounting differences can be explained by Gray's four cultural variables (see Section 2.2) plus six others (including the factors of Sections 2.3–2.7 above). However, Nobes (1998) suggests that this is problematic because (a) the cultural variables might be better seen as influencing the second six independent variables rather than directly affecting accounting, and (b) several of the second six variables (e.g. the nature of the accountancy profession) seem to be largely dependent rather than independent.

Nobes (1998) proposes that, at least for the purposes of dividing developed countries into major groups (see Chapter 3), the most important direct cause of the financial reporting differences is a two-way split of countries into: (i) those with important equity markets and many outside shareholders; and (ii) those with a credit-based financing system and with relatively unimportant outside shareholders. The equity/outsider system leads to decision-useful accounting, to a separation between tax and accounting rules, and to large auditing professions. This is also generally associated with the common law system, although the Netherlands seems to be an exception: a country with Roman law but where many other features related to accounting are like those of the United States or the United Kingdom.

Ball *et al.* (2000) suggest connections between common law and certain aspects of accounting, such as the speed of reporting of losses. As noted earlier, La Porta *et al.* (1997 and 1998) examine some connections between common law and large equity markets.

Factors that might be relevant as causes but have not been addressed above include language, history, geography, religion, education, and many others. Some of these may be too vague to be useful; for example, it is the history of equity markets or the legal system that may be particularly relevant, rather than history in general.

However, when looking at countries that are strongly culturally influenced from elsewhere (e.g. many former colonies), the best predictor of the accounting system may be that it will be like that of the former colonial power. This will usually overwhelm other factors, even the corporate financing system. For example, some former British colonies in Africa have an accounting system based on that of the United Kingdom, even though they have no equity market at all. In other cases (e.g. New Zealand), a former colony may inherit a legal system, an equity market and an accountancy profession, as well as an accounting system. For many Commonwealth countries, the British influence over accounting has now been replaced by that of the IASB.

Xiao *et al.* (2004) apply the ideas of Nobes (1998) and Ball *et al.* (2000) to the development of accounting in China. They suggest that governmental influence can slow down the rate at which an accounting system will change in response to a growing equity market. Tarca *et al.* (2005) examine the change towards IFRS in Germany and confirm the suggested link with the growth of outsider equity. Zeghal and Mhedhbi (2006) also show that, among developing countries, international standards are most likely to be adopted where there are capital markets and Anglo-American culture. However, Tyrrall *et al.* (2007) suggest that, at least in emerging economies, there is so much pressure from outside to use IFRS that Nobes (1998) no longer applies. The issue is, instead, how quickly and fully IFRS is applied.

2.9 Some examples of differences

2.9.1 Conservatism and accruals

The word 'conservatism' in the accounting literature has two different meanings. In this book we use it to mean the tendency to understate profit and assets. This is associated with the state's desire to limit dividends in order to protect creditors, and with a company's desire to limit taxable income. Another meaning (e.g. Ball *et al.*, 2000; Ryan, 2006) is the speed with which losses are reported. This is discussed further in Section 20.5.

Perhaps because of the different mix of users in differing countries, conservatism (in the former sense) is of different strengths. For example, the importance of banks in Germany may be a reason for greater conservatism in reporting. It is widely held that bankers are more interested in 'rock-bottom' figures in order to satisfy themselves that long-term loans are safe. At the same time, the consequent lack of interest in a 'fair' view reduces the need to modify conservatism.

IFRS refers to the concept of 'prudence' (as in the *Framework,* para. 37) rather than 'conservatism'. In many cases, accounting standards are the compromise treaties that settle a battle between prudence and the accruals concept. For example, it is not fully conservative to require the capitalization of some development expenditure as in IAS 38, but it may be reasonably prudent under certain conditions. A similar argument applies to the taking of profit on long-term contracts as in IAS 11. Many Anglo-Saxon countries use similar ideas. For example, although US accounting practice does not generally allow capitalization of development expenditure (SFAS 2), it does require gains to be taken on certain unsold investments (SFAS 115). Hung (2000) finds that the use of accruals in various contexts reduces the usefulness of accounting information in some countries but not in Anglo-Saxon countries.

Continental European conservatism is of a more stringent variety, as may be illustrated by a study of published financial statements. The 1998 to 2004 annual reports of BASF (i.e. pre-IFRS) will be examined here. The evidence of conservatism in such reports depends upon the events of the year and the style of the companies' reports, thus it is not possible to organize a consistent survey. However, these reports seem to be broadly representative of domestic practice in Germany. The quotations below are designed to give an impression of the company's conservatism. It should be noted that these indications survived even into the consolidated accounts, which are not relevant for taxation; and they survived even in BASF, which was influenced by international pressures, such that it stated that it complied with US rules as much as possible:

> Movable fixed assets are mostly depreciated by the declining balance method, with a change to straight-line depreciation if this results in higher depreciation rates . . .
>
> For participations acquired through December 31, 1997, goodwill is mostly amortized over a period of five years . . .
>
> Loans are stated at cost or, in the case of non-interest-bearing loans or loans at below market interest rates, at their present value . . .
>
> Uncompleted contracts relate mainly to domestic and foreign plants under construction for third parties. Expected profits are not recognized until final settlement of accounts for the projects in question: expected losses are recognized by write-downs to the lower attributable values. Inventories are carried at acquisition or production cost or the lower quoted or market value, or at such lower values as appropriate . . .
>
> The valuation is mainly based on the LIFO method (last in, first out on an annual basis). Overall, 64 (BASF Aktiengesellschaft: 91) per cent of inventories were valued by the LIFO method . . .
>
> Receivables are generally carried at their nominal value; notes receivable and loans generating no or a low-interest income are discounted to their present values . . .

There are also provisions for uncertain liabilities and anticipated losses from uncompleted transactions and deferred maintenance expenses to be incurred within the first three months of the following year . . .

Long-term foreign-currency receivables are recorded at the rate prevailing on the acquisition date or at the lower rate on the balance sheet date. Long-term foreign-currency liabilities are recorded at the rate prevailing on the acquisition date or at the higher rate on the balance sheet date . . .

This greater conservatism in continental Europe seems to be a long-run phenomenon. Davidson and Kohlmeier (1966) and Abel (1969) noted that profit figures would be consistently lower in France, Sweden, Germany and the Netherlands (when use of replacement cost was assumed) if similar companies' statements were merely adjusted for differences in inventory and depreciation practices from those used in the United States or the United Kingdom.

One way of being more precise in this area is to construct a 'conservatism index'. Gray (1980) suggested the following ratio:

$$1 - \left(\frac{R_A - R_D}{|R_A|} \right)$$

where R_A = adjusted profit, and R_D = disclosed profit. A company with a ratio above one would be using relatively optimistic accounting practices, whereas a company with a ratio of less than one would be relatively conservative.

Gray (1980) examined a number of companies from France, Germany and the United Kingdom in the early 1970s in order to produce an index of conservatism. He concluded that 'French and German companies are significantly more conservative or pessimistic than UK companies' (page 69). However, the figures disclosed by Daimler-Benz for 1992 to 1995 for adjustments from German to US principles show that, in times of deep recession, German figures can be less conservative (see Section 2.9.2 below). As noted earlier, Ball *et al.* (2000) find that continental European companies take longer to recognize losses.

Gray used estimated adjustments by analysts for his data. Another source of data is that published by those companies that reconcile to US rules (see Table 1.1). Several researchers have used such data to construct conservatism indices for countries; some researchers refer instead to 'comparability indices'. Table 2.5 shows some details of those studies. In summary, the findings are that aspects of UK and Australian accounting are less conservative than US practice, but that continental European companies are generally more conservative.

More recent data on prudence can be found by examining the reconciliations of companies from domestic rules to IFRS. Staying with the example of Germany, Volkswagen's reconciliation shows more than a doubling of equity when moving from German rules to IFRS (see Table 2.6).

One major caveat, that has not always been discussed by researchers, is that the companies that publish this data may be atypical of their countries. For example, a German company might have used the choices available in German law in order to conform to US rules as much as possible, so that there would be fewer items to adjust for on reconciliation. This means that it would be following legal but atypical German practices for its domestic accounting. This is clearly the case for Daimler-Benz in 1993 to 1995 (e.g. page 65 of the 1995 Annual Report).

Table 2.5 **Studies of reconciliations to US GAAP**

	Authors	Sample size	Countries	Period covered
1	Weetman and Gray (1991)	57	UK, Sweden, Netherlands	1986–8
2	Cooke (1993)	5	Japan	1989–91
3	Hellman (1993)	13	Sweden	1981–90
4	Norton (1995)	13	Australia	1985–93
5	Zambon and Dick (1998)	40	France, Germany, Italy	1983–96
6	Zambon (1998)	68	UK	1994–6
7	Weetman, Jones, Adams and Gray (1998)	25	UK	1988 & 1994
8	Rueschhoff and Strupeck (1998)	58	13 developing countries	1994
9	Adams, Weetman, Jones and Gray (1999)	41	UK	1994
10	Street, Nichols and Gray (2000)	33	Countries using IAS	1997
11	Whittington (2000)	2	UK and France	1988–96

Source: By kind permission of Felix Soria, adapted from an unpublished draft PhD thesis, University of Reading, 2001.

Table 2.6 **Volkswagen 2001 (opening reconciliation)**

	€m
Equity (German law) 1.1.2000	9,811
Capitalization of development costs	3,982
Amended useful lives and depreciation methods of tangible and intangible assets	3,483
Capitalization of overheads in inventories	653
Differing treatment of leasing contracts as lessor	1,962
Differing valuation of financial instruments	897
Effect of deferred taxes	−1,345
Elimination of special items	262
Amended valuation of pension and similar obligations	−633
Amended accounting treatment of provisions	2,022
Classification of minority interests not as part of equity	−197
Other changes	21
Equity (IFRS) 1.1.2000	20,918

Source: Adapted from *Volkswagen AG Annual Report 2001*. Volkswagen AG, Wolfsburg, Germany.

A further example of the protection of creditors is the use of statutory or legal reserves in several continental European countries and Japan. These are undistributable reserves that are set up out of declared profits. They are an extra protection for creditors above the normal rules on the maintenance of capital. In France, Germany and Belgium a company is required to appropriate 5 per cent tranches of its annual profit until the statutory reserve reaches 10 per cent of issued share capital (20 per cent in Italy and Spain; 25 per cent in Japan).

Table 2.7 **Words for 'provision' and 'reserve'**

UK English	*Provision*	*Reserve*
American English	*Reserve*	*[Element of equity]*
French	*Provision*	*Réserve*
German	*Rückstellung*	*Rücklage*
Italian	*Fondo*	*Riserva*

This international difference in conservatism has largely survived international harmonization of domestic rules (see Chapter 11). For example, neither EU nor international harmonization efforts have addressed legal reserves. Also, the EU Fourth Directive makes prudence an overriding principle in the German-language version (and most others) but not in the English-language version (Evans and Nobes, 1996).

2.9.2 Provisions and reserves

The area of 'provisions' and 'reserves' is fraught with linguistic difficulties. For example, in American English the word 'reserve' always means 'provision' in UK English (see Table 2.7). We will use UK English here, but this still leaves another difficulty in that the word 'provision' means two things: (i) a liability of uncertain timing or amount (e.g. 'provision for pensions') and (ii) an allowance against (or impairment of) the value of an asset (e.g. 'bad debt provision' or 'provision for depreciation'). To avoid confusion in this section, we will use 'provision' to mean the first of these, and 'impairment' to mean the second. This is IFRS usage.

Setting up a provision or making an impairment involves a charge against income, but there is an important distinction. Making an impairment is a matter of measurement relating to an asset which has already been recognized. By contrast, setting up a provision requires three stages of consideration: is there a liability? should it be recognized? how should it be measured? More attention will be given to this topic in Chapter 16.

The distinction between provisions and reserves is important for financial reporting because provisions are liabilities recognized by charges against profit, whereas reserves are elements of equity caused by undistributed gains. The influences that lead to a proliferation of provisions appear to be conservatism and generous tax regulations. Both these factors have been discussed, and their effects on provisions mentioned. The result of such provision accounting may be that the accruals convention, the definition of 'liability' and 'fairness' are partially overridden; this in turn may result in income smoothing. Provisions for risks and contingencies which fluctuate in reverse relationship with profits are examples of income smoothing.

With reference to Germany, remarks concerning provisions have already been made above. In IFRS or US GAAP, provisions for general risks are not supposed to be set up, and therefore income should not be smoothed by changing their size. In 1998, the International Accounting Standards Committee (see Chapter 4) brought some clarity to this area by requiring (in IAS 37) that a provision should be recognized when, and only when, there is a liability to a third party at the balance sheet date. Such rules would clearly outlaw BASF's provision for next year's repair expenses (see quotation in Section 2.9.1).

Another language issue is that a provision (or a reserve) should not be confused with a pile of money or investments, which should be termed a 'fund'. For example, when a company recognizes that it has a liability to pay future pensions to current and former employees, it should set up a provision. However, this merely admits the obligation. If the company wishes to go further and set aside money outside of the company in order to pay these obligations, then it needs to set up a fund. For example, in the United Kingdom and the United States, it is customary for companies to send money to a legally independent pension fund or life assurance company. The resulting fund reduces the size of the provision shown in the balance sheet. Note (in Table 2.7) that the Italian word for provision is *fondo*, and this is also the Italian word for fund, which can increase confusion here.

2.9.3 Measurement of assets

There is great international variation in the degree to which departures from a cost basis are allowed or required. In a country with detailed legal rules and a coincidence of tax and commercial accounting the predominant valuation system will involve as little judgement as possible. Flexibility and judgement would make it difficult for auditors to determine whether the law had been obeyed and might lead to arbitrary taxation demands. Thus, in a country such as Germany, the required method of valuation under domestic rules is a strict form of historical cost. This also fits with the German opposition to inflation (and to adjustments for it), resulting from the scarring experiences of hyper-inflation after each of the two world wars.

At the other extreme is the Netherlands. Some Dutch companies (e.g. Philips) published replacement cost financial statements for four decades until recently. Although this remained minority practice, during inflationary periods many Dutch companies have partially or supplementarily used replacement costs. Dutch practice reflected the influence of microeconomic theory and a striving after fairness.

Between these two extremes, UK 'rules' until recently allowed a chaotic state of affairs, where some companies revalued, some of the time, using a variety of methods. This is the story for much of the English-speaking world, except that the United States and Canada keep to historical cost (except for financial assets) in the main financial statements because of the influence of the SEC. Throughout the English-speaking world during the inflationary 1970s and 1980s there was experimentation with current cost accounting, normally via supplementary statements. Now IFRS and UK rules allow revaluation of tangible and some intangible assets, as long as it is continuous and applies to all assets of the same sort. In France, Spain and Italy, where there is much tax and other government influence, there have been revaluations from time to time, as noted earlier.

Some countries, notably in South America, have adopted forms of general purchasing power (GPP) adjusted accounting. This has occurred in countries with very high inflation, government/tax controlled accounting, and a paucity of accountants. Thus GPP satisfies the requirements of simplicity and uniformity, as a single inflation index can be used by all companies. GPP accounting is of course basically historical cost accounting with 'last minute' annual indexations.

2.9.4 Financial statement formats

Balance sheets vary in two main ways under domestic rules (see Table 2.8). First, in some countries, assets are displayed in order of decreasing liquidity (cash first), whereas in other countries there is an increasing order of liquidity (intangible fixed assets come first). The key to predicting is that the decreasing order is used by countries influenced by the United States, and the increasing order is used by countries in the EU.

The other main variation in balance sheets is the shape of them. Some combine together all the debits and then all the credits. Such balance sheets are either two-sided (with assets on the left) or in 'report form' on a single page (with assets at the top) – see the example of report form in Table 2.9. Other companies arrange the items in order to calculate totals of net current assets and net assets; this may be called a financial position format. These three shapes (with assets in order of increasing liquidity) are all allowed in the EU. There is no US requirement on the shape of balance sheets.

Table 2.9 records that the present EU model can be traced back to an earlier German format. As may be seen, the first (1971) draft of the Directive followed the previous German format quite closely. The final (1978) version of the Directive was the one included into member state laws (e.g. the UK Companies Act). The UK format shown is an option in UK law. Normally, UK companies use instead the 'financial position' form, but this starts with assets presented in the order shown in Table 2.9. Partly because it would have been difficult to reach international agreement, the IFRS on this subject (IAS 1) contains no requirements on formats; neither on the liquidity order nor on the shape.

International variation of balance sheets should not create many problems, except that a reader's attention may be drawn to different totals, e.g. total assets as opposed to net assets. The format of Table 2.9 also does not show current liabilities separately, and it can be difficult to work out this total from the notes.

Table 2.8 Usual balance sheet formats

Country	Order of liquidity	Shape
Australia	Decreasing	Financial position
France	Increasing	Two-sided
Germany	Increasing	Report
Italy	Increasing	Two-sided
Japan	Decreasing	Two-sided
Spain	Increasing	Two-sided
United Kingdom	Increasing	Financial position
United States	Decreasing	Two-sided or report

Table 2.9 The evolution of the balance sheet (abbreviated versions)

1965 German AktG (§ 151)	1971 Draft Directive (Art. 8)	UK 1981 Act (Format 2)
Assets (shown on left)		
I Unpaid capital	A Unpaid capital B Formation expenses	A Unpaid capital

II Fixed and financial
  A Fixed and intangible
  B Financial
	C Fixed assets
	  I Intangible
	  II Tangible
	  III Participations
		B Fixed assets
		  I Intangible
		  II Tangible
		  III Investments

III Current assets
  A Stocks
  B Other current
	D Current assets
	  I Stocks
	  II Debtors
	  III Securities
		C Current assets
		  I Stocks
		  II Debtors
		  III Investments
		  IV Cash

IV Deferred charges	E Prepayments	D Prepayments

V Accumulated losses	F Loss
	  I For the year
	  II Brought forward	

Liabilities and capital (shown on right)		

I Share capital	A Subscribed capital	A Capital and reserves
		  I Called up capital
		  II Share premium
		  III Revaluation reserve
		  IV Other reserves
		  V Profit and loss

II Disclosed reserves	B Reserves	
III Provisions for diminutions	C Value adjustments	
IV Provisions for liabilities	D Provisions for charges	B Provisions for liabilities and charges
V Liabilities (4 years+)	E Creditors	C Creditors
VI Other liabilities		
VII Deferred income	F Accruals	D Accruals

VIII Profit	G Profit
	  I For the year
	  II Brought forward	

For income statements, the variety is rather more of a problem for users of financial statements. Table 2.10 shows the variety for some countries. The vertical/two-sided variation should not be a difficulty for users, although non-accountants may find the two-sided version hard to understand. The real problem lies in the two ways of combining costs: by nature or by function. The by-nature format combines costs as total purchases, total depreciation, total wages, etc. The by-function format

Table 2.10 Usual income statements under national laws

Country	Shape	Cost combination
Australia	Vertical	Function
France	Two-sided	Nature
Germany	Vertical	Mainly by nature
Italy	Vertical	Nature
Japan	Vertical	Function
Spain	Two-sided	Nature
United Kingdom	Vertical	Function
United States	Vertical	Function

combines costs by stage of production: cost of sales, administrative costs, distribution costs, etc. The by-function format allows the calculation of gross profit for a manufacturing company, whereas the by-nature format does not, because there is no information on the *manufacturing* wages, depreciation etc. that would be needed for the calculation of cost of sales. Again, IAS 1 contains no requirement on formats.

This chapter has discussed the connection between accounting and the predominance of outside shareholders. Shareholder orientation spreads further than accounting principles: it affects the format of financial statements. At its most obvious, the general use of a vertical format in the United Kingdom, rather than a horizontal format as in France or Spain, suggests a greater shareholder orientation in the United Kingdom. This is because, as noted above, the financial position format of the balance sheet allows the presentation of working capital and net worth, and it contrasts net worth with shareholders' funds. The vertical format of the income statement is easier to read for non-accountants.

However, even in the double-entry version of the balance sheet (see Table 2.9), the current continental European version has greater shareholder orientation than before. For example, it shows the elements of shareholders' funds together, rather than showing the year's net profit as a separate item at the bottom of the balance sheet (or a loss at the bottom of the assets side!) as did the 1965 *Aktiengesetz* (the German rules until 1987) and practice in Spain until 1989 and Italy until 1993. The greater continental interest in the double-entry aspects of the balance sheet was demonstrated by the presentation of 'provisions for bad debts' as a liability, and 'called up share capital not paid' as the first asset. The new formats introduced to implement the Fourth Directive removed many of these differences.

SUMMARY

- A large list of proposed causes of international accounting differences can be found in the literature.
- It seems very plausible that cultural differences affect accounting. Although efforts have been made to quantify culture, it is difficult to apply this to the

measurement of accounting differences. More direct linkages can be established between accounting, legal and financing systems.

- Most countries considered in the book can be seen as either common law or codified law countries. There seems to be some linkage with types of accounting.

- Countries with large equity markets need financial reporting suited to disclosing useful information to investors. Other countries are likely to have an accounting system linked to the calculation of taxable income and distributable income.

- Tax is very closely linked with financial reporting in several countries (e.g. Germany).

- External forces affect accounting in a country, particularly in the case of former colonies. An important external force is now the IASB.

- High levels of inflation have generally led to effects on accounting but they have differed by country. Theory seems to have little influence in most countries but, in the form of conceptual frameworks, is of increasing importance.

- International variations in the strength and size of the accountancy profession may be more a result than a cause of accounting differences.

- In summary, unless colonial influence overwhelms, an accounting system is most influenced by whether or not there is a strong equity market.

- Different degrees of conservatism can be found from country to country. Greater conservatism might be expected in countries where tax and accounting are closely linked and where there are conservative users such as bankers. One way of being more conservative is to make 'unnecessary' provisions. However, these can be reversed in bad years, thereby reversing the effects of conservatism on the earnings figure.

- The measurement of assets shows important international differences. Some countries require strict historical cost, others allow revaluations of selected assets at selected times. In several countries, governments have required controlled revaluations of fixed assets from time to time.

- The formats of financial statements differ markedly internationally. This leads to some difficulties for comparisons. The degree of shareholder orientation in a country affects the formats of financial statements, the provision of cash flow statements, the disclosure of certain items, and many other accounting practices.

References

Abel, R. (1969) 'A comparative simulation of German and US accounting principles', *Journal of Accounting Research*, Vol. 7, No. 1.

Adams, C.A., Weetman, P., Jones, E.A.E. and Gray, S.J. (1999) 'Reducing the burden of US GAAP reconciliations by foreign companies listed in the United States: the key question of materiality', *European Accounting Review*, Vol. 8, No. 1.

Ali, A. and Hwang, L.-S. (2000) 'Country-specific factors related to financial reporting and the value relevance of accounting data', *Journal of Accounting Research*, Vol. 38, No. 1.

Ball, R., Kothari, S.P. and Robin, A. (2000) 'The effect of international institutional factors on properties of accounting earnings', *Journal of Accounting and Economics*, Vol. 29, No. 1.

Baskerville, R.F. (2003) 'Hofstede never studied culture', *Accounting, Organizations and Society*, Vol. 28, No. 1.

Bushman, R. and Piotroski, J. (2006) 'Financial reporting incentives for conservative account-ing: the influence of legal and political institutions', *Journal of Accounting and Economics*, Vol. 42, Nos 1, 2.

Chanchani, S. and MacGregor, A. (1999) 'A synthesis of cultural studies in accounting', *Journal of Accounting Literature*, Vol. 18.

Chanchani, S. and Willett, R. (2004) 'An empirical assessment of Gray's accounting value constructs', *International Journal of Accounting*, Vol. 39, No. 2.

Choi, F.D.S. and Meek, G.K. (2005) *International Accounting*, Prentice-Hall, Upper Saddle River, NJ.

Cooke, T.E. (1993) 'The impact of accounting principles on profits: the US versus Japan', *Accounting and Business Research*, Autumn, Vol. 23, No. 32.

David, R. and Brierley, J.E.C. (1985) *Major Legal Systems in the World Today*, Stevens.

Davidson, S. and Kohlmeier, J. (1966) 'A measure of the impact of some foreign accounting principles', *Journal of Accounting Research*, Vol. 4, No. 2.

Doupnik, T. and Salter, S. (1995) 'External environment, culture, and accounting practice: a preliminary test of a general model of international accounting development', *International Journal of Accounting*, Vol. 30, No. 3.

Doupnik, T.S. and Tsakumis, G.T. (2004) 'A critical review of tests of Gray's theory of cultural relevance and suggestions for future research', *Journal of Accounting Literature*, Vol. 23.

Evans, L. and Nobes, C.W. (1996) 'Some mysteries relating to the prudence principle in the Fourth Directive and in German and British law', *European Accounting Review*, Vol. 5, No. 2.

Flint, D. (1982) *A True and Fair View*, Gee, London.

Frank, W.G. (1979) 'An empirical analysis of international accounting principles', *Journal of Accounting Research*, Vol. 17, No. 2.

Franks, J. and Mayer, C. (2001) 'Ownership and control of German corporations', *Review of Financial Studies*, Vol. 14, No. 4.

Gray, S.J. (1980) 'The impact of international accounting differences from a security-analysis perspective: some European evidence', *Journal of Accounting Research*, Vol. 18, No. 1.

Gray, S.J. (1988) 'Towards a theory of cultural influence on the development of accounting systems internationally', *Abacus*, Vol. 24, No. 1.

Guenther, D.A. and Young, D. (2000) 'The association between financial accounting measures and real economic activity: a multinational study', *Journal of Accounting and Economics*, Vol. 29, No. 1.

Haller, A. (1992) 'The relationship of financial and tax accounting in Germany: a major reason for accounting disharmony in Europe', *International Journal of Accounting*, Vol. 27, No. 4.

Hellman, N. (1993) 'A comparative analysis of the impact of accounting differences of profits and return on equity: differences between Swedish practice and US GAAP', *European Accounting Review*, Vol. 2, No. 3.

Hofstede, G. (1980) *Culture's Consequences: International Differences in Work-Related Values*, Sage Publications, Beverley Hills.

Hofstede, G. (1984) 'Cultural dimensions in management and planning', *Asia Pacific Journal of Management*, January.

Hofstede, G. (2003) 'What is culture? A reply to Baskerville', *Accounting, Organizations and Society*, Vol. 28, Nos 7–8.

Hoogendoorn, M. (1996) 'Accounting and taxation in Europe – a comparative overview', *European Accounting Review*, Vol. 5, Supplement.

Hung, M. (2000) 'Accounting standards and value relevance of financial statements: an inter-national analysis', *Journal of Accounting and Economics*, Vol. 30, No. 3.

Jaggi, B. and Low, P.Y. (2000) 'Impact of culture, market forces, and legal system on financial disclosures', *International Journal of Accounting*, Vol. 35, No. 4.

La Porta, R., Lopez-de-Silanes, F., Shleifer, A. and Vishny, R.W. (1997) 'Legal determinants of external finance', *Journal of Finance*, Vol. 52, No. 3.

La Porta, R., Lopez-de-Silanes, F., Shleifer, A. and Vishny, R.W. (1998) 'Law and finance', *Journal of Political Economy*, Vol. 106, No. 6.

Lamb, M., Nobes, C.W. and Roberts, A.D. (1998) 'International variations in the connections between tax and financial reporting', *Accounting and Business Research*, Vol. 28, No. 3.

Nobes, C.W. (1993) 'The true and fair view requirement: impact on and of the Fourth Directive', *Accounting and Business Research*, Vol. 24, Winter.

Nobes, C.W. (1998) 'Towards a general model of the reasons for international differences in financial reporting', *Abacus*, Vol. 34, No. 2.

Nobes, C.W. and Schwencke, H.R. (2006) 'Tax and financial reporting links: a longitudinal examination over 30 years up to IFRS adoption, using Norway as a case study', *European Accounting Review*, Vol. 15, No. 1.

Norton, J. (1995) 'The impact of financial accounting practices on the measurement of profit and equity: Australia versus the United States', *Abacus*, Vol. 31, No. 2.

Parker, R.H. (1994) 'Context, diversity and harmonization', Ch. 1 in T.E. Cooke and R.H. Parker (eds), *Financial Reporting in the West Pacific Rim*, Routledge, London.

Parker, R.H. and Nobes, C.W. (1994) *An International View of True and Fair Accounting*, Routledge, London.

Radebaugh, L., Gray, S. and Black E.L. (2006) *International Accounting and Multinational Enterprises*, Wiley, New York.

Roe, M.J. (2003) *Political Determinants of Corporate Governance*, Oxford University Press, Oxford.

Rueschhoff, N.G. and Strupeck, C.D. (1998) 'Equity returns: local GAAP versus US GAAP for foreign issuers from developing countries', *International Journal of Accounting*, Vol. 33, No. 3.

Ryan, S.G. (2006) 'Identifying conditional conservatism', *European Accounting Review*, Vol. 15, No. 4.

Salter, S.B. and Niswander, F. (1995) 'Cultural influence on the development of accounting systems internationally: a test of Gray's [1988] theory', *Journal of International Business Studies*, Vol. 26, No. 2.

Soeters, J. and Schreuder, H. (1988) 'The interaction between national and organizational cultures in accounting firms', *Accounting, Organizations and Society*, Vol. 13, No. 1.

Street, D.L., Nichols, N.B. and Gray, S.J. (2000) 'Assessing the acceptability of international accounting standards in the US: an empirical study of the materiality of US GAAP reconciliations by non-US companies complying with IASC standards', *International Journal of Accounting*, Vol. 35, No. 1.

Tarca, A., Moy, M. and Morris, R.D. (2005) 'An investigation of the relationship between use of international accounting standards and sources of company finance in Germany', paper presented at the University of Sydney, 31.3.2005, under journal review.

Tucker, J. (1994) 'Capital structure: an econometric perspective on Europe', in J. Pointon (ed.), *Issues in Business Taxation*, Avebury, Aldershot.

Tweedie, D.P. and Whittington, G. (1984) *The Debate on Inflation Accounting*, Cambridge University Press, Cambridge.

Tyrrall, D., Woodward, D. and Rakhimbekova, A. (2007) 'The relevance of International Financial Reporting Standards to a developing country: evidence from Kazakhstan', *International Journal of Accounting*, Vol. 42, No. 1.

van Caenegem, R.C. (1988) *The Birth of the English Common Law*, Cambridge University Press, Cambridge.

Weetman, P. and Gray, S.J. (1991) 'A comparative international analysis of the impact of accounting principles on profits: the USA versus the UK, Sweden and the Netherlands', *Accounting and Business Research*, Autumn, Vol. 21, No. 84.

Weetman, P., Jones, E.A.E., Adams, C.A. and Gray, S.J. (1998) 'Profit measurement and UK accounting standards: a case of increasing disharmony in relation to US GAAP and IASs', *Accounting and Business Research*, Summer, Vol. 28, No. 3.

Whittington, M. (2000) 'Problems in comparing financial performance across international boundaries: a case study approach', *International Journal of Accounting*, Vol. 35, No. 3.

Xiao, J.Z., Weetman, P. and Sun, M. (2004) 'Political influence and coexistence of a uniform accounting system and accounting standards: recent developments in China', *Abacus*, Vol. 40, No. 2.

Zambon, S. (1998) 'Twin accounting? A closer look at the compatibility of accounting practices of UK companies with US GAAP', University of Reading, Department of Economics, Discussion Papers, Series D, X(57).

Zambon, S. and Dick, W. (1998) 'Alternative standards (IAS/US GAAP) and continental European accounts: evidences of a competitive process', University of Reading, Department of Economics, Discussion Papers, Series D, X(58).

Zeghal, D. and Mhedhbi, K. (2006) 'An analysis affecting the adoption of international accounting standards by developing countries', *International Journal of Accounting*, Vol. 41, No. 4.

Zysman, J. (1983) *Governments, Markets and Growth: Financial Systems and the Politics of Industrial Change*, Cornell University Press, Ithaca.

QUESTIONS

Suggested answers to the asterisked questions are given at the end of the book.

2.1∗ 'The basic cause of international differences in financial reporting practices is the different degree of interference by governments in accounting.' Discuss.

2.2∗ Assess the view that accidents of history are primarily responsible for international differences in corporate financial reporting.

2.3 If you were trying to predict which financial reporting regulations and practices would be found in various African countries, which non-accounting variables would you measure?

2.4 Explain how international differences in the ownership and financing of companies could lead to differences in financial reporting.

2.5 Do international differences in the rules for the calculation of taxable income cause accounting differences, or is the influence the other way round?

2.6 Why is it difficult to establish a causal relationship between specific external factors and international differences in accounting? Discuss the methodological problems in identifying possible causes.

2.7 How do the causal factors discussed in the chapter affect corporate governance structures in different countries?

2.8 Are the international differences in the formats of financial statements a major obstacle to comparing the statements?

2.9 Explain, using several different accounting topics, in what ways domestic German accounting rules are more conservative than IFRS.

3 International classification of financial reporting

Christopher Nobes

After reading this chapter, you should be able to:

● explain why classification can be useful in the natural and political sciences and in the study of accounting;

● outline the classifications of national accounting systems that have been developed, distinguishing between those based on influences and those based on actual practices;

● show why it is important to be clear what is being classified: practices or regulations, regulations or regulatory systems, practices of all companies or only of listed companies, measurement practices or disclosure practices, countries or sets of financial statements;

● outline which countries can be classified with which others, depending on what is being classified;

● critically appraise the classifications in the literature.

3.1   Introduction

Chapter 2 discussed the causes and nature of international differences in financial accounting practices. Already it has been useful to note similarities between groups of countries, and to divide countries into two main classes for some purposes. This chapter is devoted to a more detailed examination of whether it is possible to classify countries by their accounting similarities and differences. First, it is useful to discuss the nature of classification in natural sciences and social sciences. This is done in Sections 3.2 and 3.3, which are followed by an examination of the purpose of classification in accounting. It is possible to divide classifications into those based on external factors (Section 3.5) and those based on accounting practices (Sections 3.6 to 3.8). Section 3.10 presents a classification of the classifications.

A major introductory point is that many countries now exhibit at least two systems of financial reporting, in addition to accounting that may be done for tax or other private purposes. For example, in France, the consolidated statements of listed companies use International Financial Reporting Standards (IFRS) whereas individual French companies, whether members of a group or not, use French national rules. The majority of the research work on classification was done in a period before this development, which relates particularly to 2005 onwards. Therefore, for readers only interested in the consolidated statements of listed companies, those classification studies are primarily of historical interest.

Nevertheless, the bulk of financial reporting (i.e. all unconsolidated statements and some consolidated statements) in many countries still follows domestic rules. So, international differences are still important. Even so, the domestic rules of some countries are themselves being harmonized with IFRS or US rules so the differences are becoming less dramatic. It is important to distinguish between this process of 'convergence' and the adoption of IFRS for certain purposes within a country. More subtly, international differences may survive in the form of different interpretations of IFRS or different choices of options. This is taken further in Chapters 4 and 7.

Studying classification is a useful prelude to the study of harmonization (Chapter 4) and to the study of domestic rules (Chapter 15).

3.2 The nature of classification

Classification is one of the basic tools of a scientist. The Mendeleev table of elements and the Linnaean system of classification are fundamental to chemistry and biology respectively. Classification should sharpen description and analysis; it should reveal underlying structures and enable prediction of the properties of an element based on its place in a classification. Classification may also provide an insight into what elements once existed, might exist in the future, or do exist and wait to be discovered.

It has been said that there are four properties necessary in a classification (AAA, 1977, pages 77–8). First, the characteristics of classification should be adhered to consistently. That is, throughout any classification the characteristics used as the means of differentiating one element from another should be the same. Different purposes for a classification will lead to the use of different characteristics. Second, a good classification will potentially contain sufficient subsets to exhaust a given universe. Third, all subsets will be mutually exclusive in such a way that no element may fall into more than one of them. Last, hierarchical integrity should be observed; for example, in the Linnaean biological classification, any specific species of plant or animal is always in the bottom tier of the classification, always belongs to a genus, which always belongs to a family, and so on. Roberts (1995, pages 653–5) examines and criticizes these properties.

Different types of classification are possible, from the simplest form of dichotomous grouping (e.g. things black versus things white) or rank ordering (e.g. by height of students in a class) to more complex dimensioning (such as the periodic table) or systematizing (such as the Linnaean system). Two ways of grouping elements used in social science are 'multidimensional scaling' and 'morphological structuring'. The first uses two or more characteristics on different axes to try to find clusters of elements displaying similar characteristics. The second seeks to compose a 'morphology' that lists elements by important differentiating factors. It should then be clearer which elements are similar to each other (see, for example, Figure 3.1, overleaf).

3.3 Classifications by social scientists

Having briefly looked at the nature of classification and the techniques used to achieve it, it may be useful to examine traditional methods of classification in areas close to accounting. There have been classifications of political, economic and legal systems. For example, political systems have been grouped into political democracies, tutelary democracies, modernizing oligarchies, totalitarian oligarchies and traditional oligarchies (Shils, 1966). Economic systems have been divided into capitalism, socialism, communism and fascism. Another classification is: traditional

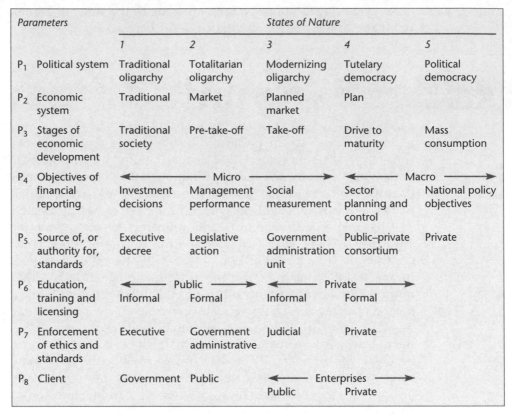

Parameters		States of Nature				
		1	2	3	4	5
P_1	Political system	Traditional oligarchy	Totalitarian oligarchy	Modernizing oligarchy	Tutelary democracy	Political democracy
P_2	Economic system	Traditional	Market	Planned market	Plan	
P_3	Stages of economic development	Traditional society	Pre-take-off	Take-off	Drive to maturity	Mass consumption
P_4	Objectives of financial reporting	←————— Micro —————→			←——— Macro ———→	
		Investment decisions	Management performance	Social measurement	Sector planning and control	National policy objectives
P_5	Source of, or authority for, standards	Executive decree	Legislative action	Government administration unit	Public–private consortium	Private
P_6	Education, training and licensing	←——— Public ———→		←——— Private ———→		
		Informal	Formal	Informal	Formal	
P_7	Enforcement of ethics and standards	Executive	Government administrative	Judicial	Private	
P_8	Client	Government	Public	←——— Enterprises ———→		
				Public	Private	

Figure 3.1 The AAA's morphology for comparative accounting systems

Source: Adapted from American Accounting Association (1977) *Accounting Review, Supplement to Vol. 52*, p. 99. Copyright © 1977 American Accounting Association. Reproduced with permission.

economies, market economies and planned economies (Neuberger and Duffy, 1976). Legal systems have also been classified (Kagan, 1955; Derrett, 1968; David and Brierley, 1985). One set of authors, while classifying legal systems, has supplied practical criteria for determining whether two systems are in the same group: systems are said to be in the same group if 'someone educated in . . . one law will then be capable, without much difficulty, of handling [the other]' (David and Brierley, 1985, page 21). Also, the two systems must not be 'founded on opposed philosophical, political or economic principles'. The second criterion ensures that systems in the same group not only have similar superficial characteristics, but also have similar fundamental structures and are likely to react to new circumstances in similar ways. Using these criteria a four-group classification was obtained by David and Brierley: Romano–Germanic, Common Law, Socialist and Philosophical–Religious.

In all the above examples, the type of classification used was rudimentary, involving no more than splitting systems into a few groups. The groups within the classifications were sometimes not precisely defined or exhaustive. Also, the method used to determine and fill the groups was little more than subjective classification based on personal knowledge or descriptive literature. These shortcomings are very difficult to avoid because of the complexity and 'greyness' in the social sciences.

3.4 Classifications in accounting

It was suggested in Chapter 2 that the expression 'accounting system' would be used to mean the financial reporting practices used by a company. Systems could be classified into groups by similarities and differences. If all or most of the enterprises in a country use very similar accounting practices, this might suggest that countries can be classified on the basis of accounting practices. Even then, the system used in the country might change from year to year. In the discussion that follows, it becomes clear that various researchers have been trying to classify various objects, not necessarily accounting systems in the above sense.

The reasons for wanting to classify financial reporting 'systems' into groups include the general reasons for classification in any science, as outlined above. Classification should be an efficient way of describing and comparing different systems. It should help to chart the progress of a country as it moves from use of one system to another, and the progress of ideas of a dominant country's system by noting the other national systems grouped around it. The activity involved in preparing a classification (e.g. multidimensional scaling or morphological structuring, as referred to above) should encourage precision. Moreover, in the social sciences, classification may be used to help shape development rather than merely to describe how and why things are. For example, classification should facilitate a study of the logic of and the difficulties facing harmonization. This should be valuable both for academics and for those organizing harmonization, or measuring it (Doupnik, 1987). Classification should also assist in the training of accountants and auditors who operate internationally. Further, a developing country might be better able to understand the available types of financial reporting, and which one would be most appropriate for it, by studying a morphology and seeing which other countries use particular systems. Also, it should be possible for a country to predict the problems that it is about to face and the solutions that might work by looking at other countries in its group.

It has also been suggested that a way for a country to change from one accounting system to another may be to adjust the economic and political parameters to those more conducive to the desired system (AAA, 1977, page 100). However, this might seem like trying to wag a tail by moving the dog.

The next section contains a summary of some classification attempts which were based on observing characteristics other than accounting practices. Such classifications may be called 'extrinsic'; for example, a classification may be based on factors influencing the development of accounting. Of course, different conclusions about which of these factors are important (see Chapter 2) will lead to different classifications.

Whether a classification is properly described as 'extrinsic' depends on what is being classified. For example, one of the classifications described as extrinsic in the next section concerns regulatory systems. This is because the central subject matter here is the accounting practices of companies and the content of the rules that control them. These are influenced by economic and other factors, and they operate within regulatory systems. By contrast, in the context of a chapter focused on regulatory systems, a classification based directly on the nature of those systems would be intrinsic.

The so-called 'intrinsic' studies of Sections 3.6 to 3.8 are also mostly at one remove from financial reporting *practices* because they are mostly based on the content of the rules of reporting rather than on the practices. Again, it is helpful to focus on what is being classified. In many cases, the objects of classification are countries, and they are classified by the nature of financial reporting rules/practices of a set of companies. As explained later, it would be better to classify financial reporting systems themselves, and to do so by their key characteristics.

3.5   Extrinsic classifications

3.5.1   Mueller's classifications

In the late 1960s, Professor Gerhard Mueller broke new ground by preparing international classifications of accounting (Mueller, 1967) and of business environments (Mueller, 1968). His classification of accounting systems into four patterns of development is a simple grouping that is not accompanied by an explanation of the method used to obtain it. However, the 'range of four is considered sufficient to embrace accounting as it is presently known and practised in various parts of the globe' (Mueller, 1967, page 2). Each group is illustrated by one or two examples. Perhaps it is not reasonable to expect a more sophisticated classification in a pioneering work, and perhaps Mueller's informed judgement was one of the best methods of classification available.

Mueller stresses that the types of accounting rules that exist in a country are a product of economic, political and other environments, which have determined the nature of the system. This also suggests that other countries' rules would not be appropriate to that country and that rules must be chosen to fit a country's needs. Consequently, doubt is cast on the possibility and usefulness of harmonization. Mueller's four groups, which are usefully summarized in a later work (Choi and Meek, 2005, Chapter 2) are as follows:

1 *Accounting within a macroeconomic framework*. In this group, accounting has developed as an adjunct of national economic policies. We might expect such financial accounting to stress value added statements, to encourage income smoothing, to be equivalent to tax accounting and to include social responsibility accounting. Sweden was said to be an example.

2 *The microeconomic approach*. This approach can prosper in a market-oriented economy that has individual private businesses at the core of its economic affairs. The influence of microeconomics has led accounting to try to reflect economic reality in its measurements and valuations. This means that accounting rules must be sophisticated but flexible. Developments such as replacement cost accounting will be accepted most readily in such systems. The Netherlands was suggested as an example.

3 *Accounting as an independent discipline*. Systems of this sort have developed independently of governments or economic theories. Accounting has developed in business, has faced problems when they arrived and has adopted solutions which

worked. Theory is held in little regard and turned to only in emergencies or used *ex post* in an attempt to justify practical conclusions. Expressions such as 'generally accepted accounting principles' are typical. Mueller recognized the accounting systems of the United Kingdom and the United States as examples.

4 *Uniform accounting.* Such systems have developed where governments have used accounting as a part of the administrative control of business. Accounting can be used to measure performance, allocate funds, assess the size of industries and resources, control prices, collect taxation, manipulate sectors of business, and so on. It involves standardization of definitions, measurements and presentation. France was cited as an example.

Mueller was not classifying financial reporting systems directly, on the basis of differences in *practices*, but indirectly, on the basis of differences in the importance of economic, governmental and business factors in the development of particular systems. However, one might expect that systems that have developed in a similar way would have similar accounting practices. To an extent, this is true. Chapter 2 of this book has suggested that the United Kingdom and United States have similar accounting practices; Mueller's developmental classification also puts them together.

Nevertheless, there are a few problems with Mueller's classification. The fact that there are only four exclusive groups and no hierarchy reduces the usefulness of the classification. The Netherlands is the only country in one of the groups and the classification does not show whether Dutch accounting is closer to Anglo-Saxon accounting than it is to Swedish accounting. Similarly, the classification cannot include such facts as that German accounting exhibits features that remind one of macroeconomic accounting as well as uniform accounting. Communist accounting was left out entirely, but this may, of course, be sensible if the classification is dealing with published financial reporting, because there was none.

Another problem has developed over time, which is that the classification is now out of date. For example, Sweden moved towards Anglo-American accounting, particularly in the 1990s; and the Netherlands largely abandoned its replacement cost accounting. However, Mueller's classification remains of historical importance.

Mueller's second classification (1968) is of business environments. He makes the point that different business environments need different accounting systems and that this should be considered when trying to change or standardize accounting. Using estimates of economic development, business complexity, political and social climate, and legal system, Mueller identifies 10 groupings. This is not a classification of financial reporting and is perhaps too general to be of help in such a classification. For example, one group – 'the developing nations of the Near and Far East' – might be argued by some to *need* similar accounting systems, but it certainly did not have them.

3.5.2 Morphologies

It has been mentioned that one way to obtain a classification is to draw up a morphology and to use empirical data with this to obtain clustering. Morphologies of accounting practice have been drawn up by Buckley and Buckley (1974) and by the AAA (1977, page 99). The latter's is reproduced as Figure 3.1. Although such parameters as the first two (political and economic systems) may seem less relevant than actual characteristics of accounting practice, it may well be important to include them in order to avoid misclassification based on temporary superficial similarities. As the AAA's Committee on International Accounting notes, 'Parameters . . . P_1 and P_2 are viewed as being pivotal to the type of accounting system which does (or can) emerge' (page 97). Unfortunately, these morphologies have not yet been taken further by combining them with empirical data.

3.5.3 Spheres of influence

There have been some 'subjective' classifications based on 'zones of influence'. Seidler (1967) suggested three groups: British, American and continental European. Also, the AAA's committee produced a subjective classification of five 'zones of influence' on accounting systems (AAA, 1977, pages 105 and 129–30). These are as follows:

1 British;
2 French–Spanish–Portuguese;
3 German–Dutch;
4 US;
5 Communist.

This classification is perhaps most useful in the context of developing countries, where cultural influences from elsewhere may be overwhelming, as discussed in Chapter 2. It seems less appropriate as a third general method of classifying financial reporting, after the direct (practices) and indirect (environment) approaches mentioned above. This is because it has no hierarchy and thus does not take account, for example, of the links between British and US accounting. Further, to call a group 'German–Dutch' seems inappropriate as a way of classifying developed financial reporting systems when examined in the light of the material in Chapters 2 and 11.

3.5.4 Cultural classification

As noted in Chapter 2, Gray (1988) uses Hofstede's (1980) cultural classification in order to propose explanations for international differences in accounting practices. Clearly, a cultural classification could then be used to propose an accounting classification, and Gray (1988, pages 12 and 13) makes preliminary suggestions along those lines. Others (e.g. Doupnik and Salter, 1995) also make use of Hofstede's factors in the context of accounting classification.

It was suggested in Chapter 2 that it may be more useful to see culture as a background influence on the causes of international accounting differences. This idea is taken up later in this chapter.

3.5.5 Classification of accounting by regulatory style

Puxty *et al.* (1987) use the work of Streeck and Schmitter (1985) to suggest that there are three limiting and ideal cases of regulation: through the 'market', the 'state' and

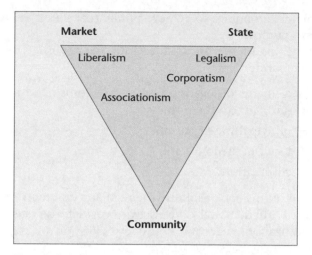

Figure 3.2 **Regulation of financial reporting**

Source: Adapted from Puxty *et al.* (1987), 'Modes of regulation in advanced capitalism: locating accountancy in four countries', *Accounting Organizations and Society*, Vol.12, p. 283. Copyright © 1987 Elsevier Science. Reproduced with permission.

the 'community'. If the process is left entirely to market forces, each company chooses its own rules, influenced only by pressures from, in particular, the capital market. To some extent this was the position in the 'unregulated economy' of nineteenth-century Britain, and in the United States before the establishment of the SEC, where some companies voluntarily published accounting information and subjected themselves to audit (Watts and Zimmerman, 1983). At another extreme the whole process can be in the hands of the 'state', an organ of which decrees which practices are to be followed and provides an enforcement mechanism. As we shall see later, this can be accomplished in a number of different ways. The third ideal case is the emergence of rules through the 'spontaneous solidarity' of the community.

Within these three extremes, Puxty *et al.* usefully distinguish what they and others term 'liberalism', 'associationism', 'corporatism' and 'legalism'. As Figure 3.2 shows, in accounting regulation, the market and the state have predominated over the community. The four modes of Puxty *et al.* form a continuum: at one extreme is liberalism, whereby regulation is provided exclusively by the discipline of the market, while companies provide information only if it is demanded commercially; at the other is legalism, which relies upon the unreserved application of state principles. Accounting practice is expected to follow the letter of the law, which is enforced by the state's monopoly of the means of coercion.

Within these two extremes are associationism and corporatism, both of which combine liberalism and legalism with a small dose of community influence. In associationism, regulation is accomplished through the development of organizations that are formed to represent and advance the interests of their members. These members form, of course, part of the community but do not represent it as a whole. Corporatism involves a greater reliance upon the state principle of hierarchical control. The state does not simply license the existence of organized interest groups but incorporates them into its own centralized, hierarchical system of regulation. The basic difference between corporatism and associationism is the extent to which the state 'leans' on interest groupings to achieve public (i.e. state), as contrasted with private (i.e. market), purposes.

Puxty *et al.* apply this framework to the United States, the United Kingdom, Germany and Sweden, as follows:

- *United States*: elements of legalism and associationism, with the latter subordinated to the former;
- *United Kingdom*: principally associationist;
- *Germany*: legalism predominant;
- *Sweden*: corporatism.

Chapters 9 and 14 of this book examine the regulatory systems in three of these (and other) countries. International differences in regulatory systems have largely survived the harmonization of accounting. A classification by regulatory style is suggested by Nobes (1992a, pages 99–103).

3.5.6 Competencies of auditors

Shoenthal (1989) purports to show that the skills of newly qualified auditors in the United Kingdom and the United States could be used as a classifying variable. However, there must be doubt whether this variable picks up anything relevant; and a two-country study can tell us nothing about classification except that the two countries are different (Nobes, 1992b; Shoenthal, 1992).

3.6   Intrinsic classifications: 1970s and 1980s

3.6.1 Introduction

Some researchers have tried to classify by measuring accounting directly, either using the data collected by others or by generating their own. In most of these cases, the data relates to accounting rules (or to a mixture of rules and practices) rather than to accounting practices alone.

An early attempt at classification and some more recent descriptions of different national systems form the background to modern intrinsic classifications. There is evidence for a three-group classification (United Kingdom, United States and Continental) being used from the beginning of the twentieth century (Hatfield, of 1911 but published in 1966). Other descriptions and analyses, such as those by Zeff (1972), Price Waterhouse (1973, 1975 and 1979), AICPA (1964 and 1975), Coopers & Lybrand (1993), Alexander and Archer (2001) and Ordelheide and KPMG (1995 and 2001), provide the raw material for intrinsic classification.

3.6.2 Classifications using clustering

Da Costa, Bourgeois and Lawson (1978) produced a classification directly based on accounting practices, using the Price Waterhouse (1973; hereafter PW) *Survey in*

Table 3.1 **Classification based on 1973 measurement practices**

British Commonwealth model	Latin American model	Continental European model	United States model
Australia	Argentina	Belgium	Canada
Bahamas	Bolivia	France	Japan
Eire	Brazil	Germany	Mexico
Fiji	Chile	Italy	Panama
Jamaica	Colombia	Spain	Philippines
Kenya	Ethiopia	Sweden	United States
Netherlands	India	Switzerland	
New Zealand	Paraguay	Venezuela	
Pakistan	Peru		
Rhodesia	Uruguay		
Singapore			
South Africa			
Trinidad and Tobago			
United Kingdom			

Source: Nair, R.D. and Frank, W.G. (1980) 'The impact of disclosure and measurement practices on international accounting classifications', *Accounting Review*, Vol. 55, No. 3, p. 429. Reproduced with permission of the American Accounting Association.

38 Countries. Clustering produced two groups: one contained the United Kingdom and nine former members of the British Empire; the other contained the United States, France, Germany, South American countries, and all others except for the Netherlands and Canada which were said to be unclassifiable.

Another researcher (Frank, 1979) used the same data and similar (though more elaborate) analysis, but produced what seems to be a much more reasonable classification. This work was extended by Nair and Frank (1980). Here the 1973 and the 1975 PW Surveys are used, and the financial reporting characteristics are divided into those relating to measurement and those relating to disclosure. This is a useful differentiation, particularly because of the effect it has on the classification of countries such as Germany that had advanced disclosure requirements. Frank (1979) classified Germany in a 'US group' but, by using 'measurement' characteristics only, Nair and Frank (1980) classify Germany in the 'continental European' group. Table 3.1 represents the classification using 1973 measurement characteristics. As yet there is no hierarchy, but the overall results do seem plausible and fit well with the analysis in previous chapters of this book. However, there are two major types of problem with these classifications that must now be dealt with, relating to the data and the methodology.

The data

Doubts have been expressed about the use of the PW data for the purpose of classification (Nobes, 1981). Four types of problem with the 1973 data were noted: (a) straightforward mistakes; (b) misleading answers; (c) swamping of important questions by trivial ones; and (d) exaggeration of the differences between the

United States and the United Kingdom because of the familiarity of these countries (and thus their differences) to the compilers of the survey questions. The examples from the 1973 survey will not be repeated here, but an error in the 1979 survey will be mentioned.

Taking consolidation practices as an example, the survey reported that for practice 209 ('consolidated statements . . . are prepared for the shareholders') the answer was 'required' in France. The reason given for this was that the *Commission des Opérations de Bourse* (COB) 'requires' consolidation. However, as the Annual Reports of the COB showed, only 305 listed companies published consolidated balance sheets and income statements in 1979 (289 in 1978). This is less than half of the listed companies, and a very much smaller proportion of 'enterprises which issue their statements to the general public', about which the survey was said to be constructed (PW, 1979, page 5).

These examples could be replicated many times over. They suggest that, at some points, the surveys reported not on actual practices but on what practices might have been if non-mandatory rules had been obeyed, or on what PW partners might have liked practices to have been. The general problem is that the publications mix rules and practices together. This and the other types of error suggest that the data were unsatisfactory for the purposes of classification. At the least, substantial caution is called for when interpreting the results.

The methodology

All the researchers cited above use cluster analysis based on the PW data and appear to consider that this may be superior to previous subjective classifications. Nair and Frank state (1980) that their research is '. . . aimed at empirically assessing the validity of international classifications proposed repeatedly in the accounting literature' (page 449).

This version of 'empiricism' must be challenged. It does not directly test a particular hypothetical classification. It classifies a mass of data that was not collected with the purpose of classification in mind. The use of this approach leads one of the sets of researchers referred to above (Da Costa *et al.*, 1978, page 79) to conclude that the country least like the UK group is the United States; in other words, accounting in Uruguay or Ethiopia was considered more like accounting in the United Kingdom than accounting in the United States was. While this may have been a statistically sound result from the PW data, it was clearly a very inaccurate representation of the real world (see Section 3.9). By itself such a result is of interest, but the researchers, who were generating a hypothesis from doubtful data rather than testing one, fell into the trap of taking their results seriously. This led them to conclude that a group of countries containing France, Germany, Belgium and Italy, among others, 'follows the lead of the United States in dissociating itself from practice common to the British model'. However, it seems highly unlikely that the makers of the company and tax laws that govern accounting in such countries bore in mind either that they should follow the United States or that they should dissociate themselves from the United Kingdom when legislating. The differences between the United States and continental European countries are known to have been great, and also suggest that there was no accidental or subconscious 'following' of the former by the latter (Chapter 15).

The problem that these examples illustrate stems from the use of data that contained errors and that were not designed for the purpose in hand. Turning to the Linnaean biological system for an analogy, to the extent that judgement and empiricism can be counterposed, the life scientists use a large measure of the former. Exactly which criteria to use for a classification of living things, and what weight to give them, is a matter of judgement. Judgement is needed to avoid such classifications as Plato's of man as a featherless biped. In fact, man is not now seen to be close to birds but to be much more closely related to most quadrupeds, and to dolphins which appear to have no feet at all. Aristotle saw this latter distinction. He referred to 'homologues', where objects similar in structure play different roles (e.g. human feet and dolphins' flippers), and to 'analogues', where similar functions are performed by quite different objects (e.g. birds' wings and bees' wings, which have entirely different structures, the former being 'arms'). It is the homologues that indicate nearness in relationship.

Looking in more detail at the Linnaean biological classification we can note that, when classifying animals, biologists largely ignore the most obvious characteristics; that is, they do not carry out factor analysis on animals by weight, colour, number of legs, nature of body covering, length of life, etc. This would merely lead to a classification of those data. It would put men with ostriches, dolphins with sharks, bats with owls, and so on. In fact, by concentrating on a subjective model that involves underlying (but less obvious) characteristics, biologists classify men, dolphins and bats more closely with each other than with any of the other three types of animal. It is then found that behaviour, intelligence, reproduction and ancestry begin to fit within the classification. The biological scientists, then, use a classification which is evolutionary and concentrates on underlying fundamental variables.

It should also be noted that botanists have had greater difficulties than zoologists. This perhaps is partly due to the lack of skeletons and comparative lack of fossil remains to look at. The modern approach to biological classification includes an analysis of the degree of similarity of the DNA of various organisms.

The analogy with classification in accounting seems clear. The danger with 'empirical' classifications is that one merely classifies data that concentrate on differences that may be ephemeral and superficial (and that may not be correctly recorded). The need is apparent for a model based on the evolution of accounting practices and upon variables that have caused differences in them. This would then have to be checked against carefully measured 'structural' practices; and one would have to be clear about the purpose of the classification.

3.6.3 Classification using a model and new data

Thus, it would be possible to criticize previous classifications for (a) lack of precision in the definition of what is to be classified; (b) lack of a model with which to compare the statistical results; (c) lack of a hierarchy that would add more subtlety to the portrayal of the size of differences between countries; and (d) lack of judgement in the choice of 'important' discriminating features. Can these problems be remedied? The author attempted to solve them in his own researches (Nobes, 1983), as explained below.

Definition

The purpose of the research was defined as the classification of countries by the financial reporting practices of their *public companies*. The countries chosen were those of the *developed Western world*; the reporting practices were those concerned with *measurement and valuation*. The date of the classification was 1980, before the implementation in EU countries of the Fourth Directive on Company Law (see Chapter 11).

It is public companies whose financial statements are generally available and whose practices can be most easily discovered. It is the international differences in reporting between such companies that are of interest to shareholders, creditors, auditing firms, taxation authorities, managements and harmonizing agencies (such as the International Accounting Standards Board or the European Commission) (Mason, 1978, Chapter 5). It was really only in developed countries that public companies existed in large numbers. However, it would be possible to include more countries by widening the definition of accounting. To some extent this has been tried (Nobes, 1992a, Appendices V and VI).

Measurement and valuation practices were chosen because these determine the size of the figures for profit, capital, total assets, liquidity and so on. Nair and Frank (1980, pages 426 and 428) point out that it is useful to separate measurement from disclosure practices.

A model with a hierarchy

The hypothetical classification similar to that shown in Figure 3.3 was based on some explanatory variables for differences in measurement practices; for example, the importance of the influence of law, or of economics. Some descriptions are included at the branching points in Figure 3.3.

The number of countries is kept to 14. All these are developed nations for reasons noted above; they are all included in the PW surveys and thus in the results of the researchers referred to earlier; and they include all the countries identified as 'vital' by Mason (1978) for the purposes of international harmonization (i.e. France, Japan, Netherlands, the United Kingdom, the United States and Germany).

Previous classifications contained separate groups (e.g. Table 3.1) but no hierarchy that would indicate the comparative distances between the groups. It may be reasonable to classify the United Kingdom and the United States in different groups, but it might be useful to demonstrate that these two groups are closely linked compared with, say, continental European countries.

Discriminating features

An attempt was made to isolate those features of a country's financial reporting practices that may constitute long-run fundamental differences between countries. The result was a selection of nine factors that, unlike the factors of most of the researchers above, are overt and thus available for inspection, criticism and amendment (see Table 3.2).

These factors were designed to be relevant for developed countries which share certain economic features. If one wished to include developing countries, it would

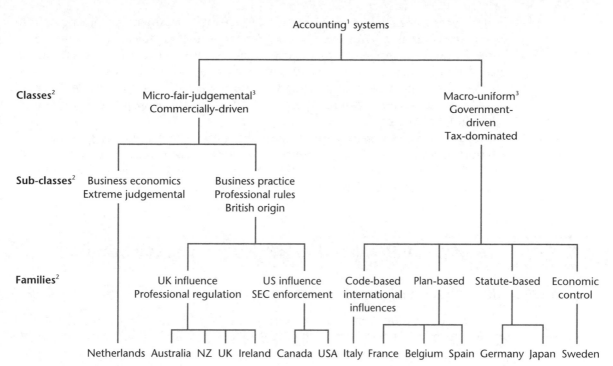

Figure 3.3 A suggested classification of accounting 'systems' in some developed Western countries in 1980

Notes:

[1] This is an abbreviated term for corporate financial reporting.

[2] These terms, borrowed from biology, should be interpreted merely as loose labels.

[3] The terms at these and other branching points are merely labels to be used as shorthand to try to capture some of the attributes of the members of the accounting systems below them. This classification has been prepared by a UK researcher and may contain usage of terms that will mislead those from other cultures.

Table 3.2 Factors for differentiation

1   Type of users of the published accounts of listed companies.
2   Degree to which law or standards prescribe in detail and exclude judgement.
3   Importance of tax rules in measurement.
4   Conservatism/prudence (e.g. valuation of buildings, stocks, debtors).
5   Strictness of application of historical cost (in the main accounts).
6   Susceptibility to replacement cost adjustments in main or supplementary accounts.
7   Consolidation practices.
8   Ability to be generous with provisions (as opposed to reserves) and to smooth income.
9   Uniformity between companies in application of rules.

be necessary to include other discriminating factors, such as the degree of development of economy or nature of economic systems. But such a process might not be sensible because there are few or no public companies in some of these other countries, so that one would have to classify something other than published financial reporting.

It was not a straightforward matter to separate measurement practices from explanatory variables. However, it was clear that at least the first two factors in Table 3.2 were examples of explanatory variables. Other factors were less clear. For example, the 'taxation' factor could have been taken as a factor explaining differences or, by asking whether particular valuations were affected by tax rules, it could have been seen as a measurement practice. All the factors except the first two were taken in this latter sense.

The 14 countries were scored on these nine factors, and then a large number of alternative arithmetical and computer-based tests were used to produce clusters. Very strong support was found for the 'micro/macro' split in Figure 3.3; and considerable support for the more detailed groupings (Nobes, 1983).

3.7   Developments related to the Nobes classification

3.7.1   Classification by degree of standardization

Further classification work has been carried out by Al Najjar (1986), using a similar approach to Nobes (1983) but applying it to a classification of countries by degree of standardization of accounting.

3.7.2   Tests

Doupnik and Salter (1993) tested the Nobes classification using their own measurements of accounting practices. One of the problems with this is that the data used to 'test' the 1980 classification relate to 10 years after it. Later, Doupnik and Salter (1995) suggest a general model about the causes of accounting differences, proposing 10 variables. However, some of the variables seem misspecified, and some seem to overlap with others. For example, Doupnik and Salter use a tax variable, measured on the basis of marginal tax rates, as a proposed cause of accounting differences. Chapter 2 of this book suggests that the international variation in the relationship between tax and accounting is more of a *result* of accounting differences than a *cause* (see Nobes 1998a for more detail). Further, the use of marginal rates seems an inappropriate measure because of the following:

● Tax rates change dramatically over time without any obvious effect on accounting. For example, the top US tax rate fell from 46 per cent to 34 per cent in 1987; and the main rate in the UK rose in 1973 from 40 per cent to 52 per cent, and has now fallen to 28 per cent.

● Many systems have more than one tax rate (e.g. in Germany in 2000, 45 per cent for retained profit but 30 per cent for distributed profit; and, in the UK in that year, 30 per cent for large companies but 20 per cent for small).

● The tax burden depends greatly on the definition of 'taxable income', not just on the tax rate.

● More importantly, in countries with a small connection between tax and accounting the tax rate will have little effect on accounting; and in countries with a close connection, the effect of tax on accounting will be in the same direction and probably almost as strong, whether the rate is 30 per cent or 50 per cent.

Despite these difficulties, Doupnik and Salter's papers provide a large degree of support for the classification in Figure 3.3, particularly for the initial two-class split.

3.7.3 Improvements

The classification in Figure 3.3 contains a hierarchy that borrows its labels from biology. This can be criticized (see below), as can the conflation of Mueller's labels 'macro' and 'uniform' (Feige, 1997a; Nobes and Mueller, 1997; Feige, 1997b). Part of the problem here is that Nobes's classification, like Mueller's, is now historical, although elements of it might survive an update.

Roberts (1995) makes a number of criticisms and clarifications relating to accounting classifications. He points out that the classification in Figure 3.3 is not really evolutionary, although its analogies with biology and use of labels such as 'species' suggest this. Also, the objects being classified appear to be countries, which seems misleading.

In order to improve upon Figure 3.3, we might make it clearer that the classification concerns accounting systems, i.e. the financial reporting practices of a particular company in an annual report. It is possible for all companies in a country at a particular date to be using the same system, or for several different systems to be in use. The most contentious labels (e.g. 'species') will be abandoned and we will admit that the classification is not evolutionary – as indeed the Linnaean system was not originally.

Figure 3.4 shows the classification of some financial reporting systems, as adapted from Nobes (1998a). Some explanation of certain features may be useful. For example, the system 'US GAAP' means the well-defined set of practices required by US regulators to be used by certain US companies (see Chapter 8). Of course, the system changes somewhat over time. Examples of users of the system are SEC-registered US companies, and certain large Japanese companies for their group statements (see Chapter 12). The figure suggests that 'US GAAP' bears a family resemblance to UK and IFRS rules (see Chapters 2 and 6), and is in a class of systems suited to strong equity markets.

3.8   Further intrinsic classification

3.8.1 New data, new classifications

D'Arcy (2001) used the data drawn from Ordelheide and KPMG (1995; hereafter OKPMG) to produce classifications including a dendrogram based on cluster analysis in which 'an Anglo-American cluster, including the UK and the US cannot be found' (page 341). D'Arcy also prepared a two-dimensional diagram derived from multidimensional scaling which shows that 'Switzerland and UK are very close'

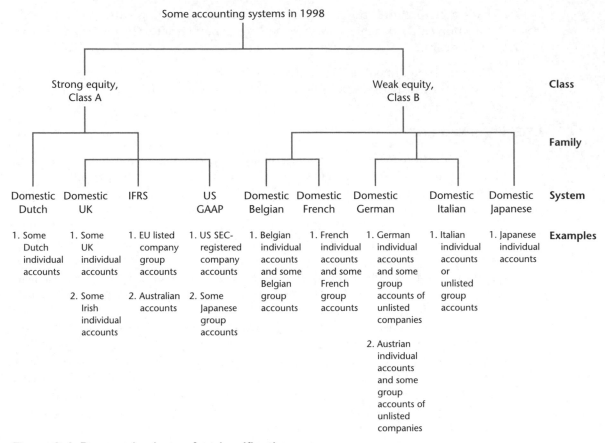

Figure 3.4 Proposed scheme for classification

(page 343), but that Australia is far removed from the UK: 'the Australian system enforces its outsider position by certain requirements and prohibitions' (page 345).

Having arrived at this counter-intuitive result concerning Australia, d'Arcy does not question the data but accepts the result and seeks to explain it. Although d'Arcy uses superior methods, this reminds one of previous classifications based on data that had not been prepared for the purpose of classification. For example, it was noted above that Da Costa *et al.* (1978) attempt to justify, rather than question, why Germany was in the same group as the US but Canada was not, and why UK accounting was apparently less like US accounting than any other in the world.

3.8.2 New data, old problems

The OKPMG data are much more recent than those of Price Waterhouse. They cover fewer countries and are more reliable. Further, they do not mix rules and practices, but are clearly based on rules alone. Nevertheless, there are problems with the data.

First, as with the PW data, the OKPMG data were not collected or designed for the purposes of classification. Therefore, important questions may be missing or may be swamped by less important ones. The second problem is that, unlike PW, the OKPMG data were not already in codable form. D'Arcy (2001) uses careful methods to code them but, according to Nobes (2004), introduces a series of errors in the process. Nobes shows that adjusted data would not lead to a classification with Australia as an outlier and would probably produce an Anglo-Saxon group.

3.9   Is there an Anglo-Saxon group?

As noted above, d'Arcy (2001) did not find an Anglo-American cluster, perhaps due to imperfect data. Cairns (1997) and Alexander and Archer (2000) also cast doubt on the two-group classification of Figures 3.3 and 3.4. Cairns argues, for example, that:

> . . . the distinction between Anglo-American accounting and Continental European accounting is becoming less and less relevant and more and more confused.
> . . . there are now probably far more similarities between American and German accounting than there are between American and British accounting.

Nobes (1998b) agreed that the distinction between the two groups was becoming less stark, partly because of some success by the EU and the IASC, particularly in harmonizing consolidated accounting. He nevertheless proposed that the two-group system still has descriptive power and recent empirical support (see Section 3.7.2 and below). The fact that large German groups are using IFRS or US rules for consolidated statements does not directly affect the German accounting rules themselves.

Alexander and Archer (2000) suggested that it is a myth that there is a coherent group of countries that was using Anglo-Saxon accounting. However, much of their discussion concerned not accounting practices but regulatory systems, which are indeed different in the UK and the US (see Section 3.5.5). The introductory chapters of this book have argued that there is a clearly definable Anglo-Saxon grouping in terms of purposes and practices. Nobes (2003) suggests that the 'Anglo-Saxon' hypothesis helps to explain the international accounting developments of the last few years.

There is another type of empirical support for the two-group classification. Guenther and Young (2000) find that accounting earnings in the UK and the US are more closely related to underlying economic activity than are accounting earnings in France and Germany. Hung (2000) finds a difference between the two pairs of countries with respect to the usefulness of aspects of accrual accounting. Ali and Hwang (2000) also find that the link between share prices and financial reporting information is less for countries with bank-oriented rather than market-oriented financial systems.

3.10   A taxonomy of accounting classifications

In order to practise what we preach, we have prepared a classification of several of this chapter's accounting classifications. This is done in order to sharpen description and analysis, and to give order to a large number of facts. The classification in

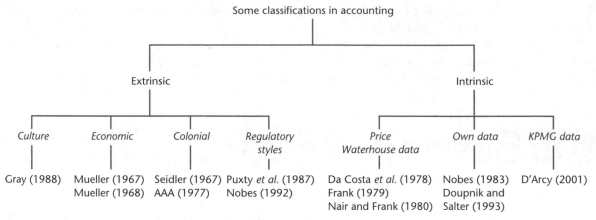

Figure 3.5 A taxonomy of some accounting classifications

Figure 3.5 first divides the classifications into extrinsic and intrinsic on the basis of whether or not their direct subject matter is financial reporting practice or the content of the rules that control it.

The extrinsic studies are then grouped by their main topic: culture, economic and related environments, colonial spheres of influence, or regulatory style. The intrinsic studies are grouped by the source of data. It would also have been relevant to group by whether the data concerned rules or practices, but in several cases there is a mixture.

SUMMARY

- Classification is of fundamental importance to natural scientists, and has also been used in many social sciences. It seems reasonable that we might gain from a classification exercise in comparative international accounting, and that similar rules of classification to those used by scientists might be appropriate. In accounting, such classification may aid understanding and training, and may help to chart the need for, and progress of, harmonization.

- There have been many attempts at classification in international accounting, and there has been much description and data gathering. Mueller's four-group classification of practices and later classification of environments were useful preliminary works. However, the classification of practices would benefit from a hierarchy.

- Other attempts have been made to construct morphologies and to identify 'zones of influence' or the effects of culture.

- Other classification studies have used the Price Waterhouse survey data of 1973–9. The results seem to vary in their plausibility, and there are doubts about the suitability of the data.

- A classification was also proposed by the author. This had a hierarchy and has been tested in a number of ways. Classification studies have been continued in the 1980s and 1990s, benefiting from a number of critiques.

- A classification using the KPMG data of 1995 repeats some of the problems of those using the Price Waterhouse data.

- Some of the classification work is now of historical interest. However, international differences remain in the many countries that have not yet adopted or converged with IFRS for all accounting purposes.

References

AAA (1977) *Accounting Review, Supplement to Vol. 52*, American Accounting Association.

AICPA (1964) *Professional Accounting in 25 Countries*, AICPA, New York.

AICPA (1975) *Professional Accounting in 30 Countries*, AICPA, New York.

Al Najjar, F. (1986) 'Standardization in accounting practices: A comparative international study', *International Journal of Accounting*, Vol. 21, No. 2.

Alexander, D. and Archer, S. (2000) 'On the myth of "Anglo-Saxon" financial accounting', *International Journal of Accounting*, Vol. 35, No. 4.

Alexander, D. and Archer, S. (2001) *European Accounting Guide*, Aspen, New York.

Ali, A. and Hwang, L.-S. (2000) 'Country-specific factors related to financial reporting and the value relevance of accounting data', *Journal of Accounting Research*, Vol. 38, No. 1.

Buckley, J.W. and Buckley, M.H. (1974) *The Accounting Profession*, Melville, Los Angeles, pp. 139–40.

Cairns, D. (1997) 'The future shape of harmonization: a reply', *European Accounting Review*, Vol. 6, No. 2.

Choi, F.D.S. and Meek, G.K. (2005) *International Accounting*, Prentice Hall, New Jersey.

Coopers & Lybrand (1993) *International Accounting Summaries*, Wiley, New York.

Da Costa, R.C., Bourgeois, J.C. and Lawson, W.M. (1978) 'A classification of international financial accounting practices', *International Journal of Accounting*, Vol. 13, No. 2.

D'Arcy, A. (2001) 'Accounting classification and the international harmonisation debate – an empirical investigation', *Accounting, Organizations and Society*, Vol. 26, Nos 4–5.

David, R. and Brierley, J.E.C. (1985) *Major Legal Systems in the World Today*, Stevens, London.

Derrett, J.D.M. (1968) *An Introduction to Legal Systems*, Sweet and Maxwell, Andover.

Doupnik, T.S. (1987) 'Evidence of international harmonization of financial reporting', *International Journal of Accounting*, Vol. 22, No. 1.

Doupnik, T.S. and Salter, S.B. (1993) 'An empirical test of a judgmental international classification of financial reporting practices', *Journal of International Business Studies*, Vol. 24, No. 1.

Doupnik, T.S. and Salter, S.B. (1995) 'External environment, culture and accounting practice: a preliminary test of a general model of international accounting development', *International Journal of Accounting*, Vol. 30, No. 3.

Feige, P. (1997a) 'How "uniform" is financial reporting in Germany? The example of foreign currency translation', *European Accounting Review*, Vol. 6, No. 1.

Feige, P. (1997b) 'Yet more misconceptions concerning the uniformity of German financial reporting', *European Accounting Review*, Vol. 6, No. 4.

Frank, W.G. (1979) 'An empirical analysis of international accounting principles', *Journal of Accounting Research*, Vol. 17, No. 2.

Gray, S.J. (1988) 'Towards a theory of cultural influence on the development of accounting systems internationally', *Abacus*, Vol. 24, No. 1.

Guenther, D.A. and Young, D. (2000) 'The association between financial accounting measures and real economic activity: a multinational study', *Journal of Accounting and Economics*, Vol. 29, No. 1.

Hatfield, H.R. (1966) 'Some variations in accounting practices in England, France, Germany and the US', *Journal of Accounting Research*, Vol. 4, No. 2.

Hofstede, G. (1980) *Culture's Consequences*, Sage Publications, Beverley Hills.

Hung, M. (2000) 'Accounting standards and value relevance of financial statements: an international analysis', *Journal of Accounting and Economics*, Vol. 30, No. 3.

Kagan, K.K. (1955) *Three Great Systems of Jurisprudence*, Stevens, London.

Mason, A.K. (1978) *The Development of International Reporting Standards*, ICRA, Lancaster University, Chapter 6.

Mueller, G.G. (1967) *International Accounting*, Part I, Macmillan, New York.

Mueller, G.G. (1968) 'Accounting principles generally accepted in the US versus those generally accepted elsewhere', *International Journal of Accounting*, Vol. 3, No. 2.

Nair, R.D. and Frank, W.G. (1980) 'The impact of disclosure and measurement practices on international accounting classifications', *Accounting Review*, Vol. 55, No. 3.

Neuberger, E. and Duffy, W. (1976) *Comparative Economic Systems*, Allyn and Bacon, Boston, pp. 96–7.

Nobes, C.W. (1981) 'An empirical analysis of international accounting principles: A comment', *Journal of Accounting Research*, Vol. 19, No. 1.

Nobes, C.W. (1983) 'A judgmental international classification of financial reporting practices', *Journal of Business Finance and Accounting*, Vol. 10, No. 1.

Nobes, C.W. (1992a) *International Classification of Financial Reporting*, Routledge, London.

Nobes, C.W. (1992b) 'Classification by competencies: a comment', *Journal of Business Finance and Accounting*, Vol. 19, No. 1.

Nobes, C.W. (1998a), 'Towards a general model of the reasons for international differences in financial reporting', *Abacus*, Vol. 34, No. 2.

Nobes, C.W. (1998b) 'The future shape of harmonization: some responses', *European Accounting Review*, Vol. 7, No. 2.

Nobes, C.W. (2003) 'On the myth of "Anglo-Saxon" financial accounting: A comment', *International Journal of Accounting*, Vol. 38, No. 1.

Nobes, C.W. (2004) 'On accounting classification and the international harmonisation debate', *Accounting, Organizations and Society*, Vol. 29, No. 2.

Nobes, C.W. and Mueller, G.G. (1997) 'How uniform is financial reporting in Germany?' *European Accounting Review*, Vol. 6, No. 1.

Ordelheide, D. and KPMG (1995) *Transnational Accounting*, Macmillan, London.

Ordelheide, D. and KPMG (2001) *Transnational Accounting*, Palgrave, New York.

Price Waterhouse (1973) *Accounting Principles and Reporting Practices: A Survey in 38 Countries*, ICAEW, London.

Price Waterhouse (1975) *Accounting Principles and Reporting Practices: A Survey in 46 Countries*, ICAEW, London.

Price Waterhouse (1979) *International Survey of Accounting Principles and Reporting Practices*, Butterworth, London.

Puxty, A.G., Willmott, H.C., Cooper, D.J. and Lowe, A.E. (1987) 'Modes of regulation in advanced capitalism: locating accountancy in four countries', *Accounting, Organizations and Society*, Vol. 12, No. 3.

Roberts, A.D. (1995) 'The very idea of classification in international accounting', *Accounting, Organizations and Society*, Vol. 20, Nos 7–8.

Seidler, L.J. (1967) 'International accounting – the ultimate theory course', *Accounting Review*, Vol. 42, No. 4.

Shils, E. (1966) *Political Development in the New States*, Mouton, The Hague.

Shoenthal, E. (1989) 'Classification of accounting systems using competencies as a discriminatory variable: A Great Britain–United States study', *Journal of Business Finance and Accounting*, Vol. 16, No. 4.

Shoenthal, E. (1992) 'Classification by competencies: a reply', *Journal of Business Finance and Accounting*, Vol. 19, No. 1.

Streeck, W. and Schmitter, P.C. (1985) 'Community, market, state – and associations', in their *Private Interest Government and Public Policy*, Sage, Beverley Hills.

Watts, R. and Zimmerman, J. (1983) 'Agency problems, and the theory of the firm: some evidence', *Journal of Law and Economics*, October.

Zeff, S.A. (1972) *Forging Accounting Principles in Five Countries*, Stipes Publishing, Champaign, IL.

QUESTIONS

Suggested answers to the asterisked questions are given at the end of the book.

3.1* In what ways might classification be useful in any field of study? Use international differences in financial reporting as an illustration of your answer.

3.2* 'The essential problems of attempts to classify financial reporting practices across the world are related to the suitability of the data upon which such classifications have been based.' Comment.

3.3 To what extent is differing national culture relevant to an understanding of the causes of accounting differences, and therefore to the process of classification of countries?

3.4 How would you judge the relative success of attempts to provide classifications in comparative international accounting?

3.5 Which of the main models of international classification of accounting do you prefer? Explain your reasoning.

3.6 When producing classifications in the field of comparative international accounting, what should one be classifying?

3.7 The countries listed below are not covered in any detail in this book. Which of the six 'vital' countries (see Section 3.6.3) does each most closely resemble so far as accounting and corporate financial reporting are concerned? Why?

Belgium	New Zealand
Brazil	Nigeria
Finland	Saudi Arabia

3.8 Do the accounting classifications suggest that there is or was such a thing as Anglo-Saxon accounting?

3.9 To what extent have the accounting classifications become irrelevant because of international harmonization?

4 International harmonization

Christopher Nobes

OBJECTIVES

After reading this chapter, you should be able to:

- assess the arguments for and against international harmonization or standardization of financial reporting;
- illustrate how harmonization can be measured;
- outline the history, purpose and activities of the International Accounting Standards Committee (IASC);
- explain how the IASC had different effects in different types of country;
- summarize the relevance of other bodies for harmonization;
- explain the structure and workings of the International Accounting Standards Board.

4.1   Introduction

The preceding (and the following) chapters make it clear that there are major differences in the financial reporting practices of companies around the world. This leads to great complications for those preparing, consolidating, auditing and interpreting published financial statements. Since the preparation of *internal* financial information often overlaps with the preparation of published information, the complications spread further. To combat this, several organizations throughout the world have been involved in attempts to harmonize or standardize accounting. Market forces also contribute to this, as will become clear.

'Harmonization' is a process of increasing the compatibility of accounting practices by setting bounds to their degree of variation. 'Harmony' is the state where compatibility has been achieved. 'Standardization' appears to imply working towards a more rigid and narrow set of rules. However, within accounting, the words have almost become technical terms, and one cannot rely upon the normal differences in their meanings. 'Harmonization' is a word that tends to be associated with the transnational legislation emanating from the European Union; 'standardization' is often associated with the International Accounting Standards Board. From now on, we will generally use 'harmony' and 'harmonization' because they have the wider meaning. It is also important to distinguish between harmonization of rules (*de jure*) and harmonization of practices (*de facto*). Tay and Parker (1990) point out that *de facto* harmonization/standardization is more useful than *de jure* harmonization/standardization. 'Uniformity' is where two or more sets of rules or practices are the same.

In principle, harmony can be achieved without uniformity, and vice versa. Let us take the example of inventory valuation, and the determination of cost according to FIFO (first in, first out) or LIFO (last in, first out). If two sets of rules require FIFO only, then they are *de jure* uniform. This will lead to uniform practice if the rules are properly obeyed. If the two sets of rules are identical and both allow FIFO and LIFO, they might be said to be uniform, but uniform practice need not result. However, if the rules require that any user of LIFO must disclose FIFO information in the notes, full *de facto* harmony might be achieved without full *de facto* uniformity, because the users of different financial statements can all come to the same conclusion about inventory values using the available FIFO information.

As has already been noted, it is possible to have *de jure* harmony without *de facto*, if companies do not comply with rules. By contrast, *de facto* harmony can be achieved without the need for *de jure* harmony when market forces persuade many companies, for example in Switzerland and Japan, to produce English-language financial reports that follow US or IASB rules.

This chapter now looks at the purposes of and obstacles to harmonization. Then, Section 4.3 examines the nature and the work of the International Accounting Standards Committee, which operated from 1973 to 2001. Some other bodies with an interest in harmonization are looked at briefly in Section 4.4, followed by a close look at the IASC's successor, the International Accounting Standards Board (IASB). The IASB's standards themselves are analyzed in Chapter 6. More detail on the EU's harmonization process is found in Chapter 11.

4.2 Reasons for, obstacles to and measurement of harmonization

4.2.1 Reasons for harmonization

The products of accounting in one country are used in various other countries. Consequently, the reasons that make national accounting standards desirable also apply internationally. The pressure for international harmonization comes from those who regulate, prepare and use financial statements.

Investors and financial analysts need to be able to understand the financial statements of foreign companies whose shares they might wish to buy. They would like to be sure that statements from different countries are reliable and comparable, or at least to be clear about the nature and magnitude of the differences. They also need confidence in the soundness of the auditing.

For this reason, various intergovernmental transnational bodies are interested, among other things, in protecting investors within their spheres of influence. Also, in cases where foreign shares are quoted on a stock exchange, that stock exchange or its regulator may demand financial statements that are consistent with domestic practices. In addition, those companies that wish to issue new shares more widely than on their domestic markets will see the advantages of harmonized practices in the promotion of their issues. International credit grantors such as the World Bank must also face the difficulties of comparison. The capital market effects of international accounting differences are examined by Choi and Levich (1990).

These pressures will also be felt by companies that do not operate multinationally. However, for multinationals, the advantages of harmonization are much more important. The great effort of financial accountants to prepare and consolidate financial statements would be much simplified if statements from all round the world were prepared on the same basis. Similarly, the task of preparing comparable internal information for the appraisal of the performance of subsidiaries in different countries would be made much easier. Many aspects of investment appraisal, performance evaluation, and other decision-making uses of management accounting information would benefit from harmonization. The appraisal of foreign companies for potential takeovers would also be greatly facilitated. Multinational companies would also find it easier to transfer accounting staff from one country to another. Above all, if accounting can be made more comparable and reliable, the cost of capital should be brought down by reducing the risk for investors.

A third group involved in harmonization are the international accountancy firms. They support harmonization partly because it is good for their large clients.

The tax authorities throughout the world have their work greatly complicated, when assessing foreign incomes, by differences in the measurement of profit in different countries. It should be admitted, however, that tax authorities have caused many of the differences, for example the influence of tax on continental European accounting (see Chapter 15) and the use of LIFO in the United States (see Chapter 8). Governments in developing countries might find it easier to understand and control the operations of multinationals if financial reporting were more uniform, particularly as this would imply greater disclosure in some cases. Other organizations that would benefit from greater international comparability of company information are labour unions that face multinational employers. All these groups might benefit from harmonization.

4.2.2 Examples of the need for harmonization

Much of this book is devoted to the analysis of international differences in accounting. The number and magnitude of the differences make clear the scope for harmonization. For example, on something as basic as inventory valuation, practices in major countries include:

● cost (FIFO, LIFO or weighted average) (e.g. some Japanese companies);

● the lower of FIFO and net realizable value (e.g. general IFRS practice in the UK);

● the lower of LIFO and current replacement cost (e.g. common US practice).

Adding all the differences together, the effects on earnings or shareholders' equity can be very large, as illustrated at the beginning of Chapter 1.

4.2.3 Obstacles to harmonization

The most fundamental of obstacles to achieving uniform practice is the size of the present differences between the accounting practices of different countries. Using the type of classifications of accounting systems discussed in Chapter 3, there are several significant differences even within the equity class, let alone between that class and the other. These differences go to the root of the reasons for the preparation of accounting information. The general dichotomy between shareholder/fair view presentation and creditor/tax/conservative presentation is an obstacle that cannot be overcome without major changes in attitudes and law.

Indeed, it is not clear that it *should* be overcome. If the predominant purposes of financial reporting vary by country, it seems reasonable that the reporting should vary. Harmonization is most useful when it concerns similar users who receive information from companies in different countries. It may be that the relevant companies should follow two sets of rules: one for domestic and another for international consumption, or one for parent statements and another for consolidated. This is discussed further at the end of Section 4.3.

Another obstacle is the lack of an international regulatory agency. The European Union is such an agency for one part of the world; and the International Organization of Securities Commissions (IOSCO) has influence for listed companies. These bodies are discussed in Section 4.4.

A further problem is nationalism. This may show itself in an unwillingness to accept compromises that involve changing accounting practices towards those of other countries. This unwillingness may exist on the part of accountants and companies or on the part of states that may not wish to lose their sovereignty. Another manifestation of nationalism may be the lack of knowledge or interest in accounting elsewhere. A rather more subtle and acceptable variety of this is the concern that it would be difficult to alter standards set outside of one's own country in response to a change of mind or a change of circumstances.

Another difficulty is the effect of 'economic consequences' on accounting standards (for example, see Chapters 5, 10 and 18). To the extent that economic consequences of standards vary by country and to the extent that they are taken into account by those who set standards, this could be a force for de-harmonization.

4.2.4 Measurement of harmonization

Statistical methods for the measurement of *de facto* harmony and harmonization were first developed by van der Tas (1988, 1992). He suggested an H (Herfindahl) index of national harmony, an I index (including a correction factor) of international harmony, and a C or comparability index. Archer *et al.* (1995) decomposed van der Tas's C index into a between-country C index and a within-country C index, and argued that the latter was superior to the corrected I index. Further discussion of the statistical properties and uses of these indices can be found in Herrmann and Thomas (1995), Archer *et al.* (1996), Krisement (1997) and Morris and Parker (1998). Other researchers making use of these indices include Emenyonu and Gray (1992, 1996). Rahman *et al.* (1996) suggest ways in which *de jure* harmonization can be measured.

Cañibano and Mora (2000) study *de facto* harmonization in Europe between 1991/2 and 1996/7. They apply a significance test to the C index and find harmonization in the period. They attribute this not to regulatory changes but to the desire of very large companies ('global players') to compete for capital in the international markets. Aisbitt (2001) examines the usefulness of the C index and uses harmonization in the Nordic region between 1981 and 1998 as a case study. She points out a series of problems, suggesting that qualitative study may be better than progressively more complex statistics.

Pierce and Weetman (2002) build on Archer *et al.* (1995) and Morris and Parker (1998) to develop a generalized formula for the between-country C index in which non-disclosure is split into cases where disclosure would be applicable and those where it would not be. They apply their methods to the harmonization of deferred tax accounting in Denmark and Ireland between 1986 and 1993. Taplin (2003) notes that previous researchers do not provide a calculation of the standard error of an index so as to give guidance on the likely values of the index in the population from which a sample was drawn. He suggests formulae for the calculation of standard errors. Taplin (2004) examines previously used indices and suggests a way of choosing the most appropriate one, for any particular piece of research, based on four criteria.

4.3   The International Accounting Standards Committee

4.3.1 History and purpose of the IASC

Arguably, the most successful body involved in harmonization has been the International Accounting Standards Committee (IASC) and its successor, the International Accounting Standards Board (IASB). These two bodies and some others are looked at in this and the following sections.

The IASC was founded in 1973 by the accountancy bodies of nine countries: Australia, Canada, France, Japan, Mexico, the Netherlands, the United Kingdom with Ireland, the United States and West Germany (Benson, 1979). A predecessor body, set up in 1966, was the Accountants' International Study Group (AISG) at which the professional bodies of Canada, the UK and the US examined their differences in accounting practices. Also relevant were the International Congresses of Accountants (see Section 4.4). The preliminary discussions towards setting up the IASC were held at meetings arranged in the margins of the Congress in Sydney in 1972. Another background factor was that the UK joined the Common Market (later EU) in 1973. Both the UK and the US professions were concerned about the draft Fourth Directive which contained unattractive accounting rules for UK companies or for the European subsidiaries of multinationals (Olson, 1982, page 226). The IASC can be seen as a countervailing force.

The original nine countries included the UK and Ireland as though they were one country. Mason (1978) had earlier suggested that there were six 'vital countries' to involve in harmonization: France, Germany, Japan, the Netherlands, the United Kingdom and the United States. He chose them partly on the grounds of the strengths of their accountancy professions and standard-setting experience. Some readers might be surprised by the inclusion of the Netherlands, but it had a long history of innovative accounting and the world's oldest stock market. It had also hosted the second international congress of accountants (see Section 4.4).

The IASC operated until 2001, when it was succeeded by the International Accounting Standards Committee Foundation (IASCF), whose operating arm is the IASB. Although the IASC set up the IASCF, it is convenient to split our consideration of the IASC/B into two parts, with a break in 2001. Section 4.5 considers 2001 onwards.

The IASC was independent from all other bodies, but from 1983 a close connection was established with the International Federation of Accountants (IFAC), which will be discussed later. The membership of IFAC and the IASC was identical, with over 150 accountancy bodies from over 110 countries by 2001. IFAC concentrates on such matters as auditing, management accounting, and the International Congresses of Accountants. The IASC was concerned only with international accounting standards. Its aim was 'to formulate and publish in the public interest accounting standards to be observed in the presentation of financial statements and to promote their worldwide acceptance and observance' (IASC, 1992).

From 1983 to 2001, the IASC's *Constitution* provided for it to be run by a Board of up to 17 members: nine or 10 from developed countries, three or four from developing countries and up to four other organizations, generally drawn from the IASC's consultative group (which included such bodies as the World Bank, the International Confederation of Trades Unions and the International Federation of Stock Exchanges). The members at 31 March 2001, after which the IASC was reformed, are shown in Table 4.1. There were never more than 16 members.

Board members of the IASC contributed much of its budget. The remaining members of the IFAC/IASC paid their subscriptions to the IFAC, which then funded another element of the IASC budget. Publication revenue and donations were also important.

Table 4.1 **Board members of IASC (at 31 March 2001)**

Australia	The Netherlands
Canada	Nordic Federation of Accountants
France	South Africa (with Zimbabwe)
Germany	United Kingdom
India (with Sri Lanka)	United States
Japan	Federation of Swiss Industrial Holding Companies
Malaysia	International Council of Investment Associations
Mexico	International Association of Financial Executives Institutes

4.3.2 The standards

A list of the standards of the IASC is shown as Table 4.2. The IASB adopted these standards *en bloc* in 2001, but made major amendments and additions from 2003. A list after those amendments is shown in Chapter 6, where the standards them-selves are examined. Standards were preceded by exposure drafts. In order to be published, an exposure draft had to be approved by a two-thirds majority of the IASC's Board; a subsequent standard by a three-quarters majority.

The IASC published a conceptual framework, which is somewhat similar to that of the FASB (see Chapter 8). There are also strong similarities with the Australian and British frameworks. The framework was also adopted by the IASB and is used when preparing standards. It is the countries influenced by the Anglo-American tradition that are most familiar with setting accounting rules in this way, and that are most likely to be able to adopt non-governmental rules. It is not surprising, then, that the working language of the IASC was English, that its secretariat was in London and that most standards closely followed, or compromised between, US and UK standards, as Table 4.3 shows. However, the degree to which the US and the UK dominated the IASC is a matter of fierce debate (see, for example, Flower, 1997; Cairns, 1997; Flower, 1998; Nobes, 1998; Alexander and Archer, 2000; Nobes, 2003).

By the late 1980s it had become clear that the substantial number of options in IASs were an obstacle to further enhancement of the status of the IASC's work. In particular, the International Organization of Securities Commissions (IOSCO), a committee of governmental regulatory bodies, held out the possibility that its members (e.g. the SEC) might accept IASs for the financial reporting of foreign com-panies listed on their stock exchanges. However, IOSCO made it clear that a reduc-tion in options was essential. This was one of the spurs to the issue of E 32, which launched the improvements/comparability project in 1989 (Purvis *et al.*, 1991).

After several years of detailed argument over the removal of options, 10 revised standards were agreed in November 1993 to come into force in 1995. Table 4.3 gives some examples of the effects. In the case of IAS 2, although E 32 proposed to remove the LIFO option, it was not possible to obtain the necessary 75 per cent majority (i.e., at that time, 11 out of 14 Board member votes). In the case of IAS 9 and IAS 22, options were removed. Furthermore, these IASs required practices that were inconsistent with US or UK practices, namely:

Table 4.2 IASC standards (late 2007)

Framework for the Preparation and Presentation of Financial Statements (1989).

IAS	Topic
1	Presentation of financial statements.
2	Inventories.
[3]	Consolidated financial statements (superseded by IAS 27 and IAS 28).
[4]	Depreciation accounting (withdrawn in 1999).
[5]	Information to be disclosed in financial statements (superseded by revised IAS 1).
[6]	Accounting responses to changing prices (superseded by IAS 15).
7	Cash flow statements.
8	Accounting policies, changes in accounting estimates and errors.
[9]	Research and development costs (superseded by IAS 38).
10	Events after the balance sheet date.
11	Construction contracts.
12	Income taxes.
[13]	Presentation of current assets and current liabilities (superseded by revised IAS 1).
[14]	Segment reporting (superseded by IFRS 8).
[15]	Information reflecting the effects of changing prices (withdrawn in 2003).
16	Property, plant and equipment.
17	Leases.
18	Revenue.
19	Employee benefits.
20	Accounting for government grants and disclosure of government assistance.
21	The effects of changes in foreign exchange rates.
[22]	Business combinations (superseded by IFRS 3).
23	Borrowing costs.
24	Related party disclosures.
[25]	Accounting for investments (superseded by IAS 39 and IAS 40).
26	Accounting and reporting by retirement benefit plans.
27	Consolidated and separate financial statements.
28	Investments in associates.
29	Financial reporting in hyperinflationary economies.
[30]	Disclosures in the financial statements of banks and similar financial institutions (superseded by IFRS 7).
31	Interests in joint ventures.
32	Financial instruments: presentation.
33	Earnings per share.
34	Interim financial reporting.
[35]	Discontinuing operations (superseded by IFRS 5).
36	Impairment of assets.
37	Provisions, contingent liabilities and contingent assets.
38	Intangible assets.
39	Financial instruments: recognition and measurement.
40	Investment property.
41	Agriculture.

Note: Square brackets denote standards superseded or withdrawn.

Table 4.3 Some international standards compared to US and UK rules (pre-1993 to 2008)

Topic	US	UK	IAS (before 1993 revisions, effective 1995)	IAS (revised)
Inventories (IAS 2)	LIFO allowed, with disclosure of FIFO.	LIFO not allowed.	LIFO allowed.	From 1995 to 2004: LIFO allowed, with disclosure of FIFO. From 2005: LIFO not allowed.
R&D (IAS 9; IAS 38)	All expensed.	Research expensed; certain development can be capitalized.	Research expensed; certain development can be capitalized.	From 1995: research expensed; certain development must be capitalized.
Goodwill (IAS 22)	To 2001: amortized over up to 40 years. From 2001: not amortized but tested for impairment.	To 1998: amortized over useful life; or (normally) written off against reserves immediately. From 1998: amortized over up to 20 years (rebuttable presumption).	Amortized over useful life; or written off against reserves immediately.	From 1995 to 1998: amortized over up to 20 years. From 1999 to 2004: amortized over up to 20 years (rebuttable presumption). From 2005: as United States.
Deferred Tax (IAS 12)	From 1992: full allocation; liability method; balance sheet basis.	Liability method; profit and loss basis. To 2001: partial allocation. From 2001: full allocation.	Partial or full allocation; deferral or liability method; profit and loss basis.	From 1998: as United States.

- IAS 9 (of 1993; absorbed into IAS 38 of 1998) *requires* suitable development expenditures to be recognized as assets. This is in conflict with US rules (SFAS 2, which does not allow such capitalization) and inconsistent with majority UK practice (SSAP 13 merely *allows* capitalization). Incidentally, it was also in conflict with practice in such countries as France, Spain or Japan, where R & D costs were usually not capitalized but where *both* could be.

- IAS 22 (of 1993) required goodwill to be capitalized and amortized over its useful life, which should not have exceeded five years unless a longer period (up to 20 years) could be justified. This was inconsistent with the then US rules (amortize over up to 40 years) and UK practice (generally to write off goodwill against reserves). Subsequently, as Table 4.3 records, both UK and IAS rules changed to be approximately in line with each other, until further US change led to further IAS change.

IAS 12 was not part of the E 32 project, but a revision in force from 1998 led to the UK and several other countries being out of line with the IAS on deferred tax.

The response of IOSCO to the revisions of 1993 was to welcome them but to call for further revisions and new IASs so that a set of 'core standards' could be accepted for the financial reporting of companies with cross-border listings. In 1995, IOSCO and IASC agreed a detailed plan to achieve this, scheduled for completion in 1998 or 1999. In the meantime, IOSCO accepted IAS 7 for cash flow reporting; and the SEC went beyond that for its foreign registrants by also accepting elements of other IASs. The IASC finished the core programme with IASs 39 and 40, published in 1999 and 2000.

The IASs that were issued or revised from 1993 onwards (see Table 4.3) contained fewer options than previous standards, although resistance to the introduction of fair value (and to taking unsettled gains) led to major options (and other opportunities) to continue to use cost in IASs 39, 40 and 41 (see Chapter 6).

A relevant development of 1996 was the IASC's decision to set up a Standing Interpretations Committee (SIC) which set out the IASC's view on certain issues that were not dealt with in sufficient detail or clarity by IASs. The work of the SIC further tightened up the IASC's requirements. The SIC has been replaced by the International Financial Reporting Interpretations Committee (IFRIC).

4.3.3 Was the IASC successful?

In order to determine whether the IASC was successful it is necessary to establish the criteria by which success should be measured. We might start by looking at the stated objectives of the IASC, though we need to confirm that these are reasonable and useful objectives before adopting them as the measure for the IASC's success. The IASC's basic objective was to publish and promote the acceptance of standards on a worldwide basis. This objective might once have been thought to be too ambitious in one respect and not ambitious enough in another.

Until fairly recently, to attempt worldwide standardization seemed a hopeless and unnecessary target. The greatest benefits come from standardization among countries where there are companies that publish financial statements and that have foreign investors, auditors, parents or subsidiaries. This means that the context of success might more sensibly have been seen as the developed West and those developing countries with which it had significant economic links. Until the 1990s, to try to bring the accounting of the Soviet Union or China into line, for example, would not only have had very few benefits but would also have been impossible. However, the IASC became an important influence on Russia and China when their communist economic systems were dismantled, and so the description 'worldwide' seems increasingly appropriate, as examined later.

Secondly, to publish and promote standards is not a sufficient aim. Fortunately, in the IASC's 1983 Preface and Constitution, the more fundamental aim of standardizing accounting practices was recognized. What is needed is progress towards an easier and surer comparability of published financial statements from different countries, or at least disclosure of the nature and significance of the differences.

The IASC can be judged against the two objectives. In terms of *issuing standards*, there was clearly success. Forty-one standards (many of them with subsequent amendments) were issued, along with a conceptual framework and other publications. Although the standards were criticized for allowing many options, this feature was probably essential to allow early progress, and it was seriously addressed in the early 1990s onwards (see Section 4.3.2).

The objectives of *promotion and observance of standards* and of general harmonization are more complex, particularly because the IASC had no authority of its own to impose its standards on companies. Success in this area up to 2001 will now be examined for four types of country: developing countries, emerging nations, continental Western Europe and Japan, and capital-market countries. The position from 2001 is looked at in Section 4.5.

Developing countries

It is perhaps in developing and newly industrialized countries that the clearest and most spectacular success for the IASC might be claimed during the 1990s. Many countries (e.g. Nigeria, Malaysia and Singapore) adopted IASs with few or no amendments as their national standards.

IASs were of importance also to many other developing countries, particularly those with a British legacy, which rely on private-sector standard-setting. These countries were members of the IASC, and some of them had been members of the Board or of working parties on particular standards. The adoption of IASs was a cheaper route for these countries than preparing their own standards and has the great advantage of making life easier for those domestic or foreign companies or accountants with international connections. The other advantage is avoidance of the politically unattractive alternative (for some countries) of adoption of US or UK standards. This use of IASs is of great value to these many countries and serves the interests of international harmonization by avoiding the creation of different rules. However, there are some doubts about the suitability of the standards for developing countries (Briston, 1978). For example, the complication of the standards and the extensive disclosures that they require might involve costs that exceed the benefits for a country with few listed companies.

Nevertheless, Saudagaran and Diga (2003) conclude, using ASEAN countries as an example, that harmonization will continue and will be based on IASB's standards. Zeghal and Mhedhbi (2006) suggest that the most likely countries to adopt international standards are those with capital markets and Anglo-American culture.

Emerging nations

Somewhat similar remarks as for developing countries may be made about those nations that moved from communist to capitalist economics, such as China and Eastern Europe. They needed a 'quick fix' to their accounting practices as they changed at breakneck speed from economies with no 'profit', no shareholders, no independent auditors and no stock markets. To some extent, institutions from the West competed to influence these countries (e.g. UK accountancy bodies, the French government, German banks, and the EU). However, the IASC as a worldwide standard-setter had advantages that enabled it to be a key influence. Further comments on this are found in Chapters 5, 11 and 12.

Continental Western Europe and Japan

Of the four types of country proposed here, it was in continental Europe and Japan that there was the greatest ambivalence towards the IASC. To some extent the IASC was seen as a Trojan horse concealing the Anglo-Saxon accounting enemy inside a more respectable international façade. The horse was wheeled into the heart of Europe and then its contents subtly contributed to the undermining of traditional continental accounting. This was perhaps the view until the late 1990s of the German or Italian accounting establishment and of elements of the European Commission.

Certainly, in 1973, the standard-setting philosophy and the dominant idea of serving capital markets with 'fair' information was largely alien to continental Europe or Japan. Nevertheless, the IASC moved forward with considerable support from these countries and remarkably little acrimony. The factors that helped this were:

● the large representation of non-Anglo-Saxon countries on the Board and working parties, and the eventual appointment of a Frenchman and then a Japanese as chairperson of the IASC;

● national delegates from these countries who had been trained in large accountancy firms or multinationals and who were not governmental bureaucrats;

● the desire in several Board-member countries to strengthen their capital markets and modernize their accounting (particularly strongly felt in France and Italy from the 1970s onwards);

● the increasing internationalization of the financial world, such that even some German and Japanese companies started to raise finance overseas;

● a desire to avoid US dominance of accounting, so that the IASC seemed the less bad alternative.

In many cases IASs were passed that were inconsistent with the letter or the spirit of some continental or Japanese rules. National delegates often voted against their own country's practices, and sometimes their country's practices subsequently changed towards the IAS. This latter feature was particularly obvious in the case of group accounting, where the EU Seventh Directive (see Chapter 11) caused dramatic changes in Europe, broadly in line with the contents of IASs. Also, the capitalization of leases and accounting for deferred tax have been seeping into continental Europe.

Indirect effects can be seen in the gradual acceptance of many IASC ideas in continental Europe and Japan. For example, during the governmental negotiations on the Seventh Directive, the existence of IAS 3 on group accounting was a point of reference, particularly as it had been passed by a Board containing so many EU members. Also, over the years, the representatives from the major countries have been engaged in continual debate at the IASC and other international bodies. This all contributes to understanding and an eventual softening of views.

The *direct* effects of the IASC on all of this are observable in two ways.

1 In some cases rule-making authorities approved the use of IASs in certain circumstances, e.g. in France or Italy for certain aspects of consolidated accounts. The Japanese regulators began a process of examining conformity of their rules with IASs.

2 Some companies chose to use IASs in part or in whole for their main or supplementary financial statements. This was seen particularly in Switzerland and, from 1994, in Germany, but it applied to several large companies throughout continental Europe.

Governments responded to this desire by large European groups to use IAS or US accounting practices. In 1998, a German law was passed allowing listed companies to use 'internationally recognized' rules for their consolidated statements in place of the national rules. There were a few conditions, such as that the rules had to be in accordance with the EU Directives. Until 2001, when IAS 39 came into force (see Table 4.2 and Chapter 6), this condition seemed to create no difficulties for the use of IASs. The Directives were amended in 2001 to ensure continued compatibility (see Chapter 11). However, there seemed to be some doubt that US rules met the condition.

As a result of the 1998 law, about half of the top 100 German groups were using IASs for their consolidated statements by 1999. Similar laws were passed in several other countries. For example, a similar law in Austria extended to all companies, not just listed ones. In France and Italy, laws similar to the German one were passed but not put into operation.

The response of the EU to all this was dramatic, as explained in Chapters 5 and 11.

Capital-market countries

The last group of countries includes former Board members such as the United States, Canada, the United Kingdom, Australia, South Africa and the Netherlands. Increasingly, however, other Board countries joined this capital-market club, especially in relation to large companies or consolidated statements (noticeably France and the Nordic Federation).

Clearly, the publication of frequent, fair, consolidated, audited information for capital markets, regulated by non-governmental standards set with the aid of a conceptual framework, is an idea associated with these countries. The content of IASs (certainly up to the improvements project) was closely consistent with practices in these countries. It seems, then, that these countries influenced the IASC, rather than the other way round. Indeed, until the late 1990s, US or UK standard-setters did not make major efforts to change their rules in those cases where there was inconsistency.

Nevertheless, IASC influence on standard-setters could be discerned. For example, the United Kingdom ASB's conceptual framework was prepared after the IASC's and is very close to it. The former ASC had begun to use the IASC's framework. Certainly, the standard-setters in the United Kingdom, Canada or Australia looked closely at the relevant IASC standards before setting or changing their own, and they were more comfortable when they are in conformity with the IASC. Several joint projects between these countries and the IASC were carried out in the late 1990s (e.g. IAS 14 revised, and IASs 33 and 37). By the late 1990s, the Australian standard-setter had begun to conform its standards with IASC (see Chapter 5).

At the level of *companies* in these countries, little direct effect of the IASC could be discerned until 2005, mainly because companies were required to use domestic rules.

Support in 2000

Major evidence of IASC success appeared in 2000. First, IOSCO recommended IASs for acceptance by its members. This improved the chances that the SEC would eventually accept IASs for the reporting by foreign listed companies on US stock exchanges. Also, the EU Commission proposed that IASs should become compulsory for the consolidated statements of all EU listed companies by 2005 (see Chapter 5). These moves should be seen in the context of the reform of the IASC (see Section 4.5) which was settled by then.

4.3.4 Empirical findings on the IASC

There has been some empirical analysis of the effects of the IASC. McKinnon and Jannell (1984), on *de jure* harmonization, concluded that 'the IASC has not succeeded in changing existing standards or setting new standards'. Evans and Taylor (1982) examined compliance with IAS standards for five of the six 'vital' countries. They suggested that the IASC had had little influence. Nair and Frank (1981) looked more widely at the degree of harmonization over the period 1973 to 1979. They arrived at no stronger a conclusion than that 'the period of the IASC's existence has coincided with a growing harmonization of accounting standards'.

Doupnik and Taylor (1985) found some increased compliance by nations with IASC standards, but their findings were disputed by Nobes (1987). Other empirical work includes that by Emenyonu and Gray (1996). Critiques of the IASC's work include those by Rivera (1989), Wallace (1990) and Goeltz (1991). However, all this work looked at practice before the improvements that came into force from 1995 onwards.

Weetman *et al.* (1998) suggested that there was increasing disharmony between UK accounting and IASC or US accounting. However, although they took account of *de jure* developments after 1995, they too studied the *practices* before that date. A survey of the conformity with IASs of the national rules in 62 countries for 31 December 2001 year ends showed a very large number of differences in nearly all the countries (Nobes, 2001). For example, there were many differences of detail for the UK and the US; many inconsistencies for several continental European countries; and many gaps in the rules of several developing and emerging countries.

Ali (2005) provides a summary of the empirical research on harmonization. Baker and Barbu (2007) provide a wider summary of research on international harmonization. The degree to which companies actually complied with IASs when they claimed to do so is discussed in Section 9.4.

4.3.5 Histories of the IASC

Two major histories of the IASC have been published: Camfferman and Zeff (2007) and Kirsch (2006). Both had varying degrees of support from the IASB, and both were written after large numbers of interviews with former participants in the IASC's work.

4.4 Other international bodies

This section looks at the nature and importance of some other bodies that were concerned, from the 1970s onwards, with international aspects of accounting.

Table 4.4 **World congresses of accountants**

1904	St. Louis	1972	Sydney
1926	Amsterdam	1977	Munich
1929	New York	1982	Mexico City
1933	London	1987	Tokyo
1937	Berlin	1992	Washington
1952	London	1997	Paris
1957	Amsterdam	2002	Hong Kong
1962	New York	2006	Istanbul
1967	Paris		

4.4.1 International Federation of Accountants (IFAC)

This body came into being in 1977 after the Eleventh World Congress of Accountants. It aims to develop a coordinated international accountancy profession. A predecessor body, called the International Coordination Committee for the Accountancy Profession (ICCAP), which had been formed in 1972 after the Tenth Congress, was wound up in favour of the IFAC.

The IFAC represents over 150 member accountancy bodies from around the world. It has a full-time secretariat in New York. Its work includes the setting of international standards for auditing (via the International Auditing and Assurance Standards Board), ethics, education and management accounting; involvement in education and technical research; and organizing the international congress every four or five years. Table 4.4 lists the congresses, from the first one in 1904.

Loft *et al.* (2006) examine the changing structure and growing importance of IFAC. They suggest that IFAC is now more influenced by experts and multinational audit firms than by national accountancy bodies.

4.4.2 The G4+1

As well as the ICCAP, another body was wound up in 1977 when the IFAC was formed – the Accountants' International Study Group. As mentioned earlier, this group had been formed in 1966 and comprised members from professional bodies in Canada, the United Kingdom and the United States. Its purpose was to study and report on accounting practices in the three countries. Twenty studies were issued, mainly on financial reporting matters.

By the early 1990s, a need for something similar was again perceived. By then, standard-setting in several of the Anglo-Saxon countries (e.g. the US and the UK, but not Canada and New Zealand) had been transferred from professional bodies to independent private-sector committees. The G4+1 group comprised the standard-setters of Australia, Canada, the UK and the US, with the IASC secretariat as observer (hence the '+1'). Later, the New Zealand standard-setter joined.

From 1995 onwards, the G4+1 issued a number of discussion papers, on such subjects as lease accounting and the measurement of performance. The members of the G4+1 shared similar conceptual frameworks and felt able to go further and faster than the Board of the IASC. This process helped to coordinate the efforts of these standard-setters.

In February 2001, after the new IASB had been appointed, the G4+1 was wound up. The discussion in Section 4.5 will reveal why the G4+1 is no longer necessary, given that so many former Anglo-Saxon standard-setters became IASB members. Street (2005) describes the work of the G4+1 and suggests that it had a major impact on the IASC and the IASB. Nobes (2006) suggests that Street exaggerates somewhat.

4.4.3 IOSCO

The International Organization of Securities Commissions was founded in 1983. It is an association of governmental securities regulators, such as the Securities and Exchange Commission of the United States. Such regulators decide whether foreign or 'international' accounting standards are acceptable for the financial reporting of domestic or foreign listed companies.

In the late 1980s, IOSCO and the IASC reached an agreement whereby IASC would improve its standards and IOSCO would consider recommending them to all their exchanges. IASC's work of the 1990s was mostly designed to satisfy IOSCO, which also joined the IASC Board meetings as an official observer.

In 2000, IOSCO endorsed the IASC's standards, particularly for use by foreign registrants. Many regulators do accept international standards for foreign companies even if domestic standards are required for domestic companies. In 2007, the SEC also accepted international standards.

IOSCO and the SEC were important contributors to the discussions that led to the creation of the IASB in 2001 (see Section 4.5).

A body that co-ordinates the European members of IOSCO was founded in 2001 and called CESR (the Committee of European Securities Regulators). It has been active in promoting enforcement agencies for the monitoring of the use of IFRS by listed companies in Europe (see Chapter 9).

4.4.4 European Union

The European Union is discussed at greater length later: in Section 5.2 concerning its requirement to use IFRS for the consolidated statements of listed companies from 2005, and in Chapter 11 concerning its efforts for the harmonization of national accounting rules in Europe since the 1970s. In both capacities the EU has been a major player in the harmonization of accounting.

4.4.5 Fédération des Experts Comptables Européens (FEE)

FEE started work at the beginning of 1987, taking over from two earlier European bodies: the *Groupe d'Etudes* (formed in 1966) and the *Union Européenne des Experts Comptables* (UEC, formed in 1951) (see McDougall, 1979).

FEE is based in Brussels and has member accountancy bodies throughout Europe. Its interests include auditing, accounting and taxation. It studies international differences and tries to contribute to their removal. Much of its work is connected with the EU, and it advises the European Commission on company law and accounting harmonization. If FEE can arrive at a consensus of European accountants, this gives it a powerful voice in Brussels, particularly if governments are disagreeing.

In 2001, FEE was the driving force behind the creation of the European Financial Reporting Advisory Group (EFRAG), which advises the EU Commission on the acceptability of new and amended IASB standards (see Chapter 5).

4.4.6 Other regional bodies

The Inter-American Accounting Association (IAA) covers the accountancy bodies of the two American continents. The Confederation of Asian and Pacific Accountants (CAPA) can be traced back to 1957, although it was not formally organized until 1976. It includes very many countries, and it may be that its members are too heterogeneous to constitute a 'viable accounting cluster' (Choi, 1981, page 31). So there may be problems in defining a region for the purpose of accounting harmonization.

In the case of CAPA countries, perhaps a more successful regional grouping involves a subset of them: the ASEAN Federation of Accountants (AFA) formed in Bangkok in 1977 (Choi, 1979). Choi (1981) suggested that one function of the AFA 'is to buffer individual ASEAN countries against the wholesale adoption of international accounting pronouncements that may not be suitable to local circumstances'. However, neither CAPA nor AFA seem to have had any effect on harmonization or the reduction of IASC or US influence. Craig and Diga (1996) examine the large differences in institutional structures in the ASEAN countries, which will hamper regional harmonization.

The Eastern, Central and Southern Africa Federation of Accountants (ECSAFA) was formed in 1990. It encourages the formation and development of accountancy bodies. It holds congresses, communicates with IFAC, and carries out other joint activities.

4.4.7 Other non-accounting bodies

One of the factors that drives accountants and their professional bodies towards better national and international standards is the possibility that governmental bodies will intervene or gain the initiative. At present, with the regional exception of the EU, such international bodies have influence rather than power. The Organisation for Economic Co-operation and Development (OECD) researched and adopted recommendations for accounting practice: the 'Guidelines for Multinational Enterprises' (OECD, 1986, page 100). This mainly concerns disclosure requirements. It is voluntary, but it may influence the behaviour of large and politically sensitive corporations. There have also been surveys of accounting practices (e.g. OECD, 1980), but no agreement as to how to achieve harmonization. It seems clear that part of the OECD's aim in this area is to protect developed countries from any extreme proposals that might have come from the United Nations, which is interested in the regulation of multinational business.

In 1977, the UN published a report in this area which proposed very substantial increases in disclosure of financial and non-financial items by transnational corporations. The UN went further and set up an 'Intergovernmental Group of Experts on International Standards of Accounting and Reporting' (ISAR) in 1979. This has published some standards on disclosures by multinationals.

Table 4.5 **Some bodies concerned with harmonization**

Sector	Scope	
	World	Regional
Governmental	UN, OECD, IOSCO	EU
Profession	IASC, IFAC	FEE
Independent	IASB	–
Mixed	–	G4+1, EFRAG

4.4.8 Classification of institutional harmonizers

Many harmonizing agencies have already been discussed in this chapter. It is useful to arrange some of these in a simple lattice (Table 4.5): by sector and by geographical scope. Table 4.5 is not exhaustive; as noted, there are other regional bodies. Further, the roles of the bodies differ markedly.

4.5   The International Accounting Standards Board

4.5.1 Reform of the IASC in 2001

The old IASC Board set up a 'Strategy Working Party' in 1997 to consider whether changes to its structure were needed after completion of the core programme for IOSCO. The working party's paper, 'Shaping IASC for the Future', was published at the end of 1998. The proposals needed approval by the Board (three-quarters majority required) and the member bodies of IASC (simple majority required).

The suggested reasons for a change included the following:

- reducing the load on the part-time Board representatives, who had been working very hard, particularly for the previous two years as the core programme was completed;

- enabling a wider group of countries and organizations to be members of the Board;

- increasing the degree of partnership with national standard-setters so as to accelerate worldwide convergence of standards.

The debate on reform concerned two competing ideas: independence and representativeness. This might also be seen as a struggle between Anglo-Saxon and continental European philosophy. The 'independence' argument is that good accounting standards are those designed in the public interest by a small group of full-time technical experts. Consequently, part-time standard-setters who work for accountancy firms or large companies are not sufficiently independent. The 'representativeness' argument is that legitimacy comes from the involvement of all interested parties, so that a large part-time Board is appropriate.

The 1998 strategy paper contained a compromise by having a small technocratic executive board and a large representative supervisory board. However, there was then a battle over which was to be more powerful. In the end, the independence argument won, partly because it was supported by the SEC, the most important member of IOSCO. Also, there was a threat that the FASB or the combined English-speaking standard-setters would try to take over world standard-setting from the IASC.

In December 1999, the Board voted unanimously to abolish itself, and in May 2000 the member bodies confirmed this. The new structure came into operation on 1 April 2001. It is headed by the International Accounting Standards Committee Foundation (IASCF) (legally registered in the United States) controlled by 22 trustees (originally 19), who have promised to operate in the public interest. The original trustees were selected by an appointments committee set up by the old Board, and chaired by the chairman of the SEC. The trustees change from time to time, including three extra members in early 2005.

The trustees are designed to be geographically representative (see Table 4.6). Their main tasks are to raise the necessary funds, and to appoint the Board of 12 full-time and two part-time members. The IASB was initially heavily dominated by former Anglo-Saxon standard-setters and former IASC Board representatives. Again, the Board changes slightly from time to time, but the initial members (see Table 4.7) were mostly still in post in 2007. Under the initial arrangements, only a simple majority was needed to pass standards, but this was increased to 9 votes in 2005.

The IASB and its secretariat remain based in London. The Standing Interpretations Committee has been replaced by the International Financial Reporting Interpretations Committee (IFRIC).

Table 4.6 Geographical backgrounds of initial IASCF trustees

	Number
US	5
Japan	2
Australia	1
Canada	1
South Africa	1
France	1
Germany	1
Switzerland	1
Brazil	1
China (Hong Kong)	1
Denmark	1
Italy	1
Netherlands	1
UK	1
	19

Table 4.7 Initial IASB members from April 2001 to early 2004

Country	Number	Comment
US	5 (or 3)*	2 former FASB + 1 former FASB trustee (and former IASC chairman) + 2 part-time
UK	2 (or 4)*	Both former ASB
Australia	1	Former AARF executive director
Canada	1	Former AcSB chair
South Africa	1	–
France	1	Former IASC Board
Germany	1	Former Daimler-Chrysler, which used US GAAP
Japan	1	Former IASC Board
Switzerland	1	Former IASC Board
	14	

Notes:
*Two board members have US work backgrounds but UK nationality.
Legend: AcSB = Accounting Standards Board of Canada.
  ASB = Accounting Standards Board of the UK.
  AARF = Australian Accounting Research Foundation, which provided the secretariat for the Australian standard-setter, the AASB.
  FASB = Financial Accounting Standards Board of the USA.

4.5.2 The IASB's initial work

The IASB adopted all the old IASs and then began its work in 2001 in three main areas:

1 a new improvements project;

2 continuing projects;

3 major reforms.

The new improvements project led to exposure drafts in May and June 2002 designed to amend 14 standards and to withdraw IAS 15 (see Table 4.2). In the resulting revised standards of 2003 and new standards of 2004, a number of options were removed, such as LIFO (IAS 2) and correction of errors through income (IAS 8). The examination of IFRSs in Chapter 6 includes these amendments.

Projects on insurance accounting and exploration costs were begun by the IASC and are being continued by the IASB. Major reforms are expected on such issues as revenue recognition and lease accounting. However, in order to allow companies to recover from the changes that came into force in 2005, the IASB has said that further substantial changes will not be compulsory until 2009, even if they are published before then.

4.5.3 Convergence with the US

Much of the activity of the IASC in the 1990s had been concerned with persuading IOSCO to endorse IASs, and in particular persuading the SEC to accept IASs for foreign registrants on US exchanges. The setting up of the IASCF and the IASB was done in close consultation with the SEC. Despite this, the SEC took until 2007 to accept IFRSs.

Nevertheless, the FASB and the IASB immediately began to work closely together. This was helped by the fact that two former FASB members (Tony Cope and Jim Leisenring) and some staff joined the IASB, and a US representative (Michael Crooch) on the old IASC Board became a member of the FASB. Then, in 2002, one of the IASB members (Bob Herz) was appointed as the new FASB chairman. Also, in 2001/2, the large companies Enron and WorldCom were surrounded by huge accounting scandals, and Andersen (the most American of the big accounting firms) collapsed. This led to heart-searching in the US (see Chapter 8), including an investigation by the FASB into whether it should adopt a more 'principles-based' approach to standard-setting (like the IASB) rather than setting detailed rules.

In late 2002, the IASB and the FASB announced a convergence project to try to eliminate as many differences as possible by 2005. IFRS 5 and IFRS 8 (see Chapter 6) were the first examples of international standards that were overtly designed to achieve convergence. It is now clear that great efforts are being made by the two standard-setters to eliminate differences and to avoid creating new ones.

As a result of all this, the SEC announced in 2007 the acceptance of IFRS statements from foreign registrants without the need for reconciliation to US accounting practices. This applies for 2007 statements, i.e. filings in early 2008. Without reconciliation, the SEC will only accept full IFRS, not EU-endorsed IFRS or any other version.

4.5.4 EU influence

As has already been mentioned in this chapter, the EU made IFRS compulsory for some purposes in 2005. The EU now sees itself as IASB's biggest 'customer' and therefore seeks influence. The increases in 2005 in the number of trustees and in the size of majority vote needed for Board decisions were requested by the EU. Also, EU threats not to endorse a standard have to be taken seriously. This is discussed in Section 5.2.

Another issue on which the EU has lobbied hard is for the creation of a simplified version of IFRS that would be suitable for small and medium-sized entities (SMEs). The IASB produced an exposure draft on this in 2007. It is discussed further in Chapter 13.

SUMMARY

- Many parties are interested in international harmonization, including shareholders, stock exchanges, multinational companies, accounting firms, trade unions and revenue authorities.

- The scope for harmonization is great because the international variations in practice are very large. However, the obstacles are important, too. The fundamental causes of differences remain and these are backed up by nationalistic inertia. At present, the lack of an international enforcement agency is crucial.

- From the 1970s, a number of bodies were working for harmonization of accounting practices and disclosures, notably the IASC, which published a substantial list of international standards.

- IASs contained many options and gaps. However, with the support of stock market regulators (IOSCO), IASs greatly improved by the end of the 1990s. They were adopted by some countries and, in other countries, by some companies.

- There are other bodies concerned with harmonization on a worldwide or regional basis. For example, in 2000, the EU Commission proposed compulsory use of IASs for the consolidated statements of listed companies. A Regulation on this was approved in 2002.

- The IASC was replaced in 2001 by a foundation and a mainly full-time IASB.

- The IASB has been particularly influenced by its relationships with the FASB and the EU.

References

Aisbitt, S. (2001) 'Measurement of harmony of financial reporting within and between countries; the case of the Nordic countries', *European Accounting Review*, Vol. 10, No. 1.

Alexander, D. and Archer, S. (2000) 'On the myth of "Anglo-Saxon" financial accounting', *International Journal of Accounting*, Vol. 35, No. 4.

Ali, M.J. (2005) 'A synthesis of empirical research on international accounting harmonization and compliance with international financial reporting standards', *Journal of Accounting Literature*, Vol. 24.

Archer, S., Delvaille, P. and McLeay, S. (1995) 'The measurement of harmonisation and the comparability of financial statement items: within-country and between-country effects', *Accounting and Business Research*, Vol. 25, No. 98.

Archer, S., Delvaille, P. and McLeay, S. (1996) 'A statistical model of international accounting harmonization', *Abacus*, Vol. 32, No. 1.

Baker, C.R. and Barbu, E.M. (2007) 'Trends in research on international accounting harmonization', *International Journal of Accounting*, Vol. 42, No. 3.

Benson, H. (1979) *Accounting for Life*, London, Kogan Page.

Briston, R. (1978) 'The evolution of accounting in developing countries', *International Journal of Accounting*, Vol. 13, No. 1.

Cairns, D. (1997) 'The future shape of harmonization: a reply', *European Accounting Review*, Vol. 6, No. 2.

Camfferman, K. and Zeff, S. (2007) *Financial Reporting and Global Capital Markets: A History of the International Accounting Standards Committee, 1973–2000*, Oxford University Press, Oxford.

Cañibano, L. and Mora, A. (2000) 'Evaluating the statistical significance of *de facto* accounting harmonization: a study of European global players', *European Accounting Review*, Vol. 9, No. 3.

Choi, F.D.S. (1979) 'ASEAN Federation of Accountants: A new international accounting force', *International Journal of Accounting*, Vol. 14, No. 1.

Choi, F.D.S. (1981) 'A cluster approach to accounting harmonization', *Management Accounting* (USA), August.

Choi, F.D.S. and Levich, R. (1990) *The Capital Market Effects of International Accounting Diversity*, Dow Jones-Irwin, Homewood.

Craig, R.J. and Diga, J.G. (1996) 'Financial reporting regulation in ASEAN: features and prospects', *International Journal of Accounting*, Vol. 31, No. 2.

Doupnik, S. and Taylor, M.E. (1985) 'An empirical investigation of the observance of IASC standards in Western Europe', *Management International Review*, Vol. 25, No. 1.

Emenyonu, E.N. and Gray, S.J. (1992) 'EC accounting harmonization: an empirical study of measurement practices in France, Germany and the UK', *Accounting and Business Research*, Vol. 23, No. 89.

Emenyonu, E.N. and Gray, S.J. (1996) 'International accounting harmonization and the major developed stock market countries: an empirical study', *International Journal of Accounting*, Vol. 31, No. 3.

Evans, T.G. and Taylor, M.E. (1982) 'Bottom line compliance with the IASC: A comparative analysis', *International Journal of Accounting*, Vol. 17, No. 1.

Flower, J. (1997) 'The future shape of harmonization: The EU versus the IASC versus the SEC', *European Accounting Review*, Vol. 6, No. 2.

Flower, J. (1998) 'The future shape of harmonization: a reply', *European Accounting Review*, Vol. 7, No. 2.

Goeltz, R.K. (1991) 'International accounting harmonization: the impossible (and unnecessary?) dream', *Accounting Horizons*, Vol. 5, No. 1.

Herrmann, D. and Thomas, W. (1995) 'Harmonisation of accounting measurement practices in the European Community', *Accounting and Business Research*, Vol. 25, No. 100.

IASC (1983) *Preface to International Accounting Standards*, London.

IASC (1992) *Constitution of the International Accounting Standards Committee*, London.

Kirsch, R.J. (2006) *The International Accounting Standards Committee: A Political History*, Wolters Kluwer, Kingston-upon-Thames.

Krisement, V. (1997) 'An approach for measuring the degree of comparability of financial accounting information', *European Accounting Review*, Vol. 6, No. 3.

Loft, A., Humphrey, C. and Turley, S. (2006) 'In pursuit of global regulation: changing governance and accountability structures at the International Federation of Accountants (IFAC)', *Accounting, Auditing and Accountability Journal*, Vol. 19, No. 3.

McDougall, E.H.V. (1979) 'Regional accountancy bodies', in W.J. Brennan (ed.), *The Internationalization of the Accountancy Profession*, CICA, Toronto.

McKinnon, S.M. and Jannell, P. (1984) 'The International Accounting Standards Committee: A performance evaluation', *International Journal of Accounting*, Vol. 18, No. 2.

Morris, R.D. and Parker, R.H. (1998) 'International harmony measures of accounting policy: comparative statistical properties', *Accounting and Business Research*, Vol. 29, No. 1.

Nair, R.D. and Frank, W.G. (1981) 'The harmonization of international accounting standards, 1973–1979', *International Journal of Accounting*, Vol. 16, No. 1.

Nobes, C.W. (1987) 'An empirical investigation of the observance of IASC standards in Western Europe: A comment', *Management International Review*, Vol. 4.

Nobes, C.W. (1998) 'The future shape of harmonization: some responses', *European Accounting Review*, Vol. 7, No. 2.

Nobes, C.W. ed. (2001) *GAAP 2001: A Survey of National Accounting Rules*, Ernst & Young for IFAD. Also available at www.ifad.net.

Nobes, C.W. (2003) 'On the myth of "Anglo-Saxon" accounting: A comment', *International Journal of Accounting*, Vol. 38, No. 1.

Nobes, C.W. (2006) 'Book review' of Street (2005), *Accounting and Business Research*, Vol. 36, No. 1.

OECD (1980) *International Investment and Multinational Enterprises*, Paris.

OECD (1986) *Harmonisation of Accounting Standards*, Paris.

Olson, W.E. (1982) *The Accounting Profession – Years of Trial: 1969–1980*, AICPA, New York.

Parker, R.H. (1996) 'Harmonizing the notes in the UK and France: a case study in *de jure* harmonization', *European Accounting Review*, Vol. 5, No. 2.

Pierce, A. and Weetman, P. (2002) 'Measurement of *de facto* harmonization: implications of non-disclosure for research planning and interpretation', *Accounting and Business Research*, Vol. 32, No. 4.

Purvis, S.E.C., Gernon, H. and Diamond, M.A. (1991) 'The IASC and its comparability project', *Accounting Horizons*, Vol. 5, No. 2.

Rahman, A., Perera, P. and Ganeshanandam, S. (1996) 'Measurement of formal harmonisation in accounting: an exploratory study', *Accounting and Business Research*, 26, No. 4.

Rivera, J.M. (1989) 'The internationalization of accounting standards', *International Journal of Accounting*, Vol. 24, No. 4.

Saudagaran, S.M. and Diga, J.G. (2003) 'Economic integration and accounting harmonization in emerging markets: adopting the IASC/IASB model in ASEAN', *Research in Accounting in Emerging Economies*, Vol. 5, pp. 239–66.

Street, D.L. (2005) *Inside G4+1: The Working Group's Role in the Evolution of the International Accounting Standard Setting Process*, Institute of Chartered Accountants in England and Wales, London.

Taplin, R. (2003) 'Harmony, statistical inference with the Herfindahl index and C index', *Abacus*, Vol. 39, No. 2.

Taplin, R. (2004) 'A unified approach to the measurement of international accounting harmony', *Accounting and Business Research*, Vol. 34, No. 1.

Tay, J.S.W. and Parker, R.H. (1990) 'Measuring harmonization and standardization', *Abacus*, Vol. 26, No. 1.

van der Tas, L.G. (1988) 'Measuring harmonisation of financial reporting practice', *Accounting and Business Research*, Vol. 18, No. 70.

van der Tas, L.G. (1992) 'Evidence of EC financial reporting harmonization: the case of deferred tax', *European Accounting Review*, Vol. 1, No. 1.

Wallace, R.S.O. (1990) 'Survival strategies of a global organization: the case of the IASC', *Accounting Horizons*, Vol. 4, No. 2.

Walton, P. (1992) 'Harmonization of accounting in France and Britain: some evidence', *Abacus*, Vol. 28, No. 2.

Weetman, P., Jones, E.A.E., Adams, C.A. and Gray, S.J. (1998) 'Profit measurement and UK accounting standards: a case of increasing disharmony in relation to US GAAP and IASs', *Accounting and Business Research*, Vol. 28, No. 3.

Zeghal, D. and Mhedhbi, K. (2006) 'An analysis of factors affecting the adoption of international accounting standards by developing countries', *International Journal of Accounting*, Vol. 41, No. 4.

Useful websites

Committee of European Securities Regulators	www.cesr-eu.org
Confederation of Asian and Pacific Accountants	www.capa.com.my
European Accounting Association	www.eaa-online.org
European Commission, Internal Market, Financial Reporting and Company Law	europa.eu.ec/ internal_market/accounting
European Financial Reporting Advisory Group	www.efrag.org
Fédération des Experts Comptables Européens (FEE)	www.fee.be
IAS Plus	www.iasplus.com
International Accounting Standards Board	www.iasb.org.uk
International Federation of Accountants	www.ifac.org
International Forum for Accounting Development	www.ifad.net
International Organization of Securities Commissions	www.iosco.org
Organisation for Economic Co-operation and Development	www.oecd.org

QUESTIONS

Suggested answers to the asterisked questions are given at the end of the book.

4.1∗ Was the IASC successful? Explain your reasoning.

4.2∗ Which parties stand to gain from the international harmonization of accounting? What are they doing to achieve it?

4.3 What arguments are there *against* the process of international harmonization of accounting?

4.4 Discuss whether the standards of the IASB should be directed to all companies or to some defined subset of companies.

4.5 Why have the UN and the OECD interested themselves in the harmonization of accounting? How have they gone about it?

4.6 Distinguish between harmony, harmonization and standardization.

4.7 Distinguish between *de jure* standardization and *de facto* standardization, giving examples of how one or both of them can be achieved.

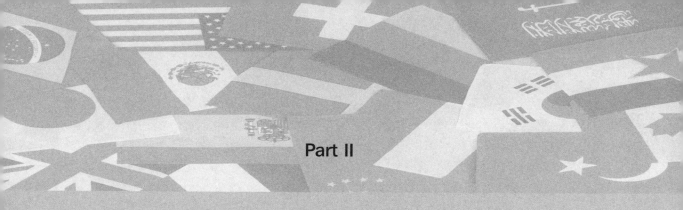

Part II

FINANCIAL REPORTING BY LISTED GROUPS

5 The context of financial reporting by listed groups

Christopher Nobes

OBJECTIVES

After reading this chapter, you should be able to:

- suggest why, and explain how, IFRS has been adopted for certain purposes in the EU;

- explain the difference between adoption of IFRS and convergence of one accounting system with another;

- give reasons why some companies list on foreign exchanges, and why some investors buy shares in foreign companies;

- illustrate the scale of differences between national and international accounting rules;

- outline both high-level and detailed differences between IFRS and US GAAP;

- outline the issues involved with the convergence of IFRS and US GAAP.

5.1 Introduction

Part II of this book (Chapters 5 to 10) examines the financial reporting rules and practices of the consolidated financial statements of listed companies. A large proportion of the world's listed companies use either IFRS or US GAAP for this purpose.

Naturally, US listed companies use US GAAP, and Canadian companies approximately do so, although Canada has announced plans to converge with IFRS by 2011. EU companies (including companies of Germany, France and the UK) use IFRS, and the same applies to Swiss, Australian and Hong Kong companies. In several cases, these companies also reconcile their IFRS statements to US GAAP because they are listed on US exchanges. As may be seen from Table 1.5, these countries contain most of the world's listed companies.

Of large exchanges, this leaves only China (except Hong Kong) and Japan but, as will be shown in Chapter 12, those two countries have been converging their rules with IFRS and/or US GAAP. Also, many Chinese companies provide IFRS data as well as data under Chinese national rules; and several Japanese companies reconcile to US GAAP.

The detailed requirements of IFRS and US GAAP are examined in Chapters 6 and 8 respectively. In between these, Chapter 7 looks at the motivations and scope for different national versions of IFRS practice. This includes listing the overt and covert options within IFRS. Chapter 9 looks at enforcement of these rules, and Chapter 10 tells the story of the pressures put on standard-setters by governments and companies. Before that, this chapter outlines some parts of the context. Section 5.2 explains the EU mechanism for requiring the use of IFRS. Section 5.3 examines the process of national convergence with IFRS. Section 5.4 examines why companies list on more than one exchange and why investors invest in foreign companies. Dual-listed companies provide reconciliations, especially to US GAAP. Section 5.5 uses some of these reconciliations to show the scale and type of differences caused by moving from national rules to IFRS or US GAAP. Section 5.6 then looks at the high-level differences between IFRS and US GAAP, including the contrast between principles-based and rules-based standards. Section 5.7 examines some reconciliations from IFRS to US GAAP, in order to illustrate the detailed differences. Lastly, Section 5.8 looks at the convergence of IFRS and US GAAP.

5.2   IFRS in the EU

By the end of the 1990s, it was clear that harmonization led by the IASC was steaming ahead but that harmonization by means of Directives was being left behind. In 2000, the EU Commission launched a new approach by proposing that, by 2005, it should be compulsory for all listed companies in the EU to use IFRS for consolidated statements, thereby outlawing European domestic rules and US rules for this purpose. This initiative was also part of a desire to strengthen the EU capital markets by establishing a standardized accounting system. Of course, US GAAP was available for this purpose but regarded as too detailed, too rules-based (see Section 5.6) and too immune from European influence to be politically acceptable.

The move to IFRS was facilitated by the growing acceptance of international standards by large European companies and therefore by governments. For example, from 1994 onwards, a number of large German companies started to use international standards or US rules for their consolidated financial statements in order to raise finance more cheaply. The position was formalized in Germany by a law of

1998 that allowed listed companies to do this without needing to comply with normal German accounting requirements.

The Commission published a draft Regulation in 2001, which was approved by the European Parliament and by the Council of Ministers in 2002. It requires EU listed companies to use international standards from 2005 for their consolidated financial statements. Member states were allowed to extend the deadline to 2007 for those companies that had already been using another acceptable set of standards (e.g. US GAAP) or whose listed securities were bonds only.

The legal and political opinion in Brussels is that future new and revised standards cannot be endorsed in advance for EU use. Therefore, the Regulation set up an Accounting Regulatory Committee (ARC) to help the Commission to consider whether changes to IFRS can be endorsed in the EU. ARC contains governmental representatives from all EU member states. This is a way of achieving EU influence over the IASB, but it has brought into existence a form of EU-endorsed IFRS that is slightly different from IFRS proper. To assist the Commission in reaching a view on new or amended IFRSs, a private-sector committee of auditors, preparers and others was established in 2001, called the European Financial Reporting Advisory Group (EFRAG). One of EFRAG's tasks is to liaise with the IASB to try to ensure that the standards take account of issues seen as important in Europe. Then, EFRAG's Technical Experts Group of twelve members considers each standard for its acceptability for endorsement in the EU. Van Hulle (2005) explains the endorsement system. In 2006, yet another feature was added to this process. The Commission set up a small body of independent experts (called the Standards Advice Review Group) to give it advice that is not influenced by governments (unlike ARC) or by audit firms and companies (unlike EFRAG).

In 2004 most of the content of IFRS was endorsed. However, the Commission refused to endorse the whole of IAS 39 on financial instruments. The Regulation does not appear to allow the Commission to amend a standard but, in effect, that is what it did. The endorsed version of IAS 39 did not contain the option to 'mark to market' any financial instruments (i.e. to value them at fair value and take the gains and losses to income). Also, the endorsed IAS 39 has more flexibility on the use of hedge accounting. However, in 2005, the IASB amended IAS 39 in order to restrict the range of instruments that can be fair valued. This was accepted by the EU, so that the difference between IAS 39 and the EU-endorsed version concerns only hedge accounting. Whittington (2005) examines the endorsement of IAS 39. Financial instruments are considered further in Chapters 8 and 16. The political aspects of this process are examined in Chapter 10.

In 2005, another problem emerged because the EU refused to endorse IFRIC 3, on accounting for emission rights. This time, rather than being a political issue, the EU considered the technical solution to be wrong. However, the IASB withdrew IFRIC 3 in June 2005, thus removing a further problem.

A further case occurred in 2007 when a motion was passed in the European Parliament, opposing endorsement of IFRS 8 (operating segments). This is discussed in Chapter 19.

The fact that EU-endorsed IFRS is not the same as IFRS has led to confusion and to audit problems. The auditors' opinion on GlaxoSmithKline's consolidated statements for 2006 is as follows:

In our opinion:

- the group financial statements give a true and fair view, in accordance with IFRSs as adopted by the European Union, of the state of the Group's affairs as at 31st December 2006 and of its profit and cash flows for the year then ended;
- the Group financial statements have been properly prepared in accordance with the Companies Act 1985 and Article 4 of the IAS Regulation; and
- the information given in the Report of the Directors is consistent with the group financial statements.

Separate opinion in relation to IFRSs

As explained in Note 1 to the group financial statements, the group in addition to complying with its legal obligation to comply with the IFRSs as adopted by the European Union, has also complied with the IFRSs as issued by the International Accounting Standards Board.

In our opinion the group financial statements give a true and fair view, in accordance with IFRSs, of the state of the Group's affairs as at 31st December 2006 and of its profit and cash for the year then ended.

Several points need to be made about this:

- The auditors refer to IFRS as adopted by the EU but, in a separate opinion, to IFRS. This is because the company has chosen not to take advantage of the extra permission to use hedge accounting in the EU version of IAS 39, so it can comply with both versions of IFRS.
- The auditors refer to the Companies Act. A company following IFRS does not have to follow national standards and most of national law on accounting. However, some aspects of law (e.g. the requirement to appoint auditors and to publish statements) are still in force.
- The auditors refer to the IAS Regulation. This is the EU Regulation of 2002 that requires listed companies to follow IFRS instead of (most of the) national rules for their consolidated statements.
- The auditors refer to the 'true and fair view'. This is because EU laws still require directors to ensure that financial statements give a true and fair view (see Sections 2.4 and 11.2), and that auditors give an opinion on that. Interestingly, IAS 1 requires instead a 'fair presentation' (see Section 6.2), but a practical assumption has been made that this is the same thing.
- The opinions on true and fair are restricted by the words 'in accordance with IFRSs'. Before 2005, UK (but not US) audit opinions referred to compliance with law *and* giving a true and fair view, as two separate matters.

The process of adoption of IFRS for Germany is examined by Haller and Eierle (2004) and for France, Germany and Italy by Delvaille *et al.* (2005).

It seems clear that compulsory use of IFRS for listed companies' consolidated statements may lead to the end of national standard-setting in some countries (an issue taken up in Section 13.3). The Regulation allows member states to extend the use of IFRSs compulsorily or optionally to unlisted companies and to unconsolidated statements, as examined in Part IV of this book.

5.3 Adoption of, and convergence with, IFRS

It is important to distinguish between IFRS adoption and IFRS convergence. At the level of a jurisdiction, adoption means that national rules are set aside and replaced by a requirement or permission to use IFRS directly. As explained in Section 5.2 this is the compulsory position for listed companies in the EU for their consolidated statements. Unlisted companies are allowed, by the EU Regulation of 2002, to adopt IFRS for their consolidated statements if a member state allows or requires this, and most have allowed it. For unconsolidated statements, the Regulation also allows member states to allow or require IFRS. The response of member states has varied, as explained later in Chapter 13. The word 'adoption' could also be used when a particular company chooses to use a set of accounting rules other than the national one.

In addition to IFRS adoption for some or all accounting purposes, countries might decide gradually to change their national accounting rules towards IFRS. This can be called 'convergence': a particular form of harmonization or standardization. The arguments for and against convergence are therefore covered in Chapter 4. Convergence of IFRS and US GAAP is examined in Section 5.8.

An interesting example of convergence is that of Australia. For 2005 onwards, all IASs and IFRSs have been turned into Australian standards (see 'AASB standards' at aasb.com.au): IFRS 1 is called AASB 1, and IAS 1 is called AASB 101, and so on. However, the AASB versions contained extra paragraphs and appendices and some original IASB paragraphs were deleted. For example, AASB 107 required the use of the direct method for the preparation of cash flow statements whereas IAS 7 also allowed the indirect method. There are also several extra standards with no IASB equivalents. The AASB standards claim that compliance will achieve compliance with IFRS. This may be true, but the Australian process seems like very close convergence with IFRS rather than exact adoption of IFRS. In 2007, the AASB changed its mind about this, partly to avoid confusion at the SEC and elsewhere about whether Australian companies comply with IFRS.

Incidentally, it was normal Australian practice for auditors to refer only to compliance with Australian accounting standards. As a result, it was not clear to foreigners that IFRS was being obeyed. However, from 2007, audit operations on full IFRS are also required.

It must be admitted that, if the Australian case is not exactly 'adoption', then perhaps neither is the EU case, because of the endorsement issue.

Chapter 15 includes an examination of those cases (e.g. the UK) where convergence of national rules with IFRS affects unconsolidated statements, in addition to the direct effects of IFRS on the consolidated statements of listed companies because they must follow IFRS.

Further cases of convergence can be found in emerging economies. Such countries were briefly considered in Section 4.3.3 in the context of the IASC. More recently, convergence has moved faster. For example, China has closely followed IFRS for its listed companies (see Chapter 11). Tyrrall *et al.* (2007) examine the use of IFRS in Kazakhstan.

Hope *et al.* (2006) empirically investigate the factors related to the adoption of IFRS in a country. They conclude that adoption tends to occur in countries that are hoping to improve investor protection and capital market access.

5.4   Foreign listing and foreign investing

5.4.1   Foreign listing

Tables 1.5 and 1.6 in Chapter 1 record the number of domestic and foreign companies listed on some major exchanges. Table 5.1 gives more detail about the origins of the 530 foreign shares on the New York Stock Exchange (NYSE). Some companies listed more than one type of share, so the numbers are larger than in Table 1.6.

Table 5.1 **Foreign listers on NYSE, 2007**

	Number
Canada	89
Bermuda	42
Europe:	
UK	54
Netherlands	31
France	18
Germany	17
Switzerland	15
Italy	11
Greece	10
Rest	44
Latin America:	
Brazil	36
Mexico	16
Chile	17
Argentina	11
Rest	7
Asia:	
Japan	19
China	21
India	10
Rest	38
Other	24
Total	530

Source: nyse.com, 9 April 2007.

As may be seen, Canada provided the largest number of foreign listers, followed by the UK. The large number of US listers based in the small island of Bermuda are mostly financial institutions enjoying a low-tax regime in a safe English-speaking country. Any particular company might be listed on many exchanges. For example, the 2000 annual report of Volvo, the Swedish car company, discloses listings on the exchanges of five foreign countries, but in 2007 there was only one: the US (the NASDAQ). Norsk Hydro, the Norwegian power company, reveals listing on seven foreign exchanges in 2000, reduced to the US, UK, France and Germany in 2007.

The above two are very large companies based in rather small countries, which suggests one of the main reasons for foreign listing: to attract extra investors and widen the pool of shareholders. For example, Norsk Hydro reports that 18 per cent of its shares are owned by US shareholders and 9 per cent by UK shareholders. Gray et al. (1994) look at foreign listings of several large European companies. Saudagaran (1988) found evidence that a company's size relative to its domestic exchange helps to explain foreign listings.

Another reason for foreign listing is that the company wishes to raise its profile in a foreign country among potential customers, employees or regulators. The first listing of a German company on a US exchange (Daimler-Benz in 1993) was related to the setting up of factories in the US and the expansion of sales. It was followed by a takeover of the US car company, Chrysler, that was presented as a 'merger of equals' for public relations and accounting reasons (see Section 8.7.2). Radebaugh et al. (1995) look in more detail at this particular case.

Of course, as well as potential benefits from foreign listing, there are also costs. These include the expenses of initially satisfying the accounting and other require-ments of the foreign exchange or its regulator, and then the continuing need to provide extra or different accounting compared to domestic requirements. Biddle and Saudagaran (1989) found evidence of the resistance to extra disclosures by MNEs from eight countries (including the UK), although Gray and Roberts (1997) found no such evidence for UK companies. The world's largest equity markets are based in New York, including the New York Stock Exchange and NASDAQ. These exchanges have their own requirements but the major problem for companies wishing to list on them is to satisfy the requirement of the Securities and Exchange Commission (SEC), including the onerous auditing and corporate governance requirements of the Sarbanes-Oxley Act. Foreign registrants could present full-scale US GAAP annual reports but generally they choose instead to file Form 20-F that contains many of the normal SEC disclosure requirements but allows non-US accounting with numerical reconciliations to US GAAP for equity and income. Unless the foreign company wishes to make a public offering, it is allowed to pre-sent reduced segment reporting using its domestic rules.

If a non-US company wishes to gain access to US markets without so much cost, it can arrange for its shares to be traded 'over the counter' (not fully listed) through American Depository Receipts (ADRs). The ADRs (which contain a package of shares) are traded, rather than the shares themselves. The SEC then accepts domestic annual reports without reconciliation to US GAAP. It is also possible to arrange for ADRs to be traded on an exchange but then reconciliation is necessary.

The world's largest exchange in terms of the number of foreign listers is London, with over 700 of them by the start of 2007, mostly from other European countries. Again, London provides greater liquidity than other European exchanges. In this case, little extra cost is involved because IFRS is used throughout the EU. Furthermore, the Sarbanes-Oxley Act does not apply. As a result, London has been taking over from New York as the place for foreign companies to make new issues or new listings. Partly for this reason, the SEC announced in 2007 that it would accept IFRS statements from foreign registrants for 2007 reports onwards (see Section 5.8).

5.4.2 Foreign investing

Having looked above at why a company might seek foreign investors, we now look at why an investor might seek foreign opportunities to invest.

It is easy, looking backwards, to identify countries where shares have risen more rapidly than in one's own country over the last one, five or 10 years. This would argue for overseas investment if the past were a good predictor of the future. Even if it is not, a large investor might wish to diversify among several countries because share price movements in different regions of the world are not strongly correlated. Gross annual purchases by foreigners of US securities in 2000 amounted to $7 trillion; and purchases by US residents of foreign securities were about half that. These figures had grown by about ten times over the previous 10 years (Griever et al., 2001).

Nevertheless, Lewis (1999) reports that investors in Europe, Japan and the US put only about 10 per cent of their investments into foreign shares, which is far below what one would expect if they considered foreign shares to be perfect substitutes for domestic ones. Choi and Levich (1990) looked at investors from the US, Japan and Europe and found that many were dissuaded from foreign investment by concern about different accounting practices. Others were put to extra expense in order to adjust the foreign statements. Later, Choi and Levich (1996) found that only about a quarter of European investors were restrained by international accounting differences. Miles and Nobes (1998) found that London-based investors did not generally adjust for the accounting differences.

Other reasons for home country bias could include currency risk, political risk, language barriers, transaction costs and taxation. Coval and Moskovitz (1999) find that investment managers show regional preferences even within the United States. On a related matter, Helliwell (1998) reports that Canadians are more than ten times more likely to trade with each other than with the US.

5.5 Reconciliations from national rules to US GAAP and IFRS

Some examples of reconciliation to US GAAP were given in Section 1.1. Further examples of reconciliation are given here relating to 2004, which was the last year for which EU listed companies produced consolidated statements under national rules. Table 5.2 shows the enormous adjustment from UK profit for Vodafone for the first half-year that it prepared IFRS information. The difference is largely due to the elimination of the expense of amortization of goodwill (see Chapter 6).

Table 5.2 **Vodafone income statement (£m)**

	UK GAAP	Presentational adjustments	Accounting adjustments	IFRS
	Six months to 30.9.2004			
Revenue	16,796	(54)	–	16,742
Operating (loss)/profit	(1,615)	(598)	6,972	4,759
Exceptional non-operating items	22	(22)	–	–
Non operating income & expenses	–	16	–	16
Net financing costs	(291)	91	(35)	(235)
(Loss)/profit before tax	(1,884)	(513)	6,937	4,540
Tax	(1,559)	865	(163)	(857)
Exceptional deferred tax credit	572	(572)	–	–
Minority interests	(324)	220	36	(68)
(Loss)/profit for the period	(3,195)	–	6,810	3,615
Basic (loss)/earnings per share	(4.77p)			5.40p

Source: Adapted from Vodafone income statement in the *Vodafone Interim Announcement, 2004*.

Another example, this time from German to US rules, is given as Table 5.3. The table combines the reconciliations for income and for shareholders' equity provided by the large German chemical company, BASF. The income reconciliation for 2004 contains some fairly large adjustments that happen to cancel out. However, for

Table 5.3 **Reconciliations by BASF from German to US rules for 2004 (€m)**

	Income	Equity
As reported income under German GAAP	1,883.0	15,765.0
Adjustments required to conform with US GAAP		
Capitalization of interest	(4.5)	472.7
Capitalization of software developed for internal use	(53.5)	128.3
Accounting for pensions	41.0	924.3
Accounting for provisions	(8.1)	244.4
Accounting for derivatives and long-term foreign currency items	194.5	3.2
Valuation of securities at market values	6.8	191.5
Valuation adjustments relating to companies accounted for under the equity method	(161.6)	39.0
Inventory valuation	(3.4)	18.9
Reversal of goodwill amortization	148.7	469.5
Other adjustments	29.8	58.6
Deferred taxes and recognition of tax effects of dividend payments	(210.4)	(810.8)
Minority interests	0.5	(345.5)
In accordance with US GAAP	1,862.8	17,159.1

Source: Adapted from the *BASF Annual Report, 2004*, p. 92. BASF SA, Ludwigshafen, Germany. Reproduced with permission.

2003, the US version of profit was 45 per cent higher than the German version. Several of these issues are taken up again in Chapters 13 and 15.

Of course, the two international benchmarks are not the same, as will now be examined.

5.6   High-level IFRS/US differences

5.6.1   Principles and rules

The collapse of Enron and its audit firm, Andersen, in 2001/2 was one of the factors that led to a reconsideration of how to set accounting standards in the United States. In 2002, the Financial Accounting Standards Board published a consultative document seeking views on whether it should move more towards principles rather than rules (FASB, 2002).

In the case of Enron, one of the main accounting issues was that many controlled entities (special purpose vehicles) with large liabilities were not consolidated. The US rule on the definition of a subsidiary (in APB Opinion 18) is based on the ownership of more than half the voting shares, rather than on the IASB's principle of 'power to govern the financial and operating policies' (in IAS 27). Furthermore, unlike in IAS 1, there is no requirement (or even permission) in the US to depart from the rules of standards on the grounds that the result is misleading. This was confirmed by the FASB in 2005 by an exposure draft on the hierarchy of principles. However, it seems unlikely that the FASB will be able to move substantially towards the IASB's style of standards because it would require the re-writing of all the US literature and the re-training of US accountants and auditors.

The issue led to an interesting academic debate. Schipper (2003) points out that the FASB tries to use principles when it is writing the rules. Nelson (2003) suggests that standards are at various points on a continuum from principles to rules. Rules include 'specific criteria, "bright line" thresholds, examples, scope restrictions, exceptions . . . implementation guidance' (page 91). Nelson suggests that rules might be useful for reducing imprecision but can lead to excessive complexity and to the structuring of transactions by companies in order to avoid a threshold (e.g. to omit something from consolidation or to escape from the capitalization of lease liabilities).

Nobes (2005) suggests that, for several standards, the quantity of rules could be reduced by identifying better principles, which would often lead to more precision and less structuring at the same time. He suggests, for example, abandoning the distinction between operating and finance leases (see, also, McGregor, 1996 and Nailor and Lennard, 1999) and treating government grants as immediate income (see, also, Westwood and Mackenzie, 1999). These can be compared to the current requirement of IFRS in Chapter 6.

Another aspect of the greater detail of US GAAP is that it contains fewer explicit options than IFRS does. There used to be more IFRS options before many were removed in 2003. Some examples of the surviving options are given in Table 5.4. For all but the first item, the US GAAP column shows no option whereas IFRS has

Table 5.4 **Some options in IFRS and US GAAP**

	IFRS	US GAAP
LIFO (Ch. 8)	No	Yes
Presenting assets in order of increasing liquidity (Ch. 2)	Yes	No
Not recognizing some actuarial gains and losses (Ch. 16)	Yes	No
Proportional consolidation for joint ventures (Ch. 17)	Yes	No
Buildings measured at fair value (Ch. 6)	Yes	No

Source: author.

one. The bracketed chapter numbers refer to the chapters in this book that cover the issues in more detail.

5.6.2 Asset measurement

A further high-level difference between IFRS and US GAAP is the greater permission or requirement in IFRS to use fair value rather than historical cost. One main example of this appears as the last item in Table 5.4; a more detailed list is shown as Table 5.5, none of which apply in the US. This is in addition to the requirements to use fair value under IAS 39 for trading financial assets and liabilities and available-for-sale financial assets (as in US GAAP).

Table 5.5 **Measurement at fair value under IFRS but not US GAAP**

IAS 16 (option)	Property, plant and equipment
IAS 38 (option)	Intangible assets with an active market
IAS 40 (option)	Investment property
IAS 41 (requirement)	Biological assets

Source: author.

5.7 Reconciliations from IFRS to US GAAP

In Section 5.5, some reconciliations from national rules to IFRS or US GAAP were presented. These illustrated the differences between national rules and the two internationally recognized systems. In Section 5.6, the high-level differences between these two systems were studied. In this section, the detailed accounting differences between IFRS and US GAAP are illustrated using published reconciliations, which were required by the SEC until 2007. The source of such data is companies using IFRS for their consolidated financial reporting that are also listed on a US exchange.

Tables 5.6 and 5.7 show reconciliations (of income and equity) for the German company Bayer, and the French company, Alcatel-Lucent. As may be seen, there are

Table 5.6 **Reconciliations from IFRS to US GAAP by Bayer, 2006 (€m)**

	Income	Equity
As reported under IFRS	1,695	12,851
Business combinations	79	950
Pensions	(168)	11
In-process research and development	(1,375)	(1,454)
Asset impairment	23	(114)
Early retirement program	(27)	74
Revaluation surplus	4	(58)
Other	(17)	2
Deferred tax effect on adjustments	67	3
Minority interest	(12)	(84)
As reported under US GAAP	269	12,181

Source: Adapted from the *Bayer Annual Report, 2006*. Bayer AG, Leverkusen, Germany. Reproduced with permission.

Table 5.7 **Reconciliations from IFRS to US GAAP by Alcatel-Lucent, 2006 (€m)**

	Income	Equity
Under IFRS	(176)	15,493
Business combinations, goodwill	(403)	4,433
Development costs	39	(146)
Restructuring	(47)	12
Sale and lease-back	(50)	(245)
Compound instruments	39	(840)
Pensions	61	837
Other	(20)	2
Tax effect	(33)	(262)
Under US GAAP	(590)	19,284

Source: Adapted from the *Alcatel-Lucent Annual Report, 2006*. Alcatel-Lucent, Paris.

several adjustments. A few companies also show reconciliations the other way, that is from US GAAP to IFRS. This particularly relates to the move by some German companies from using US GAAP to using IFRS in response to the EU Regulation of 2002. Table 5.8 shows the equity and income reconciliations of Degussa Group for 2003.

The major differences in the rules are listed in Section 8.9, after IFRS and US GAAP have been examined in Chapters 6 and 8. The largest adjustments in Tables 5.6 and 5.7 are caused by differences in consolidation rules. An earlier one of these (the amortization of goodwill under IFRS) no longer applies from 2005 onwards. These consolidation differences are also taken up again in Chapter 17.

Table 5.8 Reconciliations from US GAAP to IFRS for Degussa Group (€m)

	Income (2003)	Equity (31.12.2003)
In accordance with US GAAP	(159)	5,017
Minority interests (stated in shareholders' equity under IFRS)	–	42
Reduction in goodwill impairment	94	94
Impairment charge on property, plant and equipment	(115)	(255)
Other liabilities	–	(53)
Pension provisions	(116)	(170)
Other provisions	(97)	(316)
Deferred taxes	131	308
Other adjustments	1	(14)
In accordance with IFRS	(261)	4,653

Source: Adapted from the *Degussa AG Annual Report, 2004*. Degussa AG, Düsseldorf, Germany. Reproduced with permission.

5.8 Convergence of IFRS and US GAAP

Section 5.3 explained the difference between adoption of a set of rules and convergence with them. It also looked at convergence of national rules with IFRS. Sections 5.5 to 5.7 examined several aspects of the differences between IFRS and US GAAP. This section looks at convergence between them.

Esty and Geradin (2001) note that liberalization of markets has been a major feature of recent years. They examine, for several topics (but not accounting), the arguments for and against allowing competition between two or more sets of regulations. Competition might allow alternative solutions to be tested and refined. It might also guard against dictatorial regulatory behaviour and against inefficient bureaucracies. However, co-ordination might reduce inefficiency caused by companies having to operate under the different rules of different jurisdictions, and might guard against a competition by jurisdictions to attract companies by having the most lax rules.

In this context, it is interesting to note that US GAAP and IFRS are both amongst the world's toughest sets of rules, in terms of coverage of topics, elimination of choices, and required disclosures. Clearly, however, US GAAP is the tougher of the two. Despite this, as noted earlier, many foreign companies had listed on US exchanges although they had to comply with US GAAP.

The FASB and the IASB are volunteering to reduce regulatory competition, for the sake of continued standardization and the attendant advantages (see Chapter 4). In September 2002, the FASB and the IASB announced plans to achieve convergence in a document called the 'Norwalk Agreement'. The proposal was that some detailed differences should be removed rapidly and then other differences gradually. Table 5.9 shows examples of convergence. These issues are discussed in Chapters 6 to 8. In 2005, the SEC announced that it could now foresee the day when it would

Table 5.9 **IFRS and US convergence**

IFRS moves to US GAAP	US GAAP moves to IFRS
Discontinued operations, IFRS 5 (2004)	Exchanges of assets, SFAS 153 (2004)
Segment reporting, IFRS 8 (2006)	Accounting policies, SFAS 154 (2005)
Borrowing costs, IAS 23 (revised 2007)	Fair value option, SFAS 159 (2007)

accept IFRS statements without reconciliation to US GAAP. In 2007, this proposal was settled; to apply for the 2007 statements filed with the SEC in 2008.

Schipper (2005) examines the implications of US/IFRS convergence. She suggests that there will be pressure on the IASB to issue more detailed interpretations, and pressure for greater enforcement (see Chapter 9). De Lange and Howieson (2006) examine the institutional structures of the FASB and the IASB. They predict that the FASB will dominate standard setting and that there is little incentive for US companies to adopt IFRS.

SUMMARY

- Most of the world's listed companies use IFRS or US GAAP for their consolidated financial reporting.

- International standards have to be endorsed before adoption in the EU, and some elements of standards have not been endorsed.

- In addition to the adoption of IFRS by some countries for some purposes, the rules in some countries are being made more similar to IFRS or US GAAP.

- Over 500 foreign companies are listed on the New York Stock Exchange. One of the reasons for such foreign listings is gaining access to larger equity markets. There are also several costs.

- Some investors, similarly, seek more exciting returns overseas, but this activity is constrained by concerns about risk and various costs.

- The differences between national rules and IFRS or US GAAP can have large effects on financial statements.

- There are also differences between IFRS and US GAAP. These include a greater tendency of US GAAP to contain detailed rules and to forbid valuations above cost.

- Published reconciliations from IFRS to US GAAP illustrate some large remaining differences.

- Convergence is also under way between those two 'international' benchmarks.

References

Biddle, G.C. and Saudagaran, S.M. (1989) 'The effect of financial disclosure levels on firms' choices among alternative foreign stock exchange listings', *Journal of International Financial Management and Accounting*, Vol. 1, No. 1.

Coval, J.D. and Moskovitz, T.J. (1999) 'Home bias at home: local equity preferences in domestic portfolios', *Review of Financial Studies*, Vol. 7, No. 1, pp. 2045–73.

Choi, F.D.S. and Levich, R.M. (1990) *The Capital Market Effects of International Accounting Diversity*, Dow Jones-Irwin, Homewood.

Choi, F.D.S. and Levich, R.M. (1996) 'Accounting diversity', in B. Steil (ed.) *The European Equity Markets*, Royal Institute of International Affairs, London.

De Lange, P. and Howieson, B. (2006) 'International accounting standards and U.S. exceptionalism', *Critical Perspectives on Accounting*, Vol. 17, No. 8, pp. 1007–32.

Delvaille, P., Ebbers, G. and Saccon, C. (2005) 'International financial reporting convergence: evidence from three continental European countries', *Accounting in Europe*, Vol. 2, pp. 137–64.

Esty, D.C. and Geradin, D. (2001) *Regulatory Competition and Economic Integration*, Oxford University Press, Oxford.

FASB (2002) *Principles-based Approach to US Standard Setting*, Financial Accounting Standards Board, Norwalk.

Gray, S.J., Meek, G.K. and Roberts, C.B. (1994) 'Financial deregulation, stock exchange listing choice, and the development of a European capital market', in Zimmerman, V.K. (ed.) *The New Europe: Recent Political and Economic Implications for Accountants and Accounting*, Center for International Education and Research in Accounting, University of Illinois.

Gray, S.J. and Roberts, C.B. (1997) 'Foreign company listings on the London Stock Exchange: Listing patterns and influential factors', in T.E. Cooke and C.W. Nobes (eds) *The Development of Accounting in an International Context*, Routledge, London.

Griever, W.L., Lee, G.A. and Warnock, F.E. (2001) 'The U.S. system for measuring cross-border investment in securities: a primer with a discussion of recent developments', *Federal Reserve Bulletin*, Vol. 87, No. 10, pp. 634–50.

Haller, A. and Eierle, B. (2004) 'The adaptation of German accounting rules to IFRS: a legislative balancing act', *Accounting in Europe*, Vol. 1, pp. 27–50.

Helliwell, J. (1998) *How Much Do National Borders Matter?*, Brookings Institution, Washington, DC.

Hope, O.-K., Jin, J. and Kang, T. (2006) 'Empirical evidence on jurisdictions that adopt IFRS', *Journal of International Accounting Research*, Vol. 5, No. 2, pp. 1–20.

Lewis, K.K. (1999) 'Trying to explain home bias in equities and consumption', *Journal of Economic Literature*, Vol. 37, pp. 571–608.

McGregor, W. (1996) *Accounting for Leases: A New Approach*, FASB for G4+1, Norwalk.

Miles, S. and Nobes, C.W. (1998) 'The use of foreign accounting data in UK financial institutions', *Journal of Business Finance and Accounting*, Vol. 25, Nos. 3 & 4.

Nailor, H. and Lennard, A. (1999) *Leases: Implementation of A New Approach*, FASB for G4+1, Norwalk.

Nelson, M.W. (2003) 'Behavioral evidence on the effects of principles- and rules-based standards', *Accounting Horizons*, Vol. 17, No. 1, pp. 91–104.

Nobes, C.W. (2005) 'Rules-based standards and the lack of principles in accounting', *Accounting Horizons*, Vol. 19, No. 1, pp. 25–34.

Radebaugh, L.H., Gebhart, G. and Gray, S.J. (1995) 'Foreign stock exchange listings: a case study of Daimler-Benz', *Journal of International Financial Management and Accounting*, Vol. 6, No. 2, pp. 158–92.

Saudagaran, S.M. (1988) 'An empirical study of selected factors influencing the decision to list in foreign stock exchanges', *Journal of International Business Studies*, Spring, pp. 101–27.

Schipper, K. (2003) 'Principles-based accounting standards', *Accounting Horizons*, Vol. 17, No. 1, pp. 61–72.

Schipper, K. (2005) 'The introduction of international accounting standards in Europe: implications for international convergence', *European Accounting Review*, Vol. 14, No. 1.

Tyrrall, D., Woodward, D. and Rakhimbekova, A. (2007) 'The relevance of International Financial Reporting Standards to a developing country: evidence from Kazakhstan', *International Journal of Accounting*, Vol. 42, No. 1, pp. 82–110.

Van Hulle, K. (2005) 'From accounting directives to international accounting standards', Ch. 6.1 in C. Leuz, D. Pfaff and A. Hopwood, *The Economics and Politics of Accounting*, Oxford University Press, Oxford.

Westwood, M. and Mackenzie, A. (1999) *Accounting by Recipients for Non-reciprocal Transfers, Excluding Contributions by Owners*, FASB for G4+1, Norwalk.

Whittington, G. (2005) 'The adoption of international accounting standards in the European Union', *European Accounting Review*, Vol. 14, No. 1.

Useful websites

The websites listed at the end of Chapters 4, 6, 8 and 11 are relevant for aspects of this chapter.

QUESTIONS

Suggested answers to the asterisked questions are given at the end of the book.

5.1∗ Distinguish between harmonization, standardization, convergence, adoption and EU endorsement.

5.2∗ Using the reconciliations of this chapter and the information in Chapter 2, comment on the adjustments necessary when moving from German or UK to US or IFRS accounting.

5.3 Which sort of companies might wish to list on a foreign exchange? Is this practice increasing or decreasing, and why?

5.4 Discuss the high-level differences between IFRS and US GAAP. Is the SEC right to demand reconciliations of IFRS to US GAAP from foreign companies that are listed on US exchanges?

5.5 Explain the arguments for and against allowing the IASB and the FASB to compete in the provision of accounting standards. Which arguments are the stronger?

6 The requirements of International Financial Reporting Standards

Christopher Nobes

OBJECTIVES

After reading this chapter, you should be able to:

- outline the overall objectives of financial reporting under IFRS, including the underlying assumptions;
- discuss the meaning of relevance and reliability and how they might conflict;
- explain the definition of assets and liabilities and when such items should be recognized on statements of financial position;
- outline the valuation methods used under IFRS for various assets;
- give examples of various types of liabilities that would be recognized under IFRS;
- explain the basic features of group accounting for subsidiaries, joint ventures and associates.

6.1 Introduction

Chapters 4 and 5 examined the purposes of standardization and its progress so far. The history and structure of the International Accounting Standards Committee (IASC) and the International Accounting Standards Board (IASB) were reviewed there. However, those chapters did not deal with the detailed requirements of the standards (IFRSs), which is the province of this chapter.

A list of IFRSs (including IASs) is shown as Table 6.1. There are some numbers missing because some of the original standards have been replaced (see Table 4.2). Also, most standards have been revised since their original issue.

In some cases, IFRSs contain optional treatments because the old Board could not make up its mind or could not achieve the required majority ($^3/_4$ until 2001) without the inclusion of an option. Some of these cases are marked by calling the choices 'the benchmark treatment' and 'the allowed alternative treatment'. In only one case is the benchmark said to be preferred (proportional consolidation in IAS 31; see Chapter 17 for more detail). Many options were removed in 2003.

This chapter looks at the content of most IFRSs under five sections, each of which deals with related topics. Consequently, the coverage here is not in the numerical order of the standards. A few current standards are left out where, for example, they are related to a specialized sector (e.g. IFRS 4 on insurance contracts). However, Appendix 6.1 at the end of the chapter gives a summary of the contents of all the standards in numerical order.

6.2 The conceptual framework and some basic standards

6.2.1 Overall objective

The IASB's *Framework for the Preparation and Presentation of Financial Statements* was published in 1989. It owes much to the framework published in the United States

Table 6.1 IASB standards (January 2008)

IAS	1	Presentation of financial statements
IAS	2	Inventories
IAS	7	Cash flow statements
IAS	8	Accounting policies, changes in accounting estimates and errors
IAS	10	Events after the balance sheet date
IAS	11	Construction contracts
IAS	12	Income taxes
IAS	16	Property, plant and equipment
IAS	17	Leases
IAS	18	Revenue
IAS	19	Employee benefits
IAS	20	Accounting for government grants and disclosure of government assistance
IAS	21	The effects of changes in foreign exchange rates
IAS	23	Borrowing costs
IAS	24	Related party disclosures
IAS	26	Accounting and reporting by retirement benefit plans
IAS	27	Consolidated and separate financial statements
IAS	28	Investments in associates
IAS	29	Financial reporting in hyperinflationary economies
IAS	31	Interests in joint ventures
IAS	32	Financial instruments: presentation
IAS	33	Earnings per share
IAS	34	Interim financial reporting
IAS	36	Impairment of assets
IAS	37	Provisions, contingent liabilities and contingent assets
IAS	38	Intangible assets
IAS	39	Financial instruments: recognition and measurement
IAS	40	Investment property
IAS	41	Agriculture
IFRS	1	First-time adoption of IFRSs
IFRS	2	Share-based payment
IFRS	3	Business combinations
IFRS	4	Insurance contracts
IFRS	5	Non-current assets held for sale and discontinued operations
IFRS	6	Exploration for and evaluation of mineral resources
IFRS	7	Financial instruments: disclosures
IFRS	8	Operating segments

by the Financial Accounting Standards Board from the late 1970s onwards (see Chapter 8 for more detail). The IASB and the FASB are working jointly on a project to revise the *Framework*. A Discussion Paper relating to objectives and qualitative characteristics was published in 2006.

The IASB's *Framework* is designed for use by the Board when setting accounting standards and for preparers, auditors and users of financial statements as they interpret accounting standards.

The *Framework* assumes that the main purpose of financial statements is to give useful information to various users (typically investors) in order to improve their

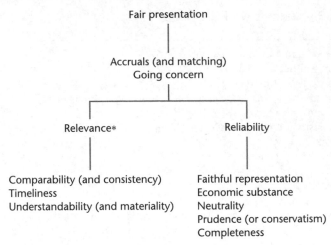

Figure 6.1 **IASB's concepts**

Note: *Although the IASB's documents show all the concepts listed on this page, they show a more complicated relationship than on the left of this figure for the three concepts shown here under relevance.

financial decisions. The *Framework* itself is not a standard, but IAS 1 (*Presentation*) turns many of its ideas into instructions. A large number of concepts, assumptions, etc. can be found in the *Framework* and in IAS 1, but they could be summarized as in Figure 6.1, although the IASB's documents do not list them so neatly into two columns.

The overall objective is to give a fair presentation of the state of affairs and performance of a business, so that users of financial statements can make good decisions. The *Framework* suggests that, in the IASB context, fair presentation could also be referred to as giving 'a true and fair view', which is the fundamental requirement in the laws of countries of the European Union (see, also, ASB, 2005). IAS 1 contains a 'fair presentation' override of the sort found in the EU Fourth Directive (see Chapter 11). However, IAS 1 also requires numerical reconciliation from any basis that departs from an IFRS to the basis required in the IFRS.

In order to achieve a fair presentation, it is important that the information presented is relevant and reliable. Most of the other concepts can be explained under those two headings.

6.2.2 Underlying assumptions

Accruals, including matching

The essence of the accruals convention is that transactions should be recognized when they occur, not by reference to the date of the receipt or payment of cash. Also, the process of profit calculation consists of relating together (matching) the revenues with the expenses; it is not concerned with relating together cash receipts and cash payments. Both ways of calculating may be relevant for prediction of the future. The balance sheet and the income statement are based on the accruals convention, but the cash flow statement is not.

IAS 1 describes the accruals basis of accounting, but notes that the application of the matching concept does not allow the recognition of items in the balance sheet which do not meet the normal criteria for the recognition of assets or liabilities. The IASB *Framework* gives primacy to the definitions of asset/liability (see below) rather than revenue/expense.

Going concern

This important convention states that, in the absence of evidence to the contrary, it is assumed that the business will continue for the foreseeable future. This convention has a major influence when evaluating particular items in the balance sheet. It allows the assumption that inventory will eventually be sold in the normal course of business, i.e. at normal selling prices. It also allows for the idea of depreciation. If the enterprise depreciates an item of plant over 10 years, then it is assuming that the plant will have a useful life *to the enterprise* of 10 years, which assumes that the enterprise will continue in operation for at least 10 years.

Proposed change

The IASB's Discussion Paper of 2006 proposes to remove the concept of 'underlying assumptions'. The accruals concept becomes part of giving relevant information. The going concern convention is not mentioned.

6.2.3 Relevance

It is clear that, in order to be useful, information must be relevant to its purpose, which is seen to be economic decision making. This requires predictions of future cash flows, which can be based partly on relevant past and present information in statements such as the balance sheet and income statement. Relevance is related to the following concepts.

Comparability, including consistency

Financial information is unlikely to be relevant unless it can be compared across periods and across companies. This requires as much consistency as possible in the use of methods of measuring and presenting numbers; it requires also that any changes in these methods should be disclosed.

Timeliness

Relevance is increased if information is up to date. This raises a common problem that there may be an inconsistency between concepts. For example, the need to ensure reliability of information may slow down its publication. The regulators of financial reporting in many countries set time limits for the publication of financial statements and require reporting more than once a year.

Understandability, including materiality

Clearly, information cannot be relevant unless it can be understood. However, in a complex world, information may have to be complex to achieve a fair presentation. The rule-makers and preparers are allowed to assume that the important users are educated and intelligent.

Connected with this is the concept of materiality, which implies that insignificant items should not be given the same emphasis as significant items. The insignificant items are by definition unlikely to influence decisions or provide useful information to decision-makers, but they may well cause complication and confusion to the user of accounts. Immaterial items do not need separate disclosure and may not need to be accounted for strictly correctly. What is 'insignificant' in any particular context may be a highly subjective decision.

6.2.4 Reliability

For information to be useful, it must be possible for users to depend on it. The several concepts below are related to this, although some of them are also clearly related to relevance.

Faithful representation

The readers of financial statements should not be misled by the contents of the statements. Transactions, assets and liabilities should be shown in such a way as to represent as well as possible what underlies them. For example, a balance sheet should not show an item under the heading 'assets' unless it meets the definition of an asset. This assumes that readers have a good grasp of the concepts used.

Economic substance

This concept is related to faithful representation. It is sometimes expressed as showing the economic substance of transactions rather than their legal form. However, this is too simple. The exact economic substance will rest on the exact legal arrangements. The issue here is to see through any superficial legal or other arrangements to the real economic effects.

To take an example, suppose that an enterprise signs a lease which commits it to paying rentals to use a machine for the whole of the expected life of the machine. This is very similar to borrowing money and buying a machine, in the sense that the enterprise (under either arrangement) has control over the operational use of the asset and has an obligation to pay money. The legal form is that the enterprise does not own the machine or have any outstanding unpaid debt owing, but the substance is that it has an asset and a liability (see the definitions in the next section).

Similarly, if an enterprise sold a machine to a financial company and immediately leased it back for most of its life, the legal form is that there has been a sale but the substance is that the enterprise still has the asset.

Neutrality

To be reliable, information needs to be free from bias, otherwise the prediction of the future will be warped.

Prudence or conservatism

The most famous bias in accounting is prudence or conservatism. There is still some room for this, despite the above requirement for neutrality.

Full-blown conservatism can still be found in some countries (see Chapter 15) in order to protect certain users (including creditors) from the risk of making the financial statements look too good, particularly given the excessive optimism of some businessmen. Recognizing that a number of estimates are involved in accounting, the accountant, according to this convention, should ensure the avoidance of overstatement by deliberately setting out to achieve a degree of understatement. This requires that similar items, some of which are positive and some of which are negative, should not be treated symmetrically.

In the IASB *Framework*, prudence is not supposed to be this overridingly strong. It is instead the exercise of a degree of caution in the context of uncertainty. In the IASB's Discussion Paper of 2006, prudence does not feature at all.

Completeness

Information needs to be as complete as possible within the constraints of materiality. Any important omissions would cause the financial statements to be misleading. However, the rule-makers (in this case, the IASB) should bear in mind that some demands for information may be too costly to the enterprise. The benefits of the information should outweigh the costs of producing it.

6.2.5 Assets and liabilities

Accounting can work on one of two bases:

Method 1

- *Expenses* of 20X1 are the costs of any period that relate to 20X1; and therefore . . .
- *Assets* at the end of 20X1 are any remaining debits.

Method 2

- *Assets* at the end of 20X1 are controlled resources that are expected to give future benefits; and therefore . . .
- *Expenses* of 20X1 are any remaining debits.

The IASB *Framework* gives primacy to the second way of defining the elements, by starting with an asset defined as follows (paragraph 49):

a resource controlled by the enterprise as a result of past events and from which future economic benefits are expected to flow to the enterprise.

This has the effect of reducing the importance of the matching concept, as noted above. If an expense is postponed in order to match it against a future revenue, it would have to be stored in the balance sheet as an asset. However, this is not allowed under IFRS unless the amount meets the definition of an asset. This restriction on the items to be shown as assets does not come from a desire to be prudent but from a desire to comply with a coherent framework.

The IASB gives similar importance to the definition of 'liability'. According to the *Framework* (paragraph 49):

A liability is a present obligation of the enterprise arising from past events, the settlement of which is expected to result in an outflow from the enterprise of resources . . .

An obligation is an unavoidable requirement to transfer resources to a third party. Many liabilities are clear legal obligations of exact amounts, such as accounts payable or loans from the bank. Some liabilities are of uncertain timing or amount. These are called 'provisions'. Depending on the nature of legal contracts, some of these provisions are also legally enforceable, such as provisions to pay pensions to retired employees or to repair machinery sold to customers that breaks down soon after sale. Some obligations are not based on precise laws or legal contracts but would probably be enforced by a court of law based on normal business practices or, at least, the enterprise would suffer so much commercial damage if it did not settle the obligation that it cannot reasonably avoid settling it.

The definition of liability is being reconsidered as part of the IASB/FASB project to revise the *Framework*.

6.2.6 Financial statements and accounting policies

Unlike some national laws, IAS 1 does not set out standard formats for financial statements. However, it does give a minimum list of headings to be shown on financial statements.

IAS 1 requires an entity to present four financial statements. First, there is the statement of financial position, often called a balance sheet in US or UK practice. In this book, we use the two terms interchangeably. If there have been any restatements (e.g. due to policy changes or error corrections), then an opening balance sheet for the earliest period presented must also be shown. If figures for two years are shown (the minimum required by IAS 1), this would mean that three balance sheets would be shown.

Next, there must be a statement of comprehensive income (SCI). This must include all items of income and expense, including revaluations. There must be no reserve movements; no gains and losses go directly to equity. However, some gains and losses (e.g. some revaluations and some foreign currency gains and losses) have traditionally been treated differently in IFRS and all national accounting systems. IAS 1 preserves this idea because these items are shown at the bottom of the SCI as 'other comprehensive income'. The total *excluding* these amounts is shown as the 'profit or loss'. The technical term 'earnings' (see Section 6.6) also excludes these amounts.

IAS 1 allows an entity to show a separate 'income statement', containing only the elements of profit and loss, before the SCI. If so, the SCI begins with the profit or loss. In this case, the entity will have five financial statements rather than four.

In this book, we will also sometimes use 'profit and loss' to refer to the parts of income excluding other comprehensive income. The equivalent UK statement is, indeed, called a 'profit and loss account'. In the US, the 'income statement' is the equivalent statement. Consequently, this book uses that term in some chapters.

Unfortunately, there is no clear principle to explain why some gains and losses are 'profit and loss' and some are not. This is discussed further in Chapter 16.

After the SCI, there is a statement of changes in equity (SCE) which shows all changes in equity in the period. These will be of three types:

1 comprehensive income (from the SCI),

2 effects of restatements (e.g. policy changes),

3 transactions with owners (e.g. share issue or dividend payments).

Lastly, there is a statement of cash flows (see below).

IFRS 5 requires an entity to identify separately those assets that are intended for sale within a year, and to show them on the balance sheet under the heading 'held for sale'. Where a major line of business is to be sold within the coming year or has been sold in the past year, its revenues and expenses should also be separated out and shown as 'discontinued operations' in the statement of comprehensive income. This is designed to help the users to predict the future.

IAS 7 requires the presentation of a statement of cash flows which classifies cash flows into operating, investing and financing flows. The total flow then reconciles to the period's change in the total of cash and cash equivalents.

IAS 8 (accounting policies, changes in accounting estimates and errors) deals with the choice of accounting policies and how to account for changes in them. It also covers the correction of errors, which are required to be corrected by adjusting the opening balance sheet rather than through current income. IFRS 1 covers the major example of full-scale change to accounting policies that occurs when an entity first adopts IFRSs. Retrospective application of the standards in force at the date of adoption is generally required.

6.2.7 Revenue

IAS 18 (*Revenue*) is another basic standard. 'Revenue' is, approximately speaking, that part of 'income' that derives from customers. IAS 18 establishes that revenue from the sale of goods should not be recognized until, among other things, the seller has transferred the significant risks and rewards of ownership to the buyer, and the revenue can be reliably measured. For services, revenue is sometimes taken before this if the stage of completion of the transaction can be measured reliably. This issue is taken further in Chapter 16.

6.3 Assets

6.3.1 Tangible and intangible fixed assets

Tangible fixed assets are covered by IAS 16 (*Property, Plant and Equipment*) and IAS 40 (*Investment Property*), and most intangible assets are covered by IAS 38 (*Intangible Assets*), although purchased goodwill is dealt with by IFRS 3 (see Section 6.5 and Chapter 17). Biological assets are the subject of IAS 41.

IASs 16, 38, 40 and 41 have similar rules on recognition. An asset should be recognized when it meets the definition of an asset (see Section 6.2), when it will probably entail future benefits and when its cost can be measured reliably. These conditions lead to a ban on the capitalization of internally generated goodwill, research costs, brands, customer lists, and so on. Similarly, expenses that do not lead to assets (e.g. formation expenses) must not be capitalized.

Assets (except biological assets) should initially be measured at their cost. Subsequently, they can continue to be measured at cost (subject to depreciation and impairment, see below). However, investment properties (basically those not owner-occupied) can instead be held at current fair value, as can other fixed assets, as long as a whole class (e.g. land, or land and buildings) is valued. The standard-setters show their suspicion of intangible assets by only allowing revaluation when there is an active market for an intangible. Since this requires homogeneous assets and public prices, most intangibles (such as brands and development costs) are excluded. The valuation (or measurement) of assets is taken further in Chapter 16.

For investment properties valued at fair value, revaluation gains and losses are taken to profit and loss, and no depreciation is charged. For any other assets, re-valued amounts are treated as replacements for the original cost. So the gains/losses on revaluation go to comprehensive income, and the calculations of depreciation and the gains/losses on sale are made by reference to the revalued amounts.

If an enterprise receives a government grant related to an asset then IAS 20 allows the grant to be deducted from the asset's cost or to be shown as deferred income. Either way, the grant is taken to income over the life of the asset, because of reduced depreciation or by gradually reducing the size of the deferred income. Frankly, this makes little sense because, if the cash is in the bank and the entity has no liability (no expected repayment of the grant), then it must have made a gain. At first sight, the spreading of the grant over the life of the asset could be defended by invoking the pre-*Framework* approach of matching. However, even that would not work because the life of the asset can be seen to be irrelevant by considering a grant for the purchase of land, which has no depreciable life. Following IAS 20 would seem to lead to never recognizing income for such a grant. The IASB is aware of this problem and has announced its intention to replace IAS 20. Another issue that can affect the recorded cost of an asset is that IAS 23 requires (from 2009) interest on the construction of assets to be capitalized.

Most assets should be depreciated over their useful economic lives. In the case of an intangible asset, the life may be difficult to estimate, so IAS 38 requires any intangible assets with indefinite lives to be tested annually for impairment rather than being amortized. Intangible assets are discussed in more detail in Chapter 16.

According to IAS 36, assets should be examined at each balance sheet date to see if there is any indication of impairment (e.g. physical damage). If not, no calcula-tions need to be done. However, if there is an indication of impairment, calcula-tions of value are necessary. If the asset's carrying amount (e.g. depreciated cost) exceeds the recoverable amount, the excess must be removed and charged as an impairment loss. The recoverable amount is measured as the higher of the value in use and net selling price. Since management have decided not to sell most fixed assets, this suggests that value in use is generally higher than net selling price, and so it is the recoverable amount. Value in use is measured by estimating the dis-counted cash flows expected from an asset.

Biological assets are measured initially and subsequently at fair value less expected point-of-sale costs, which amounts to a net selling price. Gains/losses are taken to profit and loss. At the point of harvest, the fair value becomes the cost for inventory accounting. The old IASC was able to establish this clear rule for biological assets in IAS 41 (unlike the measurement choices in IASs 16, 38 and 40) partly because most Board delegations were not directly concerned with biological assets, so there was less political opposition to fair value and to taking 'unrealized gains' to profit and loss.

6.3.2 Inventories

IAS 2 deals with most inventories and IAS 11 with construction contracts. As under many accounting systems, inventories should be valued at the lower of cost and net realizable value. Cost can be measured using FIFO or weighted average. The former option to use LIFO was removed in 2003 with effect from 2005.

Construction contracts that can be reliably measured must be accounted for on a percentage-of-completion basis.

6.3.3 Leases

Leases are divided by IAS 17 into those that transfer substantially all the risks and rewards of the leased asset to the lessee (finance leases) and those that leave them with the lessor (operating leases). The latter are treated, following their legal form, as rentals. However, finance leases must be capitalized as assets and liabilities of the lessee and shown as receivables by the lessor.

There are problems with the 'substantially all' in the above definition. First, this is rather vague. In the US and the UK, one reference point for this is 90 per cent of the fair value of the asset. So, for example, a lease involving 92 per cent of fair value would generally lead to full capitalization of the asset and matching liability, whereas a lease involving 88 per cent of fair value would not be capitalized at all. This makes little sense. Related to this is the fact that there is no 'substantially all' in the definitions of asset and liability (see Section 6.2).

The conclusion of the IASB and some other standard-setters (McGregor, 1996) is that lease accounting needs to be reformed. When a lessee signs an uncancellable lease, this always creates a liability, and presumably (for a sensible lessee) an asset. These should be recognized. So, all leases should be capitalized in proportion to the values involved, not all or nothing.

6.3.4 Financial instruments

IAS 32 deals with the definitions and presentation for financial instruments, which include financial assets, financial liabilities and equity.

IAS 32 was path-breaking when it was published in 1995 because it requires the classification of liabilities and equity to be based on the substance of the instruments not on their legal form. For example, redeemable preference shares contain a commitment to pay cash to the shareholders, so they must be treated as debt, and the dividends must be treated as interest expenses. This was not the case in the national rules of any major countries at the time, and mostly is still not.

The same point applies to convertible debentures but has the reverse effect. That is, such instruments should be treated as partly equity, with a proportion of the financial payments being re-classified from interest to dividends.

Financial assets are defined very widely to include cash and receivables as well as investments of all types. Investments should (according to IAS 39) be valued at fair value, unless they fall into one of the following categories:

● no reliable fair value (e.g. some unlisted shares);

● those intended to be held to maturity (e.g. some bonds); or

● non-traded loans originated by the enterprise (e.g. loans made by banks).

The measurement of these three types of assets (and of financial liabilities) can be based on cost, although IAS 39 allows the option of fair value for the latter two cases under certain conditions.

For the investments valued at fair value, the gains and losses should be recognized in profit and loss, except that those related to investments categorized as 'available for sale' should be put through comprehensive income. For those financial instruments not measured at fair value in the balance sheet, IFRS 7 requires note disclosures of fair value.

Financial liabilities should be 'marked to market' (i.e. held at fair value with gains and losses to profit and loss) if they are derivatives or for trading. Otherwise, they can either be held at amortized cost or some can be marked to market (see Chapter 16 for more detail).

In 2000, the IASC and other standard-setters published a 'draft standard' intended to replace these mixed valuations with a full fair value system. This reform has taken longer than hoped because of opposition from companies that do not like the resulting volatility of income.

6.4 Liabilities

The IASB's definition of a liability is set out in Section 6.2.6. Financial liabilities have already been mentioned above. Other liabilities include provisions, employee benefits and deferred tax.

6.4.1 Provisions

Provisions (according to IAS 37) are liabilities of uncertain timing or amount. Let us take the example of provisions for repair expenses. The debit side of the double entry for the creation of the liability is an expense. At a year end, it has been traditional practice under German national rules (see Chapter 15) to charge the expected repair expenses of the first three months of the following year. This has a tax advantage in Germany because a (tax-deductible) expense can thereby be charged earlier. The large German chemical company (BASF) provided an example (Annual Report, 2004):

> Maintenance provisions are established to cover omitted maintenance procedures as of the end of the year, and are expected to be incurred within the first three months of the following year.

The entries for a repair provision would be as follows, at the end of 20X1:

Debit: Repair expense of 20X1
Credit: Provision for repair expense (to be carried out in 20X2)

Suppose that the definition of an expense is the traditional one, based on matching, as outlined above (Method 1 in Section 6.2.6), then it would be easy to argue that the German practice is right. The reason for the need for repair of a machine in early 20X2 was the wearing out of the machine in 20X1. So, the expense could be said to *relate* to 20X1, although this answer is not completely clear.

However, let us now give primacy to the IASB's definition of 'liability'. In the above example of the repair, does the enterprise have an obligation to a third party at the balance sheet date to transfer resources? Probably not. If not, there is no liability at the end of 20X1; therefore, there can be no expense in 20X1; therefore the above entries should not be made.

Returning to IAS 37, when provisions are recognized, they should be measured at the best estimate and should be discounted for the time value of money.

Contingent liabilities are possible liabilities or liabilities that cannot be quantified or are unlikely to lead to outflows of resources. They should be shown in the notes, unless they are remote. Chapter 16 considers further the topics of provisions and reserves.

6.4.2 Employee benefits

IAS 19 covers employee benefits such as bonuses, and post-employment benefits such as pensions. These should be recognized on a balance sheet when they are liabilities that are likely and measurable.

The greatest complications occur when an enterprise has made commitments to pay defined benefit payments, such as pensions that depend on length of service and future salary levels. Basically, these must be accounted for as the discounted estimate of the existing obligation at the balance sheet date less the fair value of any fund set up outside the enterprise to pay the obligation.

Another important employee benefit in some companies is share-based payments. IFRS 2 deals with this. If the promised payments to employees are to be made in cash but are related in size to the company's share price, a liability and an expense are recorded over the period that the employee must work in order to earn the payment. If the payment is in shares or share options, the credit is to equity rather than to a liability.

These issues lead to very large numbers in the financial statements of many companies and are examined in more detail in Chapter 16.

6.4.3 Deferred tax

IAS 12 requires enterprises to account fully at current (or future) enacted tax rates for deferred tax assets and liabilities arising on temporary differences between the carrying values of the enterprise's assets and liabilities and their tax values. This, again, is a complex issue and is examined later (e.g. Sections 8.6 and 16.7).

6.5 | Group accounting

The topic of group accounting is discussed for the US in Chapter 8 and on a comparative international basis in Chapter 17. Here an outline of the IASB's requirements is given.

6.5.1 Business combinations

IFRS 3 requires business combinations to be accounted for as acquisitions (also called purchases). It no longer allows a method called uniting of interests (called pooling in the US or merger accounting in the UK). On acquisition, the identifiable assets, liabilities and contingent liabilities of the new subsidiary should be brought into the consolidated balance sheet at their fair values. Any excess payment is capitalized as goodwill. IFRS 3 requires annual impairment tests for the goodwill rather than amortization. This is consistent with IAS 38's requirement for intangible assets with an indefinite life. In the unusual event that negative goodwill should arise, it must be treated as income immediately because it is not a liability.

6.5.2 Consolidation

IAS 27 defines a subsidiary as an enterprise over which there is power to control the financial and operating policies. This makes the assets and liabilities of the subsidiary those of the group, so they should be fully consolidated. This applies even if the subsidiary is very dissimilar from the rest of the group. Subsidiaries should also be consolidated even if control is temporary, but they will be shown as 'held for sale' under IFRS 5.

Normal consolidation procedures (e.g. elimination of inter-company balances) are required. Minority interests must be shown as group equity (because they do not fit the definitions of asset or liability), though not as parent's equity.

6.5.3 Joint ventures

A joint venture is evidenced by a contract of joint control that requires the unanimous consent of the two or more venturers over the strategic financial and operating decisions of an entity. IAS 31 deals with the accounting in such a case.

There is little problem with joint assets or operations. They can be accounted for according to who controls them. The interesting question is what to do with a joint-venture entity. Is this in the venturer's group or not? IAS 31 allows a choice here: either proportional consolidation or the equity method. Proportional consolidation brings in to the venturer's consolidated statements its proportion of all the venture's assets, liabilities, expenses and revenues on a line-by-line basis. However, imagine a 40 per cent holding in a joint venture. Does the venturer control all of the venture's assets or 40 per cent of them? The answer appears to be: neither. None of the assets are controlled by the venturer. This suggests that proportional consolidation is inappropriate, and that the IASB will remove the choice in due course. This issue is examined further in Chapter 17.

The alternative offered by IAS 31 (the equity method) is examined below as it is the required treatment in consolidated statements for investments in associates.

6.5.4 Associates

Associates are defined by IAS 28 as entities over which an investor can exercise significant influence but not control. This vague term is given some precision by reference to a presumption that a holding of 20 per cent or more of voting shares leads to significant influence. Clearly the investor does not control, and should not consolidate, the associate's assets, etc. However, it also seems unsatisfactory to record the holding at cost and take only dividends as group income. The equity method is required by IAS 28 for consolidated statements as a sort of compromise between these extremes.

The equity method brings the investor's proportion of the associate's equity (= net assets) and income into the investor's financial statements. It is not clear whether this is supposed to be a one-line consolidation method or a proxy for showing the value of the investment. The equity method is looked at in more detail in Chapter 17.

6.5.5 Currency translation

IAS 21 deals with foreign currency transactions and balances as well as with the translation of the financial statements of foreign subsidiaries, joint ventures and associates.

Transactions should generally be translated into an enterprise's reporting currency at the rate ruling on the date of the transaction. Resulting monetary balances (foreign receivables and payables) should be translated in subsequent balance sheets at the current rate, with gains and losses taken to profit and loss.

Foreign operations should be translated after identifying their functional currencies. The rules for translation are of considerable complexity and are examined in detail in Chapter 18.

6.6   Disclosures

Each of the standards looked at above contains disclosure requirements, generally grouped together at the end of a standard. However, there are other standards that are specifically about disclosures and do not affect the recognition of assets, liabilities, equity, revenues or expenses. Two important disclosure standards are summarized below. These two are only compulsory for enterprises whose securities are publicly traded.

1 IFRS 8 requires reporting of many items (e.g. assets, sales and profit) split into the segments as reported to an entity's chief operating officer. This issue is dealt with in more detail in Chapter 19.

2 IAS 33 requires disclosure of the enterprise's basic earnings per share (EPS). The earnings is the net profit after tax, extraordinary items and preference dividends. The 'per share' number is the weighted average of the ordinary shares outstanding during the period. It is also necessary to disclose the diluted EPS by adjusting the earnings and the shares for any possible extra shares (e.g. convertible debentures) that would make the EPS look worse.

SUMMARY

- The IASB's *Framework* is closely in line with the US *Framework* which preceded it. It is oriented towards investor decision-making. Fair presentation is required and this means trying to maximize the relevance and reliability of information.

- The *Framework* gives primacy to assets and liabilities, leaving equity, revenues and expenses as derivative terms.

- Some IFRSs contain options called 'benchmark' and 'allowed alternative'; generally this does not suggest a preference for the benchmark or a requirement to reconcile to it. Several options were removed in 2003.

- IAS 1 requires a statement of comprehensive income and a statement of changes in equity.

- Most assets can be revalued under IASB's rules but there is a mixture of valuation bases and points at which gains are recognized as income. There has been a gradual move towards the use of fair values, with immediate recognition of income.

- The capitalization of leased assets and liabilities seems consistent with the *Framework*, but the split between operating and finance leases does not.

- The IASB's definition of provision is narrow compared to the meaning under some domestic laws. Provisions should be discounted, and this includes employee benefit obligations.

- Business combinations give rise to goodwill which has to be capitalized. The traditional requirement to amortize has been replaced by annual impairment measurements.

- Joint ventures can either be proportionally consolidated or equity accounted.

- IFRSs require a number of disclosures, including segment reporting and earnings per share.

References   Alexander, D. and Archer, S. (2001) *IAS Accounting Guide*, Harcourt Brace, Orlando.

Alfredson, K. *et al.* (2007) *Applying International Accounting Standards*, Wiley, Milton.

ASB (2005) *The Implications of New Accounting and Auditing Standards for the 'True and Fair View' and Auditors' Responsibilities*, Accounting Standards Board, London.

McGregor, W.J. (1996) *Accounting for Leases: A New Approach*, FASB for the G4+1, Norwalk.

Nobes, C.W. (2001) *Asset Measurement Bases in UK and IASC Standards*, ACCA.

Nobes, C.W. (2003) *Liabilities and their Measurement in UK and International Accounting Standards*, ACCA, London.

Further reading   For the full text of the IASB's standards, see the annual 'bound volume' from the IASB. For guides on how to use IFRSs, see Alexander and Archer (2001) or Alfredson *et al.* (2007). For a survey of asset and liability measurement rules under IFRSs, see Nobes (2001 and 2003). For differences between IFRSs and the requirements in various countries, see chapters of Parts II, III and IV of this book.

Useful websites

International Accounting Standards Board	www.iasb.org
IAS plus (Deloitte)	www.iasplus.com
KPMG	www.kpmgifrg.com
PricewaterhouseCoopers	www.pwc.com/ifrs

QUESTIONS

Suggested answers to the asterisked questions are given at the end of the book.

6.1∗ Explain the purposes and uses of a conceptual framework.

6.2∗ 'Neutrality is about freedom from bias. Prudence is a bias. It is not possible to embrace both conventions in one coherent framework.' Discuss.

6.3 'Substance over form is a recipe for failing to achieve comparability between financial statements of different enterprises.' Discuss.

6.4 Explain why it is necessary to define either 'asset' or 'expense' from first principles, but not both. Why has the IASB chosen to define the former?

6.5 Is it necessary and useful to have different valuation bases for different assets?

6.6 Outline all the ways that one could in principle include a joint venture in a venturer's financial statements. Which is the best?

6.7 'In recent years, the IASC/B has clearly been moving towards the use of current values rather than historical costs.' Discuss.

An outline of the content of International Financial Reporting Standards

This appendix summarizes the content of IFRSs extant on 1 January 2008.

IAS 1 Presentation of financial statements

This standard was revised in 1997 and superseded the old IAS 1, IAS 5 and IAS 13. It was revised again in 2003, in 2004 and in 2007. The components of financial statements are a statement of financial position, a statement of comprehensive income, a statement of changes in equity, a statement of cash flows, and notes (paragraph 10). If there have been any restatements, a statement of financial position at the beginning of the earliest comparative period must also be presented. An entity can show an income statement separately before the statement of comprehensive income (paragraph 12). Fair presentation is required and this may sometimes entail departure from an IFRS, which must then be disclosed including the numerical effect (paragraphs 15–24).

The going concern assumption must be assessed for each set of financial statements, and departed from (with disclosure) when appropriate (paragraph 25). Offsetting is only allowed when specifically permitted by another standard (paragraph 32). Comparative information must be given relating to the previous period (paragraph 38).

The current/non-current distinction is generally required (paragraph 60). There are no required formats but there are lists of minimum contents of financial statements (paragraphs 54 and 82). There are also illustrations of formats in an appendix.

IAS 2 Inventories

Inventories should be valued at the lower of cost and net realizable value (paragraph 9). Cost includes all costs to bring the inventories to their present condition and location (paragraph 10). FIFO or weighted average is required (paragraph 25).

IAS 3

Replaced by IAS 27.

IAS 4

Withdrawn, because the content (on depreciation) is covered by asset standards (particularly IAS 16 and IAS 38).

IAS 5

Replaced by IAS 1 (revised).

IAS 6

Replaced by IAS 15.

IAS 7 Cash flow statements

Cash flow statements are required (paragraph 1). They should classify cash flows into operating, investing and financial activities (paragraph 10). Cash and cash equivalents include short-term investments subject to insignificant risk of changes in value (paragraph 6).

Either the direct or indirect method is allowed (paragraph 18). Cash flows from taxes should be disclosed separately within one of the three headings (paragraph 35).

IAS 8 Accounting policies, changes in accounting estimates and errors

Changes in policy should follow specific transitional provisions. If none, then they should be applied retrospectively, by adjusting the earliest presented opening balance of retained earnings (paragraph 19). Changes in estimates should be absorbed in income (paragraph 36). The same applies to the correction of errors (paragraph 42).

IAS 9

Replaced by IAS 38.

IAS 10 Events after the balance sheet date

Events occurring after the balance sheet which provide additional information on conditions existing at the balance sheet date should lead to adjustment of the financial statements (paragraph 8). However, disclosure should be made for other events, if necessary for proper evaluation (paragraph 21). Proposed dividends should not be accrued (paragraph 12).

IAS 11 Construction contracts

There is no reference to the length of a contract in its definition, but there is a requirement that the contract should be specifically negotiated (paragraph 3).

When the outcome of such a contract can be estimated reliably, revenues and costs should be estimated by stage of completion. Expected losses should be recognized (paragraph 22). The conditions for reliable estimation are (paragraph 23):

(a) revenue can be reliably measured;

(b) it is probable that the benefits will flow to the enterprise;

(c) future costs and stage of completion can be measured reliably; and

(d) costs can be identified and measured reliably.

If the outcome cannot be measured reliably, costs should be expensed and revenues should be recognized in line with costs recoverable (paragraph 32).

IAS 12 Income taxes

Temporary differences are differences between the carrying amount of an asset or liability and its tax base (paragraph 5). Deferred tax assets and liabilities should be recognized for temporary differences except when relating to goodwill (unless the amortization is tax deductible) or certain transactions with no effect on tax or accounting profit (paragraphs 15 and 24). Deferred tax assets should not be accounted for unless sufficient future taxable income is probable (paragraphs 24 and 34). Certain deferred tax assets and liabilities relating to group companies should be recognized where the temporary differences will reverse (paragraphs 39 and 44).

Current and deferred tax assets and liabilities should use enacted or substantially enacted tax rates (paragraphs 46 and 47). Deferred tax assets and liabilities should not be discounted (paragraph 53).

Current and deferred taxes should be recognized in profit or loss to the extent that they relate to transactions not recognized in profit or loss (paragraph 58).

IAS 13

Replaced by IAS 1 (revised).

IAS 14 Segment reporting

Unusually for an IAS, the standard applies only to enterprises whose equity or debt is publicly traded (paragraph 3).

Business segments or geographical segments are distinguishable components of an enterprise with different risks and returns from other components (paragraph 9). An enterprise's primary segment reporting will be based on either business or geographical segments, depending on the dominant source and nature of the risks and returns (paragraph 26). Usually, management's internal financial reporting system will coincide with this (paragraph 27).

A reportable segment is one where sales to external customers or result or assets are 10 per cent or more of the total for the enterprise (paragraph 35). For primary reporting, an enterprise should disclose for each segment: revenue, operating result, operating assets, operating liabilities, capital expenditure and depreciation (paragraphs 50–8).

Segment reporting on the basis other than primary is also required for revenue, assets and capital expenditure (paragraphs 69 and 70).

Replaced (compulsorily from 2009 onwards) by IFRS 8.

IAS 15

Withdrawn.

IAS 16 Property, plant and equipment

Property, plant and equipment (PPE) should be recognized when (a) it is probable that future benefits will flow from it, and (b) its cost can be measured reliably (paragraph 7).

Initial measurement should be at cost (paragraph 15). Subsequently, one treatment is to use cost but an allowed alternative is to use an up-to-date fair value by class of assets (paragraphs 29, 30 and 36). Revaluations should be credited to comprehensive income unless reversing a previous charge to income. Decreases in valuation should be charged to profit and loss unless reversing a previous credit to reserves (paragraphs 39 and 40).

Gains or losses on retirement or disposal of an asset should be calculated by reference to the carrying amount (paragraph 68).

IAS 17 Leases

Finance leases are those which transfer substantially all risks and rewards to the lessee (paragraph 3). Finance leases should be capitalized by lessees at the lower of the fair value and the present value of the minimum lease payments (paragraph 12).

Rental payments should be split into (i) a reduction of liability, and (ii) a finance charge designed to reduce in line with the liability (paragraph 17). Depreciation on leased assets should be calculated using useful life, unless there is no reasonable certainty of eventual ownership. In this latter case, the shorter of useful life and lease term should be used (paragraph 19).

Operating leases should be expensed on a systematic basis (paragraph 25).

For lessors, finance leases should be recorded as receivables (paragraph 28). Lease income should be recognized on the basis of a constant periodic rate of return (paragraph 30). The net investment method should be used (paragraph 30).

For sale and leaseback which results in a finance lease, any excess of proceeds over carrying amount should be deferred and amortized over the lease term (paragraph 57).

IAS 18 Revenue

Revenue should be measured at fair value of consideration received or receivable (paragraph 9). Revenue should be recognized when (paragraph 4):

(a) significant risks and rewards are transferred to buyer;

(b) managerial involvement and control have passed;

(c) revenue can be measured reliably;

(d) it is probable that benefits will flow to the enterprise; and

(e) costs of the transaction can be measured reliably.

For services, similar conditions apply by stage of completion when the outcome can be estimated reliably (paragraph 20).

IAS 19 Employee benefits

For defined contribution plans, the contributions of a period should be recognized as expenses (paragraph 45).

For defined benefit plans, the liability should be the total of the present value of the obligation, plus unrecognized actuarial gains, minus unrecognized past service costs, and minus the fair value of plan assets (paragraph 55). The profit and loss charge should be the total of current service costs, interest cost, expected return on assets, actuarial gains recognized, past service cost recognized and the effect of curtailments and settlements (paragraph 62).

The actuarial valuation method is specified (one called the projected unit credit method) (paragraph 65). The discount rate used should be based on the market yield on high-quality corporate bonds (paragraph 79).

Actuarial gains and losses can be recognized on an amortization basis in profit and loss, and this can be restricted to any excess over 10 per cent of the obligation (or the fund, if greater). The amortization should be over the remaining working lives of employees in the plan, or faster (paragraph 94). Alternatively, actuarial gains and losses can be recognized immediately in full in comprehensive income. Past service cost should be recognized over the period until the benefits are vested (paragraph 98).

IAS 20 Government grants

Grants should not be credited directly to reserves but should be recognized as income in a way matched with the related costs (paragraphs 7 and 12). Grants related to assets should be deducted from the cost or treated as deferred income (paragraph 24).

IAS 21 The effects of changes in foreign exchange rates

Transactions should be translated on the date of the transaction (paragraph 21). Subsequently, monetary balances should be translated at the closing rate, and non-monetary balances at the rate which relates to the valuation basis (e.g. historical cost) (paragraph 23). Differences on monetary items should be taken to profit and loss, unless the items amount to a net investment in a foreign entity (paragraphs 28 and 32).

Financial statements of other entities whose functional currency is not the presentation currency should be translated using closing rates for balance sheets and transaction rates (or, in practice, average rates) for incomes and expenses. Differences should be taken to comprehensive income (paragraph 39).

IAS 22 Business combinations

Replaced by IFRS 3.

IAS 23 Borrowing costs

Borrowing costs on construction projects must be capitalized as part of the cost of the asset (paragraph 8), although until 2009 expensing is allowed.

In cases of capitalization, where funds are specifically borrowed, the borrowing costs should be calculated after any investment income on temporary investment of the borrowings (paragraph 12). If funds are borrowed generally, then a capitalization rate should be used based on the weighted average of borrowing costs for general borrowings outstanding during the period. Borrowing costs capitalized should not exceed those incurred (paragraph 14).

Capitalization should commence when expenditures and borrowing costs are being incurred and activities are in progress to prepare the asset for use or sale (paragraph 17). Suspension should occur when active development is suspended for extended periods, and cessation should occur when substantially all activities are complete (paragraphs 20 and 22).

IAS 24 Related party disclosures

Related parties are those able to control or exercise significant influence, though some exceptions are noted (paragraphs 9 and 11). Relationships and transactions should be disclosed (paragraphs 12 and 17).

IAS 25

Replaced by IAS 39 and IAS 40.

IAS 26 Reporting by retirement benefit plans

This standard relates to accounting and reporting by retirement benefit plans themselves, not by employers. Separate rules are set out for defined benefit plans and defined contribution plans.

IAS 27 Consolidated and separate financial statements

A subsidiary is defined as one controlled by another enterprise (paragraph 6). Certain intermediate parent companies are exempted from preparing consolidated accounts (paragraph 4).

All subsidiaries must be included, even where control is temporary due to expected sale (paragraphs 12 and 16).

The reporting dates of consolidated companies should be no more than three months different from the parent's (paragraph 26).

In parent financial statements, subsidiaries may be shown at cost or as available-for-sale investments (paragraph 37).

IAS 28 Investments in associates

An associate is an enterprise over which the investor has significant influence, i.e. the power to participate in financial and operating policy decisions (paragraph 2). This is a rebuttable presumption when there is a holding of 20 per cent or more in the voting rights (paragraph 6).

Associates should be accounted for by the equity method in consolidated statements, even when held for disposal in the near future (paragraph 13). In investor company accounts, associates can be held at cost or as available-for-sale investments (paragraph 12).

IAS 29 Financial reporting in hyperinflationary economies

Hyperinflation is indicated by several features, including cumulative inflation over three years of 100 per cent or more (paragraph 3).

Financial statements (including corresponding figures) should be presented in a measuring unit which is current at the balance sheet date (paragraph 8).

IAS 30 Disclosures by banks

Replaced by IFRS 7.

IAS 31 Interests in joint ventures

A joint venture is a contractual arrangement subject to joint control (paragraph 3). Jointly controlled *operations* should be recognized by including the assets controlled and the liabilities and expenses incurred by the venturer and its share of income (paragraph 15). Jointly controlled *assets* should be recognized on a proportional basis (paragraph 21).

In the consolidated financial statements, jointly controlled *entities* should be recognized as follows (paragraphs 30 and 38):

(i) one treatment is proportional consideration;

(ii) an allowed alternative is the equity method.

However, interests held for resale separately should be treated as investments under the rules of IFRS 5.

IAS 32 Financial instruments: presentation

Financial instruments should be classified by issuers into liabilities and equity, which includes splitting compound instruments into these components (paragraphs 16 and 28).

Treasury shares (i.e. a company's own shares that have been bought back by the company) must be shown as a deduction from equity (paragraph 33).

Financial assets and liabilities can be set off when there is a legally enforceable right and an intention to do so (paragraph 42).

IAS 33 Earnings per share

The standard applies to enterprises with publicly traded shares (paragraph 2).

Basic earnings per share (EPS) should be calculated using (i) the net profit or loss attributable to ordinary shareholders, and (ii) the weighted average ordinary shares outstanding in the period (paragraph 10). The weighted average should be adjusted for all periods presented for events (e.g. bonus issues) that change the number of shares but not the resources (paragraph 19).

Diluted EPS should adjust earnings and shares for all dilutive potential ordinary shares (paragraph 30).

Presentation of basic and diluted EPS should be on the face of the income statement (paragraph 47).

IAS 34 Interim financial reporting

This standard is not mandatory but might be imposed by stock exchange authorities, for example (paragraph 1).

The minimum contents of an interim report should be condensed comprehensive income statement, balance sheet, changes in equity, cash flow and notes (paragraph 8). Minimum contents of the statements and the notes are specified (paragraphs 10 and 16). Prior period data should be presented (paragraph 20).

The frequency of reporting should not affect the annual results (paragraph 28). In most ways, the end of a period should be treated as the end of a year (paragraphs 28, 37, and 39).

IAS 35 Discontinuing operations

Replaced by IFRS 5.

IAS 36 Impairment of assets

Enterprises are required to check at each balance sheet date whether there are any indications of impairment; several examples are given (paragraph 12). When there is an indication of impairment, an enterprise should calculate the asset's recoverable amount, which is the larger of its net selling price and value in use. The latter is equivalent to the discounted expected net cash inflows, which should be calculated for the smallest group of assets (cash generating unit) for which the calculation is practicable (paragraph 66).

If the asset's recoverable amount is less than its carrying value, an impairment loss must be recognized (paragraph 59). Impairment losses should first be allocated to goodwill (paragraph 104). Impairment losses, except those relating to goodwill, should be reversed under certain circumstances (paragraph 110).

IAS 37 Provisions, contingent liabilities and contingent assets

A provision is defined as a liability of uncertain timing or amount. For there to be a liability, there must be an obligation at the balance sheet date (paragraph 10). Provisions should be recognized unless a reliable estimate cannot be made or the possibility of outflow is unlikely (paragraph 14).

Contingent liabilities (where there is no obligation or where there is no reliable measure or no probability of outflow) should not be recognized as liabilities but disclosed in the notes, unless remote (paragraphs 10, 27, 28). Contingent assets should not be recognized (paragraph 31).

IAS 38 Intangible assets

Intangible assets should be recognized where it is probable that benefits will flow to the enterprise and cost can be measured reliably (paragraph 21).

Internally generated goodwill must not be capitalized (paragraph 48). Research and many other internally generated intangibles cannot meet the above recognition criteria (paragraphs 54 and 68). Development expenditure may sometimes meet the criteria, and must then be capitalized. More detailed guidance is given on this (paragraph 57). Costs treated as expenses cannot subsequently be capitalized (paragraph 71).

Intangible assets for which there is an active market can be carried at fair value (paragraph 75).

Intangible assets with finite useful lives should be amortized (paragraph 97). Annual impairment tests are otherwise required (paragraph 107).

IAS 39 Financial instruments: recognition and measurement

All financial assets and financial liabilities, including derivatives, should be recognized on the balance sheet (paragraphs 2 and 14).

Financial assets should be held at fair value except that the following are held at amortized cost:

(a) receivables originated by the enterprise and not held for trading,

(b) held-to-maturity investments, and

(c) assets whose fair value cannot be measured reliably (paragraph 46).

However, an option allows some assets of type (a) or (b) to be held at fair value.

Financial liabilities are held at amortized proceeds, except that fair value should be used for those held for trading and for derivatives, and that option exists for some others (paragraph 47).

Gains and losses should be recognized in profit and loss, except that gains on available for sale items are taken to comprehensive income (paragraphs 55 and 56).

Hedge accounting is permitted under certain circumstances for derivatives and (only for foreign currency risks) for other financial instruments. The hedges must be designated and effective (paragraph 88).

IAS 40 Investment property

Investment property is held to earn rentals or for capital appreciation, rather than being owner-occupied (paragraph 5).

Initial measurement should be at cost, and there should be subsequent capitalization of expenditure that improves the originally assessed standard of performance (paragraphs 16 and 20). There should then be an entity-wide choice of the fair value model or the cost model (paragraph 30). Under the first of these, gains and losses are taken to profit and loss (paragraph 35). If, under the fair value model, fair value of a particular property is not determinable at the beginning, then cost should be used (paragraph 53).

Transfers to owner-occupied property or inventory should take place at fair value (paragraph 60). Transfers to investment property should treat the initial change to fair value as a revaluation under IAS 16 (paragraph 61).

Under the cost model, fair value should be disclosed (paragraph 79).

IAS 41 Agriculture

This standard covers all biological assets to the point of harvest (paragraph 1). Such assets are measured at fair value less point-of-sale costs (paragraph 12). If fair value is not reliably determinable, then cost should be used (paragraph 30).

Agricultural produce is measured at harvest at fair value less point-of-sale costs, which then becomes the cost for inventory accounting (paragraph 13).

Gains and losses on changes in fair value should be taken to profit and loss (paragraphs 26 and 28). Government grants should be taken to profit and loss when their conditions are met (paragraph 34).

IFRS 1 First-time adoption of International Financial Reporting Standards

This standard relates to entities that, for the first time, give an explicit and unreserved statement of compliance with IFRS (paragraph 3). An entity has to prepare an opening balance sheet for the earliest period presented that is in accordance with the standards ruling at the reporting date (paragraph 6). No other versions of standards are relevant, nor are the transitional provisions of standards. A few exemptions are allowed, e.g. for business combinations (paragraph 13). A few retrospective estimates are not allowed, e.g. related to hedge accounting (paragraph 26).

A reconciliation is required from accounting under the old rules to the opening IFRS balance sheet (paragraph 39).

IFRS 2 Share-based payment

Share-based payments should be recognized as an expense unless an asset is recognized. The payments can be settled in cash or in shares. The former give rise to liabilities; the latter to equity. The recognition should take place as the goods or services are received (paragraph 7). Share-settled payments should be recognized at fair value: of the goods or services (for non-employees) or of the equity (for employees) (paragraph 10).

No adjustment should be made if shares or share options are forfeited or not exercised after vesting date (paragraph 23).

IFRS 3 Business combinations (before revisions of 2008)

All business combinations should be treated as purchases (paragraph 14). Goodwill is the difference between the fair value of the consideration given and the fair value of the subsidiary's assets, liabilities and contingent liabilities (paragraph 36). The resulting contingent liabilities should continue to be recognized despite IAS 37 (paragraph 48).

Goodwill should be tested annually for impairment (paragraph 54). Negative goodwill should be recognized as income immediately (paragraph 56).

IFRS 4 Insurance contracts

This standard applies to insurance contracts whatever sort of company holds them (paragraph 2).

Insurers are temporarily exempted from the general requirements of IAS 8 on accounting policies. This is pending a full standard on insurance contracts (paragraph 13). Changes to policies are only allowed if the resulting information is more relevant (paragraph 22). A liability adequacy test is required (paragraph 15).

IFRS 5 Non-current assets held for sale and discontinued operations

Non-current assets should be classified as held for sale if expected to be sold within one year (paragraphs 6–8). They should be shown separately on the balance sheet at the lower of carrying value and fair value less costs to sell (paragraph 15).

A discontinued operation is a separate major line of business that has been disposed of or is classified as held for sale (paragraph 32). The statement of comprehensive income should show a single amount for all items related to discontinued operations (paragraph 33).

IFRS 6 Exploration for and evaluation of mineral resources

Pending a full standard on this subject, entities are exempted from certain requirements of IAS 8 on accounting policies (paragraph 7). Measurement of assets should follow IAS 16 (paragraph 12).

A special rule on impairment applies, which allows cash generating units to be as large, but not larger than, a segment (paragraph 21).

IFRS 7 Financial instruments: disclosures

All types of entities are required to make disclosures about financial instruments on a wide range of issues, including: fair values (paragraph 25), credit risk (paragraph 36), liquidity risk (paragraph 39) and market risk (paragraph 40).

IFRS 8 Operating segments

The standard applies to listed companies (paragraph 2). Operating segments are those regularly reviewed by the entity's chief operating officer (paragraph 5). Information on operating segments should be reported when it is 10 per cent or more of all segments (paragraph 13). Many items must be reported on, including revenues, assets, interest, depreciation, tax (paragraph 23). Revenues and non-current assets should be reported by geographical segments (paragraph 33).

7 Different versions of IFRS practice

Christopher Nobes

OBJECTIVES

After reading this chapter, you should be able to:

- explain how the potential reasons for international accounting differences, as discussed in previous chapters, might still be relevant under IFRS;

- give examples of how different versions (including different translations) of IFRS can be in force at the same time;

- give examples of how gaps, choices and estimations in IFRS can lead to different practices;

- outline how international differences in monitoring and enforcement can lead to different IFRS practices;

- discuss some of the implications of the existence of different national versions of IFRS.

7.1 Introduction

The objectives of the International Accounting Standards Committee Foundation (IASCF) include the development of 'a single set of high quality, understandable and enforceable global accounting standards' and 'to promote the use and rigorous

145

application' of them (IASCF *Constitution*, para. 2). Progress continues to be made on this, as the standards become tighter and as compulsory application spreads. However, even if we concentrate on those financial statements that claim to comply with international standards (IFRS), is there uniform practice?

This chapter first (Section 7.2) examines the motivations for different practice within IFRS use. In particular, are there reasons why IFRS might be applied systematically differently from one country to another? Section 7.3 then looks at the scope for IFRS practice to vary. Included in this examination is a look at the overt and covert options included in IFRS. Study of this will help readers to understand IFRS, not just for the specific purpose of this chapter. It will also reveal the scope for different IFRS practice between companies or between industries, not just between countries.

To the extent that different versions of IFRS practice exist, several implications follow:

● Users of financial statements need to be warned that IFRS statements from different companies/countries might be less comparable than they had hoped.

● The SEC was slow to accept IFRS from foreign companies listed on US exchanges.

● 'Comparative international accounting' still exists as a field of study even within IFRS usage.

7.2   Motivations for different IFRS practice

Assuming that there is scope for different practice within IFRS (see Section 7.3), there are various motivations for this at the level of companies, industries or countries.

Companies face different circumstances, so might make different policy choices (e.g. Watts and Zimmerman, 1978). For example, some companies might like to show high profits in order to impress the stock market. Others might like to show low profits in order to bolster an argument for raising prices or for reducing dividends or wages. These different motivations can also apply between industries. For example, it is normal in public utilities, such as gas or telecommunications, to have regulated prices and therefore sometimes to want to show low profits, but this is not normal in most industries.

This chapter focuses on why companies in particular countries might want to practice IFRS differently from those in other countries. The starting point is to ask whether the factors considered in Chapter 2 are relevant. Three factors in particular are considered here: financing systems, tax systems and legal systems. Germany and the UK will be used as the main illustrations because they are important countries (i.e. Europe's two largest economies and stock markets) with clearly contrasting accounting (see Chapter 3).

As discussed in Section 2.4, it is possible to divide countries into 'insider financing' and 'outsider financing', however the starkness of the divide is reducing. For example, Germany was traditionally seen as an 'insider' country, but the largest German listed companies were already adapting to a shareholder/outsider financial culture and voluntarily using IFRS or US GAAP from the middle 1990s (Weissenberger *et al.*, 2004). However, many German listed companies waited to use IFRS until driven by compulsion from the Deutsche Börse and then the EU Regulation 1606 of 2002. Such German companies might still be dominated by 'insider' finance and might still feel no commercial need for the creative accounting and extensive disclosures seen in US or UK markets. They might therefore have motivations towards a particular style of IFRS reporting, assuming that opportunities for different styles exist.

Secondly, as discussed in Section 2.3, the literature also divides the *legal* systems of the developed world into two main types: Roman (code) law and common law (e.g. David and Brierley, 1985). This affects the regulation of financial reporting. For example, the preparation of financial statements under German national rules is largely specified by the commercial code (HGB) and tax law, whereas the detail in UK national rules is found in accounting standards written in the private sector.

For IFRS reporting in Germany and the UK, the content of the standards is now the same. However, monitoring and enforcement remain national. This includes the nature and regulation of audit, the stock exchange rules, the activities of the stock exchange regulator and of any other monitoring or review bodies. International differences in these areas continue, so the Roman/common dichotomy could still affect financial reporting practice. Section 7.3 suggests examples.

The third issue is the influence of tax on financial reporting. This was examined in Section 2.5, where the influence in Germany was seen as larger than the influence in the UK. However, does this difference remain relevant in the context of the use of IFRS for consolidated statements? At first sight, it does not, because IFRS consolidated accounting is, even in Germany, separated from tax calculations which begin with the pre-tax accounting profit of unconsolidated individual entities. However, as explained below, there are two reasons why tax practice may influence IFRS consolidated statements: convenience (in Germany) and tax conformity (in the UK).

In Germany, companies are required to continue to prepare unconsolidated financial statements under the conventional rules of the HGB for calculations of taxable income and distributable income. This is irrespective of any use of IFRS for consolidated or unconsolidated statements (Haller and Eierle, 2004). In some areas, the tax-driven accounting choices of the unconsolidated statements might flow through to consolidated IFRS statements. For example, asset impairments are tax deductible in Germany (but not in the UK), so there is a bias in favour of them. They might survive into IFRS consolidations in Germany, given the room for judgement in IFRS impairment procedures (see Section 7.3).

In the UK, IFRS is allowed for individual company financial statements and therefore as a starting point for calculations of taxable income. The tax authorities generally expect the statements of a parent and other UK group members to use the same accounting policies as group statements. To take an example, the recognition and measurement of intangible assets has tax implications. Consequently, given that IFRS requires considerable judgement in this area, individual companies using IFRS will have an incentive to make interpretations of IAS 38 (Intangible Assets) in order to minimize capitalization and therefore tax, and these will then flow through to consolidated statements.

A way of summarizing this section is to say that national accounting traditions are likely to continue into consolidated reporting where scope for this exists within IFRS rules. This is not to suggest that this continuation of practices results merely from inertia, but that the reasons for the different traditions will in some cases remain relevant. However, inertia might be a further explanation in itself, as might a company's conscious desire to disrupt its accounting as little as possible for the better understanding of internal and external users.

7.3   Scope for different IFRS practice

7.3.1   Introduction

Any motivations for different IFRS practice among companies, industries or countries would be of little importance unless there was scope for it to occur. This section examines this scope, concentrating on international differences, again often using Germany and the UK as examples.

Eight categories of scope for different IFRS practice are identified here: different versions of IFRS, different translations, gaps in IFRS, overt options, covert options, measurement estimations, transitional issues and imperfect enforcement. These are now considered in turn.

7.3.2   Different versions of IFRS

Despite adoption or alleged adoption of IFRS, international differences in the IFRS rules in force at a particular date can occur. Three cases are noted here. First, there are differences between IFRS and EU-endorsed IFRS. These were examined in Section 5.2. The second case is Australia, where direct compliance with IFRS is not required, but instead IFRS is turned closely, *but until 2007 not exactly*, into Australian standards that are then legally imposed on companies. To take an example of the differences, IAS 31 allows a group to choose between proportional consolidation and equity accounting for its holding in a joint venture entity. By contrast, AASB 131 (para. 38) required equity accounting. This was an Australian 'carve out', although the Australian standard could correctly state that compliance with it ensures compliance with IFRS. However, it meant that Australian groups did not use proportional consolidation, but German or French groups could, under IFRS, continue their previous national practices of doing so.

The third case of difference within IFRS rules concerns implementation dates and year ends. New standards generally have an in-force date of 'annual periods beginning on or after 1 January 200X'. However, early application is usually allowed, so two quite different versions of IFRS can be in-force at the same time. For example, IFRS 8 and new versions of IAS 1 and IAS 23 were available for use in 2007, but not required to be used until 2009. Another aspect of this is that the EU endorsement process can take many months. So, some parts of IFRS might be in force, but not endorsed at a particular company's year end. An EU company would be required not to obey such parts of IFRS unless they were consistent with endorsed IFRS (KPMG, 2005).

Furthermore, many companies in some countries (e.g. in Australia and the UK, but not in Germany) have accounting periods that do not begin on 1 January. Researchers might therefore find that a sample of companies with annual reports relating to years ending in 2006 are subject to different versions of IFRS. More subtly, some companies (e.g. UK retail groups) choose to have accounting years comprising exactly 52 or 53 weeks, so some have accounting years that begin on 28 December, thereby escaping a new standard that comes into force four days later.

7.3.3 Different translations

The IASCF (the parent organization of the IASB) has an official translation process for IFRS, including committees to review the quality of translations. There are official translations in many European languages and in Arabic, Chinese and Japanese.

In the case of Europe, the EU Regulation of 2002 gives the translations legal status in the various countries. EU and government representatives have been added to the IASCF's review committees, and the EU's Accounting Regulatory Committee (see Chapter 5) has also reviewed the translations.

As in any field, there is a risk that the process of translation will change or lose meaning from the original version, in this case English. Evans (2004) examines the major problems of accounting communication when more than one language is involved. Two examples are given here.

Cash flow statements are required by IAS 7, reconciling to 'cash and cash equivalents'. The term 'cash equivalents' is defined in paragraphs 6 to 9, including:

> An investment normally qualifies as a cash equivalent only when it has a short maturity of, say, three months . . .

This is an attempt to avoid writing a rule, as opposed to a principle. The Portuguese translation of IAS 7 omits the word 'say'. This improves the standard, but does not translate it accurately. As a result, it would be more difficult in Portugal than in Ireland to argue successfully that an investment with a maturity of just over three months is a cash equivalent.

As a further example, IAS 41 (para. 34) requires that an unconditional government grant related to a biological asset be recognized as income when the grant becomes 'receivable'. The Norwegian[1] version (DnR, 2006, p. 543) translates this as '*mottas*', which means 'received'. This could sometimes be an important difference.

7.3.4 Gaps in IFRS

In a sense, there are no gaps in IFRS because IAS 8 (para. 10) tells an entity how to choose accounting policies when no other part of IFRS applies. In such a case, resort is made to the general criteria of the International Accounting Standards Board

---

[1] Norway, although not an EU country, has implemented the Regulation as a member of the European Economic Area.

(IASB) *Framework*, to parts of IFRS related to the gap, and to more detailed standards of other bodies that use a similar *Framework* (most obviously, US GAAP). This leaves entities with considerable room for manoeuvre, and allows the continuation of differences in practice.

Examples in 2007 were accounting for insurance contracts and accounting for oil and gas. The general topics are addressed by IFRS 4 and IFRS 6, respectively, but a number of areas are left unresolved. Under such circumstances, national traditions might continue as a way of filling any gaps in IFRS.

7.3.5 Overt options

As noted in previous chapters, in the early 1990s there were large numbers of options in international standards. The options have been gradually removed, particularly in 1993 and in 2003 as a result of two 'improvement' exercises.

Table 7.1 shows remaining examples of overt options in IFRS in 2007. These do not include the large number of options in IFRS 1 (first-time adoption), but these are discussed in Section 7.3.8. The main issue for this chapter is whether options are exercised systematically differently from one jurisdiction to another, so that 'international accounting differences' survive.

Let us again take the examples of the UK and Germany, restricting ourselves as usual to the consolidated statements of listed companies. Tradition might be a major influence on the choices. For example (from Table 7.1):

- (IAS 1) UK groups might continue to use the financial position format of the balance sheet (see Section 2.9). For example, this is used in the model IFRS formats suggested by the UK firm of PricewaterhouseCoopers (2005). However, German groups will mostly continue to use the report format.

- (IAS 1) Under the old version of IAS 1 as in force for 2006 and available for 2007 and 2008, UK groups will present a Statement of Recognised Income and Expense (SORIE) which is similar to the UK Statement of Total Recognised Gains and Losses (see Section 15.4.1), whereas German groups will present the broader Statement of Changes in Equity.

- (IAS 2) UK groups will mainly continue to use 'first in, first out' (FIFO), whereas many German groups will use weighted average because it is common under German national practice, given that FIFO is restricted by tax law (Kesti, 2005). 'Last in, first out' (LIFO) is also found in unconsolidated statements in Germany (see Chapter 15), but not allowed by IAS 2.

- (IAS 19) UK groups will take actuarial gains and losses immediately in full to comprehensive income, whereas German groups will continue to take them to profit and loss using the corridor (smoothing) approach.

- (IAS 40) Some UK groups will continue to use fair value for investment properties, but German groups will continue to use cost.

7.3.6 Covert options

There is further scope for internationally different IFRS practice because of different interpretations, covert options or vague criteria in IFRS. This is a different matter

Table 7.1 Examples of overt options in IFRS*

IAS 1	No format requirements for statements of financial position or comprehensive income (paras 79 and 82).
IAS 2	FIFO or weighted average for the determination of the cost of inventories (para. 25).
IAS 2	Marking to market allowed for inventories of commodity broker-traders (para. 3).
IAS 7	Net basis allowed for cash flow statements (para. 21).
IAS 7	Choice of classification for interest and dividend flows (para. 31).
IAS 16	Cost or fair value measurement basis for classes of property, plant and equipment (para. 29).
IAS 19	Actuarial gains and losses can be taken (a) immediately in full to the SORIE, (b) immediately in full to the income statement, (c) in full to income over the remaining useful lives of employees in the plan, (d) in part to income over that period, or (e) in full or in part to income over a shorter period (paras 92–93A).
IAS 20	Asset grants can be shown as a deduction from the asset or as deferred income (para. 24).
IAS 23	Choice of capitalization or expensing for interest costs on constructed assets (paras 7 and 10 of old standard). Choice removed for 2009 onwards.
IAS 27	In parent statements, subsidiaries can be shown at cost or as available-for-sale investments (para. 37).
IAS 28	In investor statements, associates can be shown at cost or as available-for-sale investments (para. 38).
IAS 31	In group statements, a choice of proportional consolidation or equity accounting for joint venture entities (para. 30).
IAS 31	In venturer statements, joint ventures can be shown at cost or as available-for-sale investments (para. 46).
IAS 38	Cost or fair value measurement for some types of intangible asset (para. 72).
IAS 39	Choice of cost basis or marking to market for some financial assets and liabilities (para. 9). (Other choices are also available within para. 9.)
IAS 40	Permission to classify a property held under an operating lease as an investment property (para. 6).
IAS 40	Entity-wide choice of cost or fair value as measurement basis for investment property (para. 30).

Note: *Paragraph numbers as at 31 October 2007 unless otherwise noted.
Source: Adapted from Nobes, C.W. (2006) 'The survival of international differences under IFRS: towards a research agenda', *Accounting and Business Research*, Vol. 36, No. 3. Reproduced with permission.

from different practice caused by the inevitable estimations involved in operationalizing the standards (see Section 7.3.7). Examples of covert options or vague criteria are shown in Table 7.2. Several of the topics are taken up in more detail later in this book. As may be seen, some of these depend upon what is 'probable'. Doupnik and Richter (2004) suggest that German accountants interpret the word 'probable' (which occurs in many places in IFRS) more conservatively than US accountants.

An example of a covert option from Table 7.2 is the capitalization of development costs, as required by IAS 38. Under EU national rules, capitalization is in some cases banned (e.g. in Germany) and is in some cases allowed but not required (e.g. in the UK). EU national requirements do not generally contain a *requirement*, like that of IAS 38, to capitalize when certain criteria are met. A famous example of the

Table 7.2 Examples of covert options or vague criteria in IFRS

IAS 1	Determination of whether a liability is current on the basis of the expected date of settlement or purpose of holding (para. 60).
IAS 8	The determination of materiality for various purposes (para. 5).
IAS 11	Use of percentage of completion method only if the outcome of a contract can be estimated reliably (para. 22).
IAS 12	Recognition of a deferred tax asset for a loss carryforward only if future taxable profit is probable (para. 34).
IAS 12	Recognition of a deferred tax liability on unremitted profits from subsidiaries only if dividends are probable in the foreseeable future (para. 39).
IAS 17	Lease classification based on 'substantially all the risks and rewards' with no numerical criteria (para. 8).
IAS 21	Determination of functional currency based on a mixture of criteria (paras 9–12).
IAS 23	Cessation of capitalization of borrowing costs when 'substantially all' the activities to prepare the asset are complete (para. 22).
IAS 27	Identification of a subsidiary on the basis of 'power to control' (para. 4).
IAS 28	Identification of an associate on the basis of 'significant influence' (para. 2).
IAS 31	Identification of a joint venture on the basis of joint control of 'strategic financial and operating decisions' (para. 3).
IAS 36	Identification of an indication of impairment based on a mixture of criteria (paras 12–14).
IAS 37	Recognition of a provision based on probability of outflow of resources (para. 14).
IAS 38	Capitalization of development costs when all of various criteria are met (para. 57).
IAS 38	Amortization of intangible assets only if useful life is assessed as finite (para. 88).
IAS 39	Use of cost basis where equity instruments cannot be measured reliably (para. 46).
IAS 39	Estimation of hedge effectiveness as a condition for use of hedge accounting (para. 88).
IAS 40	Use of cost basis, despite entity-wide choice of fair value, for an investment property whose fair value cannot be measured reliably (para. 53).
IAS 41	Use of cost basis for a biological asset whose fair value cannot be measured reliably (para. 30).
IFRS 3	Identifying the acquirer in a business combination presented as a merger of equals (para. 20).
IFRS 5	Treatment of assets as held-for-sale if expected to be sold within one year (para. 8).
IFRS 8	The determination of reportable segments based on a mixture of factors (para. 11).

Source: Adapted from Nobes, C.W. (2006) 'The survival of international differences under IFRS: towards a research agenda', *Accounting and Business Research*, Vol. 36, No. 3. Reproduced with permission.

importance of this is Volkswagen's voluntary transition to IFRS from German accounting in 2001 (see Section 2.9): the increase in shareholders' equity caused by capitalization of development costs was 41 per cent. A similar large effect occurred for BMW.

Since there are no large UK car companies, no direct comparisons can be made with these German examples. However, capitalization depends on demonstrating that all of a list of vague criteria are met, such as feasibility of completion, intention to complete, and availability of adequate resources to complete (IAS 38, para. 57). Therefore, there is scope for deliberate or unconscious systematic international difference, driven by the factors discussed in Section 7.2. For example, as explained there, it is clear that German capitalization for IFRS consolidation purposes has no tax implications, whereas the position for the UK is different because tax considerations can affect accounting practice on this topic, and this could flow through to consolidated statements. On the other hand, capitalization runs far more against the German tradition of conservatism than it does against the British tradition.

More examples of possible different national approaches to measurement estimations are given in Nobes (2006), upon which this chapter is loosely based.

Another way of looking at the existence of covert options is that the existence of the IASB's International Financial Reporting Interpretations Committee (IFRIC) is evidence of the potential for different interpretations of standards. The IASB's preference for principles-based rather than rules-based standards (see Chapter 5) means that it tries to avoid detailed prescription. IFRIC publishes lists of topics that have been raised with it, but that it has decided not to deal with (e.g. IFRIC, 2007). At least two answers were thought plausible by those who raised these topics.

7.3.7 Measurement estimations

Table 7.3 gives some examples of IFRS measurement estimations (as opposed to estimates related to recognition, as in Section 7.3.6). An example of a measurement estimation is that, for depreciation, it is necessary to assess an asset's expected useful life and residual value. The depreciation method (e.g. straight line or reducing balance) is also an estimate and not a policy choice, because which method is appropriate depends on how the asset wears out.

Table 7.3 Examples of measurement estimations in IFRS

IAS 2	Net realizable value of inventories (paras 30 and 31).
IAS 11	Costs attributable to a contract (para. 16).
IAS 12	Tax rate for deferred tax calculations based on the expected manner of settlement or recovery (para. 51).
IAS 16 (and IASs 17, 38, 40)	Depreciation (or amortization) based on estimates of useful life, residual value and pattern of consumption (paras 50, 51 and 60).
IAS 16 (and IASs 38, 40)	Fair value when selected as a measurement basis (paras 31–34).
IAS 19	Pension obligations based on estimates of mortality, final salary, etc. (para. 64).
IAS 36	Discounted cash flows or net realizable values for impairments (para. 18, etc.).
IAS 37	Best estimate of provisions based on percentage likelihoods of outflows (para. 40).
IAS 39	Fair values for certain financial assets and liabilities (para. 48).
IAS 41	Fair values for biological assets (para. 12).
IFRS 2	Fair value of equity instruments (e.g. share options or shares in an unlisted company) granted to employees (para. 11).
IFRS 3	Allocation of cost of a business combination to assets and liabilities of acquiree based on fair values (para. 36).

Source: Adapted from Nobes, C.W. (2006) 'The survival of international differences under IFRS: towards a research agenda', *Accounting and Business Research*, Vol. 36, No. 3. Reproduced with permission.

Tradition, convenience and tax will all play roles here. UK tradition (FEE, 1991) is that a convenient method is used (typically for plant: straight line, zero residual value and ten-year life). This is done in the knowledge that an entirely separate scheme of capital allowances operates for tax purposes (see Sections 2.5 and 22.2). German tradition was (Haller, 1992), and for unconsolidated statements remains, to accelerate expenses by using the minimum lives allowed by tax law and the reducing balance method (but changing to straight line near the end of an asset's life).

It is clear that the tax-based useful lives and other estimates should be abandoned by German groups for IFRS purposes. For example, Volkswagen's transition showed an increase in shareholders' funds of 36 per cent as a result (see Section 2.9). Related to this, reducing balance has largely been abandoned for German IFRS statements, partly perhaps because an amendment to German law had already required the removal of tax-based policies from consolidated statements prepared under German domestic rules. However, in some other EU countries, reducing balance might continue under IFRS.

7.3.8 Transitional issues

One transitional issue has already been dealt with under Section 7.3.2: sometimes a new standard allows a period during which its requirements are merely encouraged. However, some transitional issues can lead to long-run effects on IFRS financial statements. IFRS 1 allows several options for companies moving from national rules to IFRS for the first time. One of them concerns goodwill. As explained in Section 4.3, goodwill requirements have changed greatly over the years. UK practice was generally to show goodwill purchased up to 1998 at zero, and to amortize subsequent goodwill over 20 years. In other countries (e.g. France) goodwill had always been capitalized. On transition to IFRS, the old national goodwill figures were allowed to be retained. These different national starting points will affect IFRS statements for many years to come.

7.3.9 Imperfect enforcement

The last of the suggested sources of scope for international differences, despite a requirement to use IFRS, is that the degree of enforcement of rules (and therefore compliance with them) varies internationally. As noted earlier, enforcement (including monitoring) of compliance with IFRS remains a national matter. This issue is discussed in Chapter 9, where research is summarized that shows German compliance with accounting rules to have been lower than that in the UK. If compliance is low in some countries, then practice under alleged IFRS may vary from IFRS requirements.

7.4 Conclusion

This chapter has addressed the question of whether there are motives and scope for different practice within IFRS. Although the question is relevant between individual companies or industries, the focus here has naturally been international.

Section 7.2 concluded that the motives for international difference, as examined in earlier chapters, are still applicable in modified form. Section 7.3 investigated the scope for different IFRS practice under eight headings. As part of doing this, extensive tables of IFRS overt options, covert options and measurement estimations were provided, and these can be studied as extensions of Chapter 6's coverage of the content of IFRS.

Over time, some of the scope for IFRS differences will be removed. For example, the IASB will continue to remove overt options, fill gaps and narrow possible interpretations. Also, the transitional differences will be eroded. Nevertheless, users of IFRS financial statements will have to be on their guard because, for example, a German version of IFRS practice is likely to continue to be different from a UK version.

SUMMARY

- Some aspects of the reasons for international differences in reporting still apply as motives for international differences in IFRS practice.

- Relevant factors include financing systems, legal systems and tax systems.

- Eight types of category are suggested as scope for different practice within IFRS.

- There are different national or regional versions of IFRS and different translations.

- There are also gaps in IFRS, overt options, covert options, scope for different measurement estimations, and transition options.

- Enforcement of IFRS varies internationally because it remains a national legal matter.

- The existence of different national versions of IFRS practice is a new feature of comparative international accounting. It has implications for users of financial statements and for US acceptance of IFRS statements.

References

David, R. and Brierley, J.E.C. (1985) *Major Legal Systems in the World Today*, Stevens, London.

DnR (2006) *IFRS på Norsk*, DnR Forlaget.

Doupnik, T.S. and Richter, M. (2004) 'The impact of culture on the interpretation of "in context" probability expressions', *Journal of International Accounting Research*, Vol. 3, No. 1.

Evans, L. (2004) 'Language, translation and the problem of international accounting communication', *Accounting, Auditing and Accountability Journal*, Vol. 17, No. 2.

FEE (1991) *European Survey of Published Accounts*, Routledge, London.

Haller, A. (1992) 'The relationship of financial and tax accounting in Germany: a major reason for accounting disharmony in Europe', *International Journal of Accounting*, Vol. 27, No. 4.

Haller, A. and Eierle, B. (2004) 'The adaptation of German accounting rule to IFRS: a legislative balancing act', *Accounting in Europe*, Vol. 1.

IFRC (2007) *IFRIC Update*, International Accounting Standards Committee Foundation, November, pp. 3–4.

Kesti, J. (2005) 'Germany', in *European Tax Handbook*, International Bureau of Fiscal Documentation, Amsterdam, part A.1.3.4.

KPMG (2005) 'IFRSs and the EU endorsement process: a status report', *IFRS Briefing*, Issue 37, November; see also Issue 41, December.

Nobes, C.W. (2006) 'The survival of international differences under IFRS: towards a research agenda', *Accounting and Business Research*, Vol. 36, No. 3.

PricewaterhouseCoopers (2005) *IFRS/UK Illustrative Financial Statements for 2005*, PricewaterhouseCoopers, London.

Watts, R.L. and Zimmerman, J.L. (1978) 'Towards a positive theory of the determination of accounting standards', *Accounting Review*, Vol. 53, No. 1.

Weissenberger, B.E., Stahl, A.B. and Vorstius, S. (2004) 'Changing from German GAAP to IFRS or US GAAP: A survey of German companies', *Accounting in Europe*, Vol. 1.

QUESTIONS

Suggested answers to the asterisked questions are given at the end of the book.

7.1∗ To what extent are the reasons for different European accounting systems still relevant as reasons for different European IFRS practices?

7.2∗ Give examples of options allowed in IFRS and how they might be chosen differently in different countries.

7.3 'The influence of tax on financial reporting cannot be relevant in the context of IFRS consolidated statements.' Discuss.

7.4 To what extent has the scope for different practice under IFRS declined over the past decade?

7.5 If it is found that large differences in IFRS practice exist systematically between countries, what implications does this have?

7.6 If a translation of IFRS exists in a language with which you are familiar, assess the quality of the translation.

8 Financial reporting in the United States

Christopher Nobes[1]

---

[1] This chapter is a considerably amended version of that in the first edition by Sir Bryan Carsberg and Alf Eastergard, who both worked for the Financial Accounting Standards Board at the time.

OBJECTIVES

After reading this chapter, you should be able to:

- explain the procedures for the setting and enforcement of standards in the United States, including the relationships between public and private sector institutions;
- describe the main features of the presentation of US financial statements;
- explain the main features of US accounting requirements;
- outline the main differences between US GAAP and the requirements of international standards.

8.1 Introduction

International standards (IFRS) have been examined in some detail in Chapters 4 to 7. Most of the listed companies in the world that still do not use IFRS (or a system based on it) use US accounting (or a system based on it). A volume of great length would be required to present a comprehensive description and analysis of financial reporting practices in the United States. In discussing those practices in a single chapter, we have had to be selective and have focused on topics in which the choice of acceptable practice may be expected to affect significantly the amounts of income and net worth reported by an enterprise.

US accounting was originally an export from the United Kingdom, like the American language and the American legal system. Such founding fathers of US accounting as Arthur Young and James Marwick (whose names are now incorporated into the names of the accounting firms Ernst & Young and KPMG, respectively) were expatriate Britons. The names in the other two big firms in the US (i.e. Deloitte, Price, Waterhouse, and the Cooper brothers) are all British, revealing the origins of the firms. Further, in terms of the causes and nature of differences discussed in Chapter 2, the United States and the United Kingdom are reasonably similar in a world context, although regulation of accounting differs. If countries are to be classified, these similarities suggest that the United States and the United Kingdom are in the same family. However, the view that there is such a thing as Anglo-American or Anglo-Saxon accounting has been criticized (as explained in Section 3.9).

One key similarity between UK and US accounting is the degree to which the financial reporting rules are separate from the tax rules (see Lamb *et al.*, 1998, for a detailed analysis). This means that tax rules are a minor influence on financial reporting, although the exception of LIFO (last in, first out) is noted in Section 8.6.5 below.

A more important issue now than US/UK similarity is US/IFRS similarity, not least because even British companies use IFRS, at least for consolidated statements. As noted already in this book, US influence on the accounting of other countries and on international standards has been considerable. However, from 2001, with the creation of the International Accounting Standards Board (IASB) coinciding closely with a series of accounting scandals in the United States, US accounting has been influenced from outside, especially by plans for convergence with IFRS.

After this introduction, there is an examination of the regulatory framework (Section 8.2), especially the Securities and Exchange Commission (SEC) which demands the world's most extensive disclosures from public companies. We then examine the standard-setting process (Section 8.3), leading to consideration of the conceptual framework (Section 8.4) and some detailed accounting and auditing topics (Sections 8.5 to 8.8). At the end of the chapter (Section 8.9) there is a comparison with IASB requirements.

As you read this chapter, remember that US rules are also used by companies based outside the United States. In some cases, this usage is still controlled by the SEC if, for example, the foreign company is listed on the New York Stock Exchange. In other cases, a foreign company may have approximately adopted US rules in order to impress investors.

8.2 Regulatory framework

8.2.1 Laws

The United States is a federation of individual states, each of which has its own legislative body with extensive powers to control business activity and levy taxes within its own boundaries. The setting up of companies and such issues as the distribution of profits to shareholders are controlled by state laws. The right to practise as a public accountant is also conferred by the individual states, and the requirements for conferring it differ slightly from state to state. Membership of the national body, the American Institute of Certified Public Accountants (AICPA), is not a condition for practising, and many practitioners elect not to become members. So, the number of CPAs recorded in Table 1.10 does not include all those with the right to practise.

Laws governing transactions in securities were first introduced by individual states, beginning with Kansas in 1911. Such state laws became widespread; they are generally known as 'blue sky laws', after a quip to the effect that unscrupulous Kansas dealers were trying to sell the blue sky. The laws normally require registration of any proposal to offer securities for sale, and disclosure of information; in some cases they confer on a state official the right to refuse permission for the proposal.

The most important regulations for the control of dealings in securities are enforced at the federal level under the Securities Act of 1933 and the Securities Exchange Act of 1934, which were passed after the financial crises of 1929 onwards, including the 'Wall Street Crash'. However, neither these statutes nor any others contain detailed provisions relating to financial reporting. The United States has no statutory requirements for accounting in a form that is comparable to the accounting sections of the Companies Acts in the UK or similar regulations in other EU countries (see Chapter 14). It has dealt with the need for accounting rules in a different way. The federal securities legislation established the SEC in 1934 to administer the securities regulations. The primary function of the SEC is to ensure that investors are given the information necessary for informed investment decisions. It requires publication and receives registration of prospectuses and periodic financial reports. It also has the power to prescribe the methods to be followed in the preparation of financial reports and to prescribe the form and content of those reports.

One vital point is that only a small minority of US companies (about 14,000) are SEC-registered and have to obey the SEC's accounting and auditing rules. Other companies have no compulsory audit or published financial reporting, although many companies are required to publish audited accounts by their shareholders or lenders. As noted above, a company must register with the SEC if it wants a market in its securities. Once registered, it has to publish financial statements, file reports, have CPA audits, follow the Regulations of the SEC (see below), and comply with generally accepted accounting principles (GAAP).

Originally, GAAP meant what it said; that is, a set of high-level principles endorsed by respectable companies, auditors and textbooks. However, from the 1930s onwards, rules have gradually been written down (or 'promulgated'), as explained later in this section. As a result, promulgated GAAP is now a large body of instructions: it is not 'principles' but detailed rules, and it is not 'generally accepted' but written down by bodies approved by the SEC.

8.2.2 The Securities and Exchange Commission

The Commission comprises five members appointed by the President of the United States and acts as an independent regulatory body with quasi-judicial powers. It has issued a large number of statements on accounting matters. However, these have related mainly to the details of registration rather than to accounting standards. Regulation S-X contains rules for the preparation of financial reports by registered companies. Form 10-K, containing the reports and extra information, must be filed annually within 60 days of the year end in the case of the largest companies. Form 10-Q contains quarterly reporting. Form 8-K is used to disclose (within 4 days) any interesting developments (e.g. the issue of more shares).

The Commission sometimes issues instructions on how to do accounting in 'Accounting Series Releases' or more recent 'Financial Reporting Releases'. There are also 'Staff Accounting Bulletins' (see below). However, the SEC has tended to limit the exercise of its accounting standard-setting authority to a supervisory role, permitting and encouraging the private sector, currently through the Financial Accounting Standards Board (FASB), to maintain leadership in the standard-setting process (see Section 8.3). In 1973 the SEC issued Accounting Series Release No. 150, *Statement of Policy on the Establishment and Improvement of Accounting Principles and Standards*, in which it reaffirmed its intention to maintain a supervisory role:

> In meeting this statutory responsibility effectively, in recognition of the expertise, energy and resources of the accounting profession, and without abdicating its responsibilities, the Commission has historically looked to the standard-setting bodies designated by the profession to provide leadership in establishing and improving accounting principles.

The determinations by these bodies have been regarded by the Commission, with minor exceptions, as being responsive to the needs of investors.

The body presently designated by the Council of the American Institute of Certified Public Accountants (AICPA) to establish accounting principles is the Financial Accounting Standards Board (FASB). . . . The Commission intends to continue its policy of looking to the private sector for leadership in establishing and improving accounting principles . . .

. . . For purposes of this policy, principles, standards and practices promulgated by the FASB in its Statements and Interpretations will be considered by the Commission as having substantial authoritative support, and those contrary to such FASB promulgations will be considered to have no such support.

In the course of monitoring the performance of the FASB in the standard-setting process, the staff of the SEC maintain regular communications with the staff of the FASB. The Commission might have reached different conclusions from those reached by the FASB on some of the topics on which the Board has issued pronouncements. However, the Commission has interfered publicly in matters that fall within the terms of reference of the Board only in a few special cases, notably two:

1 In March 1976 the Commission issued Accounting Series Release No. 190, requiring large public companies to disclose information about inventories, cost of goods sold, productive capacity, and depreciation expense on a replacement cost basis. That action, discussed further below, effectively (a) delayed the progress of the FASB towards establishing a requirement for the introduction of 'constant dollar accounting' (accounting for changes in purchasing power of the dollar), but (b) accelerated the progress towards an FASB requirement for the introduction of 'current cost accounting' (accounting for changes in prices of specific assets owned).

2 In 1978 the Commission effectively overruled part of an FASB standard for oil and gas accounting (Gorton, 1991). That standard (Statement No. 19) required the use of the 'successful efforts method' for measurement of the historical cost of oil and gas reserves and outlawed use of the 'full cost method'. Under Statement 19, all companies would have been required to treat the costs of abortive exploration as expenses when they were determined to have no further economic benefit. However, the SEC concluded that neither cost-based method provided information that was satisfactory for the needs of investors. It decided to study the feasibility of a method of measuring the value of oil and gas reserves and gave companies permission to use either the full cost method or the successful efforts method until a more permanent solution could be found. In 1978, the Commission adopted rules requiring oil and gas companies to present supplementary information according to 'Reserve Recognition Accounting', a method under which proven oil and gas reserves are measured at the net present value of their estimated future cash flows.

The SEC's ventures described above have been interesting for their strategic implications as well as for their direct contribution to accounting practice. Both initiatives concerned topics that were controversial. It would have been difficult for a private-sector organization to introduce the new requirements because it would need the broad support of the people who implement the requirements, and that support is not readily given for innovative types of reporting that put a burden on the preparers of financial reports. The SEC used its legislative authority to hasten the adoption of new practices; however, it made clear its wish that the FASB should take over the job of further standard-setting in the areas concerned. Nevertheless, what matters in the end to companies and auditors is how the staff of the SEC interpret an accounting standard. On many topics, the answer to this is given in a series of published *Staff Accounting Bulletins* from the SEC, which become part of GAAP.

The SEC requires foreign company registrants (e.g. German, Japanese or UK companies listed on the New York Stock Exchange or NASDAQ) either to report under US GAAP or to provide reconciliations to US GAAP using Form 20-F. It was noted in Chapter 5 that the New York exchange has the world's largest number of foreign listers. In 2000, the SEC issued a 'Concept Release' on the subject of whether to allow foreign registrants to use IFRS without reconciliation. In 2007, the SEC issued a 'Proposing Release' requesting comments on such a proposal. This was turned into a rule in 2007 with immediate effect (i.e. for 2007 reports filed in 2008). The SEC also raised the possibility that this could lead to US companies being given the same choice. The slow speed of this project may be due partly to the resignation of one chairman of the SEC when President Bush was elected in 2000, and of the next chairman after the accounting scandals of Enron and WorldCom of 2001/2 which were followed by the collapse of the Big-5 accounting firm, Andersen. These events led to the creation by Congress of the Public Company Accounting Oversight Board (PCAOB), which is overseen by the SEC (Carmichael, 2004). Also, the accounting duties of directors and the independence requirements of auditors were increased (see Section 8.8).

8.2.3 The United States Congress

The US legislative authority – the Congress – has occasionally taken a direct interest in accounting matters, although it has usually relied on the SEC to look after the public interest. However, some exceptions to that practice are illustrative. The first concerned the investment credit, a provision of tax law designed to give an incentive for the purchase of productive assets. The credit was a deduction of a percentage of the cost of new assets from the tax liability for the year in which the assets were first used. The introduction of the credit led to a controversy about the timing of its recognition in earnings. Some believed that the credit should be added to earnings in the year for which it was given; others believed that it should be spread over the life of the asset concerned. Eventually, the private-sector standard-setting authority proposed to require the use of one method – the spreading of the credit over the asset's life. However, before that proposal was finalized, the Congress passed legislation (the Revenue Act of 1971) to prevent any standard-setting body from limiting the acceptable methods of accounting for the investment credit in reports filed with any government agency, including the SEC.

This action of Congress was apparently motivated by a concern not to reduce the incentive effect of the tax credit. Congress recognized that it would be unfortunate if accounting standards were to produce an unfavourable pattern of earnings when optimal decisions were being taken, and hence to give an incentive to the taking of 'uneconomic decisions'. Today, it is widely accepted that accounting standards should, as far as possible, have a neutral effect on economic decisions. The FASB has sponsored research to estimate the economic consequences of its standards. The action of Congress may be seen as the forerunner of the concern about the neutrality of standards. Incidentally, the investment credit was abolished from 1986 as part of a general tax reform.

The 'politicization' of accounting in the United States has been commented on by Solomons (1978) and Zeff (1978), and more recently again by Zeff (1997) and Mozes (1998), who describe a major battle between standard-setters and elements of government on the subject of accounting for stock options (see Section 8.6). There was further involvement by Congress on the reform of accounting for business combinations caused by opposition from companies to the banning of pooling accounting (Beresford, 2001). These examples, and the general topic of political involvement in standard-setting, are examined in detail in Chapter 10. Zeff (2005) surveys the effects of political lobbying on US standard-setting.

8.3   Accounting standard-setters

8.3.1   Standard-setting by the profession

The first private-sector body to become involved with the systematic development of US accounting standards was the Committee on Accounting Procedure established by the AICPA in 1936 soon after the SEC was founded (Davidson and Andersen, 1987). The Committee produced 51 publications known as 'Accounting Research Bulletins' during the period 1939–59. The Committee was replaced, in 1959, by the Accounting Principles Board (APB) which published 31 Opinions and four Statements up to 1973. Pronouncements of the Committee and of the APB remain in force if they have not been amended or superseded by action of the FASB. Zeff (1972) examines standard-setting in the US and other countries in this period.

In 1971, growing dissatisfaction with the procedures for setting accounting standards led the AICPA to establish two committees to review those procedures. One source of dissatisfaction was that the APB was dominated by the accounting profession; there were insufficient provisions to ensure that the opinions of other interested parties were taken into account. The Wheat Committee was given the task of studying this problem. Its 1972 report, *Establishing Financial Accounting Standards*, led to the formation of three new bodies: the FASB, responsible for setting standards; the Financial Accounting Foundation (FAF), responsible for appointing members of the Board and for raising finance; and an advisory body, the Financial Accounting Standards Advisory Council (FASAC).

A second source of dissatisfaction with the APB was its limited progress in identifying fundamental concepts that would put the development of accounting standards on a surer foundation. The Trueblood Committee was formed to prepare a report on the objectives of financial reporting – a first step in the development of the FASB's conceptual framework project.

British readers will note that somewhat analogous reports to Wheat and Trueblood were published in the United Kingdom (Dearing in 1988 and Solomons

Table 8.1 **Standard-setting structure**

Body	US	International
Governing Trust	Financial Accounting Foundation	International Accounting Standards Committee Foundation
Board	Financial Accounting Standards Board	International Accounting Standards Board
Advisory Council	Financial Accounting Standards Advisory Council	Standards Advisory Council
Interpretation Body	Emerging Issues Task Force	International Financial Reporting Interpretations Committee

in 1989) leading to similar results, including the creation of the Accounting Standards Board. Similarly, the three US bodies (FASB, FAF and FASAC) all have their equivalents in the reforms that set up the International Accounting Standards Board (IASB) in 2001 (see Chapter 4). Table 8.1 records the US and international bodies.

Although the AICPA gave up its role as the main standard-setter, it still issues detailed guidance called 'Statements of Position', concentrating from 2003 on industry-specific guidance.

8.3.2 Financial Accounting Standards Board

Since 1973, the FASB has been the SEC's designated organization in the private sector for establishing standards of financial accounting and reporting in the United States. It is financed by voluntary contributions from public accounting firms, industry, investor and creditor organizations and various related organizations and individuals. Each annual contribution is limited to ensure the Board's independence from undue influence.

The seven members of the FASB serve full time and are required to sever all previous business or professional connections before joining the Board. They have diverse backgrounds; not all are recruited from public accounting firms.

The FASB issues Statements of Financial Accounting Standards (SFASs), Statements of Financial Accounting Concepts, and Interpretations. Statements of Standards establish new standards or amend those previously issued. Concepts Statements establish general concepts that will be used to guide the development of standards, but do not contain standards for direct application in themselves. Interpretations clarify, explain or elaborate existing standards.

Before it issues a Statement, the FASB is required by its rules to follow extensive 'due process'. In connection with each of its major projects, the Board:

- appoints a task force of technical experts representing a broad spectrum of preparers, auditors and users of financial information to advise on the project;
- studies existing literature on the subject and conducts such additional research as may be necessary;

- publishes a comprehensive discussion of issues and possible solutions as a basis for public comment;
- conducts a public hearing;
- distributes an exposure draft of the proposed statement for public comment.

The Board's operations are much more extensive, and its budget larger, than any other national standard-setter or the IASB. The substantial number of its technical staff conduct research, participate in public hearings, analyze oral and written comments received from the public, and prepare recommendations and drafts of documents for consideration by the Board. At the time of writing, the Board has published 160 Statements.

A further aspect to the workings of the FASB has been the Emerging Issues Task Force (EITF). This is a committee with members from the large accountancy firms and from companies, with the AICPA and the SEC as observers. The EITF examines newly apparent problems that require rapid guidance on what is to be generally accepted. Its conclusions are made public, and are very influential. The IASB's International Financial Reporting Interpretations Committee and the UK's Urgent Issues Task Force are somewhat similar.

In 2001/2, the difference between US 'rules-based' standards and IASB 'principles-based' standards was highlighted because of the spectacular collapses of some large companies (e.g. Enron). The FASB (2002) issued a consultative document on the issue. Despite this, the FASB issued an exposure draft in 2005 that proposes to make it even clearer than before that US GAAP does not allow departures from the rules in the name of the need to give a 'fair presentation'.

In 2002, the FASB announced a joint project (the 'Norwalk Agreement') with the IASB to remove as many differences as possible between their standards by 2005, and then to work on further convergence in the medium term. Section 8.9 looks at this and at the differences currently remaining.

Miller *et al.* (1998) examine the operations of the FASB. Zeff (1995) analyzes the mix of public and private-sector regulation in the United States.

8.3.3 Other influential parties

Particularly in the United States, there is substantial influence on standard-setting from representatives of the users of financial statements. The CFA Institute (formerly the Association for Investment Management and Research) is consulted and listened to by the FASB. One of the seven board members of the FASB is a financial analyst by training.

Naturally, a major influence on standard-setting comes from the management of large companies (the 'preparers'). It has been suggested (e.g. Watts and Zimmerman, 1978) that they will lobby the FASB on the basis of their personal interests (e.g. in trying to support a company's share price). Presumably, lobbying of senators and others explains the intervention of Congress (see Sections 8.2 and 8.6, and Chapter 10).

Academics have also played an important role. Usually, one of the Board members is a former academic, and individual academics are frequently commissioned by the FASB to conduct research on issues under discussion. The organization representing academic accountants, the American Accounting Association, comments on exposure drafts.

8.3.4 Enforcement

As already noted, the FASB's standards are officially recognized in the United States as authoritative by the SEC. Further assurance of the enforcement of FASB standards is provided by the AICPA rules. It was noted above that membership of the AICPA is not a prerequisite of the right to practise. However, state authorities that control the right to practise have generally adopted the AICPA rules. Rule 203 of the AICPA's Code of Professional Ethics states:

> A member shall not express an opinion that financial statements are presented in conformity with generally accepted accounting principles if such statements contain any departure from an accounting principle promulgated by the [FASB] . . . which has a material effect on the statements taken as a whole, unless the member can demonstrate that due to unusual circumstances the financial statements would otherwise have been misleading. In such cases his report must describe the departure, the approximate effects thereof, if practicable, and the reasons why compliance with the principles would result in a misleading statement.

The AICPA's Rules of Conduct also provide that 'the Trial Board may, after a hearing, admonish, suspend, or expel a member [of the AICPA] who is found guilty of infringing . . . any provisions of the Rules of conduct'. Accordingly, a Certified Public Accountant who condones a departure from an FASB pronouncement is subject to loss of his or her standing in the profession and, assuming that the licensing authorities concur with the conclusions of the AICPA Trial Board, loss of his or her legal authority to attest to the fairness of an enterprise's financial statement presentation.

Section 8.8 examines US audit further. Chapter 9 looks, in a comparative international way, at enforcement of rules on listed companies.

8.4   The conceptual framework

8.4.1 Introduction

The FASB devoted a significant portion of its early resources to the development of what has been referred to as a 'Conceptual Framework for Financial Accounting and Reporting'. As noted above, the need for a conceptual framework was one of the primary considerations in the studies that led to the establishment of the FASB, and the work undertaken by the Trueblood Committee made an important contribution to the development of a key statement on the objectives of financial reporting. One of the documents issued by the FASB on this subject explains the significance of that framework:

> Though many organizations, committees, and individuals have published their own constructs of conceptual framework or aspects of a framework, none by itself has come to be universally accepted and relied on in practice. Notable among those efforts is Accounting

Principles Board Statement No. 4 'Basic Concepts and Accounting Principles Underlying Financial Statements of Business Enterprises' (1970), but it purports primarily to describe the way things are and not to prescribe how they ought to be.

A conceptual framework is a constitution, a coherent system of interrelated objectives and fundamentals that can lead to consistent standards and that prescribes the nature, function and limits of financial accounting and financial statements. The objectives are to identify the goals and purposes of accounting. The fundamentals are the underlying concepts of accounting, concepts that guide the selection of events to be accounted for, the measurement of those events, and the means of summarizing and communicating them to interested parties.

Pressure for development of a conceptual framework came from many quarters, including accountants in public practice who saw it as a means of reducing the difficulty of judgements that have to be made about the relative desirability of accounting alternatives in areas that were not already covered by well-defined standards. The FASB worked on the framework continuously for a decade after its formation. The Board's conclusions about the framework are contained in concepts statements as follows:

- Concepts Statement No. 1 describes the fundamental objectives of financial reporting for business enterprises; a separate statement (No. 4) gives the objectives for non-business organizations.

- Concepts Statement No. 2 describes the qualities that make accounting information useful.

- Concepts Statement No. 3, later superseded by No. 6, gives definitions for the main elements of financial statements: components such as assets, liabilities, revenues and expenses.

- Concepts Statement No. 5 deals with criteria for recognizing and measuring the elements of financial statements, and with some of the issues that arise in relation to the presentation of information in financial reports.

In 2000, the FASB added to the framework by issuing CON 7, *Using Cash Flow Information and Present Value in Accounting Measurements*. This helps to bring the framework up to date and is part of the process of moving away from costs and towards values for certain balance sheet items.

In 2006 the FASB issued a discussion paper jointly with the IASB on proposals to revise the framework's sections on objectives and qualitative characteristics. Papers on other aspects are being prepared.

However, it is not clear whether the conceptual framework helps to force the FASB to particular conclusions in any topic area. For example, discussions about standards involve the assessment of the benefits and costs of accounting alternatives and that assessment continues to be partly subjective because of conflicts of interest and the lack of firm evidence about the level of both costs and benefits. Many papers have suggested various limitations of the framework and its use (e.g. Dopuch and Sunder, 1980; Ketz and Kunitake, 1988; DePree, 1989; Mozes, 1998).

The FASB's framework has been influential around the world. For example, the IASB's Framework (see Chapter 6) and the UK's Statement of Principles clearly derive from it. The broad conclusions of Statements 1, 2 and 6 are examined below.

8.4.2 Objectives of financial reporting

The FASB issued the first in its series of Statements of Financial Accounting Concepts in November 1978. The Statement, entitled *Objectives of Financial Reporting by Business Enterprises*, contains the following major conclusions:

1 Financial reporting is intended to provide information that is useful in making business economic decisions.

2 The objectives state that:

(a) Financial reporting should provide information that is useful to present and potential investors and creditors and other users in making rational investment, credit and similar decisions. The information should be comprehensible to those who have a reasonable understanding of business and economic activities and are willing to study the information with reasonable diligence.

(b) Financial reporting should provide information to help present and potential investors and creditors and other users in assessing the amounts, timing and uncertainty of prospective cash receipts from dividends or interest and the proceeds from the sale, redemption, or maturity of securities or loans.

(c) Financial reporting should provide information about the economic resources of an enterprise, the claims to those resources (obligations of the enterprise to transfer resources to other entities and owners' equity), and the effects of transactions, events and circumstances that change its resources and claims to those resources.

3 Information about enterprise earnings based on accrual accounting generally provides a better indication of an enterprise's present and continuing ability to generate favourable cash flows than information limited to the financial effects of cash receipts and payments.

4 Financial reporting is expected to provide information about an enterprise's financial performance during a period and about how management of an enterprise has discharged its stewardship responsibility to owners.

8.4.3 Qualitative characteristics of accounting information

The Statement on qualitative characteristics aims to identify the specific qualities that make accounting information useful. It adopts the framework of a cost–benefit test: accounting information is costly to provide and should be provided only if the benefits from use can be judged to outweigh the costs; the optimal amount of information is that which brings about the greatest possible surplus of benefits over costs. However, the Statement also acknowledges that the test can be applied only roughly at the present time, using subjective judgement.

The Statement emphasizes the importance of making accounting information understandable; but relevance and reliability are seen as the key qualities that make the information useful. Information is not worth presenting unless it has some minimum level of both relevance and reliability. Once those minima have been reached, a trade-off may be necessary: to gain relevance, some sacrifice of reliability may be required, or vice versa.

Relevance comprises three subsidiary qualities: predictive value, feedback value and timeliness. The quality of predictive value is defined in a way that echoes the main point of the Objectives Statement: information is useful if it helps the assessment of future cash flows. Feedback value is related to predictive value. Users will require information about actual results in areas where they have previously made predictions so that they can consider the efficiency of their predictive processes and improve them if they are found to be deficient. The quality of timeliness emphasizes that information must be available in good time to be useful.

Reliability also consists of three subsidiary qualities: verifiability, representational faithfulness and neutrality. Verifiability indicates that the numbers should be capable of independent checking by people using an agreed method. Representational faithfulness means that accounting information should represent what it purports to represent: in other words, it should be true. Neutrality implies the desirability of avoiding bias. Although bias may be difficult to detect in practice, at least information should not be chosen with a view to supporting the interests of some parties to the accounting process at the expense of others.

8.4.4 Elements of financial statements

Statement 6 defines ten elements of financial statements, the main ones being assets, liabilities, equity, revenues and expenses. The other definitions rest upon 'asset' and 'liability'. An asset is defined as:

> probable future economic benefits obtained or controlled . . . as a result of past transactions or events.

A liability is:

> probable future sacrifices of economic benefits arising from present obligations . . . to transfer assets or provide resources to other entities in the future as a result of past transactions or events.

Equity is the difference between assets and liabilities; and revenues and expenses are defined in terms of increases and decreases in assets and liabilities.

As noted in Section 8.4.1, use of the framework has limitations. The FASB does not always follow its framework, or may take many years to bring standards into line with it. For example, SFAS 150 of 2003 eventually required mandatorily redeemable preference shares to be classified as liabilities, many years after IAS 32 had done so. However, convertible debentures are generally classified as debt, even though they have an equity element that IAS 32 requires to be shown separately.

8.5 Contents of annual reports

8.5.1 Introduction

As explained in Section 8.2.2, the SEC requires a number of reports at various frequencies. A company must also file its financial statements (see below) and notes

Table 8.2 US terms for 'balance sheet'

	Companies
Balance sheet	577
Statement of financial position	22
Statement of financial condition	1
Total	600

Source: American Institute of Certified Public Accountants (AICPA) (2006) *Accounting Trends and Techniques* (issued annually). AICPA, Jersey City, New Jersey, p. 133. Reproduced with permission.

Table 8.3 US terms for IFRS 'income statement' or UK 'profit and loss account'

Companies	2000	2005
Operations statement*	198	255
Income statement*	284	254
Earnings statement*	108	86
Other	10	5
Total	600	600

Note: *Or statement of income, etc.
Source: American Institute of Certified Public Accountants (AICPA) (2001/2006) *Accounting Trends and Techniques* (issued annually). AICPA, Jersey City, New Jersey, p. 311 (2001), p. 295 (2006). Reproduced with permission.

with its Form 10-K. There is also a requirement for 'Management's Discussion and Analysis' which explains the company's results and financial condition.

There are three main annual financial statements for a US corporation: the balance sheet, the income statement and the statement of cash flows. Tables 8.2 and 8.3 illustrate the titles of the first two of these, as used by 600 large US corporations, drawing on an annual survey of US practice (AICPA, annual). As may be seen, the term 'income statement' has gradually been replaced in the United States. Ironically, this coincided with the move of IFRS to that term and away from the UK term 'profit and loss account'.

As explained below (Section 8.5.3), a statement equivalent to the IFRS SORIE is not required in the United States.

8.5.2 Balance sheets

There are some standard elements of US balance sheets: for example, assets are shown at the top of a vertical balance sheet (or on the left of a two-sided balance sheet). Unlike the format under European (including UK) national laws, current assets precede fixed assets. Only a small proportion of US corporations use a 'financial position' format that approximately corresponds to the standard UK format (Format 1 in Schedule 4 of the UK's Companies Act 1985; see Chapter 15), and so US formats are not especially well-adapted for reading by non-technical shareholders.

Table 8.4 **US titles for 'shareholders' funds'**

	Companies
Stockholders' equity	302
Shareholders' equity	228
Shareowners' equity	19
Shareholders' investment	8
Common stockholders' equity	7
Common shareholders' equity	4
Deficit or deficiency	25
Other or no title	7
Total	600

Source: American Institute of Certified Public Accountants (AICPA) (2006) *Accounting Trends and Techniques* (issued annually). AICPA, Jersey City, New Jersey, p. 273. Reproduced with permission.

Table 8.5 **US expressions for UK 'share premium'**

	Companies
Additional paid-in capital	330
Capital in excess of par or stated value	106
Paid-in capital	57
Additional capital or other capital	23
Capital surplus	18
Other captions	9
Sub-total	543
No additional paid-in capital account	57
Total	600

Source: American Institute of Certified Public Accountants (AICPA) (2006) *Accounting Trends and Techniques* (issued annually). AICPA, Jersey City, New Jersey, p. 278. Reproduced with permission.

The variety of terminology used can be further illustrated by looking at the equivalent of the UK term 'shareholders' funds'. In the United States, many different expressions are used, as demonstrated in Table 8.4. A further example is the remarkable diversity of terms (shown in Table 8.5) for the standard UK expression 'share premium'.

8.5.3 Income statements

US income statements tend to be somewhat more detailed than those in other countries. Their titles vary, as already shown in Table 8.3. A further difference from nearly all other countries and from IFRS is that *three* years of figures are presented; that is, the two preceding years' comparative figures. This is an SEC requirement.

In 1997, SFAS 130 introduced the requirement for information to be given on 'other comprehensive income'. This is analogous to the UK's earlier introduction of the statement of total recognized gains and losses (see Chapter 15). 'Other comprehensive

Table 8.6 Are gains or losses that were previously recorded as 'other comprehensive income' later re-classified as profit or loss?

	US	IFRS	UK*
Revaluation of financial assets	Yes	Yes	N/A
Revaluation of tangible assets	N/A	No	No
Translation of foreign statements	Yes	Yes	No

Notes: *Standards for unlisted companies.
N/A = Not applicable because practice not allowed.

income' (OCI) includes gains on the revaluation of investments that have not yet been included in net income (see Section 8.6.5) and gains or losses on the translation of foreign subsidiaries' financial statements. The IASC introduced something similar into IAS 1 in 1997; with further convergence towards SFAS 130 in 2007.

SFAS 130 allows the information on OCI to be included in the Statement of Changes in Equity (the normal US practice), to be shown as a separate second statement or as part of a single statement of comprehensive income. Another international difference is the treatment of any gain or loss on realization (e.g. on the sale of a foreign subsidiary). In other words, on disposal, is a gain that was previously recorded in equity reclassified as an increase in income and a reduction in other comprehensive income? Table 8.6 shows three different answers for the US, IFRS and the UK. Clearly, this issue needs to be addressed by the standard-setters, but despite large numbers of working parties from the late 1990s onwards, no conclusion had been reached as this book was being written.

8.5.4 Statements of cash flows

The financial statement on cash flows is required by SEC Regulations, but is a more recent arrival than the other two main statements. It is not part of the double-entry system but, as its name suggests, is another way of looking at some of the information in the balance sheet and income statement. Such a statement is also required by IAS 7 and in the United Kingdom (by FRS 1), but it was uncommon in much of continental Europe before the use of IFRS. As with the income statement, the US rules are unusual in requiring three years' figures.

Until 1987, the US requirement had been for a 'statement of changes in financial position', but this was replaced by the statement of cash flows, as outlined in SFAS 95, which concentrates on cash movements rather than on a more general notion of 'funds'. There are three main headings in the statement: 'operating', 'investing' and 'financing'. Unlike the UK's statements, SFAS 95 statements start with post-tax profit, and so tax is not shown as a use of cash.

8.5.5 Technical terms

Table 8.7 gives several examples of US/IFRS/UK differences in terminology. In many cases, these are fairly harmless. For example, most non-American speakers of English

Table 8.7 **Some US, IFRS and UK accounting terms**

United States	IFRS	United Kingdom*
Accounts payable	Payables	Creditors
Accounts receivable	Receivables	Debtors
Allowance (e.g. doubtful debts)	Impairment	Provision
Balance sheet	Statement of financial position	Balance sheet
Bylaws	–	Articles of association
Capital lease	Finance lease	Finance lease
Capital surplus	–	Share premium
Certificate of incorporation	–	Memorandum of association
Common stock	Ordinary shares	Ordinary shares
Constant dollar accounting	–	Current purchasing power
Current rate method	–	Closing rate method
Fiscal year	–	Financial year
General price level adjusted	–	Current purchasing power
Income	Profit	Profit
Income (or operations) statement	Income statement	Profit and loss account
Inventories	Inventories	Stocks
Leverage	–	Gearing
Notes	–	Bills
Paid-in surplus	–	Share premium
Par value	Par value	Nominal value
Pooling of interests	Uniting of interests	Merger accounting
Preferred stock	Preference shares	Preference shares
Property, plant and equipment	Property, plant and equipment	Tangible fixed assets
Purchase accounting	Purchase accounting	Acquisition accounting
Real estate	Land	Land
Reserve (e.g. doubtful debts)	Impairment	Provision
Reserve (e.g. pensions)	Provision	Provision
Sales	Revenue	Turnover
Stock	Shares	Shares
Stock-based compensation	Share-based payment	Share-based payment
Stock dividend	Bonus issue (small)	Bonus issue (small)
Stockholders' equity	Equity	Shareholders' funds
Stock split	Bonus issue (large)	Bonus issue (large)
Treasury stock	Treasury shares	Own shares

Note: *Terms used in the Companies Act and UK national standards.

can easily understand terms such as 'accounts receivable', 'accounts payable' or 'sales'. However, in some cases, confusion is possible. For example:

- The British Companies Act's term for 'sales' is 'turnover'. However, 'turnover' would be interpreted in the US as departure and hiring of staff.
- The most usual meanings of the UK terms 'stock' and 'shares' are translated into the US terms 'inventory' and 'stock' respectively. It would be unwise, therefore, to try to discuss with an American the use of FIFO for *stock* valuation. Consequently, IFRS uses 'inventory' and 'shares'. Worse than this, the expression

'treasury stock' would be taken to mean gilt-edged (i.e. government) loan securities in the United Kingdom, whereas in the United States it means a corporation's
own shares bought back and held in the corporate treasury. The IFRS term for
such shares is a compromise: 'treasury shares'.

- Some words, such as 'property', have subtly different meanings when they cross
  the Atlantic. In the United Kingdom, 'property' usually means land (i.e. *real*
  estate or *real* property) and buildings. In the United States, 'property' can have a
  wider meaning, encompassing any tangible fixed asset.

- Severe difficulties with the words 'provision', 'reserve' and 'allowance' occur, as
  noted earlier in Section 2.9.

8.6 Accounting principles

8.6.1 Tangible assets

North American accounting practices reflect a long-standing adherence to historical cost and to the notion that revenues and gains are recognized only when an
objective 'arm's length' transaction with another party has occurred. Accordingly,
the financial statement carrying values of property, plant and equipment or intangible assets are not increased on the basis of upward appraisals or changes in prices
because those events are not 'transactions'. This is unlike IFRS, which gives permission for revaluations in IASs 16, 38 and 40, and requires them in IAS 41.

The 'cost' of assets that have been constructed by a company for its own use must
include 'borrowing costs', i.e. the interest cost or money borrowed to finance the
project. This capitalization of interest cost is not required (and in some cases not
allowed) by most national rules (e.g. those of France, Germany or the UK). It is also
not required by IAS 23 until 2009, when a revision published in 2007 comes into force.

It is universal practice in North America to allocate the cost of tangible fixed
assets over their useful lives. Paragraph 5 of Accounting Research Bulletin (ARB)
No. 43, Chapter 9C, states the position in the United States:

> The cost of a productive facility is one of the costs of the services it renders during its use-
> ful economic life. Generally accepted accounting principles require that this cost be spread
> over the expected useful life of the facility in such a way as to allocate it as equitably as
> possible to the periods during which services are obtained from the use of the facility. This
> procedure is known as depreciation accounting, a system of accounting which aims to
> distribute the cost or other basic value of tangible capital assets, less salvage (if any), over
> the estimated useful life of the unit (which may be a group of assets) in a systematic and
> rational manner. It is process of allocation, not of valuation.

It is important to emphasize that there are no exceptions to this rule as there is,
for example, in IFRS for investment properties.

As in most countries, several methods are accepted for the computation of depreciation. The straight-line method is most common, but various methods of providing accelerated charges are also accepted including the reducing balance method
and the sum-of-the-years'-digits method.

There are also some relatively recent rules on impairment of assets, in the shape of SFAS 144 (and its predecessor, SFAS 121). This requires that assets be examined at each balance sheet date for any indication of impairment (e.g. physical damage). If there is an indication, a calculation must be made to compare: (i) an asset's carrying value with (ii) the sum of the expected future cash flows from the use and sale of the asset (undiscounted and without interest charges). If (ii) is lower than (i), then an impairment loss should be recognized. The loss is measured as the excess of the carrying amount over the fair value.

The term 'fair value' means the amount that willing buyers and sellers would exchange the asset for, in an arm's length transaction. If there is no market, the impairment loss is measured by reference to discounted cash flows as an estimate of fair value.

By contrast, IASB (and UK) rules have no test of impairment using undiscounted cash flows. If there is an indication of impairment, its size is measured by comparing carrying value with the higher of a market value and value in use (i.e. discounted cash flows). This means that more impairments will be recorded under IFRS, because many of them would be filtered out by the use of undiscounted (i.e. higher) cash flow totals under US rules.

For example, suppose the following facts about a used and damaged machine:

- carrying value (depreciated cost) = $9 million
- net realizable value = $6 million
- undiscounted net cash flows = $10 million
- discounted net cash flows = $8 million

Under US GAAP, there is no impairment because the expected cash flows ($10 million) exceed the carrying amount ($9 million). However, under IFRS, there is an impairment of $1 million because the recoverable amount (the higher of discounted cash flows and net realizable value)[2] is only $8 million.

8.6.2 Leases

For 60 years the United States has had accounting requirements dealing with leasing arrangements. They began in 1949 with a relatively simple requirement that lessees (a) disclose the amounts and timing of annual rental payments and (b) assess whether certain leases might be considered a capitalizable asset. This has evolved into a comprehensive, sometimes complex, network of accounting and reporting criteria related to leasing activities from the perspectives of both the lessee and the lessor.

Current reporting for leases is governed by FASB Statement No. 13, *Accounting for Leases*. Despite the complexity of the pronouncement, the concept is simple: if the risks and rewards associated with ownership of the leased asset accrue to the lessee, the lessor reports the signing of the lease as a sale of that asset (sales-type or direct

---

[2] IAS 36 uses the terms 'value in use' and 'fair value less costs to sell'.

financing lease), while the lessee reports it as a purchase. This is a 'capital lease'. Otherwise, both the lessee and the lessor report the lease as an 'operating lease'. The practical dividing line between capital and operating leases is set arbitrarily. One threshold for a capital lease in SFAS 13 is 75 per cent of useful life, another is that it involves at least 90 per cent of the asset value. By contrast, the IASB's standard (IAS 17) makes no reference to these numerical thresholds, relying only on the idea of transfer of 'substantially all the risks and rewards' to the lessee. This is a good illustration of a US rule contrasted to an IASB principle.

The idea that a lease should be a basis for reporting both an asset and a liability of equal amounts is designed to reflect 'substance over form', i.e. the economic reality (that the lessee has use of most of the asset) rather than the legal formality (that the lessee does not own the asset). However, this itself can be a misleading way to look at the issue, because the economic substance depends on the exact legal arrangements.

In the United States, the use of leasing agreements as a financial mechanism grew very rapidly. In certain industries (such as the manufacture of photocopiers or computers) 'leasing' overtook the traditional 'sale' as a means of marketing finished products. Because lessors know that lessee companies do not like to capitalize leases, particularly because of the liabilities that are then recognized, leases are often arranged to avoid meeting the technical criteria for being treated as capital leases. The FASB and other standard-setters are considering whether to require all non-cancellable leases to be treated as capital leases, given that the definitions of 'asset' and 'liability' seem to be satisfied (see Section 6.2). Such a move would be unpopular with companies.

8.6.3 Intangible assets

The general requirements on intangible assets are similar to those for property, plant and equipment. Most obviously, such assets must be valued at historical cost and, if they have identifiable useful lives, amortized over those lives. APB Opinion 17 had limited the useful life to 40 years, but this limit was removed by SFAS 142 in 2001. Intangible assets without definite lives (including any goodwill) should now be tested annually for impairment.

There are special rules on research and development in SFAS 2 that require such costs to be treated as expense immediately, unless of course they create physical fixed assets such as a laboratory. A specific exception to the US prohibition on capitalization concerns computer software. SFAS 86 and other statements require the costs of developing this to be capitalized under certain conditions when the technological feasibility of the product has been established.

SFAS 2 discusses the conflict between *prudence* (which would require the amounts to be treated as expense at once) and *accruals* (which suggests that the expense should be carried forward for matching). However, it concludes that, on balance, prudence and a desire for uniformity call for a straightforward prohibition on capitalization. The US requirements are more conservative than the IFRS rule (in IAS 38), which requires certain development costs to be capitalized (see more detail in Chapter 16); that is, carried forward as assets in order to be matched against future related revenues.

8.6.4 Investments

The use of a current/non-current distinction is not required in the United States, although many companies present their balance sheets classified in this way. For *measurement* purposes, SFAS 115 also ignores this distinction and requires investments to be split into *three* types, based largely on management intentions:

1 *held-to-maturity*: measure at amortized cost;

2 *trading*: measure at fair value; and

3 any others, called *available-for-sale*: measure at fair value.

The second two treatments will lead to unsettled gains and losses. These should be taken to income for item 2, and to other comprehensive income for item 3. The treatment of item 2 (i.e. fair value with gains to income) is called 'marking to market'. This also applies to any trading liabilities.

For *disclosure* purposes, SFAS 107 requires fair value information for many of the investments measured at cost. By contrast, in most countries there are no systematic disclosures of fair value; fixed asset investments are generally held at cost, and current asset investments are generally accounted for at the lower of cost and net realizable value, although financial institutions tend to hold marketable securities at market value.

In 1998, SFAS 133 extended marking to market to derivative financial instruments, both assets and liabilities. These various rules were approximately copied by the old Board of the IASC as IAS 39. However, more flexibility of use of marking to market was added to IAS 39 in 2004, and by SFAS 159 in 2007.

8.6.5 Inventories

The general rules for the valuation of inventory are to be found in Accounting Research Bulletin 43. The almost universal rule of 'the lower of cost and market' is used in the United States. However, 'market' normally means replacement cost in the United States, whereas it means net realizable value to the IASB and in the United Kingdom. Once an inventory has been reduced from cost to market, the impairment cannot be reversed if the market rises. This, again, is unlike IFRS or UK practice.

The major feature of US inventory valuation is that many companies use the last-in first-out (LIFO) method of determining the cost of inventory (see Table 8.8).

The use of LIFO means that the most recently purchased inventory is deemed for accounting purposes to be the earliest to be used up in production or sales, leaving the oldest inventory to be included in the closing inventory at the year end. When the price of a particular type of inventory is rising, this means that income is lower and closing inventory is also lower than it would be when using the alternative methods of average cost or 'first-in first-out' (FIFO).

LIFO was originally allowed for tax purposes in the United States in order to act as a relief from the taxation of inventory holding gains when prices rise. Otherwise, tax would have to be paid on income that is tied up in the extra value (despite a constant volume) of inventory. The problem for US accounting is that the tax rules require companies to use LIFO for the published income statements if it is used for

Table 8.8 Cost determination for inventory valuation, for 600 companies

	Instances of use
FIFO	385
LIFO	229
Average cost	155
Other	30
	799

	Companies
Use of LIFO by the 251 companies above:	
For all inventories	16
For 50% or more	113
For less than 50%	76
Not determinable	24
Companies using LIFO	229

Note: This table shows methods used by 600 large companies. A company may use more than one method.
Source: American Institute of Certified Public Accountants (AICPA) (2006) *Accounting Trends and Techniques* (issued annually). AICPA, Jersey City, New Jersey, p. 153. Reproduced with permission.

tax purposes. This is reminiscent of the more general effect of tax rules on accounting in some continental European countries (see Chapter 2).

As has been mentioned, many US companies take advantage of the tax reductions made possible by the use of LIFO. However, as Table 8.8 shows, most companies actually use a mixture of methods, presumably because some inventories fall in price and because the non-LIFO inventories of overseas subsidiaries are included. Those companies still using FIFO may be doing so in order to keep profits up, perhaps because management compensation is linked to declared net income. A considerable amount of empirical research (e.g. Jennings *et al.*, 1992) has been carried out but has not been able to resolve whether the market can see through LIFO's disadvantageous effect on earnings to the advantageous effect on tax payments. The rule requiring consistent application of GAAP stops frequent changes from LIFO to FIFO and back.

The effects of the use of LIFO can be very great. As far as the valuation of closing inventory is concerned, the prices involved can be *decades* old, not just slightly out of date. That is, LIFO retains costs of inventory from whenever that type of inventory was first bought. Thus, closing inventory valuations may be *very* unrealistically low. This might be more serious than out-of-date fixed asset valuations because inventory is nearer being sold and it forms a major element in liquidity ratios. Even worse, when inventories are physically reduced, perhaps because production shifts to the use of a more modern material, very old costs of inventory may pass through the income statement. This is sometimes called 'eating into old LIFO layers of inventory'. This can lead to misleadingly high income, although it could be claimed that LIFO normally gives a better picture of income because cost of sales includes more current costs.

GAAP requires companies to disclose which method of inventory valuation is being used, and the SEC requires its registrant companies that use LIFO to disclose in the Notes what the value of inventory would have been using FIFO. To take two examples:

	LIFO ($m)	Adjustment ($m)	FIFO ($m)	% Increase
General Motors (2006)	13,921	1,508	15,429	11
Caterpillar (2006)	6,351	2,403	8,754	38

In the case of Caterpillar, inventory would have been 38 per cent higher if FIFO had been chosen as the basis of valuation. This difference is very important in the context of net current assets (63 per cent) and net assets (35 per cent). So, important ratios, such as liquidity and return on net assets and gearing/leverage, are seriously affected.

The use of LIFO is one of the largest differences, in terms of millions of dollars, between US and IFRS (or UK) accounting. There is no particular international difference of theory that explains this difference in practice; it is merely that LIFO is allowed for the purposes of taxation in the United States. For example, LIFO is not acceptable for tax purposes in the United Kingdom, which made it possible for SSAP 9 to generally ban it for accounting purposes on the grounds that it will not normally give a fair view of closing inventory. The IASB banned LIFO for similar reasons in 2003.

8.6.6 Employee benefits, including stock-based compensation

One of the largest liabilities in the balance sheets of many US companies relates to employee benefits. US companies tend to promise not only pension benefits, but also post-retirement medical benefits. Such obligations must be accounted for at the discounted value of expected payments. Complications arise when the estimates change, giving rise to actuarial gains and losses. Treatment of these has been controversial for the FASB and the IASB, and a new US standard (SFAS 158) was issued in 2006. The main point is that actuarial gains and losses must now be recognized immediately in the balance sheet, whereas this is merely one option in IFRS. These matters are discussed in detail in Chapter 16.

Another way of remunerating employees beyond their salaries is to make grants (or promises of grants) of shares (or options to buy shares). This practice began in the United States and is still most widespread there. Let us take a typical example. Suppose that Company X grants an option to Employee Y, on 1 January 2007, to buy 1,000 shares in Company X at $5 per share on 31 December 2008 (or within a period starting on that date) if the employee is still working for the company on that date. On the grant date, the share price is $5.

One view is that the options are not worth anything (i.e. have no 'intrinsic value'), at least not when granted. However, they would have a *market* (fair) value because the least they can yield to the employee is zero, and they will become valuable if the share price is above $5 by the end of 2008.

Accounting on a fair value basis requires an estimation of the fair value of the options on the grant date. This is treated as an employee expense (and a credit to equity) over the two-year period. The management of companies would prefer to avoid recognizing this expense. The FASB's predecessor (the APB) issued Opinion 25, which required only disclosure of fair value. When the FASB itself tried to issue a fair value standard, it was beaten into submission by companies and Congress (see Chapter 10), such that SFAS 123 also originally allowed disclosure only. In 2004, the FASB revised SFAS 123 in order to require accounting for the fair value of stock options, but again this led to political action and postponement of the standard until 2006 when it eventually came into force. This standard is similar to the IASB's IFRS 2 that had come into force in 2005.

For a review of the theoretical issues concerning share-based payments, see Mozes (1998) and Kirschenheiter *et al.* (2004).

8.6.7 Accounting for corporate taxes

It is well known that the income of a company, measured according to generally accepted accounting principles, normally differs under Anglo-Saxon accounting (or under IASB standards) from the income on which taxes are payable. The most common reason for the difference is that various accelerated depreciation allowances are deductible in the computation of taxable income regardless of the methods used to compute depreciation expense in the income statements. Consequently, when the assets of a company are relatively new, or when a company is expanding or when prices are rising, its depreciation for tax purposes will exceed the amount charged in the published income statement. Consequently, taxable income will be lower than reported income. So, the real tax bill will be lower than the 'tax expense' shown in the income statement as calculated on the basis of the reported income. This difference is matched by a credit balance shown as a deferred tax liability in the balance sheet: a sort of postponed tax bill.

Another way of looking at this is that the asset is held at a different value for tax purposes compared with its value for accounting purposes. In the example of accelerated tax depreciation, the tax written down value is lower than the accounting written down value. This creates a deferred tax liability. Deferred tax accounting traditionally took the income statement view (see Section 8.4) (e.g. APB Opinion No. 11 in the United States, the original IAS 12 of 1979, and SSAP 15 in the United Kingdom). However, in 1991 the FASB issued SFAS 109, which moved to the balance sheet view. IAS 12 (of 1996 onwards) also takes this view, but the UK retained the income statement view in FRS 19 of 2000.

In US, IASB and UK rules, account is taken of any change in corporate income tax rates, as this affects the size of any liability (the 'liability method'). In some other countries (and under the old APB Opinion No. 11), rate changes are ignored so that the rate used is that ruling when the timing/temporary difference originated (the 'deferral method').

After many changes, US GAAP and IFRS requirements on deferred tax are now largely the same: full accounting for temporary differences using the liability method. More detail on accounting for deferred tax is given in Chapter 16. For a US overview of the historical development of deferred tax accounting, see Schultz and Johnson (1998).

8.7 Consolidation

8.7.1 The scope of the group

As for many other topics, US GAAP has tried to provide an auditable rule rather than a principle for the definition of those companies to be consolidated. The IASB's concept (in IAS 27) of 'power to control the financial and operating policies' is a clear principle, but leads to the need for judgement in some cases. The US definition of subsidiary in APB Opinion 18 rests on the ownership of more than half of the voting shares or on other legal arrangements to secure control. This enables companies to engage in a series of devices to establish entities that are in practice controlled but fall outside the scope to be consolidated. These 'special purpose vehicles' (SPVs) can then contain unconsolidated borrowings, capitalized leases and other forms of off-balance sheet finance. The most spectacular example of this was the energy trading company, Enron, which had thousands of such SPVs when it collapsed in 2001/2, taking its adviser/auditor (Andersen) with it.

The Sarbanes-Oxley Act of 2002 responded by requiring footnote disclosure of off-balance sheet liabilities. The FASB also issued Interpretation No. 46 in 2003 that requires consolidation of certain 'variable interest' entities that the group supports or receives residual returns from. The investigation by the SEC and the FASB of the merits of principles-based standards (see Section 8.3) is also related to this.

8.7.2 Accounting for business combinations

A detailed discussion of practice on the preparation of consolidated statements and on the alternative methods of accounting for mergers and acquisitions is given in Chapter 17. US accounting practices related to business combinations were determined until 2001 on the basis of APB Opinion 16, *Business Combinations*. That Opinion provided for the use of two methods of accounting: the 'purchase method' and the 'pooling of interests method'.

Under the purchase method, the accounting basis for the acquired enterprise's assets in the group financial statements is their fair value at the time of the business combination. Paragraph 11 of APB Opinion 16 described the essence of the purchase method, as follows:

> The purchase method accounts for a business combination as the acquisition of one company by another. The acquiring corporation records at its cost the acquired assets less liabilities assumed. A difference between the cost of an acquired company and the sum of the fair values of tangible and identifiable intangible assets less liabilities is recorded as goodwill. The reported income of an acquiring corporation includes the operations of the acquired company after acquisition, based on the cost to the acquiring corporation.

Under the pooling of interests method, the accounting basis of the acquired enterprise remains unchanged, and the depreciated historical cost of its assets is combined with that of the acquiring enterprise's assets. Opinion 16 described in paragraph 12 the pooling of interests method, as follows:

> The pooling of interests method accounts for a business combination as the uniting of the ownership interests of two or more companies by exchange of equity securities. No acquisition is recognized because the combination is accomplished without disbursing resources of the constituents. Ownership interests continue and the former bases of accounting are retained. The recorded assets and liabilities of the constituents are carried forward to the combined corporation at their recorded amounts. Income of the combined corporation includes income of the constituents for the entire fiscal period in which the combination occurs. The reported income of the constituents for prior periods is combined and restated as income of the combined corporation.

In periods of rising prices, the purchase method can be expected to produce the following two main differences from the pooling of interests method: first, the fixed assets will tend to be reported at greater amounts, and an intangible asset (goodwill) is usually created; and secondly, net income reported after the business combination will tend to be less under the purchase method because the depreciation of the higher carrying amounts of the fixed assets and the impairment (or, formerly, amortization) of goodwill (both of which are reported as expenses) are deducted in the determination of net income. A significant minority (about one-fifth) of US business combinations met certain conditions set out in the authoritative literature that enabled them to be accounted for under the pooling of interests method.

In 1999, the FASB announced its intention to abolish poolings, on the grounds that the method amounted to a choice in most cases. The SEC supported this position. However, that decision was very unpopular with companies because of the enormous amount of goodwill amortization expense that would have arisen if large poolings had been accounted for as purchases. For an examination of this, see Ayers *et al.* (2000). One way of reducing the opposition to the elimination of poolings was to amend the requirements on goodwill, as examined below.

The elimination of pooling was achieved by the FASB in 2001 with the publication of SFAS 141. However, poolings up to 30 June 2001 are allowed to remain in place in subsequent financial statements, so poolings will continue to be relevant for an understanding of financial statements prepared under US GAAP for many years to come. The IASB had already in the 1990s restricted the use of poolings more than in the US, but pressure was on it to follow the US and to eliminate poolings, and it did so in 2004.

8.7.3 Goodwill

There have been major international differences on the treatment of goodwill in purchase accounting. Under US and IASB rules, goodwill is calculated as the difference between the fair value of the consideration and the fair value of the net assets acquired. However, there is a major practical difference in that the United States requires (until 2009) the use of the acquirer's perspective whereas IFRS 3 takes a neutral or market perspective. The acquirer's perspective involves recognizing provisions for proposed restructurings, which writes down the net assets and increases goodwill. This reduces subsequent depreciation of assets, increases the recorded gains on sale of assets and absorbs various future expenses.

Another difference (until 2009) is that negative goodwill does not generally arise in the US because the acquired assets are written down pro rata to avoid it, whereas under IFRS negative goodwill is treated as immediate income.

The more general international difference concerns the treatment of positive goodwill. A brief outline of changes to US, UK and IASB rules reveals some of the remarkably different possibilities. US practice, under APB Opinion 17 until 2001, was to treat goodwill as an asset and to amortize it over its useful economic life (not exceeding 40 years). Many companies used 40 years, given the difficulty of estimating the life of goodwill and that this choice slowed down the expense as much as possible. However, the SEC frequently required a shorter period to be used by companies in particular sectors. By contrast, majority UK practice ('preferred' by SSAP 22) was (until 1998) that goodwill was deducted immediately from group reserves. This meant that US group assets looked larger than UK practice required, and US group income looked smaller. It has been suggested that this led to a comparative international disadvantage for acquisitive US managements (Choi and Lee, 1991).

The IASC had allowed the UK practice until 1995 but then set a maximum of 20 years for amortization. However, at the end of the 1990s both the UK and the IASC moved to a requirement to capitalize and a rebuttable presumption of a 20-year life. Any goodwill with a life in excess of 20 years had to be tested annually for impairment.

In 2001 the FASB took all this development to its logical conclusion by publishing SFAS 142, which abolished amortization, requiring instead annual impairment tests. The logic of this is that goodwill does not necessarily wear out, and the annual amortization expenses over an arbitrary life were meaningless numbers. Of course, the removal of this expense made the removal of poolings (see above) more palatable. The IASB followed the FASB's approach in 2004.

8.8 Audit

The report of independent auditors can be an important source of information for the reader of financial reports. It explains what the auditors have done to satisfy themselves as to the fairness of the financial statements and states an opinion regarding their fairness, given the context of generally accepted accounting principles. The standard form of the audit report in the United States, controlled until 2003 by the AICPA, is as follows:

> We have audited the accompanying Consolidated Balance Sheets of XYZ Company and subsidiaries (the Corporation) as of December 31, 2007 and 2006, and the related Consolidated Statements of Income, Cash Flows, and Stockholders' Equity for each of the three years in the period ended December 31, 2007. Our audits also included the Supplemental Information to the Consolidated Balance Sheets and Consolidated Statements of Income and Cash Flows and the financial statement schedules listed (collectively, the financial statement schedules). These financial statements and financial statement schedules are the responsibility of the Corporation's management. Our responsibility is to express an opinion on these financial statements and financial statement schedules based on our audits.

We conducted our audits in accordance with the standards of the Public Company Accounting Oversight Board (United States). Those standards require that we plan and perform the audit to obtain reasonable assurance about whether the financial statements are free of material misstatement. An audit includes examining, on a test basis, evidence supporting the amounts and disclosures in the financial statements. An audit also includes assessing the accounting principles used and significant estimates made by management, as well as evaluating the overall financial statement presentation. We believe that our audits provide a reasonable basis for our opinion.

In our opinion, such consolidated financial statements present fairly, in all material respects, the financial position of XYZ Company and subsidiaries at December 31, 2005 and 2004, and the results of their operations and their cash flows for each of the three years in the period ended December 31, 2005, in conformity with accounting principles generally accepted in the United States of America. Also, in our opinion, such financial statement schedules, when considered in relation to the basic consolidated financial statements taken as a whole, present fairly, in all material respects, the information set forth therein.

The key words in the opinion in the last paragraph are 'present fairly . . . in conformity with accounting principles generally accepted'. The reference to generally accepted accounting principles (GAAP) reflects a reliance on authoritative literature, including standards (see Zeff, 1990 and 1992).

In 2002, the US Congress passed the Sarbanes-Oxley Act (SOX) that requires senior management to certify the reliability of the financial statements and imposes greater independence requirements on auditors. SOX is not directly about accounting, except requiring some disclosures. It is mainly about corporate governance and audit. Its requirements are onerous and have made it more expensive to be registered with the SEC and listed on US exchanges. In 2003, the Public Company Accounting Oversight Board decided to set auditing standards itself rather than delegating this task to the AICPA, which had performed the role for over 60 years. Zeff (2003) examines how the US audit profession gradually fell from grace over a century.

As mentioned in Section 8.2.1, there is no compulsory audit for most US corporations, some of whom therefore choose instead to have an 'audit review', which is a standardized set of procedures but less than a full audit.

8.9   Differences from IFRS

As mentioned in Chapter 5, major companies throughout the world are using, or are moving towards, either US GAAP or IFRS for consolidated reporting. Consequently, the differences between the two systems are of great importance for international comparisons.

The US and the IASB largely share the same conceptual framework. In particular, both see the primary purpose of financial reporting as the provision of useful information to investors for the prediction of future cash flows; and both have similar definitions of 'asset' and 'liability', which are seen as the basic elements of financial statements. Furthermore, the FASB and the IASC/B collaborated on certain projects in the late 1990s (e.g. IAS 14 (revised) on segment reporting, and IAS 33 on earnings per share). By the late 1990s, US GAAP and IFRS had clearly become rivals for worldwide domination of financial reporting. Consequently, the FASB was keen to point out the differences in the two systems and, by implication, the weaknesses of IFRSs (e.g. Bloomer, 1999). However, the original IASB, which began work in 2001, contained two former FASB members and one former FASB trustee among its 14 members, and the chairman of the FASB appointed in 2002 had been an IASB member. Also, the SEC had signalled approval of the new IASB arrangements (see, for example, Camfferman and Zeff, 2007, ch. 13). As noted earlier, a formal convergence project was announced in 2002. As a result, cooperation is now extensive, and all major new projects are undertaken jointly. Four exposure drafts were issued by the FASB in 2004 designed to adopt certain IASB requirements. Table 5.9 shows the progress with issuing standards.

One general difference from IFRS is that US GAAP is much more detailed ('rules-based') on many topics, as discussed in Chapter 5. A hindrance to the international use of US GAAP is that it is not available in languages other than English, whereas there are now official translations of IFRS into several languages. Chapter 5 also includes some reconciliations from IFRS to US GAAP.

Table 8.9 shows some of the ways in which US rules would not allow or would not require conformity with IFRS. Looking at it the other way round, there are many areas of US GAAP on which IFRS is less detailed or allows more options; Table 8.10 shows some examples of these. The differences were charted in detail in Nobes (2001) and more recently at iasplus.com/country/compare.htm. Ernst & Young (2005) also examine them.

Table 8.9 Some ways in which US GAAP would not allow or would not require IFRS

- The setting up of provisions in the context of business combinations can be more extensive than under IFRS (see Section 8.7.3).
- Negative goodwill generally does not arise (see Section 8.7.3).
- Fewer impairments are recognized in the US because of a test involving undiscounted cash flows (see Section 8.6.1).
- Impairments cannot be reversed (see Section 8.6.1).
- Compound financial instruments are not split into debt and equity components (see Section 8.4.4).
- Inventories are reduced to current replacement cost (rather than to net realizable value) and the reduction cannot be reversed (see Section 8.6.5).
- The LIFO method is allowed (see Section 8.6.5).
- Some enterprises that are *de facto* controlled may be excluded from consolidation (see Section 8.7.1).
- Development costs (except for software) cannot be capitalized (see Section 8.6.3).

Table 8.10 Some IFRS options not allowed under US rules

- Full flexibility of balance sheet formats.
- Valuing tangible and intangible assets above cost.
- Expensing borrowing costs on construction of fixed assets (until 2009).
- Taking actuarial gains and losses gradually to the balance sheet.
- Proportional consolidation of joint venture entities (instead of the equity method).

SUMMARY

- There are many similarities between the US and IASB in terms of philosophy and practice of accounting.
- The US has no federal Companies Act but a powerful Securities and Exchange Commission.
- Private-sector standard-setting has supplied most of the content for generally accepted accounting principles. The body now setting standards is the FASB.
- The conceptual framework of the IASB is based on that of the FASB, which uses a balance sheet basis.
- There are large numbers of US/IFRS/UK differences in technical accounting terms.
- The US adheres to historical cost for tangible and intangible assets, with a different test of impairment from the IASB.
- The US invented the idea of capitalizing leases, and proposes to extend this further.
- Fair value accounting has been introduced for certain investments.
- LIFO is allowed and commonly practised for inventory valuation, which causes large reductions in balance sheet figures.
- The US method of fully accounting for deferred taxes on temporary differences was the model for the standard of the IASB.
- The pooling of interests method for accounting for business combinations was used more in the United States than in other countries, but it was banned in 2001.
- For decades, the US rule on the treatment of goodwill was that it should be capitalized and amortized over useful life. In 2001, this changed to capitalization followed by impairment reviews.
- US rules are more extensive and detailed than those of the IASB, and there are some incompatibilities.

References

AICPA (annual) *Accounting Trends and Techniques*, issued annually, American Institute of Certified Public Accountants, New York.

Ayers, B.C., Lefanowicz, C.E. and Robinson, J.R. (2000) 'The financial statement effects of eliminating the pooling-of-interests method of acquisition accounting', *Accounting Horizons*, Vol. 14, No. 1.

Beresford, D.R. (2001) 'Congress looks at accounting for business combinations', *Accounting Horizons*, Vol. 15, No. 1.

Bloomer, C. (1999) *The IASC–US Comparison Project*, FASB.

Camfferman, K. and Zeff, S. (2007) *Financial Reporting and Global Capital Markets: A History of the International Accounting Standards Committee, 1973–2000*, Oxford University Press, Oxford.

Carmichael, D.R. (2004) 'The PCAOB and the social responsibility of the independent auditor', *Accounting Horizons*, Vol. 18, No. 2.

Choi, F.D.S. and Lee, C. (1991) 'Merger premia and national differences in accounting for goodwill', *Journal of International Financial Management and Accounting*, Vol. 2, No. 3.

Davidson, S. and Andersen, G.D. (1987) 'The development of accounting and auditing standards', *Journal of Accountancy*, Vol. 163, No. 5.

DePree, C.D. (1989) 'Testing and evaluating a conceptual framework of accounting', *Abacus*, Vol. 25, No. 1.

Dopuch, N. and Sunder, S. (1980) 'FASB's statements on objectives and elements of financial accounting: a review', *Accounting Review*, Vol. 55, No. 1.

Ernst & Young (2005) *IFRS/US GAAP Comparison*, Butterworths, London. (Later versions can be found online.)

FASB (2002) *Principles-based Approach to US Standard Setting*, Financial Accounting Standards Board, Norwalk.

GAAP Guide (annual), Harcourt Brace Jovanovich, issued annually, Orlando.

Gorton, D.E. (1991) 'The SEC decision not to support SFAS 19', *Accounting Horizons*, Vol. 5, No. 1.

Jennings, R., Mest, D.P. and Thompson, R.B.II (1992) 'Investor reaction to disclosures of 1974–5 LIFO adoption decisions', *Accounting Review*, Vol. 67, No. 2.

Ketz, J.E. and Kunitake, W.K. (1988) 'An evaluation of the conceptual framework: can it resolve the issues related to accounting for income taxes?' *Advances in Accounting*, Vol. 6.

Kirschenheiter, M., Mather, R. and Thomas, J.K. (2004) 'Accounting for employee stock options', *Accounting Horizons*, Vol. 18, No. 2.

Lamb, M., Nobes, C.W. and Roberts, A.D. (1998) 'International variations in the connections between tax and financial reporting', *Accounting and Business Research*, Vol. 28, No. 3.

Miller, P., Redding, R. and Bahnson, P. (1998) *The FASB: The People, the Process and the Politics*, Irwin/McGraw Hill, Homewood.

Mozes, H.A. (1998) 'The FASB's conceptual framework and political support: the lesson from employee stock options', *Abacus*, Vol. 34, No. 2.

Nobes, C.W. (ed.) (2001) *GAAP 2001; A Survey of National Accounting Rules*, Pricewaterhouse-Coopers, London; also available at www.ifad.net.

Schultz, S.M. and Johnson, R.T. (1998) 'Income tax allocation: the continuing controversy in historical perspective', *Accounting Historians Journal*, Vol. 25, No. 2.

Solomons, D. (1978) 'The politicization of accounting', *Journal of Accountancy*, November.

Watts, R.L. and Zimmerman, J.L. (1978) 'Towards a positive theory of the determination of accounting standards', *Accounting Review*, Vol. 53, No. 1.

Zeff, S.A. (1972) *Forging Accounting Principles in Five Countries: A History and an Analysis of Trends* (Arthur Andersen & Co. Lecture Series, University of Edinburgh 1971), Stipes Publishing Co., Champaign, IL.

Zeff, S.A. (1978) 'The rise of economic consequences', *Journal of Accountancy*, December.

Zeff, S.A. (1990) 'The English language equivalent of geeft een getrouw beeld', *De Accountant*, October.

Zeff, S.A. (1992) 'Arthur Andersen & Co. and the two-part opinion in the auditor's report: 1946–1962', *Contemporary Accounting Research*, Vol. 8, No. 2.

Zeff, S.A. (1995) 'A perspective on the U.S. public/private-sector approach to the regulation of financial reporting', *Accounting Horizons*, Vol. 9, No. 1.

Zeff, S.A. (1997) 'Playing the congressional card on employee stock options', in T.E. Cooke and C.W. Nobes (eds), *The Development of Accounting in an International Context*, Routledge, London.

Zeff, S.A. (2003) 'How the US accounting profession got where it is today', *Accounting Horizons*, Vol. 17, Nos. 3 and 4.

Zeff, S.A. (2005) 'The evolution of US GAAP: the political forces behind professional standards', *CPA Journal*, January, pp. 18–27, and February, pp. 18–29.

Further reading

The accounting practices of US corporations are surveyed each year in AICPA (annual). The US GAAP requirements are summarized topic by topic in *GAAP Guide* (annual). The differences between US GAAP and IFRS are examined in detail by Ernst & Young (2005).

QUESTIONS

Suggested answers to the asterisked questions are given at the end of the book.

8.1∗ 'US accounting is the best in the world.' Discuss.

8.2∗ To what extent, if at all, is US accounting influenced by accounting in other countries?

8.3 Which US accounting practices seem out of line with those of many other countries? What explanations are there for this?

8.4 Discuss the causes of differences in financial reporting and its regulation (giving relevant examples of the effects) between your own country and the United States.

8.5 'The most important influence on US accounting has been and remains the SEC.' Discuss.

8.6 As pointed out in this chapter, the United States and United Kingdom are reasonably similar with respect to the causes and nature of differences in financial reporting. Identify and discuss factors that may account for the existing differences in practices between US GAAP and UK national rules.

8.7 Would you describe the differences between IFRS and US GAAP as 'major'? Will it be easy for the standard-setters to remove these differences?

9 Enforcement of Financial Reporting Standards

Robert Parker

OBJECTIVES

After reading this chapter, you should be able to:

● explain the various ways in which the application of financial reporting standards by listed companies can be monitored and enforced;

● compare and contrast the monitoring and enforcement bodies and processes used in the US, the member states of the EU (with particular reference to the UK, France and Germany), and Australia.

9.1 Introduction

Chapter 5 discussed in general terms financial reporting by listed companies around the world. Chapters 6 to 8 examined the accounting rules under the two main systems for listed companies: IFRS and US GAAP. This chapter discusses how, and to what extent, these and other rules are monitored and enforced. Modes of enforcement vary from country to country much more than the rules themselves do.

Enforcement comprises:

a cascade of different elements including (1) clear accounting standards (2) timely interpretations and implementation guidance (3) statutory audit (4) monitoring by supervisors and (5) effective sanctions. Each of these must work efficiently: the system will be as strong as its weakest part in delivering strong investor and creditor protection.

(Commission of the European Communities, 2000, paragraph 26)

This chapter discusses the last three of these elements, looking not at the content of accounting standards or the processes by which standards are set but at the ways in which their application is monitored and enforced.

'Enforcement' is a difficult concept to quantify and measure. Hope (2003) compiled a country enforcement index comprising five elements: audit spending, judicial efficiency, rule of law, insider trading laws and shareholder protection. He calculated the index for 21 countries. The highest value was for the US, followed by the UK, Canada, Norway, Sweden and Japan. The lowest value was obtained by Italy, followed by Spain, South Africa, Portugal and Germany. In this chapter we compare and contrast monitoring and enforcement in five countries: the US; three member states of the European Union, the UK, France and Germany; and Australia. These countries have been chosen because they have a considerable number of listed companies and a high market capitalization (see Table 1.5).

The emphasis in the chapter, as it is in these countries, is on publicly traded (listed) companies. Enforcement for other companies still tends to be limited to the lodgement of annual reports rather than the checking of their contents. In the countries discussed in this chapter, listed companies are required to follow in their consolidated financial statements (and in some cases their individual statements) either US GAAP, IFRS or standards equivalent to IFRS, all of which comprise reasonably clear standards accompanied by implementation guidance.

Section 9.2 looks at modes and models of enforcement. How enforcement operates in the five countries we have chosen is considered in Sections 9.3 to 9.5.

9.2 Modes and models of enforcement

In this section we distinguish rule-making from rule-enforcing (which includes rule-monitoring); look at the different sorts of enforcement and oversight bodies; analyze the role of auditors in the enforcement process; discuss the procedural choices of enforcement and oversight bodies; and consider the administrative and other actions available to such bodies.

Rule-making is conceptually different from rule-enforcing. The two functions may be separated institutionally or may be combined (Brown and Tarca, 2005a). At one extreme, some accounting bodies confine themselves to making rules, leaving other bodies to enforce them. An obvious example is the International Accounting Standards Board (IASB) which, as a private-sector body not backed by any national government, has no option but to leave enforcement to others. Another example is the UK Accounting Standards Board (ASB) which sets standards for non-IFRS financial reporting and whose powers depend on national legislation which does not give it an enforcement role. At the other extreme, some bodies act only as enforcers. Examples are the *Autorité des Marchés Financiers* (AMF) in France and the Financial Reporting Review Panel in the UK. There are also bodies, however, which act both as rule-makers and rule-enforcers. The best known example is the US Securities and Exchange Commission (SEC), although, as discussed in Chapter 8, most of its rule-making role is performed by the Financial Accounting Standards Board (FASB).

Enforcement of financial reporting rules can be carried out by several different sorts of bodies. These include:

- stock exchanges;
- regulators of stock exchanges;
- government departments and agencies;
- private-sector bodies.

In the US and Australia, enforcement is carried out by a stock exchange regulator. According to FEE (2001), in Europe in 2001 enforcement was carried out by stock exchanges in Norway, Sweden and Switzerland; by stock exchange regulators in Belgium, France, Italy, Portugal and Spain; by a private sector review panel in the UK; and by government departments in Denmark and the Czech Republic. There were no enforcement bodies in other European countries at that date, but since then, with the encouragement of the Committee of European Securities Regulators (CESR) and with the revision of the Eighth Directive, they have been established in Germany (see Section 9.4.4 below), the Netherlands and other member states.

There is no reason to suppose that there is an ideal model of an enforcement body to fit all countries. What kind of body is chosen, and what powers it is given, will depend in part on the overall regulatory system of the country concerned, which in turn may be regarded as a reflection of that country's culture or, more narrowly, of its political, legal and financial environment, all of which may change over time. Two of the most highly regarded bodies are the Securities and Exchange Commission (SEC) in the US and the Financial Reporting Review Panel (FRRP) in the UK. They have served as models to be followed in adapted form in other countries. The SEC model has been followed in France and Australia. A review panel has been set up in Germany. One should beware, however, of assuming that similarity of name implies similarity of function. Brown and Tarca (2007), after a comparison of the performance of the UK and Australian bodies, are unable to conclude that one model is more effective than the other.

For many countries, until recently the only monitoring mechanism was an annual audit, and auditors were not subject to much in the way of statutory control (Baker *et al.*, 2001). Although audit is a necessary component of the monitoring and enforcement process, it is unlikely to be sufficient. In large companies there is a divorce between directors and investors such that it is in the interests of both directors as agents and investors as principals that the fairness of the financial statements be assured by an independent third party. But can auditors be relied upon to be independent? Recent accounting scandals have persuaded legislators in many countries that sometimes they cannot be and that the proper conduct of an audit needs supervision. Auditors (often appointed *de facto*, if not *de jure*, by directors to whom they may provide taxation advice and management services) are perceived to have difficulty in maintaining their independence. Auditors can benefit from the backing of an enforcement body since otherwise their main means of encouraging compliance with standards is to threaten to qualify their audit opinions.

Until recently, many professional auditing bodies were self-regulating, at least in Anglo-Saxon countries, although this is now being replaced by the setting up of oversight bodies. An oversight (or supervisory) body in this context is a body independent of the audit profession which regulates the work of the auditor. The oversight body may be separate from the financial reporting enforcement body or combined with it. Examples of separate bodies are the Public Company Accounting Oversight Board (PCAOB) in the US and the Professional Oversight Board (POB) in the UK. In France and Australia the functions of the enforcement bodies (the AMF; and the Australian Securities and Investments Commission, ASIC) have been extended to include oversight.

The evidence summarized in later sections of this chapter suggests that auditors and enforcement bodies benefit from each other's activities. Enforcement bodies cannot check accounting records in detail and perforce rely on the work of external auditors in this respect. The existence of enforcement bodies strengthens the ability of the auditor to insist on compliance with financial reporting standards. In the US, auditors are appointed by directors, but both are aware that compliance with GAAP will be strictly enforced by the SEC. In the UK, directors and auditors are loath to appear before the FRRP. In Germany, by contrast, the lack of an enforcement body until recently meant that auditors accepted degrees of non-compliance from companies claiming to apply international standards.

Enforcement bodies need both to monitor compliance and to take appropriate actions in case of non-compliance. How the monitoring is done and how effective the actions will be depends on the powers granted by legislation and on available resources, both financial and human. No body has the resources to monitor every year all the financial statements of all companies subject to accounting regulation. Even the best-resourced body, the SEC in the USA, monitors only publicly traded corporations (of which there are about 14,000, or 0.3 per cent of all US corporations) and does so on a selective basis. Less well-resourced bodies have to decide whether to monitor proactively as well as reacting to complaints against companies and, if so, whether to do so using a risk-based strategy such as rotation or on a sample basis, or some combination thereof. They also need to decide whether to issue guidance statements and/or to provide advance clearance for particular accounting practices (sometimes referred to as pre-clearance); what action to take in the event of non-compliance (e.g. levying fines, taking a company to court, de-listing); and what use to make of publicity in the financial press and elsewhere.

Summing up, those responsible for setting up and operating enforcement bodies are faced with a number of choices:

- which companies to monitor;
- which company documents to monitor and when;
- whether to monitor proactively as well as reactively;
- to what extent to rely upon the opinions of company auditors;
- whether to issue guidance statements;
- whether to provide advance clearance;
- whether to take administrative or legal action in the event of non-compliance;
- what use to make of publicity.

Different enforcement bodies have come to different conclusions and some have changed their choices over time. Table 9.1 summarizes the position as of late 2007

Table 9.1 Comparison of five enforcement bodies as of late 2007

	US	UK	France	Germany	Australia
	SEC	FRRP	AMF	BaFin/FREP	ASIC
Type	Stock-exchange regulator	Private-sector regulator	Stock-exchange regulator	Govt body/private-sector regulator	Stock-exchange regulator
Date established	1934	1991	1967	2004	1998
Procedures					
Reactive investigation	Yes	Yes	Yes	Yes	Yes
Proactive surveillance	Yes	Yes	Yes	Yes	Yes
Advance clearance	Yes	No	Yes	No	No
Powers					
Publicity	Yes	Yes	Yes	Yes	Yes
Fines	Yes	No	Yes	Yes	No
Court referral	Yes	Yes	Yes	Yes	Yes
De-listing	Yes	No	No	No	No

Source: Adapted from Brown, P. and Tarca, A. (2005a) 'A commentary on issues relating to the enforcement of international financial reporting standards in the EU', *The European Accounting Review*, Vol. 14, No. 1.

for the SEC in the US, the FRRP in the UK, the AMF in France, the BaFin and FREP in Germany (see Section 9.3.4 for full names), and the ASIC in Australia. More details and explanations are given in the country sections that follow. We also explain why within the EU there is not one but several national enforcement bodies.

It is not easy to measure the success of an enforcement body. For example, the SEC undoubtedly works hard to ensure that most publicly traded corporations follow the letter of US GAAP, but it was unable to prevent the sophisticated creative accounting of Enron (Benston and Hartgraves, 2002) or even the simple (but equally devastating) accounting misstatements perpetrated at WorldCom.

More generally, it is difficult to quantify the costs and benefits of regulation and regulatory bodies and to determine their incidence (see, e.g., Gwilliam *et al.*, 2005). The direct costs borne by taxpayers are higher for a body such as the SEC than for private-sector bodies such as the FRRP. There are social as well as private costs and benefits, so the setting up of enforcement and oversight bodies concerns stakeholders of all kinds, not just shareholders, directors and auditors. For example, corporate collapses connected with accounting scandals have deprived many people, not all of them employees of the collapsed companies, of their jobs and pensions. Externalities such as these have been an additional factor in leading governments to concern themselves with compliance with financial reporting standards.

9.3 United States

Financial reporting in the US is discussed at length in Chapter 8. This section concentrates on those aspects that concern the monitoring and enforcement of financial reporting standards.

American accountants are more apt than European (including UK) accountants to assume that once a standard is passed it will be complied with. This is a perhaps unconscious tribute to the power of the Securities and Exchange Commission, an independent federal regulatory agency established in 1934 by Congressional legislation, which since inception 'has applied a heavy hand to enforcement'. US standard setters are unlikely 'to recall a time when financial reporting was not tightly prescribed, and the prescriptions not strictly enforced' (Zeff, 1995, pages 61, 64). Registration statements (prospectuses) of corporations coming to the market for the first time are reviewed in detail. Registration statements and periodic reports of other companies are reviewed selectively. Currently each company is reviewed on a three-year cycle. Discussions between the SEC and registrants are entirely confidential. The SEC does not need to use publicity in the financial press to the same extent as, say, the FRRP in the UK as a means of 'naming and shaming'. The SEC's ability to levy fines and de-register companies means that most disputes are settled without any formal action.

Strict enforcement of compliance by the SEC means that lobbying of the standard-setter (currently the FASB) is more intense in the US than in countries where monitoring and enforcement is more relaxed (see Chapter 10). The SEC has been criticized for hampering accounting innovation (which can be positive as well as negative) (Solomons, 1986, pages 194–8).

Non-US companies with a listing on a US stock exchange are required to file financial statements complying with US GAAP or that have a reconciliation to US GAAP. Most companies choose to provide a reconciliation. The requirement means that many of the world's multinationals (or at least their auditors) need to be familiar with the complexities of US GAAP. Such a reconciliation is not required by other stock exchange regulators around the world. In 2007, the SEC, perhaps conscious of the greater success of the London rather than the New York Stock Exchange in attracting listings by foreign companies (Holgate, 2007), announced that it was eliminating reconciliations for IFRS reporters and giving not only foreign investors but also US corporations a choice between US GAAP and IFRS. The SEC will no doubt seek to enforce compliance with IFRS as rigorously as it does with US GAAP.

The reputation of auditors in the US was severely dented by the Enron and other scandals. The Sarbanes-Oxley Act prohibits the provision of some non-audit services to audit clients, requires the rotation of audit lead and review partners every five years, and requires auditors to report to an audit committee not to management. As explained in Chapters 8 and 21, auditors are now supervised by the Public Company Accounting Oversight Board. The PCAOB registers auditors and has the right to conduct inspections and investigations, take disciplinary action and impose sanctions.

9.4　European Union

9.4.1　Introduction

Enforcement of financial reporting standards within the EU has been very different from that in the US. In recent years, however, it has been influenced by the Sarbanes-Oxley Act (Haller *et al.*, 2006). Little systematic research was done into compliance rates by EU companies with domestic GAAP prior to 2005 but, with the possible exception of the UK and France, it was not high. Even in France, those companies applying US GAAP or IAS tended to comply on a pick-and-choose basis (Ding *et al.*, 2003). Gebhardt and Heilmann (2004) find that not only did many German companies fail to comply fully with the accounting standard on cash flow statements (whether the German standard GAS 2, IAS 7 or SFAS 95), but not one audit opinion contained a qualification in respect of the non-compliance. However, Glaum and Street (2003) show that German companies that were listed on both that country's New Market and on a US exchange showed in their 2000 statements higher rates of compliance in their domestic reporting not only with US GAAP but also with IAS. Street *et al.* (1999), Street and Bryant (2000) and Street and Gray (2001) report a lack of compliance in a wide range of countries both within and outside the EU. Compliance by companies domiciled in EU countries such as France and Germany was worse than that by companies domiciled in countries outside the EU (notably Switzerland and China). Compliance with IAS was particularly weak in respect of disclosures relating to pensions, leasing, financial instruments and earnings per share.

It is as yet unclear to what extent compliance will improve in the near future. Weak legislation, lack of resources and an ineffective audit profession in some EU countries may make compliance with IFRS in practice voluntary. However, as shown in Table 21.2, the majority of listed companies in major EU countries are audited by the Big-4 international firms. The technical resources of the 'international desks' (centres of IFRS expertise) of these firms may play an important part in improving compliance. Companies are also likely to be under pressure to comply from the international capital market. Schipper (2005), an American academic who has been a member of the FASB, predicts increasing demand for a pan-European enforcement body, but acknowledges the considerable difficulties, political and otherwise, of setting one up. The replacement of national enforcers by a pan-European enforcer is highly unlikely in the short term. However, under the aegis of the Committee of European Securities Regulators (CESR), the national enforcers meet periodically in European Enforcers Co-ordination Sessions (EECS) to exchange views and discuss experiences. The CESR publishes extracts from its database of their enforcement decisions, but without revealing which national enforcer took which decision. Information is also shared among EU and non-EU enforcers under the aegis of IOSCO. Variation in enforcement opens up the danger of 'regulatory arbitrage' (i.e. companies choosing to list on exchanges in countries perceived to have the weakest enforcement regime) (Brown and Tarca, 2005b).

Oversight of auditors was one of the concerns when the Eighth Directive was being drafted, but in its watered-down form of 1984 it confirmed rather than changed existing practices in member states. Recent changes have been driven by accounting scandals rather than by the EU Commission. A revised Eighth Directive was approved in 2006 (see also Chapter 21). The Directive requires all member states to set up a national auditors' oversight body but does not envisage an EU-wide body. A European Group of Auditors' Oversight Bodies (EGAOB) was established in 2005 to encourage cross-border cooperation between the national regulators.

The position in the UK, France and Germany, the EU's three largest economies, is discussed in the next three sections.

9.4.2 United Kingdom

The UK system of setting, monitoring and enforcing accounting standards has changed several times in the last few decades. Before 1990 standard-setting was in the hands of the accountancy profession and had no legal backing. The position of standards was strengthened as a result of the Dearing Report (1988) and the Companies Act 1989 (now replaced by the Companies Act 2006). The Act requires directors of plcs and other large companies to disclose in their annual reports any departures from accounting standards. As discussed in Chapter 14, the Accounting Standards Committee (ASC) was superseded in 1990 by an Accounting Standards Board (ASB). The ASB was not given a monitoring or enforcement role. Instead a separate Financial Reporting Review Panel (FRRP) was established to monitor the financial statements of public and large private companies. All other companies are dealt with by the Department for Business Enterprise and Regulatory Reform (DBERR). Both the ASB and the FRRP were established as subsidiaries of a Financial Reporting Council (FRC) set up to be independent of both the profession and the government. When the Financial Services Authority (FSA), a member of CESR, was established in 2000 by the Financial Services and Markets Act to regulate the financial services industry, it was given no part in enforcing compliance with accounting standards.

Between 1991 and 2003, the Financial Reporting Review Panel played an important role in examining the financial statements of public companies and large private companies for material departures from the Act and from accounting standards. It did not attempt to monitor all companies within its remit nor to be proactive, but restricted its investigations to companies brought to its attention. It achieved its aims by persuasion, although it had the power to apply to the court for a declaration that the financial statements of a company did not comply with the requirements of the Act (including giving a true and fair view) and for an order requiring the company's directors to prepare (and personally pay for) revised statements.

Hines *et al.* (2000) discussed the workings of the Panel during its first decade and assessed its effectiveness. They concluded that it was an effective regulator, concerned to establish its legitimacy, despite its limited powers. Peasnell *et al.* (2001) researched the characteristics of companies judged by the Panel to have published defective financial statements. They show that such companies were more likely to be suffering from performance difficulties in the defect year and less likely to have a Big Five auditor. Weaker evidence suggested that the companies were less likely to have an audit committee and to have a high proportion of outside directors. Fearnley *et al.* (2002) showed that the FRRP changed the costs and benefits to auditors of permitting non-compliance. Although the Panel has regulatory authority over directors not auditors, it has motivated auditors to improve accounting compliance and has enhanced their independence.

The role of the Panel was re-considered in the light of the Enron case and other accounting scandals. The FRRP was asked by the government to become more proactive and to explore ways of working with the Financial Services Authority (FSA). From 2005 onwards one of the main tasks of the Panel has been to ensure compliance by listed companies with IFRS. The FRRP was given a wider remit and greater powers by the Companies (Audit, Investigations and Community Enterprise) Act of 2004. In particular, its operations were extended to cover interim as well as annual financial statements, the operating and financial review (OFR), and the directors' report. Its remit also covers compliance with the accounting requirements of the FSA's listing rules for publicly traded companies.

The Panel selects statements for review both proactively and reactively. It discusses with the FSA and its own Standing Advisory Group which sectors of the economy are under strain or likely to give rise to difficult accounting issues. A number of financial statements are reviewed in the sectors thus selected. The Panel is developing a risk model to identify cases where accounting problems are more likely, for example, where corporate governance is poor. It looks at topical accounting issues, and responds to complaints from the public, from the press and from the City of London. All selections take account of the risk of non-compliance and the risk of significant consequences in the event of non-compliance.

The Panel does not operate a system of advance clearance. It usually makes an announcement at the conclusion of an enquiry if the directors of a company under review have agreed that their statements were defective and have been corrected or clarified, as specified by the Panel. No announcement is usually made when a report is found not to be defective, although the Panel may, without naming companies, issue 'generic' press notices about matters that have come to its attention. The Panel publishes an annual Activity Report.

The FRRP collaborates closely with the FSA. The UK fiscal authorities (HM Revenue and Customs) are authorized to disclose information regarding company accounts to the Panel.

Turning now to auditors, formal supervision of them in the UK began with the implementation of the EU Eighth Directive in the Companies Act 1989. The Act required that company auditors must be registered auditors, i.e. have their names inscribed as qualified for appointment on a statutory register maintained by recognized supervisory bodies. The main bodies so recognized (by DBERR) were the three Institutes of Chartered Accountants and the Association of Chartered Certified Accountants. This legislation meant that the professional bodies had to supervise their members in the public interest, whilst at the same time continuing to serve the private interests of those members.

This combination of roles can lead to a conflict of interest, and in 1998 a Regulation Review Implementation Working Party of the Consultative Committee of the Accountancy Bodies (CCAB) proposed the establishment of an independent Review Board. Five bodies were set up: an Accountancy Foundation, a Review Board, an Ethics Standards Board (ESB), a re-formed Auditing Practices Board (APB), and an Investigation and Discipline Board (IDB). The Foundation was given an over-arching responsibility; the Review Board's task was to monitor the operation of the system to confirm that it met the public interest; the ESB had the role of securing the development on a profession-wide basis of ethical standards for all accountants; and the IDB dealt with disciplinary cases of public concern. The APB was re-constituted to be independent of the accountancy profession, with a full-time executive director. Dewing and Russell (2002) pointed out that the Accountancy Foundation had direct responsibility for discipline (via the IDB), indirect responsibility for auditor independence (via the ESB) but no responsibility for monitoring audit quality.

The system thus set up was not seen to operate very successfully and was reformed in 2002. Under the reformed system six operating bodies are responsible to the FRC: the ASB, the APB, the FRRP, the Professional Oversight Board (POB) and an Accountancy and Actuarial Investigation and Discipline Board (AAIDB).

The POB is independent of the accountancy profession and accountancy firms. It is currently chaired by the Comptroller and Auditor General. Its responsibilities include overseeing the regulation of auditors by the recognized supervisory bodies, monitoring the quality of the audits of economically significant entities, and overseeing the regulation of the accountancy profession by the professional accountancy bodies. It has set up an Audit Inspection Unit, which in 2005 reported on audit quality at the Big-4 firms.

The APB is responsible for the issue of, *inter alia*, auditing standards (ISAs [UK and Ireland]), ethical standards, standards for investment reporting (SIRs), and statements of standards for reporting accountants. The AIDB is responsible for administering an independent disciplinary scheme covering members of the six UK professional accountancy bodies. The Companies Act 2006 introduced a requirement that audit reports be signed for and on behalf of the audit firm by the senior statutory auditor (the partner in charge of the audit). It also allowed for the first time companies and their auditors to enter into liability limitation agreements that limit the auditors' liability to what is fair and reasonable. Rotation of auditors is not required by the Act.

Compliance with standards by individual companies is left largely to auditors and so is much more weakly monitored than compliance with IFRS by groups. Furthermore, many private companies are no longer required to be audited (see Chapter 14).

9.4.3 France

The enforcement body in France is the *Autorité des Marchés Financiers* (AMF, Financial Markets Authority), established in 2003 by the merger of the *Commission des Opérations de Bourse* (COB, Stock Exchange Commission) and two other stock exchange regulatory bodies. The AMF is responsible for the enforcement of the application of IFRS by listed companies. It is not a standard-setting body.

The AMF can draw upon the procedures set in place by COB, which was established in 1967. These have been described by Dao (2005). Acting as a stock-exchange regulator, the COB reviewed prospectuses and the documents lodged annually (compulsorily or voluntarily) by listed companies. Verification of compliance was carried out in two divisions: the *Service des Affaires Comptables et Fiscales* (SACF, Accounting and Tax Division) and the *Service des Opérations et de l'Information*

Financière (SOIF, Corporate Finance Division). The SOIF carried out a general review of the legal, economic and financial aspects of the documents. Its role was to identify issues considered to be important and then to ask legal and accounting specialists to carry out further examination. The role of the SACF was to verify the compliance of the documents with applicable accounting standards and to supervise the quality of the audit. They did not attempt to re-do the work of the auditor.

The SACF followed a proactive risk-based approach in selecting which companies to investigate, but also on occasion followed up press comments and complaints. The COB used both advance clearance and post-lodgement reviews. The reviews were not completely standardized; professional judgement was also important. Advance clearance sometimes involved consulting the *Comité d'Urgence* (Urgent Issues Committee) of the *Conseil National de la Comptabilité* (National Accounting Council, CNC) on emerging accounting issues. The COB carried out studies to identify companies likely to be affected by emerging issues. It issued recommendations, without naming companies, to notify registrants of the need to comply with particular accounting treatments or disclosures. Such recommendations are not mandatory but they are usually followed.

The COB delegated to the national body of state-registered auditors, the *Compagnie Nationale des Commissaires aux Comptes* (CNCC), the task of assessing whether company auditors have properly checked compliance with accounting standards. An annual review of audit quality of listed companies was carried out by a committee of the CNCC, the *Comité de l'Examen National des Activités* (CENA) on behalf of COB. CENA carries out its reviews on a rotation basis. The reviews are seen not just as a means of audit quality but as a means of strengthening auditors' independence from management. Note that this task was not delegated to the professional accountancy body, the *Ordre des Experts Comptables* (OEC). The role of the CNC, the CNCC and the OEC in relation to making accounting rules is discussed in Chapter 14.

The AMF has power to refuse to approve a prospectus and to require companies to make changes to their financial statements if in its opinion they did not comply with applicable standards. It can take administrative action against a company, although this rarely proved necessary. It is easier to detect non-compliance with disclosure rules than with measurement rules, which are more difficult for an oversight body to detect than for an auditor. Like the SEC, and unlike the FRRP, it does not issue press releases on the outcome of its enquiries, or name companies whose statements have been found to be defective.

Supervision of company audit is achieved in a number of ways. All auditors are required to be members of the CNCC. The *Loi de Sécurité Financière* (Financial Security Law) of 2003, enacted partly as a result of a continuing review of French commercial law but also in response to Enron and other scandals (Stolowy, 2005), set up the *Haut Conseil de Commissariat aux Comptes* (H3C, Statutory Auditing High Council), which is external to the audit profession, and only three of whose 12 members are *commissaires aux comptes*. The function of the H3C is to supervise the profession, in particular its ethics and independence. The 2003 Law also requires a new report by the auditors on internal control systems and prohibits the provision of both auditing and consulting services to the same client.

Other differences from US and UK rules include:

- auditors are appointed for a six-year term, rather than annually;
- for companies presenting consolidated as well as individual financial statements, there must be at least two auditors, drawn from different firms;
- auditors must disclose to the public prosecutor any criminal acts by an audit client of which they become aware.

French regulations as to activities regarded as incompatible with the conduct of a statutory audit have been more restrictive than those in the UK and the US, although in practice the differences have not been great (Mikol and Standish, 1998).

9.4.4 Germany

As noted in Section 9.4.1, enforcement of accounting rules has been weak in Germany, both for AGs (public companies) and GmbHs (private companies). Before 1985, only very large GmbHs were required to publish their financial statements. Since the *Bilanzrichtliniengesetz*, Accounting Directives Law, 1985, many more GmbHs have been required to do so as a result of the implementation of the EU Fourth Directive (Eierle, 2005), but many failed to do so until the German government was forced into action by the EU Commission.

Between 1998 and 2005 listed AGs, and between 2000 and 2005 all entities that raised money on the equity market, were permitted to apply either US GAAP or IASs in their consolidated financial statements instead of German rules. As noted earlier, Glaum and Street (2003) tested compliance with IAS in the year 2000 financial statements of companies listed on the *Neuer Markt* (New Market). They reported considerable non-compliance, but that the highest compliance rates related to audit by the Big-5 audit firms and companies which were also listed on a US exchange and thus subject to SEC surveillance. These results were consistent with previous research by Street and Bryant (2000) and Street and Gray (2001) (see Section 9.4.1).

These weaknesses triggered a discussion in Germany of the relative merits of the US and UK models of enforcement: the SEC and the FRRP. In 2001, the *Institut der Wirtschaftsprüfer* (IdW) proposed an enforcement body modelled on the FRRP rather than one based on the SEC. An SEC-type body was seen by the IdW as contrary to the trend in Germany towards deregulation and more private-sector involvement (Evans *et al.*, 2002). However, a compromise between the US and UK precedents was enacted in 2004. The *Bilanzkontrollgesetz* (BilKoG, Financial Reporting Control Act) and the *Bilanzrechtsreformgesetz* (BilReG, Accounting Law Reform Act) established a new regulatory framework for financial reporting (Eierle and Haller, 2004). A two-tier enforcement regime was established, with two enforcement bodies, one private, the other public. The philosophy of the legislation is that unlawful practice will be prevented by the existence of the regulatory framework rather than by the taking of specific actions. The private body was set up in 2005 as the *Deutsche Prüfstelle für Rechnungslegung* (DPR) (Financial Reporting Enforcement Panel, FREP). It reports to the *Bundesanstalt für Finanzdienstleistungsaufsicht* (BaFin, Federal Institute for the Oversight of Financial Services). The BaFin is a stock exchange regulator with similar functions to the FSA in the UK. As a public body it acts as a supervisor of FREP's activities and has the power to re-examine a company's financial statements.

A company which refuses to change its accounting treatment can be fined €50,000, an amount not large enough to act as much of a deterrent. If an audit firm's behaviour has been called into question, the BaFin can refer it to the *Wirtschaftsprüferkammer*, the private-sector body responsible for the regulation of the audit profession. The WPK deals with minor violations of professional rules; severe violations are dealt with in the criminal courts. Since 2005, all decisions of the WPK are subject to the public oversight of the Auditor Oversight Commission (*Abschlussprueferaufsichtkommission*, APAK), a body in the public sector.

9.5 Australia

The monitoring and enforcement of compliance with accounting standards by listed companies is one of the functions of the Australian Securities and Investments Commission (ASIC) (Brown and Tarca, 2007). The ASIC was created in 1998 as the successor to the Australian Securities Commission (ASC) which had been set up by the Australian federal government in 1990 on the model of the SEC. The ASIC has a close working relationship with the Australian Stock Exchange (ASX).

In carrying out its monitoring and enforcement function the ASIC has always been a proactive body, drawing on a broad range of sources of information, including its own surveillance programme. Currently, each listed company is reviewed every four years. In addition, targeted surveillance is conducted on issues considered to pose a particular risk. For example, dot.com companies were targeted in 2001.

The actions of the ASIC have generated much press publicity. The most common remedial action required has been revision of accounts, published in a subsequent annual report. Like the FRRP in the UK, the ASIC has the power to take a company to court and, unlike its UK counterpart, has done so on a number of occasions, although it prefers other remedies where possible. The ASIC has itself been taken to court by companies that disagreed with its rulings. Companies involved in ASIC cases between 1998 and 2004 were less profitable and less likely to have a Big-4 auditor than companies in a matched control sample (da Silva Rosa *et al.*, 2005).

Further discussion of the activities of the ASIC and a comparison with the FRRP is provided by Brown and Tarca (2005b, 2007). In 2003 the ASIC proposed the setting up of an Australian Financial Reporting Panel as a consensual way of resolving disputes (Pound, 2003). The panel commenced work in 2006. The intention is to complement the activities of the ASIC not substitute for them; it does not conduct surveillance; and avoids legal actions.

The Corporate Law Economic Reform Program (Audit Reform and Corporate Disclosure) Act 2004 replaced the self-regulation of auditors by the professional bodies with a system of supervision of auditors by the Financial Reporting Council and the ASIC. The former is responsible for monitoring the independence of auditors, the latter for their registration. The Act also introduced a number of changes to promote auditor independence, including restrictions on auditors being employed by an audit client, prohibition of some non-audit services for an audit client, and five-year rotation of audit lead and review partners.

SUMMARY

- Enforcement of accounting standards requires, *inter alia*, statutory audit, monitoring by supervisory bodies, and effective sanctions.

- Making rules is conceptually distinct from enforcing them but the roles may sometimes be combined in practice.

- Enforcement may be carried out by stock exchanges, regulators of stock exchanges, government departments and agencies, or private-sector bodies.

- Modes of enforcement differ from country to country, partly as a function of the local environment.

- The supervision (oversight) of auditors may strengthen the hand of auditors against directors.

- The powers and operating procedures of enforcement bodies differ from country to country.

- The strictest and best-resourced enforcement regime is that of the Securities and Exchange Commission in the US. Auditors in the US are supervised by the Public Company Accounting Oversight Board.

- There are no EU-wide enforcement or oversight bodies; enforcement and supervision are weak in many member states. Cooperation among national regulators takes place through European Enforcers' Co-ordination Sessions and the European Group of Auditors' Oversight Bodies.

- In the UK, the Financial Reporting Review Panel, a private-sector body, has been an effective enforcer of accounting standards from 1991 onwards. Recently it has adopted more proactive operating procedures and forged close links with the stock exchange regulator, the Financial Services Authority.

- In France, the enforcement body is the stock exchange regulator, the *Autorité des Marchés Financiers*, which is proactive and uses advance clearance as one its operating procedures. It has delegated review of audit quality to the *Comité de l'Examen National des Activités* of the *Compagnie Nationale des Commissaires aux Comptes*. The latter body is responsible for the registration of auditors and is supervised by the *Haut Conseil des Commissaires aux Comptes*.

- In Germany, enforcement of accounting standards is shared between the stock-exchange regulator (BaFin) and a private-sector Financial Reporting Enforcement Panel. The *Wirtschaftsprüferkammer* is responsible for the registration of auditors. It is supervised by the *Abschlussprueferaufsichtkommission*.

- In Australia, accounting standards are enforced by the stock exchange regulator, the Australian Securities and Investments Commission (ASIC), which is proactive and has taken legal action against several companies. Auditors are supervised by the ASIC and the Financial Reporting Council.

References

Baker, C.R., Mikol, A. and Quick, R. (2001) 'Regulation of the statutory auditor in the European Union: a comparative survey of the United Kingdom, France and Germany', *European Accounting Review*, Vol. 10, No. 4.

Benston, G.J. and Hartgraves, A.L. (2002) 'Enron: what happened and what we can learn from it', *Journal of Accounting and Public Policy*, Vol. 21, No. 2.

Brown, P. and Tarca, A. (2005a) 'A commentary on issues relating to the enforcement of international financial reporting standards in the EU', *European Accounting Review*, Vol. 14, No. 1.

Brown, P. and Tarca, A. (2005b) '2005. It's here, ready or not: A review of the Australian financial reporting framework', *Australian Accounting Review*, Vol. 15, No. 2.

Brown, P. and Tarca, A. (2007) 'Achieving high quality, comparable financial reporting: A comparison of independent enforcement bodies in Australia and the United Kingdom', *Abacus*, Vol. 43, No. 4.

Commission of the European Communities (2000) 'EU financial reporting strategy: the way forward', COM (2000) 359 final.

Dao, T.H.P. (2005) 'Monitoring compliance with IFRS: some insights from the French regulatory system', *Accounting in Europe*, Vol. 2.

da Silva Rosa, R., Filippetto, J. and Tarca, A. (2005) 'ASIC actions: Canaries for poor corporate governance?', working paper, University of Western Australia. Available at www.ssrn.com.

Dearing, Sir R. (1988) (The Dearing Report) *The Making of Accounting Standards, Report of the Review Committee*, presented to the Consultative Committee of Accountancy Bodies, London.

Dewing, I.P. and Russell, P.O. (2002) 'The new Accountancy Foundation: A credible form of regulation for UK listed companies?' *International Journal of Auditing*, Vol. 6, No. 3.

Ding, Y., Stolowy, H. and Tenenhaus, M. (2003) '"Shopping around" for accounting practices: the financial statement presentation of French groups', *Abacus*, Vol. 39, No. 1.

Eierle, B. (2005) 'Differential reporting in Germany – a historical analysis', *Accounting, Business and Financial History*, Vol. 15, No. 3.

Eierle, B. and Haller, A. (2004) 'Financial reporting enforcement in Germany', *World Accounting Report*, March.

Evans, L., Eierle, B. and Haller, A. (2002) 'Financial reporting in Germany – the enforcer', *Accountancy*, January.

Fearnley, S., Hines, T., McBride, K. and Brandt, R. (2002) 'The impact of the Financial Reporting Review Panel on aspects of the independence of auditors and their attitudes to compliance in the UK', *British Accounting Review*, Vol. 34, No. 2.

Fédération des Experts Comptables Européens (FEE) (2001) 'Enforcement mechanisms in Europe: a preliminary investigation of oversight systems'. Available at www.fee.be/publications/

Fédération des Experts Comptables Européens (FEE) (2003) 'European enforcement coordination'. Available at www.fee.be/publications/

Gebhardt, G. and Heilmann, A. (2004) 'Compliance with German and International Accounting Standards in Germany: Evidence from cash flow statements', in C. Leuz, D. Pfaff and A. Hopwood *The Economics and Politics of Accounting: International Perspectives on Research Trends, Policy and Practice*, Oxford University Press, Oxford.

Glaum, M. and Street, D.L. (2003) 'Compliance with the disclosure requirements of Germany's new market: IAS versus US GAAP', *Journal of International Financial Management and Accounting*, Vol. 14, No. 1.

Gwilliam, D., Macve, R. and Meeks, G. (2005) 'The costs and benefits of increased accounting regulation: a case study of Lloyd's of London', *Accounting and Business Research*, Vol. 35, No. 2.

Haller, A., Ernsberger, J. and Kraus, C. (2006) 'Extraterritorial impacts of the Sarbanes-Oxley Act on external corporate governance – current evidence from a German perspective', *Corporate Ownership & Control*, Vol. 3, No. 3.

Hines, T., McBride, K., Fearnley, S. and Brandt, R. (2000) 'We're off to see the wizard: an evaluation of directors' and auditors' experiences with the Financial Reporting Review Panel', *Accounting, Auditing & Accountability Journal*, Vol. 14, No. 1.

Holgate, P. (2007) 'Whither US GAAP?', *Accountancy*, Vol. 140, No. 1367.

Hope, O.-K. (2003) 'Disclosure practices, enforcement of accounting standards, and analysts' forecast accuracy: An international study', *Journal of Accounting Research*, Vol. 41, No. 2.

Mikol, A. and Standish, P. (1998) 'Audit independence and nonaudit services: a comparative study in differing British and French perspectives', *European Accounting Review*, Vol. 7, No. 3.

Peasnell, K.V., Pope, P.F. and Young, S.E. (2001) 'The characteristics of firms subject to adverse rulings by the Financial Reporting Review Panel', *Accounting and Business Research*, Vol. 31, No. 4.

Pound, G. (2003) 'A case for consensus', *CA Charter*, June.

Schipper, K. (2005) 'The introduction of international accounting standards in Europe: Implications for international convergence', *European Accounting Review*, Vol. 14, No. 1.

Solomons, D. (1986) *Making Accounting Policy: The Quest for Credibility in Financial Reporting*, Oxford University Press, New York.

Stolowy, H. (2005) 'Nothing like the Enron affair could happen in France (!)', *European Accounting Review*, Vol. 14, No. 2.

Street, D.L. and Bryant, S.M. (2000) 'Disclosure level and compliance with IASs. A comparison of companies with and without US listings and filings', *International Journal of Accounting*, Vol. 35, No. 3.

Street, D.L., Gray, S.J. and Bryant, S.M. (1999) 'Acceptance and observance of international accounting standards: An empirical study of companies claiming to comply with IASs', *International Journal of Accounting*, Vol. 34, No. 1.

Street, D.L. and Gray, S.J. (2001) *Observance of International Accounting Standards: Factors Explaining Non-compliance*, Association of Chartered Certified Accountants, London.

Swinson, C. (1999) 'Regulating the profession. The DTI's proposals', *Accountancy*, January.

Zeff, S.A. (1995) 'A perspective on the US public/private-sector approach to the regulation of financial reporting', *Accounting Horizons*, Vol. 9, No. 1.

Useful websites

Abschlussprueferaufsichtskommission (APAK) (Germany)	www.apak-aaoc.de
Accountancy and Actuarial Investigation and Discipline Board (UK)	www.frc.org.uk/aaidb
Auditing Practices Board (APB) (UK)	www.frc.org.uk/apb
Australian Securities and Investments Commission	www.asic.gov.au
Authority for the Financial Markets (Netherlands)	www.autoriteit-fm.nl
Autorité des Marchés Financiers (France)	www.amf-france.org
Bundesanstalt für Finanzdienstleistungsaufsicht (Germany)	www.Bafin.de
Committee of European Securities Regulators	www.cesr.eu
Compagnie Nationale des Commissaires aux Comptes (France)	www.cncc.fr
Department for Business, Enterprise and Regulatory Reform (UK)	www.berr.gov.uk
Deutsche Prüfstelle für Rechnungslegung (Financial Reporting Enforcement Panel) (Germany)	www.frep.info
European Group of Auditors' Oversight Bodies	http://ec.europa.eu/ internal_market/ auditing/egaob
Fédération des Experts Comptables Européens	www.fee.be
Financial Reporting Review Panel (UK)	www.frc.org.uk/frrp
Financial Services Authority (UK)	www.fsa.gov.uk
Haut Conseil du Commissariat aux Comptes (France)	www.h3c.org
Professional Oversight Board (UK)	www.frc.org.uk/pob
Public Company Accounting Oversight Board (US)	www.pcobus.org
Securities and Exchange Commission (US)	www.sec.gov

QUESTIONS

Suggested answers to the asterisked questions are given at the end of the book.

9.1∗ To what extent is the making of rules on financial reporting in the US separated from their enforcement? What is the historical background to the present situation?

9.2∗ What are the arguments for and against proactive surveillance by enforcement bodies?

9.3 Why is there no pan-European accounting standards enforcement body in the European Union? Ought one to be established?

9.4 Why do the US and France have stock exchange regulators as accounting standards enforcement bodies, whereas the UK does not?

9.5 Discuss the view that the costs of establishing and maintaining accounting standards enforcement bodies are likely in most countries to exceed the benefits.

9.6 'Enforcement bodies merely duplicate the work of auditors.' Discuss.

9.7 Why have several countries recently introduced auditor oversight bodies? Is this a positive or a negative development?

10

Political lobbying on Accounting Standards – US, UK and international experience

Stephen A. Zeff

OBJECTIVES

After reading this chapter, you should be able to:

- define political lobbying;
- explain the motivations of companies and governments when they lobby standard-setters;
- give examples from several countries of political lobbying in the context of particular standards;
- give examples of lobbying concerning the structure of a standard-setting body;
- explain why some standard-setters are more subject to lobbying than others.

10.1 Introduction

Standard-setters, such as the International Accounting Standards Board (IASB), the US Financial Accounting Standards Board (FASB) and the UK Accounting Standards Board (ASB), have committed themselves to act in the interests of investors (not of companies or auditors), to use conceptual frameworks (see, for example, Section 8.4) and, recently, to converge their standards. But there is a challenge: political lobbying is driven by preparer or governmental self-interest. This may cause the standard-setters to modify their positions and run the risk of diluting or abandoning the principles implicit in their standards.

The term 'economic consequences' has been used to describe the 'impact of accounting reports on the decision-making behavior of business, government, unions, investors and creditors' (Zeff, 1978). Those who have a vested interest in how this decision-making behaviour is conducted will place pressure on the standard-setter not to approve the standard containing an objectionable feature. This is lobbying, and it includes writing letters or giving oral testimony at a hearing arranged by a standard-setter to expose its tentative views to public comment. 'Political lobbying' goes beyond that, and the term is used here to describe concerted campaigns of action against a proposal, where the lobbyists make overt or covert threats to seek intervention to overturn a proposed standard or to compromise the standard-setter's reputation, independence, powers or even its existence.

Pressure induced by political lobbying might constitute threats to withdraw funding or other vital support for the standard-setter, or appeals to public opinion by carrying the dialogue into the public media. In recent decades, the pressure brought by preparers has escalated to a more intimidating level: engaging the active support of the executive and legislative branches of government. We have seen this development most particularly in the United States, but also in Europe over IAS 39 on financial instruments.

Political lobbying on proposed accounting standards has been a long-standing phenomenon in the United States (e.g. Sutton, 1984). However, other standard-setters have faced such lobbying, and recently the IASB faced lobbying on the subjects of accounting for share-based payment and financial instruments, and it seems likely to intrude as well on the future standards dealing with accounting for pensions, insurance, leases and performance reporting. The IASB Chairman, referring to the likely reaction by preparers to the board's initiatives on these topics, has been quoted as warning that there could be 'blood all over the streets' (Tricks and Hargreaves, 2004).

In what circumstances does political lobbying emerge as an issue for standard-setters? The answer to this is principally in situations where the standard-setter proposes to issue a standard on a topic not previously covered, or to eliminate or sharply reduce optional accounting treatments in an existing standard, and where a regulatory body will intervene to secure strict compliance with the standard. The likelihood of political lobbying would increase in some countries if the proposed standard were either to lower companies' earnings or make their trend of earnings more volatile. In other countries where profits[1] are linked with tax on income, such as in Germany, companies lobbied against any measures in the German implementation of the EEC's Fourth Directive that would *increase* their earnings (Ordelheide, 1993, page 87; von Wysocki, 1984, page 58).

The task for the standard-setter is to determine when, and to what extent, political lobbying raises valid issues which, in the light of its conceptual framework, require attention in the fashioning of a standard, and when it does not. Not all of the examples presented later in this chapter are of the latter kind.

After this introduction, the chapter looks (in Section 10.2) at the motivations for political lobbying. Section 10.3 then examines examples of lobbying of standard-setters up to 1990. That year is chosen as a boundary because of the increasing incidence of standard-setters' advocacy of fair value accounting, a controversial issue, in the United States and the United Kingdom and at the IASC, during the 1990s. Also, in the United Kingdom, the Accounting Standards Board replaced the Accounting Standards Committee (ASC) in that year. The examples depend on the availability of evidence. They are drawn from the United States and the United Kingdom because these countries had (and have) the largest number of listed companies, well-established private-sector standard-setters, and the best documented examples. A few documented instances of political lobbying can be found elsewhere. For example, Germany is mentioned above. Also, Zeff and Johansson (1984) report on parliamentary meddling in standard-setting in Sweden in 1977. Crandall (1983) and Scott (2003, page 270) report on the failure of lobbying in Canada in 1982 concerning the accounting treatment of grants in the oil industry.

Section 10.4 looks at national political lobbying from 1990 onwards. All the examples are from the United States. There are few well-documented cases of political lobbying of national standard-setters outside the United States from 1990 onwards. This might be partly because the United Kingdom's ASB was more independent than its predecessor (Swinson, 2004). In contrast, the international standard-setter was becoming more important during the 1990s and beyond (see Chapter 4), and therefore more prone to lobbying. Section 10.5 looks at political lobbying of the IASC/IASB.

Lobbying can also concern attempts to change the structure or mode of operation of the standard-setter. Section 10.6 examines examples of this relating to the FASB and the IASB.

The new millennium is also a new era of standard-setting in the sense that there are now two major superpowers: the IASB has joined the FASB. Section 10.7 considers political lobbying of the FASB's attempts to converge with the IASB's standards. Section 10.8 offers some concluding remarks.

10.2 Motivations for political lobbying

Why do preparers and governments engage in the political lobbying of accounting standard-setters? For listed companies operating in major capital markets, there are

---

[1] In particular, this refers to profits as prepared under national rules in the financial statements of individual entities.

several motivations, mostly related to the revenue and earnings pressures on top management. Company managers are 'held to account' by securities analysts whose publicly announced earnings forecasts raise the bar for the performance measures in companies' quarterly, semi-annual and annual reports to shareholders. If a company were to announce an earnings per share of just a few cents below the forecasted figure, its share price might be badly affected. For example, eBay, the online auction house, announced earnings for the fourth quarter of 2004 that were up by 44 per cent over its earnings for the fourth quarter of 2003. Yet, when its fourth quarter 2004 earnings fell short of Wall Street's expectations by a penny a share, the company's share price dropped by nearly 12 per cent on the announcement date.[2] In order to avoid suffering such impacts on their company's share price, top company executives wish to retain as much flexibility as possible over the 'management' of their earnings. Such flexibility also applies to managing their reported revenues, which are a key market indicator. When standard-setters propose to limit this flexibility, company managements – the preparer sector – resist with the considerable power at their disposal.[3]

The same perceived need to manage earnings arises when a company seeks to engineer a hostile takeover or is itself the object of an unfriendly takeover, each party wishing to persuade the object's shareholders that its earnings record is the superior one. The merger movement was particularly strong in the 1960s and again from the 1980s to the present.

In an active market for chief executive officers, it is a natural desire for them to flaunt their credentials as successful managers; and a record of lifting the revenues and earnings of a major company, or of maintaining a record of smoothed and growing earnings, helps their reputations. Again, top executives are motivated to build their company's revenue and earnings, and any initiative by a standard-setter that would diminish top executives' flexibility to manage these figures would be opposed.

Another motivation relates to how managers are compensated. Increasingly since the 1980s, top executives have been showered with bonuses based on earnings and with stock options whose value, it is widely supposed, is enhanced by a solid record of earnings. When executives sense that standard-setters might alter accounting in such a way as to endanger the munificence of their compensation package, they fight the change fiercely.

Very large companies that are regulated or subject to pressure from politicians (e.g. anti-trust actions) might well seek to ward off intervention in their affairs by lobbying for a standard that lowers their earnings, in order not to attract undue attention from government.[4]

When company executives register objections to standard-setting initiatives, especially when complaining to the legislative or executive branches of government for relief, they do not, of course, cite self-serving reasons to support their cause. And

---

[2] 'EBay Misses Forecast a Bit, and Shares Fall', *The New York Times*, 20 January, 2005, p. C1.
[3] A substantial empirical research literature supports the view that companies manage earnings. See, for example, Burgstahler and Dichev (1997) and Nelson *et al.* (2003). Also see the major speech by SEC Chairman Arthur Levitt, 'The "Numbers Game"' (28 September 1998), http://www.sec.gov/news/speech/speecharchive/1998/spch220.txt, as well as Bruns and Merchant (1990), Dechow and Skinner (2000) and Duncan (2001).
[4] For evidence in support of this thesis, see Watts and Zimmerman (1978).

when dealing with legislators, they do not argue in terms of accounting issues. Legislators and their staff typically know nothing, and could not care less, about accounting standards. Instead, the preparers elevate the discourse to the level of public policy, claiming, for example, that the proposed initiative would stifle entrepreneurial activity or could make it harder for established companies to expand and thrive by obtaining sufficient capital based on a promising record of revenues and earnings. When the banking community feels under threat by a standard-setter, it argues that a proposed accounting standard would project an image of instability in the banking system and might restrict the availability of credit. The standard might even force regulators to close some banks, because the balance of capital in their financial statements is below the solvency line. When their arguments are expressed in terms of public policy, preparers can more easily obtain a sympathetic hearing from legislators and others in government.

Governments have also engaged in political lobbying on proposed accounting standards. If it is believed that a proposed standard would lead to companies reporting lower or more volatile earnings, they might abandon plans for expansion by withholding investment in capital goods. A result of such a decision might be a rise in unemployment and perhaps even the closing of plants, which a government may wish to avoid at all costs, especially when the national economy is recovering from a recession.

One can easily discern from this discussion that accounting has become a pawn in a game of political chess. Using an analogy from sports, 'the way you play a game determines the way the game is played'. The scoring system influences behaviour. If, in football (called 'soccer' in the United States), it is decided that the outcome of matches with tied scores at the end of regulation play will be determined by the side having the larger number of corner kicks (as has been proposed), teams will modify their strategy to maximize the opportunities for corner kicks. In basketball, the scoring change that created the three-point line has motivated many players to shoot from the outside. Accounting scores the game of enterprise and, when the accounting rules change, those who run enterprise are motivated to change their managerial behaviour so as to restore or enhance a company's previous record of reported revenues and earnings. Those who want to change the way enterprise is conducted may find it much easier to alter the accounting rules rather than to try to persuade all company managers to change their behaviour.

10.3 Political lobbying up to 1990

10.3.1 The United States[5]

Examples of an appeal to 'economic consequences' or even attempts to bring political pressure on accounting standard-setters can be found at least as far back as

---

[5] Readers seeking a comprehensive review of the political origins and other explanations of US GAAP, from the 1930s to the 2000s, are invited to consult Zeff (2005). Online access to this article in *The CPA Journal* is free of charge.

the 1940s. This occurred in the United States before other countries for at least two reasons. First, the United States was among the very first countries to have an accounting standard-setter, and especially one that was trying to come to grips with diverse accounting practice. Second, the United States has a rigorous securities market regulator, the Securities and Exchange Commission (SEC). Since its establishment in 1934, the SEC has regularly taken strong measures to prevent listed companies from deviating from generally accepted accounting principles (GAAP).[6] As there is usually little to be gained by arguing with the SEC, which, except in rare instances, is obdurate in not tolerating such departures, companies disliking a proposed accounting standard know that they must do battle with the standard-setter instead. No other country's securities market regulator possesses either the authority or the staff to ensure such strict compliance with its national GAAP. Consequently, the US accounting standard-setter has been beset by insistent demands from the preparer sector not to change accounting standards in a way that damages their perceived interests. In some instances, the preparer community urges the standard-setter to modify an existing standard, because changing economic circumstances would enable companies, by use of the changed standard, to present their financial results in a more favourable light.

The effects of the post-war inflation (1947–9)

An interesting appeal to 'economic consequences' occurred in the late 1940s, during the serious bout of inflation of the post-war period. A number of major manufacturing companies, such as Chrysler, US Steel and Du Pont, wanted to record depreciation expense for accounting purposes at replacement cost rather than at historical cost, which was the only method allowed under GAAP. Basing depreciation expense on historical cost, which reflected the much lower pre-war prices of property, plant and equipment, was said to overstate the companies' earnings, often by a very large fraction. Depreciation expense was, for manufacturing companies, one of their largest items of expense. The companies' argument could be justified by accounting principles because of the mismatching of old dollar costs with new dollar revenues, yet the SEC and therefore the standard-setter were unflinching in their defence of historical cost accounting.

As companies saw it, an overstatement of earnings would encourage aggressive labour unions to press for higher wages and fringe benefits (such as pensions), and shareholders would demand larger dividends. Worse, the country's press would accuse the giant companies of profiteering against the best interests of the public in an already inflationary economy. Should the standard-setter try to alleviate the effects of these possible consequences? Another motivation of management was to seek Congressional approval to use replacement cost depreciation for federal income tax purposes, because the companies were convinced they were being taxed on capital. If the companies could persuade the accounting standard-setter to recognize replacement cost depreciation in their financial statements, they hoped to have success when urging an income tax reform along similar lines. In the event, neither the standard-setter nor Congress accepted the companies' argument.

---

[6] For a discussion of this role played by the SEC, see Zeff (1995).

There is no evidence that the companies put political pressure on the standard-setter, but this was one of the earliest concerted attempts to link accounting measurements with their possible economic consequences (Zeff, 1993).

The three stages of the investment tax credit (1962–71)

Perhaps the most celebrated early case of political lobbying in the setting of accounting standards occurred in three stages between 1962 and 1971. In 1962, the federal government introduced an 'investment tax credit' to stimulate the purchase of capital goods at a time of economic malaise. In its simplest form, the credit allowed a company purchasing, say, $1,000,000 of equipment or machinery to deduct 10 per cent of the purchase price as a credit against its current year's income tax liability. But how should the $100,000 be accounted for in the company's financial statements? Two competing schools of thought immediately emerged: the 'flow-through' method and the 'deferral' method. Advocates of the flow-through method argued that the $100,000 credit against taxes should be taken immediately to earnings, an approach favoured by companies that were looking for any way to boost their reported earnings. Proponents of the deferral method argued, however, that a company makes a profit by selling, not by buying. They contended that the $100,000 was, in reality, a government subsidy that should be subtracted from the purchase price for accounting purposes, and the netted purchase price of $900,000 should be treated as the effective cost of the asset, to be depreciated for financial reporting purposes over the useful life of the asset. The 20-member Accounting Principles Board (APB), the accounting standard-setter at the time, was riven by disagreement over which method should be accepted. The Big-8 accounting firms split 4–4 in the final vote, which, by an overall vote of 14 to 6, imposed a requirement to use the deferral method, under which companies must subtract the tax credit from the purchase price of the asset. The APB, by just achieving the required two-thirds majority, therefore rejected the inclusion of an option to take the tax credit immediately to earnings.

Companies made it known that they opposed the APB's decision and, behind the scenes, the Administration of President John F. Kennedy argued that the requirement to subtract the tax credit from the purchase price of the asset for accounting purposes would lead companies to report lower earnings and thus be less keen to purchase capital goods and thereby expand employment. Hence, for reasons of macro-economic policy, the Administration urged the SEC to allow both treatments. A significant number of company managements and several of the dissenting Big-8 accounting firms also entreated the SEC not to sustain the APB's opinion. In the end, probably because of the pressure brought by the Administration, the SEC announced in January 1963 that it would allow companies to use either the flow-through or deferral method. This rebuff came as a shock to the APB, which the SEC had been pressuring to 'narrow the areas of difference' in accounting practice. In the case of the tax credit, the APB had earnestly and with great difficulty settled on only one permissible method, yet the SEC overruled it and allowed both methods.

It was not publicly known at the time that political lobbying had prompted the SEC's surprising authorization to allow both treatments. The APB assumed that the SEC disagreed with it over which was the superior accounting treatment. In the end, the SEC embarrassed the APB by not backing it up, but it was not until 1967 (see below) that the APB actually learned why the SEC had overruled it. By 1964, fully three-quarters of major companies opted to take the tax credit immediately to earnings.[7]

The issue of the proper accounting treatment of the investment tax credit arose a second time, in 1967. In that year, the APB proposed once again, with apparent support from the SEC, to require that the investment tax credit be subtracted from the purchase price of the asset. But then the Assistant Secretary of the Treasury (Tax Policy) stated his view publicly that 'a mandate to defer the benefit arising from the investment credit could well blunt its effectiveness as an incentive to modernization and expansion'.[8] Once it became known that the Treasury stood against the APB's proposed standard, the SEC withdrew its support. The APB thus learned that it was the Treasury, not the SEC, which was pulling the strings, and for political and not technical accounting reasons.

The matter came up for a third time, in 1971, when the Administration of President Richard M. Nixon introduced a 'job development credit', which was the old 'investment tax credit' dressed up in new clothes, to emphasize its potential to increase employment. After the APB again issued an exposure draft proposing a requirement that the credit be subtracted from the purchase price of the asset, the Treasury took definitive action to counter its move. In the draft of its proposed legislation to enact the job development credit, the Treasury stipulated that taxpayer companies, in their financial statements filed with the SEC, would be entitled to use *any* method of accounting for the credit they preferred. Congress passed the legislation, which was promptly signed into law by the President.[9] The APB was therefore powerless, as was the SEC, being a creature of Congress. It was not until 1986 that Congress repealed the tax credit.

The three incidents involving the tax credit, especially the first and third ones, received extensive coverage in the financial press, and these news reports and editorials probably served to alert company executives to what could be achieved by lobbying the accounting standard-setter on political grounds.[10]

Business combinations (1968–70)

At the end of the 1960s, US industry and government both applied pressure on the APB from different directions, forcing it to issue a highly compromised standard on business combinations. Industry strongly opposed the elimination of 'pooling of interests' accounting, which was the APB's initial position, while government believed that its elimination might usefully slacken the pace of a merger movement that seemed to be getting out of hand. The Financial Executives Institute blanketed the nation's press with news releases criticizing the APB, and its Corporate Financial Reporting Committee urged FEI members:

---

[7] For fuller discussions, see Moonitz (1966), Keller and Zeff (1969, pp. 417–20), Horwitz and Kolodny (1982, pp. 95–7), and Seligman (2003, pp. 424–5).
[8] Stanley S. Surrey, letter to AICPA re exposure draft of APB Opinion on Accounting for Income Taxes, dated 7 November 1967, reproduced in Keller and Zeff (1969, p. 449).
[9] See Zeff (1972, pp. 178–80, 201–2, 219–21), and Zeff (1993).
[10] See, for example, 'A Matter of Principle Splits CPAs', *Business Week* (26 January 1963), pp. 50ff.

to contact your outside auditors and request a meeting with the senior partners to discuss your views on the proposed [APB] opinion, and also [the committee] strongly recommends that you seek to determine the position your audit firm is taking on this issue.[11]

This was a brazen attempt to apply pressure on the Big-8 audit firms, all of whom had a partner serving on the APB. As seen by the Big-8 firms, a decision to vote against the wishes of their major audit clients could place future engagements at risk. In the end, principle was thrown to the winds, as the APB was barely able to muster the required two-thirds majority to issue a flawed Opinion No. 16 which did not eliminate pooling (Chatov, 1975, Chs 13 and 14; Seligman, 2003, pages 419–30; and Zeff, 1972, pages 212–16).

Petroleum exploration costs, marketable securities, and leases (1971)

There were other such examples of political lobbying during the tenure of the APB (1959–73). In 1971 it scheduled three public hearings to consider accounting for petroleum exploration costs, marketable securities, and long-term, non-cancellable leases in the accounts of lessees. The petroleum industry used its might to prevent the APB from pursuing the treatment of exploration costs any further for the moment (see below) (Savoie, 1974, page 326). The mutual property and casualty insurance industry, which was opposed to the inclusion in earnings of the volatile unrealized holding gains and losses on their large portfolio of marketable securities, effectively prevented the APB from issuing even an exposure draft.[12] The leasing industry, which was making a handsome profit from bringing parties together that wanted to arrange long-term, non-cancellable leases of assets, such as aeroplanes or petrol (gasoline) stations, for which the lessee could avoid displaying the leased asset and liability on its balance sheet, fought off the APB's attempt to open formal consideration of the matter. Capitalization of the leased asset and liability would adversely affect a lessee's return on investment and its debt–equity ratio, thus making the lease arrangement less attractive. To fight the APB, the leasing industry organized a letter-writing campaign of key members of Congress so as to raise their ire towards the APB. In the letter, sent in identical format by more than 50 constituents on the same date from all parts of the country, it was stated that the APB was threatening to:

1 Raise the cost of electric power to the public by an estimated $550 million yearly towards the end of the decade.

2 Raise the cost of freight transportation to industry and the public.

3 Reduce the inventory of railroad cars and locomotives.

4 Increase the costs of air fares to the public.

5 Damage the aerospace industry.

6 Raise the costs of all goods and services to the public.

---

[11] Letter stamped 'ACTION' from J.J. Hangen, Chairman of the FEI Corporate Reporting Committee, to FEI members, dated 15 October 1969.
[12] For further discussion, see Horngren (1973). The mutual property and casualty insurance industry objected to the inclusion of unrealized holding gains and losses in earnings because of the volatility it would create. Also, see Savoie (1974, p. 326).

7 Prevent many small and growing businesses from acquiring modern cost-cutting machinery and equipment.

8 Negatively affect the present adverse international balance of trade.[13]

There was something in the letter to cause every member of Congress to hate the APB. The APB was only holding a public hearing, and no exposure draft had even been drafted, let alone issued. But the letters of concern and even outrage from members of Congress, as well as from the Secretary of Transportation, forced the APB to close down its consideration of the issue of capitalizing leases in lessees' balance sheets altogether. Politics had won again.

Segment reporting (1966–7)

When segment reporting became an issue towards the end of the 1960s, politics also intervened. During the decade, numerous mergers created conglomerate, or diversified, enterprises as well as multinational enterprises. As a result of the mergers, their operations spanned multiple product groupings and geographical regions. They opposed having to disclose the revenues and earnings associated with each of these major segments of their worldwide operations. One of their aims was to avoid 'tipping off' competitors that some of their product lines or geographical operations were especially profitable. The APB's attempt to issue a mandatory standard on segment reporting was frustrated by this political opposition. In the end, the APB could do no more than issue a non-binding Statement.[14]

Restructuring of troubled debt (1973–7)

From its foundation in 1973 onwards, the FASB also was besieged by political lobbying. During 1973–4, when the City of New York was found to be insolvent and defaulted on its long-term debt to banks across the country, the leaders of the banking community managed to restructure the City's debt by extending its maturities and reducing the interest rates. The question then arose in the minds of the FASB of how the banks should reflect this economic loss in their financial statements. The FASB held a public hearing in which it contemplated, as one solution, showing the loans receivable at market value, which meant that the banks would need to record significant losses in their own published financial statements. At the outset of the public hearing, Walter B. Wriston, the Chairman of Citicorp and the nation's leading banker, rose to make a statement that jarred the members of the FASB:

> If the banks that held the New York City obligations had been required to record an immediate write-off of say, 25 per cent of principal as a result of restructuring, that restructuring just might not have happened. Several of the banks whose cooperation was essential might not have been able to afford it, not from an economic point of view, but in terms of the way that readers of financial statements would interpret such charged earnings. Some New York banks were at that time under severe earnings pressure and the prospect of a significant additional charge with a corresponding reduction in capital would have been totally unacceptable.
>
> (Zeff, 1985, footnote 4, page 25)

---

[13] See Zeff (1985), footnote 3 on p. 24, and Savoie (1974, p. 326).

[14] See Zeff (1972, pp. 202–4). For a discussion of the SEC's involvement in this controversy, see Seligman (2003, pp. 430–8).

Should the FASB have insisted on an immediate write-down of the receivable in the banks' balance sheets and run the risk that any future such restructurings of the debt of defaulting cities or companies might thereby be jeopardized? In the end, the FASB 'pulled its punch' and did not require an immediate write-down of the receivable. The 'economic consequences' were, to the board, evidently overpowering. The board's Statement 15, finally issued in 1977 with two dissenting votes, is regarded by many as the worst it has ever issued. And the reason was politics (Zeff, 1993).

Petroleum exploration costs (1975–81)

A major political issue in the latter 1970s was accounting for petroleum exploration costs, a subject that the industry had succeeded in squashing in 1971, as noted earlier. The issue arose in the wake of the Arab Oil Embargo of 1973 and the US Government's need to develop a database for making national energy decisions. The Energy Policy and Conservation Act of 1975 instructed the SEC to establish uniform accounting standards for oil and gas exploration. Until then, most of the major producers were expensing the cost of dry holes (known as 'successful efforts costing'), while most of the small and medium-sized entities were capitalizing costs of all of the holes drilled (known as 'full costing'). The assignment given to the SEC was to establish a single method that all companies must use. As authorized in the 1975 Act, the SEC turned to the FASB for the development of a standard on which it might rely, and the board began its work in earnest. The FASB's exposure draft, issued during 1977, proposed successful efforts costing as the sole method to be used. This position so infuriated the small and medium-sized entities that they lobbied Congress to pass legislation that would preclude either the FASB or the SEC from eliminating full cost accounting as an acceptable method. A bill was drafted but, following negotiations with the SEC, it failed to gain passage (Gorton, 1991, page 32). This episode placed both the FASB and the SEC on notice about the lengths to which the powerful oil and gas industry would go to preserve its financial reporting options. Nonetheless, the FASB issued Statement of Financial Accounting Standards (SFAS) 19, by a vote of 4 to 3, which eliminated full costing as an acceptable method.

Then the SEC held public hearings in Washington and Houston, taking thousands of pages of testimony. Companies opposing SFAS 19 embarked on a frantic campaign to prevent the SEC from enforcing the standard, and they enlisted the support of members of Congress from oil-producing states to write letters to the SEC. Small and medium-sized entities feared the prospect of large year-to-year fluctuations in their earnings under successful efforts costing with the result that banks and other capital suppliers might cut them off from needed finance. The Department of Justice and the Federal Trade Commission lent support to the companies' argument by alleging that a requirement to adopt successful efforts costing would hamper their financing, and they raised fears that, as a consequence, small and medium-sized entities might have little option but to be merged into the major producers, thus reducing the number of competitors in the industry. This further concentration in the industry, they said, was not consistent with the government's anti-trust policy; therefore, they argued that full costing should be retained as an acceptable accounting method. The newly formed Department of Energy registered its opposition to SFAS 19, also for a reason having nothing to do with accounting:

The Department of Energy argued that small companies, if they were forced to use successful efforts costing, would deliberately engage in less risky drilling, in order to dampen the amplitudes in their year-to-year earnings, which was contrary to the Department's evolving policy of encouraging the exploration for oil and gas in places where it had not been discovered before.

(Zeff, 1993, page 138)

In this highly pressurized environment, the SEC decided instead that companies' proven oil and gas reserves should be reported in their financial statements at current value (known as 'reserve recognition accounting'), rather than be reflected at either successful efforts or full costing, which were predicated on the historical costs incurred. But then the major oil and gas producers aggressively complained that the use of reserve recognition accounting, under which unrealized holding gains and losses were to be taken to earnings, would, at a time when the OPEC cartel was regularly raising the price of crude, expose them to fierce criticism in the press and by the public for bloated earnings. The supply of petrol (gasoline) to consumers was severely restricted, and its price was, of course, steadily rising to unprecedented levels. Consumers were irate. This was not the time, the major producers argued, for them to be reporting record earnings in quarter after quarter. Finally, buffeted by intense criticism and lobbying, the SEC instructed the FASB to develop a current-value footnote for oil and gas reserves, and all companies in the industry were once again authorized to choose successful efforts or full costing (Van Riper, 1994, Ch. 4; Horwitz and Kolodny, 1982, pages 102–7; Miller *et al.* 1998, pages 125–7; and Zeff, 1993, pages 137–40). Politics was again the victor.

Other post-employment benefits (1987–90)

Although there were strong voices from the preparer sector foretelling disastrous consequences if the FASB were to require that a liability be placed on the balance sheet for the hitherto unrecognized cost of health benefits for all current and retired employees, the board nonetheless succeeded in doing so in SFAS 106, issued in December 1990.[15] This was an interesting case in which the preparer community failed to defeat a proposed standard. Previously, companies' health care costs were recorded as expenses when they were paid, not when they were accrued during employees' productive years of service. Employees and unions were worried that some companies, facing a mountainous liability in their balance sheets, might withdraw some health benefits from employees or seek to renegotiate collective bargaining agreements. Two years before SFAS 106 was issued, it was reported that, as a result of such a standard, 'The data show that the companies' health costs [in their income statements] are likely to jump by three to six times, an explosion that in some instances will crater earnings' (Loomis, 1988, page 108).[16] SFAS 106 allowed companies either to write off the total unfunded obligation as a lump-sum expense, classified as a 'cumulative effect of an accounting change', in the year in which the standard was adopted, or to amortize it as an ordinary expense, usually over 20 years.

---

[15] SFAS 106 formed part of the FASB's major project on pensions, which also produced SFAS 87, on employers' accounting for pensions.
[16] Also, see Dankner *et al.* (1989).

The vast majority of the adopters chose the former option, perhaps believing that the market would pay little attention to a 'cumulative effect' disclosure of a one-time, non-cash expense. Older industrial companies' balance sheets were hit particularly badly. General Motors reported a 1992 after-tax charge of $20.8 billion, compared with 1991 year-end shareholders' equity of $27 billion. Chrysler's after-tax charge exceeded the balance in its retained earnings. But the FASB was generally praised for forcing companies to account for the accrued cost of the health care benefits that they had awarded to employees, thus requiring them, many for the first time, to calculate and analyze the cost of the benefits conferred. SFAS 106 justly gave rise to the maxim, 'you manage what you measure' (Miller *et al.*, 1998, pages 136–7; Wyatt, 1990, pages 108–10; Loomis, 1988, pages 106, 108).[17]

10.3.2 The United Kingdom

Beginning in 1970, with the launch of the United Kingdom and Ireland's first standard-setting committee, the Accounting Standards Steering Committee (ASSC), companies began to take the matter of accounting norms more seriously. This was so even though there was effectively no one other than auditors to monitor on a continuing basis whether companies' financial statements gave 'a true and fair view' in accordance with the Companies Acts (see Chapter 14).

Inflation accounting (1971–5)

Political lobbying was evident in the attempt by the ASSC to set a standard on inflation accounting. At a time of rising concern over inflation, the ASSC in August 1971 issued a discussion paper, *Inflation and Accounts*, in which it outlined an argument for the use of 'current purchasing power' (CPP) accounting. This meant an indexation of the financial statements for changes in the Consumer Price Index, in a supplementary statement to the annual accounts. This paper was followed up in January 1973 by the ASSC's exposure draft, ED8, which proposed that a CPP supplementary statement become a requirement, and comments were invited during a six-month period. Whilst the public accounting firms, on balance, favoured the CPP approach, it was opposed by most of the preparers who submitted comments (Tweedie and Whittington, 1984, pages 64–73).

In July 1973, six days before the end of the comment period, the Government 'shook the accounting profession' (ibid., page 74) by announcing in Parliament that it would be setting up an independent committee of enquiry on the adjustment of company accounts for inflation, citing 'the wide range of national interests affected by the subject' (ibid., page 74). This action precluded the ASSC from converting its exposure draft into an obligatory standard. Yet in May 1974 the Councils of the six accountancy bodies sponsoring the ASSC approved Provisional Statement of Standard Accounting Practice (PSSAP) 7, which embodied the recommendations in ED8. The provisional character of the standard meant that it was not binding on companies or auditors, but instead encouraged them to use the CPP approach

---

[17] For examples of 'you manage what you measure', see Lowenstein (1996).

to account for the effects of inflation. The government's committee of enquiry had been appointed in January 1974, and the ASSC and the accountancy bodies believed that the issue of an interim, non-binding standard was desirable.

There is evidence that 'the Government had been lobbied by a number of companies which opposed the introduction of a CPP standard' (ibid., page 76; Rutherford, 2007, Ch. 4). Moreover, government was concerned that a CPP approach might institutionalize inflation, and it feared that CPP accounting might be advocated as the basis for company taxation (Tweedie and Whittington, 1984, pages 76–7). Government thus saw the ASSC's initiative as a source of potential problems in other key areas.

In the end, the committee of enquiry, known as the Sandilands Committee, issued a report[18] in September 1975, in which it backed current cost accounting (largely based on replacement costs) and rejected CPP accounting. PSSAP 7 therefore lost any practical effect it might have had.

Deferred taxes (1975–8)

Politics again intruded in 1976, after the governing Councils of the accountancy bodies sponsoring the ASSC (see Chapter 14) had approved Statement of Standard Accounting Practice (SSAP) 11 on accounting for deferred taxes. The standard would have required companies to record a liability for all timing differences between taxable income and accounting earnings. But the 1970s were an inflationary decade, and Parliament enacted two major income tax concessions: it authorized a 100 per cent first-year capital (i.e. depreciation) allowance on many fixed assets as well as stock appreciation relief for merchandise inventories, a variation of 'last in, first out' (LIFO) for tax purposes only. Because of these generous tax concessions at a time of considerable inflation, which would give rise to major timing differences, companies knew that they would be required to recognize very large deferred tax liabilities (see Chapter 16). Industry protested against the new standard vigorously, chiefly because of its adverse effects on company balance sheets.

Also, a minister in the Labour government had been advocating a gradual nationalization of industry, and some companies feared that the government might call in the notional tax liability – which industry believed would grow and grow, and never reverse – as a down-payment towards an eventual government takeover. For its part, government did not like the standard because it would oblige each company to record a much larger notional tax expense than was actually due, thus masking the significant tax concessions that government had given to enterprise. None of these were accounting arguments. They were self-interested pleading. In the end, the standard-setter was forced by these political pressures to withdraw the standard and replace it with one that allowed companies to record a much lower deferred tax liability, which could be expected to reverse in the foreseeable future (Zeff, 2002, pages 46–8; Hope and Briggs, 1982; Arnold and Webb, 1989, pages 29–30; Zeff, 1988, pages 21–2).

---

[18] *Inflation Accounting*, Report of the Inflation Accounting Committee, Cmnd 6225, Her Majesty's Stationery Office, London, 1975.

Research and development (1977)

A special pleading was also pressed on the standard-setter during the run-up to SSAP 13, issued in 1977. The aerospace industry used the following argument to persuade the standard-setter not to require the immediate write-off of development costs in SSAP 13:

> deferral should be permitted because the profit percentage allowed in government contracts was calculated on capital employed, which was defined as including development expenditure included in the balance sheet. Immediate write-off therefore would have reduced the profit calculation. In other words, the aerospace industry was worried about the possible economic effects of an accounting standard.[19]

The final standard did not require an immediate write-off of development costs.

Goodwill (1987–90)

In the last three years of the ASC's life,[20] it gamely attempted to impose some discipline on the accounting treatment of goodwill. SSAP 22, which had been issued in 1984, allowed almost unconstrained choice, and most companies continued to write off goodwill against shareholders' equity.

In ED 47, issued in February 1990, just months before it was to give way to the Accounting Standards Board, the ASC proposed a single method: amortization to be charged to expense over a maximum of 20 years. This proposal was met by intense lobbying. Industry strongly opposed a requirement of amortization, and the stream of adverse letters of comment included protests from the Confederation of British Industry and the 100 Group of Finance Directors. A member of the ASC and of its working party on ED 47 has reported that members of the ASC and the working party were subjected to political pressure from colleagues and clients.[21] All of the Big-6 audit firms expressed opposition, one explanation being the need to avoid antagonizing actual and potential clients. Owing to the intense controversy, the ASC had no choice but to pass the goodwill project on to its successor, without resolution.

10.4   US political lobbying from 1990

10.4.1   Marketable securities (1990–3)

The SEC has historically been averse to companies carrying assets in their accounts at market value – its decision in 1978 to support reserve recognition accounting in the petroleum industry being the only prominent exception before 1990. However, in the early 1990s, its Chairman argued that marketable securities should be 'marked to market'. The FASB responded with alacrity to this suggestion and began working on a draft standard that would value equity securities at market prices, with the unrealized holding gains and losses taken to earnings. The banking industry,

---

[19] Taylor and Turley (1986, p. 84). For a fuller treatment of this controversy, see Hope and Gray (1982).
[20] In 1976, 'Steering' was dropped from the committee's name.
[21] Nobes (1992, p. 154 and fn. 9). Also see the interview with Nobes in Rutherford (2007, p. 269).

abetted by its regulators, quickly reacted by mounting a campaign to oppose any such standard, as banks typically held large portfolios of securities. The industry was worried that bank earnings would become unmanageably volatile and therefore indicative, in the eyes of many observers, of instability in the banking system. No less a political figure than the Secretary of the Treasury wrote a letter to the FASB in which he asserted:

> This proposal could have serious, unintended effects on the availability of credit as well as on the stability of the financial system, and I strongly urge the FASB not to adopt it at this time. . . . [Market value accounting] could even result in more intense and frequent credit crunches, since a temporary dip in asset prices would result in immediate reductions in bank capital and an inevitable retrenchment in bank lending capacity.[22]

Under this assault from the banking industry, the FASB felt the need to craft a compromise. Equity securities would be classified as either 'trading' or 'available for sale'. Both would be marked to market, but only the unrealized holding gains and losses on the trading securities, which were to be sold in the near term, would be taken to earnings. Gains and losses accumulated on available for sale securities, usually the larger of the two portfolios, would be diverted to the shareholders' equity section, and would not affect earnings until the securities were actually sold. SFAS 115, issued in 1993, embodied this compromise, and the lion's share of unrealized gains and losses on equity securities were therefore diverted from earnings. Debt securities to be held until maturity were, as before, recorded at amortized historical cost (Kirk, 1991; Wyatt, 1991; Scott, 2003, pages 460–4). Chapter 16 takes this topic further.

10.4.2 Employee stock options (1992–5)

The best known of the recent political controversies dealt with employee stock (or share) options. On this subject, emotions were sky high, because the compensation packages of top executives were in peril. In 1993, the FASB published an exposure draft that called for the mandatory expensing of employee stock options in the income statement, using an estimate of fair value based on an option pricing model. Previously, companies recorded no expense at all when granting stock options, because, in order to secure favourable income tax treatment, their exercise price was set equal to the market price of the shares on the date of the grant, so they had no 'intrinsic value'. Top executives, especially of high-tech enterprise, were livid with the FASB. In the high-tech field, many of the small companies granted options to all of their employees, not just to favoured top executives. Companies sensed that their earnings would take a hard hit and that shareholders would be less willing to tolerate generous grants of stock options if they were accompanied by a significant drop in company earnings.

As soon as the high-tech sector concluded that the FASB was unresponsive to their criticisms and objections, they appealed to members of Congress. Bills were introduced to order the SEC not to enforce an FASB standard that required expensing of stock options. At the same time, a number of other members of Congress,

---

[22] Letter from Nicholas F. Brady to Dennis R. Beresford, FASB Chairman, dated 24 March 1992.

supporting the FASB position, tabled bills that ordered the SEC to enforce any such standard. In March 1994, the FASB held a public hearing in Silicon Valley, and a raucous 'STOP FASB' protest rally, complete with inspirational speakers and a high school marching band, drummed up a frenzy of opposition. The rally was widely covered in the local media. Six weeks later, US Senators recruited by the opponents of the FASB's proposal approved a non-binding resolution by a lop-sided vote of 88–9 to urge the FASB not to adopt the standard, as it 'will have grave economic consequences particularly for business in new-growth sectors which rely heavily on employee entrepreneurship . . . [and] will diminish rather than expand broad-based employee stock option plans'.[23]

Warren Buffett, the widely respected American investor and member of corporate boards of directors, defended the FASB and said:

> If options aren't a form of compensation, what are they? If compensation isn't an expense, what is it? And, if expenses shouldn't go into the calculation of earnings, where in the world should they go?[24]

The lines were drawn, and the stakes were high. Then, in October 1994, the same Senator who had sponsored the resolution that had sailed through the Senate introduced another bill, which, if passed, would require the members of the SEC to affirm by a majority vote any new FASB standard before it could go into effect. Such legislation would threaten the future viability of the FASB. Shortly afterwards, the SEC Chairman privately counselled the FASB to retreat from its position because of the intense heat on Capitol Hill. The Chairman, who had previously spoken out in support of the FASB's exposure draft, has since written:

> I warned [the FASB] that, if they adopted the new standard, the SEC would not enforce it. . . . In retrospect, I was wrong. I know the FASB would have stuck to its guns had I not pushed it to surrender. Out of a misguided belief that I was acting in the FASB's best interests, I failed to support this courageous and beleaguered organization in its time of need, and may have opened the door to more meddling by powerful corporations and Congress.
> (Levitt and Dwyer, 2002, page 110)

In the end, the FASB, by a vote of 5 to 2, approved SFAS 123 which favoured expensing the fair value of stock options in the income statement, but few companies adopted this treatment. The allowed alternative was a footnote disclosure of the impact that any stock options expense would have on earnings.[25]

It had been a wrenching affair, which the FASB had no desire to repeat. Yet, as will be seen in Section 10.7, it had to be repeated between 2002 and 2004, when the FASB carried out its commitment to converge with IFRS 2, Share-based Payment.

10.4.3 Business combinations and goodwill (1996–2001)

For some years, the SEC's accounting staff had wanted the FASB to tackle 'pooling of interests' v. 'purchase' accounting for business combinations (see Chapters 8 and

---

[23] *Congressional Record – Senate*, 3 May 1994, p. S 5032.
[24] *Congressional Record – Senate*, 3 May 1994, p. S 5040.
[25] For fuller discussions of this affair, see Zeff (1997), Mozes (1998), Miller *et al.* (1998, pp. 137–42) and Revsine *et al.* (2005, pp. 876–81).

17). The staff complained that 40 per cent of its time was consumed with issues relating to business combinations. The issue was finally added to the FASB's agenda in 1996. After a lengthy process of enquiry, the board resolved in a 1999 exposure draft to eliminate pooling of interests as an acceptable accounting method and to reduce the maximum useful life for amortizing goodwill and other intangibles from 40 to 20 years, which would have harmonized with IAS 22 (as revised in 1993). These positions precipitated hearings, in March and May 2000, on Capitol Hill, in the Senate and the House of Representatives. A former FASB Chairman has made the following observation on Congressional hearings called to address proposed FASB standards:[26]

> The FASB often is on the defensive because these hearings are generally convened when certain companies, industry associations, or others allege that pending FASB positions will cause serious economic harm if adopted as final accounting standards. Although parties sympathetic to the FASB are sometimes invited to speak, the deck is often stacked in favor of the opponents.

The two hearings on business combinations and goodwill were of that ilk, but the FASB stood its ground. A senior Senator, the Chairman of the powerful Committee on Banking, Housing, and Urban Affairs, held a 'Roundtable Discussion on Accounting for Goodwill' in June 2000, before the FASB's exposure draft could be converted into a standard. During the session, he directed the following remarks to the FASB's Chairman:

> In a financial snapshot at the point of an acquisition, I would argue that purchase accounting is superior to pooling of interest. The problem comes, however, in that purchase accounting requires that this goodwill be written down over time, even though, in any successful merger, we expect the value of that goodwill to rise and not to decline.
>
> The question then becomes, are the problems created by arbitrarily writing down goodwill sufficient to override the benefits in approximating reality that we get from purchase accounting? Is there a way you can develop an approximation that would allow you to assess periodically the value of goodwill and whether or not it's being preserved, whether or not it's declining, whether or not it's actually rising in value?[27]

The Chairman had expressed a very similar view in March 2000 during the hearing held by his Committee.[28]

After the FASB Chairman returned to his offices, the board proceeded to reconsider its proposed treatment of goodwill. By December, the board had concluded that, in principle, it could support a periodic impairment test for goodwill.[29] It therefore decided to issue a revised exposure draft to replace the requirement that

---

[26] Beresford (2001, p. 74). This is the best single work on the business combinations and goodwill controversy from 1996 up to 2000. Also see Zeff (2002, pp. 50–1).

[27] 'Gramm's Statement at Roundtable Discussion of Accounting for Goodwill', News from the Senate Banking Committee (14 June 2000).

[28] 'Prepared Statement of Chairman Phil Gramm', *Pooling Accounting*, Hearing before the Committee on Banking, Housing, and Urban Affairs, United States Senate, 106th Congress, 2nd Session (2 March 2000), p. 47.

[29] See 'Business Combinations – FASB Reaches Tentative Decisions on Accounting for Goodwill', *FASB Status Report*, No. 331 (29 December 2000), p. 1, and 'A Landmark Proposal from FASB', *The Accountant* (December 2000), p. 3. The board would have been aware that the UK Accounting Standards Board stated in FRS 10, issued in December 1997, that any goodwill and other intangibles with an amortizable life in excess of 20 years or not being amortized must be subjected to an annual impairment review.

goodwill be amortized over a period of up to 20 years by a requirement that goodwill be reviewed periodically for impairment. The final standard, SFAS 142, included the periodic impairment test for goodwill.

10.5 Political lobbying of the IASC/IASB

10.5.1 Elimination of LIFO (1992)

Even before the International Accounting Standards Committee's standards became requirements in several countries, a display of special-interest lobbying afflicted the board. This occurred in 1992, when the IASC board attempted to carry out one of the provisions in its *Statement of Intent*, issued in 1990, that LIFO should be eliminated as an acceptable treatment.[30] Because LIFO could be used for income tax purposes in Germany, Italy, Japan and South Korea, countries in which tax reporting and financial reporting were intertwined, the delegations to the IASC board from those countries voted against the elimination of LIFO. One supposes that the delegations aligned themselves with views expressed within their countries that nothing should be done to disturb the tax benefits conferred by LIFO. These four negative votes constituted a blocking minority, and the motion to eliminate LIFO failed. The defeat of the motion, which was unexpected, became an embarrassment to the IASC board. Interestingly, the US delegation to the board voted in favour of eliminating LIFO, despite the common use of LIFO in the US (see Chapter 8), believing that it was not a proper accounting method.

Finally, in 2003 the IASB, as part of its Improvements project, eliminated LIFO in its revision of IAS 2.

10.5.2 Share-based payment (2001)

When the IASB began work in 2001, one of the topics on its agenda was share-based payment, which included employee stock options. Prior to developing an exposure draft, the board re-exposed the G4+1[31] research report on the subject.[32] The report recommended that share options be expensed in each period in which employee services were performed, based on the fair values of the options at the end of each successive reporting period. This re-exposure precipitated a letter-writing campaign from 15 major European multinationals. The letter writers complained that a standard embodying this recommendation would place them at a competitive disadvantage compared with companies using US GAAP, which did not need to record such an expense in their accounts and thus depress their earnings. These were the companies that wrote the letters:

---

[30] *Comparability of Financial Statements*, Statement of Intent, International Accounting Standards Committee, July 1990, p. 19.
[31] See Chapter 4.
[32] Crook (2000).

Nokia (Finland)

Ericsson (Sweden)

Bayer (Germany)

DaimlerChrysler (Germany)

Océ (Netherlands)

Philips (Netherlands)

ING (Netherlands)

Jefferson Smurfit (Ireland)

UBS (Switzerland)

Nestlé (Switzerland)

F. Hoffmann-La Roche (Switzerland)

Saint-Gobain (France)

Lafarge (France)

Pirelli (Italy)

Repsol YPF (Spain)

Key passages in several of the letters were identical, suggesting that at least some of the letters were written in concert, probably organized by the European Round Table of Industrialists, a lobbying organization of major multinationals. Their argument took advantage of one of the recitals in the proposed IAS Regulation, which was then under consideration by the European Parliament (see Chapter 5), as follows:

> (15) In its deliberations on and in elaborating positions to be taken on documents and papers issued by the IASB in the process of developing international accounting standards (IFRS and SIC-IFRIC), the [European] Commission should take into account the importance of avoiding *competitive disadvantages* for European companies operating in the global marketplace, and, to the maximum possible extent, the views expressed by the delegations in the Accounting Regulatory Committee. The Commission will be represented in constituent bodies of the IASB. [emphasis added]

Despite this intervention before the IASB had even composed an exposure draft, the board succeeded in issuing IFRS 2 in February 2004, which requires that companies expense the fair value of employee stock options. At the exposure draft stage, companies had softened their opposition, perhaps because of the concern over accounting abuses arising from the widely publicized Enron and WorldCom scandals. A year later, in February 2005, the European Commission formally endorsed IFRS 2 for use in Europe. In December 2004, the FASB had issued SFAS 123(R), which converged, in large measure, with IFRS 2, but the political opposition in Congress to prevent the US standard from going into effect led to the introduction of blocking legislation (see Section 10.7).

10.5.3 Financial instruments (2002–4)

IAS 39 (revised 2003), which addresses the measurement and recognition of financial instruments, became the major political battle of the young IASB's life. The initial version of IAS 39 had been issued by the IASC in December 1998, being the last of its standards to form part of the 'core set', which the International Organization of Securities Commissions (IOSCO) endorsed in May 2000. It had been difficult enough for the IASC to agree on the standard, even though there were then comparatively few countries in the world where its standards really mattered in terms of national GAAP. The proposal by the European Commission to require all listed companies in the European Union (EU) to use international standards in their consolidated statements by 2005 was not announced until June 2000, and the relevant Regulation formally imposing this requirement was adopted by the Council of the EU in June 2002.

In 2001, the Commission encouraged the European private sector to set up a body to screen IFRSs for technical soundness. The body that shortly came into being was the European Financial Reporting Advisory Group (EFRAG). It proceeded to create a Technical Expert Group (TEG) composed of accounting experts from EU countries. The TEG sends comments to the IASB on its draft standards, and it advises the Commission on the technical propriety of IFRSs. To enable the Commission to receive advice at the 'political' level, the Regulation created an Accounting Regulatory Committee consisting of government representatives from the EU's member states. The TEG's advice is also to be sent to the ARC. The final decision to endorse IFRSs for use in Europe, and thus make them subject to the Regulation, is taken by the Commission.

The revised IAS 39 was the first serious test of this new relationship between the IASB and both EFRAG and the Commission. It was also the first standard that so infuriated an important preparer sector in Europe that it brought unrelenting pressure on the Commission to qualify its endorsement. The objections to the standard, which the IASB tried but failed fully to accommodate,[33] were twofold: its full fair value option as applied to certain liabilities, and the restriction on hedge accounting that prevented the banks from hedging their portfolio of core deposits. The loudest complaint, especially coming from the French banks, was that the standard would afflict them with unacceptable earnings volatility and that it would require them to change their risk management practices to their disadvantage. The European Central Bank argued that the full fair value option would lead to an undervaluation of bank liabilities, especially if discounted at a high interest rate reflecting the bank's weak credit standing. Moreover, the Commission asserted that the standard's full fair value option is contrary to an article in the EU's Fourth Directive on company accounts. This argument was of dubious merit, if only because the Commission itself could initiate a procedure to modify the Directive accordingly.

The objections from France reached fever pitch in July 2003, when President Jacques Chirac wrote to Commission President, Romano Prodi, that the IASB's proposed standard on financial instruments would have '[disastrous] consequences for financial stability'.[34] The European Central Bank and the Basel Committee of bank regulators also were concerned about aspects of the standard that could create artificial volatility.

For its part, the TEG recommended endorsement of IAS 39, but by a curious vote of 5 in favour and 6 against. The rules of the TEG provide that it may recommend rejection of a proposed endorsement only when at least two-thirds of its members oppose a standard. The Accounting Regulatory Committee recommended endorsement of IAS 39 in October 2004, but 'minus the provisions on full fair value

---

[33] In March 2004, the IASB issued an amendment to IAS 39, 'Fair Value Hedge Accounting for a Portfolio Hedge of Interest Rate Risk', which failed to placate the opponents of the standard.

[34] Quoted in 'IAS Unstoppable', *Global Risk Regulator Newsletter* (July/August 2003), http://www.globalriskregulator.com/archive/JulyAugust2003–19.html. In news articles containing this quotation, the English rendering of the French *néfaste* has been nefarious, but 'disastrous' is a better translation.

and portfolio hedging on core deposits'.[35] These became the two 'carve outs' of the Commission's partial endorsement of IAS 39 announced in November.[36] In June 2005, responding to criticism, the IASB issued an amendment to IAS 39 on the fair value option, which led the Commission to eliminate the 'carve out' on that subject. The 'carve out' on hedge accounting for core deposits remained.

Among the dilemmas facing the IASB was that, if it were to accommodate completely all of the objections emanating from Europe, it would, in its view, have issued a standard that was less than principled. It was essential to the IASB that the door be open for convergence with the FASB. But the FASB Chairman made it known that his board could not converge with other than a high quality standard.[37] Furthermore, the 'carve out' is believed to be a source of concern to the SEC's accounting staff,[38] which has been encouraging the FASB and the IASB to eliminate the differences in their respective standards at a high level of quality. The SEC and the IASB hope that, one day, the requirement that the SEC imposes on foreign registrants to reconcile their IFRS-based earnings and shareholders' equity to US GAAP can be dropped, but only if the convergence between US GAAP and IFRS is, in the SEC's eyes, at a high level of quality (see Chapter 5).

Questions are now being raised whether standard-setters or regulators in other parts of the world would use the precedent set by the Commission to accommodate domestic opposition to future IFRSs, by carving out objectionable passages. Although the Commission denies that its 'carve outs' of IAS 39 constitute a precedent, it could nonetheless take similar action on a future IFRS.[39]

10.5.4 Operating segments (2006–7)

In 2006, the IASB issued a new standard, IFRS 8, to replace IAS 14 on segment reporting. IFRS 8 is similar to the US standard on operating segment disclosures, and convergence was one of the IASB's objectives.

Positive endorsement advice was given by EFRAG, and the European Commission was in favour of endorsement. However, a campaign to oppose endorsement led to a motion in the European Parliament. Resolving this delayed endorsement until November 2007. More details are given in Chapter 19.

---

[35] 'EU Accounting Regulatory Opinion on IAS 39' (19 November 2004), IP/04/1385, http://www.iasplus.com/europe/0410arcopinion.pdf.
[36] 'Accounting Standards: Commission Endorses IAS 39', press release, http://www.iasplus.com.europe/0411ecias39pr.pdf.
[37] See, for example, 'US Watchdog Warns Europe: European Opposition to Derivatives Rules May Hinder Agreement on Global Accounting', *Financial Times*, 25 August 2003.
[38] In a speech on 8 March 2007, SEC Commissioner Roel Campos complained that the SEC had received only 40 sets of foreign companies' financial statements for the year 2005 which were said to be prepared in accordance with IFRS. The SEC had expected to receive some 300 such reports. Among the other 260 would have been EU companies whose auditors are required to state that their financial statements have been fairly presented in accordance with IFRS as adopted by the European Union. Even if, for companies other than banks, the carve out does not apply, the auditor and company nonetheless do not in many cases affirm that the financial statements comply with IFRS as issued by the IASB. See http://www.sec.gov/news/speech/2007/spch030807rcc.htm.
[39] 'IAS 39 Financial Instruments: Recognition and Measurement – Frequently Asked Questions (FAQ)' (19 November 2004), MEMO/04/265, http://www.iasplus.com/europe/0411ecias39faq.pdf.

10.6 Preparer attempts to control the accounting standard-setter

10.6.1 The United States

It was not enough for preparers to confront the FASB on particular accounting issues. Beginning in 1985, they took a number of steps to try to 'rein in' the FASB. In 1985, the Financial Executives Institute (FEI) urged that a second preparer be appointed to the seven-person FASB, which was done, displacing the lone former financial analyst on the board. In 1988, the Business Roundtable, composed of the chief executive officers of some 200 of the largest US publicly traded companies and banks, pressed the SEC to cooperate in setting up a board to oversee the FASB. The board would exercise control over the FASB's agenda and could reject any standards after the FASB had approved them. The SEC Chairman peremptorily rejected the proposal, saying that the SEC oversees the FASB. Then, in 1990, probably with the encouragement of the preparer lobby, the trustees of the Financial Accounting Foundation (FAF), who appoint FASB members and raise funds, changed the FASB's minimum voting rule for approving standards from 4–3 to 5–2, ostensibly to slow the board's pace.[40]

A major confrontation erupted in 1996. Shortly after the FASB approved SFAS 123 on employee stock options in the wake of the political assault from Congress (see Section 10.4), the FEI President apprised the Chairman of the FAF trustees of the FEI's strong desire to take steps to bring the FASB more under preparer dominance. That led to a move by the SEC Chairman to protect the independence of the FAF board of trustees. He insisted that the FAF board appoint four trustees who represent the public interest. Until then, all of the trustees were appointed by the FAF's sponsoring organizations, which included the FEI. Initially, the FAF board resisted, until the SEC Chairman threatened a loss of SEC support for the FASB unless it were to comply. In the end, the FAF appointed four new trustees who were well known to the SEC Chairman, increasing the size of the FAF board from 14 to 16.

This series of interventions – and there were others not mentioned above – indicates how seriously the preparer community in the United States takes the FASB as an unwelcome force in its financial affairs.[41]

10.6.2 The IASB

One of the consequences of the IAS 39 affair (see Section 10.5.3) was a move by the European preparer sector to press EFRAG to expand its role and mission so as to take expressly into account the self-interested concerns of European industry towards future IFRSs. EFRAG was therefore to venture beyond its purely accounting domain and to enter the realm of political and economic impact. An EFRAG policy statement issued in April 2004 said that, in accordance with this broadened authority,

---

[40] In 2000, the trustees quietly voted to restore the 4–3 simple majority.
[41] For a full account of the initiatives taken by the preparer community between 1985 and 1996, see Miller *et al.* (1998, pp. 179–93) and Van Riper (1994, Ch. 8).

'EFRAG, when expressing views on major issues will need to analyze their economic, legal and practical implications with the input of other stakeholders. . . . Some of these issues may give rise to political debate. . . .' Proposed IFRSs are to be 'fully discussed in the context of the "European Public Good" at an early stage'.[42] Political impact is therefore to be given a higher profile in EFRAG's deliberations. In this way, European industry could appeal to EFRAG as well as to the Commission on 'political' grounds.

From 2003, the IASC Foundation trustees, who oversee the IASB, conducted a review of its Constitution and working procedures. European industry and the Commission had been urging the IASB to improve its consultation procedures, which means to exhibit a greater willingness to accept the views of critics in the preparer community. European industry and the Commission wanted to see more representatives from adopter countries on the board of trustees as well as on the IASB, and fewer from the United States, which does not use IFRSs. They succeeded in persuading the trustees to broaden the criterion of 'technical expertise' for membership on the IASB to 'professional competence and practical experience', so that the board might become less of an 'ivory tower'. The trustees also made a change in the required minimum vote for approval of standards from a simple majority of the 14 members to 9–5. The Commission and EFRAG had argued for 10–4 and wanted the board to have more than two part-time board members.[43] To some, these reforms (effective from 1 July 1995) may be reminiscent of attempts made by preparer bodies in the United States to gain greater control over the FASB. But the standard-setter must be regarded as a fair- and open-minded arbiter by those who are affected by its decisions.

10.7 Political lobbying of the FASB's convergence with the IASB

10.7.1 Employee stock options: round 2 (2002–5)

In 2002, there were two developments in the United States on accounting for employee stock options. In the wake of the Enron and WorldCom bankruptcies and alleged frauds, pressure began to build on companies to take steps to restore public and shareholder trust. The failure of companies to expense the fair value of stock options was seized upon as an example of corporate abuse. As noted above, this treatment to record an expense was the one favoured by the FASB in its SFAS 123, issued in 1995, but all but a few companies initially opted instead to disclose the

---

[42] 'The Enhancement of the Role and Working Process of EFRAG' (28 January 2004), http://www.iasplus.com/efrag/0404enhancement.pdf.
[43] The full report by the trustees on their proposals for changes in the Constitution may be downloaded from the IASB website. A summary of these major proposed changes may be found in the entry for 23 November 2004 in the IASPLUS.com website. For a recent expression of the further constitutional changes being urged by the EC, see the letter from Alexander Schaub, Director-General of Internal Market and Services, to Tom Seidenstein, Director, International Accounting Standards Foundation, dated 7 March 2005. Letters of comment received by the Foundation in response to an Invitation to Comment issued in 2003 are posted on the IASB website.

dilutive effect on earnings of the expense in a footnote. Because of the efforts of Warren Buffett, several major companies, including Coca-Cola, the Washington Post and General Electric, announced in 2002 that they would in future record stock option expense in their income statements. The movement to adopt this treatment began to resonate with the media and with shareholders, and pressure began to build on other companies to follow their lead. The momentum proceeded apace, and by the end of 2004, more than 825 companies had made such an announcement, of which about 120 were ones whose common stock was so widely held that they were included in Standard & Poor's 500 index. But this was still a small fraction of the some 14,000 companies reporting to the SEC.

The other development in 2002 was the FASB's issue of an *Invitation to Comment*, comparing its SFAS 123, as modified, with the IASB's recently issued exposure draft on share-based payment (see Section 10.5). This initiative carried forward FASB's commitment to converge with IFRSs. The FASB knew full well that it was again headed into the path of a political storm over accounting for employee stock options. In March 2004, the FASB issued an exposure draft, calling for the required expensing of the fair value of stock options in the income statement, which was similar in many respects to its exposure draft issued in 1993 (see Section 10.4). A record number of comment letters, exceeding 14,000, were received.[44]

Propelled mostly by the high-tech sector, members of Congress quickly lined up behind a legislative proposal, known as the Stock Option Accounting Reform Act (HR 3574), designed to severely limit the applicability of any FASB standard based on the exposure draft. Under the bill, the mandatory expensing of the fair value of stock options would apply only to a company's chief executive officer and the four other most highly compensated executives. This represented a major concession to the many high-tech companies that granted stock options to most of their employees. The bill also stipulated, contrary to financial wisdom, that volatility shall be zero when using an option-pricing model to estimate the fair value of options. The House of Representatives passed the bill by a vote of 312 to 111, which was indicative of the breadth of support across party lines. However, several key Senators pronounced themselves opposed to interference with the FASB. By the time the 108th Congress adjourned in December 2004, a companion bill (S. 1890) was still pending in the Senate.

Despite this, the FASB unanimously approved SFAS 123(R) in December 2004, but its effective date was postponed until 15 June 2005 because the SEC believed that companies were already overwhelmed at year-end with implementing internal controls mandated by the Sarbanes-Oxley Act of 2002. In April 2005, the SEC extended the effective date, for most companies, by another six months.

In February 2005, a new blocking bill, the Broad-Based Stock Option Plan Transparency Act (HR 913), was introduced in the House by the same supporters of HR 3574 in the previous Congress.[45] It would require the SEC to improve the stock option disclosures in footnotes to the financial statements, including their dilutive

---

[44] *Share-Based Payment*, Statement of Financial Accounting Standards No. 123 (revised 2004) (FASB, December 2004), para. C23. This standard is referred to in this chapter as SFAS 123(R).
[45] Complete information about the transaction of business in the Congress may be found at http://thomas. loc.gov.

effect on earnings per share. At the end of three years, the SEC would be required to transmit to Congress its report on the effectiveness of these enhanced disclosures. Prior to the end of the three-year period, the SEC would not be allowed to recognize SFAS 123(R) as part of GAAP. The aim of the bill was transparent: to be the first stage in an effort to prevent the FASB's standard from ever taking effect.

Because of the unyielding opposition by two key Senators, the momentum behind the House bill petered out, and the FASB's standard went into effect for 2006. Nonetheless, initiatives such as those taken in the House, obviously driven by company lobbying, could well occur on other topics, such as leasing. Political lobbying verily represents a potential threat to the achievement of genuine international convergence of accounting standards.

10.8 Some concluding remarks

Prior to the 1990s, the US Securities and Exchange Commission was the only securities market regulator that rigorously enforced compliance with GAAP. Since the 1990s and especially in the 2000s, other countries have fortified their enforcement agencies. But the level and consistency of their performance in Europe and elsewhere is still highly variable, partly because of their insufficient budgets and weak supporting legislation. Furthermore, regulatory cultures are different in different countries. But once the standard-setter is of high quality and the regulator is also of high quality, not only will the standards potentially improve the quality of company reporting, but the increased incidence of insistent political lobbying from the preparer community could lead to diluted or compromised standards. At the least, they are likely to lead to more detailed standards, with extra paragraphs specifying provisos, exemptions, exceptions and clarifications in order to accommodate special interests pressed upon the standard-setter.

Can one deny that political lobbying is a reality of standard-setting both at the national and international levels? As the stakes get higher, the political opposition to disagreeable change will surely grow in intensity. To a considerable degree, the preparers of financial reports have become a countervailing power against a standard-setter that is seen to overstep its authority. An intelligent student of the standard-setting process must be attentive to the phenomenon of political lobbying.

SUMMARY

- Political lobbying is the bringing of pressure on standard-setters, typically by companies or governments, beyond a debate about the technical merit or compliance costs of a particular proposed standard.

- The motivations of the lobbyist can include a desire to make earnings look larger, smaller or less volatile. In the case of governments, lobbying can concern the desire to ensure that various economic incentives have more attractive accounting results.

- Lobbying of the US standard-setters up to 1990 included that on replacement cost depreciation, the investment tax credit, business combinations, petroleum exploration costs, marketable securities, leases, segment reporting, restructuring of debt, and post-employment benefits.

- UK examples include those on inflation accounting (when the government was involved), deferred tax, research and development, and goodwill.

- US lobbying from 1990 concerned marketable securities, stock options and goodwill; two of which were repeats of earlier cases.

- As the IASC/B became more important, so it was more lobbied. Examples concern LIFO, share-based payment and financial instruments.

- There were also preparer attempts to control the FASB and, later, the IASB.

- Share-based payment returned as a major topic for US lobbying when the FASB sought to converge with the IASB.

References

Arnold, A.J. and Webb, B.J. (1989) *The Financial Reporting and Policy Effects of Partial Deferred Tax Accounting*, The Institute of Chartered Accountants in England and Wales, London.

Beresford, D.R. (2001) 'Congress looks at accounting for business combinations', *Accounting Horizons*, March, pp. 73–86.

Bruns, W.J. Jr. and Merchant, K.A. (1990) 'The dangerous morality of managing earnings', *Management Accounting* (US), August, pp. 22–5.

Burgstahler, D. and Dichev, I. (1997) 'Earnings management to avoid earnings decreases and losses', *Journal of Accounting and Economics*, pp. 99–126.

Chatov, R. (1975) *Corporate Financial Reporting: Public or Private Control?*, The Free Press, New York, Chapters 13 and 14.

Crandall, R.H. (1983) 'Government intervention – the PIP grant accounting controversy', *Cost and Management*, September–October, pp. 55–9; reproduced in *Accounting Horizons*, September 1988, pp. 110–16.

Crook, K. (2000) *Accounting for Share-Based Payment*, Financial Accounting Series, No. 211-A, FASB, July.

Dankner, H., Bald, B.S., Akresh, M.S., Bertko, J.M. and Wodarczyk, J.M. (1989) *Retiree Health Benefits: Field Test of the FASB Proposal*, Financial Executives Research Foundation, Morristown, NJ.

Dechow, P.M. and Skinner, D.J. (2000) 'Earnings management: reconciling the views of accounting academics, practitioners, and regulators', *Accounting Horizons*, June, pp. 235–50.

Duncan, J.R. (2001) 'Twenty pressures to manage earnings', *CPA Journal*, July, pp. 32–7.

Gorton, D.E. (1991) 'The SEC decision not to support SFAS 19: a case study of the effect of lobbying on standard setting', *Accounting Horizons*, March, pp. 29–41.

Hope, T. and Briggs, J. (1982) 'Accounting policy making – some lessons from the deferred taxation debate', *Accounting and Business Research*, Spring, pp. 83–96.

Hope, T. and Gray, R. (1982) 'Power and policy making: the development of an R and D standard', *Journal of Business Finance and Accounting*, Winter, pp. 531–58.

Horngren, C.T. (1973) 'The marketing of accounting standards', *Journal of Accountancy*, October, pp. 63–4.

Horwitz, B. and Kolodny, R. (1982) *Financial Reporting Rules and Corporate Decisions: A Study of Public Policy*, JAI Press Inc., Greenwich, CT.

Keller, T.F. and Zeff, S.A. (eds) (1969) *Financial Accounting Theory II: Issues and Controversies*, McGraw-Hill Book Company, New York, pp. 417–20.

Kirk, D.J. (1991) 'Competitive disadvantage and mark-to-market accounting', *Accounting Horizons*, June, pp. 98–106.

Levitt, A. with Dwyer, P. (2002) *Take on the Street*, Pantheon Books, New York.

Loomis, C.J. (1988) 'Will "FASBEE" pinch your bottom line?' *Fortune*, 19 December.

Lowenstein, L. (1996) 'Financial transparency and corporate governance: you manage what you measure', *Columbia Law Review*, June, pp. 1345–52.

Miller, P.B.W., Redding, R.J. and Bahnson, P.R. (1998) *The FASB: The People, the Process, and the Politics*, fourth edn, Irwin/McGraw-Hill, Burr Ridge, IL.

Moonitz, M. (1966) 'Some reflections on the investment credit experience', *Journal of Accounting Research*, Spring, pp. 47–61.

Mozes, H.A. (1998) 'The FASB's conceptual framework and political support: the lesson from employee stock options', *Abacus*, September, pp. 141–61.

Nelson, M.W., Elliott, J.A. and Tarpley, R.L. (2003) 'How are earnings managed? Examples from auditors', *Accounting Horizons*, Supplement, pp. 17–35.

Nobes, C. (1992) 'A political history of goodwill in the U.K.: an illustration of cyclical standard setting', *Abacus*, September, pp. 142–67.

Ordelheide, D. (1993) 'True and fair view: a European and a German perspective', *European Accounting Review*, No. 1, pp. 81–90.

Revsine, L., Collins, D.W. and Johnson, W.B. (2005) *Financial Reporting and Analysis*, third edn, Pearson Prentice Hall, Upper Saddle River, NJ, pp. 876–81.

Rutherford, B. (2007) *Financial Reporting in the UK: A History of the Accounting Standards Committee 1969–1990*, Routledge, London.

Savoie, L.M. (1974) 'Accounting attitudes', in R.R. Sterling (ed.), *Institutional Issues in Public Accounting*, Scholars Book Co., Lawrence, KS.

Scott, W.R. (2003) *Financial Accounting Theory*, third edn, Prentice Hall, Toronto.

Seligman, J. (2003) *The Transformation of Wall Street: A History of the Securities and Exchange Commission and Modern Corporate Finance*, third edn, Aspen Publishers, New York, pp. 424–5.

Sutton, T.G. (1984) 'Lobbying of accounting standard-setting bodies in the U.K. and the U.S.A.: a Downsian analysis', *Accounting, Organizations and Society*, Vol. 9, No. 1, pp. 81–95.

Swinson, C. (2004) 'When politics and financial reporting don't mix', *Accountancy*, September, p. 28.

Taylor, P. and Turley, S. (1986) *The Regulation of Accounting*, Basil Blackwell, Oxford.

Tricks, H. and Hargreaves, D. (2004) 'Accounting watchdog sees trouble', *Financial Times*, 10 November, p. 19.

Tweedie, D. and Whittington, G. (1984) *The Debate on Inflation Accounting*, Cambridge University Press, Cambridge.

Van Riper, R. (1994) *Setting Standards for Financial Reporting: FASB and the Struggle for Control of a Critical Process*, Quorum Books, Westport, CT.

von Wysocki, K. (1984) 'The Fourth Directive and Germany', in S.J. Gray and A.G. Coenenberg (eds), *EEC Harmonisation: Implementation and Impact of the Fourth Directive*, North-Holland, Amsterdam.

Watts, R.L. and Zimmerman, J.L. (1978) 'Towards a positive theory of the determination of accounting standards', *Accounting Review*, January, pp. 112–34.

Wyatt, A. (1990) 'OPEB Costs: The FASB establishes accountability', *Accounting Horizons*, March, pp. 108–10.

Wyatt, A. (1991) 'The SEC says: mark to market!' *Accounting Horizons*, March, pp. 80–4.

Zeff, S.A. (1972) *Forging Accounting Principles in Five Countries: A History and an Analysis of Trends*, Stipes Publishing Co., Champaign, IL.

Zeff, S.A. (1978) 'The rise of "economic consequences"', *Journal of Accountancy*, December, p. 56.

Zeff, S.A. (1985) 'The rise of "economic consequences"', the unabridged version, reproduced in T.F. Keller and S.A. Zeff (eds), *Financial Accounting Theory: Issues and Controversies*, McGraw-Hill, New York.

Zeff, S.A. (1988) 'Setting accounting standards: some lessons from the US experience', *The Accountant's Magazine*, January, pp. 21–2.

Zeff, S.A. (1993) 'The politics of accounting standards', *Economia Aziendale* (monthly review of the Accademia Italiana di Economia Aziendale), August, pp. 130–32.

Zeff, S.A. (1995) 'A perspective on the U.S. public/private sector approach to the regulation of financial reporting', *Accounting Horizons*, March, pp. 52–70.

Zeff, S.A. (1997) 'The US senate votes on accounting for employee stock options', in S.A. Zeff and B.G. Dharan, *Readings & Notes on Financial Accounting*, fifth edn, McGraw-Hill, New York, pp. 507–17.

Zeff, S.A. (2002) '"Political" lobbying on proposed standards: a challenge to the IASC', *Accounting Horizons*, March, pp. 46–8.

Zeff, S.A. (2005) 'The evolution of US GAAP: the political forces behind professional standards', *CPA Journal*, January, pp. 18–27, and February, pp. 18–29.

Zeff, S.A. and Johansson, Sven-Erik (1984) 'The curious accounting treatment of the Swedish government loan to Uddeholm', *Accounting Review*, April, pp. 342–50.

Useful websites

Accounting Standards Board	www.asb.org.uk
European Commission	www.europa.eu.int
European Financial Reporting Advisory Group	www.efrag.org
Financial Accounting Standards Board	www.fasb.org
Financial Executives Institute	www.fei.org
International Accounting Standards Board	www.iasb.org
Securities and Exchange Commission	www.sec.gov

QUESTIONS

Suggested answers to the asterisked questions are given at the end of the book.

10.1∗ Explain the various motivations of those who politically lobby standard-setters.

10.2∗ Give examples of political lobbying of US standard-setters, explaining in what ways the lobbying went beyond arguments about the correct technical solutions.

10.3 Why might it be expected that there would be more examples of political lobbying relating to the US than to any other country?

10.4 Give examples of political lobbying of the IASC/B, explaining why and how lobbying has increased over the years.

10.5 Discuss the view that political lobbying could and should be reduced by giving preparers more say in the setting of accounting standards.

10.6 Is there a connection between the amount of political lobbying in a country and the degree of independence of the standard-setter from (a) government departments, and (b) the accountancy profession?

10.7 Discuss the role of a conceptual framework as a defence against political lobbying.

Part III

HARMONIZATION AND TRANSITION IN EUROPE AND EAST ASIA

11 Harmonization and transition in Europe

Robert Parker

OBJECTIVES

After reading this chapter, you should be able to:

- explain why harmonization of financial reporting was undertaken by the EU;
- outline the content and effects of the EU's Fourth Directive;
- contrast the process and progress of EU harmonization with that of the IASB (as outlined in Chapter 4);
- explain how financial reporting in Central and Eastern Europe responded to the transition from command economies to market economies;
- outline the problems of applying IFRS in Central and Eastern Europe.

11.1 Introduction

Part III of this book looks at accounting harmonization and transition in two major regions of the world: Europe (this chapter) and East Asia (Chapter 12). In each case, international harmonization has had major effects, but regional and national concerns still influence the financial reporting of some or all companies for many accounting issues.

The history of financial reporting in Europe provides a striking example of the influence of political and economic change on accounting rules and practices. The political map of Europe is dominated by the member states of the European Union (EU) and the successor states of the Soviet Empire. Since the admission of ten of the latter to the EU in 2004 and 2007, there has been considerable overlap between the two categories. In this chapter we discuss the effects of these political changes on first the process of accounting harmonization within the EU and then the problems of financial reporting within the transition economies of Central and Eastern Europe, both those within the EU (e.g. Poland and Hungary) and those outside (notably the Russian Federation).

In Section 11.2, the EU's efforts at harmonization, beginning in the 1960s, are examined. These remain relevant because national laws still apply compulsorily or optionally for some purposes in most EU countries. This is particularly the case for unconsolidated financial statements, which are the basis for the calculation of taxable income and distributable income. Chapter 5 has already looked at the relevance of the EU for the use of IFRS for the consolidated statements of listed companies. Section 11.3 examines the process of transition from communist to capitalist accounting that took place in Eastern Europe from the 1990s.

11.2 Harmonization within the European Union

11.2.1 Reasons for and obstacles to EU harmonization

What is now known as the EU was established on 1 January 1958 following the Treaty of Rome of 1957. The six founding members were France, the German Federal Republic, Italy and the three Benelux countries (Belgium, the Netherlands and Luxembourg). They were joined in 1973 by the UK, Ireland and Denmark, in 1981 by Greece, in 1986 by Portugal and Spain, in 1995 by Austria, Finland and Sweden, in 2004 by Cyprus, the Czech Republic, Estonia, Hungary, Latvia, Lithuania, Malta, Poland, Slovakia and Slovenia, and in 2007 by Bulgaria and Romania. The population of the EU is approximately 500 million. From an accounting and many other points of view, the early years of the EU were dominated by France and West Germany. The entry of the UK and Ireland in 1973 introduced Anglo-Saxon ideas of financial reporting. The entry of the other countries has not had much effect on the content of harmonizing Directives and Regulations, but has presented several member states with difficulties of implementation. The process of accession to the EU, with particular reference to accounting and auditing, is discussed by Day and Taylor (2005).

The drive for harmonization of accounting and financial reporting derived initially from the Treaty of Rome. The objects of the Treaty include the establishment of the free movement of persons, goods and services, and capital. This involves the elimination of customs duties, the imposition of common tariffs to third countries and the establishment of procedures to permit the coordination of economic policies. More specifically, the Common Industrial Policy of 1970 called for the creation of a unified business environment, including the harmonization of company law and taxation, and the creation of a common capital market.

The activities of companies extend beyond national frontiers and shareholders and other stakeholders need protection throughout the EU. In order to achieve this and to encourage the movement of capital, it is necessary to create a flow of reliable homogeneous financial information about companies from all parts of the EU. Further, since companies in different EU countries exist in the same form and are in competition with each other, it is argued that they should be subject to the same laws and taxation.

The obstacles to harmonization of financial reporting and company law were discussed in Section 4.2. Of particular importance here are the fundamental differences between the contexts and purposes of the various national accounting systems in the EU. They include the differences between creditor/secrecy in the traditional Franco-German systems and investor/disclosure in the Anglo-Dutch systems; and between law/tax-based rules and private sector standards. These large differences have contributed towards the great variations in the size and strength of the accountancy profession. The smaller and weaker professional bodies in Franco-German countries were an obstacle to movements towards accounting and auditing of an Anglo-Dutch type (see Chapter 2).

Sections 11.2.2 to 11.2.5 detail the slow but generally successful achievement of greater harmonization of financial reporting and auditing throughout an expanding EU during the 1960s, 1970s and 1980s. In the 1990s the European Commission turned its attention to financial services, launching a Financial Services Action Plan (FSAP) in 1999 and commissioning the Lamfalussy report of 2001. The Committee of European Securities Regulators was established in 2001.

11.2.2 Directives and Regulations

The EU attempted to harmonize company law and financial services through two main instruments: Directives, which must be incorporated into the laws of member states; and Regulations, which become law throughout the EU without the need to pass through national legislatures. The Directives and Regulations on company law and financial services relevant to corporate accounting are listed in Table 11.1, which also gives a brief description of their scope. The company law Directives of most relevance are the Fourth and Seventh (see Chapter 17 for the latter). The Fourth will be discussed in more detail below, after an outline of the procedure for setting Directives and Regulations. The Regulation of 2002 on the use of IFRS has already been examined in Chapter 5.

First, the European Commission, which among other things is the EU's permanent civil service, decides on a project and asks an expert to prepare a report. In the case of the Fourth Directive, this was the Elmendorff Report of 1967. Then an *avant projet* or discussion document is prepared. This is studied by a Commission working party and leads to the issue of a draft Directive, which is sent to the European Parliament (a directly elected assembly) and commented on by the Economic and Social Committee (a consultative body of employers, employees and others). A revised proposal is then submitted to a Working Party of the Council of Ministers. Parliament decides whether the proposal should be adopted, but the Council, consisting of the relevant ministers from each EU country, must give its final approval. In the case of a Directive, member states are required to introduce a national law within a specified period, though they often exceed it, as discussed below in the case of the Fourth Directive. Table 11.1 includes UK implementation dates, as an example. For an analysis of the process of setting accounting Directives, see Diggle and Nobes (1994).

11.2.3 The Fourth Directive

The exact effects of any Directive on a particular country will depend upon the laws passed by national legislatures. For example, there are dozens of provisions in the Fourth Directive that begin with such expressions as 'member states may require or permit companies to . . .' Given this flexibility, the effects on accounting differ country by country (see Chapter 15). However, it seems appropriate to consider here the general outline of the Directive and the process whereby it took its ultimate form.

The Directive (EC Commission, 1978) covers public and private companies in all EU countries. Its articles include those referring to valuation rules, formats of published financial statements and disclosure requirements. It does not cover consolidation; that is left for the Seventh Directive. The Fourth Directive's first draft was published in 1971, before the United Kingdom, Ireland and Denmark had entered the EU in 1973 or had representatives on the *Groupe d'Etudes* (see below). This initial draft was heavily influenced by German company law, particularly the *Aktiengesetz* of 1965. Consequently, valuation rules were conservative, formats were prescribed in rigid detail, and disclosure by notes was very limited. Financial statements were to obey the provisions of the Directive.

The influence of the United Kingdom and Ireland on the Commission, Parliament and *Groupe d'Etudes* was such that a much amended draft was issued in 1974. This introduced the concept of the 'true and fair view'. Another change by 1974 was that some flexibility of presentation had been introduced. This process continued and, by the promulgation of the final Directive, the 'true and fair view' was established as a predominant principle in the preparation of financial statements (Art. 2, paragraphs 2–5). In addition, the four principles of the UK's SSAP 2 (accruals, prudence, consistency and going concern) were made clearer than they had been in the 1974 draft (Art. 31). The translation of the 'true and fair view' and its differing effects in various countries have been extensively discussed (e.g. Alexander, 1993; Ordelheide, 1993; Nobes, 1993; Aisbitt and Nobes, 2001).

More rearrangement and summarization of items in the financial statements were made possible (Art. 4). There were also calls for more notes in the 1974 draft than the 1971 draft, and more in the final Directive than in the 1974 draft

Table 11.1 **Directives and Regulations relevant to corporate accounting**

Directives	Date adopted	UK law	Topic
First	1968	1972	*Ultra vires* rules
Second	1976	1980	Separation of public companies, minimum capital, distributions
Third	1978	1987	Mergers
Fourth*	1978	1981	Formats and rules of accounting
Fifth	–	–	Structure, management and audit of companies
Sixth	1982	1987	De-mergers
Seventh	1983	1989	Consolidated accounting
Eighth	1983, 2006	1989, 2006	Statutory audit
Tenth	–	–	International mergers of public companies
Eleventh	1989	1992	Disclosures about branches
Twelfth	1989	1992	Single member company
Accounts Modernization	2003	2006	Modernization and update of 4th and 7th Directives
Transparency	2004	2006	Transparency in EU capital markets
Takeovers	2005	2006	Cross-border takeovers within the EU
Regulations			
Societas Europaea	2004	–	European company subject to EU laws
European Economic Interest Grouping	1985	–	Business form for multinational joint ventures
International Standards	2002	–	Use of IFRSs and a mechanism for their endorsement

Note: *Special versions of the Directive for banks and insurance companies were adopted in 1986 and 1991, respectively.

(Arts. 43–46). Another concern of Anglo-Dutch accountants has been with the effect of taxation on Franco-German accounts. The extra disclosures called for by the 1974 draft about the effect of taxation are included in the final Directive (Arts. 30 and 35).

The fact that member states may permit or require a type of inflation accounting (an important topic in the 1970s) was treated in more detail than in the 1974 draft (Art. 33), although the Directive remains based in historical cost. As a further accommodation of Anglo-Dutch opinion, a 'Contact Committee' of EU and national civil servants is provided for. This was intended to answer the criticism that the

Table 11.2 **Implementation of accounting Directives as laws**

	Fourth	Seventh
Denmark	1981	1990
United Kingdom	1981	1989
France	1983	1985
Netherlands	1983	1988
Luxembourg	1984	1988
Belgium	1985	1990
Germany	1985	1985
Ireland	1986	1992
Greece	1986	1987
Spain	1989	1989
Portugal	1989	1991
Austria*	1990	1990
Italy	1991	1991
Finland*	1992	1992
Sweden	1995	1995
Norway[†]	1998	1998

Notes: *Some amendments to these laws were necessary for full implementation.
[†]A member of the European Economic Area, but not of the EU.

Directive gives rise to laws that are not flexible to changing circumstances and attitudes. The Committee looks at practical problems arising from the implementation of the Directive, and makes suggestions for amendments (Art. 52). The Fourth Directive was supposed to be enacted in member states by July 1980 and to be in force by January 1982. No country managed the former date, as may be seen in Table 11.2, which includes implementation dates for those countries that had become members of the EU by May 2004.

For the United Kingdom, Ireland and the Netherlands, the changes included compulsory formats and detailed valuation requirements (Nobes, 1983). In other countries the introduction of the 'true and fair view' as an overriding requirement, the requirements for extra disclosures, and the extension of publication and audit to many more companies were significant (see Chapter 14).

It is clear that neither asset valuation, nor formats, nor disclosure were completely standardized as a result of the laws consequent upon the Fourth Directive. However, *harmonization* was noticeable. Also, several other countries (e.g. Switzerland and Poland) made legal changes that were strongly influenced by the Directives, in some cases as preparation for membership of the EU. Members of the European Economic Area that are not part of the EU (e.g. Norway) were also obliged to implement the Directives.

In the area of valuation, there was a very loose compromise between the opinions of those countries that were in favour of adjustments for price changes (the Netherlands, at one extreme) and those that were against them (Germany, at the other extreme). Member states may allow various forms of revaluation. There is a requirement that the difference between the adjusted figures and historical cost must be shown.

European professional accountancy bodies have naturally taken a great interest in harmonization and have set up institutions to monitor and influence its progress (see Section 4.4). The most important body at present is the *Fédération des Experts Comptables Européens* (FEE), which advises the European Commission on company law and accounting harmonization. One of FEE's predecessors (the *Groupe d'Etudes*) accepted in the 1970s the dominance of 'true and fair' and the need for consolidation; this may have helped in their acceptance by the Commission.

In 1990, the EU established a Forum of European standard-setters, which discussed issues not covered by the Directives, for example, lease accounting and foreign currency translation. However, it was also made clear that further accounting Directives were unlikely; and the Forum was little more than a discussion group. It was closed down in 2001. In 1995, the EU gave public backing to the IASC, as discussed earlier (see Chapter 4 and Gornik-Tomaszewski, 2005).

In 2001, the first substantial amendment to the Fourth Directive since its adoption in 1978 allowed the requirements of IAS 39 relating to the fair valuation of financial instruments (see Chapter 6), so that EU companies could obey the Directives and the standard at the same time. In 2003, the Accounts Modernization Directive allowed more extensive use of fair values and removed all other incompatibilities with the standards of the IASB. This is a separate issue from the EU requirement for some companies directly to use IFRS for consolidated statements.

11.2.4 The European company and the EEIG

One of the Regulations in Table 11.1 concerns a totally new type of company, to be registered as an EU company and subject to EU laws. It is called a *Societas Europaea* (SE), which is Latin for European Company. Despite continued pressure from the Commission, progress in agreeing upon this Regulation was very slow, partly because member states did not wish to lose sovereignty over companies operating in their countries, and partly because member states found it difficult to agree upon a company structure with respect to worker participation on boards of directors. The Regulation was finally adopted in 2004. In 2007, the Commission was consulting business on a possible European Private Company Statute.

It was easier to agree upon proposals for a form of joint venture organization for EU companies. The Regulation on the 'European Economic Interest Grouping' is based on the French business form, the *groupement d'intérêt économique*. It provides a corporate organization that can be smaller and of shorter duration than the SE. Members of a grouping are autonomous profit-making entities, whereas the grouping itself provides joint facilities or enables a combination for a specific purpose (McGee and Wetherill, 1989).

11.2.5 Other Directives

The Second Directive concerns a number of matters connected with share capital and the differences between public and private companies (see Nobes, 1983). The Seventh Directive concerns consolidated accounting, and is considered in Chapter 17.

The original Eighth Directive was watered down from its original draft, which might have greatly affected the training patterns and scope of work of accountants, particularly in the United Kingdom. Its main effect has been to decide on who is allowed to audit accounts in certain countries that have small numbers of accountants, such as Denmark and Germany. Some changes to auditor independence and audit firms also occurred (e.g. see Evans and Nobes, 1998a and 1998b).

Partly as a result of the legislative reaction in the US and elsewhere to the Enron and other scandals, a revised Directive was approved in 2006. *Inter alia*, the revised Directive requires member states to establish auditor oversight bodies; sets out rules on professional ethics and independence; requires the use in statutory audits of international auditing standards (ISAs) endorsed by the EU; requires the establishment of audit committees by public interest entities; and the publication of transparency reports on audit firms. The Directive is discussed further in Sections 9.4.1 and 21.3.2.

Financial services Directives have been adopted on, *inter alia*, transparency in EU capital markets (2004) and cross-border takeovers (2005).

11.2.6 Research findings

Several of the empirical studies referred to in Chapter 4 applied their proposed measures of harmonization to European differences. Little harmony or harmonization was discovered within the EU. A further empirical paper on Britain and France after EU harmonization by Walton (1992) finds little evidence of harmony in a case study concerning several accounting measurement issues. Parker (1996) examines the *de jure* harmonization of the notes to financial statements between Britain and France. He finds that the notes still have a different status in the two countries, but that French notes have expanded towards the coverage of British notes.

11.3 Transition in Central and Eastern Europe

11.3.1 Introduction

It became clear in the late 1980s that the command economies of Central and Eastern Europe were failing to deliver economic growth. The inability of communist parties to hold on to political power led to the overthrow of governments (once the threat of Soviet armed intervention was lifted), the reunification of West and East Germany, and the break-up of the Soviet Union itself. This section looks collectively at financial reporting in the large number of European countries formerly under Soviet domination. They include those countries that were constituent parts of the Soviet Union (Russia, Ukraine, Belarus, Moldova and the Baltic States of Estonia, Latvia and Lithuania) as well as Poland, the Czech Republic, Slovakia, Hungary, Romania, Bulgaria, Albania, Serbia, Croatia, Bosnia, Slovenia and Macedonia. As already noted, ten of these countries became members of the EU in 2004 or 2007. On accession all had GDPs per head below the average of the 'EU of 15'. As members they are committed to enacting legislation implementing the accounting Directives and requiring their listed companies to comply with international financial reporting standards in their consolidated financial statements.

Countries aspiring to join the EU (notably Croatia) are also expected to amend their legislation and even those not so aspiring (notably Russia) are influenced by the EU. Financial reporting and accounting cannot, however, be reformed simply by the adoption of EU laws and practices, which in any case, as we have seen, are themselves by no means fully harmonized.

Enterprises in these emerging market economies, which previously relied on government finance, now need access to non-governmental sources of finance, both debt and equity. Debt, especially bank loans, is likely to be more important than equity (especially given the lack of personal savings where there has been hyperinflation), suggesting accounting rules biased towards creditor protection. On the other hand, it may be necessary for larger companies to have a financial reporting system based on Anglo-Saxon concepts in order to attract investment from overseas. Funds channelled through international agencies may be dependent upon the provision of accounting information in a recognized international format and certified by a recognized international audit firm. Although 'capitalist' accounting (whether of the Anglo-Saxon or continental European variety) is not being *imposed*, it is still, to varying degrees, a foreign implant that will need adaptation to local circumstances. It is too early to state how successful these adaptations are likely to be, especially as changes in regulations may not always be accompanied by changes in practice.

Events since the break-up of the Soviet Union and its loss of control over Central and Eastern Europe have amply demonstrated in many ways that the region is no less diverse politically, economically and culturally than Western Europe. This diversity manifests itself in financial reporting just as it does in other areas. It is neither possible nor profitable to look at every country in detail, especially as the detail of laws and regulations has been, and still is, subject to rapid change. The former German Democratic Republic is a special case. Its business enterprises now have to comply with the accounting rules established by the German Federal Republic (see Chapter 15). The economic stresses of reunification, however, as discussed elsewhere in this book, have led to changes in financial reporting by major German companies (Young, 1999).

The development of financial reporting in Eastern and Central Europe has inevitably been subject to more discontinuities than in countries such as the United Kingdom and the United States, but no country has broken completely with the past, and influences remain both from the pre-communist period and from the communist period.

11.3.2 Pre-communist accounting

Accounting in pre-communist Eastern and Central Europe (which excludes those countries that were part of the Soviet Union between the two World Wars) had, as was the case also in Austria (Nowotny and Gruber, 1995), many similarities with that in Germany. In the absence of sophisticated equity capital markets, there was an emphasis on creditor protection and tax collection, and a preference for national charts of accounts, mainly based on the pioneering work of Schmalenbach in Germany in the 1920s. Schmalenbach's chart was intended for a market economy but could be adapted to a planned economy, as happened in Nazi Germany in the 1930s and Vichy France in the early 1940s (see Chapter 14), and to a command economy, as in the Soviet Union in the 1920s. Many occupied countries in Eastern and Central Europe were forced to adopt the German chart during the Second World War, and then the Soviet chart after the War (Richard, 1995a). Business transactions were regulated by means of Commercial Codes based on the German model, which in its turn was based on the French Napoleonic Code.

In Poland, for example, during the inter-war period, economic development was slow and characterized by governmental intervention. Industrial finance was dominated by the banks, both state-owned and private. Relevant legislation on accounting, audit and companies was consolidated in the Commercial Code of 1934, which was influenced by the German code. The Accountants Association in Poland (AAP) was established in 1907, but its influence on accounting regulation was slight and the accountancy profession was weak and fragmented. There was no national chart of accounts. Such improvements in accounting practice as there were in the 1930s were mainly the result of pressure from the tax authorities. During the German occupation (1939–44) the rules of the uniform German General Plan of Accounts were in force.

11.3.3 Communist accounting in a command economy

For many decades the financial reporting and accounting practices in the communist countries of Central and Eastern Europe were very distinct from, and largely cut off from, those in Western Europe, although accounting in countries such as Hungary and Poland had, even before 1989, become more adaptive and flexible as a result of economic reform and democratization (Bailey, 1988). This distinctiveness was inevitable in the absence of privately owned enterprises and market-determined prices. The main objective of accounting systems under the command economy of traditional communism is the provision of financial statistics (often in terms of quantities rather than values) for use in higher-level budgets. There is very little emphasis on accountability, which is a crucial element in accounting in a market-based economy in which managers are delegated with the control of resources by the shareholders of companies who are granted limited liability in order to encourage investment. There is no concept of 'fair presentation' or 'true and fair view' in a command economy. Financial reporting is thus 'hierarchical' rather than 'lateral', so that reports flow upwards through the administrative structure rather than outwards into the market.

Accounting in a command economy is of relatively low status, is inflexible and does not have to respond to market innovations. For example, the Soviet accounting system used throughout Eastern Europe was largely a matter of clerical bookkeeping and was compulsory for all state enterprises. Soviet-style national charts of accounts were imposed. It was because accounting had become ever more standardized, simplified and routinized that it regressed to bookkeeping. Accounting records were much more important than financial statements.

The nature of accounting in a command economy has important consequences that impede the transition to post-communist accounting. Under communism, a sophisticated accountancy and auditing profession did not develop. The accounting worker tended to be, in the words of Bailey (1988, page 12), 'the personification of the conservative and rule-bound bureaucrat'. In Hungary, for example, accountants were regarded as low-skilled technicians during the communist period. Consequently, the profession lost its reputation, and was not able to attract young people of talent (Borda, 2001, page 1536).

In Poland, during the period of communist rule and a centrally planned economy (1944–89), accounting lessened in importance, comprising essentially a very detailed set of financial rules based on a Soviet-style national chart of accounts, although this chart was modified from time to time. There was no independent accountancy profession and no scope for innovation in accounting practice. Accounting became an instrument of central economic administration exercised through a uniform accounting system mandatory for all enterprises.

11.3.4 Problems of transition to a market economy

In a command economy the means of production are in public ownership, the state dominates the economy, and economic activity is supposed to respond to state direction. By contrast, in a market economy the means of production are mainly in private ownership, the state creates the legal framework in which economic activity takes place, and economic activity is supposed to respond to market forces. After the collapse of communist domination, the countries of Central and Eastern Europe embarked upon the ideological and practical transition from one type of economy to the other. Such a transition obviously has important consequences for accounting, which ceases to be an instrument of state economic administration and becomes instead an instrument at the disposal of the business community (Bailey, 1995).

Progress in making the transition has varied greatly from country to country. Annual macroeconomic assessments are available in the *Transition Reports* of the European Bank for Reconstruction and Development. Summing up success under the six headings of structural reform, control of inflation, privatization, economic growth, limitation of corruption (perhaps the one most related to accounting and auditing) and democracy, Aslund (2002) awarded a full score of six only to Estonia and Hungary. These were the only two with a corruption score less than the worst West European countries on the Transparency International Index.

In the transition from a command to a market economy, there has been a serious shortage of skilled accountants and auditors. The profession has had difficulty in acting as a source of improved practices and regulations, so that this function has had, paradoxically, to be performed by discredited state authorities. Ministries of Finance have acquired a dominant position in post-reform accounting regulation, reflecting not only their roles in state-directed economic planning and as tax assessors and collectors, but also, in many countries, the need to legislate accounting reforms consistent with EU Directives. This dominance of Ministries is also to be found in creditor/tax countries such as France, Germany and Japan (see Chapter 2).

In making the transition, each country has been able to make use not only of its own experience of pre-communist and communist accounting but also of the rules and practices of the outside world, in particular those of the European Union (which many of the countries joined in 2004 or 2007 or aspire to join) and its member states, and of the International Accounting Standards Board. This richness of outside examples (which may have come as a surprise to East European accountants) has not made the transition any easier, given the diversity of practice within the EU (even after the adoption of IFRSs by listed companies in their consolidated financial statements) and the fact that international standards are philosophically of Anglo-Saxon rather than of continental European origin.

Both domestic pre-communist and external non-communist sources have advantages and disadvantages. Pre-communist practices and regulations may have been tailored to the country concerned but are likely to be very outdated. Practices from outside may be much more up to date but may be of unnecessary complexity and sophistication and may be an 'inappropriate technology'.

Not surprisingly, most of the new laws retain some aspects of the old ones, especially given the lack of qualified accountants and the importance of accounting for tax collection. The latter is particularly relevant in those countries that lack capital markets on which the state can raise loans. This means both a relatively great emphasis on accounting record keeping and on charts of accounts and also, as in Germany, an extension of accounting regulation to all types of business enterprises, not just limited liability companies.

In practice, both historical and external sources were drawn upon. There was a widespread re-introduction of pre-Second World War corporate laws and commercial codes. These were originally German-based and are not incompatible with the EU Directives that, as new and aspirant member states, many former Communist countries are introducing into their legislation. However, the influence of the IASC/IASB and the Big-4 international accountancy firms (all of which have expanded vigorously into the region: Kirsch *et al.*, 2000) has brought in more Anglo-Saxon ideas of accounting. This is not necessarily inappropriate since these countries, unlike Germany until recently, do not have the strength of their economies to shield their few large companies from the demands of the international capital market. Furthermore, foreign investors may prefer to base their decisions on non-statutory financial statements reworked by an international firm rather than on statutory statements (Bailey and Alexander, 2001a). Independent corporate audit is a new concept in Eastern Europe and the Big-4 audit firms have successfully sought to obtain the audits of the largest domestic companies. The demand for local accountants trained in Anglo-Saxon accounting skills has been partly met by making the British-based ACCA qualification available to them and by the translation of teaching materials into local languages (Sucher and Zelenka, 1998, pages 730–1; Focus, 2000).

External auditing and auditor independence are not needed in a command economy and cannot, for many reasons, be established quickly in practice in a transition economy even if relevant legislation and regulations are enacted (Sucher and Kosmala-MacLullich, 2004a, 2004b). Chambers of Auditors have been set up but tend to be staffed in the first instance by accountants brought up and trained in the culture and procedures of a command rather than of a market economy. Furthermore, independence may be threatened by competition among auditors for clients, by a legal system that penalizes departures from tax rules rather than provides protection for investors, and by client companies vulnerable to collapse if they receive a qualified audit report. Audit failure has received much publicity in some countries (e.g. the Czech Republic). The Czechs have contributed the word 'tunnelling' to the international accounting vocabulary to describe the transfer (as through an underground tunnel) of assets and profits out of companies for the benefit of the managers who control them (Johnson *et al.*, 2000).

Different ex-communist countries have made different choices, which have been influenced by political as well as technical factors. In Poland, legislation was passed between 1989 and 1991 reorganizing the banking and insurance sectors, starting the process of privatization, and creating a stock exchange in Warsaw. Legislation on bankruptcy dating from the inter-war period was revived. Personal and corporate income tax Acts were passed in 1991 and 1992. The 1934 Commercial Code was revived with the start of privatization. Privatization of state enterprises proceeded slowly, partly because of the rigorous criteria imposed by the Securities Commission that was set up in 1991 (on the model of the US Securities and Exchange Commission) to regulate the stock market. A 'mass privatization' law was passed in 1994, under which some 500 medium-sized companies were allocated to 15 National Investment Funds (NIFs) set up by the state. The NIFs are the main owners of the companies. All adult Polish citizens were entitled to a 'universal' share certificate exchangeable into NIF shares (OECD, 1996, Annex IV). Transfer of ownership also took place by other means, but the residual state sector remains relatively large (OECD, 2000, page 20 and Annex V). The Warsaw Stock Exchange has about 280 domestic listed companies, most of which are audited by international accounting firms.

An Accounting Decree was issued by the Ministry of Finance in January 1991 to cover all enterprises except financial institutions. It was heavily criticized (Jaruga, 1993) both as lacking the prestige of accompanying legislation and as insisting on an unhelpful uniformity and was superseded by the Accounting Act of 1994, which was itself significantly amended in 2000 (Reczek and Lachowski, 2002).

The Act, which takes account of the seventh EU Directive, as well as the fourth, requires the presentation of a 'true and fair view', which means that the accounting rules formally (but not necessarily in practice) override the tax requirements. The true and fair view requirement is perceived in practice as compliance with legal pronouncements on financial reporting, including tax rules (Kosmala-MacLullich, 2003). The concept is treated as a formula to be complied with, without further investigation into its wording and meaning (Kosmala, 2005). In 1995 the Ministry of Finance issued a Decree specifically on consolidations.

An important innovation was the formal divorce between tax and financial reporting, with the concomitant introduction of the concept (but not yet the common practice) of deferred taxation. Deferred taxation liabilities *must* be accrued; deferred taxation assets *may* be accrued. Also important are the emphasis on prudence and the introduction of cash flow statements.

The 1994 Accounting Act does not impose an obligatory uniform chart of accounts but economic entities are required to draw up their own accounting plans. An optional Model Chart of Accounts was developed and published by the Accounting Association in Poland in 1995 (Jaruga and Szychta, 1997).

The shortage of well-tried and experienced staff is a major problem affecting the implementation of both auditing and accounting standards. Nevertheless, few audit failures have been reported (Sucher and Kosmala-MacLullich, 2004b). More information on auditing in Poland is given in Krzywda *et al.* (1998) and in Schroeder (1999).

Measurement rules in Poland have, since the days of the Second Republic, been strongly influenced by the detail of income tax legislation. This link was weakened by the Accounting Act of 1994 but is still important given that Polish accountants lack experience of financial reporting not driven by tax rules (Jaruga *et al.*, 1996). For tax purposes, but not in principle for financial reporting purposes, depreciation rates and methods (including accelerated depreciation to encourage investment), inventory valuation methods, and provisions for bad and doubtful debts are all largely determined by rules laid down by the Ministry of Finance, with little choice available to the individual company.

The Commercial Code requires the creation of a legal reserve by public companies, but contains very few disclosure requirements. This gap has been filled by the Accounting Act, which has adopted the financial statement formats of the EU Fourth Directive. The formats are reproduced in both Polish and English in Jaruga and Schroeder (2001), who also summarize the regulations in the Act relating to the form and content of published financial statements, and asset valuation and income measurement. Some of the reporting traditions of the command economy have persisted, however – for example in the definition in the Act of 'extraordinary items', which includes, for example, bad and doubtful debts and the costs of abandoned projects (Krzywda *et al.*, 1996, page 78).

An Accounting Standards Committee has been established under the Ministry of Finance with a membership representative of academia, large international and domestic auditing firms, the Securities Commission, the NCSA, the AAP, and domestic banks. The Committee aims to prepare national accounting standards for implementation as revisions and amendments to the Accounting Act.

The experience of some of the other ex-communist countries has been similar. Borbély and Evans (2006), for example, report that Hungary enacted the Law on Accounting of 1991 mainly in order to to harmonize Hungarian law with the EU Fourth Directive, although the Law contained more in the way of detailed regulation than did the Directive. The Law followed the traditions of German accounting, including an optional chart of accounts (in practice treated as obligatory), mandatory formats for financial statements, and an emphasis on prudence. The Law was amended several times during the 1990s, as the market economy developed, to implement other EU Directives (particularly the Seventh), and to take account of international accounting standards, but the emphasis in practice remained the minimization of taxation. The 1991 Law was superseded by the Law on Accounting of 2000. Its main objective was harmonization with the EU Directives, but it also showed the influence of IASs. It too has been amended several times. An Association of Hungarian Accountants was created in 1995 and the Chamber of Hungarian Auditors (similar to the WPK in Germany) was formally re-established in 1997. A full set of auditing standards (based on international auditing standards) was adopted in 1999. An Accounting Standards Board has been established. Both regulators and accountants have continued to show a preference for detailed rules.

Accounting change has been slowest in Russia and the other successor states to the Soviet Union. Russia has a large informal ('black') economy, a high degree of corruption, weak law enforcement, little demand for the provision of financial statements to outside investors, and no tradition of external auditing or of auditor independence. In practice the main role of an auditor is to ensure that there are no problems with the tax authorities, who can act at times almost as a political arm of government (Sucher and Bychkova, 2001; Sucher *et al.*, 2005). The transition to Western-style democracy and capitalism has proceeded more slowly and been accompanied by a considerable amount of economic and political chaos. In these circumstances a precipitate rate of accounting change could lead to 'accounting uniformity being displaced by accounting disarray' (Bailey and Alexander, 2001b). In Russia, unconditional adoption of the Anglo-American accounting model 'is not considered to be the best way to reform the national accounting system' (Sokolov *et al.*, 2001). Certain well-established aspects of Russian accounting, both communist and pre-communist, are likely to persist: a strong emphasis on the control function of accounting; adherence to a national chart of accounts; detailed regulations and instructions from central state authorities such as the Ministry of Finance; and a relatively weak accountancy profession (Enthoven *et al.*, 1998).

However, there have been changes as the government seeks to move Russian accounting towards IFRS. Many large listed companies now follow IFRS or US GAAP and new regulations have been enacted which bring Russian accounting rules closer to IFRS (Enthoven *et al.*, 2001; Krylova, 2003a). Although accounting for most enterprises is still in practice dominated by the uniform chart of accounts (significantly revised as from 1 January 2001), the consolidated financial statements of listed companies are required to comply with IFRSs as in the EU (Krylova, 2003a).

Although both Russia and Romania have retained compulsory national charts of accounts, they have reformed them in different ways. Russia adapted the old Soviet model to a market economy but retained a chart originally inherited from Schmalenbach's *Kontenrahmen* based on the processes of production rather than, as in France, on the financial statements. Romania, on the other hand, abandoned the old-style Soviet chart for one based closely on the French model. Richard (1995b) argues that the reasons for these differences are political rather than technical. Romanian accountants, unlike Russian accountants, regard the Soviet chart as a foreign import; some Romanian accountants were interested in strengthening their influence with French help; French accountants wanted to strengthen French economic interests in Romania; and a French-style chart is seen in Russia as moving away rather than towards US practices. Russian law, unlike Romanian law, has not been influenced by the French *droit comptable*. However, a project began in 1996, sponsored by the British Foreign Office, that was designed to help Romanian accounting to evolve in a direction closer to the capital-market style of accounting found in the Anglo-Saxon world. King *et al.* (2001) provide an inside view of how the project proceeded and why IASs were considered appropriate. In 1999 a Ministerial Order was published which enshrined both the IASC's framework and the body of the IASC's standards into Romanian legislation. Roberts (2001) examines this and notes what he considers to be a range of conflicts and confusions caused by mixing a French-based philosophy with IASC content.

One of the biggest stumbling blocks to reforming accounting in transitional economies has been the close link between financial reporting and fiscal reporting. One of the largest changes in Russia has been the amendment of tax legislation and the implementation of Chapter 25 of the Tax Code. This effectively separates financial and tax reporting. Separate accounts have to be kept for tax reporting from those for financial reporting. While this may seem to be a positive development, which will enable Russian financial reporting fully to embrace an approach based on IFRS, there is a concern about what will actually happen on the ground. It is possible that compliance with two sets of rules will be too complex and expensive for most Russian companies. Many companies may comply only with the taxation reporting rules (Krylova, 2003b). This is more likely to be so for private companies, for whom reporting to the taxation authorities and minimizing tax payments is the dominant reason for the preparation of financial statements, than for public companies. The latter have greater incentives to improve the quality of their reported earnings in order to attract outside investors. Goncharov and Zimmermann (2006) provide empirical evidence that, in Russia as elsewhere, compliance with tax rules has a greater effect on financial reporting by private companies than by public companies.

11.3.5 Applying IFRS

In anticipation of joining the EU in 2004 or 2007 most of the Central and Eastern European countries sought to implement accounting legislation that brought them into line with EU Directives and Regulations. After the initial implementation of new accounting legislation from 1989 onwards, they further updated their accounting legislation to bring it more into line with IFRS. Examples are the amendments to the Accounting Act in 2001 and 2003 and related Accounting Decrees in the Czech Republic (Sucher and Alexander, 2002; Sucher and Jindrikovska, 2004) and the Amendment to the Accounting Act 2000 in Poland (Kosmala-MacLullich, 2003; Vellam, 2004). The 2002 Regulation of the European Union on the application of IFRS, requires listed companies to prepare IFRS consolidated financial statements. Use in other financial statements is optional. As in Western Europe, the response to the Regulation in the transitional economies has been varied and complex. As shown in Table 13.3, the Czech Republic requires IFRS in the individual statements of listed companies, but bans them from the individual statements of unlisted companies. By contrast, Poland permits, but does not require, IFRS for the statements of subsidiaries of listed companies, whereas Hungary (similar to France) bans them from all but the consolidated statements of listed companies. The three Baltic states (similar to Cyprus and Malta) require IFRS for all financial statements, perhaps because they are small economies lacking their own well-developed national rules. There are considerable differences between IFRS and national accounting regulations (for Poland see Krzywda and Schroeder, 2007).

Although Russia is not a member of the EU, many large Russian enterprises, mainly in response to the demands of overseas funds providers, prepare financial statements which claim to be based on international standards. In practice these statements are often drawn up by the companies' auditors, and in particular by offices of the Big-4 accountancy firms. Sucher and Alexander (2004) suggest that compliance with international standards is often incomplete and that training in the use of IFRS is badly needed.

Implementation and enforcement of IFRS in transition economies will not be easy. The problems in the Czech Republic are discussed in Sucher and Alexander (2002) and in Sucher and Jindrichovska (2004). The implementation process has been dominated by the Ministry of Finance and the needs of the tax inspectorate. The directors of larger listed Czech companies often rely heavily on international accounting firms to prepare their IFRS financial statements, may themselves have little understanding of them, and in particular find the concept of substance over form alien. Smaller listed Czech companies, owned by local investors and audited by local firms, have more difficulty in moving to IFRS and the benefits of them doing so are less obvious. These findings probably apply to other transitional economies as well (for Poland see Jaruga *et al.*, 2007).

SUMMARY

- The world's most powerful source of change towards regional harmonization has been the EU. Harmonization of accounting is one of the many aims of its Commission as part of the overall objective to remove economic barriers within the EU.

- Harmonization is being achieved through EU Directives and Regulations. The Fourth Directive caused some change in most EU countries in formats of accounts or disclosure or valuation procedures. The Seventh Directive achieved a significant degree of harmonization of group accounting.

- Financial reporting in Central and Eastern Europe has been transformed as a result of political change and economic reforms.

- The former communist countries of Europe are very diverse and their financial reporting rules and practices reflect this. Many have adopted continental European accounting, including charts of accounts and the predominance of tax rules, but Anglo-Saxon accounting has also been influential. Accounting – and the accountancy profession – is gaining in status and influence compared with the period of communist rule.

- Ten Central and Eastern European countries joined the EU in 2004 and 2007 and the consolidated financial statements of their listed companies have to comply with IFRS. Although Russia is not a member of the EU, its listed companies are also being required to follow IFRS. In some countries, companies may be required or permitted to apply IFRS to other financial statements as well. It is uncertain how much compliance there will be in the short term.

References

Aisbitt, S. and Nobes, C.W. (2001) 'The true and fair view requirement in recent national implementations', *Accounting and Business Research*, Spring.

Alexander, D. (1993) 'A European true and fair view?', *European Accounting Review*, Vol. 2, No. 1.

Alexander, D. and Archer, S. (2001) *European Accounting Guide*, Aspen, New York.

Aslund, A. (2002) *Building Capitalism. The Transformation of the Former Soviet Bloc*, Cambridge, Cambridge University Press.

Bailey, D. (ed.) (1988) *Accounting in Socialist Countries*, London, Routledge.

Bailey, D. (1995) 'Accounting in transition in the transitional economy', *European Accounting Review*, Vol. 4, No. 4.

Bailey, D. and Alexander, D. (2001a) 'Eastern Europe: overview', in Alexander and Archer (2001), pp. 1456–63.

Bailey, D. and Alexander, D. (2001b) 'Commonwealth of independent states (CIS): overview', in Alexander and Archer (2001), pp. 1628–9.

Borbély, K. and Evans, L. (2006) 'A matter of principle: recent developments in Hungarian accounting thought and regulation', *Accounting in Europe*, Vol. 3.

Borda, M. (2001) 'Hungary', in Alexander and Archer (2001), pp. 1528–95.

Day, J. and Taylor, P. (2005) 'Accession to the European Union and the process of accounting and audit reform', *Accounting in Europe*, Vol. 2.

Diggle, G. and Nobes, C.W. (1994) 'European rule-making in accounting: the Seventh Directive as a case study', *Accounting and Business Research*, Autumn.

EC Commission (1978) *Fourth Directive on Company Law*, reprinted in *Trade and Industry*, 11 August 1978.

Enthoven, A.J.H., Sokolov, Y.V., Kovalev, V.V., Bychkova, S.M. and Semenova, M.V. (1998) *Accounting, Auditing and Taxation in the Russian Federation*, Center for International Accounting Development, Dallas, TX.

Enthoven, A.J.H., Sokolov, Y.V., Kovalev, V.V., Bychkova, S.M., Smirnova, I.M. and Semenova, M.V. (2001) *Accounting, Auditing and Taxation in the Russian Federation [An Update] 2001 Study*, Center for International Accounting Development, The University of Texas at Dallas; St. Petersburg State University, St. Petersburg; and East-West Management Institute, New York/Moscow.

European Bank for Reconstruction and Development (EBRD), *Transition Reports* (annual), London.

Evans, L. and Nobes, C. (1998a) 'Harmonization of the structure of audit firms: incorporation in the UK and Germany', *European Accounting Review*, Vol. 7, No. 1.

Evans, L. and Nobes, C. (1998b) 'Harmonization relating to auditor independence: the Eighth Directive, the UK and Germany', *European Accounting Review*, Vol. 7, No. 3.

Focus (2000) 'Focus on Central and Eastern Europe', ACCA *Students' Newsletter*, April.

Goncharov, I. and Zimmermann, J. (2006) 'Earnings management when incentives compete: the role of tax accounting in Russia', *Journal of International Accounting Research*, Vol. 5, No. 1.

Gornik-Tomaszewski, S. (2005) 'Antecedents and expected outcomes of the new accounting regulation in the European Union', *Research in Accounting Regulation*, Vol. 18.

Jaruga, A. (1993) 'Changing rules of accounting in Poland', *European Accounting Review*, May.

Jaruga, A. and Schroeder, M. (2001) 'Poland', in Alexander and Archer (2001), pp. 1596–625.

Jaruga, A. and Szychta, A. (1997) 'The origin and evolution of charts of accounts in Poland', *European Accounting Review*, Vol. 6, No. 3.

Jaruga, A., Walinska, E. and Baniewicz, A. (1996) 'The relationship between accounting and taxation in Poland', *European Accounting Review*, Vol. 5, supplement.

Jaruga, A., Fijalkowska, J. and Jaruga-Baranowska, M. (2007) 'The impact of IAS/IFRS on Polish accounting regulations and their practical implementation in Poland', *Accounting in Europe*, Vol. 4.

Johnson, S., La Porta, R., Lopez-de-Silanes, F. and Sheifer, A. (2000), 'Tunneling', *American Economic Review*, Vol. 90, No. 2, May.

King, N., Beattie, A., Cristescu, A.-M. and Weetman, P. (2001) 'Developing accounting and audit in a transition economy', *European Accounting Review*, Vol. 10, No. 1.

Kirsch, R.J., Laird, K.R. and Evans, T.G. (2000) 'The entry of international CPA firms into emerging markets: motivational factors and growth strategies', *International Journal of Accounting*, Vol. 35, No. 1.

Kosmala, K. (2005) 'True and fair view or *rzetelny i jasny obraz*? A survey of Polish practitioners', *European Accounting Review*, Vol. 14, No. 3.

Kosmala-MacLullich, K. (2003) 'The true and fair view construct in the context of the Polish transition economy: some local insights', *European Accounting Review*, Vol. 12, No. 3.

Krylova, T. (2003a) 'Accounting in the Russian Federation', in P. Walton, A. Haller, and B. Raffournier, *International Accounting*, Thomson Learning, London.

Krylova, T. (2003b) book review of Enthoven *et al.* (2001), in *International Journal of Accounting*, Vol. 38, No. 3.

Krzywda, D., Bailey, D. and Schroeder, M. (1998) 'The development of the role of the statutory audit in the transitional Polish economy', *European Accounting Review*, Vol. 7, No. 3.

Krzywda, D. and Schroeder, M. (2007) 'An analysis of the differences between IFRS and Polish accounting regulations: evidence from the financial statements of listed entities on the Warsaw Stock Exchange for the calendar years ending 2001, 2003 and 2004', *Accounting in Europe*, Vol. 4.

McGee, A. and Wetherill, S. (1989) *European Economic Interest Groupings*, Certified Bulletin No. 25, Chartered Association of Certified Accountants.

Nobes, C.W. (1983) 'The origins of the harmonising provisions of the 1980 and 1981 Companies Acts', *Accounting and Business Research*, Winter.

Nobes, C.W. (1993) 'The true and fair view requirement: impact on and of the Fourth Directive', *Accounting and Business Research*, Winter.

Nowotny, C. and Gruber, E. (1995) 'The history of financial reporting in Austria', in P. Walton, *European Financial Reporting. A History*, Academic Press, London.

Ordelheide, D. (1993) 'The true and fair view – a European and German perspective', *European Accounting Review*, Vol. 2, No. 1.

Organisation for Economic Co-operation and Development (OECD) (1996) *Economic Survey: Poland 1996–1997*, Paris.

Organisation for Economic Co-operation and Development (OECD) (2000) *Economic Survey: Poland 1999–2000*, Paris.

Parker, R.H. (1996) 'Harmonizing the notes in the UK and France: a case study in *de jure* harmonization', *European Accounting Review*, Vol. 5, No. 2.

Reczek, A. and Lachowski, W. (2002) 'Ties that don't bind', *Accountancy*, January, pp. 102–4.

Richard, J. (1995a) 'The evolution of accounting chart models in Europe from 1900 to 1945: Some historical elements', *European Accounting Review*, Vol. 4, No. 1.

Richard, J. (1995b) 'The evolution of the Romanian and Russian accounting charts after the collapse of the communist system', *European Accounting Review*, Vol. 4, No. 2.

Roberts, A.D. (2001) 'The recent Romanian accounting reforms: another case of cultural intrusion?' in Yelena Kalyuzhnova and Michael Taylor (eds), *Transitional Economies: Banking Finance Institutions*, Palgrave, London, pp. 146–7.

Schroeder, M. (1999) 'A description of the contents of the long-form statutory audit reports of a sample of Polish listed companies for 1996', *European Accounting Review*, Vol. 8, No. 1, pp. 1–23.

Sokolov, Y.V., Kovalev, V.V., Bychkova, S.M. and Smirnova, I.A. (2001) 'Russian Federation', in Alexander and Archer (2001), pp. 1642–84.

Sucher, P. and Alexander, D. (2002) *IAS: Issues of Country, Sector and Audit Firm Compliance in Emerging Countries*, Centre for Business Performance, Institute of Chartered Accountants in England and Wales, London.

Sucher, P. and Alexander, D. (2004) 'The preparation of IAS financial statements: A case study in a transitional economy', *Research in Accounting in Emerging Economies*, Supplement 2.

Sucher, P. and Bychkova, S. (2001) 'Auditor independence in economies in transition', *European Accounting Review*, Vol. 10, No. 4.

Sucher, P. and Jindrichovska, I. (2004) 'Implementing IFRS: A case study of the Czech Republic', *Accounting in Europe*, Vol. 1, September, pp. 109–41.

Sucher, P., Kosmala, K., Bychkova, S. and Jindrichovska, I. (2005) 'Introduction: Transitional economies and changing notions of accounting and accountability', *European Accounting Review*, Vol. 14, No. 3.

Sucher, P. and Kosmala-MacLullich, K. (2004a) *A Comparative Analysis of Auditor Independence in Economies in Transition*, Institute of Chartered Accountants of Scotland, Edinburgh.

Sucher, P. and Kosmala-MacLullich, K. (2004b) 'A construction of auditor independence in the Czech Republic: local insights', *Accounting, Auditing & Accountability Journal*, Vol. 7(4), pp. 276–305.

Sucher, P. and Zelenka, I. (1998) 'The development of the role of the audit in the Czech Republic', *European Accounting Review*, Vol. 7, No. 4.

Taylor, S. (2000) 'Standard bearer', *Accountancy*, August, pp. 114–16.

Vellam, I. (2004) 'Implementation of international accounting standards in Poland: Can true convergence be achieved in Poland?' *Accounting in Europe*, Vol. 1, September, pp. 143–67.

Walton, P. (1992) 'Harmonization of accounting in France and Britain: some evidence', *Abacus*, Vol. 28, No. 2.

Young, S.D. (1999) 'From plan to market: financial statements and economic transition in the East German enterprise', *European Accounting Review*, Vol. 8, No. 1.

Useful websites

European Accounting Association	www.eaa-online.org
European Commission, Internal Market	ec.europa.eu.int/internal_market
Fédération des Experts Comptables Européens (FEE)	www.fee.be
IAS Plus	www.iasplus.com
Organisation for Economic Co-operation and Development	www.oecd.org
Warsaw Stock Exchange	www.gpw.com.pl
World Bank, Reports on the Observance of Standards & Codes. Accounting & Auditing	www.worldbank.org/ifa/rosc_aa.html

QUESTIONS

Suggested answers to the asterisked questions are given at the end of the book.

11.1* Is it both *desirable* and *possible* to harmonize company financial reporting in the European Union?

11.2* In what ways have pre-communist and communist accounting affected post-communist accounting in Central and Eastern Europe?

11.3 What effect, if any, has harmonization in the EU had on *non-member* states in Europe?

11.4 Discuss the choice of national charts of accounts in post-communist Russia and Romania.

11.5 Compare the importance of the influences of Anglo-Saxon accounting and continental European accounting in Eastern Europe during the 1990s.

11.6 Why is auditor independence a problem in Central and Eastern Europe?

11.7 Why, and to what extent, has post-communist Romania adopted Anglo-Saxon rather than French-style corporate financial reporting?

11.8 Which was more successful at harmonization until 2001: the IASC or the European Union?

12 Harmonization and transition in East Asia

Christopher Nobes[1]

OBJECTIVES

After reading this chapter, you should be able to:

- outline the major foreign influences that have affected Japan and the resulting unusual features of its accounting system;

- explain the various layers of governmental requirements and the difference between Commercial Code statements and Securities Law statements;

- illustrate the main differences between Japanese practices and those used elsewhere;

- comment on the degree of international harmonization achieved and expected in Japan;

- summarize the development of accounting in China from the late 1980s;

- explain how China has fused old and new ideas in accounting;

- outline the remaining differences between Chinese practice and international standards.

---

[1] Section 12.2 is a revised version of that originally written for the second edition by Leslie Campbell.

12.1 Introduction

The last chapter concerned accounting in Europe, which includes four of the 'G7' of the world's richest nations (Germany, the UK, France and Italy). This present chapter looks at accounting in the two largest economies of the East: Japan and China. Japan has the world's second largest economy. China, at the time of writing, has recently become the fourth largest and may eventually be the largest.

Despite several unique features of Japan, its accounting has been heavily influenced from outside for more than a century, first from Europe and then from the United States. In the new millennium, the IASB has become a key factor in the development of Japanese accounting. These issues are examined in Section 12.2.

China has substituted one European-invented economic system (communism) for another (stock-market-based capitalism). This has brought dramatic changes in the purposes and operations of accounting. Again, the IASB has been of considerable importance. This is examined in Section 12.3.

The coverage of Japan is greater than that for China for two reasons. First, the importance of Japanese listed companies is currently much larger than that of Chinese ones. Secondly, Japan's accounting system has developed continuously from the late nineteenth century, although with a major change from the late 1940s, whereas China's present system is largely a product of the 1990s onwards. However, China's accounting will no doubt grow in international importance.

12.2 Japan

12.2.1 Context of accounting

This section examines the development of Japanese accounting since the introduction of Commercial Codes in the late nineteenth century. We particularly comment on the changes over the last decade, as an illustration of harmonization in accounting. In this sub-section we look at the context of accounting. Later sub-sections examine the regulatory framework, then accounting practices and differences from IFRS.

The industrialization of Japan began in earnest in 1868 after the Meiji Restoration. The government was responsible for encouraging and enabling the growth of industry. At least until the Second World War, the Japanese economy was controlled by a small number of *Zaibatsu*, industrial–political consortia usually involving a bank and originally based on noble families. The importance of banks and the existence of several closed aspects of business control still continue, although informal groupings called *Keiretsu* have replaced *Zaibatsu*.

After the Second World War, Japan developed into one of the world's economic superpowers. By the end of 1989, the market capitalization of the Tokyo Stock Exchange was greater than that in New York, though it then fell dramatically. The Nikkei index fell from a peak of 38,916 at the end of 1989 to well below a third of that in 2005. At the end of 1994, the market capitalization in Tokyo was still over three times the size of London's (*The Economist*, 1996, page 56), although by 2007 they were much nearer (see Table 1.5). For 1994/5, the common feature of the world's six largest banks was that they were all Japanese (*The Economist*, 1996, page 54); however, by the end of 1998, none of the top six were Japanese (*Financial Times*, 1999), due partly to the fall in the yen and partly to the fall in the Japanese stock market.

The massive fall in share prices and asset prices during the 1990s led to the need for bank reorganizations and rescues. It also led to an increased openness to change and outside influence in accounting.

The state has had the most significant influence on accounting in Japan (Arai and Shiratori, 1991). However, this comes from three separate sources: the Commercial Code (deriving from continental European influence); the Securities and Exchange Law (deriving from US influence); and tax law. These are examined in Section 12.2.3 below. There is little overall coordination of these sources and they sometimes have conflicting approaches to financial reporting issues.

Listed companies in Japan are subject to the requirements of the Securities and Exchange Law. The Tokyo Stock Exchange also has its own listing requirements. Although the stock exchanges are now very large (see Table 1.5), Japanese companies have normally relied heavily on debt rather than equity as their principal source of finance, and banks have been the main providers of this (Cooke and Kikuya, 1992, page 46). Short-term debt finance in Japan commonly consists of fixed interest ninety-day promissory notes. Longer-term financing may consist of an informal agreement to roll over these short-term notes for a number of years. Short-term debt often finances a substantial proportion of a Japanese company's fixed assets. In many cases, banks own a significant proportion of a client's shares, and may even be the largest shareholder. In general, shares in Japanese companies are held on a long-term basis. The heavy involvement of the banks and the long-term nature of share ownership means that there is less focus on short-term earnings information in Japan than in the United Kingdom or the United States. The banks have direct access to their clients' accounting information, and so have relatively little interest in external financial reporting. Also, there are often reciprocal shareholding arrangements between companies. These shareholders, as well as banks, may tend to have private accounting information and to vote with the company's management at annual meetings.

The Japanese accounting profession has had relatively little influence on financial reporting, because of the importance of the above governmental sources of authority. The Japanese Institute of Certified Public Accountants (JICPA) was a founder member of the International Accounting Standards Committee (IASC), but the latter had little effect on Japanese financial reporting until the late 1990s. The primary reason for this is that the IASC originally sought to implement its standards through the efforts of the national professional accounting bodies. More obvious long-term international influences on Japanese financial reporting are that of the US on the Securities and Exchange Law and that of Germany on the original Commercial Code. The US influence narrowed the space for the influence of the IASC/B. Nevertheless, from 1993 to 1995 there was a Japanese chairman of the IASC and this coincided with increased international influence in Japan. In 2001, a private-sector standard-setter was established (see Section 12.2.4) partly in order to liaise with the new International Accounting Standards Board.

12.2.2 Forms of business organization

The most common form of business organization in Japan is the *kabushiki kaisha* (KK). This is similar in many respects to the public limited company in the United Kingdom, although an even closer analogy is the German *Aktiengesellschaft* (AG) (see Chapter 14). There are approximately one million *kabushiki kaisha* in Japan. They must have a minimum issued capital of ¥10 million. Only about 2,600 of these have their stock traded publicly, and only 2,400 or so are listed on the Tokyo Stock Exchange. Consequently, although all companies whose shares are publicly traded are *kabushiki kaisha*, by far the majority have few shareholders and are relatively small.

The next most common form of business organization in Japan is the *yugen kaisha*. The nearest equivalent in the United Kingdom would be the private limited company, although the German GmbH is closer. The shareholders of a *yugen kaisha* have limited liability in the same way as the shareholders of a *kabushiki kaisha*. The main differences between a *yugen kaisha* and a *kabushiki kaisha* are restrictions on shareholders. A *yugen kaisha* cannot have more than 50 shareholders, whereas there is no upper limit on the number of shareholders of a *kabushiki kaisha*. A shareholder in a *yugen kaisha* may dispose of the shares only if the other shareholders give their consent. There is no such restriction for a shareholder in a *kabushiki kaisha*, although the articles of incorporation may require that shares be disposed of only with the approval of the directors.

There are two main types of partnership in Japan: a *gomei kaisha* is a general or unlimited partnership; a *goshi kaisha* is a combined limited and unlimited partnership, consisting of one or more limited partners and one or more unlimited partners.

12.2.3 Regulatory framework

The first source of regulation is the Commercial Code. This is administered by the Ministry of Justice and applies to all *kabushiki kaisha*. It has its roots in the German Commercial Code of the nineteenth century, which was first adapted by the Japanese in 1890. However, the German influence has diminished over time as amendments have been made.

In general, the staff in the Ministry of Justice have a legal background rather than an accounting background. Consequently, the administration of the Commercial Code is influenced, as in Germany, by the belief that the protection of creditors is at least as important as the protection of shareholders. This may explain why the specific accounting rules of the Commercial Code place greater emphasis on prudent asset valuation than on income measurement. Independent professional audit is required for companies with share capital over ¥500 million or total liabilities over ¥20 billion.

The second source of regulation is the Securities and Exchange Law. This was administered by the Ministry of Finance until 2000 and now by the Financial Services Agency (FSA), and it applies only to those *kabushiki kaisha* that are publicly traded. The Securities and Exchange Law was enacted shortly after the Second World War, when General MacArthur was responsible for the Allied administration of Japan (Chiba, 2001). The MacArthur regime took the US system of accounting regulation as the model for the revised Japanese system. The main US influences on the Japanese Securities and Exchange Law were the Securities Act of 1933 and the Securities and Exchange Act of 1934. Consequently, the functions and powers of the Ministry of Finance and now the FSA in relation to financial reporting are similar in many respects to those of the US Securities and Exchange Commission. An SEC was established by the US occupying administration in 1947 but dismantled when the Americans left in 1952.

The accounting measurement requirements and particularly the disclosure and filing requirements of Japan's Securities and Exchange Law are more extensive and specific than those of the Commercial Code (see Cooke, 1993a, for a comparison). A company must file its financial statements with the FSA and with any stock exchange on which it is listed. The financial statements (see Section 12.2.5) are available for public inspection at the Ministry and at the relevant exchanges. All companies subject to the Securities and Exchange Law must be audited.

The FSA is in charge of a reference document known as *Business Accounting Principles*, which was first issued in 1949 and is amended about once a decade. All companies that report under the Securities and Exchange Law must comply with these Principles. The financial reporting requirements of the FSA tend to place greater emphasis on income measurement and shareholder protection than on asset valuation and creditor protection, in contrast to the Code of the Ministry of Justice referred to above.

The FSA had an advisory body, called the Business Accounting Deliberation Council (BADC), whose members come from a variety of backgrounds, such as industry, the accountancy profession, government and the universities. Until the formation of the Accounting Standards Board in 2001 (see below), the BADC also published 'opinions' and 'standards' on particular issues. The BADC has been replaced by the Business Accounting Council, which is still concerned with auditing guidelines.

A kabushiki kaisha that is publicly traded is subject to both the sources of government influence described above. Consequently, it must prepare two sets of financial statements: one for the shareholders, in accordance with the requirements of the Commercial Code; and one for filing, in accordance with the requirements of the Securities and Exchange Law. Net income will be the same in the two sets of financial statements. The principal difference is the greater amount of disclosure required under the Securities and Exchange Law. Another significant difference is that there is no requirement in the Commercial Code to prepare group accounts. The Code requires KK companies to publish a condensed version of their financial statements in newspapers or an official gazette. Companies below the size criteria mentioned earlier need only publish a condensed balance sheet.

The third source of regulation arises from the tax laws and rules. These have a significant impact on financial reporting, because, as in many continental European countries, certain deductions for expenses and deferrals of income are only permitted for tax purposes if they are reflected in the company's statutory accounts as prepared under the Commercial Code. Examples of these deductions and deferrals are depreciation, allowances for bad debts, accrued employee severance indemnities, and profit from instalment sales. The general point is that the Commercial Code, Securities and Exchange Law and Business Accounting Principles are all rather vague in some areas, so tax law is often looked to for detailed rules. For example, the Commercial Code requires current assets to be valued at cost unless there is a 'substantially lower' market value. This tends to lead to use of the tax rule's meaning of a decline of 50 per cent or more (Sawa, 2003, page 179).

Companies often choose an accounting practice that maximizes the tax benefit, rather than one that more accurately reflects the underlying economic reality. Another influence that the tax laws have is that some non-deductible items, such as directors' bonuses, are charged by companies against retained earnings rather than against income.

So there are three distinct government influences on financial reporting. The influence of the FSA has increased relative to that of the Ministry of Justice. Because of the fundamental difference in the attitude of the two authorities, this change in relative influence has resulted in a move away from a 'legal' approach to a more 'economic' approach to financial reporting requirements.

12.2.4 The accountancy profession and accounting standards

The Japanese accounting profession has had relatively little influence on financial reporting compared with the government, and has far less influence than Anglo-Saxon professions have (Sakagami et al., 1999). The Japanese Institute of Certified Public Accountants (JICPA) was established by the Certified Public Accountants Law of 1948 (although there was a predecessor body established by a law of 1927). It has approximately 17,000 members. The JICPA is thus of quite recent origin and is very small compared to the Anglo-Saxon professional bodies.

Until 2001 (see below) the JICPA issued recommendations on accounting matters. A company that reports to the FSA under the Securities and Exchange Law must comply with the pronouncements because non-compliance would be considered a departure from acceptable accounting practice. If the departure were material, the FSA would require the company to amend its financial statements. However, although the JICPA pronouncements are supported by this strong sanction from the FSA, they tend to deal with relatively minor matters.

Very few members of the JICPA hold senior financial positions in industry or commerce. Consequently, the Japanese accounting profession has little influence on the preparers of financial information. This is in contrast to the United Kingdom, for example, where most of the financial directors of large companies are members of the accounting profession. As in Germany, there is a separate (and larger) profession of tax experts. As mentioned earlier, the BADC included representatives of the accounting profession. So these individual members of the JICPA could influence financial reporting by influencing the form and content of the Business Accounting Principles.

In 2001, a private-sector standard-setting authority (the Financial Accounting Standards Foundation) was set up, partly so that there would be a clear body to liaise with the new IASB. The Foundation was established by 10 private-sector organizations, including the JICPA. The objective was to transfer rule-making in accounting from the public sector (e.g. the BADC) to the private sector. Along the lines of the arrangements for standard-setting in the US, the UK and the IASB, the Japanese organization has a supervisory Board of Governors and an Accounting Standards Board (ASBJ) of 13 members (three full-time). One of the main tasks of the new Board is to assist in the convergence of Japanese practice towards international practice.

Table 12.1 Standards of the ASB Japan (early 2008)

Statement	
1	Treasury shares and appropriation of legal reserves
2	Earnings per share
3	Amendment to standard on retirement benefits
4	Directors' bonuses
5	Presentation of net assets
6	Statement of changes in net assets
7	Business divestitures
8	Share-based payments
9	Measurement of inventories
10	Financial instruments
11	Related party disclosures
12	Quarterly financial reporting
13	Lease transactions
14	Amendment to standard on retirement benefits
15	Construction contracts

Source: Prepared by the author with assistance from Tatsumi Yamada of the IASB.

By the January 2008, the ASBJ had issued 15 'Statements' and several guidance documents, which are shown in Table 12.1. Some of these (e.g. No. 8 on share-based payments and No. 11 on related party disclosures) are largely in line with IFRS. Others deal with specifically Japanese issues (e.g. No. 6 on the statement of changes in net assets). The Japanese differences from IFRS are examined in Section 12.2.9.

12.2.5 Contents of annual reports

Commercial Code requirements

The specific regulations that govern the form and content of the financial statements required under the Commercial Code are contained in the 'Regulations Concerning the Balance Sheet, Income Statement, Business Report and Supporting Schedules of Joint Stock Corporations'. The Ministry of Justice first issued these in 1963 and has subsequently amended them from time to time, including a major revision in 1982.

The financial statements prepared under the Commercial Code must include a balance sheet, an income statement and a statement of proposed appropriation of earnings. In terms of the formats discussed in Chapter 2, the Japanese balance sheet is two-sided, starting with liquid assets; and the income statement is vertical, by function. A company must also present various supplementary schedules to the shareholders' meeting, including details of changes to share capital and reserves, acquisitions and disposals of fixed assets, and transactions with directors and shareholders. The JICPA has published a specimen set of financial statements that conform to the disclosure requirements of the regulations under the Commercial Code (JICPA, 1991).

The JICPA publication mentions some key differences between the form and content of financial statements prepared under the Commercial Code and the form and content of US financial statements. These are:

1 The amount of trade notes (i.e. commercial bills) receivable is nearly always greater than the amount of trade accounts receivable in a Japanese balance sheet. Similarly, the amount of trade notes payable is nearly always greater than trade accounts payable. Japanese companies normally issue non-interest-bearing notes for accounts receivable and payable. The notes normally have terms of 90 days or 120 days.

2 Trade accounts payable in Japan include only amounts owed to suppliers of goods and materials. Amounts owed for services are included under other accounts payable or under accrued expenses.

3 The directors may make a proposal to increase or decrease the amount of the general purpose appropriation account in the retained earnings subsection. This increase or decrease would be either from or to the unappropriated retained earnings account. The proposal of the directors is subject to approval at the shareholders' annual meeting. The amount that the directors propose to leave in the unappropriated retained earnings account often represents the extent of the dividend that the directors intend to distribute in the near future.

4 The special gain or loss section of the income statement includes any credits to income that result from the reversal of a provision for a liability that the company originally set up for some specific purpose, but that the company no longer considers is necessary.

5 The special gain or loss section includes any prior-year adjustments before arriving at the profit or loss for the year. In the United States, however, companies make prior-year adjustments against the opening balance of reserves.

6 The special gain or loss section includes unusual gains or losses that arise when the company writes off deferred assets when there is no longer an expected future benefit, and other losses that arise from events or transactions that are not normal. Consequently, unusual gains or losses in Japan are not governed by the two criteria of expected non-recurrence and of unusual nature.

7 Companies in Japan are subject to three different taxes, generally all based on income: corporation tax, business enterprise tax and inhabitants tax. Companies do not report the business enterprise tax as part of income taxes, but include it in the amount of selling, general and administrative expenses.

Securities and Exchange Law requirements

The specific regulations that govern the form and content of the financial statements required under the Securities and Exchange Law are contained in the 'Regulations Concerning the Terminology, Forms and Preparation Methods of Financial Statements', issued by the Ministry of Finance in 1963. The financial statements prepared under the Securities and Exchange Law must include a balance sheet, an income statement, a statement of proposed appropriation of earnings, certain supplementary schedules and certain additional unaudited information. The supplementary schedules include details of share capital and reserves, long-term debt, fixed assets and intra-group transactions. The additional unaudited information includes details of the company's organizational structure, employees, production and cash flows.

Items such as profit and loss for the year and shareholders' equity will be the same in the financial statements that a company prepares under the Securities and Exchange Law as in those prepared under the Commercial Code. However, the regulations of the former are the more detailed on terminology, form and content of the financial statements, and will normally require a company to disclose additional details of certain items, or to reclassify certain items disclosed in the Commercial Code financial statements.

The JICPA (1991) publication mentions some of these additional requirements of the Securities and Exchange Law, including:

● Listing of assets and liabilities in decreasing order of liquidity.

● Disclosure of transactions and balances with related parties separately from other transactions and balances.

● Use of a materiality standard of 1 per cent for balance sheet accounts: for example, separate disclosure of a particular class of inventory, such as raw materials, if it exceeds 1 per cent of total assets. The materiality standards for the profit and loss account are 10 per cent and 20 per cent, depending on circumstances. For example, a company must disclose separately sales to related parties if they exceed 20 per cent of total sales. Another example is that a company must disclose separately losses from the sale of marketable securities if they exceed 10 per cent of total non-operating expenses.

● Disclosure of additional notes to the financial statements; for example, a detailed description of any material change in an accounting policy, including reasons for the change.

● Disclosure of the separate components of selling, general and administrative expenses.

Convenience translations

A foreign user of Japanese financial statements generally faces one immediate and important difficulty: the language barrier. It is obvious that, with Japanese financial statements, there are not only different *words* from English but also a different *script*. Consequently, few Western users can even guess at the key elements of a set of Japanese statements. The language barrier may be overcome in several different ways. A Western firm of stockbrokers may employ Japanese nationals to translate and comment on Japanese financial statements, and individual shareholders may benefit from this; or a user interested in the financial statements of a particular Japanese company may employ a firm or individual who specializes in translating Japanese material.

Some large Japanese multinational companies prepare English-language versions of their annual reports. For example, a Japanese company that is listed on the New York Stock Exchange must comply with the relevant requirements of the Securities and Exchange Commission (SEC). These require either a set of English-language financial statements in accordance with US generally accepted accounting principles

(GAAP) or a reconciliation from Japanese to US GAAP. Although US GAAP financial statements may be helpful to a user, the conversion means that such financial statements are not a reliable source of information about financial reporting in Japan. Nevertheless, Japanese companies are one of the largest groups of foreign SEC registrants (Godwin *et al.*, 1998), particularly of those that provide US GAAP statements rather than reconciling to US GAAP.

A Japanese company that is not listed on a foreign stock exchange may still prepare English-language financial statements. These are sometimes described as 'convenience translations'. A company may prepare a convenience translation as part of a public relations and marketing exercise. It usually includes the relevant amounts in yen, and translates the yen amounts into US dollars using the appropriate year-end exchange rate. The report normally emphasizes that the company has translated the yen amounts into dollars solely for the convenience of the reader, which does not imply that they actually have been, or could be, translated into dollars. A convenience translation normally uses income measurement principles and asset valuation principles that are in accordance with Japanese GAAP. However, a convenience translation may include additional disclosure items that are not required by Japanese GAAP, and may reclassify some financial statement items into a form that is more familiar to non-Japanese readers (Nobes and Maeda, 1990). Such reclassifications normally do not affect the values of total assets, of shareholders' funds or of the profit for the year. Convenience translations provide a useful insight into some aspects of financial reporting in Japan. However, the additional disclosures and the reclassifications referred to above mean that they also do not provide a completely accurate picture of financial reporting in Japan.

12.2.6 Accounting principles

Tangible assets and depreciation

The balance sheet of a Japanese company must show fixed assets at cost (less aggregate depreciation). The regulations do not allow revaluation with the exception of land (see below). This conservative approach is in line with German and US practice, but in contrast to permission to revalue in several IASB standards. However, in 1998 a new law (amended in 1999) allowed large companies (see Section 12.2.3) to revalue land up to March 2001. Any resulting revaluation reserve is not taxed as a gain and therefore gives rise to a deferred tax liability.

The most common depreciation method in Japan is the reducing-balance method. A survey of Japanese financial reporting (Gray *et al.*, 1984) found that 47 of the 50 companies in the survey used the reducing-balance method of depreciation (see, also, Cooke and Kikuya, 1992, page 223). Companies generally use the depreciation rates that are prescribed in the tax laws.

The capitalization of finance leases is required practice under IFRS or US rules, but capitalization of leases was rare in Japan, as would be expected for a country that concentrates on the tax rules and the legal form rather than commercial substance. However, in 1993 the BADC issued a guideline requiring 'ownership transfer' leases to be capitalized and other finance leases either to be capitalized or to be disclosed by provision of substantially the same information. This remains the position.

Intangible assets

Until fairly recently, the Commercial Code and the Business Accounting Principles generally permitted a company to defer both research and development expenditure. However, the BADC required R&D to be expensed from April 2000 onwards. Under IASB rules, capitalization is compulsory when certain criteria are met; and in the United States, companies are not permitted to defer most development expenditure. Ballon *et al.* (1976) suggested that some Japanese companies adopted a flexible deferral policy and smoothed their profits by deferring development expenditure in a bad year and writing it off in a good year. However, later surveys of Japanese financial reporting (Gray *et al.*, 1984; Cooke and Kikuya, 1992, page 224) found that 80 per cent of the companies wrote off development expenditure immediately, as incurred.

Other intangibles such as preliminary expenses and costs of issue of securities may be capitalized in Japan, but not under IFRS or in the United States. Non-consolidation purchased goodwill (*Noren*) is capitalizable, and then amortized over five years on a straight-line basis. This is tax deductible (Nobes and Norton, 1996).

Investments

Until 2000/1, financial assets were generally valued at cost or at a lower value after a major loss. Consequently, gains could be postponed for years until sale, and most falls in value were ignored. However, from 31 March 2001 balance sheets onwards, marketable financial assets are treated approximately as under US or IASB rules. That is, in summary:

- In an investor's unconsolidated statements, investments in subsidiaries, joint ventures and associates are held at cost.
- Bonds held to maturity are valued at amortized cost.
- Marketable trading securities are valued at fair value with gains and losses going to income (whether realized or not).
- Other investments are valued at fair value with gains and losses going to equity.

Inventories

Until recently, companies generally measured their inventories at cost (Cooke and Kikuya, 1992, Table 12.3). However, the Commercial Code and the Business Accounting Principles did not allow a company in Japan to measure inventories at cost where there has been a significant and irrecoverable decline in their market value. As noted earlier for current assets in general, a loss is only tax deductible if it relates to a fall of 50 per cent or more below historical cost; therefore, losses of less than this tend not to be accounted for. ASBJ Statement No. 9 (of 2006) requires the use of the lower of cost and market, where market generally means net realizable value (NRV).

In the United States, companies use replacement cost where it is lower than cost and net realizable value. Under IAS 2, the lower of cost and net realizable value must be used. The Statement allows companies to retain the lower value even when the market subsequently rises (as in the US) or to use the lower of cost and *current* NRV (as in IFRS).

Where a company cannot specifically identify the actual cost of an item of inventory, the company may choose from a variety of flow assumptions: weighted average cost, first-in first-out (FIFO), or last-in first-out (LIFO). In practice, weighted average cost is more common than either FIFO or LIFO. Naturally, as in the United States in this case, the method chosen for accounting must be the same as the method chosen for taxation. The IASB banned LIFO for 2005 onwards.

Debtors

Companies sometimes calculate the allowance for doubtful debts in accordance with what the tax laws permit. Consequently, it may be more than the amount that a comparable company elsewhere would include (JICPA, 1994, page 13). A Japanese company is allowed to record a provision in excess of that allowed for tax purposes, but the excess would not be tax deductible and so few Japanese companies do this. This is an illustration of how the tax laws influence financial reporting in Japan.

The Japanese treatment of foreign currency debtors and creditors was until 2000 different from that in most other countries. Short-term items (maturing within one year) were translated at the closing rate, but long-term items were translated at the historical rate of the transaction (except when a material loss has occurred). However, Japan has now adopted the US/IASB treatment of using closing rates for both short-term and long-term items.

Legal reserve

The Commercial Code requires a company to transfer an amount equal to at least 10 per cent of its dividends paid to a legal reserve, until the reserve equals 25 per cent of the capital stock account. This is similar to, but larger than, French or German legal reserves. The specimen balance sheet in the Appendix to this chapter shows where a company should disclose the reserve. The legal reserve is undistributable, but may be capitalized following the appropriate legal procedures, e.g. to issue bonus shares. The requirement for a legal reserve illustrates the creditor-protection orientation of the Commercial Code. The reserve is designed to ensure that the company does not adopt a profligate dividend policy at the expense of its creditors.

Deferred taxation

As already mentioned, tax laws have a significant influence on financial reporting in Japan. Material timing differences rarely arise, because the amounts in the financial accounts normally correspond closely to the amounts in the tax accounts. For example, companies normally charge in their financial accounts the same amount of depreciation as for tax purposes, i.e. the maximum amount permitted for tax purposes. Because material timing differences are rare, the practice of deferred tax accounting did not develop in Japan.

The Commercial Code does not refer specifically to deferred taxation, but its accounting rules limit the deferral of expenses to certain specified categories, not including income taxes. Consequently, the Code seemed to prohibit a company from recording a deferred tax asset, though not a deferred tax liability. However, it seems inconsistent for some companies to record a deferred tax liability when other companies are prohibited from recording a deferred tax asset. So deferred tax accounting was rarely found in financial statements prepared under the Commercial Code (JICPA, 1994, page 35).

Traditionally, deferred tax was also rarely accounted for in consolidated financial statements. However, BADC pronouncements have required full allocation of deferred tax in all financial statements for March 2000 year ends onwards. The JICPA issued an audit guideline on the recognition of deferred tax assets.

Gee and Mano (2006) review the convergence of the Japanese rules on deferred tax with US and IASB standards. They show that deferred tax assets were very important in the balance sheets of Japanese banks in 2002 to 2004.

Extraordinary items

In the profit and loss account format extraordinary items are separated out from others and shown in a separate section before corporate taxes. They include gains and losses on the sale of fixed assets, and material restatements resulting from corrections of errors. This is a much wider definition than in the United States (where such items seldom arise in practice). The IASB banned the presentation of such items for 2005 onwards.

Pensions

Traditionally, almost all Japanese companies had (unfunded) employee retirement and termination plans that allowed for amounts to be paid when employees left a company, calculated using length of service, salary and other factors. The amounts charged against profits were often limited to those allowed by tax law, which is 40 per cent of the payments that would be required if all employees voluntarily terminated at the year end. However, BADC pronouncements require full provision for employee benefits in consolidated statements for accounting years ending in March 2001 onwards. Increasingly, major companies are establishing Western-style funded, external pension plans.

Dividends paid/payable

Dividends recorded in Japanese profit and loss accounts represent only the interim dividends paid in the year. The final dividend has not been approved by the year end and so is only recorded in the appropriation account, and affects brought-forward retained earnings. By contrast, in the United States the dividends paid in the year are not shown in the profit and loss account, and there is no appropriation account.

12.2.7 Consolidation and currency translation

Group financial reporting is a relatively recent development in Japan compared with its use in the United States. Financial reporting in Japan has traditionally emphasized parent company financial statements rather than consolidated financial statements. As has been mentioned, the Commercial Code does not require consolidated financial statements; the Securities and Exchange Law required them only as supplementary information until 1992. In another change to the

Regulations in 1998, relating to listed KKs, consolidated statements became the prime basis for securities reporting.

One source of requirements dealing with consolidated financial statements is the 'Regulations concerning Consolidated Financial Statements', issued in 1976 by the Ministry of Finance, which has also issued related interpretative rules and ordinances. The Ministry could exempt a company from these requirements if, prior to 1977, it was issuing consolidated financial statements prepared in accordance with standards accepted in foreign countries. Such a company was permitted (until 2001) to continue with this. For example, some Japanese companies prepared their consolidated financial statements in accordance with US accounting principles (Cooke, 1993b).

One difference from Europe or the IASB used to be that a subsidiary was defined in Japan as an enterprise in which another owned more than half the voting shares, rather than the definition being based on the vaguer concept of 'control'. This changed in Japan for accounting years ending in March 2000 onwards (Seki, 2000). One major problem is that the informal *Keiretsu* groupings are not covered by the consolidation rules because there is no parent company.

The Regulations prescribe some specific procedures for preparing consolidated financial statements. For example, companies must eliminate intra-group balances and transactions, and must recognize minority interests in consolidated subsidiaries that are not wholly owned by the group. Japanese consolidations have, in some cases, been allowed to include numbers from foreign subsidiaries without imposing uniform policies. This is still allowed by ASBJ guidance of 2006 for certain aspects of accounting by subsidiaries under IFRS or US GAAP.

In Japan, the calculation of goodwill on consolidation used to be based on the book value of the net assets acquired, or on the fair value as in IASB rules or the United States (JICPA, 1994, page 26). However, for 2000 onwards, goodwill must be calculated by reference to the fair values of a subsidiary's net assets, approximately as under IFRS 3. There are also considerable international differences in how groups subsequently eliminate goodwill from their balance sheets. In Japan, a group must amortize goodwill over its useful economic life. The amortization period normally follows that for non-consolidation goodwill, i.e. it does not exceed five years, and sometimes goodwill is amortized in just one year. However, international harmonization can be seen again in a Japanese move to allow up to 20 years from accounting years ending in March 2000 onwards. As noted in earlier chapters, the US and IASB have since moved to an impairment-only approach for goodwill, but Japan has not yet caught up with that change. Negative goodwill is treated as a liability and amortized into income in Japan, whereas it is treated as immediate income under IFRS and seldom arises under US GAAP.

Japanese groups must use the equity method to account for associated companies in group accounts, as in the United States or under IFRS. This is also the normal practice for joint ventures.

The Japanese accounting treatment of foreign subsidiaries on consolidation was considerably different from that in the United States or under IFRS. The requirements are contained in a BADC statement known as the 'Accounting Standard for Foreign Currency Transactions', which was issued in 1979 and subsequently amended in 1984 and 1995. Until this last amendment (effective from 1996) the standard required a group to use a modified temporal method to translate the financial statements of foreign subsidiaries for consolidation purposes. Under this method, historical rates were used for assets held at historical costs and for capital and non-current liabilities, and the closing exchange rate was used for most assets and liabilities measured at current values, such as debtors, creditors and inventories carried at market value. The amended standard requires the use of the closing rate for balance sheet items and the average rate for income statement items. This is similar to US or IFRS requirements.

12.2.8 Audit

The Commercial Code requires KK companies to have statutory auditors, but these do not have to have professional qualifications. Independent professional audit is only required for companies meeting one of the two criteria that:

● either the company has share capital over ¥500 million, or

● its total liabilities amount to more than ¥20 billion.

The relative weakness of the Japanese accounting profession (see Section 12.2.5) is emphasized again by the fact that it is the BADC, not the JICPA, that controls auditing standards. However, from 1991, the BADC has recognized JICPA as the body that can prepare and issue auditing standards. The FSA has a regulation that states that the audit of financial statements for Securities and Exchange Law purposes must be conducted in accordance with generally recognized auditing practices, which shall be taken as meaning the auditing standards and working rules issued by the BADC. Consequently, the FSA has delegated the responsibility for setting auditing standards to the BADC, whose standards then have legal authority.

12.2.9 Differences from IFRS

In the last few years there have been major changes in Japan. As mentioned earlier, a private sector standard-setting body was established in 2001. Even before this, the BADC had been adjusting Japanese requirements towards those of the IASC or the US. By the accounting year end of 31 March 2001, many traditional Japanese accounting features had been abandoned. However, unlike the position in several European countries, there are no examples of Japanese companies directly using IFRS for their financial statements (Sawa, 2003, page 183). Table 12.2 lists some of the major ways in which Japanese requirements in 2008 would not allow or would not require conformity with IFRS. Table 12.3 shows some of the major differences in practice in comparative form.

In 2005, the IASB and the Accounting Standards Board Japan announced a convergence project designed to remove the major differences in the rules (IASB, 2005). The ASBJ issued a 'Statement on Japan's Progress towards Convergence' in 2006. It revealed that a number of issues were outstanding, though most of those were under review.

Table 12.2 **Some ways in which Japanese rules would not allow or do not require IFRS (March 2008 year ends)**

- Impairments are assessed on the basis of undiscounted cash flows, and reversals are not allowed.
- Leases, except those which transfer ownership to the lessee, are treated as operating leases.
- A write-down of inventory to market value can be treated as permanent.
- LIFO is allowed for the determination of inventory cost.
- Development costs cannot be capitalized.
- Pre-operating costs can be capitalized.
- The completed contract method can be used for the recognition of revenues on construction contracts.
- Provisions can be made on the basis of decisions by directors before an obligation arises.
- Provisions do not need to be discounted.
- Proposed dividends can be accrued in consolidated financial statements.
- The portion of a convertible debenture that is in substance equity is not normally accounted for as such.
- Extraordinary items are disclosed and defined widely.
- Errors and policy changes are corrected/changed through income.
- Pooling of interests is allowed for certain business combinations.
- Goodwill is amortized over life limited to 20 years.
- Associates should not be accounted for by the equity method when this would significantly mislead interested persons, and there is no guidance on when this might apply.
- No specific requirements for disclosures of:
    - a primary statement of comprehensive income;
    - the FIFO or current cost of inventories valued on the LIFO basis;
    - discontinuing operations;
    - segment reporting of liabilities.

12.3 China

12.3.1 Context of accounting

Developments related to accounting in China have been driven by dramatic economic reforms, although these have not been accompanied by major political reforms. China has moved from a planned socialist model to a 'socialist market economic system'. This process began in 1978 after the Cultural Revolution ended in 1976. Examples of these economic reforms are that:

- although ownership of business enterprises remains substantially with the government, management is now separated from ownership, so that the concept of a 'business entity' is relevant;

Table 12.3 **Some major Japan/IFRS differences**

Topic	Japan	IFRS
1 Finance leases, except those transferring ownership	Not capitalized	Capitalized
2 Inventories	LIFO allowed	LIFO not allowed
3 Construction contracts where outcome can be measured reliably	Can use completed contract (until 2009)	Percentage of completion
4 Provisions	Can be made when no obligation; generally not discounted	Only when obligation; discounted
5 Goodwill	Amortized over life up to 20 years	Annually impaired
6 Proposed dividends	Can be accrued	Not accrued
7 Convertible debentures	Generally treated as debt	Not accrued
8 Extraordinary items	Wide definition	Not allowed

- the banking system now allows for non-governmental loan funding to be important, and equity financing has also begun;
- large amounts of foreign investment capital have flowed into China (Davidson *et al.*, 1996).

Particularly relevant developments include that:

- by 1984 the National Central Bank had recognized and had begun regulating share issues (Winkle *et al.*, 1994);
- by the early 1990s, there were stock exchanges in Shanghai and Shenzhen;
- in 1992, a Chinese company (Brilliance China Automotive) made an initial public offering on the New York Stock Exchange;
- Chinese companies can now have 'A' shares (which must be owned by Chinese), 'B' shares (which can be owned by foreigners and, from 2001, by Chinese) and 'H' shares (which are listed in Hong Kong). Some Chinese companies have also listed in the USA, the UK, Singapore and elsewhere.

12.3.2 Accounting regulations of 1992

The Chinese accounting system had been adapted to the economy and was based on a Soviet system of uniform accounting. It included a chart of accounts, a balance sheet based on sources and applications of funds, and the requirement to prepare many analytical schedules. Funds were provided by the state and were classified, by reference to their application, into fixed funds, current funds and special funds.

Each source of funds had its stipulated application, which had to be adhered to. The system and the beginnings of reform are described by Enthoven (1987), Skousen and Yang (1988) and Zhou (1988).

Following the economic reforms, the government instituted accounting reforms, particularly in order to encourage foreign investors. In 1992, the Ministry of Finance issued four accounting regulations. These include instructions about profit distribution and auditing. The regulations of most relevance are the 'Accounting Regulations of the People's Republic of China for Enterprises with Foreign Investment' and the 'Accounting Regulations for Share Enterprises'. The document 'Accounting Standards for Business Enterprises' (ASBE) came into force in 1993. It imposed some basic rules (e.g. that double-entry bookkeeping must be used, that a cash or funds statement must be included in the financial statements, and that consolidated financial statements must be provided where appropriate); set out a conceptual framework (although not called that); imposed a detailed chart of accounts; and made some detailed rules of financial reporting. A translation of the ASBE is given in Tang *et al.* (1994).

The conceptual framework aspects of the regulation are reasonably close to US and IASC precedents (Davidson *et al.*, 1996). However, the regulation does not specifically identify the primary user or purpose of financial statements. Instead, a hierarchy of users includes the government, banks, the public and an enterprise's own management. This is very different from the US/IASB emphasis on financial decision making by outside investors, although it fits a country where the government is still the most important provider of corporate finance and where loan capital is more important than equity. Also of relevance is that there is still a high degree of conformity between tax and accounting figures, so that the calculation of taxable income is a major purpose of accounting. The ASBE is based on historical cost without the revaluations allowed in IASB or UK rules or the increasing use of fair value in IASB/US/UK rules. Furthermore, 'substance over form' was not established as a principle, and reliability took precedence over relevance. However, the Chinese system recognized the business entity and the related concept of owner's equity and profit.

It is important to note that the regulatory framework also remains quite unlike that of Anglo-American countries. The 'standards' come from a government ministry, and the Chinese Institute of Certified Public Accountants (CICPA) is also controlled by the ministry. CICPA was established in 1988 and has a rapidly growing membership (see a recent figure in Table 1.10).

The accounting rules of the 1992 Regulation were patchy. They included the use of historical cost for fixed assets; a choice of FIFO, LIFO, etc. for inventory valuation but no 'lower of cost and market' rule; and bad debt and depreciation provisions based on tax rules. For more coverage, see Liu and Zhang (1996) and Jiashu *et al.* (1997). In order to supplement the ASBE, a series of industry-specific 'uniform accounting systems' were implemented (Xiao *et al.*, 2004).

12.3.3 Developments after 1992

After the 1992 Regulations, the World Bank provided a US$2.6 million loan in order to help the Chinese Ministry of Finance to reform the accountancy profession and to extend the accounting standards (Davidson *et al.*, 1996). The main consultant was the international accounting firm of Deloitte Touche Tohmatsu. One of its team was a former staff member of the IASC (Cairns, 1996), and there had been several contacts between IASC and CICPA.

Thirty exposure drafts were issued between 1994 and 1996, and they were generally closely in line with the standards of the IASC. The first of the resulting standards, on disclosures of relationships and transactions with related parties, was issued in 1997.

In that year China joined the IASC, and became an official observer at Board meetings; an IASC Board meeting was held in Beijing; and the Chinese government announced its support for the IASC. Of course, also in 1997, Hong Kong, which had begun to base its standards on IASs in 1993, was reunited with China.

In October 1998, an Accounting Standards Committee (CASC) was founded within China's Ministry of Finance. It comprises academics and members of accounting firms as well as government experts. The CASC received a further World Bank grant and again used Deloitte Touche Tohmatsu as consultant. Sixteen standards were issued up to early 2005. Some of these applied to listed companies only.

Also in 1998, the Ministry of Finance issued the 'Accounting System for Joint Stock Limited Enterprises', which sets out prescribed formats for financial statements (Taylor, 2000). All listed enterprises were required to consider whether there are impairments of inventories, investments and debtors. Impairments are not allowed for other types of enterprises.

In 1999 the Accounting Law, which includes coverage of such issues as corporate governance and internal control, was amended (it had originally been issued in 1985 and amended in 1993) to enhance the protection of investors. Leading from this, the State Council (an administrative legislative body of the National People's Congress) issued 'Financial Accounting and Reporting Rules' (FARR) which updated the framework of the ASBE to be more consistent with that of the IASC (Pacter and Yuen, 2001b). Huang and Ma (2001) provide an overview of accounting transition in China from 1949 to 2000.

In 2000, an 'Enterprise Accounting System' designed for all industries was promulgated by the Ministry, and it became effective in 2002. Part 1 of this extends the requirements for impairment accounting to most assets and introduces the concept of 'substance over form'. Part 2 contains a chart of accounts (see Chapter 14) for application across all businesses in order to improve uniformity of accounting. This approach to accounting regulation exists in parallel to accounting standards.

From 2005, an 'Accounting System for Small Business Enterprises' was available for unlisted and other small entities. This had simplified rules. Then, in February 2006, the Ministry of Finance issued a new set of Accounting Standards for Business Enterprises (ASBEs): a Basic Standard and 38 specific standards, largely in line with IFRS. These ASBEs are required for listed companies from 2007 and allowed for other companies. Appendix 12.1 at the end of this chapter provides the list of ASBEs.

The arrival of the ASBEs led to large changes to Chinese accounting, but there are still differences from IFRS (see Section 12.3.6).

12.3.4 Overview of development process

It was argued by Chow *et al.* (1995) that cultural constraints would slow China down in its move towards Anglo-American accounting. The large number of remaining differences from IFRS (see Section 12.3.6) bear this out. Nevertheless, Xiao and Pan (1997) saw the adoption of a conceptual framework from the English-speaking world as a way of assisting in the reform of out-moded Chinese practices. The conceptual framework was seen as a way of continuing to improve standards.

Xiao *et al.* (2004) argue that political factors have led China to maintain a uniform accounting system (such as the Enterprise Accounting System of 2000) while simultaneously developing accounting standards.

12.3.5 Audit

The recent foundation of the CICPA was mentioned above. Audit is now required for a variety of enterprises, including foreign-funded enterprises (over 200,000 of them), limited liability companies (about 5,000) and many state-owned enterprises. The large international accounting firms have been rapidly growing in China, although there are some limits on them – for example, audit reports can generally only be signed by Chinese CPAs, although some foreign members of CICPA are allowed to sign under certain conditions (*Accountancy*, 1997).

Hao (1999) traces changes in the organization and regulation of the accountancy profession in China during the twentieth century and particularly from 1978. The state is still seen to exercise a large influence.

For an analysis of Chinese auditing standards compared to international guidelines, see Lin and Chan (2000).

12.3.6 Differences from IFRS

Cairns (1996) examines the annual reports of 18 Chinese companies listed on the Hong Kong stock exchange. As noted above, such companies have 'H' shares. They are required to publish financial statements that conform either to IFRSs or to Hong Kong rules (which are close to IFRS). Of Cairns's 18 companies, 5 chose IFRS and 13 Hong Kong rules. When compared with their original Chinese financial statements, the IAS statements exhibited only small adjustments, the most common being caused by a temporary problem of the treatment of currency unification. Adjustments from Chinese rules to US rules are rather more major in size. However, all these adjustments can be expected to decline in importance as the new standards take effect.

Chen *et al.* (1999) examine reconciliations between reported earnings under Chinese rules and IAS. They suggest that reported earnings were noticeably higher under Chinese rules. Chen *et al.* (2002) examine reconciliations from Chinese to IAS rules for 1997 to 1999 in order to discover whether the 1998 Regulation reduced the gap between the two sets of rules. They find no evidence of this, which they put down to lack of supporting infrastructure, leading to earnings management and poor audits.

The influence of the IASC/B on China has been noted above. Nevertheless, a number of differences between Chinese and IFRS rules remain (see Deloitte, 2006). Table 12.4 shows the important differences. This table relates to listed companies. For unlisted companies, the differences can be much greater.

Table 12.4 **Some ways in which Chinese rules differ from IFRS**

Incompatibilities

- ASBE 8 prohibits the reversal of all impairment losses (like US GAAP but unlike IAS 36)
- ASBE 5 generally requires measurement at cost for biological assets (like US GAAP but unlike IAS 41)

Gaps

- ASBE 9 on Employee Benefits does not deal with defined benefit plans. However, these are not widespread in China
- ASBE 11 on Share-Based Payments does not cover cases where the entity receives an asset or where the settlement is in cash. However, such payments are rare
- ASBE 4 and 30 have fewer requirements than IFRS 5 on held-for-sale assets and discontinued operations

Removal of options

- ASBE 4 and 6 do not allow a choice of fair value measurement for assets (like US GAAP but unlike IASs 16, 38 and 40)
- ASBE 2 only allows equity accounting for joint ventures (like US GAAP but unlike IAS 31 which allows proportional consolidation)
- ASBE 16 does not allow government grants to be netted against the asset (unlike IAS 20)
- ASBE 31 does not allow the indirect method for the cash flow statement (unlike IAS 7 or US GAAP)
- ASBE 30 requires the income statement to be presented by function (whereas IAS 1 and US GAAP allow it by nature)

As may be seen from Table 12.4, most of the differences concern the removal of options, mostly non-US options. As a result, compliance with ASBE should lead to compliance with IFRS.

SUMMARY

- The government is the main influence in the financial reporting environment in Japan. There are three distinct sources of government influence, namely, the Commercial Code, the Securities and Exchange Law and the tax regulations. These three sources represent different attitudes to the purposes of financial statements.

- The accounting profession in Japan is relatively small and has a lesser influence on financial reporting in comparison to the long-established and powerful accounting professions in the United Kingdom and the United States.

- Japan has some accounting requirements and practices that may appear conservative. For example, Japanese companies generally measure fixed assets at historical cost. The most common depreciation method is the reducing-balance method, which results in relatively high depreciation charges in the early years of an asset's life. Japanese companies must establish a legal reserve, which is not distributable. Many companies charge expenses in their financial accounts to the full extent permitted by the tax laws, even where this exceeds what is required by prudent accounting principles.

● Japanese rules changed extensively in the late 1990s to reduce the differences from US and IFRS practice. A private-sector standard-setter was established in 2001.

● Financial reporting in China has been transformed as a result of economic reforms. Anglo-Saxon accounting has been influential. Accounting – and the accountancy profession – is gaining in status and influence compared with the period of communist rule.

● Nevertheless, several older features of Chinese accounting have been retained, so that a fusion of ideas has resulted.

● Some differences between new Chinese standards and international standards remain.

References

Accountancy (1997) 'China's profession lets the outside in', Accountancy International, June, p. 17.

Accountancy (2000) 'More standards planned', Accountancy, June, p. 9.

Arai, K. and Shiratori, S. (1991) Legal and Conceptual Framework of Accounting in Japan, Japanese Institute of Certified Public Accountants, Tokyo.

Ballon, R.J., Tomita, I. and Usami, H. (1976) Financial Reporting in Japan, Kodansha International, Tokyo.

Cairns, D. (1996) 'When East meets West', Accountancy (international edn), August, pp. 53–5.

Chen, C.J.P., Gul, F.A. and Xijia, S. (1999) 'A comparison of reported earnings under Chinese GAAP vs. IAS: evidence from the Shanghai Stock Exchange', Accounting Horizons, June.

Chen, S., Sun, Z. and Wang, Y. (2002) 'Evidence from China on whether harmonized accounting standards harmonize accounting practices', Accounting Horizons, Vol. 16, No. 3.

Chiba, J. (2001) 'The designing of corporate accounting law in Japan after the Second World War', Accounting, Business and Financial History, Vol. 11, No. 3.

Chow, L.M., Chau, G.K. and Gray, S.J. (1995) 'Accounting reforms in China: cultural constraints on implementation and development', Accounting and Business Research, Vol. 26, No. 1, pp. 29–49.

Cooke, T.E. (1993a) 'Disclosure in Japanese corporate annual reports', Journal of Business Finance and Accounting, June.

Cooke, T.E. (1993b) 'The impact of accounting principles on profits: the US versus Japan', Accounting and Business Research, Autumn.

Cooke, T.E. and Kikuya, M. (1992) Financial Reporting in Japan, Blackwell, Oxford.

Davidson, R.A., Gelardi, A.M.G. and Li, F. (1996) 'Analysis of the conceptual framework of China's new accounting system', Accounting Horizons, Vol. 10, No. 1, pp. 58–74.

Deloitte (2006) China's New Accounting Standards, Deloitte.

Economist (1996) Pocket World in Figures 1997, The Economist, London.

Enthoven, A.J.H. (1987) 'A review and some observations', in Accounting and Auditing in the People's Republic of China, Shanghai University of Finance and Economics, and Center for International Accounting Development, University of Texas at Dallas, pp. 205–26.

Financial Times (1999) FT 500, Financial Times, 28 January, p. 23.

Gee, M.A. and Mano, T. (2006) 'Accounting for deferred tax in Japanese banks and the consequences for their international operations', *Abacus*, Vol. 42, No. 1, pp. 1–21.

Godwin, J.H., Goldberg, S.R. and Douthett, E.B. (1998) 'Relevance of US–GAAP for Japanese companies', *International Journal of Accounting*, Vol. 33, No. 5.

Gray, S.J., Campbell, L.G. and Shaw, J.C. (eds) (1984) *International Financial Reporting*, Macmillan, London.

Hao, Z.P. (1999) 'Regulation and organization of accounts in China', *Accounting, Auditing and Accountability Journal*, Vol. 12, No. 3, pp. 286–302.

Huang, A. and Ma, R., (2001) *Accounting in China in Transition: 1949–2000*, World Scientific Publishing, Singapore.

IASB (2005) *Insight*, International Accounting Standards Board, April/May, p. 2.

Japanese Institute of Certified Public Accountants (1991) *Corporate Disclosure in Japan, Reporting*, JICPA, Tokyo.

Japanese Institute of Certified Public Accountants (1994) *Corporate Disclosure in Japan, Accounting*, JICPA, Tokyo.

Jiashu, G., Lin, Z.J. and Feng, L. (1997) 'Accounting standards and practices in China', in N. Baydoun, A. Nishimura and R. Willett, *Accounting in the Asia-Pacific Region*, Wiley, Singapore.

Lin, K.Z. and Chan, K.H. (2000) 'Auditing standards in China – a comparative analysis with relevant international standards and guidelines', *International Journal of Accounting*, Vol. 35, No. 4, pp. 559–80.

Liu, K.C. and Zhang, W.G. (1996) *Contemporary Accounting Issues in China*, Prentice Hall, Singapore.

Nobes, C.W. and Maeda, S. (1990) 'Japanese accounts: interpreters needed', *Accountancy*, September.

Nobes, C.W. and Norton, J.E. (1996) 'International variations in the accounting and tax treatments of goodwill, and the implications for research', *Journal of International Accounting, Auditing and Taxation*, Vol. 5, No. 2.

Pacter, P. and Yuen, J. (2001a) 'Chinese standards in the international arena', *Accounting and Business*, March, pp. 36–9.

Pacter, P. and Yuen, J. (2001b) 'Accounting standards in China: a progress report', *Accounting and Business*, February, pp. 22–5.

Sakagami, M., Yoshimi, H. and Okano, H. (1999) 'Japanese accounting profession in transition', *Accounting, Auditing and Accountability Journal*, Vol. 12, No. 3.

Sawa, E. (2003) 'Accounting in Japan', Chapter 7 in P. Walton, A. Haller and B. Raffournier (eds), *International Accounting*, Thomson, London.

Seki, M. (2000) 'Reshaping Standards', *Accountancy*, June.

Skousen, C.R. and Yang, J. (1988) 'Western management accounting and the economic reforms of China', *Accounting, Organizations and Society*, Vol. 13, No. 2, pp. 201–26.

Tang, Y.W., Chow, L. and Cooper, B.J. (1994) *Accounting and Finance in China*, 2nd edn, Longman, Hong Kong.

Taylor, S. (2000) 'Standard bearer', *Accountancy*, August, pp. 114–16.

Winkle, G.M., Huss, H.F. and Xi-Zhu, C. (1994) 'Accounting standards in the People's Republic of China: responding to economic reforms', *Accounting Horizons*, Vol. 8, No. 3, pp. 48–57.

Xiao, J.Z., Weetman, P. and Sun, M. (2004) 'Political influence and coexistence of a uniform accounting system and accounting standards: recent developments in China', *Abacus*, Vol. 40, No. 2, pp. 193–218.

Xiao, Z. and Pan, A. (1997) 'Developing accounting standards on the basis of a conceptual framework by the Chinese government', *International Journal of Accounting*, Vol. 32, No. 3, pp. 279–99.

Zhou, Z.H. (1988) 'Chinese accounting systems and practices', *Accounting, Organizations and Society*, Vol. 3, No. 2, pp. 207–24.

Further reading

Choi, F.D.S. and Hiramatsu, K. (1987) *Accounting and Financial Reporting in Japan*, Van Nostrand, Reinhold.

Cooke, T.E. (1991) 'The evolution of financial reporting in Japan: a shame culture perspective', *Accounting, Business and Financial History*, Vol. 1, No. 3.

Cooke, T.E. (1994) 'Japan', in T.E. Cooke and R.H. Parker (eds), *Financial Reporting in the West Pacific Rim*, Routledge, London.

Kuroda, M. (2001) 'Japan – Group Accounts', in Ordelheide, D. and KPMG, *Transnational Accounting*, Palgrave, New York, pp. 1807–907.

McKinnon, J.L. (1984) 'Application of Anglo-American principles of consolidation to corporate financial disclosure in Japan', *Abacus*, June.

Oguri, T. and Hara, Y. (1990) 'A critical examination of accounting regulation in Japan', *Accounting, Auditing and Accountability*, Vol. 3, No. 2.

Sakurai, H. (2001) 'Japan – Individual Accounts', in Ordelheide, D. and KPMG, *Transnational Accounting*, Palgrave, New York.

Useful websites

Accounting Standards Board of Japan	www.asb.or.jp
Japanese Institute of Certified Public Accountants	www.jicpa.or.jp
China Securities Regulatory Commission	www.csrc.gov.cn
Chinese Institute of Certified Public Accountants	www.cicpa.org.cn
World Bank, Reports on the Observance of Standards & Codes. Accounting & Auditing	www.worldbank.org/ifa/rosc_aa.html

QUESTIONS

Suggested answers to the asterisked questions are given at the end of the book.

12.1∗ 'Unlike US accounting, Japanese accounting is not a product of its environment but of outside influences.' Discuss.

12.2∗ Which factors could have been used at the beginning of the 1990s to predict the direction in which Chinese accounting would develop?

12.3 Compare and contrast the roles of the JICPA and the AICPA.

12.4 Discuss the causes of differences in financial reporting and its regulation (giving relevant examples of the effects) between your own country and Japan.

12.5 'Japan is unique, so Japanese accounting is unique.' Discuss.

12.6 Imagine that you are a financial analyst used to US or IFRS company statements; what difficulties would be met when assessing Japanese companies?

12.7 Discuss the classification of Japanese accounting in Nobes's (1998) model (see Figure 3.4). Which features give rise to this classification, and what have Japanese accounting and its environment in common with other countries in this group?

12.8 From your knowledge of Japanese accounting, what characteristics do you think it has in terms of Gray's (1988) model?

12.9 Why did Chinese accounting develop differently from Eastern European accounting in the 1990s?

12.10 Compare the importance of the influences of Anglo-Saxon accounting and continental European accounting in Eastern Europe and in China during the 1990s.

Appendix 12.1 ASBE Standards

- Basic Standard
- ASBE 1   Inventories
- ASBE 2   Long-term Equity Investments
- ASBE 3   Investment Property
- ASBE 4   Fixed Assets
- ASBE 5   Biological Assets
- ASBE 6   Intangible Assets
- ASBE 7   Exchange of Non-Monetary Assets
- ASBE 8   Impairment of Assets
- ASBE 9   Employee Benefits
- ASBE 10   Enterprise Annuity Fund
- ASBE 11   Share-based Payment
- ASBE 12   Debt Restructuring
- ASBE 13   Contingencies
- ASBE 14   Revenue
- ASBE 15   Construction Contracts
- ASBE 16   Government Grants
- ASBE 17   Borrowing Costs
- ASBE 18   Income Taxes
- ASBE 19   Foreign Currency Translation
- ASBE 20   Business Combinations
- ASBE 21   Leases
- ASBE 22   Recognition and Measurement of Financial Instruments
- ASBE 23   Transfer of Financial Assets
- ASBE 24   Hedging
- ASBE 25   Direct Insurance Contracts
- ASBE 26   Reinsurance Contracts
- ASBE 27   Extraction of Petroleum and Natural Gas
- ASBE 28   Accounting Policies, Changes in Accounting Estimates and Correction of Errors
- ASBE 29   Events after the Balance Sheet Date
- ASBE 30   Presentation of Financial Statements
- ASBE 31   Cash Flow Statements
- ASBE 32   Interim Financial Reporting
- ASBE 33   Consolidated Financial Statements
- ASBE 34   Earnings per Share
- ASBE 35   Segment Reporting
- ASBE 36   Related Party Disclosures
- ASBE 37   Presentation of Financial Instruments
- ASBE 38   First-time Adoption of Accounting Standards for Business Enterprises

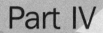

Part IV

FINANCIAL REPORTING BY INDIVIDUAL COMPANIES

13 The context of financial reporting by individual companies

Christopher Nobes

OBJECTIVES After reading this chapter, you should be able to:

- give examples of differences between national rules and the two world 'standards';
- explain why, and for what purposes, national rules are surviving;
- outline the links between financial reporting, tax and distribution of profit;
- make the case for, and explain the progress towards, special standards for small companies.

13.1 Introduction

The vast majority of companies in the world are not listed on stock exchanges. This includes nearly all the subsidiaries of listed companies. Many of these companies are required to publish unconsolidated financial statements relating to the company as an individual legal entity. The same may apply to the parent company itself in a group whose parent is listed or unlisted. Even if the individual entity does not publish financial statements, it still needs to do accounting for various purposes: for example, the calculation of taxable income, the calculation of legally distributable income or the provision of numbers for consolidation.

In many countries (e.g. most EU countries), consolidated and unconsolidated statements of unlisted companies continue to follow national rules. Even in those cases where consolidated statements are required to follow IFRS or US GAAP (see Chapter 5), the unconsolidated financial statements of individual entities are, in many cases, required or allowed to follow national accounting rules instead. In other words, the bulk of accounting going on in many countries (e.g. in most EU countries) does not follow IFRS or US GAAP. This Part of the book (Chapters 13 to 15) examines this accounting.

Chapter 14 looks at different ways in which national accounting rules are set in different countries. Chapter 15 examines the national accounting rules in several major countries, including comparisons with IFRS. Before that, this chapter provides some context. Section 13.2 outlines the scale of difference between national rules and IFRS or US GAAP. Section 13.3 summarizes the degree to which national rules are still used in some major countries. Section 13.4 examines the connections between financial reporting, tax and the calculation of distributable income. Section 13.5 looks at the arguments for having special rules for small or unlisted companies. Section 13.5 also introduces the IASB's standard for such companies.

13.2   Outline of differences between national rules and IFRS or US GAAP

Chapter 15 looks at some of the international differences in accounting rules and practices. One way of illustrating these is to look at reconciliations from national practices to IFRS or to US GAAP. This is already done in other places in this book. Several examples were shown in Tables 1.1 and 1.2 and in Section 5.4. Sections 16.2 and 16.3 include reconciliations from German rules to IFRS by Volkswagen and Deutsche Bank.

These reconciliations relate to consolidated statements. No reconciliations of unconsolidated statements are available because investors operating on an international basis would not be interested in them. For example, in the world's biggest capital market, the United States, unconsolidated statements are seldom audited or published at all. However, most of the adjustments in the reconciliations of consolidated statements apply equally for unconsolidated statements, the major exception being those related to goodwill.

Table 13.1 repeats part of the information given by BASF when reconciling from German to US accounting. The items marked with an asterisk are not consolidation issues. Another German chemical company, Bayer, explained the differences between IFRS and German requirements in the last year for which IFRS was not compulsory. Extracts of this are shown as Table 13.2. Again, only one of the issues relates to consolidation. Several of these issues are taken up in Chapter 15.

13.3   The survival of national rules

The distinction between adoption of IFRS and convergence with IFRS was examined in Chapter 5. There are several reasons why a country might not wish to adopt IFRS for some or all purposes. The most obvious case of non-adoption is the United States, where the SEC does not yet accept IFRS for domestic registrants because it

Table 13.1 Reconciling items for BASF (German to US)

	Equity (million €)
As reported stockholders' equity under German GAAP	15,765.0
Minority interests	(331.8)
Stockholders' equity excluding minority interests	15,433.2
Adjustments required to conform with US GAAP	
*Capitalization of interest	472.7
*Capitalization of software developed for internal use	128.3
*Accounting for pensions	924.3
*Accounting for provisions	244.4
*Accounting for derivatives and long-term foreign currency items	3.2
*Valuation of securities at market values	191.5
Valuation adjustments relating to equity accounting	39.0
*Inventory valuation	18.9
Reversal of goodwill amortization	469.5
*Other adjustments	58.6
*Deferred taxes and recognition of tax effects of dividend payments	(810.8)
Minority interests	(13.7)
Stockholders' equity in accordance with US GAAP	17,159.1

Note: *Items marked with an asterisk are not consolidation issues.
Source: Adapted from the *BASF Annual Report, 2004*, p. 93. BASF SA, Ludwigshafen, Germany. Reproduced with permission.

believes that US GAAP is better. It is certainly the case that US GAAP has more detailed rules and demands more disclosures than IFRS (see Part II).

Interestingly, since the SEC only imposes reporting requirements on registered companies, the great bulk of US corporations fall outside of its control. Also, the SEC is only interested in consolidated financial statements, so it imposes no requirements for accounting by the individual parent or subsidiary companies of its registrants. To the extent that US accounting is done beyond the consolidated statements of SEC-registrants, there are no publication or audit requirements. In many cases, companies nevertheless prepare full-scale US GAAP for their lenders or shareholders, and profit calculations are still necessary as the starting point for taxation (see Section 13.5).

In Japan, the feeling of national uniqueness leads to reluctance to abandon national rules. For example, the Japanese are opposed to the abolition of pooling/merger accounting (see Chapter 8) because, culturally, they like to present combinations as agreed mergers rather than as contested takeovers. This might slow down convergence with IFRS (IASB, 2005). In some parts of the EU, national pride also leads to a distaste for US GAAP or for IFRS which is seen as a Trojan horse concealing Anglo-Saxon accounting (see Chapter 4). However, there are better reasons for caution in the adoption of IFRS for unconsolidated statements. The basic point is that the purpose of accounting may differ between a listed company's consolidated report and other accounting. For example, an unlisted company may have no shareholders beyond its directors. Full-scale IFRS reporting might be disproportionately expensive for it. These issues are examined in Section 13.5.

Furthermore, the main purposes of unconsolidated accounting may be to calculate taxable income or distributable income rather than to give useful information

Table 13.2 Explanations by Bayer of differences between IFRS and German requirements

Financial statements prepared in compliance with IFRS aim to provide information on which investors can base their decisions. Accordingly, IFRS prescribes strict separation of commercial and tax accounting, provisions for expenses are not permitted, a different definition of realized gains is used in certain cases, recognition and valuation options are more narrowly defined, and more extensive notes and explanations are required.

Material differences relate primarily to the accounting treatment of securities, foreign currency receivables and payables, and derivative financial instruments, which under IFRS are stated at closing values whereas German accounting regulations apply the imparity principle. . . .

Both IFRS and German accounting rules stipulate that leased assets should be recognized on the basis of economic ownership. However, the definition of economic ownership varies. Under IFRS, leased assets should be recognized by the party that bears the attendant risks and rewards. . . .

Following the introduction of IFRS 3 (Business Combinations), which replaces IAS 22, goodwill arising on business combinations for which the agreement date is on or after March 31, 2004 may not be amortized but instead must be tested annually for impairment. German accounting standards continue to permit companies to amortize goodwill or offset it against retained earnings. . . .

Under IFRS, provisions may only be set up for liabilities to third parties. Pension provisions are calculated using the projected unit credit method, taking into account future increases in remuneration and pensions. The German tax-based method is not permitted. . . .

Deferred taxes must also be recognized for loss carryforwards if it is sufficiently probable that these loss carryforwards can be utilized. German accounting rules do not permit capitalization of deferred tax assets resulting from tax loss carryforwards.

Source: Adapted from *Bayer AG Annual Report, 2004*. Bayer AG, Leverkusen, Germany. Reproduced with permission.

to investors to help them to predict cash flows. Perhaps such accounting *should* be different from IFRS. In those EU countries where tax and financial reporting have been closely linked (see Section 13.4), there is an understandable reluctance to adopt IFRS for unconsolidated statements because the resulting profit figure is more judgemental. Also, in effect, a country would be delegating the calculation of taxable income to the IASB that has no interest in that topic.

Table 13.3 gives some examples of the response of EU countries to permission from the EU Regulation 1606/2002 to use IFRS for unconsolidated statements. Countries in the bottom half of the table are those with stronger tax/reporting links. It should be noted that these countries are on the right of the classifications in Chapter 4. To take the example of Germany, companies are allowed to use IFRS for unconsolidated reporting but only if they also prepare accounts under national rules for tax and distribution purposes (Haller and Eierle, 2004). This issue is taken further in Section 13.4, below.

Even those countries that allow the use of IFRS are still maintaining national rules. However, in some cases, for example the UK, substantial programmes of convergence with IFRS have been undertaken.

Table 13.3 **Some EU reactions to optional IFRS use for unconsolidated statements**

● Compulsory use	– Cyprus, Malta
● Listed compulsory (from 2009), unlisted optional*	– Denmark
● Optional*	– UK, Netherlands, Norway
● Listed compulsory, unlisted banned*	– Czech Republic
● Optional but only for financial reporting	– Germany
● Banned	– Austria, Belgium, France, Spain, Sweden

*Implication of two different starting points for taxable income.
Source: Compiled by authors.

13.4   Financial reporting, tax and distribution

As explained in Chapter 2, profits under normal accounting rules are the starting point for the calculation of taxable income and distributable income in any country. However, the degree of closeness varies greatly. Lamb *et al.* (1998) examine several accounting topics and suggest that reporting and tax are much closer in France and Germany than in the US or the UK. Nobes and Schwencke (2006) study how the links between reporting and tax develop over time, using Norway as an example of a country where the gap has widened.

In cases where reporting and tax rules are identical, the theoretical legal position that tax should use reporting rules tends to become reversed, such that accounting numbers are chosen with their tax effect in mind. This describes the position under German national rules (Haller, 1992). Such a close linkage also makes it impossible in practice for a country to adopt or fully converge with IFRS because IFRS profit is more subjective and the rules are beyond national control. The use of IFRS implies that the close linkage must be broken or that accounting must be done twice, which amounts to the same thing.

In countries where some or all companies have an option to choose between IFRS or national accounting rules for financial reporting, a further complication arises: a company can have two different measures of pre-tax profit and therefore two different starting points for the calculation of taxable income. Such countries are shown with an asterisk in Table 13.3. This might not be a problem for a country which has special tax rules on many accounting topics (see the discussions in Sections 2.5 and 22.2), but there could still be a difficulty where tax practice rests upon accounting rules for particular topics. For example, under IAS 32 (see Section 6.3), certain payments are re-classified as dividends rather than interest, or vice versa. The issue here is whether the amount of 'interest' that is tax deductible will follow the classification for financial reporting. The answer can vary internationally.

The amount of legally *distributable* income is also the same as the accounting profit for individual legal entities in many countries (e.g. France and Germany). Under the Fourth Directive, distributable profit is 'cumulative realised profit less cumulative realised losses'. In the UK, adjustments are made to accounting profit, for example to add back any depreciation expense caused by having voluntarily revalued assets upwards in the past. However, a move to IFRS by individual companies (which are the ones that can distribute profit) can presumably affect what is regarded as realized.

In the USA, the restraint on distributable income rests on solvency measures rather than on profits, which might be a better solution for Europe.

13.5 Special rules for small or unlisted companies

13.5.1 The case for special rules

There is a long history of 'big GAAP versus little GAAP' or 'differential reporting'. An obvious example is the SEC's imposition of US GAAP on listed companies only, as noted in Section 13.3. In the EU, small companies can be exempted from audit and publication under national laws based on the Fourth Directive. For this purpose, 'small' is related to having below 50 employees and to monetary values of turnover and total assets that have been raised from time to time (see Section 14.3).

The UK, Hong Kong and New Zealand are examples of countries that have special versions of their accounting standards for small companies. The UK's Financial Reporting Standard for Smaller Enterprises (FRSSE), originally issued in 1997, abbreviates the main standards and reduces the disclosure requirements. 'Small' is defined using the legal basis mentioned in the previous paragraph. The key issue is that the measurement rules of the main standards are not significantly affected. Also, if small companies have an accounting problem not covered by the FRSSE, they must refer to the main standards. The FRSSE needs to be revised frequently as a result of changes in other standards.

13.5.2 IASB's draft standard for SMEs

Throughout the life of the old IASC, the standards were written largely with one type of accounting in mind: consolidated statements of large listed companies. However, in the early years of the IASB, a demand began for a version of IFRS suitable for small and medium-sized entities (SMEs). IASB began the project in 2003, against the wishes of some of its board members who thought that it would divert attention from their main task.

In countries such as Australia, Cyprus, New Zealand or South Africa that have adopted (or adapted) IFRS for all purposes, an IFRS for SMEs (whether defined in terms of size or unlisted status) might be useful as a way of reducing burdens on such companies. However, it is not immediately clear why an *international* SME would be relevant for countries such as France or Germany where IFRS is only used for consolidated statements. Nevertheless, the European Commission was at the forefront in arguing for an SME version of IFRS. This is partly with a view to eventual standardization of accounting and then a common European tax base (see Chapter 22). These objectives are quite different from the IASB's aim of international comparability for investors. One result is that the Commission has wanted an SME standard to contain more simplifications (i.e. measurement differences from IFRS) than the IASB was inclined to allow.

The issue of differential measurement bases slowed down the IASB's project. Despite the project's SME title, it was decided that the key point is not size but whether the reporting entity is of public interest, and especially whether it is listed. In 2004, a Discussion Paper was issued (IASB, 2004). As a result of the feedback from this, the IASB decided, in principle, to allow some measurement differences on the basis of assessing costs and benefits.

In 2007, the IASB issued an exposure draft. At the time of writing (early 2008), the standard had not been issued. Although the draft still refers to 'small and medium-sized entities', the standard is intended for entities that are not publicly accountable, i.e. that are not listed and that do not carry out fiduciary activities such as a bank or insurance company.

The draft is about 250 pages long compared to full IFRS which is about 2,500 pages. It is also easier to read than full IFRS, not just because it is shorter. There are many reductions in disclosure requirements and some simplifications and exemptions.

In principle, any option allowed in full IFRS (see Chapter 7) is also allowed in the SME standard. Several options are not covered in detail in the SME standard, but reference is made to full IFRS for those entities that wish to take the options (e.g. measuring assets at fair value rather than cost (as in IASs 16, 38 and 40)). Other complex issues are also dealt with by reference to full IFRS (e.g. how to do equity accounting or proportional consolidation, as in IASs 28 and 31). Certain standards are omitted from the SME document (e.g. IFRS 8 on segment reporting and IAS 33 on earnings per share).

There are a few simplifications compared to full IFRS, as summarized in Table 13.4. Some commentators had argued for further simplifications, such as treating all leases as operating leases or, even, not accounting for deferred tax.

Jurisdictions, such as the member states of the EU, will be considering whether to allow or require companies to use the SME standard. If the EU or another jurisdiction believes that the IASB's standard is not simple enough, it might invent yet another level of accounting rules for the 'smallest' companies, which might mean for *most* companies.

Table 13.4 Simplifications proposed in the SME draft of 2007

Standard in full IFRS	Proposal for SME standard
IAS 12	Recognition of deferred tax liabilities on unremitted earnings of associates and joint ventures only if probably to be paid in the foreseeable future.
IAS 19	Actuarial gains and losses to be immediately recognised in income.
IAS 20	Government grants treated as income when receivable (as in IAS 41).
IAS 23	Borrowing costs on construction can be expensed (as in old IAS 23).
IAS 27	Parents exempted from preparing investor statements.
IAS 28/31	Associates and joint ventures can be held at cost.
IAS 38	All development costs can be expensed.
IAS 38/IFRS 3	Intangibles with indefinite life to be impaired when there is an 'indication', not annually.
IAS 39	No available-for-sale category of financial assets (so, only cost or marking-to-market).

SUMMARY

- Most of the accounting done in the world, for internal purposes and for publication, still uses national rather than international rules.

- There are still many accounting topics where differences survive, including accounting for intangible assets, for pensions and other provisions, and for financial instruments.

- National rules survive for several reasons, including reluctance to change and resistance to 'foreign' influences. Better reasons could include the greater suitability of national rules for tax and distribution calculations.

- Reduced requirements for smaller or for unlisted companies are a feature of some national rules.

- The IASB's draft standard on SMEs relates particularly to companies that are not publicly accountable. The standard is one-tenth of the length of full IFRS. Some measurement simplifications are included.

References

Haller, A. (1992) 'The relationship of financial and tax accounting in Germany: a major reason for accounting disharmony in Europe', *International Journal of Accounting*, Vol. 27.

Haller, A. and Eierle, B. (2004) 'The adaptation of German accounting rules to IFRS: A legislative balancing act', *Accounting in Europe*, Vol. 1, No. 1.

IASB (2004) *Preliminary Views on Accounting Standards for Small and Medium-sized Entities*, International Accounting Standards Board, London.

IASB (2005) *Insight*, International Accounting Standards Board, London, p. 1.

Lamb, M., Nobes, C.W. and Roberts, A.D. (1998) 'International variations in the connections between tax and financial reporting', *Accounting and Business Research*, Summer.

Nobes, C.W. and Schwencke, H.R. (2006) 'Tax and financial reporting links: a longitudinal examination over 30 years up to IFRS adoption, using Norway as a case study', *European Accounting Review*, Vol. 15, No. 1.

Useful websites

The websites at the end of Chapters 6, 8, 15 and 22 may be useful for various aspects of this chapter.

QUESTIONS

Suggested answers to the asterisked questions are given at the end of the book.

13.1* Using information from this chapter and earlier ones (e.g. Chapters 2, 3 and 5), give examples of accounting topics on which there are major differences between two national accounting systems or between a national system and IFRS.

13.2* Are the arguments for differential reporting convincing? Should differentiation be made on the basis of company size or using some other characteristic?

13.3 From this and earlier chapters, explain how financial reporting profit can differ from taxable income, and how this varies internationally.

13.4 Explain how the IASB's standard for SMEs differs from full IFRS. In your opinion, does it differ enough?

14 Making accounting rules for non-listed business enterprises in Europe

Robert Parker

OBJECTIVES

After reading this chapter, you should be able to:

- explain who makes accounting rules for non-listed business enterprises in France, Germany and the UK;
- explain why the forms of business enterprise subject to accounting rules differ from country to country within the European Union;
- describe the legal forms of business enterprise in France, Germany and the UK.

14.1 Introduction

Chapter 13 explained that international financial reporting standards apply compulsorily within the EU only to the consolidated financial statements of listed companies. The present chapter and Chapter 15 are concerned with the overwhelming majority of business enterprises in Europe whose accounting and financial reporting rules are *not* made by the IASB or contained in US GAAP. These chapters do not deal with listed companies or with consolidated statements. Chapter 15 looks at accounting rules and practices for individual companies. The present chapter addresses two related questions:

- Who makes accounting rules for business enterprises not listed on a stock exchange (Section 14.2)?
- Which business enterprises are subject to these accounting rules (Section 14.3)?

The answers to these questions differ quite considerably from country to country, in ways that, not surprisingly, are connected to the two legal systems of common law and codified Roman law distinguished in Chapter 2 and to sources of finance. The US and Japanese regulatory frameworks discussed in Chapters 8 and 12 provide instructive examples of the effect on financial reporting rules and practices of these two factors. In the present chapter we look in detail at the current position in France, Germany and the UK. There are good reasons for choosing these three countries. They comprise the EU's largest economies and stock markets. They have influenced law and practice elsewhere in the EU and around the world. All continue to reveal interesting differences in approach. All, not just the two continental European countries but also the UK, have regulatory frameworks strikingly different from that in the US.

14.2 Who makes accounting rules?

14.2.1 Introduction

The diversity of accounting rule-making bodies within the EU has decreased in recent decades. Indeed, superficial comparisons suggest that few differences now remain. Compare, for example, France and the UK. As member states of the EU, they have both implemented its accounting Directives by domestic legislation (see Chapter 11). Both have companies acts and secondary legislation. Both have mixed public-sector/private-sector regulatory and standard-setting bodies. It might be argued that the only difference of importance is the lack of a national accounting plan (*plan comptable général*) in the UK. When we look more closely, however, the similarities are not as great as they appear, as will be become clearer below as we look at the rule-making bodies in France, Germany and the UK in some detail.

14.2.2 France

The state has been a major influence on French accounting since at least the late seventeenth century, although often in indirect and complex ways. Colbert's *Ordonnance de Commerce* of 1673 during the reign of Louis XIV formed the basis for the Napoleonic Commercial Code (*Code de Commerce*) of 1807 (Howard, 1932). The Code spread throughout continental Europe and beyond (e.g. to Japan, see Chapter 12). The influence of the state was especially strong from 1946 to 1983 but it has since weakened under the impact of external factors such as the company law harmonization programme of the EU and the impact of increasingly global capital markets dominated by Anglo-Saxon countries and in particular by the United States.

Colasse and Standish (1998) distinguish four periods:

1 1946–57, a period of post-war reconstruction and indicative planning of the economy by the French state, during which the national accounting plan (*plan comptable général*, PCG) was established, with mainly macroeconomic aims and little input from the accountancy profession.

2 1958–73, a period of modernization and strong economic growth, during which the field of application of the PCG was extended and more closely linked to tax rules.

3 1974–83, a period of economic instability and the high point of *normalisation à la française* (accounting standardization, French style), during which the EU company law Directives were integrated into French accounting and the formal regulation of French accounting greatly increased.

4 1984–, a period of globalization, deregulation and privatization, during which the French approach was put severely to the test, accounting institutions were reorganized, the role of the accountancy profession was strengthened, and international standards emerged as a strong competitor to national standards.

The net result of all these influences has been to produce a dualism in French accounting between the financial statements of individual business enterprises and those of groups. Group accounting has had special rules since it became compulsory in 1987, so French accountants were already prepared for the idea that IFRS would apply only to consolidated statements.

The increase in the volume of French rules on accounting has led to the recognition of a *droit comptable* (a body of legal rules relating to accounting). These rules originate from a variety of sources. Those relevant to the financial statements of individual companies have been classified as follows by Raybaud-Turrillo and Teller (1998):

- *Public sources*:
  French state   laws (*lois*), decrees (*décrets*), ministerial orders (*arrêtés*), national accounting plan;
  EU   Directives (implemented by domestic legislation).

- *Mixed public/private sources*:
  national accounting council (*Conseil National de la Comptabilité*, CNC);
  accounting regulation committee (*Comité de la Réglementation Comptable*, CRC).

We adopt this classification in the discussion below and also explain the roles of tax law and of the professional accountancy body, the *Ordre des Experts Comptables* (OEC). The work of the *Autorité des Marchés Financiers* (AMF) (see Chapter 9) does not directly concern individual financial statements.

The most distinctive part of French accounting regulation is the national accounting plan (*plan comptable général, PCG*). The PCG is not merely a chart or classified list of ledger accounts but a very detailed manual on financial accounting. Included within it are definitions of accounting terms, valuation and measurement rules, and model financial statements. Many accounting textbooks are based on it. All French accountants have been trained to use it, for recording accounting transactions, for drawing up financial statements and for filling in tax returns. Standish (1997, pages 273–6) claims that the PCG has in effect created a national accounting language and that in this area the CNC plays a comparable role to that of the *Académie Française* for language in general.

Various aspects of the history of the plan are discussed by Standish (1990), Fortin (1991) and Richard (1992). The version of the plan promulgated in 1947 owed as much to German as to French ideas. The plan was revised in 1957 and again in 1982 and 1986 to take account of the Fourth and Seventh Directives of the EU (see Chapter 11). Importantly, the 1982 plan, unlike previous plans, was made compulsory for all industrial and commercial companies. The most recent version of the plan was issued in 1999. Changes are made from time to time to incorporate new rulings on, for example, such matters as long-term contracts. In particular, amendments are being made in order to bring French rules closer to those of IFRS (but see Section 15.2.2). Unlike the 1982 version, the 1999 plan excludes any reference to cost and management accounting and to consolidated financial statements. In other respects it is mainly a codification and rearrangement of the 1982 plan.

Appendix 14.1 lists the contents of the 1999 plan; Appendix 14.2 sets out the chart of accounts contained within the plan.[1] The basis of the plan is a decimalized chart of accounts. The major account classes are:

Balance sheet accounts

1 Capital (owner equity, loans and debts payable)

2 Fixed assets

3 Stocks and work in progress

4 Debts receivable and payable

5 Financial

Operating accounts

6 Charges

7 Income

There is further subdivision. For example: 211 Land; 2114 Mining sites; 21141 Quarries.

It will be noted from Appendix 14.2 that the classification of expenses and revenues is by nature not by function (see Chapter 2). This has disadvantages for some users of income statements but enables the PCG to be applied the same way by all business enterprises. Each industrial sector has its own adaptation of the PCG, the so-called *plans professionels*.

The plan is administered by the *Conseil National de la Comptabilité* (CNC). This mixed public/private-sector body was established in 1957 and extensively reformed in 1996 when its membership was reduced from 115 to 58. It comprises a president (a prominent accountant, not a civil servant as previously); six vice-presidents (including the presidents of the OEC and the CNCC); 40 persons knowledgeable in accounting (including eight nominated by the accountancy bodies); and 11 civil servants (including the president of the AMF). The membership was again reformed in 2007, giving more power to auditors and bankers, but the reform has been criticized as not going far enough to establish institutions capable of responding

---

[1] The English versions in the Appendices are adapted from the website of the CNC.

quickly and effectively to the challenges posed by the initiatives of international accounting standard-setters.

The CNC issues opinions (*avis*), most of which are submitted to the *Comité de la Réglementation Comptable* (CRC) and become regulations. Those which do not become regulations are regarded as examples of best practice. The CRC, established in 1996, is a small, high-powered mixed public/private-sector committee, chaired by the Minister of Economy and Finance or the Minister's representative. Its other members are the Justice Minister, the Budget Minister, a judge of the *Conseil d'Etat* (which adjudicates on public law), a judge of the *Cour de Cassation* (which adjudicates on private law), the presidents of the AMF, the CNC, the OEC and the CNCC, three enterprise representatives and two trade union representatives. Its membership is thus very different from that of the FASB in the US (see Chapter 8) or the ASB in the UK. Unlike the CNC, the CRC has the power to make regulations, either following proposals from the CNC or as an endorsement (*homologation*) of IFRSs or other 'internationally recognized standards'.

Tax law plays an important role in the individual financial statements of French companies and other business enterprises for two reasons: the rules for measuring reported accounting profit in such statements do not differ significantly from those for measuring taxable income; and expenses are only deductible for tax purposes if treated as expenses in the annual financial statements. The legislator has been concerned, at the level of the individual enterprise, to harmonize accounting and tax law and this has been largely achieved by formalizing a connection between the Tax Code (*Code général des impôts*, CGI) and the PCG. The Commercial Code and the Companies Act are also compatible with the PCG although they do not refer to it. However, in recent years the influence of tax rules has been under attack. Lamb *et al.* (1998) look in detail at the links between accounting and taxation in France.

Professional accountancy developed later in France than in the UK or the US. The Big-4 firms are well established in France but none of them is of French origin. The *Ordre des Experts Comptables* (OEC) was established in 1942 and reconstituted by the post-war government in 1945. Although growing in size and influence, it is a smaller, weaker and less autonomous body than, say, the ICAEW in the UK and has never been responsible for setting accounting standards. However, as already noted, it participates in the work of the CNC and the CRC. It issues opinions (*avis*) on accounting matters. The functions of the *Compagnie des Commissaires aux Comptes* (CNCC) and the *Haut Conseil du Commissariat aux Comptes* (H3C) have been discussed in Chapter 9.

14.2.3 Germany

Most German rules on accounting for individual enterprises are made by the German state and are set out in the *Handelsgesetzbuch* (HGB, Commercial Code) and in tax legislation. The HGB requires that the annual financial statements be prepared according to the principles of orderly bookkeeping (*Grundsätze ordnungsmässiger Buchführung*). To the extent that these principles are not set out in the Code, they must be deduced from it, from statements by the *Institut der Wirtschaftsprüfer* (see below) and from tax legislation, as well as from the accounting practices of enterprises.

Tax law and Federal Fiscal Court decisions are in practice major sources of accounting rules. The so-called 'authoritative principle' or conformity principle (*Massgeblichkeitsprinzip*) applies to the determination of taxable income. This principle states that tax statements are based on the commercial statements (Haller, 1992). In practice this means that any and all deductions from taxable income, for example, special depreciation, valuation allowances or provisions, must be recorded in the commercial statements as well. As tax law requires special depreciation to be recorded in the commercial statements even though this may obscure the insight into net worth, financial position and results, there is in effect a reversal of the authoritative principle. Hence, the development of accounting principles can largely be traced to the Federal Fiscal Court. However, recent changes in German tax law, especially in the area of provisions, have led to more extensive differences between financial and tax accounts. Lamb *et al.* (1998) examine in detail the closeness of the tax and accounting links in Germany, compared with the position in the United States, the United Kingdom and France. Fiscal authorities in Germany remain in general opposed to allowing accounting rules over which they have no influence to affect financial statements that form the basis for tax computations.

The influence of the auditing profession has grown in recent years, but it is still weak. The German body, the *Institut der Wirtschaftsprüfer in Deutschland e.V.* (IdW), was formed in 1931 following the provisions of the Companies Act 1931. It is smaller than the UK and French bodies and membership is voluntary, although a large majority of German *Wirtschaftsprüfer* (WPs) have joined the Institute. Membership in the *Wirtschaftsprüferkammer* (Chamber of Accountants), which was introduced by the law regulating the accountancy profession (*Wirtschaftsprüferordnung*) of 1961, is a legal requirement. The influence of the German Institute is mainly by recommendations and releases which are binding on auditors, and by consultation in the process of law making. Authorities such as the Stock Exchange and trade unions, which exercise direct influence in some other countries, are of less importance to accounting in Germany, but they take part in discussions on the setting of rules. This is also true of accounting academics – although there is a long tradition and great variety of approaches offered by German accounting theory. The German Accounting Standards Committee (GASC – in German, the *Deutsches Rechnungslegungs Standards Committee* (DRSC)) was set up in 1998 to develop standards for consolidated financial statements, not for individual company financial statements. In 2007 a *Bilanzrechtsmodernisierungsgesetz* (Accounting Law Modernization Act) was under discussion. It may bring German accounting rules closer to international rules and change the HGB rules for individual financial statements.

14.2.4 The UK

Company legislation is the means by which UK governments have made rules on financial reporting. Incorporation of companies by registration, rather than by the more cumbersome means of a royal charter or a private act of parliament, first became possible in the United Kingdom in 1844 and was coupled with the availability of limited liability in 1855. Companies Acts apply to England, Wales and Scotland and, by a separate ordinance, to Northern Ireland. During the twentieth century, the rules greatly increased in quantity and complexity. A notable landmark was the Companies Act 1947 (consolidated as the 1948 Act), which made group financial statements compulsory, distinguished between 'reserves' and 'provisions' (thus making the creation of secret reserves more difficult), introduced many new disclosure requirements, and required directors to prepare (and auditors to report on) financial statements that give a 'true and fair view'. The Act was based on the 1945 Report of the Cohen Committee on company law amendment. The accounting and audit contents of both the Report and the Act were strongly influenced by the 'Recommendations on Accounting Principles' of the Institute of Chartered Accountants in England and Wales (ICAEW), which had been issued from 1942.

The 1948 Act remained the principal Act for almost 40 years but it was amended by a series of Acts: the first in 1967, which made the disclosure of turnover (i.e. sales) mandatory, greatly expanded the information to be provided in the Directors' Report and Notes, and removed the privilege of non-disclosure for family-owned private companies; another in 1976, which tightened the legal requirements for the maintenance and publication of information, strengthened the power of auditors, and increased the disclosure of directors' interests; an Act in 1980, which implemented the EU Second Directive; and one in 1981, which implemented the EU Fourth Directive. In 1985 all these Acts were consolidated into the Companies Act 1985, a 'jumbo' Act of 747 sections and 25 schedules. The accounting and auditing provisions of the Act were amended and restated by the Companies Act 1989, which *inter alia* implemented the EU Seventh and Eighth Directives.

Despite all these amendments, UK company law was still strongly influenced by its nineteenth-century origins and, in 1998, the Department of Trade and Industry (DTI) established a Company Law Review Steering Group (CLRSG) whose Final Report was published in 2001. The Group recommended a major reworking of the whole framework of company law. Most of the recommendations in the Report were accepted by the government, and the DTI published a White Paper, 'Modernising Company Law', in July 2002. A Companies (Audit, Investigations and Community Enterprise) Act was enacted in 2004. A new Companies Act, containing many reforms, including some implementing EU Directives (see Table 11.1), but also consolidating all previous legislation, was eventually enacted in 2006. Surpassing even the 1985 Act, the Companies Act 2006 comprises 1,300 sections and 16 schedules, and is the longest Act on the UK statute book.

The accounting requirements of the UK Acts, unlike those of the American Securities and Exchange Commission (SEC), apply to the individual financial statements of all British limited companies, except those few incorporated by royal charter or special Act of Parliament. There are, however (see Section 14.3), important exemptions for small and medium-sized companies.

Apart from the state, the most important influence on the rules of financial reporting has been accountants. In 1969 the Institute of Chartered Accountants in England and Wales (ICAEW) responded to what were widely regarded as damaging examples of misleading annual accounts and some sustained hostile criticism of the profession, particularly by sections of the media. In order to defuse criticism and to be seen to address these problems and to retain its moral authority, the ICAEW set up an Accounting Standards Steering Committee, later renamed the Accounting Standards Committee (ASC) and joined by the other five main professional accountancy bodies. Membership of the ASC varied, but the committee was always relatively large (21 members at the date of its dissolution in 1990), with unpaid part-time members drawn largely, although not entirely, from the profession. At the time of its demise, there was provision for up to five members, not necessarily accountants, as representatives of users of accounts. The role of the ASC was confined to developing Statements of Standard Accounting Practice (SSAPs) with adoption and enforcement remaining the responsibility of the six professional bodies.

In 1988 the Report of the Dearing Committee accepted the criticism that arrangements closer to those in the United States (see Chapter 8) were preferable and, in 1990, the ASC was replaced by an Accounting Standards Board (ASB) comprising a full-time paid chairman, a full-time paid technical director and seven (now eight) part-time paid members. The ASB is supervised by a Financial Reporting Council (FRC), independent of the profession. Unlike the ASC, the ASB has power to issue accounting standards on its own authority.

The ASB's standards are termed Financial Reporting Standards (FRSs). The ASB also adopted the extant Statements of Standard Accounting Practice (SSAPs) of the ASC. These remain in force until replaced by an FRS. SSAPs and FRSs contain both disclosure rules (e.g. FRS 1 on cash flow statements) and measurement rules (e.g. SSAP 4 on government grants). Some standards are a mixture of both sets of rules, for example, FRS 22 that requires both the disclosure of earnings per share (not required by the Companies Act) and lays down the rules by which it is to be calculated. Most standards apply to all large and medium-sized companies, except when IFRS are applicable (see Chapter 5). Small companies need comply with only one standard: the Financial Reporting Standard for Smaller Entities (FRSSE). This standard, which is revised periodically, reduces disclosure requirements and provides a useful summary of UK standards in many areas.

Since 2002, the main task of the ASB has been to bring about the convergence of UK and International Financial Reporting Standards. Table 14.1 lists the FRSs and SSAPs extant as at early 2008. FRSs 12, 20–26 and 29 are close copies of IFRS. Some standards only apply to listed companies, which is why there are two standards on foreign currency (SSAP 20 and FRS 23). There are also non-mandatory but very influential Statements of Recommended Practice (SORPs) on matters such as the financial statements of charities and universities.

As a result of the Dearing Report, the position of accounting standards was strengthened. The Companies Act requires directors of plcs and other large companies to disclose in their annual reports any departures from accounting standards. Also, apart from the ASB, two new bodies were set up in 1990. These are the Financial Reporting Review Panel (FRRP), a subsidiary of the FRC, and the Urgent Issues Task Force (UITF), established by the ASB along the lines of the Emerging Issues Task Force of the United States (see Chapter 8). It is legal counsel's opinion (Arden, 1993) that, as a result of these changes, a court would generally find that it is necessary for financial statements to comply with accounting standards in order to give a true and fair view. The work of the FRRP has been discussed in Chapter 9.

The main role of the UITF is to assist the ASB in areas where an accounting standard or Companies Act provision exists, but where unsatisfactory or conflicting interpretations have developed or seem likely to develop. The UITF tries to reach a consensus to which companies are then expected to conform as if it were an accounting standard. This procedure has considerably speeded up rule-making in

Table 14.1 SSAPs and FRSs, as at early 2008

SSAP	
4	Accounting for government grants
5	Accounting for value added tax
9	Stocks and long-term contracts
13	Accounting for research and development
19	Accounting for investment properties
20	Foreign currency translation
21	Accounting for leases and hire purchase contracts
25*	Segmental reporting

FRS	
1	Cash flow statements
2	Accounting for subsidiary undertakings
3	Reporting financial performance
5	Reporting the substance of transactions
6	Acquisitions and mergers
7	Fair values in acquisition accounting
8	Related party disclosures
9	Associates and joint ventures
10	Goodwill and intangible assets
11	Impairment of fixed assets and goodwill
12	Provisions, contingent liabilities and contingent assets
13	Derivatives and other financial instruments: disclosures
15	Tangible fixed assets
16	Current tax
17	Retirement benefits
18	Accounting policies
19	Deferred tax
20	(IFRS 2) Share-based payment
21	(IAS 10) Events after the balance sheet date
22*	(IAS 33) Earnings per share
23*	(IAS 21) The effects of changes in foreign exchange rates
24*	(IAS 29) Financial reporting in hyperinflationary economies
25	(IAS 32) Financial instruments: disclosure and presentation
26*	(IAS 39) Financial instruments: recognition and measurement
27	Life assurance
28	Corresponding amounts
29*	(IFRS 7) Financial instruments: disclosures

Note: *Apply particularly to listed companies.

the areas to which it has been applied (e.g. accounting for currencies in countries suffering from hyperinflation).

There are far fewer standards and interpretations in the UK than there are in the United States. One reason for this is that, unlike in the US, standards are revised without changing their number. Another major difference in style is that UK (and

IASB) standards have less detail than US standards. This can be expressed as a contrast between 'principles-based' and 'rules-based' standards (see Section 5.6).

The concept of the true and fair view has played an important role. A 'true and fair view' is nowhere defined but it is an overriding requirement. To ensure that a true and fair view is given, the Act requires additional information to be provided where necessary and, in special circumstances, the detailed provisions to be departed from. Particulars of any such departure, the reasons for it, and its effect, must be given in the notes. Tweedie (1988) has shown how the true and fair concept can be used both as an aid to, and as a defence against, creative accounting. Whereas the concept was once taken for granted, it has been widely debated in recent years (see Parker and Nobes, 1994; Parker, Wolnizer and Nobes, 1996; Alexander, 1999 and 2001; Nobes, 2000). The Enron affair in the US has strengthened the hand of those who prefer 'principles-based' standards.

In practice, the true and fair override has been used more by standard-setters than companies. Unlike the IASB, UK and other national accounting standard-setters have to set standards within the constraints of domestic law. This became more difficult in the UK with the great extension of detailed rules resulting from the implementation of EU Directives, but the ASC and the ASB have been quite ingenious in using the general requirement to give a true and fair view to override particular requirements of the Act. They also, on occasion, restricted the options legally available, or effectively removed a legal option by defining it out of existence. Some illustrations are given below:

- The Act specifically permits the use of LIFO but SSAP 9 suggests that the use of LIFO will not normally lead to a true and fair view. In practice, LIFO is therefore not allowed.

- SSAP 9 was revised so that profits recognized on long-term contract work-in-progress are classified as 'amounts recoverable on contracts' rather than as part of stocks, in order to avoid the inclusion of possibly unrealized profit in the stock valuation.

- SSAP 12 (now replaced by FRS 15) was revised to remove the option, apparently permitted by the Act, of charging historical cost depreciation on revalued buildings.

- SSAP 19 requires, in the interests of a true and fair view, investment properties not to be depreciated, although the Act stated (with no exception until 2004) that all fixed assets with limited useful lives should be depreciated.

- SSAP 20 (now replaced for listed companies by FRS 23) uses the 'true and fair view' criterion to permit gains as well as losses to be recognized on unsettled long-term monetary items, although this is a departure from prudence.

- FRS 2 does not allow some of the permitted options in the Act relating to the exclusion of subsidiaries. The exclusion for dissimilar activities is in principle sometimes required but the standard claims that it is unlikely to occur in practice.

- FRS 3 effectively abolishes the concept of extraordinary items by defining ordinary items very widely.

- FRS 4 (now replaced by FRS 25) got around the constraint of the legal definition of shares by inventing a new category of 'non-equity shares'.

- FRS 5 requires quasi-subsidiaries to be treated exactly as subsidiaries, although they are not legally subsidiaries.
- The legal ban on offsetting assets and liabilities is escaped in certain cases by referring to them in FRS 5 as 'debit and credit balances'.
- FRS 10 allows the possibility that goodwill should not be amortized, but this requires an override of the Act similar to that of SSAP 19.

Most of the above have so far survived the convergence of UK standards with IFRS.

Tax law has only a minor effect on company financial reporting. It is not, as it is in many parts of continental Europe, a major determinant of the contents of and rules relating to unconsolidated financial statements. Accounting profit is not the same as taxable income, and providing for deferred taxation is standard practice. The complex relationship between tax and financial reporting is examined for the UK and some other countries by Lamb *et al.* (1998). However, the tax authorities (HM Revenue and Customs) have a policy of trying to move the calculation of taxable income nearer to the calculation of accounting net profit. Details of the United Kingdom's imputation system and the role of tax credits are given in Chapter 22.

14.3   Which business enterprises are subject to accounting rules?

14.3.1   Introduction

Which business enterprises are subject to accounting rules? There are several possibilities connected with both legal and economic criteria:

- all business enterprises;
- business enterprises with a particular legal form;
- business enterprises above a certain size;
- business enterprises whose shares are publicly traded;
- various combinations of the above criteria.

The idea that all business enterprises should be required by law to keep accounting records makes good sense if the primary objectives of account-keeping are the protection of creditors and the facilitation of tax collection. The idea was expressed first in France, in the shape of Colbert's *Ordonnance de Commerce* of 1673. The requirement to keep records has obvious advantages for state authorities overseeing bankruptcy proceedings and levying taxation. In the UK, by contrast, although the needs of creditors have not been neglected, the emphasis has been more on requiring the preparation and publication of financial statements by companies whose shareholders have limited liability and where ownership may be divorced from control. The law has treated shareholders as the primary stakeholders and aimed to protect them as principals against directors as agents. French law has placed less emphasis on the information needs of investors. Germany followed the French rather the British approach, but insolvencies in the 1960s of large partnerships without limited liability hit stakeholders of all kinds hard and led to the imposition of size criteria to determine what enterprises should disclose in their annual reports. This innovation was picked up in the EU Fourth Directive of 1978 on company law (the first draft of which in 1971 was strongly influenced by German law) and spread throughout the EU. At the other extreme, the US approach since the 1930s has been to concentrate on regulating enterprises whose securities are publicly traded on a stock exchange, ignoring the needs of stakeholders in other companies.

We now look at the selected three EU countries in more detail as illustrations of how national rules in this area can differ.

14.3.2 France

Unlike the regulations in the US or the UK, the accounting laws and decrees of the French state apply to all business enterprises, not just to companies, and cover the keeping of accounting records and the needs of the taxation authorities as well as reporting to owners and creditors. Articles L123-12 to L123-28 of the Commercial Code as restructured on 22 September 2000 provide a framework of general accounting rules, applicable to all forms of business enterprise. The emphasis of the Code is as much on the keeping of accounting records as on the preparation of annual financial statements.

The most important forms of business enterprise in France are the *société anonyme* (SA) and the *société à responsabilité limitée* (SARL). An SA is roughly equivalent to a UK public company and an SARL to a UK private company, although the SARL, originally based on the German GmbH (see Section 14.3.3), has some of the aspects of the UK partnership. The number of SAs and SARLs in existence at a given date is not published on a regular basis. In 1999 there were about 154,000 SAs and 742,000 SARLs. Also in that year about 60 per cent of French business enterprises were unincorporated. Companies are also subject to the accounting provisions of the Companies Act as incorporated in the Commercial Code (Articles L232-1 to L233-27). The Act dates from 1966 but was amended in the 1980s to implement the Fourth and Seventh Directives of the EU.

The PCG uses size measured by balance sheet total, turnover and number of employees to determine choice of permissible financial statement formats and what must be disclosed in the Notes, but the cut-off points are not the same for each. In practice most companies, irrespective of size, use the standard formats (see Section 15.2.1). Because different size criteria are used for different purposes, no simple table, such as Table 14.2 for Germany, can be presented.

French companies are not allowed to use IFRS for unconsolidated statements.

Table 14.2 **Size limits for small and medium-sized companies in Germany**

	Small	Medium-sized
Turnover	€8.03 million	€32.12 million
Balance sheet total	€4.015 million	€16.06 million
Employees	50	250

14.3.3 Germany

In Germany, as in France, all business enterprises, including sole traders and part-nerships (general or limited), are subject to the accounting requirements of the Commercial Code (HGB), although the requirements vary with legal form and size. Companies comprise primarily the *Aktiengesellschaft* (AG) and the *Gesellschaft mit beschränkter Haftung* (GmbH). The AG is the nearest analogy to a British PLC or a French SA. The decision-making power and responsibility in AGs are concentrated within the management board (*Vorstand*). In addition, there is a supervisory board (*Aufsichtsrat*), one-third of whose members (or half if the number of employees exceeds 2,000) are appointed by the workforce, and the other members by the shareholders' meeting. The *Aufsichtsrat* comprises non-executive directors. Such a board is unknown to British law but has parallels in the Netherlands, and, option-ally, in France. Its main functions are to appoint and dismiss the members of the management board, to supervise the latter body, and to approve the annual fin-ancial statements. The supervisory board may not assume management functions. Members of the management board are not eligible to join the supervisory board. The KonTraG of 1998 (see Chapter 9) passed control of audit assignments from the management board to the supervisory board, and strengthened the supervisory board in other ways.

The GmbH is quite similar to the AG in its basic legal characteristics, such as sep-arate legal personality and the nature of the company (although it has partnership aspects). However, it has some quite distinct features, particularly the less restrictive legal regulations. Accordingly, a GmbH's formation is simpler and cheaper than that of the AG. Most German subsidiaries of foreign MNEs are set up as GmbHs. There is no requirement to establish a supervisory board unless the workforce exceeds 500 or it is required by the articles of association. Unlike the UK and France, there is a separate body of private company law in Germany. A common business form is the one-person company.

Other legal forms of business enterprise include the *Einzelkaufmann* (sole pro-prietorship) as well as the OHG (partnership), KG (limited partnership) and the popular GmbH & Co. (a limited partnership with a corporation as a general partner).

Data on the number of companies are not provided by official sources. However, fairly recent data show that AGs decreased from a total of about 17,000 in 1926 to 3,000 in 1992 but rose to about 18,000 in 2006. As with PLCs and SAs, only a minority of AGs (about 650) are listed on a stock exchange. By contrast, GmbHs rose from about 15,500 in 1909 to over 814,000 in 2006. Medium-sized and small businesses seem to prefer the GmbH form, whereas the AG is mainly used by com-panies that need to raise money on the capital market. In 2001 the largest 104 industrial enterprises in Germany by turnover were 27 AGs, 31 GmbHs, one KG, five OHGs, 39 GmbH&Co.KGs and one other.

In addition to the requirements of the Commercial Code, companies must follow rules laid down in the *Aktiengesetz* (AktG, Stock Corporation Law) and the *GmbHGesetz* (GmbHG, private company law) respectively. Larger partnerships fall within the scope of the disclosure requirements of the *Publizitätsgesetz* (PublG, Disclosure Act) of 1969. The Act was introduced after the failures of some large partnerships had demonstrated that although no shareholders were involved there were major impacts on other stakeholders including governments (Eierle, 2005).

The extent to which the supplementary rules of the HGB have to be followed varies according to the size of the company. The size limits for small and medium-sized companies are shown in Table 14.2. A company has to meet at least two of the three size criteria in consecutive years. There are no exemptions for large companies. Small companies are permitted to file an abbreviated balance sheet, do not have to file an income statement, and file abbreviated Notes. Medium-sized companies are allowed to prepare an abbreviated income statement and omit an analysis of sales in their Notes. Individual companies are permitted to file IFRS financial statements, but if they do so must also prepare (but need not file) HGB statements. From 2007 onwards, all companies are required to file their financial statements electronically with the Federal Gazette, which forwards them to the local commercial Registry.

14.3.4 The UK

In the UK all business enterprises are required to keep accounting records for taxation purposes but specific financial reporting measurement and disclosure requirements apply only to companies, not to sole traders or partnerships (except limited liability partnerships, see below). Companies have been the most important form of business enterprise since the nineteenth century. The most economically significant type of company recognized by UK company law is the public company limited by shares, and the most numerous is the private company limited by shares. There are also companies limited by guarantee and unlimited companies, but these are relatively rare. Table 14.3 gives the number of public and private companies limited by shares in the UK in 2006. The status of UK companies has been indicated in their names only since the implementation of the Second EU Directive on company law in 1980. 'PLC' or 'plc' indicates a public company and 'Ltd' a private company.

The essential difference between public and private companies is that only the former have the right to make an issue of shares or debentures to the public. To be a public company is a necessary but not a sufficient condition for a Stock Exchange listing. There are about 2,600 listed domestic companies in the United Kingdom.

As a result of the implementation of the EU Fourth Directive in 1981, the most important distinction within non-listed companies for financial reporting purposes is that between large, medium-sized and small companies. Size is measured by sales

Table 14.3 **Companies limited by shares registered in the UK as at 31 March 2006**

	000s	%
Public companies	11.5	0.5
Private companies	2,118.7	99.5
Total	2,130.2	100.0

Source: Department of Trade and Industry (2006).

Table 14.4 Size limits for small and medium-sized companies in the UK

	Small	Medium-sized
Turnover	£6.5 million	£25.9 million
Balance sheet total	£3.26 million	£12.9 million
Employees	50	250

(turnover), balance sheet total (i.e. fixed assets plus current assets) and number of employees. The size limits vary from time to time. Table 14.4 sets out the current requirements, which correspond to the maxima allowed by the EU.

Large companies must file a full set of audited financial statements with the Registrar of Companies. Medium-sized companies are permitted to file and send to shareholders a balance sheet and an abbreviated profit and loss account (called an income statement in IFRS). Small companies are permitted to file an abbreviated balance sheet and are exempt from filing a profit and loss account. Subject to certain restrictions, private companies that have an annual turnover of not more than £5.6 million and a balance sheet total of not more than £2.8 million need not be audited. These limits are the maxima allowed by the EU.

The attractiveness of the private company form to, especially, small business enterprises has restricted the number of partnerships, except for professional services. Limited liability partnerships (LLPs) were introduced mainly as a result of lobbying by large accountancy firms. LLPs are similar to companies in benefiting from corporate personality and limited liability (for all the partners) but each partner is taxed individually and an LLP is not liable to corporation tax. Audited financial statements which give a true and fair view and comply with accounting standards must be filed by LLPs with the Registrar of Companies. There were 13,426 LLPs as at 31 March 2006.

SUMMARY

France

- Accounting rules are codified in a Commercial Code (*Code de commerce*) and a national accounting plan (*Plan comptable général*, PCG), both of which have been influenced by EU Directives.

- The PCG is administered by the *Conseil National de Comptabilité* (CNC), a mixed public/private-sector body.

- Tax legislation, which is compatible with the PCG, is a very important influence on the financial statements of individual business enterprises.

- The French accountancy profession is increasingly influential but has never issued accounting standards.

- Accounting rules apply to all business enterprises, the most important of which are SAs and SARLs.

Germany

- The major influences on German accounting are the Commercial Code and tax legislation. Tax law requires expenses to be recorded in the financial statements if they are to be tax deductible.
- Germany, like the UK, has no national accounting plan.
- The standards set by the GASC do not apply to individual companies.
- Germany has a wide variety of forms of business enterprise. The most important are AGs, GmbHs and GmbH & Cos.
- The Code and tax laws apply to all business enterprises.

UK

- Company law is a major direct influence on corporate financial reporting but accounting standards (FRSs and SSAPs) are also very important.
- Both law and standards have been influenced by professional accountants, EU Directives, US GAAP and, especially since 2005, international standards.
- Accounting standards cover both disclosure and measurement but disclosure requirements vary considerably according to whether a company is public or private and whether it is large, medium-sized or small.
- The recognized standard-setter is the Accounting Standards Board, which is independent of government and the professional bodies; its standards are mandatory for all companies and are converging with international standards.
- UK standard-setters have used the true and fair requirement to restrict or expand the detailed requirements of the Companies Act.
- The most important forms of business enterprise are public and private companies.

References

France

Colasse, B. (ed.) (1998) *Encyclopédie de Comptabilité, Contrôle de Gestion et Audit*, Economica, Paris.

Colasse, B. and Standish, P. (1998) 'De la réforme 1996–1998 du dispositif français de normalisation comptable', *Comptabilité, contrôle, audit*, September.

Fortin, A. (1991) 'The 1947 Accounting Plan: origins and influence on subsequent practice', *Accounting Historians Journal*, December, reprinted in Lemarchand and Parker (1996).

Howard, S.E. (1932) 'Public rules for private accounting in France, 1673 to 1807', *Accounting Review*, Vol. 7, No. 2, reprinted in Lemarchand and Parker (1996).

Lamb, M., Nobes, C.W. and Roberts, A.D. (1998) 'International variations in the connections between tax and financial reporting', *Accounting and Business Research*, Summer.

Lemarchand, Y. and Parker, R.H. (eds) (1996) *Accounting in France/La Comptabilité en France. Historical Essays/Etudes Historiques*, Garland Publishing, New York.

Raybaud-Turrillo, B. and Teller, R. (1998) 'Droit et comptabilité', in Colasse (1998).

Richard, J. (1992) 'De l'histoire du plan comptable français et de sa réforme eventuelle', in Lemarchand and Parker (1996).

Standish, P.E.M. (1990) 'Origins of the plan comptable général: a study of cultural intrusion and reaction', *Accounting and Business Research*, Autumn, reprinted in Lemarchand and Parker (1996).

Standish, P.E.M. (1997) *The French Plan Comptable*, Ordre des experts comptables and Institute of Chartered Accountants in England and Wales, Paris.

Germany

Eierle, B. (2005) 'Differential reporting in Germany. A historical analysis', *Accounting, Business and Financial History*, Vol. 15, No. 3.

Haller, A. (1992) 'The relationship of financial and tax accounting in Germany: a major reason for accounting disharmony in Europe', *International Journal of Accounting*, Vol. 27, No. 4.

Lamb, M., Nobes, C.W. and Roberts, A.D. (1998) 'International variations in the connections between tax and financial reporting', *Accounting and Business Research*, Summer.

UK

Alexander, D. (1999) 'A benchmark for the adequacy of published financial statements', *Accounting and Business Research*, Summer.

Alexander, D. (2001) 'The over-riding importance of internationalism: a reply to Nobes', *Accounting and Business Research*, Spring.

Arden, M. (1993) 'The true and fair requirement', *Accountancy*, July, reprinted in Parker and Nobes (1994).

Dearing, Sir R. (1988) (The Dearing Report) *The Making of Accounting Standards, Report of the Review Committee*, presented to the Consultative Committee of Accountancy Bodies.

Department of Trade and Industry (2006) *Companies in 2005–2006*, HMSO, London.

Department of Trade and Industry (2002) *Modernising Company Law*, Cm. 5553.

Lamb, M., Nobes, C.W. and Roberts, A.D. (1998) 'International variations in the connections between tax and financial reporting', *Accounting and Business Research*, Summer.

Nobes, C.W. (2000) 'Is true and fair of over-riding importance?: a comment on Alexander's benchmark', *Accounting and Business Research*, Autumn.

Parker, R.H. and Nobes, C.W. (1994) *An International View of True and Fair Accounting*, Routledge, London.

Parker, R.H., Wolnizer, P. and Nobes, C.W. (1996) *Readings in True and Fair*, Garland Publishing, New York.

Tweedie, D. (1988) 'True and fair v the rule book: which is the answer to creative accounting?', *Pacific Accounting Review*, December, reprinted in Parker *et al.* (1996).

Further reading | ## France

Mikol, A. (1995) 'The history of financial reporting in France', in P. Walton (ed.), *European Financial Reporting. A History*, Academic Press, London.

Raffegau, J. *et al.* (latest edition) *Mémento Pratique Francis Lefebvre Comptable*, Editions Francis Lefebvre, Paris.

Germany

Ballwieser, W. (2001) 'Germany – Individual Accounts', in Ordelheide and KPMG (2001).

Beckman, J., Brandes, C. and Eierle, B. (2007) 'German reporting practices: an analysis of reconciliations from German commercial code to IFRS or US GAAP', *Advances in International Accounting*, Vol. 20.

Fey, G. and Fladt, G. (2006) *Deutsches Bilanzrecht Deutsch-Englische Textausgabe begruendet von J. Brooks and D. Mertin – German Accounting legislation, Synoptic Translation with Introduction founded by J. Brooks and D. Mertin*, 4th edition, IDW-Verlag, Düsseldorf.

Institut der Wirtschaftsprüfer (2000) *Wirtschaftsprüfer-Handbuch*, Band I, Institut der Wirtschaftsprüfer-Verlag, Düsseldorf.

Leuz, C. and Wuestemann, J. (2004) 'The role of accounting in the German financial system', in Krahnen, J.P. and Schmidt, R.H. (2004), *The German Financial System*, Oxford University Press, London.

Seckler, G. (2001) 'Germany' in D. Alexander and S. Archer (eds), *European Accounting Guide*, 4th edn, Harcourt Brace, San Diego.

UK

Accounting Standards (texts of FRSs, SSAPs, SORPs, exposure drafts, important technical releases; published annually by the Institute of Chartered Accountants in England and Wales).

Cooke, T.E., Choudhury, M. and Wallace, R.S.O. (2001) 'United Kingdom – Individual Accounts', in D. Ordelheide and KPMG, *Transnational Accounting*, Vol. 3, Palgrave, Basingstoke.

Ernst & Young, *UK and International GAAP* (latest edition), Butterworths Tolley, London.

Lamb, M. (2001) 'United Kingdom', in D. Alexander and S. Archer (eds), *European Accounting Guide*, Aspen, New York.

Napier, C. (1995) 'The history of financial reporting in the United Kingdom', in P. Walton (ed.), *European Financial Reporting. A History*, Academic Press, London.

Useful websites for Chapters 14 and 15

France

Association Francophone de Comptabilité	www.afc-cca.com
Comité de la Réglementation Comptable	www.minefi.gouv.fr/themes/ entreprises/compta_entreprises/ directions_services-CNCompta-rcrc_modify.php
Compagnie Nationale des Commissaires aux Comptes	www.cncc.fr
Conseil National de la Comptabilité	www.minefi.gouv.fr/ directions_services/CNCompta
Ordre des Experts Comptables	www.expert-comptables.com

Germany

Institut der Wirtschaftsprüfer	www.idw.de
Wirtschaftsprüferkammer	www.wpk.de

UK

Accounting Standards Board	www.frc.org.uk/asb
Association of Chartered Certified Accountants	www.accaglobal.com
British Accounting Association	www.shef.ac.uk/baa
Chartered Institute of Management Accountants	www.cimaglobal.com

Chartered Institute of Public Finance and Accountancy	www.cipfa.org.uk
Department for Business, Enterprise and Regulatory Reform	www.berr.gov.uk
Financial Reporting Council	www.frc.org.uk
Institute of Chartered Accountants in England and Wales	www.icaew.co.uk
Institute of Chartered Accountants of Scotland	www.icas.org.uk
Registrar of Companies	www.companieshouse.gov.uk

QUESTIONS

Suggested answers to the asterisked questions are given at the end of the book.

14.1* The US, UK, France and Germany have evolved different answers to the question as to which business enterprises should be subject to accounting regulation. Which country, in your opinion, has got it 'right'?

14.2* Why do UK accounting rules for individual companies differ not simply on the distinction between public and private companies?

14.3 Is it useful to regulate, as for example in France, the keeping of accounting records, as well as the preparation of financial statements?

14.4 What are the arguments for and against a national accounting plan?

14.5 'The UK accountancy profession no longer has any influence on the accounting rules relating to individual financial statements.' Discuss.

14.6 Compare the composition and the roles of the ASB in the UK and the CRC in France.

14.7 Why has the ASB in the UK decided to converge (partially but not completely) UK standards for individual companies with IFRS?

Contents of the *Plan comptable général* (relating to financial accounting and reporting)

TITLE I – OBJECT AND PRINCIPLES OF ACCOUNTING

Chapter I – Field of application
Chapter II – Principles
Chapter III – Definition of annual accounts

TITLE II – DEFINITION OF ASSETS, LIABILITIES, INCOME AND CHARGES

Chapter I – Assets and liabilities
Chapter II – Charges and income
Chapter III – Profit or loss

TITLE III – ACCOUNTING RECOGNITION AND VALUATION RULES

Chapter I – Accounting for assets, liabilities, income and charges
Chapter II – Valuation and method of accounting for assets and liabilities
Chapter III – Particular valuation and accounting recognition procedures
Chapter IV – Valuation of assets and liabilities where value depends on foreign currency fluctuations
Chapter V – Revaluation
Chapter VI – Valuation and accounting recognition of specific assets and liabilities
Chapter VII – Valuation and accounting for specific financial transactions
Chapter VIII – Taking account of transactions extending beyond the financial year
Chapter IX – Valuation and accounting recognition of joint transactions and transactions for the account of third parties

TITLE IV – KEEPING, STRUCTURE AND FUNCTIONING OF ACCOUNTS

Chapter I – Organization of accounting
Chapter II – Recording
Chapter III – Accounting code
Chapter IV – Functioning of accounts

TITLE V – FINANCIAL STATEMENTS

Chapter I – Annual accounts
Chapter II – Annual account formats – Balance sheet – Income statement
Chapter III – Formats of annual accounts – Notes on the accounts

Adapted from http://www.finances.gouv.fr/reglementation/avis

	BALANCE SHEET				OPERATING	
Class 1	Class 2	Class 3	Class 4	Class 5	Class 6	Class 7
Capital (Owner equity, loans and debts payable)	Fixed assets	Stocks and work in progress	Debt receivable and payable	Financial	Charges	Income
10 Capital and reserves	20 Intangible assets	30	40 Suppliers and related accounts	50 Short-term investment securities	60 Purchases (except 603). 603. Change in stocks (consumables and goods for resale)	70 Sales of manufactured products, services, goods for resale
11 Profit or loss carried forward	21 Tangible assets	31 Raw materials (and supplies)	41 Customers and related accounts	51 Banks, financial and similar institutions	61 External services	71 Change in stocks of finished products and work in progress
12 Profit or loss for the financial year	22 Assets in concession	32 Other consumables	42 Personnel and related accounts	52 Short-term financial instruments	62 Other external services	72 Own work capitalized
13 Investment grants	23 Assets in progress	33 Work in progress (goods)	43 Social security and other social agencies	53 Cash in hand	63 Taxes, levies and similar payments	73 Net period income from long-term transactions
14 Tax-regulated provisions	24	34 Work in progress (services)	44 State and other public authorities	54 Expenditure authorizations and letters of credit	64 Personnel costs	74 Operating grants
15 Provisions for liabilities and charges	25	35 Product stocks	45 Group and partners/ associates	55	65 Other current operating charges	75 Other current operating income
16 Loans and similar debts payable	26 Participating interests and related debts receivable	36	46 Sundry debts receivable and payable	56	66 Financial charges	76 Financial income
17 Debts payable related to participating interests	27 Other financial assets	37 Stocks of goods for resale	47 Provisional or suspense accounts	57	67 Extraordinary charges	77 Extraordinary income
18 Reciprocal branch and joint venture accounts	28 Cumulative depreciation on fixed assets	38	48 Accrual accounts	58 Internal transfers	68 Appropriations to depreciation and provisions	78 Depreciation and provisions written back
19	29 Provisions for diminution in value of fixed assets	39 Provisions for diminution in value of stocks and work in progress	49 Provisions for doubtful debts	59 Provisions for diminution in value of financial assets	69 Employee profit share, income and similar taxes	79 Charges transferred

15 Accounting rules and practices of individual companies in Europe

Robert Parker

OBJECTIVES

After reading this chapter, you should be able to:

- compare the financial statement formats used in France, Germany and the UK;
- compare the accounting principles applicable to individual companies in France, Germany and the UK;
- describe the differences from IFRS and explain why they exist.

15.1 Introduction

Chapter 13 discussed the extent to which financial reporting by individual companies differs from that of groups of companies around the world. Chapter 14 looked at rule-making for individual companies in three contrasting EU countries, the UK, France and Germany. This chapter looks at how accounting rules and practices differ for individual companies in those countries and compares their rules and practices with IFRS. The chapter does not deal with consolidated statements. The chapter demonstrates the important differences that still exist even after several decades of harmonization within the EU and after the adoption of IFRS for the consolidated statements of listed company groups. These differences exist both for financial statement formats (covered in detail in the Fourth Directive but barely mentioned in IFRS) and for accounting principles (covered in great detail in IFRS but more broadly and selectively in the Fourth Directive). The chapter assumes a knowledge of the rule-making bodies discussed in Chapter 14. The emphasis is on France and Germany rather than the UK, as the first two countries are better examples of countries whose individual companies' accounts differ considerably from IFRS. Unlike the UK, they differ in the absence of rules in areas covered by IFRS, as well as in having divergent rules in areas covered by both domestic standards and IFRS (Ding *et al.*, 2007). In all three countries, but to varying extents, IFRS are influencing the content of national rules and practices. IFRS concepts and rules are having their greatest effect on individual companies in the UK. Their effect is beginning to felt in France but hardly at all so far in Germany.

15.2 France

15.2.1 Formats of financial statements

The primacy of the national accounting plan (PCG) in French accounting was stressed in Chapter 14. It is the PCG that regulates and sets out the prescribed formats for financial statements. These are not innovations introduced by the EU Fourth Directive, but a practice of long standing, although implementation of the Directive did bring about some changes. There are standard, abridged and extended formats, depending on size (as measured by balance sheet total, turnover and number of employees), but in practice almost all companies use the standard formats. These are set out in Appendix 15.1. Details of the composition of any item in the formats of an individual company can be found in the PCG. The standard balance sheet is usually presented in tabular (two-sided) form. The income statement may also be in this form, but most companies adopt the columnar form shown in Appendix 15.1.

Compared to the equivalent UK formats (see Appendix 15.3) more detail is shown on the face of the balance sheet rather than in the Notes. On the assets side are presented, in order of decreasing liquidity, fixed assets (classified into intangible, tangible and financial) and current assets. Excluded from fixed and current assets and shown separately at the foot of the balance sheet are the *comptes de régularisation* which represent expenditure spread over more than one period. They include prepaid expenses, deferred charges, redemption premiums and negative exchange differences, only the first of which is considered an asset under IFRS.

On the liabilities and capital side are presented shareholders' funds, provisions for liabilities and charges, and liabilities, with positive foreign exchange differences at the foot. Shareholders' funds are divided into:

1 share capital

2 share premiums

3 revaluation reserves

4 legal reserves

5 statutory reserves

6 tax-regulated reserves

7 other reserves

8 profit or loss brought forward

9 profit or loss for the year

10 investment grants

11 tax-regulated provisions.

Some of these items are typical of creditor/tax oriented accounting. The legal reserve arises from the obligation of French companies to retain 5 per cent of each year's profit, less losses brought forward, until an amount of 10 per cent of issued share capital is reached. The reserve is undistributable but may be turned into shares. Revaluation reserves arise from revaluations required or allowed by tax law. Some French company balance sheets still retain a revaluation reserve arising from the revaluation of non-depreciable fixed assets as at 31 December 1976. Tax-regulated reserves contain items such as untaxed long-term gains arising from the sale of fixed assets. Tax-regulated provisions are those which must be set up for a tax deduction when a company provides for expenses which exist only for tax purposes, such as excess depreciation. French companies sometimes publish balance sheets with one column before and one column after the allocation of profits to reserves and distributions. If only one column is shown it is before allocation.

The income statement is usually presented in columnar format, with income and expenses subdivided into operating, financial and '*exceptionnel*'. The last of these is often translated into English as 'extraordinary' but is a wider term than either extraordinary or exceptional.

The CNC recommends publication of a funds statement (*tableau de financement*) based on working capital flows. The OEC recommends a statement of cash flows (*tableau de flux de trésorerie*) more in line with international practice. Neither is mandatory for individual companies. The former is still common but is being gradually superseded by the latter.

Notes to the financial statements were not required by law in France before the implementation of the Fourth Directive in 1983 (Parker, 1996), although a number of schedules were required in addition to the balance sheet and income statement. The functions of the Notes (*Annexe*) are set out in the Commercial Code. They are:

1 completing and commenting on the information given by the balance sheet and the income statement;

2 supplying additional information, if following the rules is not sufficient to give a true and fair view;

3 mentioning, in exceptional cases, departures from an accounting requirement, if necessary to give a true and fair view;

4 describing and justifying changes in accounting policies or in the presentation of the financial statements.

All types of business enterprises, not just companies, are required to provide an *annexe*, although sole traders below a certain size are exempted. A simplified *annexe* is permitted for SAs, SARLs and partnerships below a certain size (as measured by balance sheet total, turnover and number of employees, but with different cut-off points than for formats).

The *annexe* plays an important role in connection both with the true and fair view requirement (see below) and with the close relationship between financial reporting and tax rules. Companies must disclose in the Notes material tax effects on the accounts. In practice, depreciation is the most important item affected. For a list of the items required to be disclosed in the annexe of an individual company, see Gélard (2001, pages 1098–9).

15.2.2 Accounting principles: differences from IFRS

Since the implementation of the EU Fourth Directive, French financial statements must display not only *régularité* (i.e. be in accordance with the rules) and *sincerité* (i.e. be in accordance with the spirit of the rules) but also give *une image fidèle* (the French version of a true and fair view – see Chapter 11). Regularity and sincerity are traditional French accounting concepts. Since a true and fair view is an imported concept with no precisely defined meaning even in its country of origin, there has been much discussion in France as to its meaning and significance (e.g. Pasqualini, 1992). In practice, both individual company statements, which follow accounting principles designed to satisfy the needs of creditors and the tax authorities, and group financial statements, which follow accounting principles designed to appeal to equity investors both in France and overseas (i.e. IFRS), are deemed to be capable of giving a true and fair view.

In this chapter, the emphasis is on individual companies. For these, the recognition and valuation of assets and liabilities follows a mainly 'patrimonial' approach, i.e. it is based on legal rights rather than on economic substance. The main valuation method is historical cost modified by prudence, with a tendency to understate rather than overstate profits and assets. This is what is to be expected of financial reporting driven by the needs of creditors and taxation rather than equity investment. The function of accounting in such an environment is, in a famous phrase, to act as the 'algebra of the law' (Garnier, 1947).

The CNC and the CRC have decided officially not to extend permission to use IFRS to the financial statements of individual companies. However, in practice they are doing so progressively and partially in another way: by converging French rules with IFRS on certain topics. In particular the CRC has issued regulations on provisions, depreciation, the recognition and valuation of assets, and the fair value of financial instruments, which follow closely the language of the relevant IFRS. Details of the new regulations and the extent to which they bring French rules closer to IFRS are given in Richard and Collette (2005). The new rules are inconsistent with tax law, but the tax authorities have been flexible and devices such as *amortissements dérogatoires* (see point 3 below) are used to overcome the inconsistencies.

Convergence with IFRS in some areas can only be achieved by the amendment of laws and decrees, which is not within the powers of the CNC and the CRC (see Section 14.2.2).

At the individual company level, there remain many differences of detail between French accounting principles and IFRS. These are not easy to summarize and are subject to change, but some examples are given below. More generally it should be noted that there has been no abandonment of the principles of prudence or of the classification of expenses by nature rather than by function (see Section 2.9.4).

1 Some intangible items can be recognized as intangible assets (market share, portfolio of customers) which do not meet the definition of an intangible asset under IFRS; these and some other intangible assets are not required to be amortized.

2 It is not permissible to capitalize leases, the legal form of the contract (i.e. rental) taking precedence over its economic substance (i.e. acquisition of a fixed asset). The CRC has accepted the IASB's definition of an asset but limited it to items which form part of a company's patrimony.

3 The rules for depreciation have recently been amended to follow those of IFRS rather than those of the tax authorities, but extra tax-driven depreciation (*amortissement dérogatoire*) must still be accounted for. The principle of the separation of financial and tax accounts has not been accepted.

4 Payments made for retirement benefits to employees must be recorded as an expense. The CNC has stated a preference for recording a liability in the balance sheet, but disclosure in the Notes instead is permitted and is usual.

5 The inclusion of deferred taxes in the income statement and balance sheet is permitted, but is extremely rare in practice.

6 According to the PCG, the percentage of completion method is the preferred method for long-term contracts but the completed contract method is permissible and common.

7 Unrealized losses on foreign exchange transactions are recognized in the profit and loss account but unrealized gains are not.

8 Extraordinary/exceptional items are broadly defined.

9 Prior year adjustments are not allowed.

10 There are no specific requirements for the disclosure of:
   - a primary statement of changes in equity;
   - transactions with related parties except for limited requirements;
   - discontinued operations.

Table 15.1 summarizes some of these major differences between French accounting principles and IFRS in individual financial statements. Delvaille *et al.* (2005) discuss the convergence of France (and Germany and Italy) with IFRS.

The IASB's draft standard on small and medium-sized entities (SMEs) is under discussion. It has not been welcomed, but it may lead to some changes in detailed rules.

Table 15.1 Some major France/IFRS differences in individual company financial statements

Topic	France	IFRS
1 Establishment costs	Can be capitalized	Expensed
2 Finance leases	Cannot be capitalized	Capitalized
3 Liability for retirement benefits	May be disclosed in the Notes	Must be recognized in the balance sheet
4 Presentation of an issuer's capital instruments	Based on legal form	Based on substance, including splitting instruments into debt and equity
5 Unsettled foreign currency gains	Can be deferred	Taken to income
6 Construction contracts	Can be completed contract	Percentage of completion where outcome can be measured reliably
7 Extraordinary items	Wide definition	Not allowed
8 Policy changes and correction of fundamental errors	Through income	Prior year adjustment

15.3 Germany

15.3.1 Formats of financial statements

The *Handelsgesetzbuch* (HGB, Commercial Code) sets out the duty of every business to prepare annual financial statements. All businesses generally follow the format prescribed for companies (see Appendix 15.2), even though unincorporated businesses are not bound by a specific format. Since there is no concept of materiality in German law, all the legal headings are shown in a financial statement, even if they contain only very small amounts.

The balance sheet may only take the double entry form; the income statement may only be prepared in vertical format (see Appendix 15.2). There must be identical classification of successive financial statements and arbitrary changes in the form of presentation are prohibited. Exemptions for small and medium-sized companies have been explained in Chapter 14.

As shown in Appendix 15.2, equity comprises subscribed capital, capital reserves, revenue reserves and retained income for the year. Unpaid contributions to the subscribed capital may be shown separately on the assets side or deducted directly from equity. Capital reserves result from share premiums or other capital contributions by shareholders. Revenue reserves are created by management or by shareholder resolution from income of the year or a preceding year.

AGs are required to create legal reserves. Five per cent of net income for the year must be allocated to the reserves until the legal reserve and the capital reserves (excluding other capital contributions by shareholders) together equal 10 per cent of the nominal capital or such higher amount as is provided in the articles. Such reserves, designed to protect creditors, are also found in France (as already noted) and several other European countries and Japan, but not in the Anglo-Saxon world.

Included under revenue reserves are *Sonderposten mit Rücklageanteil* (special items with an equity element). These result from the setting up of tax-related provisions and provide good examples of tax regulations determing the content of commercial financial statements. They are created, for instance, in order to store the capital gain when land and buildings are sold, in order to postpone tax. They are also used to record the additional depreciation allowed by tax law. The item should be interpreted as both equity and a future tax liability.

The income statement must be presented vertically (see Appendix 15.2). Like a French statement, the basic structure contains the subdivisions of operational income and expenses, financial income and expenses and extraordinary income and expenses. Abbreviated presentations are permitted for small and medium-sized corporations (see Chapter 14).

Two types of classification of costs are allowed. The 'total costs' method classifies expenses according to their nature (e.g. materials, wages and salaries, depreciation, etc.). Expenses are determined from a production aspect. Inventory increases and decreases as well as own work capitalized are shown as adjusting items in the calculation of total performance. This is the usual German format and, before the 1985 amendments to the HGB, it was the only format allowed. The 'cost of sales' method separates expenditure according to function, i.e. manufacture, selling, general administration, and other.

Cash flow statements are not required for individual company financial statements.

15.3.2 Accounting principles: differences from IFRS

The HGB summarizes the main accounting principles: prudence, accruals, consistency, going concern and individual valuation. Adherence to historical cost is required. Since the implementation of the EU Fourth Directive, annual financial statements must, in compliance with principles of orderly bookkeeping, present a true and fair view[1] of net worth, financial position and results. If special circumstances result in the financial statements not showing a true and fair view, additional disclosures are required in the Notes. The reference to compliance with the principles of orderly bookkeeping implies that the true and fair view concept is not overriding and does not require accounting principles to be adjusted (Alexander, 1993 and 1996; Ordelheide, 1993 and 1996). In case of doubt, observance of the concept is achieved by disclosures in the Notes.

German accounting is in general rather conservative (Evans and Nobes, 1996). The impact of the tax law largely determines accounting for individual company financial statements. As explained in Section 14.2.3, expenses are only considered to be tax deductible (in the *Steuerbilanz*) if they are also included in the commercial

---

[1] Unter Beachtung der Grundsätze ordnungsmässiger Buchführung ein den tatsächlichen Verhältnissen entsprechendes Bild . . . zu vermitteln (S. 264(2) of the Commercial Code). More literally, the last eight words could be rendered as 'to present a picture in accordance with the actual circumstances'.

accounts (*Handelsbilanz*). This may lead to considerable distortions in the presentation of net worth, financial position and results.

Haller and Eierle (2004) summarize the discussion that has taken place in Germany as to the advantages and disadvantages of the application of IFRS to individual company accounts. They characterize the activities of the government as primarily reactive (to capital market pressure and EU law), conservative and slow, but nevertheless steady and continuous. IFRS is allowed for unconsolidated statements, but only if HGB statements are also prepared for tax and dividend calculations.

Accounting principles for individual companies continue to differ in important respects from IFRS. Examples of some major features of German accounting are given below.

1 Land must be stated at acquisition cost, buildings and other fixed assets at acquisition or manufacturing cost net of systematic depreciation. Companies generally charge the maximum depreciation allowed by tax law. The reverse 'authoritative principle' applies to depreciation provided for by tax law. Hence, special depreciation is recorded in the commercial balance sheet either as a reduction of assets or as 'special items' (see Section 15.3.1); companies must disclose the effects in the Notes.

2 Tangible and intangible assets cannot be valued above cost. Intangible assets (other than goodwill) acquired must be capitalized and then depreciated according to their useful life. The costs of raising equity capital, and intangible fixed assets that were not acquired for a consideration must not be included in the balance sheet. However, companies are permitted to capitalize start-up and business expansion expenses. This is not allowed under IFRS. Development expenditure cannot be capitalized. Any goodwill acquired by an individual company (by buying the net assets of a business) may be capitalized and must then be amortized over four years or according to the anticipated period of usefulness. Since tax law requires capitalization of such goodwill and provides for straight-line depreciation over a 15-year period, this method is the one most frequently used. Stolowy *et al.* (2001) compare the German rules on intangible assets with those of France and the IASB.

3 Leases are normally classified according to tax rules, and are seldom recognized as finance leases and capitalized (Garrod and Sieringhaus, 1995).

4 Marketable securities and other financial assets are not marked to market. If there is a temporary impairment, current financial assets must be written down and non-current financial assets may be written down to the lower value. If there is a permanent impairment, both current and non-current assets must be written down to the lower value.

5 Valuation of inventories may be based on the weighted average method or by using FIFO or LIFO. Since LIFO is acceptable for tax purposes, it is commonly followed for accounting purposes in order to reduce tax. Inventories are written down to net realizable value, or if no net realizable value is available, to replacement cost. Inventory costs may include attributable portions of general overheads. For tax purposes, material and production overheads must be included in addition to direct material and production costs and, therefore, generally the cost

of inventories is based on full production-related overhead absorption. The completed contract method has to be used for long-term construction projects. Stage of completion accounting may be applied to the extent that the customer has agreed that a stage has been completed successfully. In general, the completed contract method is used for the recognition of revenues on construction contracts and services.

6 Non- or low-interest bearing receivables are discounted to present value, which is another illustration of conservatism in the German approach to accounting. General credit risk is usually covered by providing a lump-sum allowance on debtors, while uncollectable amounts are written off.

7 Creditors are stated at the amount payable. Discounting of non- or low-interest bearing liabilities is not permitted. There is generally no classification on the face of the balance sheet into current and non-current liabilities; such detail is shown in the Notes.

8 Provisions must be set up for uncertain liabilities and for potential losses from contracted transactions. They are also required for repairs and maintenance expenses to be incurred within the first three months of the following year. Provisions must be stated at the amount required according to sound business judgement. The 'prudence' concept in particular is to be observed. This wording leads to a wide variety of provisions, which are usually made as large as possible because of their significance in the determination of taxable income. Provisions may also be set up for repairs and maintenance carried out after the first three months but before the end of the following financial year, and for certain periods in respect of expenses for which a necessity will arise over a longer period, such as major repairs. These latter provisions are not tax deductible. Given that certain provisions are not tax deductible, it is possible for a company to build up discretionary provisions in good years, and to reverse this process in bad years in order to cover reductions in profit or even losses.

9 Unlike most provisions, pension provisions are discounted. Employee benefit calculations generally follow tax regulations with respect to the actuarial valuation method and discount rate; they normally do not take account of expected future salary increases. Pension commitments made after 1 January 1987 must be recorded, but accrual for earlier commitments is optional. Pension provisions are tax deductible under tax rules. In general, pension provisions are larger under US or IFRS rules, which do not take account of tax deductibility. This is an example of less conservative accounting in Germany. A further difference is that German pension obligations are often unfunded; that is, money is not set aside irrevocably to cover them. The obligation is therefore shown on the balance sheet. By contrast, UK and US companies fund their obligations by sending money to outside institutions (e.g. pension trusts) and thus fully or partially cover their obligations, which they then show as net liabilities on balance sheets.

10 A provision for deferred taxes must be set up if the taxable income of the current and prior years is lower than the commercial income before taxes, and if the resulting tax burden will probably be balanced by a correspondingly higher tax expense in later years. A deferred tax asset may be, but need not be, recorded if the taxable income of the current and prior years is higher than the

commercial income before taxes, and if the resulting tax charge will probably be equalized by a corresponding lower tax expense in later years. This item is to be shown separately with an appropriate description and is to be explained in the notes. The method used shows the net amount of positive and negative effects of all items. These are, of course, less important than in Anglo-Saxon countries, because of the closeness of German tax and accounting rules. Deferred tax is calculated on the basis of timing differences rather than temporary differences. Deferred tax assets arising on loss carryforwards must not be recognized, and most others need not be.

11 There are no specific rules for foreign currency translation or hedge accounting. Foreign currency monetary balances are generally translated at the worse of transaction and closing rates so as to avoid the recognition of gains on unsettled balances.

12 There are no specific requirements for the disclosure of:
   – a cash flow statement;
   – a statement of changes in equity;
   – related party transactions other than those with equity participants;
   – discontinued operations;
   – earnings per share.

Table 15.2 summarizes some major differences between German accounting principles and IFRS in individual company financial statements.

Table 15.2 **Some major Germany/IFRS differences for individual companies**

Topic	Germany	IFRS
1 Fixed assets	Cost or lower	Can be held at fair value
2 Goodwill	Either expensed, or capitalized and amortized	Capitalized and impaired
3 Contracts	Usually completed contract	Percentage of completion
4 Trading and available-for-sale marketable securities	Lower of cost and market	Fair value
5 Foreign currency monetary balances	Worse of transaction rate and closing rate	Closing rate
6 Inventories	LIFO common	LIFO not allowed
7 Provisions	Can be made when no obligation; not discounted	Only when obligation; discounted
8 Employee benefit provisions	Follow tax rules	Take account of expected salaries; use market discount rate
9 Deferred tax	Timing differences; some deferred tax assets not recognized	Temporary differences
10 Policy changes and correction of errors	Through income	Prior year adjustment

The IASB's draft standard on SMEs has been widely discussed in Germany, but, given the many differences between IFRS and HGB financial statements, and the unsuitability of the former for tax and dividend determination purposes, it is unlikely that the German legislator will implement the standard.

15.4 United Kingdom

15.4.1 Formats of financial statements

UK Companies Acts have traditionally laid little stress on the formats of financial statements. The basic requirements of the Companies Act, as applicable to individual companies, are that companies must prepare *either* a balance sheet and a profit and loss account that comply with the detailed regulations made under the Act, *or* accounts that comply with international accounting standards. The former are termed 'Companies Act individual accounts'; the latter 'IAS individual accounts'.

Companies Act individual accounts must comply with mandatory formats for the balance sheet and profit and loss account, and with lists of items to be disclosed in the notes and accounts. The formats (see Appendix 15.3) are derived from the EU Fourth Directive but the UK government, unlike those in some other member states (e.g. Germany), deliberately left them as flexible as possible. Thus UK companies may choose between two balance sheet formats and four profit and loss account formats (and more after the 2003 accounts Modernization Directive). The published financial statements of UK companies (especially profit and loss accounts, and again unlike those of their German counterparts) do not at first sight greatly resemble the formats in the legislation. This is mainly because, apart from main headings, much detail is allowed to be shown in the Notes and partly because the formats are sometimes followed in spirit rather than to the letter.

Two other statements are required, not by company legislation but by accounting standards. They are the statement of total recognized gains and losses (STRGL) and the cash flow statement. The function of the STRGL, required by FRS 3, is to record those gains and losses that are not included in the profit and loss account, for example those arising on the translation of foreign currency financial statements and the revaluation of assets. The origins of the statement of recognized income and expense (SORIE), an alternative in IAS 1 to the US-derived statement of changes in equity, can be traced to the STRGL, which has no equivalent in French and German domestic regulations.

Cash flow statements are required by FRS 1, except for certain small companies. The format of the cash flow statement is very different from that required under IAS 7. For example, there are three headings of cash flow under IAS 7 (see Chapter 6) but nine under FRS 1. Also, whereas IAS 7 statements reconcile to a wide total of 'cash and cash equivalents' (including investment of up to three months' maturity), FRS 1's reconciling total is 'cash' (up to 24 hours' notice deposits).

15.4.2 Accounting principles: differences from IFRS

As noted in Chapter 14, the Accounting Standards Board in the UK is following a deliberate and systematic policy of converging accounting standards, for all companies, and for both individual financial companies and groups, with international standards. The list of UK standards shown in Table 14.1 includes many that are directly based on IFRS (see FRS 20 onwards). The relationship between law and standards in the UK, including those on accounting principles, was discussed in Section 14.2.4.

Company law in the UK permits companies to choose between IFRS and UK GAAP for unconsolidated statements and for the consolidated statements of unlisted companies. The difference between IFRS and UK GAAP is, however, limited given the ASB's declared policy of convergence. Many of the remaining differences relate to consolidation issues so are not the concern of this chapter. The differences related to individual company financial statements in 2007 are summarized in Table 15.3. Some of these, for example, on deferred tax, have major effects. There are no published plans to remove most of these differences.

The content of the IASB's draft standard on SMEs is closer to existing accounting practice by UK SMEs than French and German SMEs, but it has not been greeted with much enthusiasm in the UK (Shearer and Sleigh-Johnson, 2007). It can be seen as a competitor to the FRSSE. The IASB standard may be more appropriate for medium-sized entities than small ones (see Section 14.2.4).

Table 15.3 Some UK/IFRS differences for individual companies

Topic	UK	IFRS
1 Intangible assets with indefinite lives	Can be (and usually are) amortized	Must have annual impairment test
2 Development costs meeting certain criteria	Can be capitalized	Must be capitalized
3 Investment property	Must be fair valued, with gains and losses going to the statement of total recognized gains and losses (STRGL)	Can be fair valued, whereupon gains and losses go to income
4 Actuarial gains and losses	Taken immediately to STRGL	Can be taken gradually to income
5 Deferred tax	Based on timing differences; can be discounted	Based on temporary differences; must not be discounted
6 Formats of statements	Specified by Companies Act	Not specified
7 Cash flow statements	Nine headings; reconciling to cash	Three headings; reconciling to cash and cash equivalents

SUMMARY

General

- Accounting rules and practices between countries differ more for individual companies than for groups, as illustrated particularly by financial statement formats and accounting principles.

France

- Balance sheet and income statement formats for individual business enterprises are set out in the PCG. Several items in these formats (e.g. legal reserves and tax-regulated provisions) are the product of creditor and tax oriented accounting.
- All financial statements must give a true and fair view but this largely affects the Notes not the balance sheet and income statement.
- Traditional accounting theory as applied to the financial statements of individual companies has a 'patrimonial' approach to the recognition and valuation of assets and liabilities.
- As a result, the rules relating to, *inter alia*, deferred taxation, leases, fixed asset and inventory valuation differ as between French and IFRS rules (and between French individual and group financial statements).

Germany

- Formats for balance sheets and income statements are laid down in the HGB. All items must be disclosed, whether or not they are material.
- Despite the introduction of a true and fair view requirement, the financial statements of individual companies are largely determined by tax rules.

UK

- Financial statement formats have been kept as flexible as possible within the constraints of EU Directives.
- The Accounting Standards Board is converging UK rules as far as possible with international standards. Nevertheless, there are some important remaining differences between UK GAAP and IFRS.

References

Alexander, D. (1993) 'A European true and fair view?', *European Accounting Review*, Vol. 2, No. 1.

Alexander, D. (1996) 'Truer and fairer. Uninvited comments on invited comments', *European Accounting Review*, Vol. 5, No. 3.

Delvaille, P., Ebbers, G. and Saccon, C. (2005) 'International financial reporting convergence: evidence from three continental European countries', *Accounting in Europe*, Vol. 2.

Ding, Y., Hope, O-K., Jeanjean, T. and Solowy, H. (2007) 'Differences between domestic accounting standards and IAS: measurement, determinants and implications', *Journal of Accounting and Public Policy*, Vol. 26, No. 1.

Evans, L. and Nobes, C. (1996) 'Some mysteries relating to the prudence principle in the Fourth Directive and in German and British Law', *European Accounting Review*, Vol. 5, No. 2.

Garnier, P. (1947) *La comptabilité, algèbre du droit et méthode d'observation des sciences économiques*, Dunod, Paris.

Garrod, N. and Sieringhaus, I. (1995) 'European Union harmonization: the case of leased assets in the United Kingdom and Germany', *European Accounting Review*, Vol. 4, No. 1.

Gélard, G. (2001) 'France – Individual Accounts', in D. Ordelheide and KPMG, *Transnational Accounting*, Vol. 2, Palgrave, Basingstoke.

Haller, A. and Eierle, B. (2004) 'The adaptation of German accounting rule to IFRS: A legislative balancing act', *Accounting in Europe*, Vol. 1.

Ordelheide, D. (1993) 'True and fair view: A European and a German perspective', *European Accounting Review*, Vol. 2, No. 1.

Ordelheide, D. (1996) 'True and fair view. A European and a German perspective II', *European Accounting Review*, Vol. 5, No. 3.

Parker, R.H. (1996) 'Harmonizing the Notes in the UK and France: a case study in de jure harmonization', *European Accounting Review*, Vol. 5, No. 2.

Pasqualini, E. (1992) *Le principe de l'image fidèle en droit comptable*, LITEC, Paris.

Richard, J. and Collette, C. (2005) *Système Comptable Français et Normes IFRS*, Dunod, Paris.

Shearer, B. and Sleigh-Johnson, N. (2007) 'Decision time for private company GAAP?', *Accountancy*, Vol. 139, No. 1364.

Stolowy, H., Haller, A. and Klockhaus, V. (2001) 'Accounting for brands in France and Germany compared with IAS 38 (Intangible Assets): An illustration of the difficulty of harmonization', *International Journal of Accounting*, Vol. 36 (1).

Further reading

See Chapter 14.

Useful websites

See the websites listed at the end of Chapter 14.

QUESTIONS

Suggested answers to the asterisked questions are given at the end of the book.

15.1∗ 'US accounting is better than German accounting.' Discuss.

15.2∗ Discuss the advantages and disadvantages for a country such as Germany of requiring or permitting companies to apply accounting principles based on IFRS in their individual financial statements.

15.3 Compare the influence of tax law on financial reporting in the UK with its influence in Germany.

15.4 Discuss the view that the individual company financial statements in Germany are useful only for tax purposes.

15.5 Why are leased assets accounted for differently in individual company financial statements in the UK and France?

15.6 The formats in the appendices to this chapter, relating to three EU countries, all comply with the EU Fourth Directive. Comment on the differences between them.

15.7 'German accounting rules for individual companies are ideal for domestic companies with no international connections.' Discuss.

Formats for French financial statements

STANDARD SYSTEM BALANCE SHEET FORMAT (in tabular form)

ASSETS

FIXED ASSETS

Subscribed capital uncalled

Intangible fixed assets:
    Establishment costs
    Research and development costs
    Concessions, patents, licences, trade marks, processes,
    software, rights and similar assets
    Goodwill
    Other
    Intangible fixed assets in progress
    Payments on account

Tangible fixed assets:
    Land
    Constructions
    Technical installations, plant and machinery, equipment and fixtures
    Other
    Tangible fixed assets in progress
    Payments on account

Financial fixed assets:
    Participating interests
    Debts receivable related to participating interests
    Portfolio long-term investment securities
    Other long-term investment securities
    Loans
    Other

Total I

STANDARD SYSTEM BALANCE SHEET FORMAT (in tabular form)

ASSETS	

C U R R E N T A S S E T S	Stocks and work in progress:
	    Raw materials and other consumables
	    Work in progress [goods and services]
	    Semi-finished and finished products
	    Goods for resale
	    Payments on account on orders
	
	Debts receivable:
	    Trade debtors and related accounts
	    Other
	    Subscribed capital – called but not paid
	
	Short-term investment securities:
	    Own shares
	    Other securities
	    Short-term financial instruments
	
	Liquid assets
	
	Prepayments
	
	Total II
	    Deferred charges **(III)**
	    Loan redemption premiums **(IV)**
	    Realizable exchange losses **(V)**
	    Overall total (I + II + III + IV + V)

LIABILITIES*

C A P I T A L A N D R E S E R V E S	Capital [of which paid up . . .]
	Premiums on shares issued, mergers, contributions . . .
	Revaluation reserve
	Equity accounted reserve
	Reserves:
	Legal reserve
	Statutory or contractual reserves
	Tax-regulated reserves
	Other
	Profit or loss carried forward
	Sub-total: Net position
	Investment grants
	Tax-regulated provisions
	Total I
P R O V I S I O N S	Provisions for liabilities
	Provisions for charges
	Total II
D E B T S P A Y A B L E	Convertible debenture loans
	Other debenture loans
	Loans and debts payable to credit institutions
	Loans and sundry financial debts payable
	Payments on account received on orders in progress
	Trade creditors and related accounts
	Tax and social security debts payable
	Creditors for fixed assets and related accounts
	Other debts payable
	Short-term financial instruments
	Deferred income
	Total III
	Realizable exchange gains **(IV)**
	Overall total (I + II + III + IV)

Note: *This official translation is not a good one; 'shareholders' equity and liabilities' would be better.

INCOME STATEMENT FORMAT (in columnar form)

Operating income:

Sales of goods for resale

Production sold (goods and services)

Net turnover

Change in stock of finished products and work in progress

Own work capitalized

Net period income from long-term transactions

Operating grants

Provisions (and depreciation) written back, charges transferred

Other income

Total I

Operating charges:

Purchases of goods for resale

Change in stocks

Purchases of raw materials and other consumables

Change in stocks

Other purchases and external charges

Taxes, levies and similar payments

Wages and salarles

Social security costs

Appropriations to depreciation and provisions:

Fixed assets: appropriations to depreciation

Fixed assets: appropriations to provisions

Current assets: appropriations to provisions

Liabilities and charges: appropriations to provisions

Other charges

Total II

INCOME STATEMENT FORMAT (in columnar form)

1. OPERATING PROFIT OR LOSS (I–II)

Share of joint venture profit or loss:

Profit or loss transferred **III**

Loss or profit transferred **IV**

Financial income:

Participating interests

Other financial fixed asset securities and debts receivable

Other interest and similar income

Provisions written back and charges transferred

Currency exchange gains

Net income on realization of short-term investment securities

Total V

Financial charges:

Appropriations to depreciation and provisions

Interest and similar charges

Currency exchange losses

Net charges on realization of short-term investment securities

Total VI

2. FINANCIAL PROFIT OR LOSS (V–VI)

3. PROFIT OR LOSS ON ORDINARY ACTIVITIES before tax (I – II + III – IV + V – VI)

Extraordinary income:

Operating transactions

Capital transactions

Provisions written back and charges transferred

Total VII

Extraordinary charges:

Operating transactions

Capital transactions

Appropriations to depreciation and provisions

Total VIII

4. EXTRAORDINARY PROFIT OR LOSS (VII–VIII)

Employee profit share IX

Income tax X

Total income (I + III + V + VII)

Total charges (II + IV + VI + VIII + IX + X)

Profit or loss

Formats for German financial statements

BALANCE SHEET

Fixed assets
Intangible assets
    Concessions, industrial and similar rights and assets
      and licences in such rights and assets
    Goodwill
    Payments on account

Tangible assets
    Land, land rights and buildings including buildings
      on third-party land
    Technical equipment and machines
    Other equipment, factory and office equipment
    Payments on account and assets under construction

Financial assets
    Shares in affiliated enterprises
    Loans to affiliated enterprises
    Participations
    Loans to enterprises in which participations are held
    Long-term investments
    Other loans

Current assets
Inventories
    Raw materials and supplies
    Work in progress
    Finished goods and merchandise
    Payments on account

Receivables and other assets
    Trade receivables
    Receivables from affiliated enterprises
    Receivables from enterprises in which participations are held
    Other assets

Securities
    Shares in affiliated enterprises
    Own shares
    Other securities

Cheques, cash in hand, central bank and postal giro balances, bank balances

Prepaid expenses

Equity
Subscribed capital
Capital reserves
Revenue reserves
   Legal reserve
Reserve for own shares
Statutory reserves
   Other revenue reserves

Retained profits/accumulated losses brought forward

Net income/net loss for the year

Provisions
   Provisions for pensions and similar obligations
   Tax provisions
   Other provisions

Creditors
   Loans
   Liabilities to banks
   Payments received on account of orders
   Trade payables
   Liabilities on bills accepted and drawn
   Payable to affiliated enterprises
   Payable to enterprises in which participations are held
   Other creditors

Deferred income

INCOME STATEMENT – Format 1

1 Sales

2 Increase or decrease in finished goods and work in process

3 Own work capitalized

4 Other operating income

5 Cost of materials

   Cost of raw materials, supplies and purchased merchandise
   Cost of purchased services

6 Personnel expenses
   Wages and salaries
   Social security and other pension costs

7 Depreciation
   On intangible fixed assets and tangible assets as well as on capitalized start-up and business expansion expenses
   On current assets to the extent that it exceeds depreciation which is normal for the company

8 Other operating expenses

9 Income from participations

10 Income from other investments and long-term loans

11 Other interest and similar income

12 Amortization of financial assets and investments classified as current assets

13 Interest and similar expenses

14 Results from ordinary activities

15 Extraordinary income

16 Extraordinary expense

17 Extraordinary results

18 Taxes on income

19 Other taxes

20 Net income/net loss for the year

INCOME STATEMENT – Format 2

1 Sales

2 Cost of sales

3 Gross profit on sales

4 Selling expenses

5 General administration expenses

6 Other operating income

7 Other operating expenses

8 Income from participations

9 Income from other investments and financial assets

10 Other interest and similar income

11 Amortization of financial assets and investments classified as current assets

12 Interest and similar expenses

13 Results from ordinary activities

14 Extraordinary income

15 Extraordinary expense

16 Extraordinary results

17 Taxes on income

18 Other taxes

19 Net income/net loss for the year

Formats for British financial statements

The formats below are those required by legislation. It is important to note, however, that:

1 many companies disclose items preceded by Arabic numerals in the Notes and not in the statements themselves;

2 appropriations of profit must be disclosed, although they are not in the formats;

3 letters and numerals are for reference only and are usually omitted;

4 immaterial items may be omitted;

5 many companies do not adhere absolutely and precisely to the formats;

6 for some items (e.g. called-up share capital not paid) there is a choice of position.

Balance sheet Format 2 is a horizontal version of balance sheet Format 1. Profit and loss account Formats 3 and 4 are horizontal versions of profit and loss account Formats 1 and 2. The horizontal versions are seldom used, and are not illustrated here.

BALANCE SHEET – Format 1

A   Called-up share capital not paid

B   Fixed assets

    I   Intangible assets
        1 Development costs
        2 Concessions, patents, licences, trade marks and similar rights and assets
        3 Goodwill
        4 Payments on account

    II   Tangible assets
        1 Land and buildings
        2 Plant and machinery
        3 Fixtures, fittings, tools and equipment
        4 Payments on account and assets in course of construction

    III   Investments
        1 Shares in group undertakings
        2 Loans to group undertakings
        3 Participating interests
        4 Loans to undertakings in which the company has a participating interest
        5 Other investments other than loans
        6 Other loans
        7 Own shares

C   Current assets

   I   Stocks
      1 Raw materials and consumables
      2 Work in progress
      3 Finished goods and goods for resale
      4 Payments on account

   II   Debtors
      1 Trade debtors
      2 Amounts owed by group undertakings
      3 Amounts owed by undertakings in which the company has a participating interest
      4 Other debtors
      5 Prepayments and accrued income

   III   Investments
      1 Shares in group undertakings
      2 Own shares
      3 Other investments

   IV   Cash at bank and in hand

D   Prepayments and accrued income

E   Creditors: amounts falling due within one year
   1 Debenture loans
   2 Bank loans and overdrafts
   3 Payments received on account
   4 Trade creditors
   5 Bills of exchange payable
   6 Amounts owed to group undertakings
   7 Amounts owed to undertakings in which the company has a participating interest
   8 Other creditors including taxation and social security
   9 Accruals and deferred income

F   Net current assets (liabilities)

G   Total assets less current liabilities

H   Creditors: amounts falling due after more than one year
   1 Debenture loans
   2 Bank loans and overdrafts
   3 Payments received on account
   4 Trade creditors
   5 Bills of exchange payable
   6 Amounts owed to group undertakings
   7 Amounts owed to undertakings in which the company has a participating interest

8 Other creditors including taxation and social security
9 Accruals and deferred income

I Provisions for liabilities and charges
1 Pensions and similar obligations
2 Taxation, including deferred taxation
3 Other provisions

J Accruals and deferred income

K Capital and reserves

I Called-up share capital

II Share premium account

III Revaluation reserve

IV Other reserves
1 Capital redemption reserve
2 Reserve for own shares
3 Reserves provided for by the articles of association
4 Other reserves

V Profit and loss account

Note: for group accounts, minority interests are to be inserted above or below K.

PROFIT AND LOSS ACCOUNT – Format 1

1 Turnover
2 Cost of sales
3 Gross profit or loss
4 Distribution costs
5 Administrative expenses
6 Other operating income
7 Income from shares in group undertakings
8 Income from participating interests
9 Income from other fixed asset investments
10 Other interest receivable and similar income
11 Amounts written off investments
12 Interest payable and similar charges
13 Tax on profit or loss on ordinary activities
14 Profit or loss on ordinary activities after taxation
15 Minority interests
16 Extraordinary income
17 Extraordinary charges
18 Extraordinary profit or loss

19 Tax on extraordinary profit or loss

20 Minority interests

21 Other taxes not shown under the above items

22 Profit or loss for the financial year

PROFIT AND LOSS ACCOUNT – Format 2

 1 Turnover

 2 Change in stocks of finished goods and in work in progress

 3 Own work capitalized

 4 Other operating income

 5 (a) Raw materials and consumables
   (b) Other external charges

 6 Staff costs:
   (a) Wages and salaries
   (b) Social security costs
   (c) Other pension costs

 7 (a) Depreciation and other amounts written off tangible and intangible fixed assets
   (b) Exceptional amounts written off current assets

 8 Other operating charges

 9 Income from shares in group undertakings

10 Income from participating interests

11 Income from other fixed asset investments

12 Other interest receivable and similar income

13 Amounts written off investments

14 Interest payable and similar charges

15 Tax on profit or loss on ordinary activities

16 Profit or loss on ordinary activities after taxation

17 Minority interests

18 Extraordinary income

19 Extraordinary charges

20 Extraordinary profit or loss

21 Minority interests

22 Tax on extraordinary profit or loss

23 Other taxes not shown under the above items

24 Profit or loss for the financial year

Part V

MAJOR ISSUES IN FINANCIAL REPORTING BY MNEs

16

Key financial reporting topics

Christopher Nobes

OBJECTIVES

After reading this chapter, you should be able to:

- explain the importance of intangible assets and which ones are recognized;

- outline the variations in asset measurement bases;

- critically summarize the treatment of financial instruments, including hedge accounting;

- explain the difference between provisions and reserves;

- distinguish between pension arrangements, pension provisions and pension funds, and give examples of how all these can differ from country to country;

- illustrate the causes of deferred tax and explain how there are various ways of accounting for it;

- outline the major issues involved in revenue recognition.

343

16.1   Introduction

This chapter examines some accounting areas that generate key accounting numbers that affect the making of financial decisions. We concentrate on topics that can have a large quantitative effect and which remain controversial. We consider particularly the practices of large companies using either IFRS or US GAAP.

All of our topics relate in some way to assets and liabilities, and mostly also to revenues and expenses. Accounting for assets and liabilities is a five-stage process:

1 Is the item an asset (or liability)?
2 Should it be recognized on the balance sheet?
3 How should it initially be measured?
4 How should it subsequently be measured?
5 How should it be removed (depreciation, impairment, derecognition)?

We consider, first, (in Section 16.2) the *recognition* of intangible assets, which involves one large difference between IFRS and US accounting. Goodwill acquired in a business combination is considered later in Chapter 17. Then, we look at the *measurement* of assets (Section 16.3), noting that IFRS allows much more flexibility than US GAAP. Financial instruments, both assets and liabilities, are the topic of Section 16.4. Various other sorts of liabilities are then looked at in Sections 16.5 to 16.7: provisions, employee benefits and deferred tax. Closely linked to liabilities is the recognition of revenue, the topic of Section 16.8. Then we look at the presentation of comprehensive income in Section 16.9.

16.2   Recognition of intangible assets

The recognition criteria in IFRS are that the inflows expected from an asset should be probable (i.e. more likely than not) and that the cost or value of the asset should be measurable reliably (e.g. *Framework*, paragraph 89; IAS 38, paragraph 21). To apply this, it is first necessary to distinguish between three ways of obtaining intangible assets: internal generation, purchase as part of a business combination, and separate purchase. There is little controversy over the last way: if an asset (e.g. a patent or a brand name) has been purchased, it should generally be recognized. There is greater difficulty with the other ways of obtaining such an asset.

Internally generated assets might fail to satisfy the recognition criteria of probable inflows and reliable measurement. US rules (SFAS 2) therefore require expensing of research and development, except in the special case of computer software development costs (SFAS 86). The same ban on capitalization applies to internally-generated goodwill and brands.

IFRS (in IAS 38) also requires expensing of the costs of most internally-generated intangibles but requires capitalization of development costs that meet certain criteria, which are an elaboration of the above recognition criteria. It thus becomes necessary to distinguish between 'research' and 'development', and then to use the criteria.

IAS 38's definitions are:

Table 16.1 Volkswagen 2001 (opening reconciliation)

	€m
Equity (German law) 1.1.2000	9,811
Capitalization of development costs	3,982
Amended useful lives and depreciation methods of tangible and intangible assets	3,483
Capitalization of overheads in inventories	653
Differing treatment of leasing contracts as lessor	1,962
Differing valuation of financial instruments	897
Effect of deferred taxes	−1,345
Elimination of special items	262
Amended valuation of pension and similar obligations	−633
Amended accounting treatment of provisions	2,022
Classification of minority interests not as part of equity	−197
Other changes	21
Equity (IFRS) 1.1.2000	20,918

Source: Adpated from Volkswagen AG (2002) *Volkswagen Annual Report 2001*, Volkswagen AG, Wolfsburg, Germany.

Research is original and planned investigation undertaken with the prospect of gaining new scientific or technical knowledge or understanding.

Development is the application of research findings or other knowledge to a plan or design for the production of new or substantially improved material devices, products, processes, systems or services . . . (paragraph 8)

The criteria for capitalization include the availability of resources to complete the development and the ability to show how future benefits will arise and to measure the expenditure.

Although judgement is involved in all this, Volkswagen's adjustment from German to IFRS accounting (examined in Chapter 2, but repeated here for convenience as Table 16.1) shows the large potential size of the resulting asset: an increase of 41 per cent in net assets.

Incidentally, capitalization begins from the day the criteria are met, not from the start of a project. Any previous expenditure cannot be later added to the asset. Capitalization stops when the asset is ready for use.

When intangible assets arise in the third way, acquisition as part of a business combination, further complications arise. Recent standards (SFAS 141 in the US, and then IFRS 3) are designed to persuade purchasers to recognize as many intangibles as possible, thereby reducing goodwill. For example, IAS 38 (paragraphs 25 and 33) presumes that the act of purchase satisfies the recognition criteria.

16.3 Asset measurement

If assets are to be recognized, they have to be measured. Until recently, the normal way of measuring assets, at least initially, was at their cost. This continues to be the case for several assets, such as intangible assets and property, plant and equipment

Table 16.2 Initial and subsequent measurement bases under IFRS

	Initial	Subsequent
Cost only	PPE, intangibles, investment properties, non-trading investments, inventories	Inventories, intangibles with no active market, held-to-maturity investments
Cost or fair value	Some non-trading investments	PPE, intangibles with active market, investment properties, some non-trading investments
Fair value only	Trading investments, derivatives, biological assets	Trading and available-for-sale investments, derivatives, biological assets

(PPE, which could also be called tangible fixed assets), where the 'cost' basis includes reductions for depreciation and impairment. However, if an asset is to be measured subsequently at fair value (see below), then perhaps it should initially be measured like that. IFRS now takes this view for assets that are required later to be held at fair value: certain financial assets (IAS 39) and all biological assets (IAS 41). These facts are recorded in the 'initial' column of Table 16.2.

IFRS also *allows* subsequent fair valuation for several other types of assets (see 'subsequent' column of Table 16.2), largely because the standard-setters are not yet able to decide between reliable costs and relevant fair values. By contrast, the US rules come down in favour of cost and require it, except for use of fair values for some types of investments (see Section 16.4).

Section 5.6 in Chapter 5 briefly records the various measurement bases used for the subsequent measurement of different assets under IFRS. In addition to the use of cost and fair value for various assets, impaired assets are valued at the higher of discounted cash flows and net selling price. This large range of measurement bases is recorded as Figure 16.1. That figure does not separately show depreciated historical cost, which is neither cost nor a market value. The depreciated cost moves gradually from cost (i.e. initial fair value plus costs of buying) to residual value (i.e. net realizable value) over life.

Although the 'Revalued' cost heading in Figure 16.1 refers to amounts measured at fair value, no gains are taken as profit on revaluation and the value is used as a new cost for depreciation and disposal calculations. This is quite different from the 'Fair value' heading, under which there is no depreciation.

As explained in Chapter 6, 'fair value' is used in IFRS to mean a current market exchange price between willing buyers and sellers. The FASB has decided (in SFAS 157 of 2006) that 'fair value' shall particularly be an exit value, i.e. what an entity could sell the asset for. However, since this still is not intended to be net of the costs of sale, there is generally no important practical difference between the IASB and FASB definitions.

As for the recognition of gains, let us imagine a piece of land that rises in market value. There are three possibilities for the recognition of gains in profit and loss:

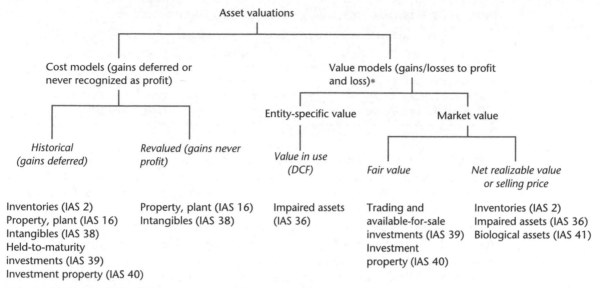

Figure 16.1 **Possible IFRS asset valuations classified by cost/value**

Note: *Except that gains/losses on available-for-sale investments are deferred.

- IAS 16/40 Cost basis: deferred until sale;
- IAS 16 Revaluation basis: never recognized (see 6.3.1 in Chapter 6);
- IAS 40 Fair value basis: immediate recognition.

It gets even more complicated when depreciation is taken into account, especially when depreciated revalued assets are then impaired. Clearly, some order needs to be brought to this. The IASB and the FASB have a project in this area, which led to the publication of a discussion paper about initial recognition in 2005.

16.4 Financial instruments

16.4.1 Financial assets

As noted in Chapter 8, the main departure from the cost basis under US GAAP relates to the valuation of financial assets that are held for trading or are available-for-sale. For them, the standard-setters were persuaded that the financial markets were liquid enough to enable a reliable measurement of market value. The IASC followed this in IAS 39. The IASB went further and amended IAS 39 in 2004 in order to allow an entity to choose to measure many other financial assets at fair value. These are called 'designated at fair value through profit or loss'. This issue caused a disagreement with the EU which took some time to resolve (see Chapter 10). In 2007, the FASB also introduced this option in SFAS 159. Table 16.3 summarizes the position.

Those assets not fair valued should be measured at amortized cost, which is a treatment exactly like that for a tangible fixed asset, i.e. the asset is initially held at

Table 16.3 Financial assets under IFRS and US GAAP

	Measurement	Gains/losses
Held-to-maturity; loans	Amortized cost	None
Available-for-sale	Fair value	Other comprehensive income
Trading; derivatives; designated	Fair value	Profit and loss

cost, then amortized down to expected residual value over its expected life. For example, imagine that a company buys a five-year government bond with maturity (face) value of $1,000 for $1,100, because the interest rate on the bond is attractively high. The asset is initially recorded at $1,100 and then amortized over five years to $1,000. The amortization expense partially sets off the interest income. Because the face value is reliable, we would also amortize *up* to it rather than merely *down* to it, as for most fixed assets.

For a bond that is held to maturity, it can be argued that fluctuations in market value are not relevant because the company will not be affected by them. At the other extreme, the same bond could be intended for short-term sale, and so the fluctuations in market value are relevant. The problem is that the intentions of directors are difficult to audit, may not be known by the directors, and can be changed. Consequently, an alternative argument is that identical bonds should be measured identically, irrespective of the alleged intentions of the directors.

The managers of companies do not generally like volatility of income, so they like to treat as few assets as possible as 'trading'. Since some financial assets clearly cannot be held-to-maturity because they have no maturity date (e.g. shares), it is common for US corporations to treat most financial assets as available for sale. In contrast, the standard-setters believe that all financial assets should be treated as 'trading' (JWG, 2000). This is why the IASB added the option to IAS 39 for other financial assets to be treated in the same way as a trading asset.

Under the national rules of countries where rules have not yet been converged with IFRS (e.g. in France or Germany), financial assets are still measured at cost or the lower of cost and market. This does not apply to banks, which have preceded other companies in their use of market values for investments.

16.4.2 Financial liabilities

The first issue here is to determine whether an item is a liability or an equity. IAS 32 broke new ground in the 1990s by requiring any item that meets the definition of a liability to be recognized as one. This applies to certain preference shares. As a reminder, the IASB definition is:

> A liability is a present obligation of the enterprise arising from past events, the settlement of which is expected to result in an outflow from the enterprise of resources embodying economic benefits.
>
> (*Framework*, paragraph 49)

Similarly, IAS 32 departed from existing conventions by requiring compound instruments (e.g. convertible debentures) to be split into elements of debt and equity based on economic substance. Most national rules base accounting on the legal form of the instrument. This applies to US GAAP except that, in 2003, SFAS 150 introduced a requirement that certain types of shares should be classified as debt because of their liability characteristics.

Once a liability is recognized, the normal procedure is to value it at amortized proceeds: the mirror image of amortized cost. However, US GAAP and IFRS require *trading* liabilities to be treated like trading assets, i.e. 'marked to market' (fair valued, with gains and losses to profit and loss). In 2004 and in 2005, IAS 39 was amended to allow certain other liabilities to be marked to market. SFAS 159 did the same for the US. This is designed to allow financial institutions to hold parts of their balance sheets, on both sides, at fair value.

16.4.3 Hedge accounting

The degree to which hedge accounting is allowed is a major topic of controversy, leading to a difference between IFRS and EU-endorsed IFRS (see Chapter 5). In IAS 39, there are 32 paragraphs (out of 110) on hedge accounting, followed by 13 pages of 'application guidance', 29 pages of 'basis for conclusions' and 108 pages of 'implementation guidance' on the subject. This sub-section can, therefore, only outline the issue.

In order to understand this topic, it is necessary to distinguish between four issues:

- hedging;
- a hedged item;
- a hedging instrument; and
- hedge accounting.

Hedging is protecting an entity from the effects of movements in prices, such as those of commodities or currencies. Items that can be hedged are an asset, a liability, a net investment in a foreign operation, a commitment or a forecasted transaction that exposes an entity to changes in fair value or cash flows that can affect profit and loss. For example, suppose that British Airways (BA) made a commitment on 1 July 2008 to buy $500 million of aeroplanes from Boeing on 31 December 2009. If BA's functional currency (see Chapter 18) is pounds sterling, this commitment in dollars exposes the company to the risk that the dollar will rise, worsening its expected cash outflows in pounds. Such an item can be hedged.

A hedging instrument is a financial asset or liability whose changes in fair value or cash flows are expected to off-set the changes of the hedged item. In the BA example, the company might buy from a financial institution, on 1 July 2008, $500 million to be delivered to it on 31 December 2009 in exchange for £270 million at that date. British Airways would then have protected itself against a rise in the dollar by buying the forward dollar contract (a derivative financial instrument).

Under the normal accounting requirements of IAS 39 or US GAAP, the derivative is marked to market. For example, if the dollar falls against the pound, the derivative contract is a liability, and a loss is immediately recorded. Paradoxically, BA's attempt to protect itself from changes in the dollar has resulted in a loss caused by a fall in the dollar. The reason is that the commitment to pay dollars to Boeing is not recorded under present accounting rules. So the fall in the pound value of the commitment is not accounted for.

In order to protect 'profit and loss' from gains and losses during the life of the hedging instrument, it is necessary to use hedge accounting. This is permission to depart from the normal accounting rules and, in this case, to record the gains and losses on the derivative as 'other comprehensive income'.

Let us suppose that the dollar continues to fall and that BA honours its commitment to buy the planes. BA can record the planes at a cost of £270 million which includes all the accumulated losses on the derivative. So, no currency losses need ever be recorded as profit and loss. Of course, if BA had not taken out the forward contract, it would record the planes at a lower cost and would then have lower depreciation expenses and higher profits over the life of the planes.

There are three main possible attitudes towards hedge accounting:

- leave it to a company's discretion (this is approximately the position in EU national laws, for example);
- allow it under certain conditions (as in IAS 39 or US GAAP, see below);
- ban it altogether (as proposed by the IASC, FASB and others: see JWG (2000)).

Using the above example, the argument for banning hedge accounting is that BA has taken a bet on the dollar. So, if the dollar falls, it has lost the bet and should recognize the loss immediately, not disguise it as depreciation expenses of some later years. Similarly, if the dollar rises, there is a gain.

Company management sees hedging in a different way (i.e. as a sort of insurance contract) and has successfully lobbied the standard-setters to include permission for hedge accounting. IAS 39 and US GAAP allow hedge accounting when a hedging instrument is expected to be fully effective against the risk (as it would be in the BA example) and when the entity documents the nature and purpose of any purchase of the hedging instrument.

The restrictions imposed on hedge accounting by IAS 39 were too restrictive for certain companies (especially French banks) who lobbied the EU successfully to have some of them removed from the version of IAS 39 endorsed by the EU in 2004.

16.5   Provisions

16.5.1 General definition

Provisions are defined by IAS 37 (in the version current in 2007 as this book is written) as liabilities of uncertain timing or amount. A good example is provisions for pensions, although they are covered by a more detailed standard (see Section 16.6). Suppose that a company promises to pay a pension to an employee when he or she retires. The pension entitlement builds up as the employee continues to work for the company. The pension will be paid every year from retirement to death, and perhaps will be equal to half the final year's salary. Such an entitlement is called a 'defined benefit pension'.

From the company's point of view, the pension is part of employee compensation; it is a current salary expense with a postponed payment date. Each year, the company should charge a pension salary expense and increase the liability to pay the pension later. It is clear that the obligation to the employee meets the above definition of liability. However, the exact amount depends on many things, such as the final salary and how long the employee will live after retirement. Consequently, the company can only *estimate* the amount, and so the liability is called a *provision*. More details on pension provisions are given in Section 16.6.

Other examples of provisions are estimates of liabilities to pay tax bills or, in the case of a mining company, to pay for cleaning up the environment after extracting minerals from the earth. Also, in most countries a company is required to recognize a provision for its obligation for future repair costs on products as a result of warranties given at the time of sale.

The particularly controversial issue in the area of provisions is the degree to which anticipated expenses and losses should be provided for. The Fourth Directive (Art. 20, as amended in 2001), on which laws in EU countries are based, states that provisions are:

1 liabilities likely to be incurred or certain to be incurred but of uncertain timing or amount; and

2 at the option of each country's lawmaker, the heading can also cover charges to be incurred in the future but with origins before the balance sheet date.

This allows the creation of provisions for trading losses, currency translation losses or repair expenses of an ensuing year, which are connected to actions of current or earlier years. Under IFRS requirements, such items generally do not meet the definition of a liability and should not be provided for. Fortunately, the EU's item 2 in the above list is only an option, so there need not be an incompatibility with IFRS.

As an example, suppose that a company has a 31 December 20X1 year end. It has had a very bad year, and its directors decide at a board meeting on 15 December 20X1 to close down half the factories and to lay off half the staff at the end of January 20X2. Detailed plans are made and minuted at the board meeting. However, in order to avoid an unhappy Christmas for the staff, the plans are kept secret until 7 January 20X2. When the financial statements for 20X1 are prepared in February 20X2, should the balance sheet record a provision for the large restructuring and redundancy costs?

The traditional (and prudent) answer to this question would be 'yes', and there would be no problem in fitting such a provision into the EU Fourth Directive's optional definition (as above). However, is there a liability at the balance sheet date? There is expected to be a future outflow of resources, but the same could be said for the wages bill of 20X2, which we would not expect to charge in 20X1. Is there an obligation to a third party on 31 December 20X1? The answer, depending on the exact circumstances, seems to be 'no'. Therefore, no provision should be recognized under IFRS requirements or under other similar sets of rules, although the notes to the financial statements must explain the situation.

Would an IFRS balance sheet give a fair presentation if it did not recognize a provision for the expenses of restructuring that had been decided upon by 31 December 20X1 and that were likely to be paid early in 20X2? In order to answer this question, it is necessary to remember that the financial statements are prepared using a series of conventions that users are expected to be familiar with. The definition of 'liability' under the IFRS regime has been the same for about two decades and is published in the *Framework* and various standards. Would it be fair to show an item under the heading 'liabilities' that clearly did not meet the definition? Probably not. Furthermore, unless everyone sticks to this clear definition, it is very difficult to stop companies from warping profits by choosing to make provisions in good years but not in bad years.

In order to inform the users, IFRS requires disclosures in the notes about any restructuring proposals when they have been announced or begun by the date that the financial statements have been authorized for issue.

Recently the requirements for setting up provisions in the US have become even stricter. SFAS 146 requires that an announcement of a detailed formal plan is not enough: there must be an event that removes discretion for the spending from the management.

When a provision is to be recognized, it becomes necessary to value it. By definition, there are estimates to make. The accountant must make the best possible estimates and be prepared to revise them at each balance sheet date in the light of better information. Provisions, such as those for decommissioning a nuclear power station, may extend decades into the future. This suggests that a fair valuation requires the use of discounting to take account of the time value of money. Discounting is now required under IFRS rules but has not been normal in the domestic rules of most continental European countries and is not required in the US.

In 2005, the IASB issued an exposure draft proposing to make major amendments to IAS 37. These were controversial and progress on the standard has been slow. However, a revised IAS 37 is still expected and is examined in Section 16.5.3 below.

16.5.2 Provisions and reserves

A major cause of confusion surrounding the issues in this chapter is an international difference in the use of the words 'provision' and 'reserve'. One source of the confusion is the use of the word 'provision' to mean a reduction in the value of an asset. It would be more helpful to call value adjustments against receivables, for example, 'allowances' or 'impairments' rather than provisions or reserves. It is also important to remember that provisions are obligations to pay money (liabilities), not funds of money (assets). By contrast, a reserve is an element of shareholders' equity. There is a vital distinction between a provision and a reserve. Setting up a provision for €1 million would involve:

Debit: Expense	€1 m
Credit: Liability	€1 m

Setting up a legal reserve (see Chapters 12 and 15), for example, would involve:

Debit: Equity (profit and loss reserve)	€1 m
Credit: Equity (legal reserve)	€1 m

Setting up a provision in the manner described above decreases profit and net assets, whereas setting up a legal reserve affects neither.

Further terminological confusion is caused because of a difference between UK and US usages. In the United Kingdom (and in IFRS), the distinction between

Table 16.4 Deutsche Bank equity (DM million)

Year	German HGB	IFRS	% increase
1994	21,198	25,875	22.1
1995	22,213	28,043	26.2

'reserve' and 'provision' is as used throughout this chapter. However, as mentioned in Chapter 2, in the United States the word 'reserve' is used to mean 'provision'. For example, Americans sometimes refer to a pension reserve rather than a pension provision. This is not confusing to Americans because they generally do not use the word 'reserve' to mean a part of equity. Indeed:

- there are no legal reserves in the United States;
- revaluation reserves relating to investments are shown as 'cumulative other comprehensive income';
- reserves caused by currency translation (see Chapter 18) are called 'cumulative translation adjustments';
- profit and loss account reserves are called 'retained earnings'.

The confusion arises when translators or analysts fail to spot this UK/US difference. Table 2.7 in Chapter 2 summarizes the words used in several languages.

Another expression that is often found, particularly under the domestic rules of prudent countries (e.g. Germany) and particularly relating to banks, is 'secret reserves' or 'hidden reserves'. These would arise because a company:

- failed to recognize an asset in its balance sheet; or
- deliberately measured an asset at an unreasonably low value; or
- set up unnecessarily high provisions.

These actions might have been taken in the name of prudence or, in some countries, in order to get tax deductions. In all three cases, net assets will consequently be understated and therefore, of course, equity will be understated. The amount of understatement could be called a secret reserve.

Most systems of accounting contain some degree of secret reserves. For example, the IFRS, German and US regimes do not recognize the internally-generated asset 'research'; and it is normal to value many assets at depreciated cost, which is often below fair value. A good time to spot secret reserves is when a company changes from one system of accounting to another. For example, in 1996 Germany's largest bank, the Deutsche Bank, disclosed for the first time financial statements under IFRS as well as under German accounting. The figures for equity are set out in Table 16.4 and illustrate a big increase in disclosed reserves under IFRS. The analysis of return on net assets or the comparison of debt to equity would have been greatly affected by this.

16.5.3 Contingent liabilities

Another point to consider here is 'contingent liabilities'. Suppose that Company X borrows €1 million from the bank but can only do so by persuading Company Y to promise to pay the loan back to the bank in the unlikely event that Company X cannot do so. Company Y has thereby guaranteed the loan. Is this guarantee a liability for Company Y? There is a legal obligation, but it is unlikely to be called upon. Where there are unlikely outflows caused by obligations or by possible obligations, these are called *contingent liabilities* and should be disclosed in the notes to the financial statements, as required by IAS 37 (at the time of writing) and under many sets of national rules.

This leads to a curious result. Suppose that an entity has two obligations as a result of past events:

- problem A is a 60 per cent likelihood of having to pay €10 million soon (and a 40 per cent likelihood of paying nothing);

- problem B is a 40 per cent likelihood of having to pay €10 million soon (and a 60 per cent likelihood of paying nothing).

How should these obligations be measured?

Under the original version of IAS 37 (still current as this book is written), the answer is that A is valued at about €6 million and B at zero. The measurement of A should be at 'the amount an entity would rationally pay to settle the obligation at the balance sheet date or transfer it to a third party' (IAS 37, paragraph 37). If A could find an insurance company to take the problem away, the price in an efficient market would be about €6 million. By contrast, problem B does not have a probable outflow so should not be recognized at all, merely noted.

IASB's exposure draft of 2005 proposes to take probability out of the recognition criteria and have it in measurement only. Consequently, problem A would continue to be measured at €6 million but problem B would be measured at €4 million. One implication of this is the removal of the concept of 'contingent liability'.

16.6 Employee benefits

16.6.1 Introduction

Pension obligations have already been referred to (in Section 16.5.1) as an example of provisions. Similar obligations also arise where an employer promises to pay an employee's medical bills after retirement. This is common in the United States, as noted in Chapter 8.

This section examines the international variations firstly in the institutional arrangements for pensions between companies and their employees, then the recognition of obligations, and then the funding of obligations. The employee benefit of share-based payments was discussed, in the context of the USA, in Chapter 8.

16.6.2 Institutional arrangements

Several types of arrangement exist for ensuring that employees have some income after retirement. These include:

- state plans,
- industry plans,
- severance indemnities,
- defined contribution plans,
- defined benefit plans.

Many countries have state pension schemes (= plans), whereby companies (and sometimes employees also) are required to pay sums to the state, which then guarantees to pay a pension after retirement or when a certain age is reached. The payments amount to a form of taxation. The monies are generally absorbed into the government's budget, and the size of the eventual pension is determined year by year. However, once the company has paid its contributions, it has no further obligation.

Industry schemes, which operate for example in some companies in the Netherlands and Sweden, work rather like a state scheme but for all the companies in a particular industry. Again, once a company has paid its annual contribution, it has no liability.

Severance indemnities operate in Italy and Japan. Here the law imposes an obligation on employers to pay amounts to employees when they leave, on retirement or for any other reason. Approximately speaking, for each year of service an employee builds up the right to be paid one month of severance indemnity. So the amount of an employer's obligation is clear at any balance sheet date.

A defined contribution plan is one where an employer (and perhaps the employee) pays specified amounts of money into the plan, which is run by a pension trust or life assurance company. The resulting eventual pension will then depend on the success of the plan's investments. The employer has no obligation once the period's contributions have been made.

Lastly, a defined benefit plan is one where the employee is promised a pension which is not fixed in terms of the contributions. For example, the pension entitlement might build up over 20 years of service to equal one half of the employee's final year salary. The obligation of the employer is then dependent upon how long the employee will live after retirement and on what the final salary will be. Such plans are fairly common in Germany, the UK and the US.

16.6.3 Accounting for defined-benefit obligations

Introduction

If an employer company has an obligation (e.g. for severance indemnities or for defined-benefit pensions), the question is how to account for it.

In Italy and Japan, the calculation of the severance obligation is precise. Under domestic Italian rules, for example, the exact amounts are recognized as provisions in balance sheets, with changes in the year charged to the income statement. The amounts are not discounted for the time value of money. The charges are tax deductible.

In the US and under IAS 19, companies are required to estimate the obligation at the balance sheet date, using a discount rate based on current market interest rates. These calculations are not relevant for tax in several countries (e.g. in the US or the

UK), because they involve so much estimation. That is, the resulting pension expense is not tax deductible. In Germany, because of the close tax and accounting link (the *Massgeblichkeitsprinzip*, see Chapter 2), the tax system specifies a discount rate and that no expected future pay rises should be accounted for. These and other assumptions generally lead to under-provision (unless the financial statements are prepared under IFRS). This is not prudent but it conforms accounting with tax.

Under the EU Fourth Directive (Art. 43 (1) (7)), it seems to be possible merely to note pension obligations rather than to provide for them in the balance sheet. Several French companies do this under domestic rules, which means that they are not accounting for some of their liabilities.

Actuarial gains and losses

A defined benefit obligation changes from year to year for many reasons, which can be divided into two types: surprises and non-surprises. The obligation increases for two unsurprising reasons: the employees keep working and therefore build up their rights to be paid pensions (this is called 'service cost'), and the obligation gets one year nearer to being paid so there is one year less discounting (this is an interest expense or the unwinding of the discount rate). These expenses are charged to profit and loss.

Then there may be 'surprising' changes. These create actuarial gains and losses. For example, the following would cause actuarial losses: the company grants larger pay rises than expected, the pensioners live longer than expected, the discount rate falls. These losses may be large. If they were recognized immediately they would cause large, surprising debits in profit and loss. Company management does not like this, because management tries to make earnings rise smoothly in the medium term. Therefore, there has been pressure to find ways of protecting profit and loss from the truth. The FASB invented two of them in SFAS 87:

(i)   if the actuarial gain or loss is small, ignore it (the limit for 'small' is set at 10% of the larger of the obligation or the fund),

(ii) if the gain or loss is not small, smooth it over the average remaining service lives of the employees.

These devices are splendid examples of 'rules' as opposed to 'principles' in an accounting standard. The IASC/B copied them in IAS 19 in order to satisfy management's complaints about volatility. However, IAS 19 also allows any faster recognition.

The UK's Accounting Standards Board invented another way of protecting profit and loss in FRS 17 of 2000: charge actuarial gains and losses in the statement of total recognized gains and losses. An option to do this (i.e. charge other comprehensive income in IFRS terms) was added into IAS 19 in 2004 (see Chapter 6). US GAAP was amended in 2006 by SFAS 158. It retains the above profit and loss treatment but requires full recognition in the balance sheet.

16.6.4 Funding of employee benefit obligations

It is important to note that provision (even full provision) does not mean that money or investments have been set aside to cover future payments to the employee. It might be a good idea to do this, but it requires the company to take deliberate action that is quite separate from accounting for the obligation. If money is sent irrevocably from the company into the hands of financial managers who will invest it so as to pay pensioners, this activity is called *funding*. For the balance sheet, the value of the accumulated fund is set off against the accumulated obligation, because the fund can only be used to pay the pensioners, so this reduces the probable size of the company's liability. The balance sheet then shows the balance of the unfunded obligation as a provision.

It is vital not to confuse a provision with a fund. A provision is an obligation to pay money. A fund is a set of financial assets (money or investments). Internationally, the scope for confusion is considerable; for example, the Italian for 'provision' is *fondo*.

In the US and the UK, it is common for companies to engage in funding designed, in the long run, to cover their obligations. Of course, an obligation is an estimate and a fund goes up and down with the markets. So, exactly full funding is unusual. Incidentally, in these two countries, contributions to funds are tax deductible because (unlike pension expenses) they are easy for the tax system to check.

Table 16.5 shows an abbreviated version of the balance sheet of the US auto-mobile giant, General Motors. In the liabilities section, there is a pension liability of $11.9 billion and a post-retirement health benefit liability of $50.1 billion. This dwarfs the stockholders' equity which was negative in 2006 and only $14.7 billion

Table 16.5 Abbreviated balance sheet of General Motors as at 31 December 2006 (US$bn)

Cash and securities		24.7
Accounts receivable		8.2
Inventories		13.9
Deferred tax		44.9
Equipment leased out		17.9
Equity in associates		9.5
Tangible assets		41.9
Intangible assets		1.1
Other		24.1
Total assets		186.2
Accounts payable		28.1
Accrued expenses and other short debt		40.9
Debt		42.5
Post-retirement benefits (not pensions)		50.1
Pensions		11.9
Other		16.9
Total liabilities		190.4
Minority interests, etc.		1.2
Common stock	1.0	
Capital surplus	15.3	
Retained earnings	0.4	
Accumulated other comprehensive loss	(22.1)	
Total stockholders' equity		(5.4)
Total liabilities and equity		186.2

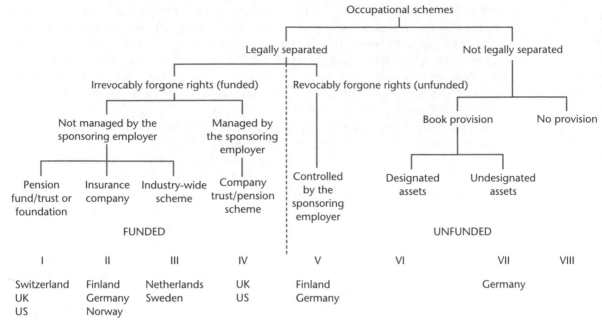

Figure 16.2 A classification of non-state pension schemes

Source: Adapted from FEE (1995) 'A classification of non-state pension schemes', in *Survey of Pensions and Other Retirement Benefits in EU and non-EU countries*. Routledge, London. Reproduced with permission of the Taylor & Francis Group, Ltd.

in 2005. The pension liability is the difference between a large obligation and a large fund. In contrast, there is little funding for the health obligations, so most of the obligation is shown as a liability.

In those continental European countries where company obligations are common (e.g. Germany and Italy), it is not usual to engage in extensive funding. The company keeps for general purposes the money that might otherwise have been set aside. Since pension provision expenses are tax deductible in these two countries, funding payments are not. Companies must ensure that they always have enough cash to pay the employee benefits falling due. The result of these practices is that large employee obligations can be seen on German and Italian balance sheets.

16.6.5 A summary for some countries

By combining the arrangements for institutions, for providing and for funding, a very varied picture emerges. Figure 16.2 shows the position for several countries. Eight types of scheme are shown in the figure, as are some countries where they are found.

16.7 Deferred tax

16.7.1 General explanation

The topic of deferred tax is one in which there have been major international differences in accounting. Deferred tax is not amounts of tax bills which the tax

Table 16.6 **Deferred tax on revaluation**

Balance sheet adjustments for Dutch company (€million)			
Fixed asset:			
cost	+3.0		
revaluation	+6.0		
	+9.0	Revaluation reserve:	+3.9
Cash:	−3.0	Deferred tax:	+2.1

authorities have allowed the taxpayer to postpone. Accounting for deferred tax is the recognition of the tax implied (but not otherwise included) by the numbers included in the financial statements.

A simple example of deferred tax would occur in the context of the revaluation of fixed assets. Suppose that a Dutch company buys a holding of land for €3 million and then revalues it in the balance sheet from €3 million to €9 million. Suppose, also, that the Dutch corporate tax rate on capital gains is 35 per cent, but that the Dutch tax rules do not tax capital gains until disposal, which in this case is not intended by the company in the foreseeable future. No tax is payable as a result of revaluing, but it is possible to see how accountants might think that the potential liability to tax of €2.1 million (i.e. €6 million revaluation × 35 per cent) relates to the period up to the balance sheet date. If so, they account for the implicitly deferred tax in the balance sheet, as in Table 16.6. Since the revaluation is not realized, there will be no gain or tax on the gain in the income statement.

In the above example, the €6 million of revaluation that is not yet relevant for tax purposes is called a 'temporary difference' under IASB or US rules. Under IAS 12 or SFAS 109, enterprises are required to account for deferred tax on temporary differences at current tax rates. A temporary difference is the difference between the carrying value of an asset or liability for financial reporting purposes and its value as recorded in the tax records. In the above example of the Dutch land, the financial reporting carrying value was €9 million and the tax value was €3 million. So, the temporary difference was €6 million.

In the US, upward revaluation of land is not allowed but current valuations of certain securities are required. In several continental countries, revaluation is legal under domestic accounting rules but would lead to current taxation. Consequently, in the individual financial statements of companies as prepared under the rules of most continental countries, deferred tax related to land would not arise, and the same applies to most accounting issues. However, particularly if a German, French, etc. group is using IFRS rules in its consolidated statements, deferred tax could arise in these countries because accounting practices might depart from tax rules for revaluation and other reasons. Furthermore, under IFRS, US GAAP and most other national rules, when a subsidiary's assets and liabilities are first consolidated, they are brought in at fair values, which are not recorded in any tax records. These all create temporary differences.

The most frequently cited cause of substantial amounts of deferred tax liabilities in Anglo-Saxon countries is depreciation. Depending on the industry sector,

Table 16.7 **Depreciation and tax**

	Accounting records			Tax calculations		
Year	Depreciation	Net book value	Year	Expense	Tax book value	Tax reduction
1	2,000	8,000	1	10,000	0	3,500
2	2,000	6,000	2	0	0	0
3	2,000	4,000	3	0	0	0
4	2,000	2,000	4	0	0	0
5	2,000	0	5	0	0	0

depreciation can be a large expense, and the tax rules can be substantially different from the accounting rules, as outlined in Chapter 2. Table 16.7 sets out a simple case, where there are 100 per cent tax depreciation allowances in the year of purchase of plant and machinery; a 35 per cent corporate income tax rate; the purchase for €10,000 of a machine which is expected to last for five years; and a country where tax and accounting are separated. The existence of 100 per cent tax depreciation is not fanciful. This applied for all plant and machinery in the United Kingdom from 1972 to 1984, to certain assets in West Berlin until the end of the 1980s, to capital investments in certain Greek islands, etc. The example would work, of course, with the less extreme tax allowances that are still common in continental Europe.

In Table 16.7, the accountants assume that the asset will have no residual value and will wear out evenly over time, irrespective of use. Consequently, for accounting purposes, they charge a depreciation expense of €2,000 per year. By contrast, the tax authorities allow an expense of €10,000 in the first year and, if the company takes this, no tax deductible expense after the first year. Consequently, there is a reduction in the tax bill of €3,500 in year 1 (i.e. an extra tax expense of €10,000 at a tax rate of 35 per cent). This cash flow advantage is designed to be the incentive to invest.

Suppose that the company uses the new asset very inefficiently or does not use it at all in the first year. In this case, depreciation may still be charged because the asset is depreciating due to the passing of time. The net effect of the inefficient capital purchase on the post-tax accounting profit of year 1 appears to be that the profit increases by €1,500 (i.e. depreciation expense of €2,000, and tax reduction of €3,500). Of course, if the company uses the asset effectively, profit will increase by much more than this, as the company should at least be able to earn enough by using the asset to cover the depreciation on it.

The above strange effect on profit is caused by deliberately charging the depreciation expense slowly but taking the tax reduction immediately. However, so far no account has been taken of deferred tax. In order to do so, under IAS 12 or US rules, it is necessary to calculate the temporary difference. This, as explained earlier, is the difference between the financial reporting carrying value of the asset and its tax value. In the case of the depreciating machine at the end of year 1, the financial reporting carrying value is cost less depreciation = €8,000, whereas the tax value is zero because there is full depreciation for tax purposes. So, there is a temporary difference of €8,000 and (at the tax rate of 35 per cent) a deferred tax liability of €2,800.

The double entry to give effect to deferred tax accounting in this case would be a debit entry under 'Tax expense' of €2,800, and a credit entry under 'Deferred tax liability' of €2,800. Then the profit for year 1 would *decrease* by €1,300 as a result of buying the asset and not using it (i.e. an extra depreciation expense of €2,000, an actual tax reduction of €3,500, but a deferred tax expense of €2,800). This is seen by most standard-setters as a more reasonable profit figure to present.

We have now seen two examples of the possible causes of deferred tax: a revaluation of assets that is not taken into account by the tax system, and depreciation running at a faster rate for tax than for accounting. Other examples include:

- the capitalization of leases, if the tax system still treats them as operating leases;
- taking profits on long-term contracts as production proceeds, if the tax system only counts profits at completion.

In order to account for deferred tax under IFRS and US rules, it is necessary to look at the values of all the assets and liabilities in the balance sheet and compare them to the tax values that would apply. Large numbers of temporary differences and resulting deferred tax assets and liabilities can arise. It is not allowed to discount the amounts to take account of the timing of the realization of the assets and liabilities.

The IFRS/US rules have changed considerably over time, and the rules vary internationally. For a review of these developments, see Schultz and Johnson (1998). One major question is whether deferred tax 'liabilities' are liabilities at all: is there an obligation to pay tax merely as a result of choosing to revalue an asset in a consolidated balance sheet (Nobes, 2003, Chapter 4)? One possible conclusion is that deferred tax should not be accounted for at all (Weetman, 1992).

16.7.2 Some international differences

In the domestic rules of several countries there are no requirements to account for deferred tax, partly because few temporary differences arise. The EU Fourth Directive does not require the recognition of deferred tax, and the Seventh Directive (Art. 29 (4)) appears to require recognition of only that deferred tax that arises as part of the process of consolidation.

Some countries (e.g. Norway) have similar rules to those of IFRS/US that were explained above. The rules in some others (e.g. France and the Netherlands) differ mainly in that deferred tax balances are sometimes discounted. In Germany and the UK, deferred tax is recognized not on temporary differences but on timing differences. The latter are measured on an income statement basis rather than by reference to assets and liabilities. Timing differences are a smaller category of things than temporary differences.

A further twist is that, in some countries (e.g. Italy and, until 2001, the United Kingdom), the recognition of deferred tax is partial in that it depends on whether payment of the amounts is likely or foreseeable.

16.7.3 Deferred tax assets

The recognition of deferred tax can lead to assets as well as to liabilities. Two of the major causes of deferred tax assets are:

- losses carried forward for tax purposes to be set against future taxable profits;
- employee benefit obligations that have been recognized for financial reporting purposes but not yet for tax.

As an example of the potential importance of deferred tax assets, Table 16.5 showed a summary of the balance sheet of General Motors. The deferred tax asset ($44.9 billion) results partly from the unfunded pension ($11.9 billion) and health benefit ($50.1 billion) obligations, multiplied by the tax rate. It should be noted again that the company's net assets (= stockholders' equity) was negative for 2006 and was only $14.7 billion for 2005.

Under US rules, deferred tax assets should be recognized when eventual realization is more likely than not. Most other rules require or imply a greater degree of probability than that. In the case of loss carryforwards, there must be doubt about realization because future profits are needed.

16.8   Revenue recognition

A credit balance can be one of three things: a liability, a revenue or an element of equity. The exact dividing lines between these three are alarmingly unclear. Section 16.4 already noted that preference shares can be seen as debt, and that convertible debentures can be seen as partly equity. Chapter 8 noted briefly that negative goodwill has sometimes been treated as a reserve (equity), sometimes as a negative asset (whatever that might be), and now under IFRS 3 as a gain. Under IAS 20, government grants can be treated as equity ('deferred income'), whereas under IAS 41 they are a gain. This section looks at the revenue/liability dividing line.

According to IAS 18 (paragraph 7):

> Revenue is the gross inflow of economic benefits during a period arising in the ordinary course of activities of an entity when those inflows result in increases in equity . . .

This definition fits with the IASB *Framework's* (paragraph 74) distinction between 'revenue' (e.g. sales) and 'gains' (e.g. on the sale of fixed assets), as pictured in Figure 16.3. However, there are severe problems. Firstly, the sale of fixed assets is also 'ordinary'. From 1993, IAS 8 greatly restricted the content of 'extraordinary'; and, from 2005, IAS 1 abolishes the concept. So, all inflows are ordinary. Secondly, some sales of fixed assets lead to increases in equity (so, are they 'revenue'?), whereas some sales of inventory lead to decreases in equity (so, are they not 'revenue'?). If the IASB would reply that one must consider the gross effect, then the words are redundant because any sale (whether of current or fixed assets) has some inflow. Presumably the definition is supposed to say that revenue is the gross income from selling things to customers. This could still be ambiguous but at least it would not be manifestly wrong.

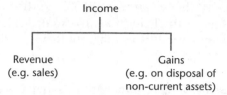

Figure 16.3 **IASB's definitions related to income**

Incidentally, it then becomes clear that 'revenue' is sometimes *associated* with 'income' and sometimes not. Indeed, 'revenue' is not a type of 'income', but its occurrence usually means that some income or loss needs to be recognized.

Under IAS 18, revenue from sales (and therefore income) should not be recognized until 'the entity has transferred to the buyer the significant risks and rewards of ownership [and control]'. For example, a binding sales contract is not yet 'revenue'.

Under US GAAP, the hurdles for the recognition of revenue are even higher, and toughly enforced by the SEC. Staff Accounting Bulletin 104 does not allow revenue recognition until all four of the following conditions are satisfied:

(i)   persuasive evidence of an arrangement;

(ii) delivery;

(iii) price is fixed or determinable; and

(iv) collectibility is reasonably assured.

Traditionally, the domestic laws of most countries have been silent on this issue, so a move to IFRS or, even more, to US GAAP may lead to later revenue recognition.

Strangely, when moving to contract accounting, the above logic and rules are abandoned. For example, IAS 18 and IAS 11 require the stage-of-completion method for those uncompleted contracts which can be estimated reliably and look profitable. Let us take the example of an apparently profitable five-year contract to build electric trains. Suppose that there has been no delivery to the customer because all the trains are half complete. Should we take profit so far? Yes. Has there been any transfer of risks and control to the customer? No.

Let us take a simpler example. Imagine a magazine publisher who sells £100 non-refundable subscriptions on 1 January 200X, and promises to supply 12 magazines in the year. Taking all the other customers into account, the average cost of production and delivery for the total of the 12 magazines is expected to be £75. When should the publisher recognize profit? The traditional answer is that the £25 profit should be recognized gradually over the year. Therefore, to start with, the £100 is recorded as a liability. The modern answer is (on 1 January):

(i)   Is there an asset? Yes, £100 in the bank.

(ii) Is there a liability? Yes, the obligation to provide 12 magazines at an expected cost of £75.

(iii) Therefore, there is an immediate gain of £25.

Note that there cannot be a liability of £100 (although one is recorded under conventional accounting) because there is no probable outflow of £100. Note, also, that we should distinguish between the 'revenue' of £100 and the 'income' of £25. Apart from the fact that this result fits the *Framework*, it also makes some sense: the difficult bit for the publisher is not producing magazines but finding customers prepared to pay £100. Once the latter is done, 'performance' has been effectively achieved.

In 2004, the IASB and the FASB began grappling with this major issue. At the time of writing, we are still waiting for a discussion paper, which may have explosive results on conventional accounting.

16.9 Comprehensive income

Beginning in the UK in 1993 (with FRS 3), standard-setters have ensured that all gains and losses are recorded in a primary statement rather than any being lost as 'reserve movements'. The UK statement is called a statement of total recognized gains and losses (STRGL). This is equivalent to an IFRS or US statement of comprehensive income. Such a statement is required by IAS 1, but not under US GAAP, which allows the elements of other comprehensive income to be disclosed in the statement of changes in equity.

As explained in Chapter 6, IFRS and US GAAP allow an entity to present an income statement that excludes other comprehensive income. This is widespread practice. Under US GAAP, if an entity does not show an income statement, it must show a Statement of Comprehensive Income (SCI). Table 16.8 shows the required statements under IFRS (as revised in 2007) and some national rules.

Under IFRS, the components of other comprehensive income are:

- revaluations of assets (under IASs 16 and 38);
- fair value adjustments on available-for-sale financial assets (under IAS 39);
- gains and losses on cash flow hedges (under IAS 39);
- foreign currency gains and losses on translation of financial statements (under IAS 21 – see Chapter 18);
- actuarial gains and losses (optionally under IAS 19).

All of these, apart from the first, are also relevant under US GAAP. IAS 1 requires an entity to show the tax related to each component in the SCI.

Table 16.8 **Required statements**

Statement	Required in:			
	IFRS	**US**	**UK**	**France/Germany**
Income statement (or profit and loss account)	No	No	Yes	Yes
SCI (or STRGL)	Yes	No	Yes	No
Statement of changes in equity	Yes	Yes	No	No

Table 16.9 **Are gains and losses previously recorded as 'other comprehensive income' later reclassified as profit or loss?**

	IFRS	US	UK*
Revaluation of tangible and intangible assets	No	N/A	No
Fair valuing available-for-sale financial assets	Yes	Yes	N/A
Gains and losses on cash flow hedges	Yes	Yes	N/A
Actuarial gains and losses	No	Yes	No
Translation of foreign statements	Yes	Yes	No

Notes: * = Standards for unlisted companies.
N/A = Not applicable because not covered by standards.

There is no principle that can explain why the above components are not included in 'profit or loss'. They all meet the definitions of 'income' or 'expense'. The explanation is *not* that they are 'unrealized', because gains on unsold investment properties or forests *are* included in profit or loss. Anyway, the concept of 'realized' does not appear in IFRS, and its meaning is unclear in EU laws.

The IASB has been trying to find a principle to classify income, but has not yet succeeded. A related issue is whether gains and losses, once recorded in other comprehensive income, are ever reclassified as profit or loss. This issue was introduced in Chapter 8, and an expanded version of the table there is shown here as Table 16.9. It reveals another set of rules for which no principle can be discovered. The political explanation is that standards influenced by the US have reclassification, whereas those influenced by the UK do not. The SCI has to show any reclassifications.

SUMMARY

- Intangible assets are very important in many fast-growing companies. Recognition of them varies between IFRS and US rules.

- The measurement of assets is mostly based on cost under US GAAP, but IFRS allows many departures from this.

- Financial assets are divided into three types, based on management's intentions.

- In most countries, the classification of financial instruments is based on legal form, and discounting of liabilities is unusual.

- Hedge accounting is permitted under some circumstances in IFRS and US GAAP.

- The degree to which provisions are recognized for future expenses varies internationally. Under IASB rules, an obligation must exist at the balance sheet date.

- Care needs to be taken when translating such terms as provision, reserve, allowance and fund.

- The institutional arrangements for post-retirement benefits vary from country to country. Accountants need to identify the degree to which a company has obligations.

- IFRS contains several devices to protect profit and loss from volatility caused by actuarial gains and losses.

- Funding arrangements also differ, with full funding often found in the United States and the United Kingdom but not in continental Europe.

- The IFRS/US rules use a balance sheet basis for deferred tax calculations (temporary differences), whereas some other rules use an income statement basis (timing differences).

- Deferred tax liabilities may be caused by accelerated tax depreciation and by the revaluation of assets.

- There are international variations in the use of discounting for deferred tax balances and in the degree to which all temporary/timing differences are accounted for.

- 'Revenue' is defined confusingly by the IASB. The recognition of revenue is the topic of much current debate.

- There are no principles to explain which income and expense is 'other comprehensive income' or which parts of that should be later reclassified as profit or loss.

References

FEE (1995) *Survey of Pensions and other Retirement Benefits in EU and non-EU Countries*, Routledge, London.

JWG (2000) *Draft Standard: Financial Instruments and Similar Items*, FASB, IASC and others.

Nobes, C.W. (2001) *Asset Measurement Bases in UK and IASC Standards*, ACCA, London.

Nobes, C.W. (2003) *Liabilities and Their Measurement under UK and International Accounting Standards*, ACCA, London.

Schultz, S.M. and Johnson, R.T. (1998) 'Income tax allocation: the continuing controversy in historical perspective', *Accounting Historians Journal*, December.

Weetman, P. (1992) *SSAP 15: Accounting for Deferred Taxation*, Institute of Chartered Accountants of Scotland, Edinburgh.

QUESTIONS

Suggested answers to the asterisked questions are given at the end of the book.

16.1∗ 'Secret reserves make a company stronger, so they should be encouraged.' Discuss.

16.2∗ Under IAS 32, some shares are treated as liabilities and some apparent liabilities are treated as partly equity. Is this a good idea?

16.3 Under what circumstances should next year's wages and next year's repair expenses be charged as expenses this year?

16.4 Are intangible assets recognized sufficiently under IFRS and US rules?

16.5   Explain how assets are measured under IFRS. How could this be improved?

16.6   Explain the difference between 'hedging' and 'hedge accounting'. In each case, what are the arguments in favour of doing them?

16.7   Explain the differences between an allowance, a liability, a contingent liability, an obligation, a provision, an accrual, a fund and a reserve. State which set of accounting rules you have been using as the context for your answer.

16.8   Compare the degrees of prudence found in accounting for employee benefits in Germany, Italy and the United States.

16.9   Explain, using various examples, the causes of deferred tax assets and deferred tax liabilities under US accounting rules.

16.10 Examine whether a deferred tax liability arising from temporary differences on the revaluation of an asset meets the IFRS/US definition of a liability.

17 Consolidation

Robert Parker and Christopher Nobes

OBJECTIVES

After reading this chapter, you should be able to:

- explain why the United States and the United Kingdom adopted consolidated financial statements before the countries of continental Europe;

- discuss the different concepts of a 'group' and how they are reflected in IFRS and US GAAP;

- outline the effects on consolidated financial statements of the harmonization programmes of the European Union and the International Accounting Standards Board;

- describe how publication requirements differ between the United States, the United Kingdom, Germany and France;

- discuss the varying approaches in IFRS and US GAAP to purchase accounting, pooling (uniting) of interests, proportional consolidation, the equity method and the consolidation difference.

17.1   Introduction

Both theory and practice in the field of consolidation accounting have differed substantially from country to country. The differences have been of four kinds:

1 differences in the rate of adoption of consolidated financial statements;
2 differences in the concept of a group for consolidation purposes;
3 differences in what is published by companies;
4 differences in the techniques of consolidation.

The harmonization activities of the International Accounting Standards Board (IASB) and the European Union have substantially narrowed these differences, but they are unlikely to be removed entirely. The main aim of this chapter is to describe the differences and, so far as is possible, to explain them.

Discussion in the chapter deals mainly with the IASB, the European Union and the United States. Consolidation practices in Japan are dealt with in Chapter 12. Australia has, in effect, adopted international standards; China and Canada are converging with them.

17.2   Rate of adoption

Consolidated financial statements were first produced in the United States. A number of US companies published such statements before the beginning of the twentieth century (Bores, 1934; Hein, 1978; Mumford, 1982) but it was the United States Steel Company, which was chartered in New Jersey in 1901 and published consolidated statements from its inception, that set a pattern.

The faster rate of adoption in the United States than elsewhere can be explained in part by the earlier development there of the holding company. This was connected to the fact that each state has a separate legal system, so that combinations of businesses from more than one state were more easily achieved by leaving the separate legal entities in place. One consequence of the wave of mergers in the United States at the turn of the twentieth century was that groups of companies, not individual companies, carried out commercial and industrial activities. There were no legal or regulatory barriers to hold up new accounting techniques and a social climate existed in which innovation was highly regarded.

In Britain and continental Europe, both holding companies and consolidated statements were a later development. In the United Kingdom it was not until the second wave of merger activity (1916–22) that holding companies became an important form of business organization. The earliest consolidated statements appear to date from 1910 (Edwards and Webb, 1984). The first British book on the subject, *Holding Companies and their Published Accounts* by Gilbert Garnsey, was published in 1923, by which time consolidation had, as Garnsey himself pointed out, become almost universal in the United States. When UK company law was extensively reformed in 1929, consolidated financial statements were not introduced as a legal requirement. Dunlop Ltd led the way during the 1930s, but consolidations still remained relatively uncommon (Bircher, 1988) although in 1939 the London Stock Exchange required consolidated statements as a condition of new issues. The Second World War then intervened and it was not until 1947 that group accounts (normally in the form of consolidated financial statements) were finally required by law.

Thus, both the need for the new technique (the rise of the holding company) and its recognition came more slowly in the United Kingdom than in the United States. Garnsey stated that 'the natural reluctance of the people of this country to change is too well known to require any comment' and he placed the blame on the directors who were, under British law, responsible for published accounts. It is possible that the obligation (not present in the United States) to publish the holding company's own balance sheet may have acted as a deterrent to the publication of a consolidated balance sheet.

Consolidated financial statements developed even later in continental Europe. The earliest Dutch example, according to Bores (1934), was Wm H. Müller & Co. of the Hague in 1926 (see also, Zeff *et al.*, 1992). German companies did not start consolidating until the 1930s and none was obliged by law to do so until 1965. French companies were even slower. According to the 1968 annual report of the *Commission des Opérations de Bourse*, only 22 French companies published a consolidated balance sheet for 1967. As late as 1983 only about 75 per cent of French listed companies published consolidated statements and they were not legally bound to do so until 1986. Consolidated statements were still very rare in the 1980s in such countries as Italy, Spain, Greece and Luxembourg. This, however, changed in the 1990s as a result of the EU Seventh Directive (see Section 17.4 below).

In some other countries, consolidation is still either non-existent or at a very primitive stage. For example, consolidated statements are not required in Morocco and were not required in India until 2001 or in Turkey until 2003.

17.3 The concept of a 'group'

The production of consolidated financial statements assumes that a group of enterprises can be regarded as a single accounting entity. In defining the boundaries of such an entity, it is necessary to ask, first, for whom is information about the entity intended, and, second, for what purpose the information is to be provided. The US and IASB conceptual frameworks assume that financial statements are particularly designed for existing and potential investors. Furthermore, the emphasis has, until recently, been on the shareholders of the parent or holding company, at the expense of any minority shareholders in the case of less than wholly owned subsidiaries. This is the 'parent company' concept of a group.

Such a concept has a number of weaknesses. For example:

● It assumes that a group consists of a parent company that dominates a number of dependent or subsidiary companies. It does not allow for the possibility that the group has been formed by the merger of two or more companies of approximately equal size; nor does it allow for companies dominated jointly by more than one company, or for companies over which another company exercises a significant influence but not control.

- It treats all interested parties other than equity shareholders of the parent as unimportant users, so minority interests are shown outside of shareholders' funds.

The 'parent company' concept is based on legal control. This is usually achieved by majority shareholder voting rights, but it can also be attained (where company legislation permits, as it does in Germany) by the use of 'control contracts' whereby one company places itself under the legal domination of another.

A possible alternative is the 'entity' concept of a group. This emphasizes the economic unity of all enterprises in the group and treats all shareholders similarly, whether majority or minority. This way of looking at a group is also, it can be argued, more appropriate for such users as employees and managers. A group that consists of, say, two equally large companies can also be accommodated more easily under the entity concept. Even before the adoption of IFRS, minority interests were shown as part of equity under Australian, German and Italian practice. This makes sense because they clearly do not meet the definition of liabilities (see Chapter 6). IAS 27 originally stated that minority interests should not be shown as parent company equity but allowed them to be shown as group equity. A revision of 2003 requires this latter treatment, which is in line with the entity concept.

Whichever of the two concepts is being used, the group is defined in principle as a set of entities that operate together because they are owned or controlled by the same parties. Neither the parent company concept nor the entity concept, however, takes account of enterprises that are linked to the group but where there is neither legal dominance nor an economic unit. These situations are, however, covered by the 'proprietary' concept, which emphasizes not legal control nor economic unity but ownership or proprietorship, which gives the possibility of exercising 'significant influence' over commercial and financial policy decisions. Under this concept a proportionate share of the profit or loss for the year and a proportionate share of the assets and liabilities are brought into the consolidated statements, either item by item ('proportional consolidation') or on a 'one-line' basis (the 'equity method').

All three concepts need to be invoked to explain the IASB standards and US GAAP.

17.4 Harmonization from the 1970s onwards

The two major attempts at harmonization of group accounting by the IASC/B and the EU were very different in nature, but they came together when all EU listed companies were required (from 2005 with a few exceptions) to use IFRS for their consolidated statements.

The International Accounting Standards Committee began by concentrating with some success on producing a standard that would encourage consolidation in countries where it was still underdeveloped, and on drawing up a list of practices acceptable to both US and UK accountants. The Committee deliberately excluded from the original standard (Consolidated Financial Statements, IAS 3, 1976) two areas – pooling of interests (merger accounting) and the treatment of goodwill on consolidation – where practice was divergent. Later the IASC produced a more comprehensive set of standards: IAS 22 (amended in 1993 and 1998 and replaced by IFRS 3 in 2004) on acquisitions and mergers; IAS 27 to replace IAS 3; IAS 28 on associated entities; and IAS 31 on joint ventures. Further amendments were made by the IASB in 2003, 2004 and 2008.

IAS 22 restricted the use of pooling/merger accounting (see Section 17.7 for more detail) to those rare cases where it was impossible to identify an acquirer. For acquisitions, IAS 22 required capitalization of goodwill and its amortization over its useful life. Until 1998, IAS 22 had limited the useful life to 20 years; however, the standard was revised in that year to allow longer periods to be used, approximately as in the United Kingdom's FRS 10 of 1997. Under IFRS 3, the pooling method is abolished and goodwill is to be tested annually for impairment rather than being amortized. This harmonizes with US practice since 2001.

IAS 27 bases its definition of a subsidiary on the existence of control and does not permit the exclusion of subsidiaries on the grounds of dissimilarity or for any other reason. IAS 28 requires the use of equity accounting for associates; and IAS 31 has a choice of proportional consolidation (benchmark treatment) and equity accounting (allowed alternative) for joint ventures. In areas of measurement, this amounts to a stricter set of rules than that of the EU Seventh Directive (see below), although the Directive has more detailed definitions of a subsidiary and more detailed format requirements.

In addition to the effect on companies that comply directly with IFRS, the various international standards on group accounting have affected those many countries where domestic rules are based exactly or closely on IFRSs. Some major European companies also used IFRSs, particularly for their group statements. For example, this was noticeable in France and Italy in the 1980s, and in the 1990s in Switzerland and Germany. As noted in Chapter 11, the existence of IAS 3 probably had an impact on the negotiations relating to the Seventh Directive.

The European Union tackled the difficult task of producing rules that were enforceable by statute and acceptable to countries of such diverse practices as the United Kingdom, Germany, France, the Netherlands and Italy. The origins of the Seventh Directive can be traced back to a supplementary paper to the Elmendorff Report (see Chapter 11). The early draft (e.g. as published by the European Commission in 1976) was closely based on German rules. This influence was gradually much reduced by the addition or substitution of many Anglo-American features (Diggle and Nobes, 1994). Adoption of the Seventh Directive in 1983 was a notable event in the history of consolidated accounting. National laws implementing the Directive were required to be enacted by 1988 and their provisions were to apply by 1990. However, these requirements were not met (see Table 17.1).

Table 17.2 lists the main provisions of the Directive and the major source country for each provision.

The Directive was a compromise between the 'parent company' concept and the 'entity' concept, with a leaning towards the former. The financial statement formats

Table 17.1 Implementation of the Seventh EU Directive by pre-2004 EU members

	National laws	In force (year ends)
France	1985	1986 (Listed); 1990 (Others)
Germany	1985	1990
Greece	1987	1990
Luxembourg	1988	1990
Netherlands	1988	1990
Spain	1989	1991
United Kingdom	1989	1990
Belgium	1990	1991
Denmark	1990	1992
Austria	1990*	1994
Italy	1991	1994
Portugal	1991	1991
Ireland	1992	1993
Finland	1992*	1993
Sweden	1995	1997
Norway[‡]	1998	1998

Notes:
*Less than complete implementation.
[‡]Member of the European Economic Area, not the EU.

Table 17.2 Main provisions of the Seventh EU Directive

	Article no.	Some source countries
1	Subsidiaries are defined largely in terms of *de jure* rather than *de facto* criteria	UK
3	Consolidation to include foreign subsidiaries	UK, NL, F
4	Consolidation irrespective of legal form of subsidiary	G
4	Consolidation by all types of company	UK, NL
7	Exemption from preparation of group accounts by wholly owned subsidiaries	UK, NL, F
13	Subsidiaries may be excluded on various grounds	UK
14	Compulsory exclusion of certain dissimilar subsidiaries [deleted 2003]	UK
16	True and fair view	UK, NL
17	Uniform formats to be used	G, F
19	Goodwill to be calculated at date of first consolidation	UK, NL
19	Goodwill to be based on fair values	UK, NL
29	Tax-based valuations to be 'corrected' or at least disclosed	–
30	Goodwill to be depreciated or written off	UK, NL
33	Equity method for associated companies	UK, NL, F

of the Fourth Directive apply 'without prejudice to the provisions of this Directive and taking account of the essential adjustments resulting from the particular characteristics of consolidated accounts as compared with annual accounts' (Art. 17).

One of the purposes of a Directive on group accounting is clear: as for other aspects of accounting, harmonization should enable easier international comparison of financial statements (whether of multinationals or not) and easier preparation of financial statements for multinationals. However, it is also clear that the Seventh Directive on company law had two additional purposes behind it. First, if harmonization of practices had been the only aim, the simplest method would have been to have no consolidation, for this was the prevailing practice throughout much of the European Union in the early 1970s when drafting began. Thus, one aim of the Seventh Directive was to 'improve' practice by requiring consolidation for all subsidiaries of groups above a certain size. A second aim was particularly apparent in the drafts of the Directive: the disclosure of information to assist in the control of multinationals by host countries.

The 'control' aim of the Directive is far less visible in the adopted version than it was in the drafts of 1976 and 1978. It is clear in these drafts that the European Commission had uses in mind for consolidated financial statements additional to the appraisal of groups by shareholders and investors. There were proposals for consolidation by groups under the control of unincorporated businesses, and by EU companies that were unconnected except for their common control by an undertaking outside the Union. In the former case, it was suggested by some that the various worldwide commercial interests of the Roman Catholic Church would have to be consolidated because they were controlled by the Pope! In the second case, a 'horizontal consolidation' would be required from the various EU subsidiaries of Ford, although none of them owned or controlled any of the others. Which EU shareholders or investors would benefit from these consolidations? What would it have to do with harmonization of accounting? Persistent asking of these questions no doubt helped to remove the mandatory status of these provisions.

Returning to harmonization, it should be clear that the aim was not uniformity. Harmonization does not imply the imposition of a rigid and narrow set of rules. There is no doubt, however, that the Directive was a major step towards the production by European companies not only of more consolidated statements but also of more comparable ones. It also had the effect of bringing continental European practice more into line with that of Anglo-Saxon countries. Nevertheless, the Directive was only adopted as the result of lengthy discussion and a series of compromises, and many options are available to member states.

The impact of the Directive was greatest on those member states such as Greece, Italy, Luxembourg, Portugal and Spain, where consolidations had been rare. A detailed survey of the options adopted in the member states is provided by FEE (1993). The Directive also affects the new member states of the EU, except to the extent that IFRS is required or optional for consolidated statements.

Some countries closely associated with the European Union have implemented laws based on the Fourth and Seventh Directives; for example, Switzerland (Zünd, 1993) implemented a law based loosely on the Seventh Directive in 1991. In the case of the non-EU members of the European Economic Area (e.g. Norway), implementation was also required.

17.5 | Definitions of group companies

The concept of a group was discussed in Section 17.3. In this section we discuss the definitions of subsidiaries, associates and joint ventures.

17.5.1 IFRS

International standards make use of all three concepts of a group (see Section 17.3). The definition of a subsidiary is based on 'control', which is defined in IAS 27 as the power to govern the financial and operating policies of an entity, including an unincorporated entity, so as to obtain benefits from its activities. Control is presumed to exist where the parent owns more than half of the entity's voting power. Control is also deemed to exist where the parent owns half or less of the voting power, but has power:

- over more than half of the voting rights by virtue of an agreement with other investors;
- to govern the entity's financial and operating policies under a statute or an agreement;
- to appoint or remove the majority of the members of the board of directors or equivalent governing body and control of the entity is by that board or body;
- to cast the majority of the votes at meetings of the board of directors or equivalent governing body and control of the entity is by that board or body.

An IFRS Interpretation (SIC 12) reminds us that we should look at the substance of the arrangements with other entities and that there may be other ways of achieving control than those mentioned above from IAS 27.

Since the revision of IAS 27 in 2003 and the publication of IFRS 5 in 2004 there are no grounds under which a group may exclude any of its subsidiaries from consolidation. IFRS 5 requires the net assets of subsidiaries that are intended to be sold to be shown on the balance sheet as 'held for sale'. More disclosures are needed if the subsidiary is large enough to be a discontinued operation.

IAS 31 (as revised in 2003) defines a joint venture as a contractual arrangement whereby two or more parties undertake an economic activity that is subject to joint control. Joint control is the jointly agreed sharing of control over an economic activity. It exists only when the strategic financial and operating decisions require the unanimous consent of all the venturers. The standard distinguishes between jointly controlled operations, jointly controlled assets and jointly controlled entities. Whether joint venture entities should be seen as part of 'the group' is unclear from either IAS 31 or the IASB's conceptual framework, which does not deal with the definition of a reporting entity. This ambivalence leads to the availability of a choice between proportional consolidation and equity accounting (see Section 17.7).

IAS 28 defines an associate as an entity over which an investor has significant influence and that is neither a subsidiary nor an interest in a joint venture. Significant influence is the power to participate in the investee's financial and operating policy decisions, but is not control or joint control over those policies. Significant influence is presumed where an investor has 20 per cent or more of the voting power of the investee. Similarly, if the investor has less than 20 per cent, the presumption is that there is no significant influence. However, these presumptions are rebuttable. Again, it is not clear whether the associate should be seen as part of the group. Certain aspects of the treatment of associates (see Section 17.7) suggest that it is.

17.5.2 United States

US practice is based on the parent company concept plus the use of the propriet-ary concept for corporate joint ventures and for associates. However, until 2001, extensive use was made of 'pooling of interests' which is discussed further in Section 17.7. This would seem to be based upon the entity concept and is difficult to reconcile with a parent company approach. Its use in the United States probably owed more to management's need to boost earnings per share than to theoretical considerations.

The US definition of a subsidiary, like that in IFRS, is based on the concept of 'control'. Accounting Research Bulletin No. 51 states that the purpose of con-solidated statements is to present, primarily for the benefit of the shareholders and creditors of the parent company, the results of operations and the financial position of a parent company and its subsidiaries essentially as if the group were a single company with one or more branches or divisions. A holding of more than 50 per cent of the voting shares of another company is a condition pointing towards con-solidation. This is different from the somewhat wider IFRS or European concept of *de facto* control. It enabled 'special purpose vehicles' (SPVs) to be set up that were controlled but not majority owned. These could then be used to hide liabilities, as was the case with Enron. Until 1988 there could also have been exceptions in the case of finance-related subsidiaries; however, SFAS 94 (and later amendments) makes it compulsory to consolidate all subsidiaries, except those that are not controlled despite being majority owned. In 2003, the FASB issued an interpreta-tion (FIN 46) that requires the consolidation of certain SPVs called variable interest entities.

It is somewhat clearer in US GAAP than in IFRS that joint ventures and associates are not part of 'the group', though this is not explained anywhere, even in the conceptual framework.

17.6 Publication requirements and practices

As explained in Chapter 5, listed companies in the EU must use IFRS for their con-solidated statements. Member states may give permission for unlisted parents to use IFRS for consolidated statements also, and this has generally been done. For the par-ent company's unconsolidated statements, some countries insist on IFRS for listed companies (e.g. the Czech Republic), some allow IFRS for any parent (e.g. the UK) and some ban IFRS for unconsolidated statements (e.g. France). Chapter 13 gives more detail on this. Consequently, publication rules and practices vary between the EU member states and the United States. For example:

● US companies publish consolidated balance sheets, income statements, statements of changes in equity, and cash flow statements, but do not publish any parent company statements.

● UK companies still using domestic rules publish the same consolidated statements as American companies (with a statement of total recognized gains and losses), plus the unconsolidated balance sheet, but not the profit and loss account, of the parent company.

● In France and Germany, a full set of parent statements is required under domestic rules, in addition to a full set of consolidated statements (under IFRS or not).

In the EU, member state laws (based on the Seventh Directive) exempt some smaller groups from preparing consolidated statements. The size criteria for exemption from consolidation are subject to change and are not uniform across the member states of the EU. However, all are based on sales, balance sheet total and number of employees. The first two measures can be 'gross' (i.e. an aggregation without consolidation adjustments) or 'net' (i.e. after appropriate consolidation adjustments). Some member states use gross measures, some net measures and some a combination of both.

US consolidation practice is governed by the rules of its SEC and by relevant accounting standards. Consolidated financial statements must be filed each year by all companies subject to SEC jurisdiction (see Chapter 8). Financial statements of any unconsolidated subsidiaries must also be filed. Article 4 of Regulation S-X sets forth the SEC's requirements as to the form and contents of consolidated and combined financial statements. It requires, *inter alia*, that consolidated statements clearly exhibit the financial condition and results of operations of the registrant and its subsidiaries. It further requires the consolidation of majority-owned subsidiaries only; the reasons for inclusion and exclusion of subsidiaries; separate disclosure of minority interest in capital, in retained earnings and in consolidated income for the year; and elimination of inter-company transactions and items.

17.7   Techniques of consolidation

17.7.1 Introduction

There have been considerable differences in the techniques of consolidation used in the EU and the US, although these differences have been substantially lessened by the implementation of the Seventh Directive and the influence of IFRSs. In summary, the most important points are:

1 Under IFRS and US GAAP, all business combinations are treated as purchases by one party of the other(s).

2 Pooling of interests (also known as uniting of interests and merger accounting) was a fairly common accounting practice only in the United States and the United Kingdom. It is no longer permissible under either IFRS or US GAAP.

3 Proportional consolidation is common in France and in some other continental European countries, but is relatively rare in the United Kingdom and the United States.

4 The equity method has been used in varying ways.

5 The treatment of the 'consolidation difference' varies from country to country.

These issues are now discussed in turn.

17.7.2 Purchase accounting

Purchase (or acquisition) accounting assumes that one party (often the parent company of a group) is buying a controlling interest in another entity. This often corresponds well with the facts of a business combination.

Under the purchase accounting method of consolidation, the group is seen as buying all the individual assets and liabilities of the new subsidiary. It is therefore necessary to establish the 'cost' to the group of each of these. This is unlikely to be the carrying value that was recorded for the assets and liabilities in the financial statements of the subsidiary. The 'cost' to the purchaser is measured by estimating the fair values (current market values) of the items.

Often, because the acquirer expects to make better use of the assets than the acquiree, the acquirer pays more for the net assets than their total fair value. This gives rise to the recognition of goodwill (see Section 17.7.6).

Both US GAAP and IFRS require a group to identify as many intangible assets as possible, leaving as little as possible to be called goodwill. Consequently, it would be normal to put a value on purchased brand names. It is also necessary to value contingent liabilities although not, as yet, contingent assets.

17.7.3 Pooling (uniting) of interests

As explained in Chapter 8, a subsidiary acquired by a US company through an exchange of shares had (until 2001) in some cases to be consolidated as a pooling of interests. In a pooling there was no revaluation of assets to fair values at the date of acquisition (as there normally would be in other methods) and no goodwill on consolidation. The investment in the subsidiary in the acquiring company's books was valued at the nominal value of shares issued. The consolidated retained profits were simply the sum of the retained profits of the companies concerned. No distinction was drawn between pre- and post-acquisition profits because, of course, there was deemed to be no acquisition. For the same reason, the subsidiary's profits were included in the consolidated profit and loss account as from the first day of the year of acquisition.

It is clear that a pooling of interests was likely to result in lower reported expenses (since depreciation was calculated on historical, not revalued, figures and there was no goodwill to be amortized or impaired) and thus higher reported annual earnings per share. Retained earnings and thus the group's distributable reserves were also higher. A share premium was not recorded by the parent company as a result of the merger.

In the US, Opinion No. 16 (1970) specified the elaborate criteria by which, until 2001, a pooling was to be distinguished from a purchase. Pooling could not be applied where shares were acquired for cash; it *had to be* applied in certain specified circumstances where shares were acquired for a consideration other than cash. *Accounting Trends and Techniques* (AICPA, 2000) reported 54 new business combinations accounted for as poolings of interests and 343 accounted for by the purchase method, from a sample of 600 companies. Figures for the previous three years showed somewhat smaller numbers of poolings and purchases.

Because the pooling method led to more attractive financial statements, there was pressure from large groups to use it. Great ingenuity was used in order to qualify for the method. As a result, standard-setters and regulators considered removing the method. In 2001, the FASB issued SFAS 141 which bans the use of the pooling method, so all business combinations must be treated as purchases. There are criteria for identifying the purchaser if it is not obvious.

The United Kingdom is the only country in the EU where pooling of interests (merger accounting) has been of any importance. The method was retrospectively legalized in 1981 and was the subject of an accounting standard (SSAP 23) in 1985. SSAP 23 was replaced in 1994 by FRS 6, which was designed to make merger accounting rare by only allowing it when it was impossible to identify an acquirer or an acquiree.

The IASB's requirements were contained in IAS 22, which had similar rules to FRS 6. In 2004, uniting of interests was abolished by IFRS 3.

17.7.4 Proportional consolidation

As noted earlier, IAS 31 requires proportional (proportionate, pro rata) consolidation for jointly controlled operations and assets, and makes it the benchmark treatment for joint venture entities. Nevertheless, for joint venture entities (i.e. joint ventures that are themselves separate entities), it can be argued that proportional consolidation may not be appropriate because the venturer does not control any of the venture's assets (Milburn and Chant, 1999), although it does have significant influence over their use. An obvious disincentive to the use of proportional consolidation is that, compared with the equity method, it increases the recorded amount of the group's liabilities. On the other hand, it increases the consolidated cash and sales figures. It is likely that the IASB will remove proportional consolidation for joint venture entities (see exposure draft of 2007).

Before the adoption of IFRS for many consolidated statements in 2005, use of the method in consolidated statements varied considerably within the EU. Under domestic French rules the method is required for joint ventures. In Germany, proportional consolidation was not allowed before the implementation of the Seventh Directive. The Accounting Directives Law permitted, but did not prescribe, proportional consolidation for joint ventures, and the method was used by some groups. In the United Kingdom, proportional consolidation is not allowed by FRS 9 for joint venture entities.

17.7.5 Equity method

IAS 28 requires use of the equity method for associates in consolidated statements. An associate is valued in the balance sheet at cost plus a proportionate share of the retained profits since the date of acquisition. The income statement does not include the detailed revenues and expenses (as would be the case for a subsidiary company or under proportional consolidation). Instead, there is a figure for the proportionate share of the associate's profit. IAS 31 permits but does not require the use of the equity method for joint venture entities. The alternative is proportionate (or proportional) consolidation (see above).

In the United States, APB Opinion No. 18 stipulates that the equity method should be used to account for investments in unconsolidated subsidiaries, for investments in corporate joint ventures and for investments in companies in which at least 20 per cent but not more than 50 per cent of the voting stock is held and the investor has the ability to exercise significant influence over the operating and financial policies of the investee. US practice also allows the equity method to be used in parent company financial statements (not that these are often published) as well as in the consolidated financial statements.

Nobes (2002) examines the international spread of the equity method over time. He suggests that most of the uses of the equity method are inappropriate; and that the 20 per cent threshold for significant influence (see Section 17.5.1) was arrived at by accident. In particular, assuming that the group is the parent plus its controlled entities, the group's share of an associate's profit is not realized in (and could not be successfully demanded by) the group. So why is it included in the group's income? A possible alternative to the equity method is the use of fair values for the investment. Where reliable fair values are not obtainable, the equity method might be regarded as a proxy.

17.7.6 Consolidation difference

'Consolidation difference' refers to the difference that arises on consolidation because the amount paid by the investor company is greater or less than its proportionate share of the tangible and identifiable intangible net assets of the investee.

Under IFRS and US GAAP, it is standard practice to make this calculation at the date of acquisition, to take in the net assets at their 'fair value' at that date, and to refer to the resulting balancing figure as 'goodwill on consolidation'. One important difference is that US calculations (until 2009) are required to take account of the acquirer's intentions, whereas IFRS 3 does not allow this. For example, suppose that a group pays €100 million to purchase all the shares in a new subsidiary. The fair value of the net assets of the subsidiary at the date of acquisition is assessed by the acquirer at €80 million. The acquirer also expects to spend €15 million on restructuring the subsidiary soon after its purchase. Under IFRS 3, goodwill is measured as €20 million (i.e. €100 million − €80 million). Under US GAAP it would be €35 million (i.e. €100 million − [€80 million − €15 million]). Given that the calculation is supposed to compare the cost of the subsidiary with *its* net assets, the IFRS treatment is the better one. The €15 million was not a liability of the subsidiary at the date of acquisition.

Having calculated goodwill, US practice, until 2001, was to amortize it over a period of not more than 40 years (APB Opinion No. 17), although the SEC required a shorter period in certain industries. Now, under SFAS 142, instead of amortization, there must be annual impairment tests. IFRS has also changed over the years. Up until 1998, IAS 22 allowed a group to write goodwill off immediately against reserves. This was then a common practice in the UK and Germany, for example. In 1998, IAS 22 was amended to require capitalization, amortization, a rebuttable presumption of useful life of up to 20 years, and annual impairment tests if a life of over 20 years was used. In 2004, the IASB replaced IAS 22 by IFRS 3, converging with US GAAP by abolishing amortization and requiring annual impairment calculations.

US and IFRS practice also differ in the treatment of negative goodwill on consolidation. Under IAS 22, negative goodwill was required to be credited against positive goodwill, and then credited to income against the anticipated losses or over the life of fixed assets purchased. IFRS 3 requires that negative goodwill be credited to income. In the United States (until 2009) it is allocated proportionately against the fair values of fixed assets other than investments. However, that is not the end of the possibilities. Under French and German national rules, negative goodwill is shown as a reserve; and under the UK's FRS 10 it is a negative asset.

For associates and joint ventures accounted for by the equity method or proportional consolidation, goodwill is also identified and then annually tested for impairment. Under IAS 28, the goodwill amount remains as part of the investment but this is separately disclosed in the notes. Under US GAAP, it is included with other goodwill.

The adoption of IFRS within the EU has continued the general effect of the Seventh Directive to harmonize the originally very diverse treatments of the consolidation difference within EU member states, largely using the Anglo-Saxon rather than the former continental European model. A study of goodwill practices for a wide selection of countries in the 1990s was provided by Nobes and Norton (1996). Whether international differences in goodwill rules affect the behaviour of companies is examined by Choi and Lee (1991), who found some evidence that UK companies were prepared to pay more for subsidiaries than US companies were because UK companies did not then need to amortize goodwill, as US companies did.

SUMMARY

- Consolidated financial statements were adopted first by the United States, followed by other Anglo-Saxon countries, then the Netherlands, Germany and France.

- The main concepts of the 'group' are the parent company concept based on legal control, the entity concept based on economic unity, and the proprietary concept based on ownership.

- Harmonization of consolidated financial statements was successfully attempted both internationally (IASs 22, 27, 28 and 31, IFRS 3) and within the European Union (the Seventh Directive). Listed companies in EU countries follow international standards from 2005.

- Some differences remain between IFRS and US GAAP. The differences cover, *inter alia*, rules and practices relating to: what constitutes a group; publication requirements; techniques of consolidation (e.g. the equity method, proportional consolidation, difference on consolidation).

References

American Institute of Certified Public Accountants (2000) *Accounting Trends and Techniques*, New York, p. 94.

Bircher, P. (1988) 'The adoption of consolidated accounting in Great Britain', *Accounting and Business Research*, Winter, pp. 3–13.

Bores, W. (1934) 'Geschichtliche Entwicklung der konsolidierten Bilanz (Konzernbilaz)', *Zeitschrift für handelswissenschaftliche Forschung*, Vol. 28.

Choi, F.D.S. and Lee, C. (1991) 'Merger premia and national differences in accounting for goodwill', *Journal of International Financial Management and Accounting*, Vol. 3, No. 3.

Diggle, G. and Nobes, C.W. (1994) 'European rule making in accounting: the Seventh Directive as a case study', *Accounting and Business Research*, Autumn.

Edwards, J.R. and Webb, K.M. (1984) 'The development of group accounting in the United Kingdom', *Accounting Historians Journal*, Spring, pp. 31–61.

FEE (1993) *Seventh Directive Options and Their Implementation*, Routledge, London.

Garnsey, G. (1923) *Holding Companies and Their Published Accounts*, Gee, London.

Hein, L.W. (1978) *The British Companies Acts and the Practice of Accountancy 1844–1962*, Arno Press, New York.

Higson, C. (1990) *The Choice of Accounting Method in UK Mergers and Acquisitions*, ICAEW, London.

Milburn, J.A. and Chant, P.D. (1999) *Reporting Interests in Joint Ventures and Similar Arrangements*, G4+1 Standard Setters, Norwalk.

Mumford, M. (1982) 'The origins of consolidated accounts', University of Lancaster Accounting and Finance Working Party Series, No. 12, September.

Nobes, C.W. (2002) 'An analysis of the international development of the equity method', *Abacus*, Vol. 38, No. 2.

Nobes, C.W. and Norton, J.E. (1996) 'International variations in the accounting and tax treatments of goodwill, and the implications for research', *Journal of International Accounting, Auditing and Taxation*, Vol. 5, No. 2.

Zeff, S.A., van der Wel, F. and Camfferman, K. (1992) *Company Financial Reporting*, North-Holland, Amsterdam, Chapter 2.

Zünd, A. (1993) 'Group accounting in Switzerland', in S.J. Gray, A.G. Coenenberg and R.D. Gordon (1993) *International Group Accounting*, Routledge, London.

Further reading

Walker, R.G. (1978) *Consolidated Statements*, Arno Press, New York.

QUESTIONS

Suggested answers to the asterisked questions are given at the end of the book.

17.1* Discuss different possible interpretations of the concept of a group, and how these may relate to differences in styles of corporate governance and of company financing.

17.2* 'The EU Seventh Directive was a much more useful harmonizing tool than the EU Fourth Directive.' Discuss.

17.3 Why did the practice of consolidated reporting arise in the United States earlier than in France?

17.4 Compare, as between US GAAP and IFRS, the consolidation of subsidiaries and the calculation and treatment of goodwill on consolidation.

17.5 To what extent did the EU Seventh Directive harmonize consolidation accounting between Germany and the United Kingdom?

17.6 One of the original aims of the Seventh Directive was to assist with the control of multinational enterprises by their host countries. Examine and discuss arguments for and against such a desire for control.

17.7 Explain the alternative uses of the equity method and how these differ as between US GAAP and IFRS.

18 Foreign currency translation

John Flower

OBJECTIVES

After reading this chapter, you should be able to:

- outline the nature of the foreign currency translation problem and the choice between historical rates and closing rates;
- explain the difference between the translation of transactions and the translation of financial statements;
- summarize the different ways in which transactions can be translated;
- set out the three traditional methods of translating financial statements and the arguments for and against each;
- understand the principal provisions of US GAAP and IFRS on currency translation;
- show how translation gains and losses can be accounted for;
- briefly summarize the purchasing power parity (PPP) theorem and the Fisher effect.

18.1 | Introduction

18.1.1 Terminology

First, it is necessary to define the word 'translation'. When used by accountants it has a special technical meaning, namely the process whereby financial data expressed in terms of one currency is restated in terms of another. The meaning of 'translation' will be illustrated with a simple example. A British company, which draws up its financial statements in pounds sterling, has among its assets a $100 bill (bank note). In order for this asset to be included in the company's balance sheet (or statement of financial position), it must be expressed in terms of pounds: one cannot add together dollars and pounds and arrive at a meaningful result. If the current exchange rate is £1 = $1.78, it would be reasonable to calculate the pound value of the $100 bill as £56.18 ($100 × £1/$1.78), so that the asset '$100' can be included in the balance sheet at the value of £56.18. Using the accountant's terminology, the asset has been 'translated' from dollars to pounds.

A clear distinction should be made between 'translation' and 'conversion'. With conversion, the asset is actually changed from one currency to another, as when dollars are exchanged for pounds in a *bureau de change*. With 'translation' the asset remains unchanged; the dollar bill itself remains the same; only the basis of measurement is changed. English-speaking accountants have borrowed the term 'translation' from the linguists to describe their procedure, but this undoubtedly confuses many non-accountants who assume that the accountants are referring to language translation. French accountants use the term '*conversion*' which also causes confusion when, in the English version of French reports, the French term is incorrectly rendered as 'conversion'. The German term is '*Währungsumrechnung*' (literally, currency recalculation), which is unambiguous as it is used only for the accountant's procedure. However it, too, is often rendered incorrectly as 'currency conversion' in the English version of German reports. It would seem that the accountants' nice distinction between 'translation' and 'conversion' is often not appreciated by laypersons.

This chapter examines the financial accounting aspects of foreign currency translation. We examine the arguments in favour of various methods, and then concentrate on the requirements of US GAAP and IFRS. The management of foreign exchange is another subject, which is dealt with to some extent in Chapter 23 and in other textbooks (e.g. Buckley, 2004).

18.1.2 The translation problem

Translation presents problems because exchange rates are not fixed. If, for example, the exchange rate between the pound and the dollar were always that £1 was equal to $1.78, there would be no grounds for differences of opinion as to the translated pound value of a US asset with a dollar value of $100. However, exchange rates are not fixed. Table 18.1 shows the exchange rate of the pound against the US dollar and the German and Brazilian currencies over a 30-year period. The table presents the number of units of the foreign currency that could be bought with one pound

Table 18.1 The value of £1 sterling in three other currencies

Date	US dollar	German mark (euro from 1999)	Brazilian cruzeiro/ cruzado/real
31.12.70	2.39	8.73	11.85
31.12.75	2.02	5.29	18.34
31.12.80	2.38	4.67	156.22
31.12.84	1.15	3.66	3,622.00
31.12.85	1.44	3.56	15,152.81
31.12.86	1.47	2.86	21,970.05
31.12.87	1.87	2.96	135.22*
31.12.88	1.81	3.22	1,384.81
31.12.89	1.62	2.73	18.24*
31.12.90	1.93	2.88	341.37
31.12.91	1.87	2.84	1,999.40
31.12.92	1.51	2.44	18,729.90
31.12.93	1.49	2.56	471.28*
31.12.94	1.56	2.42	1,319.76
31.12.95	1.55	2.22	1,508.06
31.12.96	1.70	2.64	1.76*
31.12.97	1.65	2.96	1.85
31.12.98	1.66	2.78	2.01
31.12.99	1.62	1.61	2.89
31.12.00	1.49	1.60	2.91
31.12.01	1.46	1.64	3.50
31.12.02	1.61	1.54	5.70
31.12.03	1.78	1.42	5.11
31.12.04	1.93	1.41	5.13
31.12.05	1.72	1.46	4.02
32.12.06	1.96	1.49	4.18

Note: *Introduction of new currency: one unit equal to one thousand units of old currency.
Source: International Monetary Fund.

on the foreign exchange market at various dates. It can be seen that there have been very substantial fluctuations over the period; for example, in 1970 one pound bought $2.39; by 1984, this had fallen to $1.15; but by 1990 it had recovered to $1.93; a value to which it returned in 2004 after some intermediate falls. In the 1970s and 1980s, exchange rates were very volatile. In recent years, particularly since 1996, this volatility has dampened down somewhat, with the consequence that, whereas in the 1970s and 1980s foreign currency translation was a very 'hot' topic, more recently the interest in the subject has declined.

In 1999, 12 member states of the European Union agreed to set up a currency union, with the euro as the common currency. At the time of writing, the countries in the euro currency zone are Austria, Belgium, France, Finland, Germany, Greece, Italy, Ireland, Luxembourg, the Netherlands, Portugal, Slovenia and Spain. The consequence is that, for many companies of continental Europe, foreign currency translation is no longer a problem as long as they have dealings only with companies in the euro zone.

The fact that exchange rates are not fixed creates two problems for the accountant:

1 What is the appropriate rate to use when translating an asset/liability denominated in a foreign currency?

2 How should one account for the gain or loss that arises when exchange rates change?

To illustrate these two problems, the example of the $100 bill will be further developed by adding the facts that the British company acquired it on 31 December 2003, when the exchange rate was £1 = $1.78, and still held it on 31 December 2004, when the exchange rate was £1 = $1.93. When considering what exchange rate to use to translate the $100 bill, for the purpose of including this asset in the balance sheet at 31 December 2004, two possible rates suggest themselves:

- *The exchange rate at the time when the $100 was acquired.* Using the exchange rate of £1 = $1.78 gives a translated value of £56.18, which is, in effect, the historical cost of the asset in terms of pounds. The exchange rate at a past date is known as the 'historical rate'.

- *The exchange rate at the balance sheet date.* Using the rate of £1 = $1.93 gives a translated value of £51.81, which is, in effect, the current value of the asset at 31 December 2004. The exchange rate at the balance sheet date is known as the 'closing rate'.

When the historical rate is used for translation, the asset's value in terms of pounds is frozen at the time of acquisition. In the above example, the dollar bill would be valued at £56.18 on 31 December 2003 when it was acquired, and this would not alter. However, when the closing rate is used, the translated value varies over time. On 31 December 2003 the dollar bill is valued at £56.18 and on 31 December 2004 at £51.81. This decrease of £4.37 is caused solely by the process of translation since the dollar value of the asset is unchanged. Hence, it is customarily termed 'gain/loss on translation', or sometimes more neutrally 'translation difference'. This gain or loss has to be recognized in some way in the financial statements.

To summarize, there are two major problems connected with translation:

1 Which rate of exchange should be used to translate the foreign currency value of assets and liabilities: the historical rate or the closing rate?

2 If the closing rate is used, how should the change in the translated value of the asset (the gain/loss on translation) be reported?

The first problem is the more significant, since it concerns the value to be placed on the assets and liabilities of the company. This affects not only the balance sheet but also, ultimately, the calculation of income. For this reason more attention is given to this problem in this chapter.

The second problem is largely concerned with presentation – how should the gain or loss be described, and where should it be placed in the financial statements? This problem is considered principally in Section 18.9. The treatment to be accorded to the loss or gain in the financial statements will affect many important accounting variables such as net profit and earnings per share.

18.1.3 Translation of transactions versus translation of financial statements

The accountant is faced with the problem of translation in two broad areas:

- *The translation of transactions*. This refers to the recording of transactions denominated in foreign currency in the books of account of an individual company, and the subsequent preparation of the financial statements of that company from these books of account.

- *The translation of financial statements*. This refers to the preparation of the consolidated financial statements of a group of companies, where the financial statements of the parent company and those of one or more of its subsidiaries are not denominated in the same currency.

In 'translation of transactions' there is only one set of accounting records (and one set of financial statements), which are denominated in the company's reporting currency, hereafter termed 'home' currency. The question of 'translation of transactions' is considered in the next section.

The problem of 'translation of financial statements' arises when a parent company owns an interest in an entity (such as a subsidiary company), which maintains its books of account and draws up its financial statements in a foreign currency. Typically this entity will be located in a foreign country and will carry out its principal activities there. The problem of translation arises at the end of the period, when the foreign currency financial statements are translated in order to enable them to be incorporated into the consolidated financial statements which are generally denominated in the parent company's 'home' currency.

Most of this chapter is given over to a consideration of the problem of translation of financial statements, in other words translation in the context of the consolidated statements of multinational groups. There are a number of reasons for this emphasis. Firstly, it is a very important problem in material terms: the amounts involved can run into millions of dollars or euros. Secondly, historically, much attention has been given to this area, as will be apparent when, later in this chapter, historical developments are considered. Thirdly (and the most compelling reason for the author), the fact that there are several fundamentally different ways of translating financial statements gives rise to a fascinating area of empirical and theoretical study, to which this chapter is, at best, only an introduction.

18.2 Translation of transactions

18.2.1 The issue

As explained in the previous section, the 'translation of transactions' concerns essentially the treatment of foreign currency transactions in the books of account and the financial statements of the individual company. The books of account are usually denominated in the company's home currency. Therefore, before a transaction that is denominated in a foreign currency can be recorded in the books of account, it must first be translated. The practical necessity of recording a transaction in the books of account gives rise to the very simple rule that transactions denominated in a foreign currency are translated at the exchange rate ruling at the date that the transaction is recognized and recorded.

Translation at the current exchange rate is also consistent with general valuation principles of historical cost accounting. In the case of an asset acquired through the outlay of foreign currency, the cost to the company is the home currency forgone because it is no longer able to dispose of the foreign currency; that is, the amount of home currency received if it had sold the foreign currency (where it already holds the foreign currency) or the amount of home currency spent in acquiring the foreign currency; in both cases the amount may be considered to be the opportunity cost of the asset at the time the asset was acquired – that is, its historical cost in terms of home currency. In the case of debtors and creditors, and other monetary assets and liabilities, they are valued, at the date that they arise, at the amount of home currency that would be received or spent if they were to be liquidated at that time.

Non-monetary assets are entered in the books of account at their historical cost in terms of home currency. All subsequent adjustments to this figure follow the normal rules of accounting, e.g. systematic depreciation in the case of fixed assets and reduction to lower market value (as measured in home currency) in the case of inventory. In effect, the fact that the assets were acquired by an outlay of foreign currency is no longer relevant, once the assets have been recorded in the books of account in terms of home currency.

On occasions, a non-monetary asset is reported at a value other than historical cost, for example replacement cost or realizable value. Where this value is measured in foreign currency, it is appropriate to translate the foreign currency amount at the exchange rate ruling at the time that the valuation was made.

In the case of monetary assets and liabilities that are denominated in a foreign currency, the historical cost in terms of home currency may no longer be the appropriate value to place on these items when a balance sheet is drawn up at a later date.

In principle, one can conceive of three different ways in which these monetary assets and liabilities may be translated:

1 *At the historical rate*. With this method, the home currency amount of these items is left unchanged and no translation gain or loss is reported.

2 *At the closing rate*. Translation at the balance sheet rate gives the current value of these items in terms of home currency, i.e. the amount of money that would be received on the balance sheet date if the monetary asset were to be converted into home currency (*mutatis mutandis* for liabilities). When the closing rate is different from the historical rate, a translation difference arises, which is generally taken as a gain or loss in the income statement.

3 *At the lower (higher) of the historical rate and the closing rate for assets (liabilities)*. When this method is used, assets are stated at the lower of two possible values and liabilities at the higher. The closing rate is only used if it gives rise to a loss on translation, which is charged to the income statement.

Of the three methods, the first method is rarely used. Some accountants might justify its application on the grounds that, in a period of fluctuating exchange rates, the historical rate is as good a guide as the closing rate to the rate at which the debtor or creditor will be settled. Particularly in respect of long-term monetary assets and liabilities, it is considered premature to report a gain or loss arising from a fluctuation in exchange rates, which may be reversed in a future period. However, in the author's opinion, this argument is invalid. It is contrary to basic accounting principles to report monetary assets at higher than their current values and liabilities at lower than their current values.

However, there are good arguments, well-grounded in accounting theory, for both the second method and the third method. The second method is based on the 'accruals principle' and the third on the 'prudence principle'. So, in deciding between the second and third methods, a judgement has to be made on the relative weight to be given to these two fundamental principles of accounting.

18.2.2 The 'accruals principle' versus the 'prudence principle'

The 'accruals principle'

The IASB Framework explains the 'accruals' principle in the following terms: 'under this basis, the effects of transactions and other events are recognized when they occur (and not as cash or its equivalent is received or paid) and they are recorded in the accounting records and reported in the financial statements in the periods to which they relate'.

If the accruals principle is followed, the accountant should not wait until the foreign monetary asset or liability has been turned into cash (in home currency) before recognizing the change in its value. Provided that there is objective evidence of the current value (given by the exchange rate quoted on the market) the accountant should recognize the changed value now. The loss or gain that arises from the recognition of the current value relates to the current period since it was caused by the change in exchange rates that occurred during that period. It does not relate to the future period when the monetary asset or liability will be liquidated.

The 'prudence principle'

However, the preparers of financial statements have to contend with the reality that they cannot establish the value of assets and liabilities with complete certainty. Hence, the need for prudence in financial reporting. The IASB Framework defines prudence as 'the inclusion of a degree of caution in the exercise of the judgements needed in making the estimates required under conditions of uncertainty such that assets or income are not overstated and liabilities or expenses are not understated'. Given the need for prudence, some accountants are not prepared to recognize gains resulting from the increased value of a foreign monetary asset (following a rise in the foreign currency) or the reduced value of a foreign liability (following a fall in the foreign currency). They claim that the realization of these monetary assets/liabilities in terms of (home) cash cannot be assessed with reasonable certainty. A future change in exchange rates may well cancel out a gain made in the current period. Hence, it would be imprudent to report this gain; as it is unrealized, it may well disappear in the future. As is to be expected, this method is applied under the national rules in those countries that give priority to the prudence principle, notably Germany.

A conclusion

Since both methods are soundly and rationally based on (different) generally accepted accounting principles, it is impossible to choose between them on grounds of logic or theory. The author's view is that there is something to be said for both methods. In general, the method based on the accruals principle gives the more relevant information, as may be illustrated with the following example. The calculations are given in Table 18.2. On 31 December 1990, a British company borrowed one million Brazilian cruzeiros. At 31 December 2000 the loan was still outstanding and had to be reported as a liability in the company's balance sheet. Translation at the historical rate gives a value of £2,929; the translated value at the closing rate is only £0.34, which is the amount that it would cost if the loan were to be paid off at that date. There can be no doubt that £0.34 is by far the better measure of the burden of the liability in 2000. Given the continuous fall in the exchange value of the cruzeiro, year after year, there is no reasonable chance that it will ever in the future regain its 1990 value.

Table 18.2 **Example based on the 'accruals principle'**

31 December 1990:	British company borrowed one million Brazilian cruzeiros
	Translated value at exchange rate current at that date:
	$1,000,000 \text{ Cr} \times \dfrac{£1}{341.37\text{Cr}} = £2,929$
31 December 2000:	Translated value at closing rate:
	$1,000,000 \text{ Cr} \times \dfrac{£1}{2.91\text{Cr} \times 1,000 \times 1,000} = £0.34$

Table 18.3 **Example based on the 'prudence principle'**

Translated value of $1,000
31 December 1995 $1,000 × £1/$1.55 = £645
31 December 1996 $1,000 × £1/$1.70 = £588
31 December 2000 $1,000 × £1/$1.49 = £671

However, the prudence principle acts as a necessary check on the optimism of management, which is always trying to present the results of its endeavours in the best possible light. For the consolidated statements of listed companies, this often means attempting to increase profit. This will be illustrated with a counter example, the calculations for which are given in Table 18.3. On 31 December 1995, a British company borrowed $1,000 repayable on 31 December 2000. The liability was initially recorded in its books at £645, using the exchange rate at 31 December 1995. A year later, at 31 December 1996, the value of the loan at the closing rate was £588. Should the company take credit for a gain of £57 arising from the fall in value of the liability? When one considers the subsequent fluctuations in the pound/dollar exchange rate, it might seem rather premature to report any gain. In the succeeding years, the pound fell against the dollar, leading to an increase in the value of the liability in terms of pounds. In fact, when the loan was finally repaid on 31 December 2000, the pound had fallen below its 1995 value, so that overall a loss of £26 was made on the loan. Many accountants would claim that the translation gain calculated for 1996 should not be regarded as realized. If the 1996 'gain' had been distributed to shareholders, the company would subsequently have been obliged to ask for its money back if it had wanted to maintain its capital.

A compromise that takes something from both methods is to value monetary assets and liabilities at the closing rate, but to defer the transfer of any gain to the income statement (i.e. to the 'profit and loss' part of comprehensive income) until the foreign currency asset/liability is realized.

Another way of looking at this is to take a balance sheet view, which is increasingly common in IASB or US standards. Under this, the foreign currency debtors or creditors should be shown at their most realistic value, and any gains or losses are 'profit or loss'. In this case, this is consistent with the result of using the accruals principle.

18.2.3 The translation of transactions: rules and practice

As explained more fully elsewhere in this book (see, particularly, Chapters 5 and 13), there are three principal sources of the rules that govern the financial reporting of the world's companies:

1 The IASB. The IASB's standards provide the rules for major companies registered in the countries of the European Union and in some other countries that are important in international trade, such as Australia.

2 US GAAP provides the rules for major US companies.

3 National rules: Rules set by national regulators govern the financial reporting of companies in many other countries. The position in the countries of the European Union is special in two respects:

(a) In most EU countries the IASB's rules apply compulsorily only to the consolidated financial statements of listed companies, which however are those that are most significant for the capital market. Other financial statements, that is the single entity statements (the 'individual accounts') of listed companies and of their subsidiaries, and both the consolidated statements and the individual statements of non-listed enterprises (the great majority of enterprises in number) are, in most cases, prepared under national rules.

(b) The rules set by national regulators have to comply with the EU's Directives on company accounting.

In respect of the translation of transactions, there has, historically, been some agreement on the basic principles. This is in sharp contrast to the position with respect to translation of financial statements, which is dealt with later in this chapter. All three sources (IASB, US GAAP and national rules) endorse the basic principle (set out in Section 18.2.1 above) that a transaction denominated in foreign currency is recorded in the 'home' currency at the exchange rate ruling at the time that the transaction is recognized. The principal differences concern the subsequent reporting of monetary assets and liabilities, notably the exchange rate to be used and the reporting of any translation difference following a change in exchange rates.

Monetary assets: the exchange rate

Both the IASB and US GAAP require that monetary assets that are denominated in a foreign currency be translated at the closing rate at the balance sheet date. The relevant standards are IAS 21 'The effects of changes in foreign exchange rates' and SFAS 52 'Foreign currency translation'.

With regard to the national rules of EU countries, the EU's Directives lay down no specific rules relating to translation. Consequently national regulators have considerable discretion in setting the rules, especially as the Directives include both the accruals principle and the prudence principle. Given the conflict between these two principles (as outlined in the previous section) it is unsurprising that in the field covered by national rules (notably the individual financial statements) there is no uniformity of national rules and practice within the European Union.

In most EU countries, the national rules require that monetary assets be translated at the closing rate. However, in Germany, the rules require that monetary assets be translated at the lower of the historical rate and the closing rate; they are reported at the lower of the two possible values in home currency. Liabilities are translated at the higher of the two rates. The theoretical justification for this rule is that there is a need for a prudent valuation of assets and liabilities (assets should not be overstated, liabilities should not be understated) to avoid reporting an unrealized profit. However, the author suspects that the prime motivation is the desire of companies to delay payment of tax until the foreign currency item has been realized, given that, in Germany, the amount of tax that a company pays is computed on the profits reported in its unconsolidated financial statements. Since, listed companies are required (and others are allowed) to apply the IASB's stand-ards for their consolidated statements, most larger companies apply the prudent German rules only in their individual statements.

The reporting of the translation gain or loss

In general a translation gain or loss arises only in respect of monetary assets, since non-monetary assets will normally be valued on the basis of the historical rate. The IASB and US GAAP are in accord on the reporting of this difference: it must be reported as part of profit or loss, i.e. in the income statement or in the first part of a statement of comprehensive income. The justification for this treatment was set out very clearly in the following statement by the British standard-setter:[1]

> In order to give a true and fair view of results, exchange gains and losses on . . . monetary items should normally be reported as part of the profit or loss of the period in accordance with the accruals concept of accounting; treatment of the items on a simple cash move-ment basis would be inconsistent with that concept. Exchange gains on unsettled trans-actions can be determined at the balance sheet date no less objectively than exchange losses; deferring the gain whilst recognizing the losses would not only be illogical by denying in effect that any favourable movement in exchange rates has occurred but would also inhibit fair measurement of the performance of the enterprise in the year.

This quotation makes clear that the British standard-setter placed more emphasis on the accruals principle than the prudence principle.

Within the European Union, this principle is followed for the national rules in those countries that adopt an Anglo-Saxon approach to financial reporting, being, for example, (apart from Britain) Ireland, the Netherlands and the Scandinavian countries. In other countries (such as France and Germany), it is the practice to report negative translation differences as an expense in the income statement. With respect to positive translation differences (gains), the position is more varied. In Germany, these gains do not arise (at least in the individual statements), because, if translating a monetary item at the closing rate would lead to a translation gain, the item continues to be translated at the historical rate. In some other European countries, it is a common practice to defer a translation gain and to transfer it to income when settled or over the life of the monetary item to which it relates. A sur-vey of European companies, which is reported in Ebbers (1997), indicates that in most EU countries of the time some companies deferred translation gains and that, in France, Spain, Italy and Belgium, a majority of companies did so. It must be emphasized that this practice is now permitted only in the financial statements of non-listed companies and the individual statements of listed companies.

Exceptions to the general rules

The general rules that have been just been outlined are subject to a number of exceptions, of which two are of particular importance: hedging and fixed assets financed through a foreign currency loan:

---

[1] Paragraph 10 of the British standard, SSAP 20, which was replaced by a UK version of IAS 21 for some com-panies in 2005.

(a) *Hedging*. Where a foreign currency debtor or creditor is hedged through a forward contract, it is commonly translated using the exchange rate specified in the contract and not the closing rate. However, US GAAP and IAS 39 specify a different treatment: the foreign currency monetary item should be translated at the closing rate and the forward contract reported at fair value, with all value changes reflected in current income. Both treatments will have the same effect of reporting no significant net gain or loss in respect of a foreign currency debtor or creditor that is hedged by a forward contract.

(b) *Fixed assets financed through a foreign currency loan*. Where a fixed asset has been financed through a foreign currency loan, it has been the practice in some countries to capitalize any translation loss on the loan as part of the acquisition cost of the fixed asset. In this way, no loss is reported in the income statement. However, this treatment is not permitted in the USA and Britain, and, in 2003, the IASB revised its standard so as to achieve convergence on this matter with the USA. Hence, capitalization of translation losses is now only permitted by the national rules in a few countries, notably Spain and Italy.

This brief introduction to the subject of translation of transactions does not deal with all the complications that may arise. For further information on this topic, readers should consult the 'further reading' suggested at the end of this chapter. This concludes the discussion on translation of transactions. The remainder of this chapter is devoted to the translation of financial statements.

18.3 Introduction to the translation of financial statements

18.3.1 The problem

As already stated in Section 18.1.3 the translation of financial statements arises when a company owns an interest in an entity that maintains its books of account and draws up its financial statements in a foreign currency. Typically this entity will be located in a foreign country.

Multinational groups are exceedingly common. Virtually all major US and European companies have foreign subsidiaries. The special problem of consolidation faced by such multinational groups is that the component financial statements are denominated in different currencies. To prepare the consolidated balance sheet of a group consisting of a British parent company and its US subsidiary, the two balance sheets must be denominated in the same currency. One cannot add together the parent company's assets valued in terms of pounds and the subsidiary company's assets valued in terms of dollars – one of the currencies must be changed. It is normal to denominate consolidated financial statements in the currency of the parent company, since the main users of the consolidated statements are the shareholders and the creditors of the parent company who are usually based in the parent's country. Therefore, in this case, it is the financial statements of the subsidiary that are translated from dollars to pounds. The methods used by accountants to achieve this will now be considered.

18.3.2 The three traditional translation methods

In practice, assets and liabilities of foreign subsidiaries are translated using either the historical rate or the closing rate. However, a generation ago, at the start of the 1970s, there was no basic agreement throughout the world as to which rate should be used to translate which type of asset. Three different translation methods were in widespread use:

1 the closing rate method, which used the closing rate for all assets and liabilities;
2 the current/non-current method, which used the closing rate for current assets and current liabilities, and the historical rate for all other assets and liabilities;
3 the monetary/non-monetary method, which used the closing rate for monetary items (i.e. money and amounts to be received or paid in money – debtors, creditors, loans etc.) and the historical rate for non-monetary items (i.e. most fixed assets and inventory).

18.3.3 An example

The application of these three methods is illustrated with a simple example, which uses the rates of exchange of the 1970s. On 31 December 1976, the German subsidiary of an American company acquired the assets and liabilities listed in the first column of Table 18.4. To ease the exposition, it is assumed that no transactions

Table 18.4 Example illustrating the three translation methods

| | Foreign subsidiary balance sheet at 31 Dec 1976 and 31 Dec 1977 (Note: no transactions in 1977) Local currency | Foreign subsidiary's translated balance sheet at 31 December 1977 | | | | | |
| | | Closing rate method | | Current/non-current method | | Monetary/non-monetary method | |
		Exchange rate	Translated value	Exchange rate	Translated value	Exchange rate	Translated value
Fixed assets (plant)	DM100,000	CR 0.50	$50,000	HR 0.42	$42,000	HR 0.42	$42,000
Current assets							
Inventory	DM30,000	CR 0.50	$15,000	CR 0.50	$15,000	HR 0.42	$12,600
Debtors	DM20,000	CR 0.50	$10,000	CR 0.50	$10,000	CR 0.50	$10,000
Total assets	DM150,000		$75,000		$67,000		$64,600
Long-term liabilities	DM130,000	CR 0.50	$65,000	HR 0.42	$54,600	CR 0.50	$65,000
Net worth at 31 December 1977 (Total assets less total liabilities)	DM20,000		$10,000		$12,400		($400)
Note:							
Net worth at 31 December 1976	DM20,000	0.42	$8,400	0.42	$8,400	0.42	$8,400
Gain (loss) on translation			$1,600		$4,000		($8,800)

Notes: Exchange rate at 31 December 1976, HR (Historical Rate) $1 = DM 0.42; at 31 December 1977, CR (Closing Rate) $1 = DM 0.50.

took place in the following year, so that the subsidiary's balance sheet in terms of local currency (at the time, Deutsche Marks) at 31 December 1977 (drawn up in accordance with the historical cost convention) is identical to that of a year earlier. Table 18.4 shows how the subsidiary's balance sheet is translated into dollars using each of the three methods described above.

The net worth of the subsidiary in terms of dollars is found by deducting the translated value of the liabilities from that of the assets. It can be seen that the three methods give widely differing figures for the subsidiary's net worth at 31 December 1977: closing rate method, $10,000; current/non-current method, $12,400; monetary/non-monetary method, minus $400. The net worth of the subsidiary at 31 December 1976 was $8,400. There is no dispute over this figure. Since all the assets and liabilities were acquired on 31 December 1976, the closing rate and the historical rate at that date are the same. The change in the subsidiary's net worth during 1977 represents a gain (closing rate method and current/non-current method) or a loss (monetary/non-monetary method). This gain (loss) clearly arises from the translation process, since no gain or loss is shown in the subsidiary's local currency financial statements. Therefore it is described in Table 18.4 as 'gain (loss) on translation'.

18.3.4 The translation gain examined

It is startling to note the wide variations in the gain or loss on translation: a loss of $8,800 under the monetary/non-monetary method, compared with a gain of $1,600 under the closing rate method and an even bigger gain of $4,000 under the current/non-current method. It is instructive to examine these gains and losses a little more closely. At the start of 1977, one mark was worth $0.42, and at the end of the year $0.50. Hence the parent company records a gain of $0.08 for every mark-denominated asset that it held during 1977. This is clearly the case where the asset involved is cash (e.g. a one-mark coin). However, where the book value in terms of marks of an asset, such as plant or inventory, remains constant over the year in accordance with accounting convention, then the exchange rate change will lead to the recording of a dollar gain in respect of this asset. In the same way a loss of $0.08 will be recorded for each mark owed.

Table 18.5 explains how this gain or loss arises under each of the three translation methods:

Table 18.5 Net gains and losses on translation

Method of translation	Assets/liabilities subject to translation gain (loss)	Net amount of relevant assets less liabilities	Gain (loss) per DM of net assets	Net gain (loss)
Closing rate	All assets/liabilities	+DM 20,000	$0.08	$1,600
Current/non-current	Current assets/liabilities	+DM 50,000	$0.08	$4,000
Monetary/non-monetary	Monetary assets/liabilities	−DM 110,000	$0.08	($8,800)

1 Under the closing rate method, all the assets and liabilities are revalued at 31 December 1977 using the new closing rate. Hence the gain is calculated on the whole of the holding company's net investment in the subsidiary.

2 Under the current/non-current method, the non-current assets and liabilities, being translated at historical rates, retain their original value in terms of dollars. Hence, no translation gain is recorded in respect of these assets and liabilities. The gain is recognized only in respect of current assets and liabilities.

3 In the case of the monetary/non-monetary method, a similar principle is followed: the gain is calculated only on the monetary items. Since, in this example, the net monetary assets are negative (the liabilities exceed the monetary assets), a loss is reported.

The three methods produce widely differing figures for the translation loss because of different assumptions as to which classes of assets and liabilities are affected by changes in exchange rates.

18.4 The US initiative

18.4.1 The temporal method

The existence of these three methods of translation, which produced such widely different valuations of foreign assets and losses or gains on translation, represented a disturbing state of affairs. Clearly not all three methods could be correct for the same purpose.

The Americans were the first to do something concrete about the problem. The American Institute of Certified Public Accountants set about tackling it in a systematic way. First it commissioned a member of its research staff, Leonard Lorensen, to undertake a thorough study (Lorensen, 1972). This was one of the best pieces of academic research applied to a major practical problem in accounting; and one of the most influential. The report established and clearly set out a universally applicable 'temporal method'. Under historical cost accounting this turns out to be very similar to the monetary/non-monetary method.

The essence of the temporal method is that the valuation methods used for the subsidiary's assets and liabilities in its own balance sheet should be retained in the translated financial statements. There are several different methods used in valuing assets in the balance sheet. They may be classified as follows:

1 Historical cost: the amount of cash (or resources of equivalent value) actually paid out in the past in order to acquire the asset.

2 Current replacement cost (CRC): the amount of cash that would have to be expended by the company at the balance sheet date to acquire a similar asset.

3 Net realizable value (NRV): the amount of cash that the company would receive (net of expenses) if it were to sell the asset at the balance sheet date.

4 Value of future receipts: debtors and other amounts receivable are stated at the amount of cash that the company expects to receive in the future. Similarly,

creditors and other liabilities are stated at the amount of cash that the company expects to be obliged to pay out in the future in order to redeem the liability.

For each of these four methods of valuation, a particular date pertains to the money amount at which a subsidiary's asset is valued, and this shows the exchange rate to be used in its translation. These are:

1 historical cost: the date of the acquisition of the asset, hence, the historical rate is appropriate;

2 **and** 3 CRC and NRV: the balance sheet date, hence the closing rate;

4 value of future receipts: the future date on which the asset or liability will be converted into cash, hence, the future rate. However, Lorensen came to the conclusion that the closing rate, and not the future rate, should be used for the translation of assets (liabilities) valued at the amount of future receipts (payments). There are a number of reasons for this decision – some pragmatic, some more theoretical. The appropriate future rate is often not known when the balance sheet is being prepared, and the best (or at least the most objective) estimate of it is the closing rate. Furthermore, if a future (or forward) rate is quoted on the foreign exchange market, which is different from the current (or spot) rate, the difference between the two rates will normally be offset by differences in interest rates; that is, interest rates will be higher in a country where the forward rate is lower than the spot rate (see the discussion on the 'Fisher effect' in Section 18.10.2). In order for interest charges to be allocated to the right period, the closing rate should be used to translate loans. If the future rate were used, interest would be anticipated. For example, a company could record instant profits simply by investing in bonds denominated in a currency whose forward rate stood at a premium in relation to its spot rate.

Finally, if there were a change in exchange rates between the balance sheet date and the date when the debt or liability were liquidated, it can be argued that the gain (or loss) would be caused by an event of the later period (i.e. when the rate changes) and should be recorded in that period. For all these reasons, the closing rate and not the future rate is used in the application of the temporal method.

18.4.2 The generalizability of the temporal method

The temporal method is generally consistent with the monetary/non-monetary method under historical cost accounting. With the temporal method, assets measured on a current or future basis (including monetary assets) are translated at closing rate, and assets that are stated at historical cost (as is generally the case with non-monetary assets) are translated at historical rates. The main difference is that with the monetary/non-monetary method inventories measured at net realizable value would be translated at a historical rate. However, the beauty of the temporal principle is that it is not tied to the historical cost convention. It provides the rules for the translation of financial statements prepared in accordance with other valuation conventions. Thus, if certain of the subsidiary's assets are valued at current replacement cost as at the balance sheet date, then clearly the closing rate should be used. The same principle applies when assets are stated in terms of net realizable value at the balance sheet date. A rather more complicated situation arises when the subsidiary's fixed assets are revalued as at a date that is not the same as that of the closing balance sheet. However, clearly the historical rate at the date of revaluation should be used.

A further justification of the temporal method is that it ensures that a company reports identical numbers for assets and liabilities irrespective of the method that it uses to finance a foreign operation: whether directly or through a subsidiary. Consider the example of a British company that plans to acquire a warehouse in the USA. It could purchase the building directly, transferring funds to the USA for the purpose. Using the rules for the translation of transactions as set out in Section 18.2, the British company would then report the building as an asset in its own balance sheet, stated at the building's dollar cost translated into pounds at the exchange rate ruling at the time that the building was acquired. Alternatively, the British company could acquire the building through a subsidiary registered in the USA. The subsidiary would maintain its books of account and draw up its financial statements in dollars: at the end of the year these financial statements would be translated into pounds using the temporal method. The value reported for the building in the British company's statements[2] would be the same irrespective of the method used to acquire the building. Hence, the temporal method respects one of the fundamental principles of financial reporting, that transactions that are essentially similar should be reported in a similar fashion.

It is the general applicability of the temporal principle that makes it so attractive to many accounting theorists and that has convinced them, on essentially *a priori* grounds, that it provides the correct solution to the translation problem.

18.4.3 FAS 8

The Financial Accounting Standards Board (FASB) of the United States accepted the recommendations of the Lorensen Study with few reservations. In October 1975 it issued 'Statement of Financial Accounting Standards No. 8' (FASB, 1975), which made the use of the temporal method obligatory for financial statements relating to accounting years beginning on or after 1 January 1976. No alternative methods were permitted.

FAS 8 caused a furore, particularly from companies that found themselves obliged to report substantial losses on translation in their consolidated statements. Under the terms of FAS 8, these losses were a charge against consolidated profits and thus reduced earnings per share. In the mid-1970s the dollar weakened against many major currencies, such as the yen, the mark and the pound. With the application of the temporal method, American multinationals were obliged to report translation losses on foreign currency borrowings (even long-term borrowings), whilst no translation gain could be reported in respect of the foreign fixed assets that had been acquired with the proceeds of these borrowings. Under other translation methods no such net loss is reported: under the current/non-current method, no gain or loss is reported on either the fixed assets or the long-term liabilities; under

---

[2] The individual statements if the building is acquired directly by the British company and the consolidated statements if it is acquired through a subsidiary.

the closing rate method, the gain on the assets offsets the loss on the liabilities. This point is illustrated in Table 18.4; in 1977 the US dollar lost value against the mark, which resulted in the reporting of a substantial translation loss with the monetary/non-monetary method, which in the example is identical to the temporal method.

Many US companies did not like the enforced change. Thus, after 1975, there began a spirited public debate over the temporal method, that started in the United States and spread to the rest of the world. This is the subject of an excellent article by Nobes (1980). In this debate it was soon agreed by most parties that the current/non-current method should be rejected, and thus the issue was reduced to a straight fight between the temporal method and the closing rate method.

18.5 The temporal method versus the closing rate method

The opposition between the temporal method and the closing rate method throughout the accountancy world is probably the most important aspect of the translation problem. Note, however, that this opposition would not arise under current value accounting, when the two methods would give the same results. It is the author's opinion that, for the reasons set out in Section 18.4.2, only the temporal method can be justified for use with historical cost accounting. The fundamental objection of the accounting theorist to the closing rate method under historical cost accounting can be stated very simply. The closing rate method, when applied to an asset stated in the foreign subsidiary's balance sheet at historical cost, produces a translated figure that has no meaning: it is not the historical cost in terms of the home currency; neither is it the current replacement cost or the net realizable value: 'The number is in fact nothing except the product of multiplying two unrelated numbers' (Lorensen, 1972, page 107). The leading German theorist, Büsse von Colbe, makes the same point rather more politely: 'translation of historical costs, expressed in foreign currency, at the current rate does not result in a valuation that can be interpreted in any meaningful sense' (Gray *et al.*, 1993, page 327). This fault of the closing rate method is so fundamental that, in the opinion of many accounting theorists, it makes the use of the method quite unacceptable.

The case for the closing rate method was set out by the British Accounting Standards Committee (ASC) in ED 21 (issued in 1977), notably paragraphs 9 and 10:

9 The closing rate method is based on the concept that a reporting company has a net investment in a foreign operation and what is at risk from currency fluctuations is the net investment . . .

10 The closing rate method possesses the following advantages:

   (a) It deals effectively with the situation where fixed assets located overseas have been financed by foreign currency borrowings and a change in the exchange rate results in offsetting gains and losses.

   (b) The relationship existing between balances in accounts as originally prepared in a foreign currency is preserved in the translated accounts, whereas this is not the case where historical rates are used for translating certain assets.

18.5.1 Preservation of relationships in the subsidiary's financial statements

Paragraph 10(b) from the above quotation refers to an interesting and somewhat disturbing aspect of the temporal method, namely that the process of translation can change the relationship between individual items in a financial statement. This arises because different exchange rates are used to translate different items: the historical rate is used for fixed assets and the closing rate for most other items. Thus the relative weight of fixed assets in the translated balance sheet will be different from that shown in the subsidiary's foreign currency balance sheet. This will affect, among other matters, the debt/equity ratio. More significantly, in the translated income statement, the weight given to depreciation (derived from fixed assets translated at a historical rate) will be different from that shown in the foreign currency statements. If the foreign currency has fallen in value (relative to the home currency) since the fixed assets were acquired, this will have the effect of increasing the relative importance of the depreciation expense in the translated income statement. This could well turn a profit reported in the subsidiary's foreign currency statements into a loss in the translated statements. This point is demonstrated in a detailed example presented in Table 18.6.

There are other circumstances in which a profit may be translated as a loss, notably when there have been significant changes in both exchange rates and profits over the year. For example, a subsidiary records a loss in the first half of the year, followed by a bigger profit in the second half, giving a profit for the whole year. In the translated statements, suppose that the loss is translated at a more favourable exchange rate than that applied to the profit, making the translated loss larger than the translated profit, giving a loss for the whole year.

Table 18.6 Example of how the temporal method translates a profit as a loss

	Foreign currency statements ($)	Translation factor	Translated statements (£)
Income statement for 1996			
Trading profit	105,000	£1/$1.68	62,500
Less depreciation	100,000	£1/$1.55	64,516
Net profit/(loss)	5,000		(2,016)
Balance sheet at 31 December 96			
Fixed assets: costs	1,000,000	£1/$1.55	645,161
less depreciation	100,000	£1/$1.55	64,516
	900,000		580,645
Current assets (cash)	200,000	£1/$1.68	119,048
Total assets	1,100,000		699,693
Less long-term liabilities	500,000	£1/$1.68	297,619
Net worth (equity)	600,000		402,074

Note: Debt/equity ratio =   1 : 1.20   1 : 1.35
Data: The foreign subsidiary bought all its fixed assets at 31.12.95.
   All transactions assumed to take place at year end.
   Exchange rates: 31 December 1995 £1 = $1.55; 31 December 1996 £1 = $1.68.

To proponents of the temporal method, this is a highly awkward result and they need all their ingenuity to explain how it is right for a profit in one currency to be turned into a loss when translated into another currency. However, there are good arguments to be made. First, it should be stressed that the purpose of translation is to permit the preparation of consolidated financial statements. As a general rule, the translated figures of the subsidiary's assets, liabilities, revenues and expenses are aggregated with those of the parent company in the consolidated statements; the foreign subsidiary's separate entity is lost in the consolidated statements. Hence, the fact that it has a certain debt/equity ratio as an individual company is irrelevant from the viewpoint of the consolidated financial statements. Conversely, if a person (e.g. a minority shareholder or a creditor of the subsidiary) wishes to examine the financial position of the foreign subsidiary as a separate entity, then he or she should look to its separate local currency statements; the group statements are irrelevant for this purpose. The creditor of a subsidiary company cannot normally demand repayment of the debt from the parent company, nor can a minority shareholder expect dividends to be paid out of group profits.

However, while the above argument goes part of the way towards explaining why the relationships in the subsidiary's financial statements are irrelevant for the consolidated statements, it is still uncomfortable that a profit in the subsidiary's own (local currency) income statement can be translated into a loss in the consolidated statement. One may legitimately ask the question: which financial statement presents the true and fair view – the subsidiary's statement or the translated version incorporated into the consolidated statement? If the temporal method is correct, then the answer to this question must be that both financial statements are true and fair. The subsidiary's own financial statements present a true and fair view for its creditors and shareholders; the consolidated financial statements (incorporating the subsidiary's translated statements) present a true and fair view for the shareholders of the parent company. How is this possible?

It will be recalled that a profit can be translated into a loss only when certain assets (i.e. fixed assets and inventory) are valued in the balance sheet at historical cost. When this convention is followed the persons for whom the statements are prepared (i.e. the shareholders) should interpret the book value of the assets as being the amount of finance that is tied up in these assets. The amount tied up in the fixed assets is expressed in terms of the currency in which the finance was provided. In the case of a parent company owning assets abroad via a subsidiary, the position is that ultimately these assets have been financed by the parent company's shareholders. When the assets were acquired these shareholders made a financial sacrifice. It is of no consequence for the argument whether this sacrifice was voluntary or involuntary, or whether the acquisition of the assets was facilitated by a remittance of cash from the parent company or by a reduction in the dividend from the subsidiary. The essential point is that in a past year the parent company's shareholders made a financial sacrifice and that this sacrifice is measured in terms of the amount of home currency forgone in that year. This is the justification for stating the subsidiary's assets in the consolidated financial statements at their historical cost in terms of the home currency. The position of minority shareholders of the foreign subsidiary is rather different. Their sacrifice was in terms of their own currency. When, subsequently, the local currency falls in value relative to the home currency, the sacrifice made by the parent company's shareholders will become valued rather more highly than that made by the subsidiary's minority shareholders; hence the paradox of a profit being translated into a loss.

To summarize, the response to the ASC's paragraph 10(b) is, first, that the relationships in the foreign subsidiary's financial statements are largely irrelevant for the consolidated financial statements. Second, where they are relevant, the relationship produced by the application of the temporal method is the correct one from the viewpoint of the shareholders of the parent company.

Finally, the '*coup de grâce*': the closing rate method suffers from the same problem, in that it can also lead to a profit being translated as a loss. It is correct that if (as implied by the name of the method) the closing rate were to be used to translate income and expenses, then the translated income statement would be a linear transformation of the original, which excludes the possibility of a profit being translated as a loss But, in fact, as explained in more detail in Section 18.8, the closing rate is not generally used for the translation of the income statement under the closing rate method. IAS 21 specifies that the income and expenses should be translated using the exchange rates at the dates of the transactions. Hence, in the example given previously of a subsidiary that reported a loss in the first half of the year and a profit in the second half, the closing rate method would also translate a profit as a loss.

18.5.2 The 'net investment' concept

Next, the ASC's paragraph 10(a) has to be considered. This is closely tied up with the statement in ASC paragraph 9 (see earlier quote) that the closing rate method is based on the concept that a reporting company has a net investment in a foreign operation and what is at risk from currency fluctuations is that net investment. This statement is rather brief. The full line of reasoning can be presented as follows:

1 In many cases, in practice, foreign subsidiaries are largely autonomous; decisions as to which assets to acquire or hold, and on trading operations, are taken by the local board of directors.

2 Additionally, these foreign subsidiaries are often largely self-financing, using local loans and retained profits.

3 In these circumstances, the parent company's main interest in the subsidiary is the annual dividend. If this is satisfactory, the parent company will not concern itself in detail with the subsidiary's financial position or operations.

4 Hence, the parent company is not interested in the detailed assets, liabilities, revenues and expenses of the subsidiary; its interest is in the net investment in the subsidiary that is the source of the only tangible benefit, the annual dividends.

5 The value of this net investment is best reflected in translating the net worth at the closing rate.

6 Since the net worth is to be translated at the closing rate, all the other items in the balance sheet must be translated at the same rate if the balance sheet is to balance.

This line of reasoning appears very strong when one considers the case of a devaluation of the home currency, as is demonstrated in the example in Table 18.4. In the normal situation of a foreign subsidiary with net monetary liabilities (i.e. total liabilities exceeding monetary assets), the application of the temporal method will lead to a fall in the value of the subsidiary's translated net worth, because the translated value of the fixed assets will remain unchanged but the translated value of net liabilities will increase. This hardly seems logical. After the devaluation, the foreign currency is worth more in terms of the home currency than before; the net investment that is expressed in terms of the foreign currency should also be worth more. An alternative argument is that, following the devaluation, the annual dividend from the subsidiary will probably be worth more in terms of the home currency. This will certainly be the case if one makes the reasonably conservative assumption of no change in the annual dividend in terms of the foreign currency. The net investment in the foreign subsidiary, the source of these dividends, should therefore be worth more on the principle of an investment being valued as the net present value of future receipts. This is essentially the case set out in paragraph 10(a).

This argument appears both logical and coherent. However, the answer of the proponents of the temporal method is simple. The above procedure may be appropriate where the parent company's investment in the foreign subsidiary is presented in the parent company's balance sheet as a single item, that is, in the same way that the interest in an associated company is commonly presented. However, it is not appropriate where the assets, liabilities, revenues and expenses of the subsidiary are incorporated as such in the group's consolidated financial statements. Essentially the above line of argument falls down in two places. First, the method of valuation that is appropriate for the net worth is not necessarily appropriate for each of the individual assets and liabilities: this line of reasoning leads directly to the nonsense of the historical cost of an asset being translated at the closing rate. Second, if a subsidiary is, in fact, a largely independent entity, then it is not appropriate to consolidate fully this subsidiary in the group's consolidated financial statements.

The IASB defines consolidated financial statements as those of 'a group presented as those of a single economic entity'.[3] The EU's Seventh Directive (Art. 26) states that 'the consolidated accounts shall show the financial position of the undertakings included in the consolidation as if the latter were a single undertaking'. The use of the terms 'single economic entity' and 'single undertaking' is very significant. It is clear that the existence of a single entity is a precondition for the preparation of consolidated financial statements. Thus, the closing rate method, which is based on the concept of the parent company having a net investment in a semi-autonomous foreign subsidiary, should not be used in the preparation of consolidated financial statements. The conclusion is escapable:

- *either* the foreign subsidiary is largely autonomous, in which case fully consolidated statements should not be prepared (and in this case the parent company's investment in the subsidiary would normally be presented in its balance sheet as a single item – perhaps using the equity method);
- *or* the parent company and the foreign subsidiary may be considered a single entity, in which case the appropriate translation method to use is the temporal method which, as explained in Section 18.4.3, reports the transactions of subsidiaries as

---

[3] IAS 27, paragraph 4.

if they had been carried out by the parent company (that is making no distinction between the members of the group, which is treated as a single entity).

However, although the author is personally convinced on this matter, the argument has been settled in favour of the closing rate method. In December 1981 the FASB finally gave way to the considerable pressure to which it had been subjected and issued a new standard, FAS 52 (FASB, 1981), which effectively reversed FAS 8 and prescribed the use of the closing rate method under most circumstances.

The demise of FAS 8 was a most significant event in the history of standard-setting. FAS 8 was a product of pure reason. Leonard Lorensen, sitting in his ivory tower, worked out the principles to be followed for foreign currency translation solely through the application of logical reasoning. However, many influential actors in the American financial community (principally preparers but also some auditors and users) objected to FAS 8, not because it contained any logical flaw, but because they did not like the numbers that resulted from its application. They applied pressure on the FASB to change the standard and the FASB was obliged to give way. The whole incident demonstrated vividly that standard-setting is essentially a political process, in which reason sometimes plays a minor part (see, also, Chapter 10).

18.6   FAS 52

Even the most convinced opponents of FAS 8 admit that FAS 52 is not a very impressive document. The intellectual basis for most of its provisions is unclear, reflecting the fact that the statement is based not so much on research and reasoning as on the opinions of the preparers and users of statements. FAS 52 was adopted by the FASB by the smallest possible majority: by four votes to three, the minority including the Chairman of the Board. In fact, the most stimulating part of the statement is the note of dissent written by the three dissenting members. However, for good or ill, FAS 52 has for many years been the effective standard in the United States.

In the introduction to FAS 52, the FASB states (1981, page 3) that the objectives of translation are twofold:

1 to provide information that is generally compatible with the expected economic effects of a rate change on an enterprise's cash flows and equity; and
2 to reflect in consolidated statements the financial results and relationships of the individual consolidated entities as measured in their functional currencies in conformity with US generally accepted accounting principles.

In setting these objectives the FASB clearly had in mind the two major criticisms of the temporal method that are discussed in Section 18.5: the first objective refers to the paradox that an upward revaluation of the foreign currency may lead to a loss on translation, and the second objective refers to the paradox of a profit being translated as a loss. Therefore, even at the stage of setting the objectives the FASB appears to have made up its mind against the temporal method.

The first objective is remarkable for the proposition that financial statements should reflect *expected* economic effects. In the author's opinion, this was a revolutionary departure from the generally accepted accounting principles of the time, which were based on the principle of measuring reality as evidenced by the past (in the case of historical cost) or by the present (in the case of replacement cost or realizable value). When the second objective is analyzed more closely, it becomes clear that it is virtually identical with the imposition of the closing rate method. For in order to preserve in the consolidated financial statements the results and relationships of the subsidiary's own statements, it is necessary that every item should be multiplied by the same factor (i.e. the translated statements should be a linear transformation of the foreign currency statements). If the same factor has to be used for all items, then clearly it has to be the closing rate.

Given these objectives, it was inevitable that FAS 52 should come to the conclusion that the financial statements of foreign entities, as expressed in their 'functional currencies', must be translated at the closing rate. The new concept of 'functional currency' was given the following definition: 'an entity's functional currency is the currency of the primary economic environment in which the entity operates' (FASB, 1981, page 3). It seems clear that, for the great majority of foreign entities, the functional currency will be the local currency; for these cases, FAS 52 provides for the straightforward application of the closing rate method.

There are two main exceptions to the general imposition of the closing rate method:

1 where the foreign operations are a direct and integral component or extension of the parent company's operations – in this case it is stated that the primary economic environment is that of the parent company and therefore the functional currency is that of the parent company;

2 where the foreign entity operates in a 'highly inflationary' economy (defined as one where prices double in three years) – in this case, FAS 52 prescribes the completely arbitrary rule that the functional currency is to be that of the parent company.

In these exceptional cases, where the financial statements of the foreign entity are not expressed in its functional currency, they must be translated into the functional currency using the temporal method. FAS 52 uses the term 'remeasurement' for this process, which is very confusing as it differs in no way from other forms of translation.

Although the use of the dollar as the functional currency of a non-US subsidiary may be exceptional, it is certainly found in practice. For example, the Caterpillar company states in its 2006 annual report that:

> The functional currency for most of our Machinery and Engines consolidated companies is the US dollar. The functional currency for most of our Financial Products and equity basis companies is the respective local currency.

Similarly, the German company, BASF, in its US GAAP report (of 2004, the last before converting to IFRS) says:

> The local currency or the US dollar is the functional currency of BASF subsidiaries and jointly operated companies in North America, Japan, Korea, China, Brazil, Malaysia and Singapore. Translation therefore takes place using the current rate method. . . . The euro is the functional currency for the remaining companies. Remeasurement therefore takes place using the temporal method.

The 'remaining companies' would include European subsidiaries outside the euro area, for example, in the UK.

Hence, FAS 52 sometimes requires the continued use of the temporal method and, to this extent, does not resolve the problems arising from the coexistence of more than one accepted translation method. The FASB claims that it has prescribed one single translation method, namely that based on the concept of the functional currency; however, this claim should be dismissed as sophistry on the grounds that the concept of the functional currency seems to have been invented by the FASB precisely to obscure the fact that it was continuing to permit two different translation methods.

The FASB retained the temporal method for subsidiaries that are integrated with their parent to ensure that a subsidiary's assets would be reported in the consolidated balance sheet at the same amounts as these assets would be reported if they had been acquired directly by the parent, that is that essentially similar transactions should be reported in the same way (as argued in Section 18.4.2). Where a subsidiary is closely integrated with its parent, it is probable that direct acquisition of the assets by the parent would be a feasible alternative. Where a subsidiary is relatively independent, this would rarely be the case.

In effect, FAS 52 is based on the principle that, in most cases, the parent company and its foreign subsidiaries should be considered as distinct and separate entities. The consolidated balance sheet is nothing more than the arithmetic sum of the balance sheets of these distinct entities, adjusted for intra-group items. Although, in order to perform the arithmetic, the balance sheets of the foreign subsidiaries must first be translated at the closing rate, in no sense does the currency of the parent company predominate over those of its subsidiaries. Essentially, all the currencies are treated as equal. The proof of this proposition can be demonstrated by the following exercise: prepare consolidated financial statements that are unconventional in that they are denominated in the subsidiary's local currency and in which the parent company's assets, etc. are translated using the closing rate. The relationships in these consolidated statements would be identical to those in the conventional consolidated statements (denominated in the parent company's currency) and, if these consolidated statements were to be retranslated back into the parent company's currency using the closing rate, they would be identical to the conventional statements. With the closing rate method, the valuation of the assets of the foreign subsidiaries remains based in their foreign currencies. The consolidated balance sheet is based on multiple functional currencies. FAS 52 rejects the concepts used by the author in Section 18.5 to justify the temporal method: that the consolidated statements are prepared for the benefit of the shareholders of the parent company and should present the returns on investments in terms of the currency provided by these shareholders. The main reason for the dissent of three members of the FASB was that they did not agree with this rejection: they believed that more meaningful consolidated results were attained by measuring costs, cost recovery and exchange risk from a home currency perspective rather than from multiple functional currency perspectives.

The FASB resolved the closing rate versus temporal method argument by changing their view of the consolidated statements of multinational companies. It took this step to resolve the problem facing US companies in the exceptional foreign exchange conditions of the late 1970s, but the resulting standard remains in place.

18.7 IAS 21

Given the diversity of accounting practice around the world, it is not surprising that the International Accounting Standards Committee had difficulties in preparing a standard on the subject of translation. It was not until July 1983 that it published IAS 21, *Accounting for the Effects of Changes in Foreign Exchange Rates*. It is no accident that this appeared after FAS 52, for the IASC had to wait until the FASB had made up its mind. IAS 21 was clearly based on FAS 52 and followed it on all important matters. In 2003, the IASB, the IASC's successor, revised IAS 21, making a few changes of substance and considerable changes in terminology. It is this latest version that is analyzed here.

For persons who have some knowledge of developments in the field of foreign currency translation over the past 30 years, the standard is puzzling and confusing. For example, the term 'temporal method' is not mentioned and, at first sight, the standard specifies only one translation method – the closing rate method. However, in fact, the temporal method survives (if only just); the difficulty with the standard stems from the terminology used. Three terms are of particular importance:

1 *functional currency*, which is defined as the currency of the primary economic environment in which an entity operates;

2 *foreign currency*, which is defined as a currency other than the functional currency of the entity;

3 *presentation currency*, which is defined as the currency in which the financial statements are presented.

A large part of the standard is taken up with the definition of functional currency. It seems clear that, for the great majority of entities, this will be the currency of the country in which they are based and carry on their business. These companies will maintain their accounting records and draw up their financial statements in this currency. If they have transactions that are denominated in the currency of another country (that is in a foreign currency), these transactions will be translated using the standard's rules for translation of transactions, which are essentially those set out in Section 18.2, with monetary assets translated at the closing rates and all translation gains and losses reported in the income statements.

However, IAS 21 leaves open the possibility that the functional currency of an entity may not be that of the country in which it is based. This would occur where the entity's revenues and costs are mainly influenced by another country and by that other country's currency. For example, suppose that the Chinese subsidiary of an American parent has as its main activity the sale of goods shipped to it by the parent, where the selling price is fixed in dollars by the parent and the sales proceeds are remitted back to the parent. In this case, the subsidiary's functional currency would be the American dollar. IAS 21 requires that an entity should record its transactions and draw up its financial statements in its functional currency. Hence, the Chinese subsidiary would have to prepare statements, at least internally, denominated in US dollars. Note that, according to IAS 21, for the Chinese subsidiary, the Chinese currency is a foreign currency, which is really rather a bizarre idea. IAS 21 (para. 21) requires an entity to *record* the amount of a foreign currency transaction in its functional currency using the exchange rate of the date of the transaction. Normally the IASB sets rules for the financial statements and not for the bookkeeping from which the financial statements are derived. In fact, it is unreasonable to expect the Chinese subsidiary to maintain its books of account in dollars. So the IASB's rule as to recording transactions will often be ignored. However, it is reasonable to require the Chinese subsidiary to prepare financial statements denominated in dollars by translating its Chinese currency statements. This point is covered in IAS 21 (para. 34) which prescribes rules for this process that are essentially the temporal method. Hence, one can summarize that the temporal method is used to translate financial statements *into* the functional currency (generally from the currency in which the entity keeps its books of account). However there will be few foreign subsidiaries whose basic financial statements are not already denominated in their functional currency. Hence the temporal method will be used only rarely. Incidentally, IAS 21 allows the Chinese company to *present* its financial statements in its own currency even if its own currency is not functional. So 'prepare' here does not necessarily imply presentation of statements (i.e. publication) in the same currency.

Although it is rare for an entity's functional currency to be different from that of its country, examples can be found. For instance, Bayer, the German pharmaceutical company notes in its 2006 IFRS report:

> The majority of consolidated companies outside the euro zone are to be regarded as foreign entities since they are financially, economically and organizationally autonomous. Their functional currencies according to IAS 21 (The Effects of Changes in Foreign Exchange Rates) are thus the respective local currencies.

The fact that only 'the majority' of non-euro companies have the foreign currency as functional tells us that some have the euro as functional, i.e. the temporal method is used.

Another German pharmaceutical company, BASF, makes this even clearer in its 2006 IFRS report:

> For certain companies outside the euro or US dollar zone, the euro or US dollar is the functional currency.
>
> The temporal method is therefore used to make the translation: long-term assets, excluding loans, and paid-in capital, are translated using historical rates. Other assets, liabilities and provisions are translated using year-end rates. Equity is then calculated as the balancing figure. Expenses and income are converted at monthly average rates and accumulated to year-end figures, except for those items derived from balance sheet items converted at historical rates. Assets and foreign exchange gains or losses resulting from the conversion process are reported as other operating expenses or other operating income.

For the great majority of foreign subsidiaries, the functional currency will be the currency of the country in which they are based. For the preparation of the consolidated financial statements, their financial statements (which are denominated in their functional currency) have to be translated into a different presentation currency (that is the currency of the consolidated statements, which is normally the parent's currency). For this procedure IAS 21 specifies the closing rate method. Hence, one can summarize that the closing rate method is used to translate statements *from* the functional currency to a different presentation currency.

18.8   Translation of comprehensive income

In order to present a complete set of consolidated statements it is necessary to translate the foreign subsidiary's comprehensive income. The procedure to be followed differs according to the method used to translate the balance sheet.

18.8.1 The temporal method

With the temporal method it is easy to discover the principle to be followed: for each item of income and expense, the rate of exchange to be applied is that ruling at the date when the underlying transaction is recognized in the books of account. For sales, this will normally be the date of delivery; for goods and services paid for in cash, this will be the date of payment; for goods and services obtained on credit, it will be the date when the goods or services were received since, if a balance sheet were drawn up at this date, the amount owing would be translated at the rate on that date. In theory, every transaction should be translated at its appropriate rate; in practice, a reasonably close approximation will often be obtained by using the average rate for the period, or a weighted average where there are marked seasonal fluctuations.

Two elements of expense require special attention:

1 *Depreciation.* The rate of exchange to be used for the translation of depreciation expense is clearly the same as that used for the translation of the underlying asset – that is, the historical rate for assets valued at historical cost, and the closing rate for assets valued at current value. The 'transaction' date that determines the exchange rate is that of the original purchase of the asset: depreciation not being a transaction. This procedure is one of the main causes of the 'profit translated as a loss' paradox that was referred to in Section 18.5.1.

2 *Cost of goods sold.* The cost of goods sold will normally include an element of inventory, which should be translated at the rate of exchange appropriate for this asset.

In addition, a gain or loss on translation must be shown in respect of monetary assets and liabilities over the period between the date that they are first recorded in the accounts and the balance sheet date. This gain or loss is reported only in consolidated income; it is not an element of the subsidiary's income, which, in the absence of inflation accounting, does not report any such gain or loss in respect of monetary items.

18.8.2 The closing rate method

There has also been debate about how to translate income and expenses when the closing rate method is used to translate the balance sheet. When it revised IAS 21 in 2003, the IASB considered two alternative methods:

Method 1. Translation at the closing rate. This method has the advantages that it is very simple to implement and understand, that the translated financial statements are a linear transformation of the original statements because the same rate is used for both comprehensive income and the balance sheet, and that, hence, ratios involving income and balance sheet items (such as return on assets) are translated correctly.

Method 2. Translation at the date of the transactions, with the understanding that, in most cases, the average rate for the period will provide a good approximation. This method has the advantages that it provides a better representation of the value in the home currency of the foreign currency flows and that the end of year financial statements are consistent with the interim statements. It has the disadvantages that the translated statement of comprehensive income may not be a strict linear transformation of the foreign currency statement (since in principle different rates may be used to translate different items of income and expense), and, more seriously, that the relationship between the balance sheet and the income and expenses in the translated statements may differ from that in the foreign currency statements, because the rate used to translate the balance sheet may differ from those used to translate income and expenses. This will affect ratios (such as return on assets) that compare the balance sheet and income. It should be noted that, with Method 2, for the reasons given in Section 18.5.1, it is possible for a profit to be translated as a loss. This is not possible with Method 1.

The IASB decided to reject Method 1 and to adopt Method 2. IAS 21 requires that income and expenses should be translated at exchange rates at the date of the transaction, but accepts that the average rate for the period may be used, unless clearly inappropriate (for example when there have been significant fluctuations). It gave the following reason:

> This method [Method 2] results in the same amounts in the presentation [that is, translated] currency, regardless of whether the financial statements of the foreign operation are (a) first translated [using the temporal method] into the functional currency of another group entity (e.g. the parent) and then into the presentation currency [using the closing rate method], or (b) translated directly into the presentation currency [using the closing rate method].

> (IAS 21, Basis for Conclusions, para. BC18;
> the explanations in square brackets have been added)

In fact, this statement is misleading, even incorrect, in three ways:

1 The method only gives the same amounts if the foreign currency markets are perfect in the sense that the cross rates between currencies are logically consistent. For example, if the exchange rate between the pound and the euro is £1 = €1.60 and the exchange rate between the pound and the dollar is £1 = $2.08 then the exchange rate between the euro and the dollar should be €1.60 = $2.08, that is €1 = $1.30 (2.08/1.60). In fact, exchange rates are rarely 100 per cent consistent, although significant inconsistencies are usually quickly eliminated by traders exploiting them to make arbitrage profits.

2 The IASB statement refers to two different processes: the first requiring two successive translations and the second only one. These processes will yield the same amounts (subject to point 1 above) if all the rates used for the translations pertain to the same day. For example, consider the translated value of £100, which is translated into dollars in two ways: firstly directly and secondly by

being translated into euros and then the euro amount being translated into dollars. Using the exchange rates quoted in the previous paragraph, the direct translation would give $208 (£100 × $2.08/£1); the second translation would give €160 (£100 × €1.60/£1), which when translated into dollars would give $208 (£100 × €1.60/£1 × $2.08/€1.60), which is mathematically identical to the amount when translated directly from pounds to dollars. However, if average rates are used (as with method 2), the identity only holds if the average is taken as the geometric mean and not the arithmetic mean (which is the more common way of expressing an average).

3 The IASB's claim that the two processes yield the same amount is correct for revenues and expenses that are translated using the same rates with the temporal method and the closing rate method 2; for example the average rate may be used by both methods for sales, wages and other cash expenses. However, depreciation expense is translated at the historical rate of a previous year with the temporal method and with the average rate for the current year with the closing rate method 2. Thus, for this expense item, the translated amounts will not normally be the same.

Hence, the reason that the IASB gives for preferring method 2 over method 1 does not stand up to scrutiny. A further problem with method 2 is that it does not specify the rate to be used to translate the expense item 'depreciation' since it is by no means obvious that the date of the 'transaction' of depreciation is in the current year at all.

For the translation of income and expenses, as for the translation of assets and liabilities, the IASB followed closely the USA. FAS 52 specifies the use of the exchange rate at the date when the revenues and expenses are recognized but, since this is generally impractical, it permits the use of an appropriate weighted average. The author suspects that the real reason that the IASB chose method 2 was to achieve convergence with the USA, and not the spurious reason that is quoted above.

In the author's opinion these problems concerning the rate to be used for the income statement is a clear indictment of the lack of theoretical basis for the closing rate method. The proponents of the method have no basic principles to which they may turn for a solution to this problem.

18.9 Accounting for translation gains and losses

18.9.1 The problem

Translation gains and losses can arise in respect of both translation of transactions and translation of financial statements. In the first case, there is general agreement that the gain or loss should be reported as profit or loss, i.e. in the income statement or in the first part of a statement of comprehensive income. This is the position of both the IASB and US GAAP. As explained in Section 18.2.3, under the national rules of a few countries, the reporting of a gain is sometimes deferred. But ultimately it will be reported as profit or loss.

The reporting of the translation difference that arises from the translation of financial statements has generated much more controversy. It might be felt that there is no problem: since income may be defined as the increase in value of net assets (ignoring any transactions with owners), it follows that, if the translated value of an asset or liability is different from its previous translated value, a gain (or loss) is automatically created that must be shown as an element of the profit for the year. The temporal method follows this reasoning and requires that all translation gains and losses be included in the income statement. This simple rule did not find favour. It was the aspect of FAS 8 that was criticized more than any other.

Although the closing rate method was introduced to alleviate what were perceived as the malign side-effects of the temporal method, it did not eliminate translation differences. When there have been wide fluctuations in exchange rates, as has been the general experience over the past decades, translation gains and losses can be very substantial for a group with significant foreign interests. If reported as profit or loss, they could be the largest single item in the income statement, turning a loss into a profit or vice versa. Therefore, attention has been given as to how the effects of translation gains and losses may be tempered.

18.9.2 The translation difference under the closing rate method

One possible way of dealing with translation gains and losses would be to report them separately in the income statement, for example as extraordinary items, but this approach has not been adopted anywhere.

Instead, the approach has been to exclude such gains and losses from the income statement. FAS 52 and IAS 21 both specify that the gain or loss arising on translation under the closing rate method should be treated as other comprehensive income.

One of the main reasons why both FAS 52 and IAS 21 exclude translation gains and losses from the income statement is the belief of those who drew up these standards that these amounts are not 'real' gains and losses but rather a difference thrown up by the translation process. Hence, FAS 52 refers to them as 'translation adjustments' and IAS 21 as 'exchange differences'.

The British standard-setter gave the following explanation for its treatment of exchange differences:[4]

> The results of an operation of a foreign enterprise are best reflected in the group profit and loss account by consolidating the net profit or loss shown in its local currency financial statements without adjustment . . . If exchange differences . . . were introduced into the profit and loss accounts, the results from trading operations, as shown in the local currency financial statements, would be distorted. Such differences may result from many factors unrelated to the trading performance or financial operations of the foreign enterprise; in particular, they do not represent or measure changes in actual or prospective cash flows. It is therefore inappropriate to regard them as profits or losses and they should be dealt with as adjustments to reserves.

The author accepts the point that it may well be appropriate to exclude the 'exchange difference' when assessing the performance of foreign subsidiaries, but

---

[4] SSAP 20, paragraph 19.

he rejects the notion that this 'exchange difference' does not represent a genuine gain or loss to the holding company. Once a holding company has decided to place certain values on its foreign-based assets and liabilities (which it has no hesitation in including in its consolidated balance sheet as the appropriate values), it cannot deny that the gain or loss that stems automatically from this decision is also genuine.

The reasoning in FAS 52 is much more difficult to understand, because the four members of the FASB who voted in favour of it could not agree on the nature of translation adjustments. The disagreement is set out in paragraphs 112–15 of FAS 52, where it is stated that there are two views. The first view is that 'the translation adjustment reflects an economic effect of exchange rate changes . . . an unrealized component of comprehensive income . . . that should be reported separately from net income'. The second view is that the translation adjustment is 'merely a mechanical by-product of the translation process'. The author has some sympathy with the first view but not with the second view, which seems to imply that items may be included in the balance sheet that have no real meaning.

Under IAS 21 or FAS 52, when a foreign subsidiary is sold, the cumulative amount of translation gain or loss relating to it should be transferred out of the 'separate component of equity' into the income statement, being reported as part of the gain or loss on liquidation. This is called the 're-classification of gains'. Incidentally, this is not allowed in the UK standard (SSAP 20),[5] on the grounds that the gains or losses have already been recognized in comprehensive income (Whittington, 2005).

18.9.3 Translation gains and losses on transactions

When a company holds a monetary asset or a liability that is denominated in a foreign currency, it will report a translation gain or loss in its individual financial statements when the exchange rate changes. If that company is a subsidiary, this translation gain or loss will be incorporated in the consolidated income statement. This can lead to the reporting of some very strange gains and losses, as is illustrated in the following example for which the calculations are set out in Table 18.7.

The Dutch subsidiary of an American parent holds two assets: bank deposits of $100 and of £100. It reports euro translation gains on its holdings of dollars and pounds in its individual financial statements, which are denominated in euros. This is fully in accordance with the rules for the reporting of monetary assets that were set out in Section 18.2. When the Dutch company's income statement is translated using the closing rate method for incorporation into the consolidated financial statements, these translation gains are translated from euros to dollars using the average exchange rate for the year, giving translation gains of $16.70 on the dollar deposit and of $23.88 on the pound deposit. These translation gains which are reported in the consolidated income statement are very strange. The American parent reports in its consolidated income statement a gain of $16.70 in respect of the $100 that is held by a member of the group. In the author's opinion, this gain is a complete fiction; it is impossible to make a gain expressed in dollars on a holding of dollars. However,

---

[5] This standard was still in force in 2007, except for listed companies who are required to follow FRS 23, which is based on IAS 21.

Table 18.7 An example of gains and losses on monetary balances

An American company owns a Dutch subsidiary, which holds only two assets: a bank deposit of $100 and a bank deposit of £100. Assume that, during the year 200x, there were no transactions and that the market exchange rates were:

> At start of year: £1 = €1.60 = $2.08
> At end of year: £1 = €1.80 = $1.98
> Average for the year: £1 = €1.70 = $2.03

At the end of the year the Dutch company reports the following translation gains in its individual financial statements:

> On the bank deposit of $100
> Value at start: $100 × €1.60/$2.08 = €76.92
> Value at end: $100 × €1.80/$1.98 = €90.91
> Difference = gain of   €13.99
> On the bank deposit of £100:
> Value at start: £100 × €1.60/£1 = €160
> Value at end: £100 × €1.80/£1 = €180
> Difference = gain of   €20

These translation gains are translated into dollars using the average exchange rate and are reported in the American company's consolidated income statement at the following amounts.

> Gain on bank deposit of $100: €13.99 × $2.03/€1.70 = $16.70
> Gain on bank deposit of £100: €20 × $2.03/€1.70 = $23.88

If the American company had held the £100 directly, it would have reported the following loss:

> Value at start: £100 × $2.08/£1 = $208
> Value at end: £100 × $1.98/£1 = $198
> Difference = loss of $10

the gain of $23.88 on the holding of £100 is even more bizarre, for the pound's exchange value against the dollar fell during the year, so that, from the viewpoint of the American shareholders, the £100 was worth $10 less at the end of the year then it was at the start. It seems quite unacceptable that the group should report a gain of $23.88 in respect of an asset whose dollar value fell during the year.

It should be noted that these anomalies arise only when the closing rate method is used. With the temporal method, the consolidated income statement reports no gain or loss in respect of the $100 holding, and a loss of $10 on the £100.

This example illustrates the implications of the multiple functional currencies approach, on which the closing rate method is based. The Dutch subsidiary makes a gain on its holdings of dollars and pounds, when they are measured in its functional currency, the euro. The translation of this gain from euros to dollars does not change the basis of its calculation which remains in the functional currency (the euro). It is only the presentation of this gain that has changed (from euros to dollars): hence, IAS 21's term presentation currency. This is the reason why it is considered perfectly acceptable for the American group in the example to report a gain in respect of dollars – the gain has been made by its Dutch subsidiary as measured in euros and once so calculated is not changed.

In effect, in the consolidated financial statements of a multinational group that is made up of many foreign subsidiaries, the profits of each subsidiary are calculated in its functional currency. In order to prepare the consolidated statements, these profits are restated in terms of a common presentation currency. However, this does not change their basis of calculation. In the author's opinion, this presentation in a common currency is purely cosmetic. It does not change the fundamental facts that the different subsidiaries' profits are calculated in different ways and that it makes no sense to combine them. In the author's opinion, combining them by translating into a common presentation currency is the equivalent of adding together apples and oranges.

18.9.4 Translation differences on intra-group loans

IAS 21 does not deal with the anomalies exposed in the previous section, except in the special case of a loan from one group member to another. For example, suppose that a parent makes a loan to a foreign subsidiary. If the loan is denominated in the subsidiary's functional currency, the parent will report a gain or loss on translation when there is a change in the exchange rate. In the consolidated financial statements, the loan will not be reported (the parent's asset will be off-set against the subsidiary's liability). However, what is to be done about the translation gain or loss that was reported by the parent in its individual statements? IAS 21 covers this matter in para. 45 as follows:

> . . . an intra-group monetary asset (or liability) . . . cannot be eliminated against the corresponding liability (or asset) without showing the results of currency fluctuations in the consolidated financial statements. This is because the monetary item represents a commitment to convert one currency into another and exposes the reporting entity to a gain or loss through currency fluctuations. Accordingly, in the consolidated financial statements of the reporting entity, such an exchange difference continues to be recognised in profit or loss . . .

In the author's opinion, the reasoning set out in the above quotation is faulty. The IASB claims that a group should report a gain or loss in respect of an intra-group transaction. This is contrary to the fundamental principle that intra-group profits and losses should be eliminated in the consolidated financial statements. In the case of an intra-group sale, the profit on the sale (which is correctly reported in the individual statements) is eliminated in the consolidated financial statements. The same principle applies to the gain or loss on the intra-group loan that is reported in the parent's individual statements.

The fault in the IASB's reasoning will be explained with the aid of an example, the details of which are set out in Table 18.8. A German parent owns an American subsidiary. The subsidiary owns assets of $100,000 financed by equity of $20,000 and a loan of $80,000, both provided by the parent. Assume that the group owns no other assets and that there were no transactions in 2004. During 2004 the exchange rate fell from $1 = €0.80 at the start of the year to $1 = €0.73, a loss €0.07 per dollar. The German parent therefore reported a loss of €5,600 ($80,000 × €0.07/$1) on its loan in its individual financial statements. The American subsidiary's balance sheets

Table 18.8 An example of intra-group loans

	Balance sheets of the US subsidiary		
At 1.1.2004	$	Translation factor	€
Assets	100,000	€0.80/$1	80,000
Loan	80,000	€0.80/$1	64,000
Equity	20,000	€0.80/$1	16,000
At 31.12.2004	$		€
Assets	100,000	€0.73/$1	73,000
Loan	80,000	€0.73/$1	58,400
Equity	20,000	€0.73/$1	14,600

at the start and end of 2004, both in the subsidiary's functional currency ($) and the presentation currency (€), are presented in Table 18.8. The translated value of the subsidiary's equity fell from €16,000 at the start of the year to €14,600 at the end, a translation loss of €1,400. The total loss suffered by the group during 2004 may be calculated by comparing the value of the group's assets at the start (€80,000) with their value at the end (€73,000), an overall loss of €7,000. According to the IASB's reasoning this loss is made up of:

Translation loss on the subsidiary's equity	€1,400
Translation loss on the loan	€5,600
Total loss	€7,000

Hence, it is claimed that it is necessary to include the translation loss on the loan in the consolidated income statement, in order to report correctly the full amount of the loss.

However, in the author's opinion, the translation loss on the subsidiary's equity should be decomposed into its constituent elements leading to the following calculation:

Translation loss on the subsidiary's assets	$100,000 × €0.07/$1	€7,000
Less translation gain on loan	$80,000 × €0.07/$1	€5,600
Equals translation loss on subsidiary's equity		€1,400
Translation loss on loan		€5,600
Total translation loss		€7,000

The two amounts of €5,600 should be set off against each other, which makes clear that the total translation loss of €7,000 relates solely to the subsidiary's assets.

In the author's opinion, the IASB's presentation of the total loss is wrong, because it gives the impression that the group suffers a loss arising from a transaction between its members. Furthermore since, according to IAS 21, the translation loss on the loan is a charge in the consolidated income statement, whereas the other translation losses are transferred direct to reserve, the effect of the IASB's presentation is to reduce the reported profit. The IASB justifies its treatment on the grounds that 'the monetary item represents a commitment to convert one currency into another and exposes the reporting entity to a gain or loss through currency fluctuations'. In the author's opinion, this is wrong. Any loss suffered by one group member arising from the monetary item will be exactly offset by the gain accruing to another member. The reporting entity (the group) makes no profit or loss from a contract made between its members.

Accounting students will no doubt find it rather alarming that such a distinguished body as the IASB can make such a patently incorrect statement. However, one should always treat the pronouncements of 'experts' with caution. Status does not confer infallibility.

18.10 Research findings

18.10.1 Walker

Economists and some accountants criticize the translation methods described in the previous sections as leading to the calculation of asset values and exchange gains and losses that are not in accordance with economic reality. Walker (1978) argues that the foreign subsidiary's value should be taken as the net present value of future cash flows. He states that 'economic analysis recognizes that a devaluation of the foreign subsidiary's local currency will not automatically reduce the parent currency value of the foreign subsidiary's net assets as is suggested by the accounting approach'. But although he analyzes in detail the effect of devaluation on a foreign subsidiary's cash flow, he is unable to arrive at any general rule. There are practical difficulties of estimation, but 'despite these difficulties, the economic analysis of exchange risk is clearly the right approach'.

In fact, one suspects that most accountants would not take exception to Walker's two main conclusions: that balance sheet values of assets determined in accordance with generally accepted accounting principles are poor indicators of economic values; and that it is very difficult to estimate future cash flows. Most accountants would probably add that it is not intended that the conventional balance sheet should reflect economic values.

18.10.2 Aliber and Stickney

A startling view was proposed by Aliber and Stickney (1975). By the use of two economic theories, they prove that changes in exchange rates have no effect on the values of foreign subsidiaries. The two theories are:

1 the Purchasing Power Parity (PPP) theorem, which states that changes in the exchange rate between two countries are proportional to changes in the relative price levels;

2 the 'Fisher effect', which states that, between two countries, the differential in the interest rates earned on similar financial assets is equal to the expected change in the exchange rate.

The implications of the PPP theorem can be examined using a simple example. At the start of a year, a British company constructs two identical factories: one in Britain costing £100,000 and one in Ruritania costing $100,000, the exchange rate at that time being £1 = $1. It has undertaken the investment in the expectation of a 20 per cent annual return, anticipating an annual cash flow in real terms in perpetuity of £20,000 in Britain and $20,000 in Ruritania, after charging the annual cost of replacing worn-out plant. During the next 12 months, prices in Ruritania rise by 50 per cent. The anticipated annual cash flow from the Ruritanian factory is now $30,000. Prices in Britain rise by 10 per cent; the anticipated annual cash flow there is now £22,000. The new exchange rate, as predicted by the PPP theorem, is £1.10 = $1.50. The future cash flows of the two factories at this new exchange rate are identical; hence, the factories' values are identical. The change in the exchange rate has not affected the value of the Ruritanian factory.

The implications for translation are most interesting. If historical cost is used as the basis of valuation of assets, the British factory will be shown in the balance sheet at £100,000. For the Ruritanian factory to be shown in the consolidated balance sheet at the same value, the historical cost in terms of local currency ($100,000) must be translated at the historical exchange rate. If assets are stated at the net present value of future cash flows, the situation is a little more complex: the British factory has a value of £110,000 (i.e. £22,000 × 100 ÷ 20) and the Ruritanian factory a value of $150,000 (i.e. $30,000 × 100 ÷ 20). To achieve identical values, the Ruritanian factory's present value must be translated at the current exchange rate. If the PPP theorem is correct, this analysis proves to be a convincing justification of the temporal method (historical cost translated at historical rates; present values translated at current rates).

The 'Fisher effect' will be illustrated using the same example. The two factories, one in Britain and the other in Ruritania, are each financed by a local loan. Lenders demand a 5 per cent real return after taking into account the expected rates of inflation as before. Hence the nominal rate of interest will be 15.5 per cent in Britain and 57.5 per cent in Ruritania. After 12 months, the exchange rate will have moved from £1 = $1 to £1.10 = $1.50. This is all as predicted by the 'Fisher effect': the interest rate differential (1.575 ÷ 1.155 = 1.36) is identical to the change in the exchange rate (1.50 ÷ 1.10 = 1.36). In other words, a person with £100,000 who invested it in Britain at the start of the year would be exactly as well off as if he or she had invested it in Ruritania. In the first case he or she would have £115,500 at the end of the year; in the second case he or she would have $157,500 which, at the current exchange rate of £1 = $1.36, is worth £115,500. If this were not the case – if, for example, the return in Britain were higher – arbitrage between the two markets should cause the gap to close; investors would invest less in Ruritania, lend more in Britain, bringing about lower interest rates in Britain and higher interest rates in Ruritania as the markets adjusted to the relative shortage and glut of funds.

The implications for accounting are interesting. Since the real rate of interest is the same for both loans, one would expect their financing cost, as reported in the consolidated income statement, also to be the same. Since the interest costs of the Ruritanian loan are so much higher than those of the British loan, this can only be achieved by deducting from the interest cost of the Ruritanian loan the fall in its sterling value, i.e. by translating the loan at the closing rate. If this is done, the financing cost of the Ruritanian loan, in terms of sterling, can be calculated as follows:

Interest: 57.5% of $100,000 = $57,500 × £1 ÷ $1.36 =   £42,167
Less fall in value of loan:
    Start of year:
        $100,000 × £1 ÷ $1 = £100,000
    End of year:
        $100,000 × £1 ÷ $1.36 = £73,333   £26,667
              Total financing costs   £15,500

The net cost of the Ruritanian loan (£15,500) is, of course, equal to the interest cost of the British loan.

The temporal principle is again vindicated. In this case it is the rather old-fashioned current/non-current method that is shown to be incorrect. Also the example shows that the practice of excluding translation gains and losses from income is wrong, since the true cost of financing a foreign loan can be established only after taking into account both the interest payments and the exchange loss or gain relating to the capital value of the loan.

It should be noted that Aliber and Stickney (1975) were in error in stating that their analysis of the 'Fisher effect' showed the temporal principle of translation to be wrong. They were correct in stating that it showed that financial liabilities were not subject to exchange risk, since the total financing cost will be the same no matter where the liability is located; however, they inferred from this that the capital value of a foreign loan should not be adjusted for changes in the exchange rate, and this is incorrect. Only by taking into account the loss (or gain) on the loan can the true cost of financing be shown.

The misleading impression given by charging translation losses on loans to the reserves is well illustrated by the case of the British company Polly Peck, which collapsed spectacularly in 1990 (Gwilliam and Russell, 1991). Polly Peck had invested heavily in bank deposits in Turkey that earned a rate of interest of 30 per cent per year, whereas its borrowings were principally in dollars and sterling on which it paid around 10 per cent per year. The interest rate differential can be explained entirely by the 'Fisher effect'. The Turkish lira was expected to fall against the dollar and sterling by around 20 per cent per year, as it had done in the past. The interest received and paid was reported in the income statement; the loss on translation on the bank deposits in Turkey was charged against the reserves. The net result was that in 1989 Polly Peck reported in its income statement a surplus of £12 million of interest received over interest paid, despite the fact that, at the end of 1989, its monetary liabilities exceeded its monetary assets by over £700 million. In charging the translation loss on its foreign deposits to reserves, Polly Peck was following the letter of the relevant standard (SSAP 20) but it was undoubtedly presenting a very misleading picture of its financing costs.

18.10.3 Beaver and Wolfson

Probably the most rigorous analysis of the translation problem has been made by Beaver and Wolfson (1982). They analyzed the effect of three translation methods with respect to two properties of the translated consolidated financial statements:

- economic interpretability, which occurs when:
  - the book values reported in the balance sheet are equal to the present values of the future cash flows of the assets, liabilities and net worth of the firm; and
  - the reported return on investment (net income divided by beginning-of-year assets) is equal to the nominal rate of return on investments, denominated in terms of the domestic currency.
- symmetry, which occurs when:
  - two economically equivalent investments (one foreign, one domestic) produce the same financial statement numbers when translated into a common currency.

The translation methods that were analyzed were:

- H/H: historical cost financial statements translated at historical rates of exchange, i.e. one application of the temporal method.
- H/C: historical cost statements translated at the current rates of exchange, i.e. one application of the closing rate method.
- C/C: 'comprehensive market value accounting' translated at current rates of exchange, i.e. a second application of the temporal method and of the closing rate method.

These three methods were analyzed using a rigorously defined mathematical model. The conclusions come as no surprise:

1 The H/H method possesses symmetry but not economic interpretability. The symmetry occurs because, under the temporal method, the accounting principles that underlie the foreign currency financial statements are retained in translation. The economic interpretability is lacking because it does not exist in the foreign currency statements; under historical cost accounting, the book values of assets are normally not equal to their present values. One cannot, through translation, import a characteristic into the translated statements that is lacking in the foreign currency statements.

2 The H/C method possesses neither symmetry nor economic interpretability.

3 The C/C method possesses both symmetry and economic intepretability.

These conclusions represent a resounding confirmation of the temporal method and a thorough condemnation of the closing rate method. They also form the rigorous proof of the author's statement in Section 18.5 above that the translated value of the historical cost of an asset under the closing rate method is meaningless.

18.10.4 Louis

Louis (2003) empirically examines the change in a company's value compared to the size and direction of its disclosed foreign currency translation numbers. He looks particularly at US manufacturing companies, and finds that the accounting rules generally produce results opposite to the economic effects of exchange rate changes. Again, evidence piles up against the propriety of existing accounting practices.

18.11   An alternative to exchange rates?

So far in this chapter it has been assumed that the conversion factor to be used in translation should be an exchange rate: either a historical rate or a current rate. However, there is a school of thought that rejects the use of exchange rates; instead it proposed the use of a purchasing power parity index (PPPI), which is defined as:

$$\frac{\text{The purchasing power of the domestic currency}}{\text{The purchasing power of the foreign currency}}$$

Purchasing power is measured in much the same way as the price level. A representative basket of goods and services is priced, first in the domestic currency (in the home country) and secondly in the foreign currency (in the foreign country). The ratio of the two numbers is the PPPI.

The principal advocate of this approach was Patz (1977), who argued that the purpose of translated statements is:

> . . . to express the economic power and results of the operations of the foreign firm, viewed as a viable concern expected to continue to operate for the foreseeable future in its present setting, in terms of that setting. The objective of the firm is the maximization of command over goods and services locally, not maximization of command over domestic currency. Consequently the focus of reporting should be on this local command over goods and services.

Given these assumptions, the use of a PPPI is logical. In theory the substitution of a PPPI for an exchange rate would be simple. The whole of this chapter could be rewritten, substituting 'PPPI' for 'exchange rate' wherever it occurs, for example a distinction could be made between historical and current PPPIs.

For the moment, the use of PPPIs in translation remains a completely theoretical issue. They are not permitted by any accounting standard, and, to the author's knowledge, no company uses them for its income statements. Certainly, if ever the use of PPPIs were to become acceptable then attention would need to be given to the practical problem of constructing objective and accurate indices. It is by no means obvious how one would compare the cost of fish and chips in London with that of sauerkraut in Berlin or that of chilli in Rio de Janeiro!

SUMMARY

- Translation is the process whereby financial data expressed in terms of one currency is restated in terms of another currency. It becomes necessary in two situations:
  - *Translation of transactions*, when transactions denominated in foreign currency are accounted for in the books of account and financial statements of an individual company.

423

– *Translation of financial statements*, when a parent company owns a foreign subsidiary and needs to incorporate its foreign currency statements in consolidated statements.

● For translation of transactions, there is general agreement that the historical rate should be used for the translation of non-monetary assets. For monetary assets and for liabilities, the closing rate is generally used, except under the national rules in some countries that prefer the prudence principle to the accruals principle.

● Under US GAAP and IFRS, gains and losses on the translation or settlement of monetary balances are treated as profit or loss.

● The traditional methods of translation of financial statements are: (a) the closing rate method, which uses only current rates; (b) the current/non-current method (CNC), which uses historical rates for non-current balances; and (c) the monetary/non-monetary method (MNM), which uses historical rates for non-monetary balances. Naturally, as exchange rates change, different methods lead to different results, including the size of gains and losses on translation.

● A new approach was made in the early 1970s by the AICPA, leading to FAS 8 which introduced the temporal principle under which a balance is translated at the exchange rate ruling when its valuation basis was established. Under historical cost accounting, this leads to results similar to the MNM method. However, the temporal principle applies equally well for current value or any other system of accounting.

● Under the temporal method, translation gains and losses are recorded as profit and loss. Under the closing rate method, they are shown as other comprehensive income.

● There was considerable opposition to the enforced application of the temporal method in the United States, particularly from companies that preferred to use the closing rate method. In 1981 the FASB issued FAS 52, which made the closing rate method the normal standard; the temporal method was only to be applied in certain well-defined, exceptional circumstances. The same line was followed by the IASC (in IAS 21).

● FAS 52 and IAS 21 refer to an entity's 'functional currency'. If a subsidiary has a different functional currency from the currency of the group's financial statements, the closing rate method is used for translation. If the subsidiary has the same functional currency as used in the group's financial statements, the temporal method is used if the subsidiary's statements are in another currency.

● Academic research relating to translation concludes that, from a theoretical viewpoint, the temporal method is to be preferred to the closing rate method.

References

Aliber, R.Z. and Stickney, C.P. (1975) 'Measures of foreign exchange exposure', *Accounting Review*, January.

ASC (1977) 'Exposure Draft 21, Accounting for Foreign Currency Transactions', Accounting Standards Committee, *Accountancy*, October.

ASC (1983) SSAP 20, *Foreign Currency Translation*, CCAB, London. (Printed in *Accountancy*, May 1983).

Beaver, W.H. and Wolfson, M.A. (1982) 'Foreign currency translation and changing prices in perfect and complete markets', *Journal of Accounting Research*, Autumn.

Buckley, A. (2004) *Multinational Finance*, Prentice Hall, Harlow.

Ebbers, G. (1997) 'Foreign currency reporting in Europe: consensus and conflict', in Flower (1997).

FASB (1975) *Statement of Financial Accounting Standards No. 8: Accounting for the Translation of Foreign Currency Transactions and Foreign Currency Financial Statements*, Financial Accounting Standards Board, Stamford.

FASB (1981) *Statement of Financial Accounting Standards No. 52: Foreign Currency Translation*, Financial Accounting Standards Board, Stamford.

Flower, J. (ed.) (1997) *Comparative Studies in Accounting Regulation in Europe*, Acco, Leuven.

Flower, J. and Ebbers, G. (2002) *Global Financial Reporting*, Palgrave, Basingstoke.

Gray, S.J., Coenenberg, A.G. and Gordon, P.D. (1993) *International Group Accounting*, Routledge, London.

Gwilliam, D. and Russell, T. (1991) 'Polly Peck: where were the analysts?', *Accountancy*, January.

IASB (2003) *IAS 21, The Effects of Changes in Foreign Exchange Rates*, International Accounting Standards Board, London.

Lorensen, L. (1972) *Accounting Research Study No. 12: Reporting Foreign Operations of US Companies in US Dollars*, AICPA, New York.

Louis, H. (2003) 'The value relevance of the foreign translation adjustment', *Accounting Review*, Vol. 78, No. 4.

Nobes, C.W. (1980) 'A review of the translation debate', *Accounting and Business Research*, Autumn.

Parkinson, R.M. (1972) *Translation of foreign currencies*, a Research Study, CICA, Toronto.

Patz, D. (1977) 'A price parity theory of translation', *Accounting and Business Research*, Winter.

Radebaugh, L.H. and Gray, S.J. (2002) *International Accounting and Multinational Enterprises*, Wiley, New York.

Walker, D.P. (1978) 'An Economic Analysis of Foreign Exchange Risk', Research Committee Occasional Paper No. 14, ICAEW, London.

Whittington, G. (2005) 'The adoption of international accounting standards in the European Union', *European Accounting Review*, Vol. 14, No. 1.

Further reading

For an introduction to translation, see IAS 21 (IASB, 2003).

For an analysis of the temporal and other methods, see Lorensen (1972).

For a defence of the closing rate method, see Parkinson (1972).

For an analysis of the USA's and the IASB's regulatory systems, see Flower and Ebbers (2002).

For the economic aspects of translation, see Walker (1978) and Aliber and Stickney (1975).

For a review of the translation debate, see Nobes (1980).

For the case in favour of purchasing power parity, see Patz (1977).

For the translation of transactions, see Radebaugh and Gray (2002, Chapter 9).

For an analysis of the rules and practice in continental Europe, see Ebbers (1997).

QUESTIONS

Suggested answers to the asterisked questions are given at the end of the book.

18.1∗ Why has there been so much controversy over currency translation methods for group accounting? Which method do you prefer?

18.2∗ Why has it been difficult, particularly in the United States, to create a satisfactory accounting standard on foreign currency translation?

18.3   Are gains on unsettled foreign currency balances realized? When should they be recognized as income?

18.4   Is there a single best method of currency translation?

18.5   Does accounting translation exposure matter? Explain your reasoning.

18.6   Discuss how different attitudes to prudence can affect foreign currency translation policies.

18.7   Discuss the effect of the temporal method on ratio analysis.

19 Segment reporting

Clare B. Roberts[1]

OBJECTIVES

After reading this chapter, you should be able to:

- explain the nature and purposes of segment reporting;
- outline the development of segment reporting from the 1960s onwards;
- describe the segment disclosure requirements of the IASB and the United States;
- outline the major practical problems met when trying to identify segments or trying to write rules on this subject; and
- explain the contributions of research to the understanding of the benefits and costs of segment reporting.

19.1 What is segment reporting?

It has long been recognized that users of financial statements need consolidated information. However, consolidated statements do not provide all the information needed, and the annual report of any large company will typically include much

---

[1] This is a revised version of the chapter in previous editions by Clare Roberts and Sidney Gray.

Table 19.1 Caterpillar's geographical disclosures

| Information about geographic areas: | External Sales & Revenues | | | Net property, plant and equipment | | |
| | | | | | December 31, | |
	2006	2005	2004	2006	2005	2004
Inside United States..............................	$19,636	$17,348	$14,198	$5,424	$4,725	$4,424
Outside United States..........................	21,881	18,991	16,108	3,427	3,263	3,258
Total..	$41,517	$36,339	$30,306	$8,851	$7,988	$7,682

Source: Adapted from Caterpillar Inc. (2007) *Caterpillar Inc. General and Financial Information 2006*, Caterpillar, Inc., Peoria, Illinois, p. A-36.

more information than this. For example, it will include non-financial or narrative disclosures describing the activities of each of its divisions or each major part of the company. This information may be broken down by different types of industry, different parts of the world, a combination of industry and geographical areas, or any other basis that the company thinks helpful for the reader. Also included, usually in the notes to the financial statements, will be disaggregated or segmented financial information, commonly referred to as segment reporting.

Segment reporting involves breaking down the enterprise into its constituent parts or segments and reporting financial information for each of these. A company can segment its operations in a number of ways, but the most common are segmentation by industry or type of business (often called line of business, or LoB), by geographical area (either in terms of location of operations or location of customers) or by a combination of both of these. An example of a very simple set of geographical segment disclosures is given in Table 19.1, which reproduces some of the disclosures made by the US company Caterpillar (this shows the US requirements for secondary segments, as discussed below). As can be seen, Caterpillar disaggregates its sales or turnover and its net property, plant and equipment into two segments – Inside United States and Outside United States.

Rather more information is provided by the Japanese company Honda Motor, as illustrated in Table 19.2. This company discloses external sales, internal sales, operating income and segment assets for its five geographic segments.

If we instead look at the UK company, Vodafone, in Table 19.3, we can see that it segments its operations into two lines of business which are further segmented into six and two geographical segments, respectively. Extensive information is provided including, for example, profits from joint ventures and associates, and impairments, goodwill amortization and depreciation. This is all required under IFRS. Vodafone also reports on bad debts and share-based payments, which are voluntary disclosures.

The rest of this chapter looks at why segment reporting is useful (Section 19.2), what the requirements are in the United States and under IFRS (Section 19.3), and at research findings on the usefulness of segment reporting (Section 19.4).

Table 19.2 **Honda's geographical disclosures**

	Yen (millions)	
Years ended or at March 31	**2005**	**2006**
Net sales and other operating revenue:		
Japan		
Sales to unaffiliated customers	¥1,983,182	¥2,021,999
Transfers between geographical segments	2,155,756	2,415,874
Total	4,138,938	4,437,873
North America		
Sales to unaffiliated customers	4,585,650	5,475,261
Transfers between geographical segments	119,904	141,064
Total	4,705,554	5,616,325
Europe		
Sales to unaffiliated customers	858,936	1,001,177
Transfers between geographical segments	184,136	188,341
Total	1,043,072	1,189,518
Asia		
Sales to unaffiliated customers	773,753	856,892
Transfers between geographical segments	86,810	140,501
Total	860,563	997,393
Others		
Sales to unaffiliated customers	448,584	552,667
Transfers between geographical segments	17,373	19,023
Total	465,957	571,690
Eliminations	(2,563,979)	(2,904,803)
Consolidated	¥8,650,105	¥9,907,996
Operating income:		
Japan	¥184,899	¥370,950
North America	321,154	353,943
Europe	41,243	26,305
Asia	60,692	64,999
Others	33,193	57,163
Eliminations	(10,261)	(4,455)
Consolidated	¥630,920	¥868,905
Assets:		
Japan	¥2,480,052	¥2,737,454
North America	5,202,980	6,026,342
Europe	649,547	800,786
Asia	541,331	717,933
Others	203,605	309,209
Corporate assets and eliminations	239,455	(20,043)
Consolidated	¥9,316,970	¥10,571,681

Source: Adapted from Honda (2007) *Honda Annual Report 2006*, Honda, Tokyo, Japan, p. 63. Reproduced with permission.

Table 19.3 Vodafore's disclosures

31 March 2006	Mobile telecommunications								Other operations		Group
	Germany	Italy	Spain	UK	US	Other mobile	Common functions	Total	Germany	Other	
	£m	£m	£m	£m	£m	£m	£m	£m	£m	£m	£m
Service revenue	5,394	4,170	3,615	4,568	–	8,530		26,277	1,320	19	27,616
Equipment and other revenue	360	193	380	480	–	720		2,133	–	–	2,133
Segment revenue	5,754	4,363	3,995	5,048	–	9,250		28,410	1,320	19	29,749
Subsidiaries	5,754	–	3,995	5,048	–	7,812		22,609	1,320	–	23,929
Joint ventures	–	4,363	–	–	–	1,470		5,833	–	19	5,852
Less: intra-segment revenue	–	–	–	–	–	(32)		(32)	–	–	(32)
Common functions							145	145			145
Inter-segment revenue	(64)	(44)	(105)	(65)	–	(121)	(19)	(418)	–	–	(418)
Net revenue	5,690	4,319	3,890	4,983	–	9,129	126	28,137	1,320	19	29,476
Less: revenue between mobile and other operations	(91)	–	–	–	–	(1)		(92)	(34)	–	(126)
Group revenue	5,599	4,319	3,890	4,983	–	9,128	126	28,045	1,286	19	29,350
Segment result	(17,904)	(1,928)	968	698	–	1,296		(16,870)	139	4	(16,727)
Subsidiaries	(17,904)	–	968	698	–	933		(15,305)	139	–	(15,166)
Joint ventures	–	(1,928)	–	–	–	363		(1,565)	–	4	(1,561)
Common functions							215	215			215
Share of result in associated undertakings					1,732	712	8	2,452	(24)		2,428
Operating (loss)/profit	(17,904)	(1,928)	968	698	1,732	2,008	223	(14,203)	139	(20)	(14,084)
Non-operating income and expense											(2)
Investment income											353
Financing costs											(1,120)
Loss before taxation											(14,853)
Tax on loss											(2,380)
Loss for the year from continuing operations											(17,233)

Operating loss	(17,904)	(1,928)	968	698	1,732	2,008	223	(14,203)	139	(20)	(14,084)
Add back											
Impairment losses	19,400	3,600	–	–	–	515	–	23,515	–	–	23,515
Non-recurring items related to acquisitions and disposals	–	–	–	–	–	(20)	(12)	(32)	–	–	(32)
Adjusted operating profit	1,496	1,672	968	698	1,732	2,503	211	9,280	139	(20)	9,399
Non-current assets	24,360	19,422	12,596	8,743	–	17,200	1,907	84,228	754	64	85,046
Investment in associated undertakings	–	–	–	–	17,898	5,182	37	23,117	–	80	23,197
Current assets	669	888	443	743	–	1,555	79	4,377	266	13	4,656
Total segment assets	25,029	20,310	13,039	9,486	17,898	23,937	2,023	111,722	1,020	157	112,899
Unallocated non-current assets:											
Deferred tax assets											140
Trade and other receivables											231
Unallocated current assets:											
Cash and cash equivalents											2,789
Trade and other receivables											79
Taxation recoverable											8
Assets included in disposal group for resale											10,592
Total assets											126,738
Segment liabilities	(753)	(1,370)	(914)	(827)	–	(2,638)	(1,458)	(7,960)	(362)	(26)	(8,348)
Unallocated liabilities:											
Current taxation liabilities											(4,448)
Deferred tax liabilities											(5,670)
Trade and other payables											(219)
Short-term borrowings											(3,448)
Long-term borrowings											(16,750)
Liabilities included in disposal group for resale											(2,543)
Total liabilities											(41,426)
Other segment items:											
Capitalised fixed asset additions	592	541	502	665	–	1,456	112	3,868	129	8	4,005
Expenditure on other intangible assets	–	1	–	11	–	4	–	16	–	–	16
Non-cash items:											
Depreciation	653	398	281	486	–	1,113	6	2,937	140	2	3,079
Amortisation of intangible assets	514	190	114	438	–	186	183	1,625	–	–	1,625
Impairment of goodwill	19,400	3,600	–	–	–	515	–	23,515	–	–	23,515
Bad debt expense	39	5	41	9	–	64	–	158	10	–	168
Share-based payment	6	7	5	18	–	17	54	107	2	–	109

Source: Adapted from Vodafone Group Plc (2007) *Vodaphone Group Plc Annual Report 2006*, Vodaphone Group Plc, Newbury, England, pp. 79–80.

Table 19.4 **Segment sales of European companies, 2006**

Company	No of LoB segments	Sales of largest as % of total	No. of geog. segments	Sales oflargest as % of total		Domestic sales as % of total
BP (UK)	4	85	4	USA	35	20
Royal Dutch Shell (UK/Netherlands)	4	69	4	Europe	43	N/A
Gazprom* (Russia)	5	57	3	Europe	66	24
Total (France)	3	61	5	Europe excl. France	46	24
GlaxoSmithKline (UK)	2	86	4	USA	48	6
Novartis (Switzerland)	8	65	3	Americas	47	1
Roche (Switzerland)	4	73	9	EU	32	1
Sanofi-Aventis (France)	2	91	3	Europe	45	N/A
Vodafone (UK)	2	95	4	Germany	35	25
Nestlé (Switzerland)	6	26	6	Americas	34	N/A

Notes: *Gazprom figures based on 2005 reports and geographic segments relate only to gas sales.
N/A = not available
Source: Relevant 2006 annual reports.

19.2 The need for segment information

Table 19.4 gives some information about the reported segments of the ten largest European non-financial companies.[2] As can be seen, all these companies report more than one LoB segment, with the maximum being six. The largest LoB segment comprises anything from 95 per cent down to 26 per cent of total sales. Similarly, they all report geographical segments, with the largest ranging from 66 per cent down to 32 per cent of total sales. Even more striking is that neither the home country nor even Europe is always the largest segment. For example, in the case of the Swiss companies Novartis and Roche, home sales account for only 1 per cent of the total sales, while for GlaxoSmithKline, UK sales make up 6 per cent of total sales. Indeed, for none of these companies do domestic sales account for more than 25 per cent of total sales.

Many users of financial reports will be interested in the performance and prospects of one particular part of the enterprise rather than the enterprise as a whole. For example, employees' security of employment, pay and conditions will generally be more directly dependent upon the performance of the specific division they work for than the performance of the group as a whole. Similarly, host governments will be primarily interested in the performance of that part of the group that is located in their countries. Customers, suppliers and creditors will instead be most interested in the subsidiary that they have contracted with. All of these users will therefore want disaggregated *and* consolidated information. For example, employees may want information about the entire group because companies may sell off a profitable subsidiary to generate cash to protect less profitable domestic or

---

[2] As measured by market capitalization, taken from FT Europe 500, 2006.

core operations. However, they will also want information at the individual plant level. Host governments will want information at the country level; and creditors will want information at the level of the legal entity. Segment information, while not perfect, goes some way towards meeting these needs. Such information will be especially important for users such as trade unions and developing country host governments who may lack the power to demand it.

Shareholders, in contrast, invest in the company (and its group) as a whole and it is therefore the performance and prospects of the entire group that they are interested in, rather than those of the individual segments. As such, it might be argued that segment reports are of little relevance or interest to shareholders. But this is to misunderstand the purpose of segment reports. A group is made up of its constituent parts, and to understand fully its performance and prospects it is necessary to consider the performance and prospects of these parts. This can be seen in the illustrations above. For example, in Table 19.2, operating income to sales varies across Honda's geographic segments from 4.5 per cent in Japan to 7.3 per cent in Asia, while in Vodafone, in Table 19.3, operating income after impairment to sales varies from 38.7 per cent for Italian mobiles to 10.9 per cent for German other operations. Enormous differences are seen once impairment is included with German mobiles: the return now being −320 per cent. This illustrates the point that different segments may have very different profit potentials, growth opportunities, capital needs, and degrees and types of risk. Therefore, the past performance of a company and its future prospects can usually only be understood if the user also has information about each segment of the business.

Thus, for example, the US standard on segment reporting (SFAS 131) states that:

> The objective of requiring disclosures about segments of an enterprise and related information is to provide information about the different types of business activities in which an enterprise engages and the different economic environments in which it operates to help users of financial statements:
> a. Better understand the enterprise's performance
> b. Better assess its prospects for future net cash flows
> c. Make more informed judgments about the enterprise as a whole.
>
> (Objectives, para. 3)

The international standard (IAS 14) contains a very similar description of the objectives of segment reporting as being to:

> Help users of financial statements
> (a) better understand the enterprise's past performance
> (b) better assess the enterprise's risks and returns, and
> (c) make more informed judgments about the enterprise as a whole.
>
> (Objective)

19.3 Disclosure regulations

19.3.1 Introduction

Requirements to disclose segment information are particularly relevant for listed companies. As explained in Chapter 5, companies listed on most of the world's large stock exchanges now use either US GAAP or IFRS. The requirements under these two sets of rules are examined below.

There is a complication with respect to IFRS because two different standards have been available for 2006 to 2008 reports: IAS 14 and IFRS 8. Therefore, the two standards are examined separately here.

19.3.2 Requirements in the United States

Disclosure requirements were first introduced in the United States in 1969 when the Securities and Exchange Commission (SEC) required the disclosure of LoB information in registration documents. A year later they extended this to cover similar disclosures in the annual Form 10-K, while from 1974 all companies that filed statements with the SEC also had to disclose this information in their annual reports.

The standard SFAS 14 'Financial Reporting for a Segment of a Business' (FASB, 1976) considerably extended the disclosure requirements. Firstly, it required two types of segments – LoB and geographical. Secondly, the amount of information required was increased. For both types of segments, companies had to disclose revenues from unaffiliated customers, intra-group transfers, operating profit/loss or net income or other profitability measures, and identifiable assets. For LoB segments, disclosures also included depreciation, capital expenditures, and equity in the net income and assets of associates. Finally, companies had to disclose, where material, export sales from the domestic segment, sales to any single customer, to all domestic government agencies and to all foreign governments. Sales were defined as material if they were at least 10 per cent of total sales, and this level of materiality has been retained in subsequent US and international standards.

However, SFAS 14 received much criticism from a number of sources. The standard contained relatively little guidance with respect to a number of areas including segment identification and how to measure the items reported. It also ignored the internal structure of an enterprise. If the internal structure is not organized along a geographical or LoB basis, it can be very expensive to produce the required information as it might even require the redesign of information systems. In addition, it is not clear that LoB and geographical segment information is always particularly useful. It might be that the enterprise is organized in a different way for good reasons and that reporting on that basis would be more useful.

These problems are compounded because the interests of users are often different from those of the company. Managers may be concerned not only with the direct costs of disclosure, but also that disclosing segment data may highlight particularly poor or good performance. Indeed, this question of the competitive disadvantage of reporting segment information was claimed to be a major problem by a significant number of companies (Edwards and Smith, 1996).

Companies in the United States were often disclosing relatively few segments while analysts were demanding more disaggregated information. A major impetus for change was therefore the establishment in 1991 of the American Institute of Certified Public Accountants' Special Committee on Financial Reporting (the Jenkins Committee). Among its recommendations was a call for improvement in segment reporting including the suggestion that the information reported should be consistent with the manner in which the enterprise is organized and with the information used by management to run the business. Thus, the Canadian and US standard-setting bodies set up, in consultation with the International Accounting Standards Committee (IASC) (see Section 19.3.3), a joint project to review their segment standards which resulted in new standards: CICA Handbook Section 1700, and SFAS 131 (FASB, 1997), respectively.

SFAS 131 marked a major move away from the earlier standard as segmentation rules are no longer based upon the 'risks and return' approach used for determining LoB and geographical segments, but instead use the 'managerial' approach. The main basis of segmentation is determined not by reference to external features of the environment, but instead to the internal operating structure of the enterprise. The standard thus refers to an 'operating segment' which is identified as:

> . . . A component of an enterprise:
> a. That engages in business activities from which it may earn revenues and incur expenses (including revenues and expenses relating to transactions with other components of the same enterprise),
> b. Whose operating results are regularly reviewed by the enterprise's chief operating decision maker to make decisions about resources to be allocated to the segment and assess its performance, and
> c. For which discrete financial information is available. (para. 10)

While the internal structure, and therefore the reporting, of an enterprise will commonly be based upon either industry or geography, it may instead use a combination or indeed any other basis. The segments now reported are the same as those reviewed by the 'chief operating decision maker'. This emphasis on internal information and decision making means that users have the information used by the company itself and the segments disclosed are more likely to be the same as those discussed in the narrative part of the annual review and report. This means that users should have a better understanding of that particular company and of the information that the chief operating officer uses when deciding upon future corporate strategy. From the perspective of the company this approach also means that the information required should be quicker, easier and cheaper to provide.

Once the operating segments are identified, the company must decide if they are reportable. Segments may be combined into larger units if this does not result in the loss of useful information. This is the case if there are no significant differences in each of the following areas:

> a. the nature of the products and services,
> b. the nature of the production processes,
> c. the type or class of customer for their products and services,
> d. the methods used to distribute their products or provide their services, and
> e. if applicable, the nature of the regulatory environment, for example, banking, insurance, or public utilities.

Individual segments may also be combined if they are immaterial in terms of revenues, or profit or loss, or assets, provided that individual operating segments make up at least 75 per cent of total revenues.

The idea of reporting the information seen by the company's chief operating decision maker extends even into the rules for the disclosure of specific items. Thus all companies must disclose the segmented profit or loss and total assets as reported internally. In addition, the following must be disclosed if they are included in the calculation of either of these two items.

- external and internal revenues;
- interest both paid and received;
- depreciation, depletion and amortization;
- unusual items;
- equity in the net income of associates;
- income taxes;
- extraordinary items;
- investment in associates; and
- expenditure on long-lived assets, excluding financial instruments and similar.

Table 19.5 provides an illustration of such disclosures.

While the disclosures under SFAS 131 mean that users can see the information that forms the basis of internal decision making, this may be at the cost of a loss of consistency and comparability both across the segments of the company and across different companies. Different companies and even different segments of the same company may use different accounting rules and different definitions of profits or assets. To some extent the problem of lack of comparability within any one enterprise is minimized by the additional requirement that companies must also disclose, where relevant, a reconciliation explaining the differences between aggregate segment and consolidated figures. However, this does not address the problems of lack of comparability across companies.

In addition to reporting extensive information on operating segments, companies must also disclose a much smaller amount of enterprise-wide information

Table 19.5 Segment disclosures by Lakeside (US) for 2006* ($000)

	US Wholesale	US Retail	International	Unallocated Corporate	Consolidated
Revenue	$795,240	$290,434	$605,224	$ –	$1,690,898
Depreciation and amortization	764	2,680	4,506	14,553	22,503
Operating income/(loss)	277,957	27,213	63,257	(129,602)	238,825
Interest expense	–	–	–	884	884
Other, net	–	–	–	(828)	(828)
Income/(loss) before income taxes	277,957	27,213	63,257	(129,658)	238,769
Total assets	157,089	28,064	152,691	300,827	638,671
Goodwill	6,804	794	6,565	–	14,163
Expenditures for capital additions	3,190	2,339	5,555	9,848	20,932

Note: *This relates to a fictitious company. Comparatives for 2004 and 2005 omitted.

about industry and geographical segments and major customers. This entails the disclosure of the revenue from:

- each product and service or group of products and services;
- external customers located in the enterprise's country of domicile;
- external customers in all foreign countries in total;
- external customers from individual countries if material;
- any single customer accounting for 10 per cent or more of revenues.

With the move from SFAS 14 to SFAS 131, the amount of information disclosed for each segment and the number of segments disclosed appear to have increased (Herrmann and Thomas, 2000; Street *et al.*, 2000) and analysts are more confident of their forecasts (Maines *et al.*, 1997). However, problems remain. The amount of geographical disclosure has decreased, particularly the number of companies disclosing geographical segment earnings (Herrmann and Thomas, 2000), although more country-specific data is provided (Nichols *et al.*, 2000) including many companies using a materiality cut-off of significantly less than 10 per cent (Doupnik and Seese, 2001). In addition, a significant minority of companies still provide operating segment disclosures that are inconsistent with the disaggregated information provided in the Management Discussion and Analysis or with other parts of the annual review (Street *et al.*, 2000).

19.3.3 IAS 14

The IASC issued a standard on segment reporting (IAS 14) in 1981. This followed the then American standard (SFAS 14) fairly closely. It required, for both LoB and geographical segments, information on: turnover, with internal and external revenues shown separately; operating results; identifiable assets (in either absolute or relative terms); and, if necessary, a reconciliation statement, explaining any differences between the sum of the segment sales, profits or assets disclosed and the total or consolidated figures. In addition, companies were required to describe the activities of each line of business, the composition of each geographical segment and the basis used to determine the value of intra-group transfers.

As described above, there were a number of problems with SFAS 14 and therefore with IAS 14. This led the IASC, in consultation with North American standard-setters, to review its standard, and a revised IAS 14 was issued in 1997. This was then further amended in December 2003 to ensure consistency with a number of other revised and new standards. While the revisions did not go as far as SFAS 131, the revised IAS 14 involved some substantial changes to the method of identification of segments and to the disclosure requirements.

Under IAS 14, the internal operating and management structure must be used as the initial basis for identifying the primary segments, which should be either the geographical or LoB segments. In those relatively few cases where the management structure is organized on neither a geographical nor industrial basis, the primary segment reporting must still be based on one or the other. In those cases where the company's risks and returns are strongly affected by differences in both geographical areas and industries, then both types of segments are regarded as primary segments. If the primary segments are geographical, then LoB segments become the secondary segments, and vice versa.

It can sometimes be difficult to determine appropriate industry and geographic segments if these differ from the basis of segmentation used for internal purposes. Several criteria are desirable. Firstly, each reported segment should reflect distinct parts of the enterprise so that the reported figures reflect meaningful parts of the enterprise and there are not extensive cost or revenue allocations. Secondly, to ensure that the information is not redundant, the segments should have different risk, return and growth characteristics. Thirdly, to aid predictions, they should also be disaggregated on the same basis as used for reporting external industry or geographic data. Finally, they should be consistent both over time and with those reported by other companies. However, it is very unlikely that these four criteria can be met simultaneously and companies then have to decide which are the most important.

IAS 14 therefore lays down detailed guidance on the identification of segments. It defines a business segment as 'a distinguishable component of an entity that is engaged in providing an individual product or service or a group of related products or services and that is subject to risks and returns that are different from those of other business segments'. To determine whether a business segment meets this definition, a company should consider:

- the nature of the products or services;
- the nature of the production processes;
- the type or class of customer for the products or services;
- the distribution channels for the products;
- any separate legislative framework relating to part of the business, for example, a bank or an insurance company (para. 9).

Thus, the same criteria as in the United States are used to determine whether or not segments can be combined.

IAS 14 similarly states that a geographical segment is:

> a distinguishable component of an enterprise that is engaged in providing products or services within a particular economic environment and that is subject to risks and returns that are different from those of components operating in other economic environments. Factors that should be considered in identifying geographical segments include:
> (a) similarity of economic and political conditions;
> (b) relationships between operations in different geographical areas;
> (c) proximity of operations;
> (d) special risks associated with operations in a particular area;
> (e) exchange control regulations; and
> (f) the underlying currency risks. (para. 9)

In a similar manner to SFAS 131, a company must then decide if the segments identified are also reportable. A 10 per cent materiality rule for sales, assets, and profit and loss is again used so that smaller segments can be combined into an unidentified segment. However, again this segment must not exceed 25 per cent of total sales.

Once the primary segmentation basis has been decided upon and the reportable segments identified, the following must be disclosed for each primary segment:

- external and internal revenues;
- operating results (with separate disclosure of continuing and discontinued operations);
- total carrying amount of segment assets;
- total segment liabilities;
- capital expenditures;
- total amount included in the segment results for depreciation and amortization (unless cash flows are disclosed);
- significant non-cash flow expenses deducted in arriving at segment results (unless cash flows are disclosed); and
- share of profit or losses of associates, joint ventures and investments.

The disclosure requirements on the secondary basis are less onerous, namely:

- external revenues;
- carrying amounts of assets; and
- capital expenditures.

IAS 14 defines segment earnings and assets (these must include all items that are directly attributable or reasonably allocable) and, unlike SFAS 131, it requires that the accounting policies used should be the same across all segments and the same as those used for external reporting.

While the reporting criteria are relatively unambiguous, no detailed rules on the above issues can compensate for problems caused by inadequately or incorrectly defined segments. Although the standards provide guidance on segment identification, it is clear that discretion is still left to companies. This means that, perhaps inevitably, companies that wish to provide either minimal disclosures or 'good news' may be able to manipulate their segment disclosures to achieve these objectives. The scope for this has been reduced but not removed. IAS 14 (like SFAS 131) therefore also requires the disclosure of changes in the segments reported. Thus, if a company changes the policies adopted, it must disclose the nature of the changes, the reasons for them and their effect. If it instead changes the segments disclosed, the comparative tables should be restated to reflect the changes.

As might be expected, the revision of IAS 14 appears to have led to an increase in the number of items disclosed. There is also evidence of increasing consistency between segment disclosures and other information in the annual report, although a significant number of companies still report segments that appear to conflict with other information provided. In addition, geographic segments too often remain vague and poorly defined (Street and Nichols, 2002).

19.3.4 IFRS 8

As discussed in Chapter 5, as a part of the convergence of accounting standards internationally, the International Accounting Standards Board (IASB) and Financial Accounting Standards Board (FASB) started, in September 2002, a short-term project aimed at reducing differences in their standards that could be resolved in a relatively short period. This included segment reporting. The IASB identified apparent advantages in SFAS 131, namely:

(a) entities will report segments that correspond to internal management reports;
(b) entities will report segment information that will be more consistent with other parts of their annual reports;
(c) some entities will report more segments; and
(d) entities will report more segment information in interim financial reports.

(IFRS 8, para. BC 9)

Therefore, the IASB decided, in January 2005, to converge with SFAS 131 and to adopt the management approach both for the identification of reportable asserts and with respect to the information reported. IASB also felt that this had the advantage that:

> . . . the proposed IFRS would reduce the cost of providing disaggregated information for many entities because it uses segment information that is generated for management's use.
>
> (IFRS 8, para. BC 9)

The project led to ED 8, Operating Segments, in January 2006, and to IFRS 8 in November 2006. The standard applies for all financial years starting on or after 1 January 2009 and optionally before that. IFRS 8 is very similar to SFAS 131 except for three relatively minor issues. Firstly, although both standards require information disclosure on long-lived assets, if these are reported to the chief operating decision maker, SFAS 131 refers to tangible assets only, whereas IFRS 8 applies also to intangible assets. Secondly, IFRS 8 additionally requires the disclosure of segment liabilities if this is regularly provided to the chief operating decision maker. Finally, the rules for determining operating segments when a matrix form of organization is used internally are slightly different.

As discussed above, the two major changes from IAS 14 to IFRS 8 are that segments are to be identified using the management approach and that most of the specific items disclosed and the accounting rules used are to be those used internally, and so are not necessarily consistent either across segments or with the consolidated figures. The exposure draft generated 182 comment letters, or 102 if those concerned only with the requirement to disclose information about single countries are excluded. Of these 102 letters, the approach adopted by SFAS 131 was most popular, with 51 per cent of respondents supporting it. IAS 14's approach was supported by 18 per cent. As might be expected, these respondents argued that using risk and return criteria and consistent accounting rules meant that the information disclosed would be more comparable, less subject to manipulation, and based upon IFRS rules. It should therefore be easier to understand and less misleading for users. It was also argued by some of these respondents that there was no need to consider the issue of segments in the comparability project. The standard is essentially a disclosure standard and it will not affect the issue of the comparability of the main financial statements and whether or not a reconciliation is required for foreign companies listed in the United States. These views were also taken by the two IASB board members who offered a dissenting opinion. Other respondents (19 per cent) preferred the management approach for segment identification, but consistent rules for disclosure. However, some argued that there was less and less need for a standard to require consistent accounting rules. With international standards becoming used in more and more countries, multinational companies would increasingly use international standards for each country of operations and therefore also for internal purposes. The few remaining differences would generally be fairly minor. Finally, 12 per cent said nothing about this issue.

Two other issues were raised by the respondents. The Quoted Companies Alliance (QCA), a UK association of the smaller (non-FTSE 350) UK quoted companies, and 10 of its supporters, wrote about their concerns that segment information could be commercially sensitive for smaller companies who either had a few major clients, or who competed against much larger companies with much larger and less informative segments, or against private US companies who do not have to follow SFAS 131. The arguments these companies used are encapsulated in the following quotation found in this or a similar form in all the letters:

> We are very concerned that these proposals do not provide an exclusion for commercially sensitive information. As a smaller quoted company it is sometimes very important that the results of new business streams are not directly evident to our competitors, until they are well established.
>
> We wish to suggest that an opt-out based on a 'comply or explain' basis is made available to smaller quoted companies to avoid damage to growing businesses.

Eighty comment letters came from supporters of the Publish What You Pay (PWYP) campaign. This is a campaign started in June 2002 by George Soros with the aim of helping citizens in resource-rich developing countries to hold their governments accountable for the management of revenues from oil, gas and mining industries. It has therefore called for the disclosure of payments made by the companies in those industries to governments on a country-by-country basis. These 80 supporter organizations all sent the same, or very similar, letters, the main points of which are shown in the following quotation:

> As a supporter of Publish What You Pay, an international campaign backed by a coalition of over 300 civil society organisations from more than 50 countries worldwide, our organisation advocates greater transparency in the management of revenues paid by the oil, gas and mining industries to governments in developing or transitional countries that are resource-rich. There is a growing international consensus that increased transparency is an essential step towards combating corruption, improving governance and promoting sustainable development in such countries.
>
> We call for country-by-country disclosure requirements to be incorporated into international accounting standards so that information on payments to individual governments is available in companies' annual financial accounts. Because we believe this issue to be of such importance to the extractive industries we are convinced that disclosure of country-by-country payments will be of benefit to users of financial statements in other sectors who need decision-useful information about the scale and location of all reporting entities' international activities.
>
> In submitting our views on ED8, we note that the role of the IASB is 'to develop, in the public interest, a single set of high quality, understandable and enforceable global accounting standards' with the aim to 'address a demand for better quality information that is of value to all users of financial statements . . . and the public' (IASB Due Process Handbook, April 2006).
>
> In our view – one shared by many other stakeholders – the publication of information on revenues paid by extractive industry operators and other companies to governments on

a country-by-country basis is in the interests of all users of financial statements and the public at large. Both investors and civil society organisations in developed and developing countries are users of company financial statements. Information on payments to governments is vital for comparing the costs of production or operation in various countries. For civil society, greater disclosure will enhance their monitoring of revenue expenditure and budgetary processes more generally.

Neither of the campaigns by QCA nor PWYP had a discernible effect on the final standard, although the IASB promised to talk to PWYP about disclosures at the country level.

Despite these concerns, it might have been expected that the replacement of IAS 14 by IFRS 8 would be fairly uncontentious given that SFAS 131 had been in place with apparently little concern in the United States since 1997. However, this is not the case. The European Financial Reporting Advisory Group (EFRAG) recommended in 2007 that the European Commission should accept IFRS 8, which it agreed to do. But concern was expressed in both the European and UK parliaments. In the UK the Labour MP Austin Mitchell put down an early day motion in April 2007, on the accountability of multinational companies. An early day motion is a formal motion laid down by an MP which other MPs can then add their names to, showing their support. Although very few are actually debated, they offer a way to publicize issues and to show the level of support for them. The following motion with 37 signatures appeared to be reasonably well supported:

> That this House finds International Financial Reporting Standard (IFRS) 8, concerning disclosure of operating segments by multinational corporations, totally unacceptable because it gives company directors carte blanche to decide what they disclose and how they disclose it and does not require consistency of disclosure either between periods or between companies and therefore fails to create a clear standard for disclosure to help investors, abolishes previous requirements for geographical disclosure and allows different accounting rules to be applied to segment information from that used in the rest of a company's financial statements; and therefore urges the UK Government and the European Commission to carry out their own urgent and in-depth impact assessments on IFRS 8 and require multinational companies to adopt, in addition to any segment data they disclose, full country-by-country disclosures of all activities in each geographical jurisdiction in which they operate, together with details of turnover, profits and taxes paid in each of those territories.
>
> (EDM 1369)

This motion reflects a similar motion in the European Parliament a week earlier.

B. whereas, within the process of convergence between IFRS and US GAAP, the IASB has proposed to replace the IAS 14 with the IFRS 8,

1. Is concerned about the Commission's proposal to endorse IFRS 8 through which it intends to incorporate US SFAS 131 into EU law and thus impose it on the listed EU companies;

2. Points out that such endorsement of IFRS 8 would imply moving from a regime which clearly defines how listed EU companies should define and report on segments to an approach that permits management itself to define operating segments as management finds suitable and which furthermore requires a lower level of disclosure and could thus lead to a lack of consistency in reporting;

3. Believes that the adopted standard should include a defined measure of segment profit or loss, as IAS 14 does;

4. Highlights that the IFRS 8 standard, which does not require companies to use IFRS measures in their disclosure about operating segments, may have a negative impact on the comparability of financial information and thus may pose difficulties for users (e.g. investors);

5. Is concerned that the Commission is proposing, contrary to the principles of better regulation, to import into EU law an alien standard without having conducted any impact assessment;

6. Expresses its concerns about the impact that such a move would have for the EU preparers and users of financial statements and stresses the urgent need to conduct such an impact assessment;

7. Calls on the Commission to urgently carry out an in-depth impact assessment before endorsing the standard;

8. Stresses that, should the Commission fail to do so, Parliament will carry out its own impact assessment;

9. Instructs its President to forward this resolution to the Council and Commission, and the parliaments and governments of the Member States.

(European Parliament, Session document B6–0157/2007)

After agreeing to carry out an impact assessment, the Commission endorsed IFRS 8 in November 2007.

19.4 Evidence on the benefits of segment reporting

19.4.1 Introduction

It is clear that segment information has the potential to help users to understand a company's past performance and to predict its likely future cash flows. However, these benefits may not exist in practice and the segment disclosures actually provided by companies may be of little use to users. The expected benefits of segment disclosures may not materialize for a number of reasons. As discussed above, existing requirements have been criticized for leaving too much discretion to companies in identifying reportable segments. The lack of unambiguous rules for segment identification means that companies may report relatively few broad segments, each of which covers a number of quite different and distinct countries or industries. For example, Harris (1998) found that the operations in less competitive industries were less likely to be reported, perhaps due to a desire to protect either abnormal profits or market shares, while Hayes and Lundholm (1996) provide a model demonstrating that companies are more likely to report segments if all segments have similar results. Even where companies do not deliberately attempt to disclose the least amount of information possible, the segment disclosures may still not be particularly useful. If a company is highly integrated, with its segments very dependent upon each other, the success or otherwise of any one segment will be more dependent upon the rest of the company than it is upon the economic or political characteristics of the industry and country it operates in. This will happen if the company is vertically integrated with segments selling much of their output internally. Combining segment information with external information will be of little practical use and the company should only be considered in its entirety.

Similar problems may occur if the company allocates significant amounts of common costs, because the reported earnings of each segment will be highly dependent upon the cost allocation policy adopted. Finally, it may not be possible to combine the information provided with external information, or the segments may not be comparable to the segments reported by other companies. This is more likely to be a problem with the operating segment approach where the segments may encompass a range of countries and industries that owe more to historical accidents than to rational organizational structuring of current operations.

Even if none of these problems exists, the information may still be of little value to users if it lacks any element of surprise because all the information is, for whatever reason, already known to users before it is published in the annual report. It is therefore not sufficient simply to make a theoretical case for the usefulness of segment information. The issue must also be explored from a practical perspective and evidence must be sought regarding the usefulness of the actual segment disclosures made by companies.

The benefits of segment disclosures have been examined using a number of different approaches. Many of the earliest studies simply asked users whether or not they wanted segment information. This may offer some insights, but if potential users are unfamiliar with segment data they are unlikely to be able accurately to assess its usefulness. They also do not directly bear the costs of the disclosure. Users will therefore have an incentive to overstate the usefulness of segment information. More direct tests of usefulness are required. These fall into three types: analysis of user decision making; comparisons of the predictive ability of different types of forecasts; and stock market reaction tests.

Analysis of user decision making is concerned with how decisions are affected by different types of information. These tests may be artificial, laboratory-type tests that give people different kinds of information and ask them to make various types of decisions. Alternatively, they may look at the actual decisions made by users, including the accuracy of analysts' forecasts. Predictive ability tests compare the accuracy of mechanical or mathematically generated forecasts of sales, earnings or other accounting variables using consolidated information with similar forecasts based instead upon segment information. The final approach, that of testing stock market reactions, generates results that are the least ambiguous with regard to the implications that can be drawn. They test to see if segment disclosures have an effect upon share prices or market risk measures. If such reactions exist, the information was somehow used and it must therefore be useful. If, instead, segment disclosures had no measurable effect then it is concluded that either they are not used by stock market participants or the information must have already been obtained from other sources. However, this does not, of course, imply that segment information has no value, since it may still be used by other groups of report readers such as governments, trade unions or employees.

19.4.2 Studies of user decision making

Various approaches have been taken to looking at the question of whether, and how, users make use of segment information. The most direct tests look at the actual decisions being made and the types of information used in making them.

Unfortunately, it is very difficult to gather accurate data on actual investment decisions and the factors that influence them. An alternative approach is therefore to look at the forecasts made to assess whether or not they are more accurate in those periods, or for those companies, for which segment information is available. The obvious group to study is that of financial analysts. Not only is this group relatively sophisticated, but their forecasts are very often publicly available, especially in the United States.

This approach was adopted by Baldwin (1984) who looked at analysts' forecasts of the earnings per share of US companies after they first started to disclose LoB segment data. He found that these disclosures appeared to help analysts to make more accurate forecasts. Similar results were also found in later studies by Lobo *et al.* (1998), who also looked at LoB segment disclosures, and by Nichols *et al.* (1995), who instead looked at the impact of geographical segment disclosures on analysts' earnings forecasts.

In other countries, analysts' forecasts are not so readily available, thus necessitating a somewhat different approach to the same issue. For example, Emmanuel *et al.* (1989) looked at the forecasts made by UK analysts when presented with specially constructed case data. Having found that the majority of analysts changed their forecasts both in terms of point and range estimates when they were presented with more segment data, the results clearly support the conclusions of the more direct US studies.

Returning to US evidence, the usefulness of segment disclosures appears to depend upon the specific characteristics of the segments. Thus, Doupnik and Rolfe (1990) conducted a similar type of experiment, which involved giving analysts various types of geographic segment data. The information provided varied in terms of the number of segments and the extent to which they were similar or dissimilar to each other. They found that the perceived risk of the proposed investments was clearly linked to the number of segments disclosed. More importantly, the segment disclosures were really only of benefit when the segments disclosed were perceived to be dissimilar from each other in terms of having different risk profiles.

19.4.3 Studies using researchers' forecasts

There have been a large number of predictive ability studies in which the researcher(s) create their own forecasts of company performance. While these studies have generated some interesting conclusions it should be recognized that this approach is based upon an implicit assumption that at least some market participants are not only capable of using, but actually do use, segment information in this way. Whether or not this is the case is not clear and, therefore, care has to be taken when drawing conclusions from these types of studies.

The first attempt to use LoB segment data for forecasting purposes was by Kinney (1971) who forecast the earnings of 24 companies. Using four models, two based upon aggregated data, one using segment sales information and the final model using segment sales and segment profit data, he concluded that the most accurate forecasting model was that which used LoB sales and profits. While this model was significantly more successful than either of the consolidated models, it was only marginally more successful than the model combining segment sales with a consolidated earnings margin. Although these results were promising, they may have depended crucially upon the particular sample chosen (in this case both small and self-selecting, in that all the companies voluntarily disclosed segment data) and the models used (the specific models used were criticized by later studies). Therefore, before concluding that LoB segment disclosures are useful, further evidence is required using different samples and different models.

The next important study in this area was by Collins (1976) who increased the number of companies used to a random sample of 96 companies that disclosed LoB data after it was made compulsory in the United States. Actual sales and profits and first differences (the change from one period to the next) were forecast for 1968 to 1970, using seven models based upon consolidated information. Sales were also forecast using LoB segment sales multiplied by the expected change in sales of the relevant industries. For earnings, two segment models were used. Firstly, the forecasted sales of each segment were aggregated to obtain a forecast of company sales and this was then multiplied by the prior year consolidated profit margin. Secondly, the forecasted sales of each segment were multiplied by the prior year profit margin for that segment and the resultant segment profit forecasts aggregated to obtain a forecast for the entire company. For sales, both actual and first differences, the segment model significantly outperformed six of the seven consolidated models. The segment profit-based forecasts were even more successful in that, for both the level and first differences of earnings, the segment models were significantly better than all the consolidated models. In addition, as found by Kinney, the use of segment profit margins, rather than segment sales and consolidated profit margins, led to only a marginal improvement in predictive ability. Similar results have also been found when quarterly data was used to predict earnings (Silhan, 1983).

In a similar study using United Kingdom rather than United States companies, Emmanuel and Pick (1980) forecasted sales and earnings of 39 companies for 1973 to 1977. They reached similar conclusions when they found that segment-based sales and earnings forecasts were more accurate than a consolidated random walk model, which assumes that next year's sales or earnings will be the same as this year's. However, their results differed slightly from the US studies in that they found that the addition of segment profit did not lead to even a marginal improvement over forecasts based upon segment sales.

While these studies clearly support the conclusion that sales and earnings forecasts can be improved if segment sales data is used, they all ignore many company-specific factors. In particular, they ignore the number of segments reported and the size of the company. There is some evidence that forecasts increase in accuracy as the number of segments increases (Silhan, 1982). In addition, any gain in predictive power due to the addition of segment data is more common for smaller companies (Silhan, 1984). Indeed, only for smaller companies were segment-based forecasts always found to be more accurate, irrespective of the number of segments disclosed. The relative superiority of LoB-based forecasts is also likely to depend upon the specific industries that a company operates in. If it operates in industries whose growth rates mirror the growth pattern of the entire economy, then there should be little additional benefit in using industry-specific forecasts. Similarly, if a company is highly industrially diversified, the overall growth rate of the company is likely to mirror the growth in the economy as a whole. Using these types of arguments, Garrod and Emmanuel (1987) found evidence that the relative success of LoB-based forecasts did indeed appear to depend upon the diversification patterns of companies.

Until recently, less interest was shown in the usefulness of geographical segment data. This is probably because it is more difficult to combine corporate geographic segment data with external economic data. It is relatively easy to obtain forecasts of growth rates for a large number of industries in the United States and to a lesser extent the United Kingdom. These forecasts of industry growth rates can then be combined with segment LoB data to obtain forecasts of segment growth rates. (This assumes that either all sales are generated domestically or, if made abroad, the relevant growth rate is the same as that which applies to domestic operations.)

If a similar approach is to be taken with geographical segments, then forecasts must be generated for the geographical segments disclosed. This presents a number of problems. External economic forecasts are generally available for individual countries only and not for the geographical segments disclosed, which are usually groups of countries such as 'North America', 'The Americas', 'Europe' or 'Middle and Far East'. The problem of how to combine forecasts of individual country growth rates into forecasts for groups of countries is magnified because most companies do not disclose which specific countries they operate in. For example, a company that discloses a segment entitled 'Europe' will generally operate in a limited but unspecified number of European countries. Thus, some assumption must be made regarding the specific countries that a company operates in. In addition, a foreign subsidiary will operate in its own local currency and its results then have to be translated into the parent currency. Therefore, the forecaster may have to incorporate country-specific forecasts of expected real GNP growth, inflation and exchange rate changes into the forecasts for each geographic segment. Despite these problems, there have been studies exploring the usefulness of geographical disclosures in both the United Kingdom and the United States.

In the United Kingdom, Roberts (1989) used a sample of multinational companies that disclosed both segment sales and segment earnings and, using this information, forecasted earnings for the period 1981 to 1983. Two basic segment models were used: expected segment earnings and expected segment sales multiplied by the consolidated profit margin. Expected segment earnings and sales were based upon prior periods' segment earnings or sales adjusted for the expected growth in the GNP of each of the relevant geographic segments, with it being assumed that each company operated in all countries in each reported segment in proportion to the GNP of that country. Four forms of each of the two basic segment models were then generated, each based upon a different assumption about expected inflation rates. Expected changes in exchange rates were ignored in these models which were then compared to two consolidated models. The conclusions reached were very similar to earlier LoB studies. The segment-based models generally significantly outperformed the consolidated models. In addition, while the segment earnings-based models were generally more accurate than the segment sales-based models, the difference in forecast accuracy was not significant in most cases.

Balakrishnan et al. (1990) conducted a similar study regarding the accuracy of earnings forecasts generated from the geographical segment data of 89 US companies. The models used were somewhat different. Expected exchange rate changes were included in the models. In addition, each model took two forms. Firstly, they used forecasts of the relevant economic variables (GNP and exchange rates). The second form of each model instead assumed perfect economic forecasting and so used actual economic variables. When economic forecasts are used, the success of the final predictions depends upon two factors: the segment data provided and its usefulness, and the economic forecasts used and their accuracy. Using *ex post* economic data or perfect forecasts means that these two factors can be separated. While the methodology was somewhat different from that used by Roberts, the conclusions reached were very similar, namely that geographic segment data appears to be useful for forecasting earnings. They also found that the available economic forecasts were, as might be expected, less than perfect. Thus forecasts using geographic earnings data and actual or *ex post* economic data were more accurate than forecasts using geographic earnings data combined with forecasts of expected GNP and exchange rate changes.

Further evidence on the usefulness of available economic forecasts has been provided by a number of later studies. For example, Herrmann (1996) found that economic forecasts of exchange rate changes, GNP changes and inflation were all useful in predicting sales and gross profits but were not useful in predicting earnings. However, the findings of Johnson (1996) suggest that it is probably not sufficient to talk of the usefulness of geographic segment disclosures without considering the actual segments reported. This is because, when she looked at the usefulness of forecasts of exchange rate changes, she found that the results were dependent upon both the countries and industries that a company operates in. This is not surprising. The impact of changes in economic factors such as inflation and exchange rate changes will vary depending upon the specific characteristics of a company. The industry it operates in and its internal organizational structure will crucially affect the extent to which a company can change its operating plans to minimize any unexpected adverse impacts or to take advantage of any unexpected beneficial impacts of changes in the economic environment facing the company. Finally, Behn *et al.* (2002) demonstrate that the move from SFAS 14 to SFAS 131 has increased the predictive ability of geographic segment information.

19.4.4   Stock market reactions to segment disclosures

Studies of the stock market effects of segment information fall into two main categories: market reactions to segment disclosure and comparisons of the success of investment made with and without segment information. Again, the earliest studies tended to look at LoB disclosures while later studies have examined geographic segment disclosures.

Looking, first, at market reaction studies, the results have generally supported the conclusion that the market finds segment data useful. For example, Simonds and Collins (1978) using analysis of variance to test for changes in market risk or companies' betas, found that disclosure of LoB data had the effect of significantly reducing risk. Very similar results were also found when a more sophisticated moving beta test was used instead (Collins and Simonds, 1979).

Rather than examining the impact of LoB disclosures on market betas, an alternative approach is to examine the relationship between betas and the specific segment disclosures, to see whether or not the two are related. Following the early work of Kinney (1972), Mohr (1983, 1985) used LoB data to estimate companies' relative investments in each type of industrial activity. These tables were then used to compute an accounting-based measure of beta which was regressed on the market beta of 56 companies. She found a significant positive linear relationship between the two risk measures, with the strongest association being between market beta and an accounting beta based upon LoB asset data rather than either LoB sales or earnings.

Rather than looking at the impact of segment disclosures on risk or return measures, an alternative approach is to compare the returns generated by two investment strategies, one based solely on consolidated data and the other based upon segment data. The first of these studies was by Collins (1975). His sample consisted of 92 companies following the introduction of the 10-K disclosure requirements in the United States, which required companies to disclose prior period LoB data. The investment strategy consisted of buying shares if segment-based forecasted earnings exceeded those from consolidated models, and selling short if the reverse held. The segment-based strategy yielded significant gains in both 1968 and 1969 of between 1.44 per cent and 1.51 per cent per month for companies that had not voluntarily disclosed segment information. In contrast, insignificant gains were made for those companies that had previously voluntarily disclosed LoB turnover data, implying that the market had used this segment information when it was first disclosed.

Prodhan (1986) examined 15 UK companies that had disclosed geographic segment information from at least 1973 and 21 companies that instead disclosed such information for the first time in December 1977. Using interrupted time-series analysis, he found that changes in beta were significantly related to segment disclosures. In the period 1973 to 1977, those companies which had disclosed segment data (the treatment companies) had significantly higher betas than those companies which did not (the control group). After 1977, when both groups disclosed segment data, there was no difference in their betas. Similar results were also found when a rather larger group of US companies were examined in a later study (Prodhan and Harris, 1989). These conclusions are also supported by a rather different type of analysis carried out by Senteney and Bazaz (1992). Instead of looking at betas, they looked at the association between unexpected share price changes or cumulative abnormal returns (CARs) and changes in annual consolidated earnings. They found that the association was weaker after companies disclosed geographic data following the US standard, SFAS 14. They concluded that the explanation for this lies in the better earnings predictions that the market could make once geographic data were available to it. Given the more accurate forecasts made possible by the disclosure of segment information, the surprise value of the annual report disclosures will be less and the share price reaction to these disclosures will therefore be smaller.

Rather than comparing the CARs of two groups of companies (those that did and those that did not disclose geographic data), Boatsman *et al.* (1993) tried to explain the size of the CARs of companies that disclosed segment information. They regressed CARs against the unexpected earnings made by companies in five geographic areas (Asia, Europe, the United Kingdom, South America and Canada). Prather-Stewart (1995) extended this work by looking at the association between CARs and unexpected geographic sales (in Asia, Europe, South America, North

America and the United States) and the number of segments disclosed. Boatsman *et al.* found that all segments were significant with the one exception of South America, while Prather-Stewart found that all regions except South America and Asia were significant.

These findings suggest not only that foreign segment information is used by the market, but also that foreign profits or sales are capitalized at lower multiples than domestic or US sales or earnings. The one exception to this appears to be the United Kingdom, in that Boatsman *et al.* (1993) found that UK earnings were valued more highly than were US earnings. However, it is interesting to note that, in contrast, Garrod and Rees (1998) found, when exploring a sample of UK companies, that US-based operations were more highly valued than all other operations including UK-based operations. Thomas (2000) also extended the work of Boatsman *et al.*, not only in terms of improving its methodology but also by extending the period examined. Specifically, he regressed leading period returns (i.e. market returns for the current and past periods combined up to a length of five years) on current geographic earnings. The results suggest that geographic segment information reflects information used by market participants for return intervals of three or more years. Again, segment earnings appear to be valued approximately in accordance with the risk and growth characteristics of each segment. Later work by Hope *et al.* (2004) suggests that the quality of the segment disclosures helps to explain the results found, with the mispricing of foreign operations decreasing as the number of segments and the amount of disclosure of performance measures increase.

A similar approach of regressing stock market measures against segment data was also used by Pointer and Doupnik (1996) who looked at the relationship between both market betas and operating risk and various measures of international diversification, all based upon geographic segment data. Using a far larger sample of US companies over a six-year period they also concluded that there is a significant relationship between geographic segment information and market risk measures.

SUMMARY

- The growth of large diversified companies has presented problems for users of financial reports, especially in terms of assessing the future cash flows of a company and the risk or uncertainty associated with those cash flows. Segment reporting goes some way towards meeting the information needs of investors and other users.

- Not all companies willingly disclose adequate segment information. Many argue that the costs of disclosure outweigh the benefits. The alleged costs include the costs of compiling, processing and disseminating information as well as competitive disadvantage.

- Given the lack of adequate voluntary disclosures, accounting regulators have increasingly required companies to disclose segment information. US and IFRS requirements have been built up over a number of years culminating in accounting standards requiring relatively extensive disclosures.

- Concern has been expressed that senior management have been given too much discretion to choose the appropriate segments. Such discretion may have been used to reduce the amount of information provided or even to provide potentially misleading information. Given these considerations, the FASB and the IASB have made changes to their segment standards and both now use the operating structure of the enterprise as the basis for determining the primary basis of segmentation.

- Until 2009, an old standard (IAS 14) that does not use the operating segment approach is still allowed under IFRS.

- Segment reporting has been a rich field for academic research. Studies have been made of how analysts use segment data, of whether researchers can make better forecasts with such data, and of whether share prices change.

- The results of predictive ability studies have shown that both LoB and geographic segment data are more useful than consolidated data for the prediction of earnings. While all studies appear to agree that segment turnover data is useful, there is less agreement over whether or not there are additional benefits to be gained from the disclosure of segment earnings data. In most studies, even when it was found that predictions were more accurate if they were based upon segment earnings instead of segment turnover data, the differences in accuracy were relatively small and often not significant.

- There is also evidence that the accuracy of forecasts is dependent upon the specific industries that a company operates in; and the accuracy of the forecasts is greater for smaller companies and for companies that disclose more segments.

- Studies that looked at the market reaction to segment data also clearly suggest that both LoB and geographical segment data are useful to the market. Specifically, segment disclosures are significantly associated with CARs and generally result in a decrease in market beta, at least in the United States and United Kingdom equity markets.

References

Balakrishnan, R., Harris, T.S. and Sen, P.K. (1990) 'The predictive ability of geographic segment disclosures', *Journal of Accounting Research*, Autumn.

Baldwin, B.A. (1984) 'Segment earnings disclosure and the ability of security analysts to forecast earnings per share', *Accounting Review*, July.

Behn, B.K., Nichols, N.B. and Street, D.L. (2002) 'The predictive ability of geographic segment disclosures by US companies: SFAS No 131 vs SFAS No 14', *Journal of International Accounting Research*, Vol. 1.

Boatsman, J.R., Behn, B.K. and Patz, D.H. (1993) 'A test of the use of geographical segment disclosures', *Journal of Accounting Research*, Supplement.

Collins, D.W. (1975) 'SEC product line reporting and market efficiency', *Journal of Financial Economics*, June.

Collins, D.W. (1976) 'Predicting earnings with sub-entity data: Some further evidence', *Journal of Accounting Research*, Spring.

Collins, D.W. and Simonds, R. (1979) 'SEC line of business disclosure and market risk adjustments', *Journal of Accounting Research*, Autumn.

Doupnik, T.S. and Rolfe, R.J. (1990) 'Geographic area disclosures and the assessment of foreign investment risk for disclosure in accounting statement notes', *International Journal of Accounting*, No. 4.

Doupnik, T.S. and Seese, C.P. (2001) 'Geographic area disclosures under SFAS 131: materiality and fineness', *Journal of International Accounting, Auditing and Taxation*, No. 2.

Edwards, P. and Smith, R.A. (1996) 'Competitive disadvantage and voluntary disclosures: The case of segmental reporting', *British Accounting Review*, June.

Emmanuel, C.R. and Pick, R. (1980) 'The predictive ability of UK segment reports', *Journal of Business Finance and Accounting*, Summer.

Emmanuel, C.R., Garrod, N.W. and Frost, C. (1989) 'An experimental test of analysts' forecasting behaviour', *British Accounting Review*, June.

Financial Accounting Standards Board (1976) *SFAS 14; Financial Reporting for Segments of a Business Enterprise*, December.

Garrod, N.W. and Emmanuel, C.R. (1987) 'An empirical analysis of the usefulness of disaggregated accounting data for forecasts of corporate performance', *Omega*, No. 5.

Garrod, N.W. and Rees, W. (1998) 'International diversification and firm value', *Journal of Business Finance and Accounting*, November/December.

Harris, M.S. (1998) 'The association between competition and managers' business segment reporting decisions', *Journal of Accounting Research*, Spring.

Hayes, R.M. and Lundholm, R. (1996) 'Segment reporting to the capital markets in the presence of a competitor,' *Journal of Accounting Research*, Vol. 34, No. 2.

Herrmann, D. (1996) 'The predictive ability of geographic segment information at the country, continent and consolidated levels', *Journal of International Financial Management and Accounting*, Spring.

Herrmann, D. and Thomas, W.T. (2000) 'An analysis of segment disclosures under SFAS 131 and SFAS 14', *Accounting Horizons*, September.

Hope, O-K, Kang, T., Thomas, W.B. and Vasvari, F. (2004) 'The effect of SFAS 131 geographic segment disclosure on the valuation of foreign earnings', Working paper, December.

Johnson, C.B. (1996) 'The effect of exchange rate changes on geographic segment earnings of US-based multinationals', *Journal of International Financial Management and Accounting*, Spring.

Kinney, W.R. (1971) 'Predicting earnings: Entity versus subentity data', *Journal of Accounting Research*, Spring.

Kinney, W.R. (1972) 'Covariability of segment earnings and multisegment company returns', *Accounting Review*, April.

Lobo, G.L., Kwon, S.S. and Ndubizu, G.A. (1998) 'The impact of SFAS 14 segment information on price variability and earnings forecast accuracy', *Journal of Business Finance and Accounting*, September/October.

Maines, L.A., McDaniel, L.S. and Harris, M.S. (1997) 'Implications of proposed segment reporting standards for financial analysts' investment judgements', *Journal of Accounting Research*, Special issue.

Mohr, R.M. (1983) 'The segment reporting issue: A review of empirical research', *Journal of Accounting Research*, 1983.

Mohr, R.M. (1985) 'The operating beta of a US multi-activity firm: An empirical investigation', *Journal of Business Finance and Accounting*, Winter.

Nichols, D., Tunnell, L. and Seipal, C. (1995) 'Earnings forecasts accuracy and geographical segment disclosures', *Journal of International Accounting, Auditing and Taxation*, No. 2.

Nichols, N.B., Street, D.L. and Gray, S.J. (2000) 'Geographic segment disclosures in the United States: Reporting practices enter a new era', *Journal of International Accounting, Auditing and Taxation*, No. 1.

Pointer, M.M. and Doupnik, T.S. (1996) 'The relationship between geographic segment information and firm risk', *Advances in International Accounting*, Vol. 9.

Prather-Stewart, J. (1995) 'The information content of geographical segment disclosures', *Advances in International Accounting*, Vol. 8.

Prodhan, B.K. (1986) 'Geographical segment disclosures and multinational risk profile', *Journal of Business Finance and Accounting*, Spring.

Prodhan, B.K. and Harris, M.C. (1989) 'Systematic risk and the discretionary disclosure of geographical segments: An empirical investigation of US multinationals', *Journal of Business Finance and Accounting*, Autumn.

Roberts, C.B. (1989) 'Forecasting earnings using geographic segment data: Some UK evidence', *Journal of International Financial Management and Accounting*, June.

Senteney, D.L. and Bazaz, M.S. (1992) 'The impact of SFAS 14 geographic segment disclosures on the information content of US-based MNEs' earnings releases', *International Journal of Accounting*, Vol. 27, No. 4.

Silhan, P.A. (1982) 'Simulated mergers of existent autonomous firms: A new approach to segmentation research', *Journal of Accounting Research*, Spring.

Silhan, P.A. (1983) 'The effects of segmenting quarterly sales and margins on extrapolative forecasts of conglomerate earnings: Extension and replication', *Journal of Accounting Research*, Spring.

Silhan, P.A. (1984) 'Company size and the issue of quarterly segment reporting', *Journal of Accounting and Public Policy*, Fall.

Simonds, R. and Collins, D. (1978) 'Line of business reporting and security prices: An analysis of a SEC disclosure rule: a comment', *Bell Journal of Economics*, Autumn.

Street, D.L., Nichols, N.B. and Gray, S.J. (2000) 'Segment disclosures under SFAS 131: Has business segment reporting improved?' *Accounting Horizons*, September.

Street, D.L. and Nichols, N.B. (2002) 'LoB and geographic segment disclosures: an analysis of the impact of IAS 14 revised', *Journal of International Accounting, Auditing and Taxation*, No. 2.

Thomas, W.T. (2000) 'The value-relevance of geographic segment earnings disclosures under SFAS 14', *Journal of International Financial Management and Accounting*, Autumn.

QUESTIONS

Suggested answers to the asterisked questions are given at the end of the book.

19.1∗ Explain why standard-setters have difficulty in drafting segment reporting standards.

19.2∗ How could one demonstrate that the benefits of segment reporting outweigh the costs?

19.3 'Research shows that line-of-business reporting is much more useful than geographical segmental reporting.' Discuss.

19.4 Using segment reporting as an example, explain how standard-setters could use research when planning to impose extra disclosure requirements.

19.5 A number of companies voluntarily prepare segment reports beyond what is required by regulation. Given the difficulties faced by regulators in developing rules for segment reporting, is regulation really necessary and/or desirable?

19.6 Discuss to what extent segment reporting is beneficial to different user/stakeholder groups.

19.7 Discuss the view that IFRS 8 ignores the needs of many stakeholders.

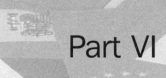

Part VI

ANALYSIS AND MANAGEMENT ISSUES

20 International financial analysis

Stuart McLeay[1]

OBJECTIVES

After reading this chapter, you should be able to:

- discuss the impact of different social, financial, tax and legal systems on accounting;

- explain why there may be differences in financial reporting behaviour between internationally listed multinationals and domestic-only listed MNEs;

- describe the several ways in which MNEs attempt to provide additional information for foreign readers of their financial reports;

- show how 'convenience currency translations' may produce apparently different indications of movements on sales and profits;

- explain why companies do not report a standard set of ratios calculated in accordance with standard definitions;

- explain the use of benchmark ratios;

- discuss the factors affecting analysts' forecasts of the future earnings of MNEs.

---

[1] For this chapter, the author has used data provided by Thomson, Worldscope and IBES.

20.1 Introduction

This chapter is concerned with the interpretation of financial statements in an international setting, which could involve:

- the analysis of the operations of a multinational company, where the financial statements result from a process of aggregation of underlying transactions that have been carried out in a number of countries and denominated in various currencies; or
- transnational comparison between companies that are based in different countries but do not necessarily have multinational activities; or, by contrast,
- the geographical spread not of companies but of the users of corporate reports, where the analysis is carried out by residents of different countries – Italian investors, American bankers, or Japanese fund managers, for instance – with their own particular expectations about corporate activity.

Whilst each of these distinctive 'international' dimensions of financial statement analysis is important, the basic process of financial communication remains the same. Essentially, we are concerned in each case with financial information that has crossed national boundaries at some stage. In so doing, financial statistics are restated and financial terminology is translated. For instance, some of the information disclosed by a multinational has already been restated using an alternative set of accounting methods and translated into a different language and currency during the consolidation of financial statements. In the case of a transnational comparison of two or more companies, it is the financial analyst who is most likely to confront the problems of restating financial statistics and translating financial terminology. Indeed, some of the key issues in international financial analysis are concerned with the restatement and translation of financial reports that describe operations conducted in one environment but that are the subject of review and analysis in another.

Accordingly, in this chapter, we shall consider ways in which a company's financial disclosures may be influenced by its operating environment, how companies report on these issues and, finally, how analysts deal with the issues that are raised.

20.2 Understanding differences in accounting

It is not necessary here to provide evidence that inter-country differences in accounting exist; there is a substantial literature on this subject (see Chapters 1 to 3, for example). However, in an international context, it is important to understand why country-to-country differences in accounting persist, and whether they merely reflect divergence of opinion on an aspect of accounting policy over which there is a choice or whether they reveal deeper structural differences attributable to the legal and social system and to the financial environment in a given country. Set out below are a number of illustrations of this point.

Table 20.1 **The impact of different remuneration schemes on funds generated from operations**

	United Kingdom (£)	France (€)	Italy (€)
Earnings	1,000	1,000	1,000
Add back:			
Depreciation of fixed assets	2,500	2,500	2,500
Provision for employee pensions	800	–	–
less: funds applied in the current year	(800)	–	–
Share of profits attributable to employees	–	800	–
less: funds applied in the current year	–	(700)	–
Deferred employee remuneration	–	–	800
less: funds applied in the current year	–	–	(300)
Funds generated from operations	3,500	3,600	4,000

20.2.1 Different social systems

Table 20.1 shows how long-term employee entitlements can influence the computation of funds generated from operations for three companies in countries where the commercial practices differ (one British company, one French and one Italian). We start in column one with the British company, which is likely to channel all deferred employee benefits into a pension scheme and, in this case of course, the 'funds' in question leave the company immediately. For a company operating in France, part of the company's profits may be allocated for the benefit of employees, with eventual reinvestment in external assets. In the short term, we could consider that there is an element in 'Funds generated from operations' (+€800 in the example), which relates to the allocation for the current period, whilst the only outflow is the cash placed in external investments (–€700), which relates to the share in prior profits.

Now compare these two approaches with the situation in Italy, where employees are entitled on leaving a company to termination pay equal to about one month's salary at current rates of pay for each year in service. There is no requirement for the company to place funds in earmarked investments, although the appropriate provisions must be made. Thus, 'Funds generated from operations' includes the provision (+€800) net of the payment to retiring employees (–€300).

Of course, there are many ways of constructing a funds or cash flow statement, and the example is not uncontentious. However, it shows that the issues of accounting and social structure are related. Indeed, we are drawn into a debate about the nature of the entity – what sort of funds are these, and what are the broader implications of providing for employee shares in profit and deferred employee entitlements? We might easily imagine an Italian company whose net assets are funded not only by shareholders' equity and interest-bearing debt, but also by an additional substantial stake neither bearing interest nor sharing in profits but nevertheless with an accumulator based on wage inflation. It certainly throws the simple notion of 'gearing' into some confusion. And the confusion arises because the simplistic model of a company financed by debt and equity no longer seems to fit the social circumstances.

The example above shows that, when we compare the funds generated by companies in different countries, an important part of the explanation of the variability in levels of self-financing lies in the different social systems within which the companies operate. Differences in accounting policies for the recognition and measurement of deferred employee entitlements also exist (see Chapters 15 and 16).

20.2.2 Different financial systems

In spite of the moves in the European Union to bring about an integrated financial system (see Chapter 5), there exist aspects of corporate financing that are idiosyncratic. For example, it is commonplace in many European countries for the extension of trade credit to be supported by a discountable bill, where a company may either allow a trade debt to run to maturity or, alternatively, discount the bill receivable. In the latter circumstance, whilst the company's liquid funds will increase, a contingent liability to the discounting bank exists until the debt has been realized. For example, a trade debt of €1,000 could appear in any one of the following balance sheet lines:

Accounts receivable	€1,000
or:	
Bills receivable	€1,000
or:	
Cash at bank	€975

where, in the latter case, it is assumed that the discount is €25. One interpretation is that discounting effectively restates trade debt at current values, rather than being stated at the amounts collectable at some future date (although the difference is likely to be relatively trivial for short-term items). Of more importance is the effect on the total of liquid funds, and it could be argued that bills receivable, which are immediately realizable, should be included.

Clearly, the 'liquidity' of a company depends to some extent on the mechanisms that exist within a financial system to provide liquidity, and bill discounting is one such mechanism that is commonplace in some European countries and not in others. Hence, we can conclude that differences in liquid funds are in part explained by the nature of the financial systems in which companies operate.

20.2.3 Different tax systems

Taxation is an area where national governments are keen to preserve their autonomy, and the consequent variety amongst taxation systems has a substantial effect on company finances. Disentangling effective tax rates in this context presents a number of problems. First, basic tax rates vary from country to country, and taxation at higher rates can also be levied. Second, tax computations vary from one jurisdiction to another, and the treatment of tax losses and tax credits also differs. Third, there exist a number of approaches to accounting for taxation, particularly

Table 20.2 **The impact of different tax systems: analysis of effective tax rates published by Eridania Béghin-Say SA**

Legal tax rate in France	33.3
French temporary surtax	4.5
Effect of lower tax rates in foreign countries	(5.5)
Utilization of tax losses carryforwards	(1.0)
Investment tax credits and other tax credits	(4.7)
Permanent differences	(2.6)
Effective tax rate	**24.0**

with respect to deferred taxation issues such as the certainty of income realization and the treatment of temporary and permanent differences between earnings and taxable income. These topics are considered further in Chapter 16. Table 20.2 shows how one firm, the French company Eridania Béghin-Say, has quantified the effect of some of the above-mentioned factors that characterize different tax systems in reconciling the legal tax rate applicable in its domicile (France) with the effective tax rate arising as a result of its international operations.

In some circumstances, the particularities of a local tax system will have such an important effect on company financial statements that a proper understanding of the tax arrangements in the country in question is required in order to carry out any kind of meaningful financial analysis. Consider the situation in Sweden, where a particular feature of accounting has been the use of untaxed reserves. Companies may allocate part of income before taxes to such reserves, and in previous years the government sometimes made it obligatory to make allocations to these reserves. For example, at one point companies were required to allocate 20 per cent of income before taxes to a special investment reserve and also to deposit funds equal to a portion of the allocation in a non-interest-bearing account with the Central Bank of Sweden. These funds could be withdrawn from the Bank of Sweden when approved investments were made in property, plant and equipment. These blocked accounts still appear in Swedish balance sheets.

The fiscal implications are substantial. Over the years, Swedish companies have been able to reduce tax payments by making tax-deductible allocations to untaxed reserves, such as the investment reserve described above, or a tax equalization reserve. The allocations are recognized in determining net income for the year, and corresponding credits are made to untaxed reserves in the balance sheet. The impact on financial structure can also be important. Untaxed reserves may be viewed as a combination of shareholders' equity and deferred taxation, where the latter is similar to interest-free debt for an indefinite period. Indeed, this is the treatment now found in consolidated financial statements in Sweden. Again, the conventional simplistic notions of leverage are thrown into some confusion by this alternative approach to company financing where the state acts as a major financial partner.

20.2.4 Different legal systems

A key issue in international financial analysis is whether or not the information in financial reports is reliable. We expect good regulation and effective accounting standards to increase the precision of financial statements. To achieve this, regulators and standard-setters eliminate options and restrict the number of rules that require judgements, and include more detail to provide guidance in those cases where judgements on accounting policy have to be made. But when laws and standards are weak, this gives managers opportunities to mask their firm's economic performance, either upwards or downwards, by overstating earnings and assets in order to conceal unfavourable circumstances or by understating them in order to create reserves that will cushion future costs.

Investor protection laws are important in this respect. These enable shareholders to hold managers accountable for their actions, at least by forcing them to communicate poor results fully in current earnings. In highly competitive circumstances, it is not surprising that managers might try to defer loss recognition to future periods, because in the long run this will shift the consequences on to subsequent generations of managers beyond their own tenure. So strong investor protection tends to make earnings lower, because losses have to be recognized immediately whereas gains are recognized only when they are realized.

The protection of minority shareholders can also have an impact on the quality of reported financial results. In firms with closely held shares, the interests of the managers and the majority shareholders are likely to be aligned and the shareholders will not necessarily rely on financial reporting in order to monitor the managers, as they have access to sources of information within the firm. Also, if the managers and controlling owners are able to dominate the firm, they will have incentives to conceal their own benefits, especially if these have a negative effect on the minority shareholders and other parties. Indeed, such managers are likely to use earnings management to conceal the firm's performance from outsiders, especially by overstating earnings in order to conceal unfavourable losses that would prompt outside interference. So earnings management is expected to be more pervasive in countries where the legal protection of outside investors is weak.

A recent international accounting study that sheds light on this is Leuz *et al.* (2003). Figure 20.1 shows one of their results. Here, we compare countries in Europe with the USA, highlighting Germany and Italy on the one hand and the UK and USA on the other. It is indeed the case that earnings management seems to be more prevalent when the legal protection of shareholders is weaker and ownership concentration is higher. For example, Germany and Italy score low on investor protection and high on ownership concentration, and the Leuz *et al.* (2003) measure of earnings management is relatively high in these circumstances. Nevertheless, we should try to disentangle accounting manipulations by way of creative accounting from those changes to earnings that are caused by real transactions, which are undertaken in order to achieve the desired earnings figure. Interestingly, the level of 'real' earnings management may be expected to increase with the reduction of discretion through tighter regulation and standards. When the legal system restricts the scope for accounting creativity, this will increase the marginal benefit of real earnings management (see Ewert and Wagenhofer, 2005).

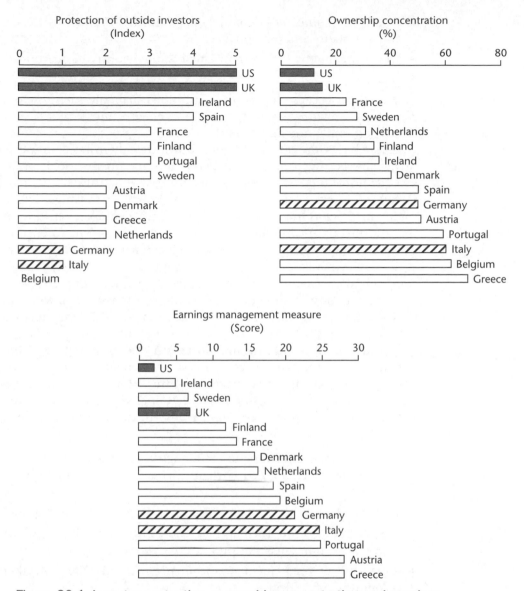

Figure 20.1 Investor protection, ownership concentration and earnings management

20.3 Disclosure practices in international financial reporting

20.3.1 Mandatory and voluntary disclosures

The examples given above demonstrate clearly that the analysis of financial statements in an international context requires information about:

- aspects of a company's domestic operating environment that exert an influence on its structure and performance;
- accounting methods that are peculiar to the country in question.

Companies experiencing a demand for this information may respond by supplying it, sometimes because regulatory institutions mandate such disclosures (as is the case in the United States, if they do not prepare a full set of accounts based on US rules), and sometimes on a voluntary basis.

Research by Gray *et al.* (1995) has shown that there are significant differences in financial reporting behaviour between internationally listed and domestic-only listed multinational companies, a conclusion that had also been arrived at by Cooke (1989) in his review of disclosure levels by Swedish companies. Exposure to the US capital market has had a considerable impact. By comparison with other countries, the information environment in the United States seems to encourage more frequent and more timely disclosure, with greater pressure to do so by analysts, and with a capital market regulator in the background that actively discourages information asymmetries (Frost and Pownall, 1994; see also Section 20.2.4).

Participation in international capital markets is associated with substantial additional voluntary disclosure in areas such as research and development, future prospects, acquisitions and disposals, director and employee information, and segmental data. According to Choi and Levich (1990), reporting on interviews with executives of multinational companies, the benefits of lower cost of capital are likely to outweigh the costs of providing the information (including the potential effects on competitivity arising from additional voluntary disclosure).

Companies adopt various approaches to transnational financial disclosure, including:

- the use of notes explaining to the foreign reader the peculiarities of the domestic accounting principles used, perhaps with a glossary of the technical expressions used;
- a restatement of the results in the currency used by the foreign reader;
- a direct translation of their annual report into other languages, or publication of a condensed translated version for foreign users;
- some kind of restatement of the financial results using an alternative set of accounting principles;
- the disclosure of comparable indicators, such as financial ratios.

20.3.2 Notes and glossaries for the foreign reader

Some of the larger international companies go to considerable lengths to inform their foreign report users of the particularities of the company's operating environment. Some even include a small lexicon within their report, explaining (amongst many other things) their distinctive approach to aspects of accounting measurement. For many years, Volvo included a separate Reader's Guide to the English language and French language editions of its annual report, along with illustrative examples of the intricacies of Swedish accounting. Other companies include supplementary notes to the financial statements, which appear solely in foreign-language versions of the annual report and which tend usually to describe the domestic tax and accounting regulations as well as any particular features of the social, legal and financial system(s) within which the company operates.

20.3.3 Translation into foreign currencies

Foreign currency translation was examined in detail in Chapter 18. It is an area where analysts are likely to focus particular attention because there is evidence of a significant impact on company valuation. In a study of multinationals, Pinto (2001) shows that foreign currency translation adjustments can be used successfully in the prediction of earnings per share, especially when factors such as size, industry, location of direct foreign investment and capital intensity are included.

In addition to the translation issues discussed in Chapter 18, there is another type of translation: some companies publish 'convenience currency translations' to re-express the financial results in another currency merely for the convenience of the reader. A more interesting case, however, is Unilever, as the Dutch parent company that reports in euros and the United Kingdom parent company that reports in British pounds are linked by an equalization agreement, and they combine their results to present consolidated figures for the group as a whole. Note, for instance, the group net profit figures reproduced in Table 20.3 and Figure 20.2 (overleaf) from the 2003 and 2004 quarterly reports. The movements in the euro and the pound sterling, and the US dollar, clearly have an interesting effect on the representation of Unilever's earnings in different currencies.

As the data for Unilever show, currency translation will influence the levels of reported earnings. In this example it can be seen that the exchange rate assumption (i.e. constant rate or current rate) produces a consistent bias in the results, the direction of which depends on the currency used. Many companies make it clear that foreign currency reports are presented 'solely for the purpose of convenience'. Indeed, the present regulations of the United States' SEC do not permit translation into US dollars but require the financial statements to be presented in their source currency. However, in their annual reports, we find that companies will use one of a number of different approaches in this unregulated area, such as the following:

Table 20.3 Unilever quarterly net profit

(Millions)		2003 Q1	2003 Q2	2003 Q3	2003 Q4	2004 Q1	2004 Q2	2004 Q3
In UK pounds	– Constant rates	433	395	574	507	366	532	611
	Current rates	426	397	578	508	352	501	582
In euros	– Constant rates	670	573	830	733	530	770	883
	Current rates	637	564	831	730	515	749	867
In US dollars	– Constant rates	705	645	934	825	597	866	994
	Current rates	683	641	933	852	644	907	1061

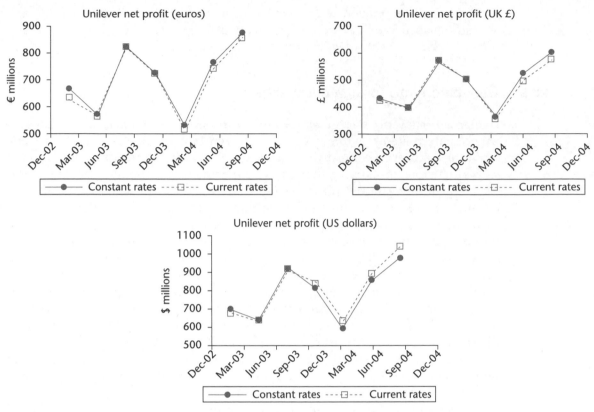

Figure 20.2 **Unilever's quarterly net profit in euros, pounds sterling and US dollars, 2003–04**

- average rates for income statement items and year-end rates for assets and liabilities;
- average rates for all amounts;
- year-end rates for all amounts where, in some cases, the rate for the current year end is applied not only to the current year's figures but also to the corresponding figures for the previous year.

20.3.4 Linguistic issues

When a company reports to an international audience, it will tend to translate its financial statements into a foreign language. Because of some of the issues mentioned earlier concerning social structures and other cultural barriers, this is problematic; after all, it is unlikely that real equivalence will be achieved in translation. The question is: what is lost and what is gained in translation? Some companies indicate an awareness of the potential pitfalls that can arise in international financial communication, where translation from a source language to another language occurs. For example, in the English-language version of its financial report, one leading Dutch company notes that 'in the event of a conflict in interpretation, reference should be made to the Dutch version of this Annual Report' and there is an even bolder declaration in the English-language report of a German MNE, disclaiming responsibility for translation equivalence: 'the auditors' report applies to the *German* version of the Financial Statements and Business Report'.

One of the reasons for this concern about equivalence in translation is that accounting terminology is particularly idiomatic. Terms such as 'net working capital' or 'liquid funds' are charged with idiosyncratic meaning that may be shared by the professional community that takes an interest in financial reporting but can be an obstacle to others. Even for the professional analyst, the language barrier is a significant problem in international financial analysis. After all, when we consider the phrase 'true and fair view', the English analyst has to travel no further than France before meeting the surrealistic notion of *'une image fidèle'*, to be contrasted with the rather loose translation *'ein den tatsächlichen Verhältnissen entsprechendes Bild'* in audit reports on German financial statements.

We meet a similar problem with financial ratio terminology. The German *Innenfinanzierungsspielraum* implicates both the notion of 'internal financing' and that of 'capacity', as indeed it is the ratio of operating cash flow to new investment. We find an equally idiomatic version in the French *taux d'autofinancement*, but the notion of 'self-financing' is not in common use in English. In some cases, the idiom is preserved in translation, as in the French *rotation des stocks* (stock turnover), and there are other cases where the metaphor is shared such as *Anspannungskoeffizient*, which conveys in German the Newtonian notion of leverage (i.e. gearing, or total debt to capital employed). However, French speakers will be aware of the influence of the *Académie Française*, and will not be surprised to hear of the entry in the Official Journal of the Republic where, in addition to pointing out that *le software* would be more appropriately described as *le logiciel*, it is noted that the preferred version of *le PE ratio* is *le coefficient de capitalisation des résultats*. What further evidence could be required to demonstrate that foreign financial terminology is in reality a Trojan horse that brings with it its own social structures and cultural connotations than the reactions of the guardians of the purity of the French language!

20.3.5 Restatement of results in accordance with internationally recognized accounting principles

It would seem that the process of international standardization of accounting principles should facilitate comparability between the financial statements of companies operating in different countries. At present, however, many companies, whose financial statements are drawn up in accordance with local regulations, volunteer (or are required) to assist their foreign report users by restating the statements using internationally recognized accounting principles. For example, the reconciliations in Table 20.4 appeared in the annual report of the Swedish company Volvo, which, like many international companies, provided restated figures using accounting principles that are generally accepted in the United States. Whilst certain stock exchanges, such as the London Stock Exchange, make some requirements for listing by foreign companies, the major influence is the United States' SEC, which stipulated that foreign registrants must file a set of financial statements prepared using US GAAP or reconciled to it. This still applies unless the registrant complies with IFRS (see Chapter 5).

A point to note is that not all international companies include their supplementary restated figures in the annual report, even the annual report prepared

Table 20.4 **Financial information regarding consolidated net income published by Volvo (Sweden) in accordance with US GAAP (SEK millions)**

Net income	2002	2003	2004
Net income in accordance with			
Swedish accounting principles	**1,393**	**298**	**9,355**
Items increasing (decreasing) reported net income			
Derivative instruments and hedging activities	1,772	882	228
Business combinations	1,094	556	826
Investments in debt and equity securities	(9,616)	4,007	5,157
Restructuring costs	–	–	311
Post-employment benefits	669	(651)	(273)
Software development	(212)	(211)	(119)
Product development	(1,236)	(352)	(828)
Entrance fees, aircraft engine programs	(219)	(20)	(392)
Other	447	2	(60)
Income taxes on above US GAAP adjustments	(357)	(532)	211
Net increase (decrease) in net income	(7,658)	3,681	5,061
Net income (loss) in accordance with US GAAP	**(6,265)**	**3,979**	**14,416**

Source: Adapted from the *Volvo Group Financial Report, 2004*. AB Volvo, Göteborg, Sweden. Reproduced with permission.

for US investors. This is certainly an area where the analyst may obtain fuller information by consulting the full set of reports prepared by a company, including its SEC filings.

A detailed analysis of the impact of different accounting principles on profits is given in Weetman and Gray (1991). They find that UK GAAP and Dutch GAAP are less conservative than US GAAP in terms of the impact on profits. Norton (1995) compares Australia with the United States; and Weetman *et al.* (1998) examine reconciliations from UK to US rules, finding an increasing gap, due particularly to differences in accounting for goodwill, deferred tax and pension costs (see also Whittington, 2000).

Ashbaugh (2001) has investigated the voluntary use of International Accounting Standards for international reporting, finding that IAS tend to be preferred to US GAAP whenever translation into US GAAP would require more accounting policy changes. In other words, firms are motivated to provide more standardized financial information at the international level, but at a cost that is as low as possible. Interestingly, a listing in the US increases the extent of compliance with IAS as well as the overall level of disclosure (Street and Bryant, 2000), and there is some evidence that the impact of accounting differences between IAS and US GAAP was narrowing (Street *et al.*, 2000), even before convergence was formally agreed in 2002 (see Chapter 5).

Other research has also considered the differences between US GAAP, IAS/IFRS, and other domestic GAAP. For instance, Barth and Clinch (1996) find that, in Australia and the United Kingdom, reported net income provides incremental explanatory power in explaining share price changes compared with income calculated using US GAAP, but this is related negatively to share returns. Amir *et al.* (1993) also discuss this issue, and Harris and Muller (1999) provide further evidence that earnings reconciliation adjustments are value-relevant. Indeed, IAS reconciliation adjustments seem to be more highly associated with prices, and US GAAP adjustments with price changes.

20.3.6 Financial ratios

The interpretation of financial statements is generally based on ratio analysis or on more intricate statistical techniques using ratios. There is frequent reference to financial ratios in published annual reports and, in some countries, it is usual for a set of ratio indicators to be published. In Table 20.5, an extract from the report of the Finnish company, Nokia, illustrates this disclosure practice.

There has been pressure to introduce sets of standardized reported ratios elsewhere, and one reason given is that the information needed for uniform computation may not be available in a company's annual report. Another reason is that information intermediaries frequently use different formulas for ratios with similar descriptions. In the United States, for instance, in *Annual Statement Studies* published by Robert Morris Associates, inventory turnover is computed by dividing cost of sales by inventory, whilst in 'Ratios of Manufacturing' published in *Dun's Review* the inventory turnover ratio is computed by dividing net sales by inventory (see Gibson, 1980). But there is also considerable inconsistency in the way companies compute the ratios that they choose to disclose. For instance, from a sample of 100 companies, Gibson reported eight different ways in which the profit margin is computed.

Table 20.5 **Ratio disclosure by Nokia (extract from five-year summary 2000–4)**

Key ratios and economic indicators	2000	2001	2002	2003	2004
Return on capital employed, %	58.0	27.9	35.3	34.7	31.6
Return on equity, %	43.3	19.1	25.5	24.4	21.8
Equity ratio, %	55.7	56.0	62.5	64.8	64.4
Net debt to equity, %	−26	−41	−61	−71	−78

Calculation of key ratios

$$\text{Return on capital employed, \%} = \frac{\text{Profit before taxes and minority interests} + \text{interest and other net financial expenses}}{\text{Average shareholders' equity} + \text{short-term borrowings} + \text{long-term interest-bearing liabilities (including the current portion thereof)} + \text{minority shareholders' interests}}$$

$$\text{Return on shareholders' equity, \%} = \frac{\text{Net profit}}{\text{Average shareholders' equity during the year}}$$

$$\text{Equity ratio, \%} = \frac{\text{Shareholders' equity} + \text{minority shareholders' interests}}{\text{Total assets} - \text{advance payments received}}$$

$$\text{Net debt to equity (gearing), \%} = \frac{\text{Long-term interest-bearing liabilities (including the current portion thereof)} + \text{short-term borrowings} - \text{cash and other liquid assets}}{\text{Shareholders' equity} + \text{minority shareholders' interests}}$$

Source: Adapted from *Nokia in 2004: The Annual Report of the Nokia Group*. Nokia Group, Espoo, Finland, p. 50.

There is also evidence of selective reporting by companies. Perhaps the point to be emphasized here is that the 'self-interest' of managers may affect the scope and computation of financial indicators published by a company and that the response of analysts could well be to ignore the summary indicators published by companies.

20.4 | Interpreting financial statements

20.4.1 Drivers of performance

So far, this chapter has emphasized the need to understand the aspects of international business operations that determine the profitability and structure of a firm, suggesting that financial statements should be interpreted in the context of the company's operating environment(s) and illustrating how some international companies actually report on these issues.

To understand the dynamics of business performance, financial analysts have developed approaches to financial statement analysis that identify various value *drivers*, including the firm's ability to use its asset base to generate sales revenue, the sales profit margin that can be achieved, and the way in which capital sources can be mixed effectively in financing the operations. Following this approach, the analysis of Return on Equity (ROE) may be based on the following financial ratio decomposition (the notation is explained in the simplified balance sheet and income statement in Table 20.6):

Return on Equity = Return on Assets × (1 − Income Gearing)/(1 − Capital Gearing)
where   Return on Assets = Operating Margin × Asset Turnover

$$\frac{E}{SE} = \frac{OI}{NA} \times \left[\left(1 - \frac{IC}{OI} \right) \Big/ \left(1 - \frac{TD}{NA} \right) \right], \; where \; \frac{OI}{NA} = \frac{OI}{S} \times \frac{S}{NA}$$

Table 20.6 Simplified financial statements and financial ratios

Balance Sheet		Ratios	
Shareholders' Equity	SE	*Profitability*	
+ Total Debt	TD	Return on Equity	E/SE
= Net Assets	NA	Return on Net Assets	OI/NA
Income Statement		Return on Sales	OI/S
Sales	S	*Efficiency*	
− Operating Costs	OC	Net Asset Turnover	S/NA
= Operating Income	OI	*Leverage*	
− Interest Charged	IC	Income Gearing	IC/OI
= Earnings	E	Capital Gearing	TD/NA

Note: To simplify matters, the tax shield has been ignored in this table and in the example that follows. Operating income is defined as the net income before preference dividends and interest expense. Income Gearing is the ratio of interest charged to operating income, and therefore IC/OI + E/OI = 1. The balance sheet equivalent of Income Gearing is Capital Gearing, the ratio of short and long term debt to total capital, TD/NA. Total capital, i.e. net assets, is defined such that TD/NA + SE/NA = 1. Therefore, E/SE = OI/NA × E/OI × NA/SE.

It can be seen that *Return on Equity* (E/SE) is driven by:

- operating activities that produce operating income (OI) from net operating assets (NA) – this is summarized in the *Return on Net Assets* ratio (OI/NA); and

- financing activities that incur interest expense – these leverage effects arise jointly from *Income Gearing* (expressed here in terms of the ratio of interest charged to earnings before interest, IC/OI) and *Capital Gearing* (expressed here in terms of the ratio of total debt to the total capital employed in funding net operating assets (TD/NA)).

In turn, *Return on Assets* is driven by:

- the profit margin that is indicated by the *Return on Sales* ratio (OI/S); and

- the efficient usage of capital employed to generate revenues, as summarized by *Asset Turnover* (S/NA)).

Table 20.7 shows the results of a ratio analysis for three European vehicle manufacturers: Fiat, Volkswagen and Volvo. An interfirm trend comparison is plotted in the graphs in Figure 20.3 (overleaf). We can see that Fiat recorded substantial net losses during the period. In addition, Volkswagen's return on equity dropped gradually between 2000 and 2004, whilst Volvo's increased. Fiat's trend is the classic 'sharp-bender' that has bounced back from its low point in 2002, although it still remains relatively low. Interestingly, Fiat and Volvo increased their asset turnover over the five years, whilst Volkswagen's declined steadily. Fiat's problems are associated with its greater reliance on a higher proportion of debt, which prevents return on equity from reflecting the improvement in operating results. The analysis shows how Fiat's gearing is consistently higher than that of its competitors, whilst Volvo's is consistently lower. Income gearing was very volatile in this period – when greater

Table 20.7 **Ratio analysis: Fiat, Volkswagen and Volvo**

	Year	Return on equity	Income gearing	Capital gearing	Return on net assets	Net operating margin	Net asset turnover
Fiat	2001	−3.34	1.29	0.71	3.34	2.67	1.25
	2002	−46.85	−1.11	0.77	−5.01	−3.38	1.48
	2003	−25.46	4.27	0.75	1.97	1.20	1.64
	2004	−27.67	5.44	0.77	1.46	0.77	1.90
Volkswagen	2001	12.15	0.36	0.64	6.81	4.95	1.37
	2002	10.49	0.19	0.65	4.56	3.56	1.28
	2003	4.48	0.59	0.69	3.35	2.95	1.13
	2004	2.84	0.69	0.72	2.58	2.46	1.05
Volvo	2001	−1.72	−1.82	0.49	0.48	0.43	1.14
	2002	1.78	0.43	0.48	2.15	1.74	1.24
	2003	0.41	0.14	0.51	1.49	1.19	1.25
	2004	13.48	0.12	0.47	8.07	5.03	1.60

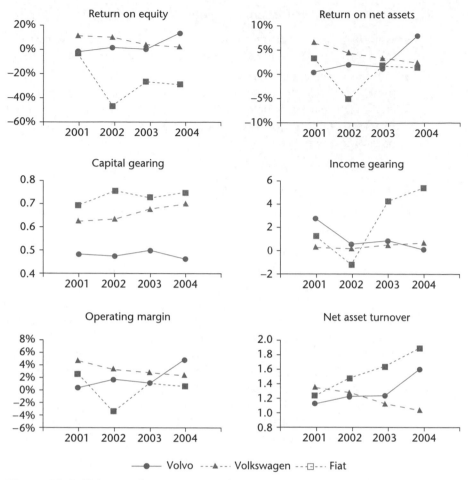

Figure 20.3 **Drivers of return on equity**

than one, this means that there was insufficient income from operations to cover interest charges.

20.4.2 Benchmarks

One way of placing a company in its operating context is to compare its financial ratios with aggregate indicators for the economy or sector. These benchmark ratios may serve as characteristic values and thus provide a way of assessing the country or sector effect, i.e. the mean effect for all companies in the reference group. Analysts have at their disposal a number of sources of such benchmarks. Indeed, given the development of electronic financial information networks, industry-wide and economy-wide statistics are readily available. Information intermediaries such as Thomson, and products such as Worldscope, provide benchmarks for peer review that are regularly updated as new results are published.

But care should be taken when drawing inferences about 'mean effects' within a given country (or sector) using the commercial financial information services, because the benchmarks in question are often obtained from subsamples that have not been constructed for this purpose. Also, there is an important theoretical issue here. A ratio computed from meaningful sector aggregates (e.g. total cash flow from operations in the sector to total sales) is likely to differ substantially from the average ratio for the individual companies in the sector, and depend on the size distribution of firms, the growth of firms and other aspects of industrial structure (McLeay and Fieldsend, 1987; McLeay and Trigueiros, 2001). A more detailed critique of the misuse of ratios in international financial analysis can be found in Choi *et al.* (1983).

A simple but effective approach to benchmarking is to plot performance against the median ratio. In the case of the three companies analyzed above, the relevant peer groups comprise the main industrial and consumer firms in Italy (Fiat), Germany (Volkswagen) and Sweden (Volvo), as the aim is to assess performance in the context of other firms domiciled in the same country. To establish upper and lower reference points, the ratio quartiles are also plotted. Figure 20.4 displays the results. It can be seen that, in 2001 and 2002, there were substantial numbers of Swedish and German firms that reported significant net losses. Against this background, we can also see that Volkswagen's ROE trend was not attributable to its German domicile, as its ROE moved from the upper quartile of German companies

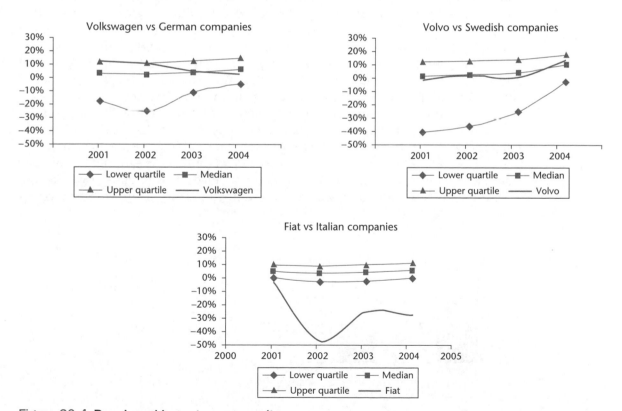

Figure 20.4 **Benchmarking return on equity**

to below the median over the four years. Volvo, however, followed much the same trend as other Swedish companies. In contrast, Fiat's performance was particularly anomalous in the context of other firms based in Italy.

20.5 Financial analysis and the capital market

The relevance of financial disclosures, and corporate earnings in particular, varies from one stock market to another (Alford *et al.*, 1993; Saudagaran and Meek, 1997). In Europe, the harmonization process of the 1980s did little to iron out these differences. Research by Joos and Lang (1994) considered the effect of the accounting Directives on the relationship between earnings and stock prices, investigating other indicators as well, such as Return on Equity, the Price to Earnings multiple and the Book to Market ratio. Changes in the accounting environment seem to have had a minimal effect in capital markets at the time, as these authors report no evidence of convergence in the value-relevance of earnings and other accounting numbers after the implementation of the Directives into national legislation.

In the case of German firms, the investment analysts' association (DVFA) attempted to address these shortcomings by devising a formula to arrive at adjusted profit figures for use in market valuation. Research by Pope and Rees (1992) and by Harris *et al.* (1994) found that DVFA adjustments significantly increased the explanatory power of earnings in the period following the changes in German accounting law. In a study of London-based analysts, Miles and Nobes (1998) report on the adjustments that are made for international accounting differences. They find that adjustments are often not made for many important differences, even though, as noted in Section 20.3, the regular publication of reconciliations to IFRS and US GAAP provides more detailed information in this respect.

An important task undertaken by the financial analyst is to provide investors not only with 'superior' earnings per share (EPS) figures when the quality of reported figures is deemed to be low, but also with estimates of *future* EPS. For example, the forecasts made by a number of different analysts regarding the earnings of Nokia are summarized in Figure 20.5, which shows the average estimates given by IBES both for the year ahead (FY1) and two years ahead (FY2). A comparison with the average

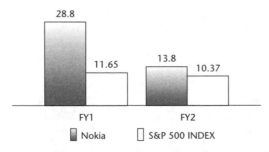

Figure 20.5 Analysts' earnings forecasts, Nokia

forward earnings for the S&P 500 firms is also shown. It is sometimes argued that analysts' forecast errors (i.e. the difference between the forecasted earnings and the actual earnings that are reported at a later date) are too large for investors to rely on analysts' predictions. The evidence suggests, however, that analysts are able to provide estimates of future EPS that can assist in market valuation. Such forecasting requires a sense of where a business and its competitors are going, and the results of a survey carried out by Moyes *et al.* (2001) indicate international differences in the relative importance of the various factors taken into account. These authors point to a more international focus by the UK analysts and a greater reliance on guidance from management in the United States, but clearly the accuracy with which analysts are able to forecast EPS will also be affected by a number of other issues, as discussed below.

Forecasting will be more difficult when earnings are volatile, and the behaviour of reported EPS will also be influenced by accounting practices that either smooth or exaggerate the underlying earnings behaviour. Figure 20.6 shows how the earnings of European firms are at their most volatile in Italy and at their least volatile in the Netherlands. Research by Capstaff *et al.* (2001) demonstrates that analysts' earnings forecasts generally outperform naïve forecasts but are typically optimistic and increasingly inaccurate the longer the forecast horizon. These researchers also find that analysts' forecasts are at their best for firms in the Netherlands and least successful in the case of firms in Italy. This is consistent with the volatility ranking in Figure 20.6.

The frequency and timing of financial disclosure also affect analysts' forecasts. Disclosure takes different forms, not only the legally required annual report but also additional mandatory disclosures to the capital market, interim reports for investors and other announcements such as preliminary earnings statements. As mentioned

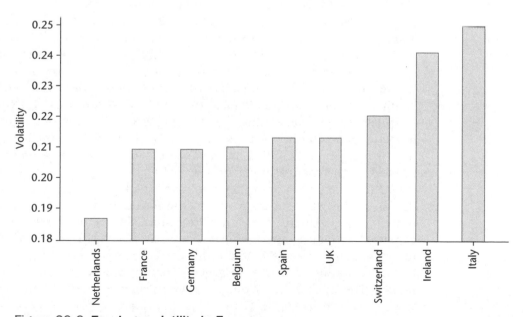

Figure 20.6 **Earnings volatility in Europe**

previously, analyst pressure encourages more frequent and timely disclosure. For instance, for large international companies, Frost and Pownall (1994) document a 39-day average reporting lag between the year end and the report release date in the United States, and a 48-day lag in the United Kingdom. On the other hand, some firms will report with considerable delay in accordance with the maximum time limit allowed. For annual reporting, these limits vary considerably – up to nine months in Germany.

Forecasting accuracy has also been found to vary with the complexity of the task (Hope, 2003). In particular, in countries where there is strong enforcement of accounting standards, which encourages managers to follow the prescribed rules, this seems to reduce analysts' uncertainty, which in turn leads to more accurate forecasts. Finally, differences between local and international accounting standards are also known to be related to the accuracy of analyst earnings forecasts, and a study by Ashbaugh and Pincus (2001) shows that the adoption of IFRS is associated with a reduction in these prediction errors.

It is important to recognize that value relevance is likely to be conditional on institutional conditions in the jurisdictions involved. In this context, Ali and Hwang (2000) ask whether the usual culprits will cause financial disclosures to be less relevant to investors. Is the financial system bank-oriented, for instance? Is the government the source of accounting rules and regulations? Is the accounting system aligned with taxation? A useful approach in this respect is to consider the incentives related to these institutional factors and how these might predictably affect accounting income. For example, when governments establish and enforce national accounting standards, this is typically with representation from business associations, banks and employee organizations. At the firm level, this is reflected in stakeholder governance. Ball *et al.* (2000) contrast stakeholder and shareholder governance. Under the former, where payouts to stakeholders are likely to be more closely linked to accounting income than otherwise, managers will have greater discretion in deciding when gains and losses will be incorporated in accounting income, and direct communication with insider groups should solve the information asymmetry between managers and stakeholders. In contrast, under a shareholder governance model, where greater reliance is placed on external monitoring in the capital market, there will be more demand for *timely* public disclosure, and *conservative* earnings computation should make managers more immediately accountable.

Timeliness and conservatism are key properties of accounting numbers that differ between accounting regimes (Pope and Walker, 1999). Timeliness is the extent to which current accounting income incorporates economic income, which can be proxied by the change in market value of equity. Conservatism is defined as the extent to which losses are recognized more quickly than gains, i.e. that unrealized decreases in asset value are written off immediately whereas unrealized gains are not recognized. Figure 20.7 shows the relationship between market price changes expressed as returns and earnings expressed as an earnings yield, based on the results in Ball *et al.* (2000). Accounting conservatism is indicated by a steeper slope for bad news in the market (a negative return) relative to good news (a positive return). The situation in Germany is of particular interest. It has been widely presumed that accounting in Germany is particularly conservative because increases in asset values cannot be written into the financial statements. Also, in the past,

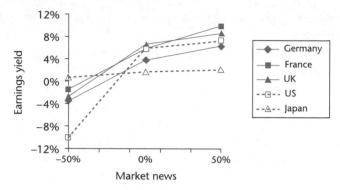

Figure 20.7 **Accounting conservatism and timeliness**

provisioning has provided ample discretion to smooth earnings by reducing income in good years (Gray, 1980). However, Germany should no longer be characterized as an extremely conservative regime in this market-based analysis.

In Japan, another typical insider system, accounting is neither timely nor conservative. Earnings do not incorporate economic income at all, the negative and positive slopes being close to zero. At the other extreme, in the United States (a typical outsider system), accounting is seen to be more timely and the most conservative.

In conclusion, international comparison of financial statement information requires a good understanding of the way in which judicial systems, securities laws and ownership structures can create incentives that influence the managers of firms in the way they draw up their financial statements, and lead to contracting and monitoring demand for credible accounting information. In this context, Bushman and Piotroski (2005) show that firms in countries with high quality judicial systems reflect bad news in reported earnings faster than firms in countries with low quality judicial systems, that strong public enforcement of securities law discourages optimism by slowing recognition of good news in earnings, and that diffuse equity holding that separates the ownership of capital from the management of capital is also consistent with more conservative earnings. However, as firms increasingly exploit the integrated global market, these national accounting differences tend to have less effect (Raonic *et al.*, 2004). But the differences still exist: foreign firms that cross-list in the USA still show more evidence of earnings management, and less evidence of the timely recognition of losses than their counterparts in the USA (Lang *et al.*, 2003).

SUMMARY

- Proper account must be taken in international financial analysis of the effects of the local operating environment on a company's reported results. Somehow or other, the analyst needs to be able to allow for the effects that are attributable to the company's country (or countries) of operations in assessing the residual performance or structure of the company itself.

- It is also necessary to allow for the differences in accounting method, but it has been shown that to some extent the latter may well be a function of, and will even interact with, the legal, social and financial systems within which a company operates.

● Some companies provide information that might assist the foreign user of accounts to understand the particularities of national accounting rules and tax legislation, and other matters such as the constraints of local financing.

● Financial analysts can take account of these matters by assessing a company's performance and structure by reference to an appropriate peer group, recognizing that forecasting accuracy and market valuation are greatly influenced by international accounting differences.

References

Alford, A., Jones, J., Leftwich, R. and Zmijewski, M. (1993) 'The relative informativeness of accounting disclosures in different countries', *Journal of Accounting Research*, Vol. 31 (Supplement), pp. 183–223.

Ali, A. and Hwang, L.S. (2000) 'Country-specific factors related to financial reporting and the value relevance of accounting data', *Journal of Accounting Research*, Vol. 38, No. 1, pp. 1–22.

Amir, E., Harris, T. and Venuti, E.K. (1993) 'A comparison of the value-relevance of US versus non-US GAAP accounting measures using Form 20-F reconciliations', *Journal of Accounting Research*, Supplement.

Ashbaugh, H. (2001) 'Non-US firms' accounting standard choices', *Journal of Accounting and Public Policy*, Vol. 20, No. 2, pp. 129–53.

Ashbaugh, H. and Pincus, M. (2001), 'Domestic accounting standards, international accounting standards and the predictability of earnings', *Journal of Accounting Research*, Vol. 39, No. 3, pp. 417–34.

Ball, R., Kothari, S.P. and Robin, A. (2000) 'The effect of international institutional factors on properties of accounting earnings', *Journal of Accounting and Economics*, Vol. 29, No. 1, pp. 1–51.

Barth, M. and Clinch, G. (1996) 'International accounting differences and their relation to share prices', *Contemporary Accounting Research*, No. 1.

Bushman, R. and Piotroski, J. (2005), 'Financial reporting incentives for conservative accounting: the influence of legal and political institutions', *Journal of Accounting and Economics*, forthcoming.

Capstaff, J., Paudyal, K. and Rees, W. (2001) 'A comparative analysis of earnings forecasts in Europe', *Journal of Business Finance and Accounting*, Vol. 28, No. 5–6, pp. 531–62.

Chang, L.S., Most, K.S. and Brain, C.W. (1983) 'The utility of annual reports: an international study', *Journal of International Business Studies*, Spring/Summer, pp. 63–84.

Choi, F.D.S. and Levich, R.M. (1990) *The Capital Market Effects of International Accounting Diversity*, Dow Jones Irwin, IL.

Choi, F.D.S., Hino, H., Sang, K.M., Sang, O.N., Ujiie, J. and Stonehill, A.I. (1983) 'Analyzing foreign financial statements: the use and misuse of international ratio analysis', *Journal of International Business Studies*, Spring/Summer, pp. 113–31.

Cooke, T.E. (1989) 'Voluntary corporate disclosure by Swedish companies', *Journal of International Financial Management*, Summer, pp. 171–95.

Ewert, R., and Wagenhofer, A. (2005), 'Economic effects of tightening accounting standards to restrict earnings management'. *Accounting Review*, October.

Frost, C. and Pownall, G. (1994) 'Accounting disclosure practices in the United States and the United Kingdom', *Journal of Accounting Research*, Vol. 32, No. 1, pp. 75–102.

Gibson, C.H. (1980) 'The need for disclosure of uniform financial ratios', *Journal of Accountancy*, May, pp. 78–84.

Gray, S.J. (1980) 'The impact of international accounting differences from a security-analysis perspective', *Journal of Accounting Research*, Spring, pp. 64–76.

Gray, S.J., Meek, G.K. and Roberts, C.B. (1995) 'International capital market pressures and voluntary annual report disclosures by US and UK multinationals', *Journal of International Financial Management and Accounting*, Vol. 6, No. 1.

Harris, T.S., Lang, M. and Möller, H.P. (1994) 'The value relevance of German accounting measures – an empirical analysis', *Journal of Accounting Research*, Vol. 32, No. 2, pp. 187–209.

Harris, M.S. and Muller, K.A. (1999) 'The market valuation of IAS versus US-GAAP accounting measures using Form 20-F reconciliations', *Journal of Accounting and Economics*, Vol. 26, No. 1–3, pp. 285–312.

Hope, O. (2004) 'Variations in the financial reporting environment and earnings forecasting', *Journal of International Financial Management and Accounting*, Vol. 15, No. 1, pp. 22–.

Joos, P. and Lang, M. (1994) 'The effects of accounting diversity: evidence from the European Union', *Journal of Accounting Research*, Vol. 32, Supplement, pp. 141–75.

Lang, M., Raedy, J. and M. Yetman (2003), 'How representative are firms that are cross-listed in the United States? An analysis of accounting quality', *Journal of Accounting Research*, Vol. 41, No. 2, pp. 363–86.

Leuz, C., Nanda, D. and Wysocki, P.D. (2003), 'Earnings management and investor protection: an international comparison', *Journal of Financial Economics,* Vol. 69, pp. 505–27.

McLeay, S.J. (1986) 'The ratio of means, the mean of ratios and other benchmarks: an examination of characteristic financial ratios in the French corporate sector', *Finance – the Journal of the French Finance Association*, Vol. 7, No. 1, pp. 75–93.

McLeay, S.J. and Fieldsend, S. (1987) 'Sector and size effects in ratio analysis – an indirect test of ratio proportionality', *Accounting and Business Research*, Spring, pp. 133–40.

McLeay, S.J. and Trigueiros, D. (2002) 'Proportionate growth and the theoretical foundations of financial ratios', *Abacus*, Vol. 38, No. 3, pp. 297–316.

Miles, S. and Nobes, C.W. (1998) 'The use of foreign accounting data in UK financial institutions', *Journal of Business Finance and Accounting*, April/May, pp. 309–28.

Moyes G.D., Saadouni B., Simon J. and Williams, P.A. (2001) 'A comparison of factors affecting UK and US analyst forecast revisions', *International Journal of Accounting*, Vol. 36, No. 1, pp. 47–63.

Norton, J. (1995) 'The impact of financial accounting practices on the measurement of profit and equity: Australia versus the United States', *Abacus*, September.

Pinto, J.A. (2001) 'Foreign currency translation adjustments as predictors of earning changes', *Journal of International Accounting, Auditing and Taxation*, Vol. 10, No. 1, pp. 51–69.

Pope, P.F. and Rees, W. (1992) 'International differences in GAAP and the pricing of earnings', *Journal of International Financial Management and Accounting*, No. 3.

Pope, P. and Walker, M. (1999) 'International differences in the timeliness, conservatism, and classification of earnings', *Journal of Accounting Research*, Vol. 37, Supplement, pp. 53–88.

Saudagaran, S.M. and Meek, G.K. (1997) 'A review of research on the relationship between international capital markets and financial reporting in multinational firms', *Journal of Accounting Literature*, Vol. 16, pp. 127–59.

Raonic, I., McLeay, S. and Asimakopoulos, I. (2004), 'The timeliness of income recognition by European companies: An analysis of institutional and market complexity'. *Journal of Business, Finance and Accounting*, Vol. 31, Nos. 1 & 2, pp. 115–48.

Street, D.L. and Bryant, S.M. (2000) 'Disclosure level and compliance with IASs: A comparison of companies with and without US listings and filings', *International Journal of Accounting*, Vol. 35, No. 3, pp. 305–29.

Street, D.L., Nichols, N.B. and Gray, S.J. (2000) 'Assessing the acceptability of international accounting standards in the US: an empirical study of the materiality of US GAAP reconciliations by non-US companies complying with IASC standards', *International Journal of Accounting*, Vol. 35, No. 1, pp. 27–63.

Weetman, P. and Gray, S.J. (1991) 'A comparative international analysis of the impact of accounting principles on profits: the USA versus the UK, Sweden and the Netherlands', *Accounting and Business Research*, Autumn, pp. 363–79.

Weetman, P., Jones, E.A.E., Adams, C.A. and Gray, S.J. (1998) 'Profit measurement and UK accounting standards: a case of increasing disharmony in relation to US GAAP and IASs', *Accounting and Business Research*, Summer.

Whittington, M. (2000) 'Problems in comparing financial performance across international boundaries: a case study approach', *International Journal of Accounting*, Vol. 35, No. 3, pp. 399–413.

Useful websites

Fortune Global 500	http://money.cnn.com/magazines/fortune/global500
Share prices, company information and analyst recommendations	http://finance.yahoo.com
Online annual reports and company home pages	www.irin.com/cgi-bin/main.cgi
Major stock exchanges	www.tdd.lt/slnews/Stock_Exchanges/Stock.Exchanges.html
Currency conversion	www.oanda.com/convert/classic

QUESTIONS

Suggested answers to the asterisked questions are given at the end of the book.

20.1∗ In an unharmonized world, how do preparers and users of annual financial statements of listed companies cope with international differences?

20.2∗ What are the major difficulties met by analysts when trying to compare companies' annual reports internationally? Which areas of financial reporting could be most usefully improved to aid such analysis?

20.3 'The best thing for users of annual accounts is to steer clear of foreign companies.' Discuss.

20.4 Into what languages do multinational companies translate their annual reports? Why?

20.5 Two approaches to measuring conservatism are discussed in the chapter: the comparison of profit figures under different GAAPs; and asymmetric recognition of good and bad news. What are the advantages and disadvantages of each approach?

20.6 Identify and discuss cultural and institutional factors which an analyst will have to consider before being able to isolate and examine the 'residual' behaviour attributable to a company's policies and characteristics.

20.7 Is worldwide application of IFRS going to solve the problems of international financial analysis?

21 International auditing

Jan Buisman and Graham Gilmour[1]

OBJECTIVES

After reading this chapter, you should be able to:

- explain why and how auditing has been internationalized, with particular reference to the role of MNEs, international capital markets, international accounting firms and harmonization;

- explain why and how IFAC has become the principal setter of international standards on auditing (ISAs);

- discuss the role of ethics, technical standards and quality control in international auditing;

- describe the stages of the international audit process;

- discuss the audit expectations gap in an international context.

---

[1] The first version of this chapter in an earlier edition was co-authored by Jan Klaassen of the Free University of Amsterdam.

21.1 Introduction

This chapter's title, 'international auditing', seems new as a phrase. The chapter explains that auditing now really is international. 'Auditing' as an activity was defined by the American Accounting Association's Committee on Basic Auditing Concepts in *A Statement of Basic Auditing Concepts*, published in 1973, as:

> a systematic process of objectively obtaining and evaluating evidence regarding assertions about economic actions and events to ascertain the degree of correspondence between those assertions and established criteria and communicating the results to interested users.

The assertions about economic actions and events are normally specified as accounting data, stored in information systems, and are used to produce financial reports. Such data are the representations of economic actions, for example transactions or events such as changes in market prices.

Auditing is a systematic process, which involves steps such as:

- acceptance and defining the terms of engagement;
- planning and risk assessment;
- gathering evidence; and
- reporting.

The process outlined above could be used for a much wider variety of engagements, for example, reporting on non-financial information. There are currently many projects around the world looking at how companies report on types of non-financial information, and how auditors can provide attestation or assurance services on that information. In the context of this chapter, however, we will discuss only the audits of financial statements.

Public accountants or external auditors are those who independently perform audits of financial statements in order to be able to express an opinion on whether those financial statements provide a true and fair view (or are fairly presented) and are drawn up in accordance with the applicable financial reporting framework. External auditors generally evaluate financial statements for external stakeholders, such as investors and creditors. However, in some countries the functions of external auditors can be somewhat different from their functions in others. As mentioned in Chapter 8, in the United States, as well as in most other Anglo-Saxon countries, the opinion of the external independent auditor is included with the published financial statements to add credibility to the financial statements for investors and creditors. As indicated for Germany in Chapter 13, financial reporting for legal purposes and tax reporting are closely connected; as a consequence, the audit in Germany has historically been focused more on legal acceptability and acceptability for tax purposes than on true and fair presentation for the benefit of external stakeholders. A suggestion that the comparison between Anglo-Saxon countries and Germany is not so stark as is often presented is made by Vieten (1995).

The international aspect of auditing refers to the harmonization of auditing standards and rules across countries as well as referring to the practice of auditing, based on one or more set of auditing rules, of the financial information prepared by multinational corporations.

When companies confined their activities within national borders and shareholders of a company were largely domiciled in the country of operations, auditing philosophies and techniques were determined by auditors in a national context and by the actions of national accountancy bodies building their own traditions. Consequently the role of auditors and their responsibilities towards stakeholders of a company – i.e. shareholders, investors, management and other interested parties – developed within the context of societal developments of each individual country. These influences are also reflected in the education process of auditors. In certain countries, prospective auditors received their education mainly in the economics or business departments of universities, while in others a large part of the auditors' education took place by way of on-the-job training supported by formal training in special educational institutions.

In addition, as a result of the different historical purposes of financial reporting between countries, the auditing profession historically played different roles in relation to company management, banks and investors, and the tax authorities. In this chapter we deal only with the activity of independent auditing for the purpose of expressing an opinion to shareholders on published financial reports of companies. Other types of auditing, for example tax auditing, internal auditing, and auditing within governmental organizations, remain outside the scope of this chapter.

The internationalization of auditing started when multinational enterprises began preparing consolidated financial statements. Such statements normally needed to be based on one set of accounting principles. In order to achieve this, a head office had to instruct subsidiaries on the accounting principles to be applied. This also induced the auditors of the parent company to set rules to ensure the quality of the subsidiaries' audits. After some time, a need became apparent for the international auditing profession to harmonize the working methods of auditors in different countries and to develop international auditing rules.

Factors which have contributed to the internationalization of auditing have included:

- the emergence of multinational enterprises;
- the increasing internationalization of capital markets;
- the growth of international accounting firms, with common approaches to audit methodology, training and quality review;
- the convergence around common international frameworks for accounting and audit.

In the following section we will discuss these factors. Section 21.3 deals with the role of international bodies including the International Federation of Accountants (IFAC) in the promulgation of international auditing standards. Section 21.4 describes in more detail the international audit process.

21.2   Reasons for the internationalization of auditing

21.2.1   The role of multinational enterprises

The emergence of multinational enterprises has to a large extent triggered the internationalization of auditing. First, multinational enterprises deal with foreign operations and these need to be audited. Generally, when multinational enterprises prepare consolidated financial statements, they will need audits of those statements on the basis of the rules of the home country of the multinational enterprises.

So, a headquarters will require that the auditors set certain standards for the quality of the audit in foreign countries. This alerts the auditors of the parent company to provide instructions to auditors in the countries where the subsidiaries are located concerning the requirements for the audit in order for them to be able to report to top management on a worldwide basis and to accept the responsibilities for the audit and to report on the truth and fairness of the consolidated financial statements. Not only have the auditors a stake in the quality of local audits, which are performed on the accounts of subsidiaries of the multinational corporations, but also central corporate management wants to be sure that the local audits are sufficient to provide credibility to the information from the local management of subsidiaries. This requires local auditors to perform audits in such a way that these are satisfactory to central management and to the auditor of the parent company. These developments led to the introduction of new auditing techniques in certain countries and new methods of communication with local and central management.

The emergence of multinational corporations has also triggered developments in the roles of audit firms and has led to international mergers among firms, partly in order to enable them to remain independent from the multinational corporations. Generally, the audit profession believes that the size of audited companies should not be allowed to become a threat to audit independence. Furthermore, very large companies can only be properly served by large accounting firms, with the appropriate technical and geographical capabilities.

In this respect it is important to note that accounting firms have tried to continue to serve their multinational clients as they have grown and extended their activities to foreign countries. Some firms have done this by establishing offices in the countries where their major clients are located; Post *et al.* (1998) examine this process for the large Dutch audit firms. Other firms have merged with foreign audit firms in order to maintain their ability to serve their clients worldwide. In both cases this has enabled the audit firms to propose to their multinational clients that one audit firm could perform all the audit work in all or most of the countries where the multinational corporation is located. This has led to centralization of certain decisions on the extent and depth of the audit worldwide and on the priorities to be set (for instance, materiality levels to be used, which may result in limited reviews to be performed on minor subsidiaries, etc.). Also, discussions on audit fees worldwide are conducted in the context of using the services of one audit firm throughout the world.

In addition to the need for audits for consolidation purposes, the need remains for statutory audits of local subsidiaries. In such cases, the audit process required for the statutory audit will be combined with that needed for consolidation purposes. Since the harmonization of accounting has not yet reached the state that one set of accounting principles could also be used to prepare statutory accounts in all the countries where a multinational company operates, national accounting rules often prevail for statutory audits. So, in many cases where the audit process has been internationalized, this takes place in conjunction with maintaining the practice of applying national rules for financial reporting for the statutory accounts of local companies.

21.2.2 Demand for international auditing from international capital markets

The demand for international audits can also be explained to a certain extent from the point of view of users of financial statements of those companies for which financing is arranged on international capital markets. For investors in international capital markets, the audit report and the quality of the audit work done are important to justify the credibility of the financial statements and other financial information that are used as an input to investment and credit decisions.

In international capital markets, investors and creditors are faced with capital demands from foreign companies whose published financial statements are drawn up in accordance with foreign laws and regulations. To some extent additional disclosures satisfy the need for comparable information. In some markets, regulators require a lot of additional information. In order to be able to rely on financial information reported by foreign companies, not only is the extent of disclosure important but so also is the quality of the audit. As a consequence, from the point of view of the regulators of capital markets and of investors in foreign equity and debt instruments, it is important that the significance of the audit report and the quality of the audit performed are in accordance with the expectations of the markets where the capital is raised. In order to achieve such a quality, the foreign auditors should be familiar with the auditing and reporting requirements of the country where the foreign capital market is located and should meet those requirements when auditing financial statements to be filed abroad. Also, the wording of the audit report is important for the effective communication of the auditor's opinion. There have been differences between auditors' opinions among countries, taking into account the differences in emphasis on 'true and fair view' (Nobes, 1993) and the importance attached to financial statements being in accordance with laws and regulations. In order to communicate properly in international capital markets, there is a need for a more or less uniform international set of wordings to characterize the auditors' opinions expressed in the audit reports.

The International Organization of Securities Commissions (IOSCO) is taking an interest in removing barriers for international capital markets (see Chapter 4). It has close consultations with the IFAC concerning international standards on auditing, to achieve uniform quality levels of audits and to promote effective international communication through audit reports. As noted in Section 21.3, IOSCO is monitoring the development of International Standards on Auditing to determine whether these should be endorsed for use for cross-border listing purposes.

21.2.3 The role of international audit firms

Internationalization of auditing has largely taken place within international audit firms. During the past few decades many local audit firms have merged into

Table 21.1 **Growth and mergers of large international auditing firms (revenues in US $m)**

Name	1992		2000		2006	
	World	US	World	US	World	US
PricewaterhouseCoopers			19,566	8,299	21,986	6,922
(formerly Coopers & Lybrand	5,350	1,557				
and Price Waterhouse)	3,761	1,370				
Arthur Andersen	5,577	2,680	8,400	3,600	–	–
Ernst & Young (formerly Arthur						
Young and Ernst & Whinney)	5,701	2,281	9,200	4,271	18,359	6,890
KPMG (formerly Peat Marwick						
and Klynveld Main Goerdeler)	6,153	1,820	13,500	4,724	16,880	4,802
Deloitte (formerly Deloitte Haskins						
& Sells and Touche Ross)	4,800	1,955	12,508	5,838	20,000	8,769

Sources: Compiled from *International Accounting Bulletin*, December 1992, December 2000, February 2007; *Accountancy* June 2007 (some figures are estimated). Andersen and Ernst & Young revenue figures for 2000 reflect the disposal of the consulting parts of those firms, otherwise figures would have been higher. No revenue figures are presented for Andersen for the final period because of the cessation of the business in 2002. PwC figures for 2006 exclude revenues from PwC Consulting following the disposal of that part of the firm.

international groups, as shown in Table 21.1. There were four very big mergers between international audit firms during the 1980s and 1990s, resulting in the emergence of five (now four) very large international firms in the marketplace. (The revenue figures in the table do not exhibit a uniform growing trend owing to the recent disposal by some firms of their consulting practices.)

The most important international audit firms have grown from their home base, either in the United Kingdom or the United States; however, the firms vary in character. This is clear from their approaches to activities as well as from their organizational forms. Their modes of operations have historically varied from a centralized approach (Andersen) to a rather decentralized approach (KPMG). However, increasingly, a unified approach is applied for international work. In a centralized firm many functions are executed at the central level, whereas in the decentralized firm it is mainly marketing strategy decisions and certain technical functions that are centralized.

As far as their organizational form is concerned, most large international firms operate as an international network of member firms, often sharing common technical and operating standards, methodologies, training and technology. However, each national member firm is a separate and independent legal entity.

The international character of all the big audit firms is evident from:

● an international approach to auditing;

● international quality control systems;

● product developments;

● international marketing and communication strategies.

The international approach to auditing generally takes the form of a single audit methodology, in which different steps are narrowly defined and which contains detailed prescriptions for the approach to auditing; for instance, descriptions of the planning process, the process of evaluating risks, the approach to testing (e.g. substantive testing – reliance on documents for the validation of assertions – or reliance on systems). A description of the process of reporting and communication of the outcomes of the audit is also part of such an international audit process.

The international process of auditing serves two main purposes:

1 Multinational clients are assured that, all over the world, members of the audit firm will apply a common set of policies and procedures to ensure the quality of the audit.

2 Consistency of the main elements of the audit process on an international scale enables the firms to increase the efficiency and effectiveness of the audit process worldwide. A common audit approach worldwide also enables easy communication on technical issues, such as the level of materiality to be taken into account in certain audits.

Through the use of an international approach to auditing, some cost savings can be achieved because the audit programme can be tailor-made on an international scale, which will prevent the level of detail applied in auditing certain subsidiaries from not being in accordance with the international approach. However, to the extent that local statutory audits are mandatory, and to the extent that regulation differs in each of the territories in which the audited company has major operations or in which it raises capital, such cost savings can be very limited.

One other advantage of internationalization is that audit firms can more easily exchange personnel between countries than if a different methodology were applied in each country, and this enhances efficiency. Furthermore, an international approach can help the auditor to set priorities concerning the level of attention paid to certain risks worldwide.

Although the approach to the audit may be internationalized within audit firms when auditing multinational clients, this is not yet the case for accounting. Of course, a multinational client has to apply accounting rules which are valid in the country in which the parent company is located. For consolidation purposes, all subsidiaries have to comply with the rules issued by the parent company concerning valuation and disclosure. However, most subsidiaries also have to prepare local financial statements applying local accounting principles.

In order to perform international audits, sufficient people within local offices of the international accounting firms have to be familiar with accounting rules applied in certain foreign countries. For example, to audit foreign subsidiaries of US multinational enterprises, the US generally accepted accounting principles (GAAP) are used by local audit offices of the big accounting firms in many countries. A significant number of multinational companies are now applying IFRS, partly as a result of the requirement for all EU listed companies to prepare their consolidated accounts in accordance with IFRS from 2005. The major accounting firms have therefore developed programmes to train their staff in these internationally used accounting frameworks.

International product development is an important tool for international audit firms. Apart from the audit process, the firms develop software for international use and establish international networks and methodologies, for example, to be able to participate in advising clients on listings on international stock exchanges, and to advise on international mergers and acquisitions.

An important characteristic of the internationalization of auditing is the establishment of international quality control criteria within the big international accounting firms. Quality control takes place at three levels: client engagements, offices and each individual country. Through the systems of quality control, an international group of firms can establish that its national member firms apply proper procedures to ensure work of a high quality. As discussed in Section 21.4.4, the quality measures taken by the large firms have now been formalized in the International Standards on Quality Control (ISCQ). In addition to review of work done for certain audits, other measures are taken to improve the quality of the audits in certain countries. One of the quality control measures is to station expatriate personnel in certain countries to enable parent companies and their auditors to communicate effectively on the audit of local subsidiaries.

Another important aspect of international quality control is the need for international education of the technical personnel of the audit firms. In order properly to introduce new techniques and new support systems, and also to guarantee a certain level of familiarity with the accounting rules of multinational clients, much internal education and training is given. Most of it is done on an international scale since this enables companies to achieve economies.

A new body, the Forum of Firms, was launched in 2001 as a significant step by IFAC and the large firms to increase the contribution of the firms to the development of professional standards and to give greater emphasis to audit quality. Member firms need to observe the Forum's membership obligations which, with respect to transnational audits, commit firms to:

- maintain appropriate quality control standards in accordance with International Standards on Quality Control issued by the International Auditing and Assurance Board (IAASB) in addition to relevant national quality control standards; and conduct, to the extent not prohibited by national legislation, regular globally co-ordinated internal quality assurance reviews;

- have policies and methodologies for the conduct of such audits that are based, to the extent practicable, on ISAs;

- have policies and methodologies which conform to the IFAC Code of Ethics for Professional Accountants and national codes of ethics.

The abovementioned aspects clearly show that it is generally advantageous for multinational enterprises to hire international audit firms for their audits. Table 21.2 shows the market share in 2004, in terms of numbers of audits, of the Big-4 accounting firms. The relative strength of the Big-4 among countries is shown in Table 21.3, in which the largest firms in certain countries are indicated by an asterisk.

Table 21.2 **Audit market share (%) based on number of appointments to major companies held by Big-4 in selected countries, 2004**

	USA	Japan	UK	Germany	France
PwC	34	30	33	42	17
KPMG	17	13	23	38	11
Deloitte	22	23	23	6	17
EY	27	29	15	5	28
Others	0	5	6	9	27

Source: Adapted from FT Global 500, FT Euro 500, FT UK 500.

Table 21.3 **Two largest firms in selected countries, 2004, based on revenues**

	USA	France	Germany	Australia	Japan	Canada
PwC		✓	✓	✓		
KPMG			✓		✓	✓
Deloitte	✓				✓	✓
EY	✓	✓		✓		

Source: Compiled from *International Accounting Bulletin*.

21.3 Promulgating international standards

21.3.1 Introduction

A common requirement of international audits is that the auditor of a group expresses an opinion on the consolidated or group financial statements, thus accepting responsibility for the audit of all the material components of those group financial statements.

In order to be able to accept such responsibility, the group auditor has to ensure that all of the detailed work has been performed at a level of quality sufficient to give the same level of assurance for each part as is required for the whole of the group. In general this can be achieved in three ways:

1 The group auditor gives detailed instructions to the other auditors on the audit procedures to be performed.

2 The group auditor requires the other auditors to adhere to the auditing standards applicable to the group auditor (e.g. requiring that all audits are performed in accordance with International Standards on Auditing).

3 The group auditor requires that all of the audit work is performed on the basis of a set of auditing principles and procedures that is common to all the auditors (e.g. the audit manual of the international firm to which they all belong).

Because an international group consists of legal entities in various countries, the financial statements of each component of the group may have to be audited both in accordance with the local regulations prevailing in the country of registration and in accordance with any requirements of the group auditor. It is self-evident that it would be in the interest of all concerned if there were no such differences in audit requirements. This is the reason for various attempts to achieve harmonized auditing standards on a worldwide scale.

21.3.2 International standard-setters

Setting standards at an international level requires a body that has the authority to do so. Such supranational bodies are created by governments or by regional or international organizations created within the accountancy profession itself. The most significant body involved in international audit standard-setting is the International Federation of Accountants.

International Federation of Accountants

The International Federation of Accountants was founded in 1977. IFAC is a non-profit, non-governmental and non-political organization of accountancy bodies. Membership is open to accountancy bodies recognized by law or consensus within their countries as being substantial national organizations of good standing within the accountancy profession. At present over 150 accountancy bodies in more than 100 countries are members of IFAC. The broad mission of IFAC is 'to strengthen the worldwide accountancy profession and contribute to the development of strong international economies by establishing and promoting adherence to high-quality professional standards, furthering the international convergence of such standards and speaking out on public interest issues where the profession's expertise is most relevant'.

IFAC's Council consists of one representative from each member body. The Council, which convenes once a year, elects the Board. The Board, comprising representatives from 15 countries, has the responsibility for implementing the work programme of IFAC, which is carried out by smaller working groups or committees. IFAC has a number of standing committees, including Education, Ethics, International Auditing and Assurance Standards, and Public Sector.

The International Auditing and Assurance Standards Board (IAASB), which succeeded the International Auditing Practices Committee (IAPC) in 2002, is the most significant of the committees. It develops pronouncements on auditing and reporting practices. In contrast to other committees, IAASB has the authority to issue pronouncements without the approval of the Board. The due process includes the issue of exposure drafts, which allows the public – including investors, regulators, national accountancy bodies and other stakeholders – a period in which to comment on them. Both the exposure drafts and the final pronouncements require the affirmative vote of at least two-thirds of the members. A list of International Standards on Auditing (ISAs) current as at June 2007 is shown in Table 21.4. IAASB also issues standards on review engagements (ISREs), assurance engagements other than audits or reviews of historical financial information (ISAEs) and other related services (ISRSs).

Table 21.4 International Standards on Auditing

Subject matter numbers and ISA document title

200–299	**General Principles and Responsibilities**
200	Objective and General Principles Governing an Audit of Financial Statements
210	Terms of Audit Engagements
220	Quality Control for Audits of Historical Financial Information
230	Audit Documentation
240	The Auditor's Responsibility to Consider Fraud in an Audit of Financial Statements
250	Consideration of Laws and Regulations in an Audit of Financial Statements
260	Communications of Audit Matters with Those Charged with Governance
300–499	**Risk Assessment and Response to Assessed Risks**
300	Planning an Audit of Financial Statements
315	Understanding the Entity and its Environment and Assessing the Risks of Material Misstatement
320	Audit Materiality
330	The Auditor's Procedures in Response to Assessed Risks
402	Audit Considerations Relating to Entities Using Service Organizations
500–599	**Audit Evidence**
500	Audit Evidence
501	Audit Evidence – Additional Considerations for Specific Items
505	External Confirmations
510	Initial Engagements – Opening Balances
520	Analytical Procedures
530	Audit Sampling and Other Means of Testing
540	Audit of Accounting Estimates
545	Auditing Fair Value Measurements and Disclosures
550	Related Parties
560	Subsequent Events
570	Going Concern
580	Management Representations
600–699	**Using the Work of Others**
600	Using the Work of Another Auditor
610	Considering the Work of Internal Auditing
620	Using the Work of an Expert
700–799	**Audit Conclusions and Reporting**
700	The Independent Auditor's Report on a Complete Set of General Purpose Financial Statements
701	Modifications to the Independent Auditor's Report
710	Comparatives
720	Other Information in Documents Containing Audited Financial Statements
800–899	**Specialized Areas**
800	The Independent Auditor's Report on Special Purpose Audit Engagements

Following a review in 2001 of the structure, responsibilities and due process of the former body, the IAPC, the membership of IAASB draws on a wider range of experience. The 18-person board comprises 10 members nominated by IFAC's member professional bodies, five nominated by the large firms through the Forum of Firms, and three public interest members. There are plans to further increase the proportion of public interest members on the board, with a consequent reduction in the number of members from the profession, though the Board will continue to have a significant degree of practitioner input. The review also resulted in more resources being made available for standards development – in particular the significant effort to update the whole suite of ISAs under the 'Clarity' project (see below), which was seen as necessary if ISAs are to be endorsed by IOSCO and the European Commission.

In addition to the audit standards, IAASB issues authoritative guidance on specific industry and audit issues known as International Audit Practice Statements (IAPSs). These include guidance on auditing banks and small enterprises. Important recent practice statements have included IAPS 1012 on 'Auditing Derivative Financial Instruments' and IAPS 1014 on reporting on IFRS financial statements.

Although harmonization of standards is easily achieved if standards are set at the lowest common denominator, this is not the policy of IFAC. The standards and guidance are set at the level that experienced accountants view as the best that should be achieved by the profession. Although IAASB representatives may be nominated by particular constituencies, they are expected to work and vote towards the achievement of standards that are the best for the worldwide profession.

Historically, International Standards on Auditing (ISAs) have been structured and have a level of detail very much like the auditing standards of the United Kingdom or the Netherlands. US generally accepted auditing standards are usually more detailed. Beginning in late 2004, the IAASB commenced a project (commonly referred to as the 'Clarity project') to re-examine the structure of its standards. Important considerations include the extent to which the standards include explanatory guidance as well as requirements, and the language used to describe steps that are expected to be performed. The project involves wide consultation with stakeholders, as the decisions taken will shape future ISA standards at a critical point in their development – when they are being considered for endorsement by the EU and while the possibility of greater convergence of standards (particularly US PCAOB standards) is being assessed. As at the time of writing, 12 revised standards had either been released in their 'close-off' pre-Clarity form, or redrafted in their Clarity format. However, the intention is not to make the Clarity standards effective until at least 2009, so that they can be adopted as a complete set with appropriate lead time.

IFAC itself has no authority to require that its pronouncements are adhered to, as it has no jurisdiction over individual accountants. However, national professional accountancy bodies, which are the members of IFAC, do. For this reason, a member body undertakes to subscribe to the IFAC Constitution and abide by a Statement of Member Obligations (SMO) which includes a requirement to demonstrate how they have used best endeavours to implement the International Standards on Auditing (recognizing that in some countries national audit standard-setting is now undertaken independently of the profession). In many countries ISAs have been adopted as the national standards and they have been translated into several languages.

In its 2007 work programme, IOSCO noted that it was closely monitoring the evolution of the ISAs, in particular the IAASB's Clarity project, to consider whether a future endorsement of the standards for use for cross-border listing purposes would be justified. Endorsement by IOSCO would be important for the globalization of the capital markets, as it would mean that stock exchanges would accept audits of financial statements and other documents from other countries that are audited in accordance with the International Standards on Auditing. The European Commission (see below) has also embarked on a process of review and endorsement of the standards, with a view to requiring member states to adopt ISAs as their national standards.

Regional organizations of IFAC

Regional organizations of accountancy bodies have been established in many parts of the world. Among the most important are the:

- Arab Society of Certified Accountants (ASCA);
- Confederation of Asian and Pacific Accountants (CAPA);
- Fédération des Experts Comptables Européens (FEE);
- Interamerican Accounting Association (IAA);
- Eastern, Central and Southern Africa Federation of Accountants (ECSAFA).

As most of these organizations have adopted the International Standards on Auditing from IFAC, they are not standard-setters themselves. Nevertheless, they play an important role in making the international standards available in other languages (Arabic and Spanish, for instance) and in the enhancement of the profession in their regions through education, congresses and harmonization. FEE has a particularly important role in representing the views of the European profession on public policy matters to the European Commission.

European Union

Within the European Union, the Council of the European Communities has issued Directives on the preparation, publication and audit of annual reports, namely the Fourth and Seventh Directives, in order to harmonize legislation within the Union. The Eighth Directive sets the qualification and education criteria for auditors. Historically, none of these has contained requirements on the methods of conducting an audit. See Chapter 11 for more details.

The European Commission published a Communication 'Reinforcing the statutory audit in the EU' in May 2003, setting out the Commission's strategy on audit matters for the next few years, including the need to modernize the Eighth Directive, strengthen public oversight of the profession and to establish appropriate regulatory structures at EU level. A draft revised Eighth Directive was published in March 2004 and, following extensive consultation and review by committees of the European Parliament, received final approval in April 2006. The revised Directive requires the use of ISAs for statutory audits in the EU – once those standards have been subject to an endorsement procedure. Member state authorities can only impose additional requirements in certain defined circumstances.

The European Commission has yet to determine the mechanism to be used for endorsing the ISAs for use in Europe – it may differ from that used to endorse IFRS accounting standards. In the meantime, a body called the European Group of Audit Oversight Bodies (EGAOB) has been set up and a committee of the EGAOB has been reviewing and commenting on the IAASB's Clarity standards as they are developed.

Evans and Nobes (1998a and 1998b) examined the limited harmonization brought about by the original version of the Eighth Directive between Germany and the United Kingdom in the areas of the structure of audit firms and independence.

US Public Company Accounting Oversight Board (PCAOB)

This chapter is not generally concerned with describing the activities of *national* standard-setters. However, the US PCAOB, established following the Sarbanes-Oxley Act of 2002 (see Chapter 8), is unusual because of its potential influence on audit standards and practice in other parts of the world. The PCAOB was established to set standards for, and to monitor the quality of, audits of companies listed on the US capital markets. Although its primary focus is domestic US listed companies and their auditors, its remit extends to audits of foreign registrant companies.

The PCAOB has begun to issue its own audit standards in addition to the existing body of US GAAS standards issued by the AICPA. In particular, it has issued Auditing Standard No. 2 (AS2) which deals with the auditor's responsibilities in relation to internal control (under section 404 of the Sarbanes-Oxley Act) in conjunction with an audit of financial statements. Following significant public debate the PCAOB has issued Auditing Standard No. 5 (AS5) which will replace AS2 from November 2007. Auditors of foreign private issuers listed on US markets are affected by the PCAOB's standards.

It is still too early to gauge the extent to which the PCAOB will affect the setting of audit standards at an international level, as well as on the work performed in practice on international audits. Foreign audit firms (that is, auditors of foreign issuers listed on US markets) have been required to register with the PCAOB. It remains to be seen the extent to which the PCAOB will directly inspect the quality of work of foreign auditors or whether it will seek to rely on the pre-existing external audit review procedures in some countries. However, it seems clear that the PCAOB will have a growing influence on the environment for international auditing.

Other organizations

A number of other international organizations, such as the OECD, United Nations Council on Trade and Development (UNCTAD) and World Bank, have issued pronouncements on financial reporting issues. However, they are not directly involved in audit standard-setting at the technical level.

Some of these other international organizations, as well as IOSCO, the Basel Committee of bank regulators and the European Commission, are represented on the Consultative Advisory Group (CAG) that meets to provide input to the IAASB on its standard-setting programme.

In late 2003, IFAC, with the support of member bodies and international regulators, approved a series of reforms to increase confidence that the standard-setting activities of IFAC are properly responsive to the public interest. These included: a more transparent 'due process' for standard-setting; greater public and regulatory input into those processes; regulatory monitoring; and public interest oversight. IFAC's Public Interest Oversight Board (PIOB) was officially established in February 2005.

The PIOB, comprising eight members appointed by regulatory organizations, oversees standard-setting activities in the areas of audit and assurance, ethics and independence and education. It also oversees the member body compliance programme. The European Commission appoints two observers to the Board but has indicated that in due course its observers will be nominated for appointment as full members of the PIOB. The PIOB issues annual public reports on its oversight activities.

21.4 The international audit process

21.4.1 Introduction

The following description of an international audit process gives a brief overview of what an international audit looks like. It is based on the International Standards on Auditing issued by IFAC. International firms of accountants have similar processes described in their audit methodologies. These are similar but not identical because the basic principles and essential procedures will be tailor-made to accommodate the firm's own approach. For instance, one firm might have a tendency towards a more systems-based approach or towards an approach that places more reliance on analytical review or sampling. Before moving to the details of the audit process, one should consider the environment in which audits take place, as shown in Figure 21.1.

The objective of an audit is to enable the auditor to express an audit opinion (reasonable assurance) on whether the financial statements give a true and fair view or fair presentation in accordance with the 'applicable financial reporting framework'

Figure 21.1 **The environment of the audit**

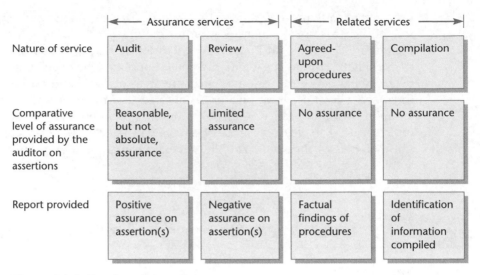

Figure 21.2 **Services by auditors**

(i.e. the set of rules being used, e.g. IFRS). In forming this opinion, the auditor carries out procedures designed to obtain sufficient appropriate evidence as to the reliability of an assertion that is the responsibility of one party for use by another party. The auditor's opinion helps to establish the credibility of the financial statements by providing a reasonable, but not absolute, level of assurance that these are free of material misstatements. Absolute assurance is neither attainable nor required by the users of financial statements. Audits cannot provide absolute assurance because of such factors as the need for judgement, the use of testing, the inherent limitations of any internal control system, and the fact that much of the audit evidence is persuasive rather than conclusive. Users do not require absolute assurance because, for their decision making, a 'fair' view of the financial position and the results and trends in it are more relevant than the exact amounts. Preparing financial statements involves the selection of accounting policies, and the making of accounting estimates and judgements, which necessarily cannot be exact.

Auditors can also be engaged to provide other types of assurance services, which are distinguished from audits in the IFAC's framework as shown in Figure 21.2. A 'review' is defined as an engagement in which an auditor is asked to carry out procedures that provide a limited level of assurance on financial information, being a lower level of assurance than that provided by an audit. The procedures, consisting primarily of inquiry and analytical review, are performed to provide auditors with a reasonable basis for stating whether anything has come to their attention that causes them to believe that the financial statements do not give a true and fair view in accordance with the applicable financial reporting framework. Auditors are often engaged to perform reviews of interim (e.g. half-yearly or quarterly) financial information. 'Agreed-upon procedures' refers to the situation in which an auditor is engaged to apply the procedures that the auditor and client have agreed on to individual items of financial data, a financial statement or set of financial statements. The auditor is only required to present the evidence collected to the user, and the report of factual findings provides no assurance on assertions. The user has to draw his or her own conclusions from the auditor's findings. Examples of this type of service are due diligence reports in the context of merger and acquisition activity and reviews of compliance with contractual arrangements. A 'compilation' involves collecting, classifying and summarizing financial information. In this case, the auditor is engaged in his or her capacity as accounting expert and is not required to test underlying assertions or to provide assurance.

21.4.2 Ethics

IFAC's Code of Ethics for Professional Accountants sets standards for conduct and states the fundamental principles that have to be observed. Performing audits in accordance with International Standards on Auditing requires adherence to the Code of Ethics. A distinguishing mark of a profession is acceptance of its responsibility to the public. The public relies on the objectivity and integrity of the accountancy profession for the orderly functioning of commerce. This reliance imposes a public interest responsibility on the profession.

1 The Code of Ethics recognizes that the objectives of the accountancy profession are to work to the highest standards of professionalism, to attain the highest levels of performance and generally to meet the public interest requirement set out above.

The Code of Ethics states the fundamental principles that apply to all professional accountants as follows:

- integrity;
- objectivity;
- professional competence and due care;
- confidentiality;
- professional behaviour.

The above list of required characteristics can be expanded upon. 'Integrity' requires the professional accountant to be straightforward and honest. 'Objectivity' requires the professional accountant not to allow bias, conflict of interest or undue influence of others to override professional judgement. The principle of 'professional competence and due care' is that providing professional services implies a level of competence necessary to perform these services and that the knowledge, skill and experience are applied with reasonable care and diligence. This also requires the auditor to keep his or her knowledge up to date. 'Confidentiality' implies that the auditor does not use or disclose information acquired without proper authority. The duty of confidentiality may be overridden by legal or professional duties (or rights). Confidentiality is one of the strictest rules in auditing firms. Especially when the firm is large, it can hardly avoid serving competing clients. The firms have well-established procedures which prevent engagement teams for one client from acquiring information about another. 'Professional behaviour' means complying with relevant laws and regulations and avoiding any action that discredits the profession – most firms' practice manuals elaborate this requirement to protect the name of the firm.

The section of the Code for accountants in public practice addresses not only independence but also such topics as fees and commissions, incompatible activities, clients' monies, advertising and solicitation, and relations with other accountants in public practice. The latter addresses both working relations between auditors and their communication on changes of auditors.

The independence rule in the Code states that independence should be interpreted as independence of mind (the state of mind that permits the provision of an opinion without being affected by influences that compromise professional judgement, allowing an individual to act with integrity and exercise objectivity and professional scepticism) and independence in appearance (the avoidance of facts and circumstances that would cause a reasonable and informed third party to conclude that integrity, objectivity or professional scepticism had been impaired).

Partly in response to recent corporate scandals and a perception of conflict of interest on the part of many of the groups involved (including boards, auditors, analysts, investment banks and regulators), a new version of the Code of Ethics was introduced in 2004. Significantly, the Code also applies to assurance assignments other than simply audit engagements. The Code follows a conceptual approach to independence. It is designed to assist auditors in (i) identifying threats to independence; (ii) evaluating whether the threats are significant; and (iii) identifying and applying appropriate safeguards to eliminate or reduce the threats to an acceptable level. Safeguards include such measures as the use of second 'review' partners and rotating the engagement partner after a specified number of years. In situations where no safeguards are available to reduce the threat, the only possible action is to eliminate the activities or interest creating the threat, or to refuse to accept or continue the engagement. Further guidance is included in the Code on situations that impair independence, such as financial involvement with the client, appointments to managerial positions in the client (before or after the audit), the provision of non-assurance services to assurance clients (such as consulting or bookkeeping), and personal relations.

In practice, international firms have more detailed regulations, such as listings of publicly held audit clients in which no investments are allowed by all or part of the partners and staff, together with procedural guidance to ensure adherence to the requirements.

In early 2007 the International Ethics Standards Board for Accountants consulted on further potential revisions to the Code of Ethics for professional accountants. These may result in further refinements to the Code in respect of partner rotation requirements and the requirements related to provision of non-assurance services, and extension of the independence requirements to the audits of a wider range of public interest entities.

21.4.3 Technical standards

IFAC's Code of Ethics requires that, in performing professional services, auditors should act diligently in accordance with applicable technical and professional standards. These may be the standards promulgated by IFAC (e.g. the pronouncements of its committees such as the International Standards on Auditing), the auditor's professional body or other regulatory bodies and relevant legislation.

The audit methodologies of most of the large international network firms are based on ISAs. However, the basic methodology is supplemented by national requirements, to the extent that these vary or go beyond those in ISAs. Technical standards in firms' manuals are also generally more detailed than the ISAs. For example, an audit firm might set out more detailed requirements on which audit working papers should be completed or which documentation should be kept on the files. Detailed requirements ensure that audits are carried out in a similar manner all over the world and allow international review for quality-control purposes.

21.4.4 Quality control

International audit firms work all over the world under the same name. Therefore, users expect the same quality internationally. IFAC has issued important pronouncements on audit quality both at the firm level and at the engagement level. ISQC 1 'Quality Control for Firms that Perform Audits and Reviews of Historical Financial Information and Other Assurance and Related Services Engagements' specifies the measures to be taken at firm level, and codifies many of the practices that the large firms were already following. For example, in most large network firms a programme of quality-control reviews of national firms is conducted, normally including participation from other member firms, in order to ascertain adherence to the international firm's standards by its separate national member firms. Ordinarily this is on the basis of a rotation scheme, so that all member firms are reviewed over a period of years. These reviews address national quality-control procedures and could include reviews of files on a test basis. Poor performance would result in remedial action; in the worst cases it could result in excluding a national firm or partner from the international firm.

The objective of a quality-control system at firm level is to provide reasonable assurance that the firm and its personnel comply with professional standards and applicable regulatory requirements, and that reports issued by the firm are appropriate in the circumstances. ISQC 1 specifies that the system of quality control in the firm is required to include documented policies and procedures addressing:

- *Leadership responsibilities for quality within the firm*: it is a responsibility of the firm's leadership to promote a culture of quality and to communicate quality-control policies and procedures.

- *Ethical requirements*: compliance with IFAC's Code of Ethics should be embedded in the firm's system of quality control.

- Acceptance and continuance of client relationships and specific engagements: detailed policies and procedures should be established in this area.

- *Human resources*: the firm should establish procedures to assign sufficient staff with the technical and other competencies necessary to perform its engagements in accordance with professional standards.

- *Engagement performance*: procedures are needed to ensure engagements are performed in accordance with professional standards (including procedures for staff supervision, consultation on contentious matters, and resolution of differences of opinion).

- *Engagement quality-control review*: listed company engagements should be subject to review by a second review partner.
- *Monitoring*: firms should have an internal inspection programme for ensuring the work of individual offices and partners is reviewed on a regular basis.

In addition to the firm-wide requirements in ISQC 1, engagement-level requirements are specified in the revised audit standard ISA 220 'Quality Control for Audits of Historical Financial Information'. These requirements mirror, at the level of the individual audit, those of ISQC 1 (e.g. requiring the engagement partner to be satisfied that potential threats to independence have been assessed, appropriate engagement acceptance procedures have been followed, and the work of the engagement team has been adequately supervised and reviewed).

Given the litigious environment of the accountancy profession in many countries, most firms have further strengthened their quality-control procedures and incorporated schemes of risk management, which include stricter rules on the acceptance and retention of clients and the abandonment of some services and clients that are judged to carry unacceptably high risks. Regulators and other interested parties have expressed interest in knowing more about the quality-control processes operated by the firms. For example, the EU Eighth Directive includes a provision for firms to disclose publicly more details of their processes around audit quality. Recently, a number of the large firms have issued on a voluntary basis 'Transparency' reports at a global level, explaining some of the quality-control policies and procedures adopted in the global networks.

21.4.5 The audit process

The four main stages of an audit process are:

- acceptance and defining the terms of engagement;
- planning, including assessment of audit risk and materiality;
- gathering audit evidence; and
- reporting.

International auditing firms may use different names for the stages, but in principle all audit processes come down to these steps, which are discussed below under these headings.

Acceptance and defining the terms of engagement

As part of their quality control, firms will apply specific procedures before accepting an engagement. These normally require involvement and agreement by more than one partner and are implemented to safeguard the audit firm's independence and ensure its ability to serve the client properly. A major consideration is the integrity of the client's management, directors and principal owners.

It is normal practice to set out the terms of engagement in an engagement letter, drafted by the auditor and signed for agreement by the client. The engagement letter is designed to document and confirm the client's understanding of the auditor's appointment, the scope of the auditor's work, the extent of the auditor's responsibilities and the form of any reports. ISA 210 describes the principal contents of an engagement letter, and its appendix contains an example of a letter. The ISA also discusses the limited circumstances in which an auditor may subsequently accept a change in the terms of an engagement.

Planning and risk assessment

Planning is the process of developing a general strategy and a detailed approach for the expected nature, timing and extent of the audit work. The planning should result in an efficient and effective audit, carried out in a timely manner.

The general strategy or overall audit plan describes the expected scope and conduct of the audit. It is not uncommon for the overall plan to be discussed and agreed with the client, for instance with an audit committee. The auditor, however, has to remain in command, as he ultimately has to decide what work has to be performed to provide the basis on which he can issue the opinion.

At the planning stage, consideration is given to the following:

- knowledge of the business (general economic factors and industry conditions affecting the client's business; important characteristics of the client, its business, financial performance and reporting requirements; the level of competence of management);
- accounting and internal control systems (accounting policies adopted; the effect of new accounting or auditing pronouncements; the auditor's cumulative knowledge of the accounting and internal control systems);
- risk and materiality (see below);
- the nature, timing and extent of procedures (including possible changes in emphasis between audit areas, the effect of IT on the audit, and the consideration of the work of internal auditors);
- coordination, direction, supervision and review (staffing requirements, involvement of experts and the coordination and instruction of the other auditors of components of the group).

Knowledge of the business is critical to all stages of the audit, as regulation of business is increasingly on industry sector lines. Accounting and reporting requirements are developed for specific industries, such as banking and insurance. Even more 'mainstream' businesses, such as energy and telecommunications, are today heavily regulated, and a modern audit often requires a significant degree of specialist knowledge and expertise.

Other matters that would have to be considered at the planning stage are factors that may affect the ability of the company to continue as a going concern and the impact of changes in laws and regulations on the client or the audit.

For a multinational company, with locations in many countries, the planning process and in particular the timely instruction of and communication with auditors in these countries are very important. International audit firms can handle this complex area more easily as they have the procedures, understanding of each other's responsibilities and the networks in place.

The planning process results in an overall audit plan, sufficiently detailed to serve as a basis for the preparation of the detailed audit programme. It could be viewed as breaking down the financial statements of the company and its underlying business processes and related information systems into areas of attention for the audit. A preliminary choice is made as to the likelihood of the mix of audit procedures, such as substantive testing for accounting estimates or non-routine transactions, relying on internal control or IT systems for routine transactions (generally the day-to-day transactions such as sales, purchases and payroll), and the need to use specialists in the audit team. On international audits, it is not uncommon to rotate the emphasis – for example, on the less important subsidiaries, between full audits in one year and limited reviews in subsequent years.

Audit risk and materiality

The concepts of materiality and audit risk, their interrelationship and the application of these concepts are the most significant for the auditor in order to perform an audit. They are used when planning and conducting an audit and when evaluating the results of the procedures.

Information is material if its omission or misstatement could influence the economic decisions of users taken on the basis of the financial statements. The assessment of materiality is a matter of the auditor's professional judgement and is considered at both the overall financial statement level and in relation to individual account balances and disclosures. Audit risk is defined as the risk that an auditor may give an inappropriate opinion on financial information that is materially misstated.

Audit risk and materiality are interrelated, as can be seen from the definition of audit risk. The higher the materiality threshold, the lower the risk. The auditor cannot raise the materiality level as he or she desires, as it rests on judgement of what the users of financial statements would view as relevant information. Disclosure guidelines in reporting frameworks such as IFRS may help in forming this judgement. An audit in accordance with generally accepted auditing standards requires the auditor to keep audit risk at an acceptably low level.

Audit risk has three components: inherent risk (the risk that there is an error), control risk (the risk that internal control procedures do not discover the error), and detection risk (the risk that the auditor fails to detect an error). Inherent risk and control risk are assessed in combination: if management feels that the inherent risk is high, it will normally implement stronger internal controls.

The auditor needs reasonable assurance that the accounting system is adequate and that all the accounting information which should be recorded has been recorded. Internal controls normally contribute to such assurance, although there are inherent limitations in any system of internal control. The auditor's work therefore includes obtaining an understanding of the entity's process for identifying business risks relevant to financial reporting, and of the information system and related processes (including control activities) relevant to financial reporting. The auditor reports to management any material weaknesses in the design or implementation of the internal control systems which have come to the auditor's attention. The auditor's assessment of control risk is then used to determine the nature, timing and extent of audit procedures (which may include substantive testing) so as to restrict detection risk to an acceptably low level. The relationship between the assessments of inherent and control risks to substantive procedures is described in the auditing standards by indicating that some substantive procedures should always be performed and reassessed as the components of audit risk change.

Gathering audit evidence

The planning stage of the audit, including the assessment of the components of audit risk, results in a detailed audit programme. This is the set of instructions for the audit team as to the procedures that should be performed to conduct the audit. Performing these procedures – both the tests of controls and substantive procedures – can be seen as a process of gathering audit evidence. Tests of controls are tests performed to obtain audit evidence about the design and operation of the accounting and internal control systems. Substantive tests or procedures are performed to obtain audit evidence to detect material misstatements in the financial statements, and they are generally of two types: (a) analytical procedures, or (b) tests of details of transactions and balances, which may involve the use of sampling.

Audit evidence is information obtained by the auditor in arriving at the conclusions upon which an opinion on the financial information is based. Ordinarily, the auditor will have to rely on audit evidence that is persuasive rather than conclusive. The auditor will therefore often seek evidence from different sources of a different nature to support the same assertion. The procedures for obtaining audit evidence are:

- inspection (of records, documents or assets);
- observation (of an internal control procedure);
- inquiry and confirmation (asking and corroborating);
- computation (of a provision or checking calculations);
- analytical procedures.

The last in the list, analytical procedures, consist of the analysis of significant ratios and trends, including the resulting investigation of relationships and fluctuations that are inconsistent with other relevant information or deviate from predicted amounts. Relationships can be very stable (e.g. between cost of sales and sales if there is a fixed margin) and may therefore be powerful tools for the auditor.

Accounting estimates and fair values. An 'accounting estimate' is defined as an approximation of the amount of an item in the absence of a precise means of measurement. Management is responsible for making accounting estimates based upon its judgement of the uncertain outcome of events that have occurred or are likely to occur. This can be a difficult and highly sensitive area. The auditor is responsible for evaluating the reasonableness of estimates, but due to the approximation inherent in accounting estimates, such an evaluation cannot be made as accurately as in other areas of the audit. The increasingly systematic use of fair values in financial accounting (e.g. under the IFRS framework) means that auditors are having to understand and assess the processes used by management to determine fair value measurements.

Management representations. Auditing standards indicate that representations by management cannot be a substitute for other audit evidence that could reasonably be expected to be available. However, the auditor should also obtain written representations from management that it acknowledges its responsibility for the financial statements, and on matters material to the financial statements when other sufficient appropriate audit evidence cannot reasonably be expected to exist. Examples of items on which specific representation might be sought include the completeness of related party information, contingent liabilities and guarantees, subsequent events, and the existence of unassessed claims.

Internal audit. The internal audit function constitutes a separate component of internal control undertaken by specially assigned staff within an entity. An objective of the internal auditor is to determine whether internal controls are well designed and properly implemented. Much of the work of the internal audit department may be useful to the independent auditor for the purpose of examination of the financial information.

Reporting

The reporting stage of the audit comprises two parts: firstly, reviewing and assessing the conclusions drawn from the audit evidence obtained in order to ensure that the audit risk is at an acceptably low level; and, secondly, the review of the financial statements in order to ensure that these comply with the relevant financial reporting framework.

The Auditor's Report on the financial statements is often the only publicly available report. It is, however, not necessarily the only report issued by the auditors. Depending on legal circumstances and/or the terms of the individual engagements, the auditor would report his or her findings in more detail to management and those responsible for the governance of the entity, such as an audit committee or any supervisory directors.

Increasingly, audit committees, composed wholly or mainly of independent non-executive board directors, are becoming the primary focus for the company's relationship with the external auditors. The committee's responsibility is to oversee on behalf of the board the integrity of the financial reporting controls and procedures implemented by management, and of the published financial information itself. A study by PricewaterhouseCoopers (2003) found that 16 of the world's 41 major economies now have mandatory requirements for audit committees. A further 14 countries have voluntary arrangements.

Recognizing this shift in the relationship between the external auditor and the client, the IAASB issued an audit standard ISA 260 'Communication of Audit Matters with Those Charged with Governance'. The standard lists those matters that the auditor would ordinarily report to the audit committee, including:

- scope of the audit and any limitations placed thereon;
- significant accounting policies;
- the potential effect on the financial statements of significant risks and exposures;
- audit adjustments, whether or not recorded by the client;
- going concern issues;
- disagreements with management;
- expected modifications of the audit report;
- material weaknesses in internal control.

In an international audit of a diversified group, the auditor can also gather information on, for example, the financial controls in the various subsidiaries that is useful to the senior management of the group. Such information, which is normally called an Interoffice Memorandum, is, after being discussed with local management, reported to the parent's auditor, who will compile an overall report to top management. Thus, in addition to the formal auditor's report, in many cases a tailor-made report will be issued to management containing information relevant for financial analysis and for control of the business.

The International Standards on Auditing provide guidance on the form and content of the auditor's report issued in connection with the independent audit of the financial statements of an entity. The 'unqualified' (or 'clean') opinion is the most familiar one and should be expressed when the auditor concludes that the financial statements present fairly or give a true and fair view in accordance with the applicable financial reporting framework. An unqualified opinion also indicates implicitly that any material changes in accounting principles or in the method of their application, and the effects thereof, have been properly determined and disclosed in the financial statements.

Figure 21.3 (overleaf) gives an illustration of an unqualified auditor's report taken from the latest version of ISA 700, effective since December 2006, incorporating the basic elements discussed above. In circumstances where the auditor is not satisfied with the audit evidence or with the compliance of the financial statements with the identified framework, a qualified or adverse opinion or a denial of opinion (often referred to as a 'disclaimer') will be issued.

Some other remarks on the auditor's responsibility

The extent of the auditors' responsibilities in specific areas is often misunderstood by management and by financial statement users. This contributes to the 'expectation gap' – that users expect more from the audit than auditors can practically or reasonably deliver. Such a gap will always exist in a dynamic society because stakeholders may change (in the past, only shareholders were viewed as the legitimate stakeholders) and may have information requirements that are not (or not yet) addressed by management (such as information on control systems or environmental behaviour) and hence not yet part of the financial statements and the audit. This section sets out some of these expectation gap considerations in relation to fraud and error, compliance with the law, subsequent events and going concern.

The responsibility for the prevention of fraud and error rests with management. The auditor should plan the audit so that there is a reasonable expectation of detecting material misstatements resulting from fraud and error. The auditor should carry out additional procedures when he or she has an indication that fraud or error may exist. The auditor has specific reporting duties to the directors (and in some countries to regulators) and may ultimately have to consider withdrawing from the engagement if management chooses to allow fraud to continue or, more seriously, if management actively colludes in the fraud.

When planning and performing audit procedures and in evaluating and reporting the results thereof, the auditor should recognize that non-compliance by the entity with laws and regulations may materially affect the financial statements. The auditor does not have the skills or the requirement to consider all laws and regulations, but

INDEPENDENT AUDITOR'S REPORT

To the Shareholders and Board of Directors of the ABC Company

Report on the Financial Statements

We have audited the accompanying financial statements of ABC Company which comprise the balance sheet as of 31 December 200X and the income statement, statement of changes in equity and cash flow statement for the year then ended and a summary of significant accounting policies and other explanatory notes.

Management's Responsibility for the Financial Statements

Management is responsible for the preparation and fair presentation of these financial statements in accordance with International Financial Reporting Standards and with the requirements of Country X company law. This responsibility includes: designing, implementing and maintaining internal control relevant to the preparation and fair presentation of financial statements that are free from material misstatement, whether due to fraud or error; selecting and applying appropriate accounting policies; and making accounting estimates that are reasonable in the circumstances.

Auditor's Responsibility

Our responsibility is to express an opinion on these financial statements based on our audit. We conducted our audit in accordance with International Standards on Auditing. Those Standards require that we comply with ethical requirements and plan and perform the audit to obtain reasonable assurance whether the financial statements are free from material misstatement.

An audit involves performing procedures to obtain audit evidence about the amounts and disclosures in the financial statements. The procedures selected depend on the auditor's judgment, including the assessment of the risks of material misstatement of the financial statements, whether due to fraud or error. In making those risk assessments, the auditor considers internal control relevant to the entity's preparation and fair presentation of the financial statements in order to design audit procedures that are appropriate in the circumstances, but not for the purpose of expressing an opinion on the effectiveness of the entity's internal control. An audit also includes evaluating the appropriateness of accounting policies used and the reasonableness of accounting estimates made by management, as well as evaluating the overall presentation of the financial statements.

We believe that the audit evidence we have obtained is sufficient and appropriate to provide a basis for our audit opinion.

Opinion

In our opinion, the accompanying fiancial statements give a true and fair view of (or 'present fairly, in all material respects,') the financial position of the Company as of 31 December 200X, and of its financial performance and its cash flows for the year then ended in accordance with International Financial Reporting Standards and with the requirements of Country X company law.

Report on Other Legal and Regulatory Requirements [if applicable]

[Form and content of this section of the auditor's report will vary depending on the nature of the auditor's other reporting responsibilities.]

[For example]

The Directors are also responsible for preparing the Corporate Governance Statement and the Directors' Remuneration Report in accordance with applicable law.

As required by [applicable requirement], we have also audited the information in the Directors' Remuneration Report that is described as having been audited, set out in pages [XX] to [YY].

We are also required by [applicable requirement] to assess whether the Corporate Governance Statement reflects the company's compliance with [for example the Country X Corporate Governance Code], and to report if it does not. We are not required to consider whether the board's statements on internal control cover all risks and controls, or form an opinion on the effectiveness of the group's corporate governance procedures or its risk and control procedures.

Auditor's signature

Date
Address

Figure 21.3 **Sample unqualified opinion by an auditor**

his or her knowledge of the business of the entity and inquiries with management on how compliance is controlled by the entity will help in planning the audit. The auditor has no detection responsibility for non-compliance but should act if he or she discovers indications that it may exist, and has specific reporting duties to those charged with governance (and may in some countries have additional responsibilities to report to regulatory and enforcement authorities). The auditor may ultimately have to consider withdrawing from the engagement if management chooses to continue the non-compliance.

The date of the auditor's report sets the boundary for the auditor's responsibility in relation to subsequent events, such as significant events occurring after the balance sheet date and facts emerging after the financial statements have been issued. The auditor generally performs specific steps to identify subsequent events until the date of the auditor's report.

In discharging their responsibilities in relation to going concern, the auditors would consider the process undertaken by management to assess the appropriateness of the 'going concern' assumption as a basis for the preparation of financial statements. Management, and the auditors, would normally consider the 'foreseeable future' – usually taken to be a period of not less than one year after the balance sheet date. The general notion is that an entity's continuance as a going concern is assumed in the absence of information to the contrary. If there is significant doubt, the auditor must perform procedures to confirm or dispel that doubt and should particularly ensure that the entity complies with the requirements of the financial reporting framework in such situations.

SUMMARY

- Auditing is a systematic process of objectively obtaining and evaluating evidence regarding assertions about economic actions and events to ascertain the degree of correspondence between those assertions and established criteria, and communicating the results to interested users.

- International auditing can be seen as referring to the harmonization of auditing standards and rules across countries as well as referring to the practice of auditing, based on one or more sets of auditing rules, the financial information prepared by multinational corporations.

- The process of internationalization of auditing developed after the Second World War. This process was triggered by the development of multinational corporations, which need an efficient and effective audit supporting their information and control systems. Until the middle of the twentieth century, most audit firms operated largely within national borders. However, the need to serve ever-growing clients has caused a movement of mergers and strategic alliances between auditing firms to be able to serve their largest clients worldwide. Auditing practice changed from an activity dominated by local traditions and roles to a process of investigation and reporting which takes place on an international scale.

- The globalization of capital markets has shown the need for a clearly defined role for auditing as a means to add credibility to the financial information provided by companies seeking finance in international capital markets. In order to define this role clearly, International Standards on Auditing have been developed by IFAC. Its standards are increasingly recognized by the business community, users and regulators as setting the benchmarks for audits.

References

American Accounting Association, Committee on Basic Auditing Concepts (1973) *A Statement on Basic Auditing Concepts*, Sarasota.

Evans, L. and Nobes, C.W. (1998a) 'Harmonization of the structure of audit firms: incorporation in the UK and Germany', *European Accounting Review*, Vol. 7, No. 1.

Evans, L. and Nobes, C.W. (1998b) 'Harmonization relating to auditor independence: the Eighth Directive, the UK and Germany', *European Accounting Review*, Vol. 7, No. 3.

Nobes, C.W. (1993) 'The true and fair view requirement: impact on and of the Fourth Directive', *Accounting and Business Research*, Winter.

Post, H., Wilderom, C. and Douma, S. (1998) 'Internationalization of Dutch accounting firms', *European Accounting Review*, Vol. 7, No. 4.

PricewaterhouseCoopers (2003) *Audit Committees – Good Practices for Meeting Market Expectations*, PricewaterhouseCoopers, London.

Vieten, H. (1995) 'Auditing in Britain and Germany compared: professions, knowledge and the state', *European Accounting Review*, Vol. 4, No. 3.

Further reading

Arens, A.A. and Loebbecke, J.K. (2000) *Auditing: An Integrated Approach*, Prentice Hall, Englewood Cliffs, NJ.

Barrett, M., Cooper, D.J. and Jamal, K. (2005) 'Globalization and the coordinating of work in multinational audits', *Accounting, Organizations and Society*, Vol. 30, No. 1.

Center for International Financial Analysis and Research (1993) International Accounting and Auditing Trends, 1995, 4th edn, Princeton.

Davidson, S. and Anderson, G.D. (1987) 'The development of accounting and auditing standards', *Journal of Accountancy*, March.

Dunn, L.J., III (2002) 'Harmonization of financial reporting and auditing across cultural boundaries: An examination of 201 company financial reports', *International Journal of Auditing*, Vol. 6, No. 3.

Gangolly, J.S., Hussein, M.E., Seow, G.S. and Tam, K. (2002) 'Harmonization of the auditor's report', *International Journal of Accounting*, Vol. 37, No. 3.

IFAC News.

International Accounting Bulletin.

Margerson, J. and Moizer, P. (1996) 'Auditor licensing in the European Union: a comparative study based on cultural differences', *European Accounting Review*, Vol. 5, No. 1.

Needles, B.E., Ramamoorti, S. and Shelton, S.W. (2002) 'The role of international auditing in the improvement of international financial reporting', *Advances in International Accounting*, Vol. 15.

Richard, C. (2006) 'Why an auditor can't be competent and independent: a French case study', *European Accounting Review*, Vol. 15, No. 2.

Schilder, A. (1996) 'Research opportunities in auditing in the European Union', *Accounting Horizons*, December.

Useful websites

Deloitte — www.deloitte.com
Ernst & Young — www.ey.com
IFAC Forum of Firms — www.ifac.org/Forum_of_Firms

International Auditing and Assurance Standards Board   www.ifac.org/IAASB
KPMG   www.kpmg.com
PricewaterhouseCoopers   www.pwc.com
Public Interest Oversight Board   www.ipiob.org

QUESTIONS

Suggested answers to the asterisked questions are given at the end of the book.

21.1* Why is it necessary to have international auditing standards?

21.2* Would it be better if international auditing standards were set by the United Nations rather than under the existing system?

21.3 Why do auditing standards differ internationally?

21.4 In what senses can certain aspects of auditing be described as 'international'?

21.5 Is it easier to reach agreement on international standards on auditing than on international accounting standards? If so, why?

21.6 Discuss the effect that the growth of multinational enterprises has had on audit firms.

21.7 The IFAC's Code of Ethics for professional accountants lists a number of fundamental auditing principles. Discuss to what extent such principles may mean different things in different countries.

21.8 What effect did the Enron affair have on the International Standards on Auditing?

22 International aspects of corporate income taxes

Christopher Nobes

OBJECTIVES

After reading this chapter, you should be able to:

- outline the main ways in which corporate income taxes can vary internationally;
- show, with examples from various accounting topics, how the tax base is very close to the accounting base in Germany, less close in France and even less close in the US and the UK;
- explain the objectives of companies and tax authorities in the area of international tax planning, including transfer pricing;
- contrast the purposes and the workings of classical and imputation systems of corporate taxation;
- briefly outline the purposes and progress of EU harmonization of corporate taxation.

22.1 | Introduction

22.1.1 The relevance of this chapter

This chapter has close connections with the material in other parts of this book, and with subjects beyond its scope. Firstly, even in Anglo-Saxon countries, corporate taxation obviously has some significant effects on net profit figures and other financial reporting matters. More importantly, it has been shown that, in some continental European countries and in China and Japan, the rules relating to corporate income taxation have a dominant effect on several aspects of financial reporting under national rules for unconsolidated statements. Secondly, an understanding of the differences between corporate taxation in different countries is a necessary introduction to a study of international business finance and management accounting. However, it is often poorly covered or omitted from books on these subjects. Hence, it was decided to provide a fairly detailed introduction here. Thirdly, the classification and harmonization aspects of taxation are useful further illustrations of the processes described in Chapters 3 and 4.

Although, for some tax purposes, parts of a group can be considered together (see Section 22.1.2 below), tax generally works on an individual company basis rather than on a group basis. Consequently, the move in the EU and elsewhere to the use of IFRS for consolidated statements does not affect tax calculations unless IFRS is extended to unconsolidated statements. For example, in France and Germany, accounting and tax for individual companies remain closely linked and largely unaffected by adoption of IFRS for other purposes.

22.1.2 Differences in taxes

There are two fundamental areas of difference between corporate income taxes in different countries or at different times: tax bases and tax systems. The international differences in corporate income tax bases (or definitions of taxable income) are very great. Although in all countries there is some relationship between accounting income and taxable income, in France and Germany the relationship is much closer than it is in the United Kingdom and the United States. Further, it has been pointed out throughout this book that the underlying measurement of accounting income itself varies substantially by country. These two points, which are of course linked, mean that similar companies in different countries may have vastly different taxable incomes (see Section 22.2).

Because taxes are internationally different, there are ways in which multinational companies might suffer or benefit. Trying to minimize taxes in this context is called international tax planning. This is the subject of Section 22.3. One aspect is that multinational companies will try to move taxable profits from operations in high-tax countries to operations in low-tax countries. One way of doing this is to set high transfer prices for intra-group goods with final customers in low-tax countries, so that low profits appear to be made by the group companies in those countries. The issue of transfer pricing is introduced in Section 22.4.

The second basic type of difference lies in tax systems. Once taxable income has been determined, its interaction with a tax system can vary, in particular with respect to the treatment of dividends. Corporations, unlike partnerships whose business income in most countries is taxed as though it were all distributed at the end of each tax year, may have both retained and distributed income for tax purposes. If business income is taxed only at the corporate level and only when it is earned, then different shareholders will not pay different rates of personal income tax. If income is taxed only on distribution, taxation may be postponed indefinitely. On the other hand, if income is taxed both when it is earned and when it is distributed, this creates 'economic double taxation', which could be said to be inequitable and inefficient (see Section 22.5).

These differences in tax bases and tax systems could lead to several important economic effects: for example, on dividend policies, investment plans and capital raising methods. Such matters are not dealt with extensively here; and neither (except in passing in Section 22.3) is the important issue of international double taxation, which in practice helps to determine total tax liabilities.

Tax bases and tax systems are examined in Sections 22.2 and 22.5, respectively. Of course, there are other important international differences. For example, the rates of taxation differ internationally and tend to change very frequently. Another international difference is in the approach of the tax authorities to groups. In all countries, tax operates basically company by company, rather than group by group, because the company is the legal taxable entity, and because groups contain overseas subsidiaries which use different accounting and tax rules. However, most countries allow some form of reliefs for losses or dividends arising or passing within groups. (For more detail, see James and Nobes, 2007 and Section 22.2.6 below.)

The definition of a group for tax purposes may vary within a country for different topics. As examples, the tax group is 75+ per cent domestic subsidiaries in the United Kingdom, and 80+ per cent domestic subsidiaries in the United States. In other words, the tax group has little connection with the accounting group and is generally smaller. Amongst the most complicated arrangements are those in France, where there are several options:

- *Parent/subsidiary system (régime des sociétés mères et filiales).* Under this system, companies in the group are basically taxed separately, but only 4 per cent of dividends are taxed if they are from companies that are 5+ per cent owned.

- *Integrated system (régime de l'intégration fiscale).* Under this, all French companies in the group can be treated as a single entity for tax purposes. However, in this case, 'group' means the parent and 95+ per cent subsidiaries. Within this group, therefore, profits and losses flow around and intra-group dividends are untaxed.

- *Consolidated worldwide basis* (with the permission of the Ministry of Finance). On this basis, the profits and losses of all 50+ per cent subsidiaries are added to the parent's and taxed on a French basis, with credit given for foreign taxes paid. This has been adopted by several large French groups.

- *Restricted worldwide basis* (with the permission of the Ministry of Finance). On this basis, worldwide consolidation with a narrower definition of subsidiary is used.

It should be noted that *none* of the bases actually uses the consolidated financial statements. This is because all the definitions of 'subsidiary' for tax purposes differ from the accounting one. Also, the amortization or impairment of goodwill on consolidation appears in the group income statement but does not affect taxable income.

For more detail on tax groups, see Lamb (1995).

22.2 Tax bases

22.2.1 Introduction

The obvious way to classify corporate income taxation bases is by degrees of difference between accounting income and taxable income. As should be clear from Chapters 2 and 14, the direct influence of taxation on accounting varies from the small in the United States to the dominant in Germany (at least, for unconsolidated accounting in Germany; see below). Such is the importance of this difference for accounting that a simple classification of tax bases would look much like a simple classification of national accounting systems. For example, a two-group classification in either case might put the United Kingdom, the United States in one group, and France, Germany and Japan in the other.

In the former group the requirement for financial accounting to present a 'fair' view to shareholders generally overrides the use of taxation rules for financial reporting. Consequently, many adjustments to accounting profit are necessary in order to arrive at the tax base: taxable income. In the other group of countries, the needs of taxation have been dominant in the evolution of accounting and auditing. Consequently, the tax base corresponds closely with accounting profit.

Hoogendoorn (1996) summarizes the relationships between tax and accounting for 13 European countries. Lamb *et al.* (1998) examine in detail the linkages between tax and financial reporting in the United States, the United Kingdom, France and Germany. They particularly concentrate on individual companies, examining the rules and practice for a number of accounting topics. For many issues, such as wages or sales, the tax system relies on accounting rules in all the countries. However, for the United Kingdom and the United States, there are issues where tax rules and financial reporting rules are different, whereas for Germany the rules or practice of tax and accounting are the same. In contrast, in Germany there are some issues where tax rules seem to override good financial reporting, whereas these are rare in the United Kingdom and the United States. The conclusion is that it is possible to distinguish the UK and the US from Germany and France.

Over time, countries can change. Nobes and Schwencke (2006) suggest that if the purpose of financial reporting in a country moves from tax-related towards investor-related, then financial reporting will gradually be separated from tax. They observe this happening in Norway over a century.

In Germany, some differences between tax and financial reporting have arisen since the study of Lamb *et al.* (1998). For example, for tax purposes, impairments are only allowed if they are expected to be long lasting. Also, long-term provisions should be discounted. Neither of these is normal financial reporting practice for German unconsolidated statements.

For consolidated statements, it is much easier for reporting to escape tax influence. Lamb *et al.* (1998) note this for France. The use of IFRS for consolidated reporting should greatly reduce or even eliminate the effects of taxation. However, tax influence is still possible where accounting choices in unconsolidated accounting are made for tax reasons and those choices flow through to consolidated statements.

In many countries, IFRS has been adopted or converged with for the purposes of *unconsolidated* financial reporting (see Chapter 13). This implies the necessity for extensive disconnection of tax from financial reporting. Otherwise, every time the IASB changes a standard, taxable income might change. Disconnection is especially important in countries (e.g. the UK or Denmark) where companies have a choice of using IFRS or national rules, leading to two different profit figures. Without disconnection, companies could choose their taxable income. Differences between a company's tax base and its financial reporting lead to the accounting topic of deferred tax. This is dealt with in Chapter 16.

Tax bases have been discussed elsewhere, country by country (James and Nobes, 2007, Chapters 12 and 14; IBFD, yearly; Picciotto, yearly; PricewaterhouseCoopers, 2000; Commerce Clearing House, yearly). Here, it is intended to discuss some of the differences between countries by topic. We generally use France, Germany, Japan, the UK and the US as examples.

22.2.2 Depreciation

Naturally, in all the countries studied in detail in this book, the tax authorities take an interest in the amount of depreciation charged in the calculation of taxable income. This concern varies from fairly precise specification of rates and methods to be used (as in most countries), to an interference only where charges are unreasonable. As has been pointed out in earlier chapters, the vital difference for financial reporting is that accounting depreciation must usually be kept the same as tax depreciation in Franco-German countries but not under Anglo-Saxon accounting.

Examples of the specification of rates and methods for depreciation of fixed assets for tax purposes are shown below:

- In the United Kingdom for 2007/08, machinery is depreciated at 25 per cent per year (or 40 per cent for small companies) on a reducing balance basis. A 6 per cent rate applies to assets with lives of over 25 years. There is a complete separation of this scheme of 'capital allowances' from the depreciation charged by companies against accounting profit. Unlike other countries, the United Kingdom does not give any depreciation tax allowance for most commercial buildings.

- In the United States, there are depreciation ranges for different assets. Normally, fixed assets are written off for tax purposes using the 'modified accelerated cost recovery system'. The most common form of this involves three-, five- or seven-year classes. These are depreciated by the declining balance method, using twice the straight-line rate. Commercial buildings have a 39-year life on a straight-line basis since 1993 changes in tax law.

- In France, depreciation is allowed by tax law on a straight-line basis for nearly all assets at the following typical rates: industrial and commercial buildings 2–5 per cent; office or residential buildings 4 per cent; plant and fixtures 10–20 per cent;

and vehicles 20–25 per cent. It is possible to use a reducing balance basis for plant. The rates to be used are expressed as multiples of the straight-line rates depending on the asset's life. It is possible to change the basis. Accelerated depreciation is allowed for R&D, certain regions, anti-pollution and energy-saving assets.

- In Germany and Japan, depreciation rates are specified by tax law. Straight-line and reducing balance methods are available, except that straight-line is mandatory for buildings. The following straight-line rates are typical in Germany: built in 2003 or later, buildings 2 per cent; plant, 6–10 per cent; and vehicles, 11–16 per cent. It is possible to change methods only from reducing balance to straight-line. Accelerated allowances were, until 1990, available for assets in Berlin and Eastern border areas and are now in eastern Germany, and for anti-pollution investment. Extra depreciation is also allowed for certain assets in Japan.

22.2.3 Allowances for inflationary gains on inventories

The second largest adjustment made during the calculation of corporate income tax liabilities in the United Kingdom between 1978 and 1984 was 'stock appreciation relief' (James and Nobes, 1992, Chapter 13). This partially allowed for the fact that, during periods of inflation, an important element of accounting and taxable profits is an unrealized gain due to holding trading stocks. This is not part of 'current operating profit' and there may be liquidity problems if it bears tax.

In the United States and Japan, the last-in first-out (LIFO) system of inventory costing is allowed as long as it is used for both financial and tax accounting. During periods of inflation, this reduces stock valuation and increases the cost of sales expense, thus reducing accounting and taxable profits. LIFO was freely allowed in Germany from 1990 to 2002, and it is now allowed in Germany except for fast-moving inventories; but in France, only in group accounts prepared under national rules (and, therefore, not for tax purposes). However, in France a *provision pour hausses des prix* is allowed when inventory prices rise by more than 10 per cent in the year. This reduces profit (and therefore taxable profit) and creates an untaxed reserve (*provision réglementée*).

22.2.4 Capital gains

The taxation of corporate capital gains varies somewhat by country, but is always based on realization. In Germany, Japan, the United Kingdom and the United States, capital gains are generally added to taxable income. In Germany, capital gains on non-trading investments in other companies are not taxable from 2001. In France, short-term capital gains (under two years) and most long-term gains are fully taxed, but a few types of long-term capital gains are taxed at a reduced rate. Roll-over relief provisions (whereby the taxation of gains can be postponed by re-investing) also vary internationally. In some countries (e.g. Malaysia) there is generally no tax on capital gains.

22.2.5 Losses

Different treatment of losses can have important effects on taxable profits. These are illustrated in Table 22.1. As may be seen, the rules differ markedly from country to

Table 22.1 **Operating loss reliefs (years)**

	Carry back	Carry forward
United Kingdom	1	No time limit
United States	2	20
France	3	No time limit
Germany	1	No time limit
Japan	1	5

country. As usual, a table cannot capture all the complications. For example, the German rules set maximum amounts that can be carried back and forward. More countries used to have limits on carrying forward (e.g. the limit in France was five years until 2004).

22.2.6 Dividends received

The degree to which the dividends received by a company must be included has an important effect on its taxable income. In the United Kingdom, Japan and (from 2001) Germany, domestic dividends are generally not taxed in the hands of a recipient company. In the United States, dividends from companies in the affiliated tax group (i.e. 80+ per cent holdings) are not taxed. However, 30 per cent of dividends from other companies are taxed. In France, dividend income is fully taxed unless there is a holding of at least 5 per cent (see Section 22.1.2).

22.2.7 Long-term contracts

In most countries, the tax authorities require or accept the completed contract method for the calculation of taxable income. This method tends to postpone the recognition of profit but involves less estimation. In France, Germany and Japan, the tax systems follow the accounting method used, and companies generally choose (or are required to use) the completed contract method for both purposes. By contrast, in the United Kingdom and the United States, the percentage-of-completion method is used for *accounting* purposes under appropriate circumstances. In the United States, the tax authorities use the completed contract method, so this gives rise to a difference between accounting and taxable income, which will reverse later.

22.2.8 Expenses

In the United Kingdom and the United States, a number of expenses deducted in the calculation of profit may not be allowed in the calculation of taxable income. In France and Germany, what is deducted for financial accounting generally depends on what is allowed for tax purposes. Most countries are more generous than the United Kingdom in allowing expenses for taxation. For example, most of them allow for some entertainment expenses to be deducted. However, most countries do not allow fines or non-business expenses to be deducted.

The expense for increasing an impairment of debtors is allowed for tax where it is specific but not if it is general (e.g. an impairment equal to 5 per cent of receivables is not allowed in the UK or the US or even in France). However, in Germany, a general provision for bad debts is tax deductible, so the tax system has to monitor the size of such provisions. In Italy and Spain, the tax law specifies maximum levels of deduction which tend to be used for financial reporting.

22.2.9 Other taxes

A very important complicating factor in determining overall tax burdens is the existence, and degree of deductibility for national corporate income tax purposes, of other types of taxes on companies. In most countries there is some form of payroll tax or social security tax. In the United States, there are state taxes on corporate income in most states. In the United Kingdom there are local property 'business rates'. In Germany there are regional income taxes and capital taxes. In France there is a business licence tax. In Italy there is a regional corporation tax. In general, these taxes are deductible in the calculation of national corporation tax. However, because of these taxes, the total tax burden is much higher than might be thought at first sight in countries, such as Germany, where regional taxes are important.

22.3 International tax planning

International tax planning is exceptionally complex but can involve enormous rewards in terms of lower taxes for multinational companies (and in terms of fees for tax lawyers and tax accountants). Multinationals will be trying to:

- move profits from high-tax countries to low-tax countries;
- avoid the taxation of the same income in two countries;
- get tax deductions twice for the same expenses;
- arrange for some income to be taxed nowhere.

The first of these issues is the field of transfer pricing, which is addressed in the next section. International double taxation is partially addressed by bilateral tax treaties between countries. Generally, it is possible to get a credit in one country for tax paid on the same income in another.

The third point above (getting tax deductions twice) is sometimes called 'double dipping'. For example, suppose that a British company obtains machinery on a finance lease (see Chapter 6) from a French financial institution. In the UK, the tax system approximately follows the accounting system for this purpose and grants capital allowances to the lessee. However, in France, leases are not capitalized in individual financial statements or for tax. So, the French lessor gets tax depreciation. Consequently, the lessor may charge an attractively low lease payment, and the lessee benefits twice. As usual, there are other complications, such as the treatment of the UK lease rental payments. However, there is at least scope for tax advantage.

The fourth point (untaxed income) is sometimes referred to as 'white income'. As an example, suppose that a compound financial instrument (see Chapter 16) is treated as a debt in the country of the issuing company but mostly as a share in the country of the owner of the instrument. The issuer's payment of interest will be tax deductible, but the owner's receipt may be treated as a non-taxable dividend.

22.4 Transfer pricing

When transactions take place between units within a company, it is necessary (at least for management accounting purposes) to set a 'transfer price' for them. When the units are separate companies within a group, the transfer pricing is necessary for financial reporting and for the calculation of taxable income. When the companies or units are in different tax jurisdictions, the issue becomes important because of different accounting rules, tax rates and so on. UNCTAD (1997) suggested that the value of goods and services being transferred within MNEs was greater than the value of all other exports from one country to another. The discussion below assumes the context of multinational enterprises (MNEs).

The way in which transfer prices are set depends upon the policies of the MNE, but it is quite common to use an approximation of arm's length market prices. Indeed, this is probably a good idea for the assessment of performance of units within the group, particularly to protect any minority shareholders. Nevertheless, an MNE may choose artificial prices in order to move profits around the group, perhaps in order to move profits away from high-tax countries. The charging of royalties, interest or management fees is another mechanism for moving profits.

On the theoretical side, McAulay and Tomkins (1992) and Leitch and Barrett (1992) examine the variables that might affect transfer pricing behaviour. These include such issues as financial markets, government intervention and administrative procedures. Elliott and Emmanuel (2000) look at the organizational issues in an international context. Lin *et al.* (1993) examine the relationship between taxes and tariffs. They point out the importance of withholding taxes in the context of Asian Pacific countries. Emmanuel (1999) creates a model, using the institutional arrangements of the United States, Taiwan and Greece. He suggests that different rates of tax are the most important variables in enabling the minimization of post-tax group income.

Research differs about what MNEs actually do. Plasschaert (1985) suggested that manipulation of transfer prices is more common in developing countries, where governments are poorly equipped to monitor MNEs. Al-Eryani *et al.* (1990) found that, for US MNEs, there was strong compliance with laws and that larger companies were more likely to use a market-based approach. Harris (1993), Klassen *et al.* (1993) and Jacob (1996) suggested that US-based multinational companies move income around the world in response to changes in tax rates. Oyelere and Emmanuel (1998) studied the practices of UK-based enterprises controlled from abroad. They also found evidence of significant shifting of income. Hung Chan and Lo (2004) find that the market-based approach is used where management believes that relationships with local partners and host governments need to be good.

Of course, tax authorities are alert to the problem of transfer pricing, which has become more important as globalization proceeds. Consequently, governments have empowered tax authorities to make adjustments to the calculation of taxable income to try to correct for transfers that are not at arm's length. The result of the adjustments may be that there is double taxation of some income of MNEs. The United States took the lead in regulations in this area. Section 482 of the Internal Revenue Code, which is the basic transfer pricing rule, has led to many regulations and tax cases. In 1992, extensive documentation requirements and penalties were introduced (US Treasury, 1992). In the United Kingdom, statutory requirements for detailed documentation on transfer prices were introduced in 1999/2000 (Rust and Graham, 2000). In some cases, governments have taken a different approach and have required apportionment of worldwide profits of the MNE (the 'unitary' or 'global' method). However, there is no international consensus on this rather broad-brush approach.

So as to add order to this area, governments have made tax treaties with each other on the subject of transfer prices. These are generally based on model tax treaties, such as those prepared by the Organisation for Economic Co-operation and Development (OECD, 1979 and 1995/6) and the United Nations. Deloitte (2002) summarize the transfer pricing rules for several countries.

22.5   Tax systems

22.5.1   Introduction

Section 22.2 has shown that the definition of taxable income varies greatly by country. The way in which taxable income is taxed depends upon the tax system. This also varies by country. Systems that are used or have been used in the recent past in the countries studied in this book can be classified into three types:

1   classical systems;
2   imputation systems;
3   split-rate systems.

These, and other ways to mitigate the double taxation of dividends, are described further below.

22.5.2   Classical systems

'Classical' tax systems are perhaps the simplest and easiest to explain. This simplicity leads to the alleged defects that other types of systems are designed to correct. Under a classical system, like most others, dividends paid are not deductible in the calculation of taxable income. However, these dividends are fully taxable in the hands of the recipients. Interest payments, as in most systems, are usually tax deductible, though this is not an essential feature of classical systems. The United States, the Netherlands and Sweden have been using classical systems for many years. The United Kingdom used such a system from 1965 to 1973. Several other

Table 22.2 **Some EU corporation tax systems in 2007/8**

(1) Country	(2) System	(3) Corporation tax rate %[a]
Austria	Classical (Split Rate to 1988)	25
Belgium	Classical (Imputation 1963–89)	33[b]
Denmark	Classical[c] (Imputation 1977–91)	28
Finland	Classical (Imputation 1990–2005)	26
France	Classical (Imputation 1965–2004)[d]	34.43
Germany	Dividend partially exempt[d] (Imputation 1977–2000)	26.38[e]
Greece	Dividend Exempt (Dividend deductible to 1992)	25
Ireland	Classical (Imputation 1976–99)	12.5
Italy	Classical (Imputation 1977–2003)	33[f]
Luxembourg	Classical[g]	22[h]
Netherlands	Classical	29.6
Portugal	Dividend partially exempt (Imputation 1989–2001)	25
Spain	Classical (Imputation 1986–2007)	30
Sweden	Classical	28
UK	Imputation (1973+)	30

Notes:
[a] Withholding taxes have been ignored throughout.
[b] This includes an austerity surcharge.
[c] With reduced rates of income tax for resident shareholders.
[d] Half of dividends are taxable.
[e] Including a social surcharge.
[f] This includes a regional tax.
[g] 50% of dividends are not taxable for resident shareholders.
[h] Including business tax.
Source: Compiled from various sources, including *Europe-Corporate Taxation* of the International Bureau of Fiscal Documentation.

EU countries have moved to (or back to) the classical system (see Table 22.2, which covers EU countries before the expansions of 2004 onwards).

There are two main criticisms of classical systems. Both rest upon what has been called the 'economic double taxation' of dividends, whereby distributed income is taxed both to corporate income tax (hereafter called corporation tax) and then to personal income tax. First, this double taxation is said to be inequitable when compared with the treatment of the distributed income of unincorporated businesses. Income of such businesses, whether physically distributed or not, bears no corporation tax but bears current income tax in the hands of the owners of the businesses. Such single taxation would not be so easy to arrange for corporations.

This is because retained profit does exist, both in reality and for tax purposes, and so if there were no separate corporation tax, taxation could be indefinitely postponed if companies delayed distribution. The alternative of taxing income only at the corporate level would mean that all individual recipients would have borne the same rate of tax. This would be unacceptable as part of an otherwise progressive income tax system. Thus, double taxation of the distributed income of corporations results from a desire by governments to ensure proper taxation of retained income.

The second case against economic double taxation is that it introduces a bias against the distribution of dividends. Since both total income and then distributed income are fully taxed, the larger the distribution, the larger is the total tax borne by a company and its shareholders. It might be thought that such an encouragement to retain profits would promote investment. However, more subtle economic thinking might suggest that profitable and efficient investment would be more likely to follow if companies distributed their profits and then shareholders allocated these funds through the new issue market to the most profitable companies. Unfortunately it is not proven that companies with a good earnings record will remain the most profitable.

It should also be noted about this second argument that, even if there were no effective corporation tax on distributed income (i.e. no double taxation), there would still be a bias against distribution if there were an income tax which had to be paid only when dividends were distributed. The two cases against the economic double taxation of dividends have given rise to other systems of taxation that are designed to mitigate these effects of classical systems.

22.5.3 Imputation systems

A frequently used way of mitigating the effects of economic double taxation is to impute to the recipients of dividends some of the tax paid by a corporation on the income out of which the dividends are paid. Imputation systems have been used in many EU countries (see Table 22.2), and also in Australia and Canada. Tables 22.3 and 22.4 illustrate the contrast between a classical system and an imputation system. The exact rates shown here are not important, but they happen to be those of the UK systems before 1973 and for 1979–83 respectively. Suppose that there is a 'basic rate' of income tax, which is the marginal rate for a majority of taxpayers; it has been assumed that this is 30 per cent, that the classical corporate tax rate is 40 per cent, and that the imputation rate is 52 per cent. Also, for simplicity, accounting and taxable income are assumed to be equal, as they might be in Germany but are generally not in the United Kingdom. The tax credit in the United Kingdom is linked to the basic rate of income tax for administrative simplicity. From 1979/80 to 1985/6, when the basic rate was 30 per cent, the tax credit was 30/70 or 3/7. Under the pre-1973 system there was a withholding of standard rate income tax at source.

A comparison of Tables 22.3 and 22.4 shows that, for shareholders who pay only basic rate income tax, the UK imputation system fully removes the double taxation of dividends. The total tax (£5,200 in the tables) under the imputation system does not alter as the level of dividends rises. However, the case is different when there are shareholders who pay a higher rate of personal income tax. Then there is still a

Table 22.3 Classical and imputation systems (low payout)

		Classical £		Imputation £
Company				
Income (say)		10,000		10,000
Corporation tax (40%)		4,000	(52%)	5,200
Distributable income		6,000		4,800
Distribution (say) gross		2,000		
Less income tax deducted at source (30%)	600			
Net	1,400		Cash	1,400
Retained income		4,000		3,400
Shareholders (basic rate)				
Dividend: cash received		1,400		1,400
Income tax deducted at source		600		0
Tax credit received (3/7)		0		600
Gross dividend		2,000	'Grossed up' dividend	2,000
Income tax liability (30%)		600		600
Less tax already deducted		600		0
Less tax credit		0		600
Tax due		0		0
Total tax	(4,000 + 600)	4,600		5,200

Table 22.4 Classical and imputation systems (high payout)

		Classical £		Imputation £
Company				
Income (say)		10,000		10,000
Corporation tax (40%)		4,000	(52%)	5,200
Distributable income		6,000		4,800
Distribution (say) gross		5,000		
Less income tax deduction (30%)	1,500			
Net	3,500		Cash	3,500
Retained income		1,000		1,300
Shareholders (basic rate)				
Dividend: cash received		3,500		3,500
Income tax deducted at source		1,500		0
Tax credit received (3/7)		0		1,500
Gross dividend		5,000	'Grossed up' dividend	5,000
Income tax liability (30%)		1,500		1,500
Less tax already deducted		1,500		0
Less tax credit		0		1,500
Tax due		0		0
Total tax	(4,000 + 1,500)	5,500		5,200

Table 22.5 Classical and imputation systems (higher-rate taxpayers)

	Classical £		Imputation £
Low payout			
Company (as Table 22.3)			
Shareholders (50% marginal rate)			
Dividend: cash received	1,400		1,400
Income tax deducted at source	600		0
Tax credit received (3/7)	0		600
Gross dividend	2,000	'Grossed up' dividend	2,000
Income tax liability (50%)	1,000		1,000
Less tax already deducted	600		0
Less tax credit	0		600
Tax due	400		400
Total tax (4,000 + 600 + 400)	5,000	(5,200 + 400)	5,600
High payout			
Company (as Table 22.4)			
Shareholders (50% marginal rate)			
Dividend: cash received	3,500		3,500
Income tax deducted at source	1,500		0
Tax credit received (3/7)	0		1,500
Gross dividend	5,000	'Grossed up' dividend	5,000
Income tax liability (50%)	2,500		2,500
Less tax already deducted	1,500		0
Less tax credit	0		1,500
Tax due	1,000		1,000
Total tax (4,000 + 1,500 + 1,000)	6,500	(5,200 + 1,000)	6,200

double taxation and the bias against distribution remains. Table 22.5 illustrates this by reworking the bottom halves of Tables 22.3 and 22.4 for shareholders who pay higher rates of tax. In this case, the total taxation is higher when there is a larger payout, not only under the classical system but also under the imputation system.

The present UK system, like most existing imputation systems, involves partial imputation. That is, only part of the corporation tax paid by companies is imputed to shareholders. In 2007/08 it was 26 per cent, as Table 22.6 shows.

The partial imputation system of France was broadly similar to that in the United Kingdom. However, only the UK system bases the size of the tax credit on an income tax rate. A summary of rates is shown as Table 22.2.

Most continental European systems of taxation also contain 'withholding taxes', whereby some proportion of dividends is deducted at source. The presence of such a tax is not a differentiating feature for the classification of tax systems; eventual tax burdens are generally not affected, since the withholding tax can be set against tax liabilities or reclaimed by most recipients of dividends. The main purpose of withholding taxes is to reduce evasion, particularly by holders of bearer shares and by foreign shareholders.

Table 22.6 UK partial imputation, 2007/8

	£
Company	
Income	1,000
Corporation tax	300
	700
Dividend	700
	0
Shareholders	
Cash receipt	700
Tax credit (10/90)	78
'Grossed up' dividend	778
Partial imputation = (78/300) =	26%

22.5.4 Split-rate systems

A second way to reduce the effects of double taxation is to charge a lower rate of tax on distributed income than on retained income. The West German system until the end of 1976 was a split-rate system, with a 51 per cent rate for retained income and a 15 per cent rate for distributed income. From 1977 to 2000, Germany had an imputation system with two rates. Austria had a split-rate system until 1989.

It is possible to reorganize a partial imputation system into a split-rate system with identical tax liabilities and therefore, presumably, identical economic effects (Nobes, 1980). Therefore it could be said that, for the purposes of classification, split-rate systems and partial imputation systems are in the same category.

22.5.5 Other ways to mitigate double taxation of dividends

There are many other ways to reduce double taxation. In the United States, for example, the classical system is modified in that there are allowances of a certain amount of investment income received by an individual each year which is exempted from personal income tax. In Germany from 2001 and in France from 2005, only half of dividend receipts are taxed. Dividends are also partially exempt in Portugal. In Greece, dividend receipts are exempt from tax. The 'primary dividend' system, which once operated in Sweden and Iceland, allows companies to deduct some proportion of dividends in the calculation of their taxable incomes.

22.5.6 A note on tax rates

Table 22.2 shows the rates of tax for a particular year, but many changes occur around the world from year to year. The trend in rates is downward. For example, President Reagan's US administration lowered rates in the late 1980s, and President Bush's administration continued that process. The composite German rate for retained profit was over 50 per cent in 1998 but fell to about 26 per cent for 2001. In Ireland the rate fell to 16 per cent in 2002 and 12.5 per cent in 2003 onwards.

22.6 | Harmonization

The existing differences between effective taxation burdens in different countries give rise to great difficulties for the revenue authorities that tax multinational enterprises. These companies themselves put considerable effort into reducing overall taxation by moving capital and profits around the world (see Sections 22.3 and 22.4). These are also matters of international business finance and management accounting. The existence of these differences has not yet given rise to the same plethora of proposals and committees for international harmonization as have the differences between accounting systems. However, within the European Union, harmonization of taxation is in progress. Many Directives on the harmonization of value added tax and other forms of indirect taxation have been passed. Direct corporate taxation, which we are concerned with here, has also been the subject of proposals for harmonization. Progress in this area has been even slower than in company law and accounting because of the reluctance of governments to lose any control over direct taxation.

The Treaty of Rome calls for the elimination of customs duties between member states, the introduction of common tariffs with third countries, and the removal of barriers to the free movement of persons, capital, goods and services. The interest in taxation shown by the European Commission, which is the guardian of the Treaty of Rome, stems from this desire to promote free movement. The free movement of goods and services implies particularly the harmonization of indirect taxes. Similarly, the free movement of people and capital implies the harmonization of direct taxes. If there were no harmonization of taxes and if barriers to movement were eliminated, there might then be encouragement or obstruction of flows of people, capital and so on to particular countries within the European Union for purely fiscal reasons.

It is the aim of harmonization (Burke, 1979) that the conditions of competition and the returns to capital and effort should not be significantly affected by differences in effective tax burdens. Just by having looked briefly at the corporate taxation systems in some EU countries, it should be clear that the scope for harmonization is considerable. The European Commission's proposals have covered tax systems and tax bases. The Commission's activity in the area of direct corporate taxation will now be outlined. Far more effort has been directed to value added taxes.

In 1962, the Neumark Committee (1963) recommended to the European Commission that a split-rate system should be adopted. Later the van den Tempel Report (1970) described the three types of corporation tax systems, and recommended the classical system. However, the Commission's draft Directive (EC Commission, 1975; Nobes, 1979) on the harmonization of corporate taxation proposed the imputation system. This must be partly due to the fact that a majority of EU countries were already using such a system or had plans to introduce one. In 1975, Belgium, France and the United Kingdom were using an imputation system. After that, Germany, Denmark, Ireland and Italy introduced one. However, most countries have returned to the classical system (see Table 22.2).

Some of the reasons for choosing an imputation system have been mentioned. They include the fact that the tax credit reduces the bias against distribution and favours small investors (lower-rate taxpayers). Also, the system should reduce the incentive for evasion by lowering the effective marginal rate of tax on dividends. In addition, since the corporation tax rate tends to be higher under an imputation system, there is a fairer comparison between the rates of tax borne on company retained profits and partnership profits (*European Taxation*, 1976; OECD, 1974).

Article 3 of the draft Directive of 1975 proposes that there shall be imputation systems in operation with a single rate of tax between 45 and 55 per cent. Also, Article 8 proposes that imputation credits shall be between 45 and 55 per cent of the corporation tax that would have to be paid on a sum equal to the taxable income out of which the dividend could be paid (i.e. on the dividend increased by the corporation tax; see Table 22.6). The rates in force in the EU in 2007/8 are shown in Table 22.2, which reveals that little notice has been taken of these proposals. Other proposals within the draft Directive are that there should be a withholding tax of 25 per cent unless shares are registered, as in the United Kingdom (Arts 15–17); and that tax credits should be available to shareholders irrespective of their member state (Art. 4). This last requirement is clearly designed to promote the free movement of investors' capital. These various requirements would necessitate important adjustments in some EU countries, as Table 22.2 suggests.

The draft Directive was criticized on many grounds. The omission of a proposed treatment for capital gains was important. Unless their taxation is also harmonized, there will be much wasteful manoeuvring in order to create capital gains in favourable member states rather than income in any state or capital gains in unfavourable states. Another criticism was that other corporate taxes, like net worth, turnover and local taxes, must be included in the harmonization. More generally, the different rules relating to the calculation of taxable income need attention if total effective tax burdens are to be harmonized. A further criticism was that some countries in the European Union are intrinsically less attractive to companies for economic, geographical and political reasons; and that these countries need advantageous corporate tax regimes if they are to encourage investment and employment. Therefore, to harmonize taxation without altering these other factors might give rise to undesirable regional side-effects.

The 'opinion' of the European Parliament (Official Journal, 1979) on the draft Directive stressed the need to include the problem of different tax bases as well as tax systems. Partly as a result of this and partly because member states are not enthusiastic about changing their tax systems or losing flexibility, the 1975 draft Directive was significantly delayed. In 1988, there was an unpublished draft of a Directive on the tax base (Kuiper, 1988). Eventually, in 1990, the Commission abandoned its plans for general harmonization, in order to concentrate on those details that particularly affect cross-border activity.

In 1990, a parent/subsidiary Directive was adopted by the EC (EC Council, 1990) that requires relief for outgoing dividends from withholding taxes and for incoming dividends of further corporate taxation. This applies to holdings of 25 per cent or more. In 1992, a major report on tax harmonization was published by the Commission (see Bovenberg *et al.*, 1992; Hamaekers, 1992; Kopits, 1992; Messere, 1993; Vanistendael, 1993). This Ruding Report (EC Commission, 1992) was somewhat overtaken by political events, such as the difficulties with the Maastricht treaty, so that only modest tax harmonization proposals are likely to be taken forward by the Commission in the short or medium term.

In 2001, the Commission established a policy to move towards a 'common consolidated tax base' in the EU. In 2003, it proposed using IFRS accounting as the starting point for the tax base. However, the whole project has generated opposition from companies who fear an attack on the competitiveness of Europe, and from particular member states (e.g. Ireland) that operate especially attractive tax regimes, so progress on this will be slow.

SUMMARY

- Corporate taxation plays an important role in some countries' financial accounting practices. Also, a knowledge of corporate taxation is important for international business finance.

- Tax bases differ in their treatment of depreciation, inventory holding gains, capital gains, losses, dividends received, certain expenses and many other matters. The importance of taxes other than national corporate income taxation also varies.

- Tax systems differ mainly in respect of their treatment of dividends. Classical systems treat corporations and their owners quite separately, giving rise to 'double taxation' of dividends.

- Other systems try to mitigate this for equity and efficiency reasons. For example, imputation systems give shareholders credit for some or all of the corporation tax underlying their dividends. Such systems are now predominant in the European Union and favoured by the European Commission.

- Split-rate systems achieve a similar effect by taxing distributed income at a lower rate than retained income.

- Harmonization of systems was proposed by the European Commission in a 1975 draft Directive, on which progress was exceedingly slow. A piecemeal approach has been taken more recently.

References

Al-Eryani, M., Alam, P. and Akhter, S. (1990) 'Transfer pricing determinants of US multinationals', *Journal of International Business Studies*, 3rd Quarter.

Bovenberg, A.L., Crossen, S., Vanistendael, F. and Westerburgen, J. (1992) *Harmonization of Company Taxation in the European Community: Some Comments on the Ruding Committee Report*, Kluwer, Amsterdam.

Burke, R. (1979) 'Harmonization of corporation tax', *Intertax*, June–July.

Commerce Clearing House (yearly editions) *United States Master Tax Guide*, Commerce Clearing House, Chicago.

Deloitte (2002) *Strategy Matrix for Global Transfer Pricing: Comparison of Methods, Documentation, Penalties, and Other Issues*, Deloitte Touche Tohmatsu, New York.

EC Commission (1975) *Proposal for a Directive Concerning the Harmonization of Systems of Company Taxation and of Withholding Taxes on Dividends*, COM(75) 392 final, Brussels.

EC Commission (1992) *Report of the Committee of Independent Experts on Company Taxation*, reprinted in *European Taxation*, Vol. 32, No. 4/5.

EC Council (1990) *Council Directive of 23 July 1990 on the Common System of Taxation Applicable to Parent Companies and Their Subsidiaries of Different Member States*, 90/435/EC.

Elliott, J. (2005) 'International transfer pricing', Ch. 11 in Lamb *et al.* (2005).

Elliott, J. and Emmanuel, C.R. (2000) *International Transfer Pricing: A Study of Cross-border Transactions*, Chartered Institute of Management Accountants, London.

Emmanuel, C.R. (1999) 'Income shifting and international transfer pricing: a three-country example', *Abacus*, Vol. 35, No. 3.

European Taxation (1976) International Bureau of Fiscal Documentation, Amsterdam, Vol. 16, Nos. 2, 3, 4, pp. 41–51.

Hamaekers, H. (1992) 'The EC on the brink of full corporation tax harmonization', *European Taxation*, Vol. 32, No. 4/5.

Harris, D.G. (1993) 'The impact of US tax law revision on multinational corporations' capital location and income shifting decisions', *Journal of Accounting Research*, Vol. 31, Supplement.

Hoogendoorn, M. (1996) 'Accounting and taxation in Europe – a comparative overview', *European Accounting Review*, Vol. 5, Supplement.

Hung Chan, K. and Lo, A.W.Y. (2004) 'The influence of management perception of fundamental variables on the choice of international transfer-pricing methods', *International Journal of Accounting*, Vol. 39, No. 1.

IBFD (yearly) *The Taxation of Companies in Europe*, Guides to European Taxation, International Bureau of Fiscal Documentation, Amsterdam.

Jacob, J. (1996) 'Taxes and transfer pricing: income shifting and the volume of intrafirm transfers', *Journal of Accounting Research*, Vol. 34, No. 2, Fall.

James, S.R. and Nobes, C.W. (1992) *The Economics of Taxation*, Prentice Hall, Hernel Hempstead.

James, S.R. and Nobes, C.W. (2007) *The Economics of Taxation*, Prentice Hall, Harlow.

Klassen, K., Lang, M. and Wolfson, M. (1993) 'Geographic income shifting by multinational corporations in response to tax rate changes', *Journal of Accounting Research*, Vol. 31, Supplement.

Kopits, G. (ed.) (1992) *Tax Harmonization in the European Community: Policy Issues and Analysis*, International Monetary Fund, Occasional Paper No. 94.

Kuiper, W.G. (1988) 'EC Commission proposes a Directive on the harmonisation of rules for the determination of taxable profits of enterprises', *European Taxation*, Vol. 28, No. 10.

Lamb, M. (1995) 'When is a group a group? Convergence of concepts of "group" in European Union corporation tax', *European Accounting Review*, Vol. 4, No. 1.

Lamb, M. (2005) 'Taxation research as accounting research', Ch. 4 in Lamb *et al.* (2005).

Lamb, M., Nobes, C.W. and Roberts, A.D. (1998) 'International variations in the connections between tax and financial reporting', *Accounting and Business Research*, Summer.

Lamb, M., Lymer, A., Freedman, J. and James, S. (2005) *Taxation: An Interdisciplinary Approach to Research*, Oxford University Press, Oxford.

Leitch, R.A. and Barrett, K.S. (1992) 'Multinational transfer pricing: objectives and constraints', *Journal of Accounting Literature*, Vol. 11, pp. 47–92.

Lin, L., Lefebvre, C. and Kantor, J. (1993) 'Economic determinants of international transfer pricing and the related accounting issues, with particular references to Asian Pacific countries', *International Journal of Accounting*, Vol. 28, No. 1.

McAulay, L. and Tomkins, C.R. (1992) 'A review of the contemporary transfer pricing literature with recommendations for future research', *British Journal of Management*, Vol. 3, pp. 101–2.

Messere, K. (1993) 'A personal view on certain aspects of the Ruding Report and the EC Commission's reaction to it', *European Taxation*, Vol. 33, No. 1.

Neumark Committee (1963) *EEC Reports on Tax Harmonization*, International Bureau of Fiscal Documentation, Amsterdam.

Nobes, C.W. (1979) 'Fiscal harmonisation and European integration: comments', *European Law Review*, August.

Nobes, C.W. (1980) 'Imputation systems of corporation tax in the EEC', *Accounting and Business Research*, Spring.

Nobes, C.W. and Schwencke, H.R. (2006) 'Tax and financial reporting links: a longitudinal examination over 30 years up to IFRS adoption, using Norway as a case study', *European Accounting Review*, Vol. 15, No. 1.

OECD (1974) *Theoretical and Empirical Aspects of Corporate Taxation*, Paris.

OECD (1979) *Transfer Pricing and Multinational Enterprises*, Paris.

OECD (1995/6) *Transfer Pricing Guidelines for Multinational Enterprises and Tax Administrations*, Paris.

Official Journal of the EC (1979) C140; see also report in *Intertax*, October 1979.

Oyelere, P.B. and Emmanuel, C.R. (1998) 'International transfer pricing and income shifting: evidence from the UK', *European Accounting Review*, Vol. 7, No. 4.

Picciotto, S. (1992) *International Business Taxation*, Weidenfeld and Nicolson, London.

Plasschaert, S.R.F. (1985) 'Transfer pricing problems in developing countries', in A.M. Rugman and L. Eden (eds), *Multinationals and Transfer Pricing*, St. Martin's Press, New York.

PricewaterhouseCoopers (2001) *Corporate Taxes, Worldwide Summaries*, New York.

Rust, M. and Graham, P. (2000) 'Transfer pricing – is your house in order?' *Accounting and Business*, April.

UNCTAD (1997) 'Overview' in *World Investment Report – Transnational Corporations, Market Structure and Competition Policy*, United Nations, Geneva.

US Treasury (1992) *Regulation S.1.6662* of the Internal Revenue Code, Washington, DC.

van den Tempel, A.J. (1970) *Corporation Tax and Individual Income Tax in the EEC*, Commission of the EC, Brussels.

Vanistendael, F. (1993) 'Some basic problems on the road to tax harmonization', *European Taxation*, Vol. 33, No. 1.

Further reading

For a more detailed account of tax systems, see PricewaterhouseCoopers' annual world tax summaries, and James and Nobes (2007).

For discussions on the effects of different tax systems, see *European Taxation* (1976) and OECD (1974).

For a survey of accounting research connected to taxation, see Lamb *et al.* (2005).

Useful websites

American Taxation Association	www.atasection.org
Institute for Fiscal Studies	www.ifs.org.uk
International Bureau of Fiscal Documentation	www.ibfd.nl
National Tax Association	www.ntanet.org

QUESTIONS

Suggested answers to the asterisked questions are given at the end of the book.

22.1* 'Corporate tax systems differ internationally more than accounting systems differ, so it is impossible to classify them into groups.' Discuss.

22.2* 'There is no point in harmonizing tax systems and tax rates without harmonizing the calculation of taxable income.' Discuss.

22.3 In which countries does taxation tend to have a major influence on published company accounts? Discuss how this influence takes effect and what the position is regarding the treatment of taxation in *consolidated* accounts.

22.4   In what ways might classification be useful in any field of study? Use international differences in financial reporting and in corporate taxation as illustrations of your answer.

22.5   'The classical system of corporation tax is useful because it causes companies to retain more profit for investment purposes.' Discuss.

22.6   Relating to the taxation of corporate income, examine international differences in:

(a) the calculation of taxable income;
(b) the 'system' of taxation (e.g. classical, imputation);
(c) the effect of taxes on accounting valuation and measurement; and
(d) the calculation of the tax numbers shown in financial statements.

22.7   Explain how the international differences in tax rules might be used to advantage by a multinational company.

23 Managerial accounting

Stephen Salter

OBJECTIVES

After reading this chapter you should be able, within a comparative and multinational context, to:

- discuss the choice, by companies, of a strategic objective;

- outline the budgeting process within multinational companies;

- explain how multinational companies attempt to avoid foreign currency translation, transaction and economic exposures;

- explain the differences between behaviour control, outcome control and clan control;

- explain the impact of the US Sarbanes-Oxley Act on global control.

23.1   Introduction

The field of managerial accounting and control in a global business environment has the interesting property of being a mixture of two disciplines. The first is the relatively soft art of management which, at least as far as 'international' is concerned, finds its origins in anthropology and psychology and attempts to provide a perspective on the unique behavioural problems of controlling a business entity. The second part, 'accounting', deals with the technical side of recording and manipulating information to provide what may be described as an optimal package or set of information. This chapter attempts to look at both areas as they relate to doing business in various countries.

The need for management accounting and control arises from the strategy of the firm. Management accounting serves both to provide information to management and to be used by management as a tool for ensuring that employees' actions and objectives are aligned with those of the firm. The basic challenges of management accounting within a firm can be formalized as follows:

1 What is the strategic objective of the firm?
2 What types of resources does the firm need and where does it anticipate getting them in the short term (operating budgets) and in the longer term (capital budgets)?
3 Is there a system in place that tells the firm whether it is going off track and needs to make corrections?
4 How does the firm know that it has arrived at where it wants to go?
5 How does the firm evaluate and reward the performance of its managers?

Figure 23.1 suggests the links that occur within a strategy and control system in diagrammatic form.

Section 23.2 looks at a popular method for assessing whether objectives have been met. In the international area, meeting objectives is made more complicated by different currencies and cultures. Sections 23.3 and 23.4 address the currency issue, and Section 23.5 looks at the role of culture. Section 23.6 examines control and performance.

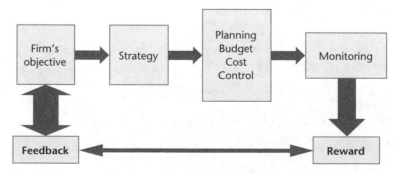

Figure 23.1 Strategy and control: an overview

23.2 The balanced scorecard as an overview tool

In attempting to approach the multi-level objectives of any firm described above, one tool that has come to the fore is the balanced scorecard (Kaplan and Norton, 1992). The idea of this control tool is that firms that both derive successful strategies and implement them within a coherent and controlled framework develop and maintain advantages over their competitors.

Organizations face an increasingly global, competitive environment. This trend has influenced strategic choices, such as what businesses and markets to be in. Taking advantage of global strategies also includes structuring decisions. For instance, the degree of centralization versus decentralization becomes an integral part of the strategy implementation process. In line with this thinking, going global entails increasing complexity with regard to management control systems. Unfortunately, typical, traditional, financial-only measures do not provide sufficient information for managers of international firms to implement global strategies. To address this problem, the balanced scorecard (BSC) can be used as a complement to the existing organizational control systems and as a means to better communicate and thus implement strategy. Robert Kaplan and David Norton introduced the technique in a 1992 *Harvard Business Review* article.

Since 1992, the BSC has gained immense popularity in the United States. Bain and Company conducts an annual survey to determine the popularity of various management techniques in the United States. They reported that about 50 per cent of *Fortune 1000* firms use balanced scorecards (Furnald, 2001). A study by Marr (2004) of 780 CEOs and CFOs from large US organizations is more conservative and finds that 35 per cent of those surveyed use a balanced scorecard. Internationally the results vary as well. In a survey of internal auditors across 34 countries, Melville (2003) concludes that the BSC has been widely adopted and forms a strong basis for internal control and commitment to the firms' strategies. This commitment includes using some of the softer objectives that are not typically associated with accountants. A study of senior executives by Franco *et al.* (2004) finds that while 35 per cent of Australian organizations use a BSC to measure performance, only 18 per cent of major UK companies do. In the United Kingdom, the preferred tool is Key Performance Indicators (KPI) which are quantifiable measurements, agreed to beforehand, that reflect the critical success factors of an organization, but tend to be hard, such as financial ratios, rather than soft.

The traditional balanced scorecard is shown in Figure 23.2 (overleaf). As can be seen, the balanced scorecard is limited to four perspectives at different parts of the organization's value adding process. Landry *et al.* (2002) have suggested that a fifth perspective could be added in order to monitor the organization's uniquely global issues such as political risk, transfer pricing, exchange rate risk and protection and market demographics. This would supplement the standard domestic balanced scorecard. A possible five-perspective card is illustrated in Figure 23.3 (overleaf).

Finally, Landry *et al.* (2002) have suggested how this might be applied to General Electric, a leading US multinational (see Table 23.1).

Figure 23.2 A traditional balanced scorecard: four perspectives

Figure 23.3 A traditional balanced scorecard adapted for international organizations

Source: Landry, S., Chan, W. and Jalbert, T. (2002) Balanced scorecard for multinationals, *Journal of Corporate Accounting and Finance*, September/October, p. 38. Copyright © 2002 John Wiley & Sons. Reproduced with permission.

Table 23.1 What the international perspective might look like for a global company

---

General Electric international perspective of balanced scorecard (hypothetical)

Perspective	Critical success factors[1]	Performance measures
International	Customer support	– International customer satisfaction
		– International customer retention
		– Quality international customer service
	Investment in global capabilities	– Number of new international markets entered
		– Number of products introduced into international markets
		– Production plants opened and/or expanded in foreign countries
	Creation of strong and global teams	– Intensify hiring of indigenous personnel
		– Cross-cultural training
		– Cultural as well as job rotation
		– Language training

Note: [1] General Electric's 2001 Annual Report noted these factors under the 'Globalization' route to accelerated growth.
Source: Adapted from Landry *et al.* (2002) 'Balanced scorecard for multinationals', *Journal of Corporate Accounting and Finance*, p. 38. Copyright © 2002 John Wiley & Sons, Inc. Reprinted with permission.

23.3   Currency and control

23.3.1 Introduction

Exchange rate movements, just as in financial accounting, have an influence on management accounting, particularly on budgeting and performance measurement. From a manager's point of view this is particularly important. In theory, non-domestic managers should be evaluated after taking account of differences in environment, such as currency fluctuations. However, Borkowski (1999) finds that multinational enterprises (MNEs) evaluate domestic and foreign subsidiary managers without compensating for these. A good understanding of the interactions of foreign exchange and management control systems can help the manager to deal with, or at least assess, the risks of a non-domestic venture.

23.3.2 Types of exposure

Defining the risks starts by understanding that movements in exchange rates between the home and other currencies leads to three types of exposure: translation, transaction and economic.

Translation exposure

'Translation exposure' is an accounting issue. It exists because, upon consolidation, assets in one currency have to be re-expressed in another. Balance sheet and income statement items, whose value remains constant in local currency, will change as they are translated into that of the parent company. This translation effect influences budgets. First, in budgetary planning, an initial rate must be chosen to prepare projected statements. This may be the current rate at the time the budget is prepared, a forward rate for the beginning or end of the budget, or some series of multiple rates. During the period for which the budget has been prepared, exchange rate variances occur. These can cause differences between actual and budgeted revenue and expenditure figures. If the temporal method (see Chapter 18) is used for translation, items such as depreciation and amortization, which are related to historical cost assets, would be budgeted using historical exchange rates, and actual costs would be translated at those same rates. Using the current rate method, by holding the assets acquired through operations to the end of the year, there will be an additional effect from exchange rate movements. Also, assets held since the beginning of the year will be affected by the exchange rate movement for the entire year. These effects on shareholders' funds are known as the cumulative translation adjustment.

These variances are, to some extent, dependent on the initial rate chosen. For performance evaluation purposes, some of the impacts of exchange movements can be removed if an individual manager is not responsible for exchange management. However, there may be indirect effects such as:

- the need to adjust selling prices and plans for out-of-country inputs;
- positive or negative changes in volume from the impact of changes in exchange rates on domestic and export markets;
- deviations from standard input efficiencies because alternative domestic and foreign suppliers, who become more price competitive as a result of exchange changes, were employed.

To remove all of the effects of foreign exchange rate fluctuations, a separate exchange rate may be required in budgeting for each revenue and expense item, making planning even more complex.

Transaction exposure

'Transaction exposure' results from unhedged contracted cash flows (see Section 16.4). Usually a separate budget for international cash flows may be prepared to assess whether the volume of unhedged cash flows is significant. Such a budget will facilitate the planning, controlling and evaluating of hedging activities and policies. While this can be done at the local level, the vast majority of companies appear to do it in global or regional treasury departments, and such departments will plan a hedging strategy. However, hedging expenses will need to be included in the income and expense budgets prepared both for the company as a whole and for the divisions.

Economic exposure

'Economic exposure' is the third impact of foreign exchange rate variations on corporations and corporate budgeting. It involves uncontracted and unplanned changes in future cash flows generated from operations and foreign investments as a result of a change in exchange rates. Decisions involved in dealing with this type of exposure are primarily long-term and include choosing market and production facility locations. Other decisions include pricing strategy, sales mix, how operations are financed and personnel rewards. The impact of each of these decisions will clearly be part of the profit planning and control structures. In the case of budgeting, if the budget is to be at all realistic, these 'economic impacts' of foreign exchange variations may determine the base decisions which in turn generate the most basic numbers for the budget.

23.3.3 The need to translate

While each of the types of foreign exchange exposure influences budgeting in the multinational, the question then becomes: 'Why bother to translate at all, why not simply leave operational budgets in local currency, much as a domestic firm would do?' In fact, if a company has a long-established tradition of being a collection of relatively independent operations, each raising capital on the local capital markets, there may well be a strong case for doing just that.

However, there are several arguments for choosing a base foreign currency rate and then translating budgets and targets into a common currency. Comparability of branch operations is the major reason to budget and control using information trans-lated into a single currency. As foreign exchange controls have fallen away in most countries, planning for a business has become similar to selecting a portfolio of foreign shares. Each of these shares must, in the end, be compared with the other members of the portfolio for maximum return to the shareholder. Companies using this strategy find it necessary to have a common basis for decisions if they are to evaluate where the foreign operation fits into their portfolio. While this may be grossly unfair to the individual managing a foreign subsidiary, this information is necessary to calculate deviations from anticipated returns on investment (ROI) worldwide. Companies, after all, must be responsible to their shareholders, and global ROI in the parent cur-rency is likely to have a major effect on dividends and share prices.

Another reason to budget using translated information is the notion of holding management responsible for dealing appropriately with exchange rate movements. In countries where the currency is depreciating against the currency of the home country, management of the foreign subsidiary may be responsible for repatriating cash as it becomes available through income, at least within the limits of the local law. Thus, management might be charged with getting cash home within those limits to reduce exchange losses. Budgeting and control with translated information can help to explain the success or failure of that policy. Finally, the accounting rules in many countries require significant global consolidation, and the use of a single master currency is likely to facilitate the process of year-end consolidation and reconciliation of management's internal and external financial data.

23.3.4 Operational budgeting under foreign exchange fluctuations

So we return to the question, what exchange rate should be used for budgeting and control? The budgeting process begins well before the budget year. This provides three clear choices for exchange rates: the rate at the time of budget completion; the rate at the beginning of the budget year; and an estimate of the average rate during the budget year (a forward rate). The choice may be made by looking at interim information during budget preparation and at who assumes responsibility for exchange management.

Consider a simple example of what can happen. Suppose that a company in South Africa is budgeting for its subsidiary in Australia for the calendar year 2007.

At the beginning of the budgeting process on 1 September 2006, the rate is 5.6 rand per dollar. This could certainly be used as the rate for the complete budgeting process. However, perhaps results have shown a steady weakening of the rand over the previous 12 months. The company could attempt to anticipate the effect of this continued depreciation by preparing several scenarios, and if this depreciation continues, both budgetary and real action may have to be taken to stabilize profits. An example of such action would be at the start of the financial year, for example, to enter into a long-term hedge until 31 December 2007 which would protect the anticipated Australian dollar profits based upon this exchange rate. This would also require a budget planning adjustment at that time.

If the South African management wants the Australian management to assume responsibility for protecting the exchange rate change, then a budget based on the beginning of 2007 rate might be appropriate. In this case, the Australian management is only responsible for exchange rate gains and losses beginning with 1 January 2007. Alternatively, the head office may budget using a September 2007 rate and should take a 90-day hedge for the period 1 October 2007 to 31 December 2007 to protect the budget until the starting point where the Australian management takes over. Once January 1 arrives the Australian management would probably enter into a hedge to protect against the exchange rate movement during the budget year.

A final strategy for selecting a budget exchange rate involves only theoretical rather than real actions in the budget process. In this case, although no foreign exchange actions are taken, the South African head office's estimate of the average rate or a forward rate for the year could be used to develop the budget, and deviations from that rate actually become the responsibility of either the forecasting department or are shared with the subsidiary's management by giving them the task of managing changes beyond the forecasters' predictions.

23.3.5 Capital budgeting

Capital budgeting is the longer-term version of the operational budgeting discussed above. However, many of the considerations discussed – particularly as they relate to economic exposure – continue to apply. As in short-term planning or budgeting, long-range planning or capital budgeting must take into consideration anticipated exchange rate movements for discounting future cash flows. This becomes part of the risk involved in choosing the discount rate, along with any environmental uncertainty. Environmental uncertainty can be mild, such as the risk of unexpected heavier taxation, or severe, such as the risk of expropriation. In general, the risk is greater in less developed countries than in wealthier trading partners, but even in the latter there are many adverse events that are unpredictable. For a discussion of this problem, see Kobrin (1979) and Edmunds and Ellis (1999).

Whether or not standardized reporting practices are used in a multinational company, it is necessary to consider whether foreign operations and their managers should be evaluated on a global basis or merely on a national basis. Comparing ROIs or net profit is a primary method to evaluate both individual operations and individual managers on a standardized or global basis. But can effective decisions be arrived at in this manner? Sometimes, when environmental factors are used in long-term strategic decisions, the outcome may appear to be at odds with the quest for strong ROIs on a year-to-year basis. Therefore capital budgeting may require even more judgement than operational budgeting. In any case, the assignment of budget responsibility should be treated seriously. It also leads us to the significant issue in the management control area, namely that of control and performance evaluation, together with an allied reward structure.

23.4 Variances and foreign exchange

We have discussed in the budgeting section how changes in the value of a local currency can affect budgeting and decisions. It can equally affect performance evaluation. The key link is a formal system of variance analysis, which can be a useful analytical tool telling management where problems lie. Consider a South African Company, Zambezi Boards, which is attempting to arbitrage the lucrative trade in high end surfboards between South Africa and Australia. Zambezi Boards forms an Australian Subsidiary (Ozboards) to sell its products in Australia. As can be seen from Table 23.2, in 2007 Ozboards suffers a number of unfortunate occurrences.

Table 23.2 Analyzing variances in the sales budget of Zambezi Boards in 2007

Basic data	Reference	Value	Calculations	Results
Exchange rate used budget (R/$)	A	R 5.66		
Exchange rate end of budget yr in R/$	B	R 5.88		
Average exchange rate (R/$)	C	R 6.01		
Budgeted sales price ($)	D	$349		
Budgeted volume (units)	E	10,000		
Sales budget ($)	F		D × E	$ 3,490,000
Sales budget (R)	G		D × E × A	R 19,755,843
Results				
Actual sales (units) at OZBOARDS Australia	H	7500		
Actual Sales Price $ OZBOARDS Australia in AUD	I	$275		
What went wrong in OZ: Australian $ variance calculations untranslated sub in $.				
Actual sales ($)	J		H × I	$ 2,062,500
Actual sales (units) × budgeted (std) price	K		H × D	$ 2,617,500
Sales price variance (minus sign is unfavourable)	L		J – K	–$ 555,000
Sales volume variance (minus sign is unfavourable)	M		K – F	–$ 872,500
What did the exchange rate do to Zambezi Boards: translated variance calculations in R				
Actual sales R at average exchange rate (R/$)	N		H × I × C	R 12,395,625
Actual sales (units) × actual price ($) × budgeted (std) exchange rate	O		H × I × A	R 11,675,194
Exchange rate variance (minus sign is unfavourable)	Q		N – O	R 720,431
You can recompute variances from above				
Actual sales (units) × budgeted (std) price × std exchange rate	P		H × D × A	R 14,816,882
R Sales price variance (minus sign is unfavourable)	R		O – P	–R 3,141,689
R Sales volume variance = (Actual sales (units) × budgeted (std) price × std exchange rate) – Sales budget (R)	S		P – G	–R 4,938,961

Due to continued personal imports by Australian surfies buying their boards directly from South African traders, Ozboards is less successful than expected. First sales volume (in units) has dropped which, even if prices had remained the same as budgeted in Australian dollars, would have resulted in a drop in sales of $872,500 (see item M). However, sales price per unit has also fallen from $349 to $275, enough to reduce revenue by a further $555,000 (item L). These variances would be the same whether Ozboards was a domestic company or the subsidiary of a multinational. Fortunately, the South African currency, the rand, has depreciated and the company gets 6 per cent more rand than originally budgeted for each Australian dollar. The net result is that, when the South African managers examine their operations, they find that these variances are offset by the foreign exchange variance. This exchange variance, however, is insufficient to offset the drop in sales price and volume. Problems therefore lie with the Australian market, and Zambezi boards needs to decide how to price its boards for next year. Similar calculations can be made for direct and indirect expenses.

23.5   Culture and management accounting

23.5.1   Overview of culture and control

Many reasons can be cited for transnational differences in management accounting and management control systems (MCS), for example, history or economic conditions. However, these reasons can be distilled into a system of beliefs broadly referred to as 'culture'. Many authors have attempted to define what culture is and to classify countries by culture. Few have been more successful or accepted than Hofstede (1980, 1984, 1991), whose work was examined in Chapter 2.

How would a senior manager begin to address the issue of making MCS culturally effective? He or she may wish to start by examining whether the cultural values matter in management accounting. The answer is far from clear. Granlund and Lukka (1998) argue that, at a macro level, management accounting practices (including concepts, ideas, techniques, system designs) and the technical aspects of the purpose of management accounting have converged globally and are no longer subject to cultural forces. However, Granlund and Lukka see culture having effects at the micro level of behavioural patterns and styles of information use. There is considerable evidence that cultural attitudes are reflected in the different ways in which information is processed and how persons react to MCS in different countries (see Harrison and McKinnon (1999) for a summary and Section 23.5.3 for more detail). Existing evidence, as summarized in Chow et al. (1999), suggests that many multinationals respond to these cross-national differences in information processing by creating unique aspects for the MCS for each national subsidiary. In addition, Borkowski (1999) indicates that there is some shifting of performance goals by US, Japanese and Canadian multinationals for subsidiaries operating in another country. Table 23.3 illustrates the Borkowski (1999) findings for the US firms at home and abroad.

In order to understand how cultural values might cause MCS to need international modification, one first needs to understand how culture may determine what

Table 23.3 Rating for key performance measures for US firms only

Performance goal	US domestic	Canadian subsidiaries	Japanese subsidiaries	German subsidiaries	UK subsidiaries
Cost reduction	1	2	2	2	2
Sales growth	2	1	1	1	1
Profit margin	3	4	4	3	3
Goal attainment	4	2	3	5	4
Budget adherence	5	5	5	4	5

Note: Rank of 1 = most utilized by firms surveyed.
Source: Extracted from Borkowski, S. (1999) 'International managerial performance evaluation: a five country comparison', *Journal of International Business Studies*, Vol. 30, No. 3, pp. 543–4.

an appropriate management control system is. Harrison and McKinnon's (1999) review provides a good summary of the considerable research that has been done thus far (see Table 23.4). They conclude that, while some relationships have been demonstrated between culture and MCS, the broad concept remains unproven. Similarly Chenhall (2003, p. 153) concludes:

> Overall, the research has provided mixed results as to whether culture does have effects across aspects of MCS. There are few areas where consensus can be drawn. This is because studies have examined different combinations of cultural dimensions and have considered aspects of MCS in different ways. As a consequence there is little overlap between studies to enable themes to be drawn or comparisons made and generalizations developed.

Both of these studies seem rather pessimistic and the next sections look at how culture has been perceived as playing a role in firms' strategic and other control decisions. The corporate objectives discussed in Section 23.1 should be borne in mind as these studies are explored.

23.5.2 Choosing a strategic objective

A great deal has been written on strategy for the multinational (see, for example, Gupta and Govindarajan, 1991; or Edmunds and Ellis, 1999). Most companies, in setting strategic objectives, focus on choosing a suitable numerical target. This can be in terms of a particular budget number or financial ratio, and it seems to vary considerably from country to country and from business unit to business unit. Possible targets include:

- sales;
- cost reduction;
- quality targets;
- market share;
- profitability;
- budget to actual.

Table 23.4 Harrison and McKinnon's cross-cultural studies in management control system design after 1990

Study	Country (sample size)	Method	MCS characteristic(s)	Cultural dimension(s)/values
Chow, Shields and Chan (1991)	Singapore (96) USA (96)	Experiment	Work flow interdependence Pay interdependence	Individualism
Frucot and Shearon (1991)	Mexico (83)	Survey questionnaire	Relation between locus of control, budgetary participation, performance, job satisfaction	Power distance Uncertainty avoidance
Vance, McClaine, Boje and Stage (1992)	Thailand Indonesia Malaysia, USA 707 > 68% response	Survey questionnaire	Formality of structures and controls Individual vs. team development Employee involvement in appraisal Intrinsic versus extrinsic rewards Feedback frequency	Uncertainty avoidance Power distance Individualism
Harrison (1992)	Singapore (115) Australia (96)	Survey questionnaire	Relation between budgetary participation and reliance on accounting performance measures (budget emphasis) in manager evaluation	Power distance Individualism
Harrison (1993)	Singapore (115) Australia (96)	Survey questionnaire	Reliance on accounting performance measures in superior evaluative style	Power distance Individualism
Ueno and Sekaran (1992) Ueno and Wu (1993)	USA (205) Japan (247)	Survey questionnaire	Formalizing communication and coordination in budgetary planning processes	Individualism Uncertainty avoidance
Harrison, McKinnon, Panchapakesan and Leung (1994)	USA (104) Australia (140) Singapore (65) Hong Kong (55)	Survey questionnaire	Organizational design: Decentralization Responsibility centres Planning and control: Use of quantitative techniques Planning time horizon Group vs. individual decision making Formalization	Power distance Individualism Confucian dynamism
Chow, Kato and Shields (1994)	USA (54) Japan (39)	Experiment	Organizing: Environmental uncertainty, hierarchy height, centralization, interdependencies, formal rules Planning: Top-down planning, standard difficulty Evaluating: Controllability filters, relative evaluation Rewarding: Individual-based rewards, preset pay	Power distance Individualism Uncertainty avoidance Masculinity

Table 23.4 (*Cond't*)

Study	Country (sample size)	Method	MCS characteristic(s)	Cultural dimension(s)/values
Lau, Low and Eggleton (1995)	Singapore (112)	Survey questionnaire	Relation between budget emphasis, budgetary participation and task characteristics affecting job related tension and performance	Power distance Individualism
Merchant, Chow and Wu (1995)	Taiwan (23) USA (54)	Open ended, in-depth interviews	Size of performance-dependent rewards Group vs. individual-based performance rewards Long-term performance incentives Subjective vs. objective performance evaluations	Power distance Individualism Collectivism Confucian dynamism Uncertainty avoidance Masculinity
O'Connor (1995)	Singapore (125)	Survey questionnaire	Participation in budget setting Participation in evaluation	Power distance
Chow, Shields and Wu (1996)	Taiwan (155)	Survey questionnaire	Decentralization, structuring of activities, participative budgeting, standard tightness, performance rewards, controllability filters, reliance on accounting performance measures, participative performance evaluation	Power distance Individualism Confucian dynamism Uncertainty avoidance Masculinity
Chow, Kato and Merchant (1996)	USA (54) Japan (28)	Survey questionnaire	Control tightness Procedural controls Controls through Directives at meetings	Collectivism Power distance Uncertainty avoidance

Source: Derived from Harrison, G. and McKinnon, J. (1999) 'Cross-cultural research in management control systems design: a review of the current state', *Accounting, Organizations and Society*, Vol. 24, p. 486 where full references to cited papers are given. Reproduced with permission from Elsevier.

Each of these has its value. In basic management accounting theory the most appropriate method to be used in a multinational is best defined by the focus of the unit for which the target is being set. Sales or market share is particularly relevant for a unit that has no control over its input costs and whose primary purpose is to sell the goods of some other unit. Profitability, measured as a ratio or some other measure, is most appropriate for a fully fledged strategic business unit (i.e. a unit within a group of companies that makes its own business decisions at all levels, e.g. a major division or subsidiary). In addition, targets for a unit may be linked not only to its objective, but also to that part of its operations that it controls.

Turning from companies as a whole to an analysis of companies by country of origin, there is considerable evidence that suitable targets vary across countries.

Table 23.5 Selected empirical studies of corporate objectives and managerial performance evaluation

Author(s)	Year	Sample Country	N.	Findings
Robbins and Stobaugh	1973	US MNEs vs domestic firms	150	Same objectives for both. ROI supplemented by budget to actual
Morsicato	1980	US MNEs vs domestic firms	70	Same objectives for both. ROI supplemented by budget to actual
Abdallah and Keller	1985	US MNEs vs domestic firms	66	Same objectives for both. ROI supplemented by profits
Demirag	1987	Japanese MNEs in the UK vs UK	105	Same objectives for both. ROI supplemented by budget to actual
Borkowski	1993	US MNEs	247	Within a firm both international and domestic subsidiaries shared the same objectives of goal achievement but international units focused more on sales growth/cost reduction
Kopp	1994	EU MNEs	23	Performance evaluation measures
		JAPAN MNEs	34	vary across international operations
		US MNEs	24	by home country of the MNE
Keating	1997	US MNEs	78	Divisional accounting criteria are the most important goal rather than overall accounting measures

Source: Adapted from Borkowski, S. (1999) 'International managerial performance evaluation: a five country comparison', *Journal of International Business Studies*, Vol. 30, No. 3, p. 539.

Borkowski (1999) provides a good summary of studies prior to that year (see Table 23.5). A few studies listed in the Table 23.5 stand out as classics. In an early study using some 200 US multinationals, Robbins and Stobaugh (1973) identified ROI as the primary target used by US multinationals. However, because of the problems of calculating ROI, some supplementary measure, usually a comparison of actual results to budget, was often used. In a sample of 70 US chemical multinationals, Morsicato (1980) found that multiple measures were used, including in descending order of use: profit, ROI, and budgeted-versus-actual for profit and sales. Abdallah and Keller (1985) found similar results.

Additional studies worth mentioning are those of Bailes and Assada (1991) and Demirag (1994). Contrasting major listed US and Japanese firms (256 Japanese and 80 US), Bailes and Assada (1991) found that most Japanese firms (86.3 per cent) preferred to use sales volume as their overall objective, with net profit after corporate overhead being a poor second (44.7 per cent); American companies, by contrast, tended to use ROI most often as the divisional budget goal (68.4 per cent) followed by controllable profit (51.8 per cent). Demirag (1994) similarly found that Japanese

Table 23.6 **Top objectives by country**

	Canada	Germany	Japan	UK	US
Net income	4	3	1	>5	5
Return on assets	>5	>5	>5	>5	5
Market share	>5	4	>5	>5	>5
Cost reduction	2	5	>5	1	1
Profit margin	1	2	4	1	3
Sales growth	2	1	2	>5	2
Budget adherence	>5	>5	5	3	5
Goal attainment	5	>5	3	3	4

Source: Summarized from Borkowski, S. (1999) 'International managerial performance evaluation: a five country comparison', *Journal of International Business Studies*, Vol. 30, No. 3, p. 545.

companies in the United Kingdom tended to use sales and market share targets over the longer term.

The Borkowski (1999) study not only reviewed the available information but also examined the performance goals of 261 multinational companies drawn from samples of global companies in Canada, Germany, Japan, the United States and United Kingdom. Borkowski found that firms from Canada, Germany, Japan, the United States and United Kingdom each have different objectives in their own countries (see Table 23.6). In Japan net income is the most important measure of performance. German and Japanese companies also focus quite heavily on sales growth. Canadian companies pay attention to sales, but their premier goal is profit margin. UK companies' premier measures of success are cost reduction and profit margin. For US companies, cost reduction is the number one goal along with sales and profit growth.

These results are quite different for Japan and the United States from those of Bailes and Assada (1991). According to Borkowski (1999) the focus of US companies appears to have shifted from ROI to profit margin (gross margin) as the primary goal, and sales growth from controllable profit as a secondary goal. Japanese companies had shifted their focus to net income rather than market share.

In summary, these studies on corporate objectives tell us that corporate goals vary across nations and that companies need to be aware that their competitors may not be playing for the same objectives. Controllers also need to adapt goals, and the MCS for each national subsidiary to attempt, by socialization or selection, to create a common corporate culture that overrides national culture. Some of this uniqueness may be reflected in the budget process to which we now turn.

23.5.3 The budget process across countries and other MCS issues

The budget process involves taking the firm's objectives and setting them out in a series of formal plans for both the short term and the long term. The issues that generally need to be resolved are:

- Is there a formal budget setting process?
- Who participates in the budget process and how?

- What style of communication (formal versus informal) should be used?
- How are the budget objectives set?

Other more general issues are, for example:

- What period should be covered (short term versus long term)?
- Should there be a specific monetary objective for the plan or would a non-quantitative objective be more appropriate?

It is intrinsically likely that Asian countries, which have a higher long-term orientation (LTO) score, will take a longer-term perspective and produce budgets that cover a longer period. Therefore, one might expect an Asian entity to use yardsticks for measuring budget performance that are less clear in their immediate impact on profits but potentially valuable in the long run. Examples of such longer-term targets are upward mobility for quality standards, increased market share, and/or sales.

Evidence seems to support theory. Ueno and Sekaran (1992), for example, report that Japanese firms indeed prefer longer budgeting horizons than US firms. A few of the findings of Ueno and Sekaran (1992) run contrary to the view of Bailes and Assada (1991) and Hawkins (1983). Despite having a longer performance reward period, Japanese managers did not have an appreciably longer planning horizon than US managers. One must remember, however, that much very long-term planning takes place outside the formal numerical atmosphere of a budget. Comparing the perspectives of over 400 managers in Australia, the United States, Singapore and Hong Kong, Harrison *et al.* (1994) concluded that Anglo-Saxon managers prefer shorter-term but more quantitative budget objectives.

Taking a slightly different angle, Ueno and Wu (1993) find that collective societies are likely to plan and reward at the group level, whereas individualist cultures might set up a series of budgets that, when linked together, become a contract linking reward and performance for each employee. This has two immediate implications. Firstly, in terms of time scale, group rewards and performance often take longer to emerge, and so group planning as found in a collectivist society will be longer term. Secondly, there is less need in a collectivist society for individual 'cover' provided by documentary evidence of the budgeting process. Employees in a collectivist society may well use communication channels and forms that are more informal in the design of budgets. This indicates that the employees feel more comfortable with each other and seek the best way to defeat a common external enemy. This does not preclude the existence of a very detailed set of budgetary documents as the output, but does reduce the documentation of the consultative process. Finally, if there is less need to assign blame or reward to a particular individual within a group or company, there is a proportionally lower need to define which part of the budget plan is controllable by a particular office or office holder.

Turning to participation in budgeting, Anglo-American practice in budgeting assumes that participation matters. If managers are permitted to participate in setting their own budget targets, they not only feel better about them but also tend to perform better. This type of behaviour was documented in a series of experiments by Brownell (1982), who suggests that, for participation to work fully, managers must feel like 'insiders', i.e. that their participation will actually influence decisions and have some impact on the outcome. This concept of insider/outsider is described as 'locus of control'. Hofstede's (1991) power–distance dimension appears to be relevant primarily in determining who is involved in budget setting. A high power–distance society is one where those who are ruled tolerate and expect power to come from above. This would seem to preclude the kind of consultative and participative budgeting more common in Anglo-American societies where power is expected to be evenly distributed.

The results from tests of the interaction of participation and budgeting are unclear. Frucot and Shearon (1991) conducted a study using Mexican managers to test this. Mexico was graded as a culture that is high on power distance and low on individualism. The researchers anticipated that, given this cultural profile, Mexican managers would not favour participation even given insider status, i.e., they would rather be dictated to. Frucot and Shearon's (1991) results appeared to indicate that no culture effect had been found. All members of the firms studied initially appeared to be motivated by participation regardless of position. However, when the sample of Mexican managers was divided by company rank, only higher-level managers displayed the American model and lower-level managers seemed to prefer a less participative style. This is as one would expect, given Mexico's culture.

Similarly, comparing high power–distance Asian societies with low power–distance Australia, Chow *et al.* (1999) and Salter and Schulz (2005) find that participation and information sharing is culture dependent but that the effects are much more subtle than expected. Overall, managers from lower power–distance societies share more information but this can often be confounded by sub-cultural issues such as saving face (and machismo in Latin America).

23.5.4 Are US management control practices a 'parochial dinosaur'?

Boyacigiller and Adler (1991) argue that organizational sciences, including management control, have relied primarily on US theorists, reflecting its development during a time when the US economy dominated world economic activity. Both theory and practice of US multinationals are based on predetermined cultural assumptions. In management control and the fundamental ideas of structure and information flow that underlie it, the question that has bedevilled academics is how exportable are different elements of a US control system. More specifically, do they work in Chinese-based and other emerging markets?

There is, frankly, no clear answer, as examining four studies shows. Harrison *et al.* (1994) draw on the national cultural dimensions of power–distance, individualism and Confucian dynamism to predict and explain differences in philosophies and approaches to organizational design, management planning and control systems in Australia, the United States, Singapore and Hong Kong. They used questionnaires mailed to senior accounting and finance executives in 800 organizations to collect their data. The results support the importance of national culture in influencing organizational design and management planning and control systems. In particular, the cultural values of Anglo-American society are associated with an emphasis on decentralization and responsibility centres in organizational design, and an emphasis on quantitative and analytical techniques in planning and control. By contrast, the cultural values of East Asian society are associated with a greater emphasis on long-term planning and on group-centred decision making.

Using a longitudinal study, Wickramasinghe and Hopper (2005) test similar ideas, i.e. that organizational controls only work in their country of origin or similar countries. They describe successive attempts to impose conventional management accounting in a Sri Lankan jute mill as control shifted between the state and foreign private owners and again to the state. In all cases the control system failed due to workers' resistance. While results initially improved after privatization and the imposition of commercial budgeting practices, problems of cultural asymmetry were inflamed by a coalition of workers and local managers against foreign owners, who fled when financial irregularities were discovered. The government resumed ownership and budgeting practices of previous eras returned. The lesson is that, while 'more sophisticated' methods work in some cultures, they fail in others.

Two recent studies contradict the view that culture is everything and present a picture of globalization of the approach to management control driven by economic reality. Waweru *et al.* (2004) examined retail enterprises in South Africa and found that considerable changes in management accounting systems within South Africa increased the use of Anglo-American contemporary management accounting practices, notably activity-based cost allocation systems and the balanced scorecard approach to performance measures. These changes were a direct result of government reform/deregulation and increased global competition. Similarly, O'Connor *et al.* (2004) studied the adoption of Western management accounting/controls by China's state owned enterprises (SOEs). O'Connor *et al.* (2004) used both interviews (focusing on 1995–7) and a survey (focusing on 1996–9). They found that:

1 China's SOEs had increased their use of management accounting/controls.

2 This change reflected a purposeful move towards more formal and transparent management accounting controls.

3 The main objectives of the change were to improve decision making and to increase performance accountability.

4 The increase in the use of Western management techniques was a response to:

    (a) an increasingly competitive environment;

    (b) institutional factors such as joint venture experience and stock exchange listing;

    (c) the percentage of employees on limited-term employment contracts and the availability of training.

5 Obstacles to change included:

    (a) government or holding company interference;

    (b) withholding of decision rights;

    (c) managers' lack of ability;

    (d) individual employees' resistance to erosion in job security;

    (e) the ability to rely on informal business relationships.

The results of all the studies are important to managers in global organizations. They need to understand that, while some Anglo-American global techniques can work, cultural factors cannot be wholly ignored in control system design. This is particularly true in Asian and Latin American nations which represent large potential areas for expansion of business, trade and inward foreign direct investment.

Further, as a result of Japanese and Chinese investments in Europe and North America, many Westerners are experiencing the joys and frustrations of dealing with a control system based on completely different values.

23.5.5 Culture and control: a summary

The literature seems to indicate that many aspects of management control are affected by the culture of the organization. However, Harrison and McKinnon (1999) severely criticized the way in which these studies were conducted. Specifically, they suggested that the research did not take into account that many dimensions of culture may be operating simultaneously, nor did it compensate for the possibility that, in any one country, a particular dimension of culture may be core to how people react to information and MCS. This would make other cultural constructs pretty much irrelevant to a decision. This ongoing area of study will become even more relevant as management control moves from the relatively concrete reporting area to the more subjective information sharing to extract the maximum value from staff.

23.6 Control and performance

23.6.1 International aspects

In a multinational corporation, steps must be taken to ensure that the control system implemented does not become more complicated than the operation itself. An overly complex system may result in suspicion of (and by) the executives, frustration among middle managers, and wasted management time. A parent company must not request information simply because the cost of providing it is borne by the subsidiary. The amount of useful feedback to the subsidiary must be made commensurate with the level of information requested from it.

Let us take the example of a sales plan. As part of this, a corporation will manage and monitor the manufacturing process through the production budget. A variety of decisions enter into the production budget, including the level of inventory required to minimize costs and stock-outs. A multinational corporation involved in inventory planning must consider and examine transportation, customs procedures, import restrictions, supply problems (e.g. dock strikes, embargoes), import duties and foreign exchange rate changes.

One possible approach to international planning involves establishing a simple decentralized control system while centrally monitoring other important information that is readily available. Flexible budgeting is useful for budget control in a foreign environment where a large degree of uncertainty exists. Many of the uncontrollable influences of the international environment can be isolated to provide a better picture of management's performance. Flexible budgeting allows management to forecast the effects of a variety of scenarios so that strategies can be prepared and implemented if necessary.

A major question that arises in the control and performance literature is what internal (transfer) prices should be charged by one division to another. At first glance, this seems to be an unusual question. By treating each division as a cost centre, one could simply pass along the total cost to the next division – and each subsequent division would do the same. When the final product came to be sold, revenue would accrue to the company and not to specific divisions; control would be achieved through cost control. However, this is not normally the case among Anglo-American companies. Divisions are generally treated as profit centres, and internal sales are recorded. This practice may have its roots in a variety of sources, for example, cultural norms, previous practice and the experience base of the comptroller (most tend to be from a finance or public accounting background). In order to create suitable reports for divisions, corporations are faced with determining market-based or other profit-inclusive internal prices.

In addition to these economic questions, internationally there may be political issues in play within the company or within the country. For example, Chan and Lo (2004) studied large Foreign Investment Enterprises (FIEs) in China which had investors from the United States, Japan, and Europe. They found that the more important management perceives the interests of local (Chinese) partners and the maintenance of a good relationship with host (Chinese) government to be, the more likely it is that the FIE will use a market-based transfer-pricing method. On the other hand, the more important the management perceives foreign exchange controls in transfer-pricing decisions, the more likely it is that the FIE will choose a cost-based method. Finally, there is a moderate consistency between US and non-US FIEs on the relative importance that they give to these environmental variables. Transfer pricing thus is a control, culture and taxation issue. More discussion of transfer pricing is contained in Chapter 22.

23.6.2 Philosophies and models of control

Ouchi (1979, 1980) proposed three models of control (behaviour control, outcome control and clan control) in which the optimal type of control was a function of the nature of task or process to be controlled. Behaviour control comprises participation in decision making, hierarchy of authority, job codification and rule observation. Outcome controls are typically accounting measures. Clan control, however, is exercised through personnel policies that ensure that individuals with the appropriate training, values and norms are selected into the organization. Abernethy and Brownell (1994) used Ouchi's framework to test the effectiveness of various types of control in R&D organizations in the United States and Australia. Their main findings were that, for their pooled sample (they did not report differences between the two groups), clan controls were most effective in an environment of high task uncertainty.

Based on Ouchi's framework and given the uncertainty of overseas operations, one would expect that international control would initially centre on behavioural or clan systems of control. This would allow time to determine what an appropriate measure of performance is. It may also give information on how such performance might be maximized, given cultural constraints. In fact, the primary forms of control, at least in Anglo-American countries, are outcome controls, usually measured by accounting returns matched to a particular objective. Therefore, as shown by Bailes and Assada (1991), US companies tend to focus on ROI or budget variances to set reward structures. Given this predilection when evaluating a foreign operation, the Anglo-American research literature emphasizes that a company must base performance measurement only on areas that a manager controls.

Large manufacturing companies often have separate departments or divisions that manufacture a product for another division. In some cases, this is the only activity of a division. The receiving division continues manufacturing the product and then either passes it on to yet another division or sells the finished product in the market. The only item that the first division appears to control is its costs. However, overall strategy dictates that a market price comparison needs to be made to ensure that divisions continue to be competitive. A good example of how this might be conducted is the significant savings that companies such as Volkswagen in Germany and General Motors in the United States have achieved by switching comparisons from internal cost-plus transfer pricing to market-based competitive pricing.

23.6.3 Sarbanes-Oxley and global control

The Sarbanes-Oxley Act (SOX), enacted in the US in July 2002, created new standards for corporate accountability and stiff new penalties for acts of wrongdoing. SOX requires companies to implement new data retention policies and outlaws changing or destroying financial records. This applies both to US companies, wherever located, and to non-US companies, such as BP, that are listed on US capital markets (see Chapter 5).

While SOX is primarily focused towards auditors, management accountants need to be aware that section 404 of the SOX Act directs the Securities and Exchange Commission to adopt rules requiring each company's annual report to contain a statement of management's responsibility for establishing and maintaining an adequate internal control structure, and management's assessment of the effectiveness of the company's internal control structure and procedures.

Section 404 also requires the company's auditor to attest to, and report on, management's assessment of the effectiveness of the company's internal controls. SOX, designed for a post-Enron US financial reporting environment, has begun to affect management control in other countries that may not be subject to the unique problems of the US legal and business environment. Thus, auditors in other countries may end up certifying the control system of a wholly local company that happens to raise capital in the US. KPMG Canada's website on SOX[1] is a good example of how SOX may affect another country's reporting.

23.7 Looking forward

The relentless pace of global business and the continuous updating of information systems technology is likely to continue to have a large impact on the development of

---

[1] http://www.kpmg.ca/en/services/audit/sarbanes.html

internal reporting systems. Just-in-time inventories, computer-integrated manufacturing systems, and job shop workstations have all altered traditional product costing. The introduction of activity-based costing, where overhead is made more of a direct cost by finding cost drivers for costs and assigning overhead to products using these drivers rather than by plant-wide or department overhead rates, has altered many firms' views of where to produce goods globally. This often leads to results that may not seem intuitive, such as the production of goods in relatively high-wage countries because efficiency, as well as raw cost, becomes a driver in overhead allocation.

Firms in the Anglo-American world are seeking to find a way of incorporating into budgets and performance appraisal non-quantitative or more culturally appropriate means of control. The openness to change that this demonstrates is perhaps one of the more interesting features that globalization has brought to what, until the early 1980s, was a stable discipline of management accounting. The changing legal environment with SOX, and the changing management structures that will be needed to manage loose confederations of outsourcers, pose challenges to the management control system globally.

One interesting and quite forward-looking perspective is the use of a major control tool, the Balanced Scorecard to monitor corporate social responsibility (CSR). While this is not strictly international, firms which operate in nations where this is a particularly important issue may wish to include such goals. A recent article by Crawford and Scaletta (2005) argues that such a focus may not only increase positive perceptions of the firm but may increase profits. They present as an example Dow Chemical's scorecard, which is reproduced as Figure 23.4.

Another ongoing question is the role of software in 'flattening' the world. Friedman (2007) has argued that the internet and other tools have created a 'flat world' where routine functions including accounting can be carried out anywhere in the world. One of the drivers of this is the use of enterprise reporting systems (ERPs) to allow managers at all levels and countries to see into the very core of the business. This should in theory flatten the business as managers work together in this virtual world. However, Quattrone and Hopper (2005) provide evidence in a case study that this effect is company specific. They find that the ways in which ERP was configured in corporations created different forms of distance and relations between headquarters and the scattered subsidiaries. In one organization the ERP reproduced existing structures and distance which permitted conventional accounting controls based on action at a distance to be maintained. The second organization used ERP to collapse distance through real-time information in a matrix structure. This did not increase centralization but rather produced constantly changing loci of control and managerial feelings of 'minimalist' control. These organizations were also from different countries indicating that more work needs to be done at the interaction points of centralization and national origin.

Finally, building on the themes of Friedman (2007), research is needed into the role that culture and religion play in designing control in countries such as India, which are major players in outsourcing, but about which almost nothing is known in the Anglo-American literature. Readers are encouraged to go further in the area of international management accounting and control, using the list of references at the end of this chapter.

Balanced Scorecard Perspective	10 Market Forces (Objective)	GRI Measure: How success or failure is measured using the triple bottom line (A common framework for sustainability reporting)	Target: The level of performance or rate of improvement required
Financial	'Green' consumers	Energy consumption footprint (annualized lifetime energy requirements) of major products	Annual reduction in energy footprint for new products
Financial	Energy crunch	Direct energy use segmented by source	100% renewable energy
Financial	Financial	Increase/decrease in retained earnings at end of period	Percentage
Internal	Pollution and health	Standard injury, lost day and absentee rates and number of work-related fatalities (including subcontractors)	No lost-time injuries and fatalities, or long-term illnesses
Internal	Climate change	Total greenhouse gas emissions	Annualized reduction
Internal	Governments and regulators	Incidents and fines for non-compliance with all laws and regulations	No incidents or fines
People and Knowledge	Civil society/NGOs	Policies, guidelines and procedures to address needs of indigenous people	Number of Indigenous employees
People and Knowledge	Activist shareholders	Business units currently operating or planning operations in or around protected or sensitive areas	Number of employees trained in environmental management practices
Customer	Erosion of trust/transparency	Policy to exclude all child labour	No child labour
Customer	Globalization backlash	Supplier performance related to environmental commitments	Use of 100% organic cotton or coffee

Figure 23.4 **Examples of how to integrate CSR into the Balanced Scorecard's four perspectives**

Source: Crawford, D. and Scaletta, T. (2005) 'The balanced scorecard and corporate social responsibility: aligning values for profit', *CMA Management*, October. Reproduced with permission.

SUMMARY

- Major challenges in the management accounting and control area are affected by the two most basic problems of doing business internationally, namely that countries have different currencies and different cultures.

- With regard to preparing budgets for a subsidiary operating in another country, it is necessary to select appropriate budgeting currency and exchange rate tools. Some argue that local managers should be left alone to budget in local currency, given that they have little control over foreign exchange management.

- Since most companies do their budgeting in the home currency, the primary question is what rate to use for planning and control. The path of least resistance would be to use the rate at the date of planning. However, this is often so far in advance of the actual budgeted year that actual results are significantly different from budgeted results. If managers are responsible for profit in home currency terms, this results in an unfair distribution of rewards.

● Thus, some companies use forward rates or continuously updated rates. Using a special form of the traditional domestic price and volume variances, firms can ascertain what part of the problem is occurring because of movements in currency values.

● The first question concerning control systems relates to differences in the strategic objective of the firm. Anglo-American firms generally prefer shorter-term and more profit-based objectives, but return on investment is declining as a measure. Asian firms, by contrast, have a longer-term objective and seem to be satisfied with more indirect objectives.

● Culture has also been found to play a role in budgeting and control. The budget process in Asia is longer term and less formal than that of Western countries. Outside the Anglo-American world, there is resistance to formal participation, particularly in authoritarian cultures such as that of Mexico. However, cultural research has many flaws, and economic need or experience with non-national entities may lead to common global standards of control.

● The introduction of the Sarbanes-Oxley Act in the United States has created a new legal environment for management accounting that stretches beyond the borders of that nation.

References

Abdallah, W. and Keller, D. (1985) 'Measuring the multinational's performance', *Management Accounting*, October, pp. 26–31.

Abernethy, M. and Brownell, P. (1994) 'Accounting, behavior and clan controls: The design of effective management and control systems', presented at the American Accounting Association Annual Meeting, New York, NY.

Bailes, J. and Assada, T. (1991) 'Empirical differences between Japanese and American budget and performance evaluation systems', *International Journal of Accounting*, Vol. 26, pp. 131–42.

Borkowski, S. (1999) 'International managerial performance evaluation: A five country comparison', *Journal of International Business Studies*, Vol. 30, No. 3, pp. 533–55.

Boyacigiller, N. and Adler, N. (1991) 'The parochial dinosaur: Organizational science in a global context', *Academy of Management Review*, Vol. 16, pp. 262–90.

Brownell, P. (1982) 'A field study examination of budgetary participation and locus of control', *Accounting Review*, Vol. 57, pp. 766–77.

Chan, K. and Lo, A. (2004) 'The influence of management perception of environmental variables on the choice of international transfer-pricing methods', *International Journal of Accounting*, Vol. 39, No. 1, pp. 93–110.

Chenhall, R. (2003) 'Management control systems design within its organizational context: findings from contingency-based research and directions for the future', *Accounting, Organizations and Society*, Vol. 28, pp. 127–68.

Chow, C., Harrison, G., McKinnon, J. and Wu, A. (1999) 'Cultural influences on information sharing in Chinese and Anglo-American organizations: An exploratory study', *Accounting, Organizations and Society*, Vol. 24, pp. 561–82.

Chow, C.W., Kato, Y. and Merchant, K.A. (1996) 'The use of organizational controls and their effects on data manipulation and management myopia: a Japan vs. US comparison', *Accounting, Organizations and Society*, Vol. 21, pp. 175–92.

Chow, C.W., Kato, Y. and Shields, M.D. (1994) 'National culture and the preference for management controls: an exploratory study of the firm–labor market interface', *Accounting, Organizations and Society*, Vol. 19, pp. 381–400.

Chow, C., Lindquist, T. and Wu, A. (1996) 'National culture and the implementation of continuous improvement performance standards: An empirical investigation', paper presented at the American Accounting Association Annual Conference, Chicago, IL.

Chow, C.W., Shields, M.D. and Chan, Y.K. (1991) 'The effects of management controls and national culture on manufacturing performance', *Accounting, Organizations and Society*, Vol. 16, pp. 209–26.

Chow, C.W., Shields, M.D. and Wu, A. (1996) 'The importance of national culture in the design of and preference for management controls for multinational operations', paper presented at the Accounting, Organizations and Society Comparative Management Accounting Conference, University of Siena, Italy, November.

Chow, C., Shields, D. and Wu, A. (1999) 'The importance of national culture in the design and preferences for management controls for multi-national operations', *Accounting, Organizations and Society*, Vol. 24, pp. 441–61.

Crawford, D. and Scaletta, T. (2005) 'The balanced scorecard and corporate social responsibility: aligning values for profit', *CMA Management*, October.

Demirag, I. (1994) 'Management control systems and performance evaluations in Japanese companies: A British perspective', *Management Accounting*, Vol. 72, No. 7, pp. 18–20.

Edmunds, J. and Ellis, D. (1999) 'A stock market driven reformulation of multinational capital budgeting', *European Management Journal*, Vol. 17, No. 3, pp. 310–17.

Friedman, T.L. (2007), *The World Is Flat Updated and Expanded: A Brief History of the Twenty-first Century*, Farrar, Straus and Giroux.

Franco, M., Bourne, M. and Huntington, R. (2004) *Strategic Performance Measurement Reward Systems Survey – Result 2004*, Cranfield School of Management/Watson Wyatt, Cranfield.

Frucot, V. and Shearon, W. (1991) 'Budgetary participation, locus of control, and Mexican managerial performance and job satisfaction', *Accounting Review*, Vol. 66, No. 1, pp. 80–99.

Furnald, G. (2001) 'On balance almost 10 years after developing the balanced scorecard, Robert Kaplan and David Norton share what they've learned', *CFO Magazine*, Vol. 17, No. 2, February 1, pp. 72–7.

Granlund, M. and Lukka, K. (1998) 'It's a small world of management accounting practices', *Journal of Management Accounting and Research*, Vol. 10, pp. 153–79.

Gupta, A. and Govindarajan, V. (1991) 'Knowledge flows and the structure of control within multinational corporations', *Academy of Management Review*, Vol. 16, No. 4, pp. 770–86.

Harrison, G. (1992) 'The cross-cultural generalizability of the relation between participation, budget emphasis and job related attitudes', *Accounting, Organizations and Society*, Vol. 17, No. 1, pp. 1–15.

Harrison, G.L. (1993) 'Reliance on accounting performance measures in superior evaluative style: the influence of national culture and personality', *Accounting, Organizations and Society*, 18, pp. 319–39.

Harrison, G. and McKinnon, J. (1999) 'Cross-cultural research in management control systems design: A review of the current state', *Accounting, Organizations and Society*, Vol. 24, pp. 483–509.

Harrison, G., McKinnon, J., Panchapakesan, S. and Leung, M. (1994) 'The influence of culture on organizational design and planning and control in Australia and the United States compared with Singapore and Hong Kong', *Journal of International Financial Management and Accounting*, Vol. 5, No. 3, pp. 242–61.

Hawkins, C. (1983) *A Comparative Study of the Management Accounting Practices of Individual Companies in the United States and Japan*, UMI International, Ann Arbor, MI.

Hofstede, G. (1980) *Culture's Consequences: International Differences in Work-related Values*, Sage Publications, Beverly Hills, CA.

Hofstede, G. (1984) 'Cultural dimensions in management and planning', *Asia Pacific Journal of Management*, January, pp. 81–99.

Hofstede, G. (1991) *Culture and Organizations: Software of the Mind*, McGraw-Hill, Maidenhead, UK.

Kaplan, R.S. and Norton, D.P. (1992) 'The balanced scorecard measures that drive performance', *Harvard Business Review*, January/February, pp. 71–9.

Kobrin, S.J. (1979) 'Political risk: a review and reconsideration', *Journal of International Business Studies*, Vol. 10, No. 1, pp. 67–80.

Landry S., Chan W. and Jalbert, T. (2002) 'Balanced scorecard for multinationals', *Journal of Corporate Accounting & Finance*, September/October, pp. 31–40.

Lau, C.M., Low, L.C. and Eggleton, I.R.C. (1995) 'The impact of reliance on accounting performance measures on job-related tension and managerial performance: additional evidence', *Accounting, Organizations and Society*, 20, pp. 359–81.

Marr, B. (2004) *Business Performance Management – the State of the Art*, Hyperion Solutions, Cranfield School of Management, Cranfield.

Melville, R. (2003) 'The contribution internal auditors make to strategic management', *International Journal of Auditing*, Vol. 7, No. 3, pp. 209–22.

Merchant, K., Chow, C. and Wu, A. (1995) 'Measurement evaluation and reward of profit centre managers: A cross-cultural field study', *Accounting, Organizations and Society*, Vol. 20, No. 7/8, pp. 619–38.

Morsicato, H. (1980) *Currency Translation and Performance Evaluation in Multinationals*, UMI Research Press, Ann Arbor, MI.

O'Connor, N.G. (1995) 'The influence of organizational culture on the usefulness of budget participation by Singaporean-Chinese managers', *Accounting, Organizations and Society*, Vol. 20, pp. 383–403.

O'Connor, N., Chow, C. and Wu, A. (2004) 'The adoption of "Western" management accounting/controls in China's state-owned enterprises during economic transition', *Accounting, Organizations and Society*, Vol. 29, pp. 349–75.

Ouchi, W. (1979) 'A conceptual framework for the design of organizational control mechanisms', *Management Science*, September, pp. 833–48.

Ouchi, W. (1980) 'Markets, bureaucracies and clans', *Administrative Science Quarterly*, March, pp. 129–41.

Quattrone, P. and Hopper, T. (2005) 'A "time–space odyssey": management control systems in two multinational organizations' *Accounting, Organizations and Society*, Vol. 30, No. 7–8, pp. 735–64.

Robbins, S. and Stobaugh, R. (1973) 'The bent measuring stick for foreign subsidiaries', *Harvard Business Review*, September/October.

Salter, S. and Schulz, A. (2005) 'Examining the role of culture and acculturation in information sharing', *Advances in Accounting Behavioral Research*, Vol. 8 (forthcoming).

Ueno, S. and Sekaran, U. (1992) 'The influence of culture on budget control practices in the USA and Japan: An empirical study', *Journal of International Business Studies*, 4th Quarter, pp. 659–74.

Ueno, S. and Wu, A. (1993) 'The importance of national culture in the design of and preference for management controls for multi-national operations', *Accounting, Organizations and Society*, Vol. 24, pp. 441–61.

Vance, C.M., McClaine, S.R., Boje, D.M. and Stage, D. (1992) 'An examination of the transferability of traditional performance appraisal principles across cultural boundaries', *Management International Review*, Vol. 32, pp. 313–26.

Waweru, N., Hoque, Z. and Uliana, E. (2004) 'Management accounting change in South Africa: case studies from retail services', *Accounting, Auditing & Accountability Journal*, Vol. 17, No. 5, pp. 675–704.

Wickramasinghe, D. and Hopper, T. (2005) 'Cultural political economy of management accounting controls: A case study of a textile mill in a traditional Sinhalese village', *Critical Perspectives on Accounting*, Vol. 16, No. 4, pp. 473–503.

QUESTIONS

Suggested answers to the asterisked questions are given at the end of the book.

23.1∗ Explain how and why the objectives of multinational enterprises vary depending on their home countries.

23.2∗ What various models of control could be used to describe the organization of multinational companies? Which ones are found in practice?

23.3 In what ways does managerial accounting change by adding an international dimension?

23.4 What problems are created for performance measurement in multinationals by the existence of foreign currencies?

23.5 Starting with Table 23.2, prepare Zambezi Board's next year's sales budget and variance report for 2008. Assume that Zambezi plans that its 2008 results in Australia will mirror those actually achieved in 2007. However, the company is again wrong. Strong demand from Australians who cannot afford to travel to South Africa to import boards personally raises demand to 12,500 boards. Prices are as budgeted in Australian $ but the rand strengthens and, on average, the Australian $ is now worth 5.56 rand.

23.6 Explain how and why the process of budgeting used by multinational enterprises varies depending on the enterprise's home country.

23.7 How, and to what extent, does culture provide a more useful tool for the analysis of international differences in managerial accounting than it appears to do for financial reporting?

Glossary of abbreviations

This glossary contains abbreviations of bodies, documents, etc. We include international terms and those relating to the countries that we refer to in detail in Parts II to IV of the book.

Australia

AARF	Australian Accounting Research Foundation
AAS	Australian Accounting Standard
AASB	Australian Accounting Standards Board
ASIC	Australian Securities and Investments Commission
ASRB	Accounting Standards Review Board
AuASB	Auditing and Assurance Standards Board (of the AARF)
AUP	Statement of Auditing Practice
CPAA	CPA Australia
FRC	Financial Reporting Council
ICAA	Institute of Chartered Accountants in Australia
LRB	Legislation Review Board (of the AARF)
SAC	Statement of Accounting Concepts
UIG	Urgent Issues Group

East Asia

AFA	ASEAN Federation of Accountants
BADC	Business Accounting Deliberation Council (Japan)
CICPA	Chinese Institute of Certified Public Accountants
CSRC	China Securities Regulatory Commission
HKICPA	Hong Kong Institute of Certified Public Accountants
JICPA	Japanese Institute of Certified Public Accountants
KICPA	[South] Korean Institute of Certified Public Accountants
KK	Kabushiki Kaisha (Japanese joint stock company)
YK	Yugen Kaisha (Japanese private company)

France

AMF	Autorité des Marchés Financiers
CENA	Comité de l'Examen National des Activités
CNC	Conseil National de la Comptabilité

CNCC	Compagnie Nationale des Commissaires aux Comptes
COB	Commission des Opérations de Bourse
CRC	Comité de la Réglementation Comptable
CGI	Code général des impôts
H3C	Haut Conseil du Commissariat aux Comptes
OEC	Ordre des Experts Comptables
PCG	Plan comptable général
SA	Société anonyme
SARL	Société à responsabilité limitée

Germany

AG	Aktiengesellschaft
AktG	Aktiengesetz
APAK	Abschlussprüferaufsichtskommission
BaFin	Bundesanstalt für Finanzdienstleistungsaufsicht
BiLiRiG	Bilanzrichtliniengesetz
BilKoG	Bilanzkontrollgesetz
BilReG	Bilanzrechtsreformgesetz
DPR	Deutscheprüfstelle für Rechnungslegung
DRSC	Deutsches Rechnungslegungs Standards Committee
EStG	Einkommensteuergesetz
EStR	Einkommensteurerrichtlinien
FREP	Financial Reporting Enforcement Panel
GmbH	Gesellschaft mit beschränkter Haftung
GmbHG	Gesetz über Gesellschaften mit beschränkter Haftung
GoB	Grundsätze ordnungsmässiger Buchführung
HGB	Handelsgesetzbuch
IdW	Institut der Wirtschaftsprüfer
KapAEG	Kapitalaufnahmeerleichterungsgesetz
KG	Kommanditgesellschaft
KonTraG	Gesetz zur Kontrolle und Transparenz im Unternehmensbereich
OHG	Offene Handelsgesellschaft
PublG	Publizitätsgesetz
WP	Wirtschaftsprüfer
WPK	Wirtschaftsprüferkammer

United Kingdom and Ireland

ACCA	Association of Chartered Certified Accountants
AIDB	Accountancy Investigation and Discipline Board

APB	Auditing Practices Board
APC	Auditing Practices Committee
ASB	Accounting Standards Board
ASC	Accounting Standards Committee
CCAB	Consultative Committee of Accountancy Bodies
CGAA	Co-ordinating Group on Audit and Accounting Issues
CIMA	Chartered Institute of Management Accountants
CIPFA	Chartered Institute of Public Finance and Accountancy
CAICE	Companies (Audit, Investigations and Community Enterprise) Act 2004
DBERR	Department of Business, Enterprise and Regulatory Reform
DTI	Department of Trade and Industry
ED	Exposure Draft
FRC	Financial Reporting Council
FRED	Financial Reporting Exposure Draft
FRRP	Financial Reporting Review Panel
FRS	Financial Reporting Standard
FRSSE	Financial Reporting Standard for Smaller Enterprises
FSA	Financial Services Authority
FSMA	Financial Securities and Markets Act 2000
ICAEW	Institute of Chartered Accountants in England and Wales
ICAI	Institute of Chartered Accountants in Ireland
ICAS	Institute of Chartered Accountants of Scotland
PLC	Public limited company
POB	Professional Oversight Board
SAS	Statement of Auditing Standards
SIRS	Statement of Investment Circular Reporting Standards
SORP	Statement of Recommended Practice
SSAP	Statement of Standard Accounting Practice
UITF	Urgent Issues Task Force
UK GAAP	UK Generally Accepted Accounting Practice
UKSIP	UK Society of Investment Professionals

European

ARC	Accounting Regulatory Committee
CESR	Committee of European Securities Regulators
EECS	European Enforcers Co-ordination Sessions
EEIG	European Economic Interest Grouping
EFRAG	European Financial Reporting Advisory Group
EGAOB	European Group of Auditors' Oversight Bodies

EU	European Union
FEE	Fédération des Experts Comptables Européens
FSAP	Financial Services Action Plan

United States

AAA	American Accounting Association
AICPA	American Institute of Certified Public Accountants
AIMR	Association for Investment Management and Research
APB	Accounting Principles Board
ARB	Accounting Research Bulletin
ASR	Accounting Series Release (of the SEC)
CFA	Chartered financial analyst
EITF	Emerging Issues Task Force
FAF	Financial Accounting Foundation
FASB	Financial Accounting Standards Board
FRR	Financial Reporting Release
GAAP	Generally accepted accounting principles
GAAS	Generally accepted auditing standards
GASB	Government Accounting Standards Board
IRS	Internal Revenue Service
PCAOB	Public Company Accounting Oversight Board
SAB	Staff Accounting Bulletin (of the SEC)
SARBOX	Sarbanes-Oxley Act
SEC	Securities and Exchange Commission
SFAC	Statement of Financial Accounting Concepts
SFAS	Statement of Financial Accounting Standards
SOX	Sarbanes-Oxley Act

International

AAC	African Accounting Council
AISG	Accountants' International Study Group
CAPA	Confederation of Asian and Pacific Accountants
ECSAFA	Eastern, Central and Southern Africa Federation of Accountants
IAA	Interamerican Accounting Association
IAASB	International Auditing and Assurance Standards Board
IAPC	International Auditing Practices Committee
IAPS	International Audit Practice Statement
IAS	International Accounting Standard
IASB	International Accounting Standards Board

IASC	International Accounting Standards Committee
IASCF	International Accounting Standards Committee Foundation
ICCAP	International Coordination Committee for the Accountancy Profession
IFAC	International Federation of Accountants
IFAD	International Forum for Accounting Development
IFRIC	International Financial Reporting Interpretations Committee
IFRS	International Financial Reporting Standard
IOSCO	International Organization of Securities Commissions
ISA	International Standard on Auditing
ISAE	International Standard on Assurance Engagements
ISQC	International Standard on Quality Control
ISRE	International Standard on Review Engagements
ISRS	International Standard on Related Services
OECD	Organisation for Economic Co-operation and Development
PIOB	Public Interest Oversight Board (of IFAC)
SIC	Standing Interpretations Committee (of the IASC)
SME	Small and medium-sized entity
UNCTAD	United Nations Council on Trade and Development
UNO	United Nations Organization
WTO	World Trade Organization

Principles, methods and financial statements

CCA	Current cost accounting
CNC	Current/non-current
FIFO	First-in, first-out
HCA	Historical cost accounting
LIFO	Last-in, first-out
MNM	Monetary/non-monetary
MD&A	Management's discussion and analysis
OCI	Other comprehensive income
OFR	Operating and financial review
SCI	Statement of comprehensive income
SORIE	Statement of recognized income and expense
STRGL	Statement of total recognized gains and losses

Further reading

More definitions and abbreviations may be found in:
Nobes, C.W. (2006) *The Penguin Dictionary of Accounting*, Penguin, 2nd edn, London.
Parker, R.H. (1992) *Macmillan Dictionary of Accounting*, Macmillan, 2nd edn, London.

Suggested answers
to some of the end-of-chapter questions

CHAPTER 1

1.1

Question What effects have the major political events in the world since the end of the Second World War had on accounting and financial reporting?

Answer The domination by the US of the non-communist post-war world has meant that capitalist countries have been strongly influenced by US GAAP, especially as propagated by the international accounting firms. Countries such as Canada and Australia have been especially open to US influence. However, despite the break-up of the British Empire, British-style accounting has continued in countries such as India and Nigeria. Similarly, former colonies of France and other European countries continue to follow the accounting styles of the former imperial power.

The creation and expansion of the European Union from 1958 onwards has helped to preserve continental European accounting concepts and practices, albeit increasingly diluted after the entry of the UK in 1973. The creation of the International Accounting Standards Committee (now the International Accounting Standards Board), also in 1973, can be seen politically both as an attempt to counter US influence and as an attempt to infiltrate Anglo-Saxon concepts and practices. The UK in this respect, as in many others, has found itself torn between the USA and Europe.

Central and Eastern European countries dominated by the USSR, the other post-war political superpower, used communist accounting until the collapse of Soviet power from 1989 onwards. All have undergone rapid accounting change and many joined the EU in 2004 and 2007. They have both reverted to continental European accounting and imported IFRS for their listed companies. An incidental effect of the political imperative of the reunification of West and East Germany was a weakening of the German economy, a consequent greater need to seek capital on world capital markets, and the adoption of US GAAP or IFRS by German multinationals.

In East Asia, US-style institutions were introduced into occupied Japan after the Second World War, but were much modified after Japan regained its political and economic independence. The political decision of the Chinese government to move its economic system closer to capitalism has led to corresponding changes in its accounting systems.

1.2

Question Why have the major accounting firms become 'international'? From what countries have they mainly originated? Why?

Answer The major firms are 'international' because, in order to stay in the top group of firms, they have had to follow their multinational clients around the world, either by setting up local offices or by merging with or taking over existing local firms. The firms mainly originate from those home countries of MNEs that have well-developed accountancy professions, notably the United Kingdom and the United States. Other home countries of MNEs and international accounting firms are Canada, the Netherlands, Germany and Japan (see Table 1.11 in the text). The last two do not have such well-developed accountancy professions; the first two countries are much smaller commercially than the United Kingdom or United States.

A more sophisticated answer will be possible after study of Chapter 21 (International auditing).

CHAPTER 2

2.1

Question 'The basic cause of international differences in financial reporting practices is the different degree of interference by governments in accounting.' Discuss.

Answer Accounting and financial reporting practices in any given country may differ because the needs of users of accounting information differ. For example, tax authorities may stress objectivity, banks with secured loans may stress conservatism, and shareholders may stress the predictability of future cash flows. Unlike loan creditors and shareholders, tax authorities have the force of government power to back up their demands and are likely to dominate financial reporting if unopposed. In countries such as the United States and the United Kingdom, the needs of capital markets have been more influential but, where the market is perceived to fail, as in the United States in the years after 1929 and in the United Kingdom in the 1960s, governments have 'interfered' on behalf of shareholders. Nevertheless, the style of financial reporting imposed by government bodies will probably reflect the strength of the capital markets.

Furthermore, strong capital markets may lead to commercial accounting largely outside of government control. For example, in Germany in 1998, the law was changed to allow listed companies to depart from normal German principles in their consolidated statements.

Within the EU, the national differences are now confined largely to unconsolidated financial reporting. Governments, through the EU legal apparatus, have interfered jointly to require IFRS for the consolidated statements of listed companies.

Professional accountants as well as governments can be seen by some observers to be interfering in financial reporting practices. In the words of a former French finance (later prime) minister, as reported in the OECD's *Harmonization of Accounting Standards*, 1986, pages 9–10:

> Standardization procedures vary from country to country. Sometimes specific standards applying to each of the main problems taken in isolation are worked out by the accounting profession, which may consult other interested parties but remains solely responsible for the decisions taken. On the contrary, accounting may be purely and simply government-regulated. Lastly, an intermediate method is adopted in some countries, including France, with systematic consultations among all the parties concerned. In many cases a consensus can be reached. Where this is not possible, government intervention preserves the public interest. It seems to us to be perfectly reasonable that the government should have the last word in deciding on the main points of standardization and make sure that no one interest group can 'lay down the law' to others.

2.2

Question Assess the view that accidents of history are primarily responsible for international differences in corporate financial reporting.

Answer Some international differences can, indeed, apparently be explained only by 'accidental' or 'exogenous' historical factors unconnected with accounting. Examples are:

- the 'import' of apparently unsuitable financial reporting practices from colonial powers (compare, for example, the former British and French colonies in Africa);
- acceptance of 'alien' accounting ideas by EU member states as part of a political package;
- influence of occupying powers (e.g. Germany on France, United States on Japan).

For a country that is heavily influenced by another (e.g. because of a former colonial relationship), this single 'accident' may be the major influence on the style of accounting found in a country. However, in other countries, accounting may be driven by the type of capital market and the nature of regulation. (See also the answer to Question 2.1.)

CHAPTER 3

3.1

Question In what ways might classification be useful in any field of study? Use international differences in financial reporting as an illustration of your answer.

Answer As the chapter suggests, classification might be helpful to:

(a) sharpen description and analysis;

(b) reveal underlying structures;

(c) enable prediction of properties of an item from its position in a classification;

(d) predict missing items;

(e) trace the evolution of items.

In international accounting, this might mean that a classification would help to:

(i) summarize the mass of data on differences;

(ii) provide a feel for the accounting of one country based on analogies with others;

(iii) estimate the difficulties of harmonization;

(iv) chart the progress of harmonization;

(v) predict problems by analyzing similar countries;

(vi) identify where to look for similar countries that might have already solved one's own problems.

3.2

Question 'The essential problems of attempts to classify financial reporting practices across the world are related to the suitability of the data upon which such classifications have been based.' Comment.

Answer Many classifications have been based on data which were not compiled for the purpose of classification. For example, reliance on data in Price Waterhouse surveys, with all questions given equal weight, might lead to the problem that important questions are swamped by unimportant ones. Also, one has to ask whether the data relates to all companies or mainly to Price Waterhouse (as it was then) clients. Further, it seems likely that different questions would be asked by a German compiler of questions compared with an American compiler. There are also many examples of errors in these databases. The net result may be merely classifications of the curious data rather than of the countries' accounting systems.

Of course, not all classifications have used this sort of data. Scientists in other areas put a great deal of judgement into choosing which characteristics to measure for the purpose of classifications. Some accounting studies have also done that. Correct data on relevant criteria will lead to better classifications.

The question asks about 'essential problems'. There are, of course, problems other than data. For example, it is vital to decide what the purpose of the classification is, and what exactly is being classified. These points are even more 'essential'.

CHAPTER 4

4.1

Question Was the IASC successful? Explain your reasoning.

Answer Success could be looked for in several areas. This question is fairly well covered in the chapter in the text. The question implies that we should study the period up to 2001, when the IASC was replaced by the IASB.

An answer might include reference to whether we look at the IASC's stated objectives or invent our own criteria for success. Indications of success might be sought in the following places:

(a) issue of standards;

(b) refinement of standards;

(c) backing from other international bodies (e.g. IOSCO endorsement in 2000);

(d) backing from national bodies (e.g. London Stock Exchange, CONSOB and SEC);

(e) use of IASs as a basis for rule-making by some national standard-setters (e.g. Hong Kong, Singapore, Nigeria);

(f) use of IASs by certain large companies in the absence of national rules (e.g. fully in Switzerland, and partially in Italy);

(g) use of IASs by certain large companies for consolidated statements instead of national rules (e.g. Germany);

(h) acknowledgement of conformity with IASs by companies (e.g. in Canada);

(i) influence of IASC in shaping the debate elsewhere (e.g. EU Seventh Directive);

(j) compulsory use in the EU for the consolidated statements of listed companies (already announced as a proposal by the Commission in 2000).

4.2

Question Which parties stand to gain from the international harmonization of accounting? What are they doing to achieve it?

Answer This question is addressed in the chapter in the text. The beneficiaries might be split into (a) users and (b) preparers. Governments might be seen to be users for the purposes of tax collection, but they also might wish to help users and preparers. The same applies to inter-governmental organizations, such as the EU.

Users include investors and lenders who operate across national borders. These would include institutions, such as banks. Companies, in their capacity as purchasers of shares in other companies or as analysts of suppliers or customers, would also gain from harmonization.

Preparers of multinational financial statements would gain from simplifications, and they would also benefit as users of their own accounting information from various parts of the group. Accountancy firms are sometimes seen as beneficiaries but at present they gain work as auditors and consultants from the existence of international differences.

In terms of who is doing what to bring about harmonization, the picture is initially confusing, because the greater beneficiaries seem to be doing little. That is, users are not sufficiently aware or sufficiently organized to address the problem. Preparers are too busy to act because they are trying to cope with, or to take advantage of, all the differences. However, some senior businessmen put public and private pressure on accountants to reduce differences. This is most notable in the case of companies such as Shell which are listed on several exchanges and try to produce one annual report for all purposes.

Governments are acting. For example the harmonization programme in the EU was active in the 1970s and 1980s. Also, the International Organization of Securities Commissions (IOSCO) is a committee of government agencies which began in the late 1980s to put considerable backing behind the IASC.

Perhaps the harmonizing body with the highest profile in the 1990s was the IASC which was a committee of accountancy bodies, largely controlled by auditing professions. Of course, the international differences do severely complicate the work of some auditors. However, there is an element of paradox in the fact that auditors are the most active in trying to remove lucrative international differences. However, the IASC was set up and run by very senior members of the worldwide profession, who might be seen to be 'statesmen' and to be acting in the public interest and in the interests of the long-run respectability of the profession. In 2001, the profession handed over responsibility for international standard setting to the IASB, an independent body.

The IASB is supported by donations from large companies, audit firms and investor organizations.

CHAPTER 5

5.1

Question Distinguish between harmonization, standardization, convergence, adoption and EU endorsement.

Answer 'Harmonization' and 'standardization' have often been used interchangeably. However, standardization implies a narrowing down to one policy for any accounting topic, whereas harmonization implies that differences could be allowed to remain as long as the users of financial statements have a means of getting similar information from different statements.

In both cases, the '-ization' suffix tells us that there is a process towards a state rather than necessarily an achieved state. Both harmonization and standardization can refer to rules (*de jure*) or to practices (*de facto*). Chapter 4 discusses these issues.

'Convergence' is a more recent term, having much the same meaning as standardization. However, it is more elegant to say 'the convergence of two sets of standards' than 'the standardization of two sets of standards'. 'Convergence with IFRS' would normally mean gradually changing a set of domestic rules towards IFRS. However, in the context of US GAAP and IFRS, it means changing both so that the differences gradually disappear.

Adoption of IFRS means abandoning national rules as opposed to changing them. EU endorsement is the process of adopting IFRS, but not necessarily all of it.

5.2

Question Using the reconciliations of this chapter and the information in Chapter 2, comment on the adjustments necessary when moving from German or UK to US or IFRS accounting.

Answer The reconciling items reveal the most important practical differences. These depend on the year in question, and of course on the GAAP that one starts from.

In the case of the UK and Germany, one major reconciling item is the absence of goodwill amortization under US or IFRS rules. Adjustments for minority interests are large but, confusingly, German and IFRS rules are the same (treat them as part of equity) and US and UK rules were the same (show them outside equity).

When moving from UK or German rules to US GAAP (and IFRS from 2009) interest on construction projects is capitalized rather than expensed, so equity rises. Also, under UK or German rules, financial assets are generally held at cost or lower, whereas many of them are marked to market (held at market value with gains and losses taken to the income statement) under US GAAP or IFRS.

These and the other differences are explained by the companies in the notes attached to the reconciliations (see the companies' annual reports on their websites).

CHAPTER 6

6.1

Question Explain the purposes and uses of a conceptual framework.

Answer The main purpose of a conceptual framework is to guide the standard-setters when setting accounting standards. It may be useful because it limits the scope for disagreement and for political interference. This is achieved by establishing the definitions of terms (such as 'asset') and the purposes of financial reporting. If all standards can be made to comply with the framework, then they are more likely to fit together coherently. Nevertheless, certain features of the existing frameworks are vague, so disagreements can continue even among adherents to them. Naturally, sometimes the standard-setters question elements of their own frameworks, and sometimes they override the frameworks for political or other reasons.

Another purpose of frameworks is to enable preparers of financial statements to interpret standards, to choose from among options in them, and to establish accounting policies in the absence of standards. The auditors and interpreters of statements may also benefit from understanding this context.

6.2

Question 'Neutrality is about freedom from bias. Prudence is a bias. It is not possible to embrace both conventions in one coherent framework.' Discuss.

Answer There certainly would be a problem for neutrality if prudence were an overriding concept, as it seems to be in the EU's Fourth Directive. However, in the IASB's Framework, prudence is instead a state of mind used when exercising judgement when making estimates. It has to be admitted that this does sound like a bias, but the Framework's version of neutrality (paragraph 36) would only be contravened if this prudence was used 'in order to achieve a predetermined result or outcome'. Prudence still seems a reasonable convention to constrain management's optimistic predictions.

CHAPTER 7

7.1

Question To what extent are the reasons for different European accounting systems still relevant as reasons for different European IFRS practices?

Answer The suggestion from Chapter 2 is that the main reason for difference is different financing systems, with supplementary effects from tax systems, legal systems and external influence such as colonization. Some of the reasons could be summed up as cultural differences. These reasons might still exist, in reduced form, as motivations for different IFRS practice. If we confine ourselves to the consolidated statements of listed companies, there may be little difference in the main purpose of financial reporting across Europe. Nevertheless, listed companies in Germany or Italy may still be dominated by insider shareholders (e.g. government, banks and families), which might reduce their enthusiasm for the optional use of fair values or for extensive disclosures.

There is still scope for tax influence, if choices available for unconsolidated statements are tax-relevant and are also available under IFRS. This includes covert options, such as the identification and measurement of impairments. In such a case, the tax-driven unconsolidated choices might flow through to consolidated IFRS statements.

Different legal systems lead to different enforcement mechanisms and therefore to different degrees of compliance with IFRS.

7.2

Question Give examples of options allowed in IFRS and how they might be chosen differently in different countries.

Answer Assuming that the question refers to overt options, the easiest way to answer the first part of the question is to refer to Table 7.1. However, it would be worth noting that there are also covert options and measurement latitude in Tables 7.2 and 7.3.

The motivations for different choices are given in the answer to Question 7.1 above; to which might be added the inertia of carrying on with previous national practices. So let us assume that the question refers to examples of the choices rather than examples of the method of choosing.

A simple example is the order of assets in a balance sheet: with inertia suggesting European increasing liquidity, but Australian declining liquidity. Similarly, inertia might suggest greater use of the SORIE in the UK than in continental Europe; greater use of proportional consolidation in France than in the UK (or than in Australia where it is not allowed). Inertia and different equity-market pressures might explain greater use of the option to charge actuarial gains and losses to the SORIE in the UK than in Germany; greater use of the option to revalue investment properties in the UK than in Belgium, Germany, Italy or Spain; and greater use of the macro-hedging option in France than in the UK.

CHAPTER 8

8.1

Question 'US accounting is the best in the world.' Discuss.

Answer If good accounting is largely about disclosure, and more disclosure is better than less disclosure, then perhaps it is easy to agree with the quotation. An examination of full-scale US annual reports (including Form 10-K and other documentation) shows that the sheer volume of information is considerably greater than in any other jurisdiction. Analysts and academic proponents of the efficient markets hypothesis often argue that disclosure is more important than particular accounting rules.

However, it should be noted that these full-scale rules apply compulsorily only to about 14,000 SEC-registered corporations, although many other US corporations adopt some or all of these procedures. In terms of the proportion of companies publishing audited annual reports, the UK's regime is more extensive than that of most countries, despite recent increases in audit exemptions.

Another potential meaning of 'best' is 'leading'. Here, again, it is hard to deny that accounting developments tend to start in the United States and then travel elsewhere. This includes consolidation, lease accounting, segment reporting and many detailed accounting practices.

A potential criticism of US rules is that they are so numerous and detailed that accountants and auditors are left with no scope for judgement, and that the accounting is therefore sometimes wrong. This can be called a preference for 'rules-based' rather than 'principles-based' standards. For example, the detailed technical definition of a subsidiary allowed Enron to hide liabilities in thousands of unconsolidated but controlled entities.

One other concern about US accounting is its traditional opposition to current value information and to the capitalization of certain intangibles (e.g. development expenditure). This may deprive the user of accounts of helpful information. However, recent changes to US rules (e.g. SFAS 115) required the use of current values for certain investments, and this was the beginning of a trend.

It should be noted that certain features of US accounting could be criticized (e.g. the permission to use LIFO). Also, it would be easy to argue that UK cash flow statements are better than US ones.

8.2

Question To what extent, if at all, is US accounting influenced by accounting in other countries?

Answer Clearly, just as the US language and legal system are British in origin, so is the US accounting system. This is a strong influence. However, for most of the twentieth century, the United

States has seen itself as a leader rather than a follower, and so influences from abroad may have been slight. Also, the United States has generally had an enormously larger population of academic accountants than other countries. This has provided both ideas and criticisms.

In the last few years, the SEC and the FASB have acknowledged the importance of international differences in accounting. The contacts between the FASB and the IASC/B and other national standard-setters have grown greatly. The SEC has shown an interest in overseas companies, and has done its part in IOSCO to bring some backing for the IASC/B.

In 1997 major liaison between the IASC and the FASB led to changes, on both sides, to standards on earnings per share and segmental reporting. From 2001, it is clear that the FASB and the IASB have been trying to move together on projects. This was given formal agreement by the two boards in 2002. Several exposure drafts have been issued by the FASB designed to adopt aspects of IFRS. The first became standards in 2005.

CHAPTER 9

9.1

Question To what extent is the making of rules on financial reporting in the US separated from their enforcement? What is the historical background to the present situation?

Answer Both the making and the enforcement of financial reporting rules for publicly traded companies in the US is the responsibility of the Securities and Exchange Commission (SEC), set up as a federal agency in the early 1930s as a result of the stock market crash of 1929. From the start the SEC has exercised a strict enforcement role but has preferred to supervise standard-setting by an authorized private-sector body (currently the Financial Accounting Standards Board) rather than making the rules itself. This strategy has the advantages of leaving the technical details to the experts and shielding the SEC from criticism. Since the standards will be enforced, there is extensive lobbying, but it is usually the FASB that is lobbied rather than the SEC. If IFRSs are accepted in the US, the SEC is likely to enforce them more literally than is the case in other countries.

9.2

Question What are the arguments for and against proactive surveillance by enforcement bodies?

Answer Proactive surveillance requires an organizational set-up and budget which may not be initially available to an enforcement body. Further, resources may be used in investigating companies unlikely to be breaching the rules. On the other hand, awareness that all listed companies may be investigated may deter companies from transgressing and may strengthen the hands of their auditors. All enforcement bodies are, at least, reactive but solely reactive surveillance may result in 'shutting the stable door after the horse has bolted'.

CHAPTER 10

10.1

Question Explain the various motivations of those who politically lobby standard-setters.

Answer The answer depends on which country we are talking about. In a tax-dominated setting (e.g. the rules for unconsolidated accounting in Germany), lobbying might concern an attempt to reduce earnings in order to reduce tax bills. Earnings reduction may also be relevant for regulated industries in any country. However, most of Chapter 10 is set in the context of the consolidated statements of listed companies in major capital markets. Here, the lobbying mostly concerns trying to increase or stabilize earnings. This is connected to management's perceptions of the effects of this on share prices, remuneration and reputation.

10.2

Question Give examples of political lobbying of US standard-setters, explaining in what ways the lobbying went beyond arguments about the correct technical solutions.

Answer The chapter lists examples in 10.3.1, 10.4, 10.6.1 and 10.7. The meaning of 'correct technical solutions' needs to be discussed. This might mean accounting standards that are consistent with the conceptual framework and that lead to relevant and reliable information, subject to a cost/benefit constraint.

One clue that lobbying is going beyond technical issues is that reference is made to the supposed economic consequences of a standard or proposed standard. Here, the several stages of the debates on the Investment Tax Credit and Employee Stock Options are interesting.

Another clue to political lobbying is that different groups of companies lobby in different ways, predictable on the basis of how they are affected. Inflation Accounting and Petroleum Exploration Costs are examples here.

CHAPTER 11

11.1

Question Is it both desirable and possible to harmonize company financial reporting in the European Union?

Answer The desirability of harmonization should be related to the beneficiaries: shareholders, lenders, companies and others. The European Union's aim of freedom of movement of capital is relevant. However, harmonization brings costly changes. It is arguable that harmonization is only really cost-effective for multinational enterprises. One should also ask whether perhaps accounting ought to remain different in different countries for various national reasons. The costs and benefits differ for large/small companies, for listed/unlisted companies, and for consolidated/unconsolidated statements.

The possibility of harmonization needs to distinguish between (i) the consolidated statements of listed companies, and (ii) other types of financial reporting. For (i), a large degree of harmonization seems possible through the EU Regulation of 2002 requiring IFRS. For (ii), discussion could proceed under the headings of (a) the process of Directives, etc., and (b) the progress so far in *de facto* harmonization. These issues are examined in the chapter.

It should be noted that it is not only the EU institutions that are helping with harmonization in the EU. The IASC had some effects in the European Union and capital market pressures led many European companies away from traditional practices. The EU Regulation of 2002 on the use of IFRS has greatly increased harmonization for the consolidated statements of listed companies, although there may still be somewhat different national interpretations of IFRS.

11.2

Question In what ways have pre-communist and communist accounting affected post-communist accounting in Central and Eastern Europe?

Answer Post-communist accounting in Central and Eastern Europe has been affected by pre-communist accounting in that there has been a widespread reintroduction of pre-war German-based corporate law and commercial codes, which are, *inter alia*, seen as compatible with EU Directives.

It has been affected by communist accounting in that the low status of accounting in a command economy meant that accountants acted mainly as bookkeepers processing routine transactions, so that both advanced accounting (e.g. consolidations) and a sophisticated accountancy and auditing profession have had to be built up almost from scratch. The profession therefore has had difficulty in acting as a source of improved practices and regulations which has meant that Ministries of Finance have had to play a dominant role.

CHAPTER 12

12.1

Question 'Unlike US accounting, Japanese accounting is not a product of its environment but of outside influences.' Discuss.

Answer The answer needs to address whether US accounting is solely a product of its environment and whether Japanese accounting is solely a product of outside influences. Of course, the quotation contains a grotesque exaggeration, but is there anything in it?

The US part of the question can be answered with the help of the answer to Question 8.2 above.

Turning to Japan, it is clear that there has been much outside influence. The regulatory framework of the Commercial Code is closely based on nineteenth-century Western European models. This involves, also, a dominance of tax considerations and a traditional lack of interest in disclosures or consolidation.

Overlaid on this is US influence after the Second World War in the setting up of Securities and Exchange Laws, which particularly relate to corporations with publicly traded securities.

The textbook chapter describes many German and US features of Japanese accounting. Nevertheless, the particular mix of Japanese rules was unique to Japan, and it had its own interesting variations on goodwill write-offs, currency translation and post-retirement benefits. However, in the 1990s, Japan seems to have become more interested in international acceptability of its accounting output, and the IASC became more influential. By 2001, many of the Japanese differences from US or IFRS accounting had been removed. Since then, a formal convergence process between the IASB and the Japanese ASB has been in progress.

12.2

Question Which factors could have been used at the beginning of the 1990s to predict the direction in which Chinese accounting would develop?

Answer By the beginning of the 1990s, the Chinese economic reforms were already well under way. 'Capitalist' development areas had been created, and plans for stock markets were well advanced. Another easily predictable change was the return of Hong Kong to Chinese control in 1997.

Also, it has always been clear that the Chinese are good at operating markets, wherever they are allowed to do so around the world. All these factors suggest the emergence of a powerful quasi-market economy containing major stock markets. This suggests the sort of accounting suitable for such economies, i.e. Anglo-American accounting.

Since US President Nixon's rapprochement with China in the 1970s, American influence has grown, and British influence has always been strong, through Hong Kong. Perhaps one could have foreseen that the Chinese government would accept assistance from Big Five firms when reforming accounting. Hong Kong's adoption of International Accounting Standards (in place of British standards) in 1993 was a typically canny move, which also might have been foreseen. This eased the way for acceptance of IASs in China for certain purposes in 1997, and then for more complete convergence from 2007.

CHAPTER 13

13.1

Question Using information from this chapter and earlier ones (e.g. Chapters 2, 3 and 5), give examples of accounting topics on which there are major differences between two national accounting systems or between a national system and IFRS.

Answer Particularly important topics include pensions, goodwill and deferred tax. In many cases, most of the deferred tax difference is caused by the other adjustments. That is, for example, if a pension liability is increased, then a deferred tax asset is created to go with it.

The pension issue is complicated. It has been looked at in Chapter 6 and will be further examined in Chapter 16. Normally an adjustment from German accounting to US or IFRS would require an increase in pension expense and liability. BASF (see Table 5.3) is unusual in showing the reverse, because it has a pension fund that is not shown in its HGB consolidation. The fund is in surplus, so improves the look of the financial statements when consolidated (as explained in the notes to the reconciliation in its annual report).

The goodwill adjustment is simpler to explain. Under German or UK national rules, goodwill was generally amortized. However, under US or IFRS rules, goodwill is not amortized but annually tested for impairment. This removes a large expense but, in bad years, might create an even larger impairment expense.

13.2

Question Are the arguments for differential reporting convincing? Should differentiation be made on the basis of company size or using some other characteristic?

Answer The key issue is whether the purpose of financial reporting is different for different types of company, and any different purpose requires different accounting. The size of a company, in itself, does not seem to be a relevant issue, although size might be associated with something else, e.g. being listed or not.

The listed/unlisted distinction is the obvious candidate for differentiation. It is relatively easy to define, although even the exact definition of 'listed' can be a matter of debate. Listed companies have more 'outsider' owners (see Chapter 2), so there is a greater need for published information. If a company is not listed, perhaps the users of information (e.g. banks) can be relied upon to demand the information they need, so that no publication or audit rules are necessary for such companies, as in the US. Also, unlisted companies tend to be smaller, so perhaps should be relieved of the cost of publication, or at least of some of it.

The issue of whether unlisted companies should be allowed simpler recognition/ measurement rules is contentious. It is unclear, for example, that lenders really need different information from that needed by shareholders.

CHAPTER 14

14.1

Question The US, UK, France and Germany have evolved different answers to the question as to which business enterprises should be subject to accounting regulation. Which country, in your opinion, has got it 'right'?

Answer It is unlikely that there is one 'right' answer that fits all countries in all political and economic circumstances. Subjecting all businesses to accounting regulation (as in France and Germany) implies an interventionist state seeking control of accounting records for taxation and insolvency purposes and also desirous of protecting all stakeholders. However, sufficient resources may not be available for this to work in practice. At the other extreme (as in the US), a non-interventionist state may wish only to protect the investors in publicly traded enterprises. This ignores the interests of other stakeholders but can be achieved within the resources likely to be available. The UK has followed a middle course, attempting to protect all stakeholders (but especially shareholders and creditors) for all companies (but not partnerships and sole traders). In practice, enforcement has been weak for non-listed companies, partly through lack of resources.

14.2

Question Why do UK accounting rules for individual companies not differ simply on the distinction between public and private companies?

Answer The distinction between public and private companies was originally introduced in the early twentieth century to enable the Companies Act to include stricter disclosure rules for companies with the right to issue shares to the public without imposing them on all companies. Most private companies were small and not part of groups but some were not. Exempt private companies were invented in 1948 to distinguish family companies from the subsidiaries of public companies. Implementation of the Fourth Directive brought in the German innovation of distinguishing companies by size as measured by sales, balance sheet total and number of employees. These measures are relevant for all stakeholders not just shareholders. UK rules now typically assume that all public companies are large and grant exemptions to small companies below sizes that vary according to the particular regulation. The possibility of sending shareholders summary instead of full financial statements is limited to listed companies, as is the enforcement of accounting standards by the Review Panel. It appears that the UK legislator is pragmatic, using whatever distinction is available and suitable for a particular purpose.

CHAPTER 15

15.1

Question 'US accounting is better than German accounting.' Discuss.

Answer The question needs to address: 'better' for what purpose? Certainly, for the information of investors who wish to make financial decisions, US accounting does seem to be better, not least because there is more disclosure. Of course, US accounting is very expensive to operate, requiring regulators, standard-setters, auditors, massive annual reports, quarterly reporting, etc. This might be an unnecessary luxury for a country such as Germany which has limited capital markets. Consequently, US accounting might be *worse for Germany*. In particular, if the main purposes of German financial reporting are to calculate a conservative distributable profit and to calculate taxable profit, it seems appropriate to tie accounting to the tax rules. In the United States, tax calculations have to be done separately from financial reporting which adds another layer of expense.

US financial reporting produces a much more volatile series of earnings figures than German accounting does. This may suit users related to active stock markets but may not suit a longer-term view, which is traditionally associated with German financiers and managers.

From 2001, it was normal practice for large listed companies in Germany to use US or IFRS accounting for their consolidated statements. IFRS is required from 2005, although groups that were already using US GAAP were allowed to continue this until 2007. So, IFRS is used for one purpose in Germany, and HGB accounting for another.

15.2

Question Discuss the advantages and disadvantages for a country such as Germany of requiring or permitting companies to apply accounting principles based on IFRS in their individual financial statements.

Answer Supporters of not moving to IFRS argue that Individual statements are mainly prepared for the determination of tax liabilities and distributable income, not to give information to capital markets. Existing German rules are thought to be better suited for tax and distribution purposes than are IFRS, and the changeover could lead to higher tax bills. In reply it can be argued that commercial figures could be used as the starting point for tax calculations and that adjustments could be made outside the accounting records as in the UK. There is no reason for total corporate taxation to go up, although its incidence might change.

A further argument against is that Germany would lose control of accounting standard setting, handing it over not to an EU institution but to an unelected private sector body dominated by Anglo-Saxon accountants. This may be an acceptable price to pay for German multinationals requiring access to international capital markets but there is no need to accept it for the great mass of German business enterprises.

It will be difficult for two diverse sets of rules to exist side by side and there will be pressures to harmonize them. Given that Germany finds it difficult to influence IFRS, local rules are likely over time to move towards IFRS (albeit more slowly than in the UK and France) rather than IFRS to move towards German rules.

CHAPTER 16

16.1

Question 'Secret reserves make a company stronger, so they should be encouraged.' Discuss.

Answer Secret reserves can be achieved in various ways, such as by deliberately not recognizing or by undervaluing assets, or by setting up unnecessary provisions. All these activities make the balance sheet look worse, and therefore there are hidden reserves. Of course, on the subject of provisions, which ones are necessary is a controversial issue. According to IAS 37, provisions should only be set up when there is a liability.

The creation of hidden reserves may make the company stronger by reducing the amount of dividends paid, because profits look lower. In the case of banks, building up a reputation for secret reserves may protect a bank from speculative pressures in times of economic difficulty. However, perhaps it would be even better protected by disclosing its strength (assuming that it actually is strong).

The main problem with secret reserves, from a financial reporting point of view, is that their existence seems to reduce the chance that the financial statements will give a true and fair view. How can anything hidden give a fair view?

16.2

Question Under IAS 32, some shares are treated as liabilities and some apparent liabilities are treated as partly equity. Is this a good idea?

Answer This question concerns truth and fairness in presentation. Once a definition of a liability has been promulgated, it seems appropriate for accounting practice to be made to fit this. Otherwise, the readers of financial statements will find that some items shown as liabilities fit the established definition and some do not.

In the case of certain types of shares, they fit the IASB's definition of liability because they involve an obligation to pay amounts from the issuer to the holder of the shares. The issuing company has deliberately chosen this type of shares rather than ordinary shares because of their different legal features. So, it makes sense to account for them differently.

The treatment of hybrid securities is more complicated. It could be argued that an issuer must decide whether such a security contains any obligations and, if so, account for it as a liability. However, IAS 32 requires the issuer to treat such securities as partly shares and partly liabilities. An investment bank would be able to split a convertible debenture into these two parts, and could easily put a value on them. So, the IAS 32 treatment is practical and perhaps leads to fuller information.

CHAPTER 17

17.1

Question Discuss different possible interpretations of the concept of a group, and how these may relate to differences in styles of corporate governance and of company financing.

Answer The parent concept of a group is based on legal control, which in turn relies on majority voting rights and shareholdings. In some countries, control can also be achieved by contract. The entity concept has the advantage that it does not treat minority shareholders differently from majority shareholders; rather, it attempts to look at all enterprises in the group as part of the same economic entity. It also appears to have advantages for user groups other than shareholders, such as employees. The proprietary concept can more easily than the previous two accommodate cases where an enterprise's membership of a group is less clear-cut, e.g. where an enterprise only partly belongs to a group or belongs to more than one group (i.e. where neither a parent nor legal dominance can be identified). Here, ownership and the right to exercise 'significant influence' are decisive factors.

The reason that different concepts of a group have arisen, and appear to 'fit' the patterns in some countries better than in others, can be linked to historical economic developments and patterns in corporate financing. For example, the economic climate in the US at the turn of the twentieth century encouraged commercial activity and expansion; as a result companies were formed and began to carry out their activities in groups. Holding companies were established earlier than elsewhere. While groups or networks of companies were also established early in, for example, Japan or continental European countries such as Germany, the different form of company financing and corporate governance (including supervisory boards) encouraged the growth of informal networks of companies and providers of finance such as banks, with cross-shareholdings (and 'cross-directorships' on each other's supervisory boards where these existed).

17.2

Question 'The EU Seventh Directive was a much more useful harmonizing tool than the EU Fourth Directive.' Discuss.

Answer From an Anglo-Saxon viewpoint, it can certainly be argued that the publication of consolidated accounts by many European companies that did not previously publish them transformed financial reporting practice. Note that the Seventh Directive could not have been adopted if the fourth was not already in place, and that capital market pressures were already pushing large European multinationals towards consolidation.

The Fourth Directive, it could be argued, established as law some not very useful formats and inflexible measurement rules which would better have been left to accounting standard-setters.

The Seventh Directive perhaps achieved more harmonization of concepts and techniques than the Fourth Directive. Major issues were either not covered in the Fourth Directive (e.g. leasing and long-term contracts) or were then handled as options (e.g. valuation of assets). The Seventh Directive contains clear rules on several issues, e.g. equity accounting, some elements of the goodwill calculation, and the definition of a subsidiary. Of course, there are still options (e.g. the treatment of goodwill, and the use of proportional consolidation).

For listed companies, the Seventh Directive has now been overtaken by the EU's Regulation on IFRS of 2002.

CHAPTER 18

18.1

Question Why has there been so much controversy over currency translation methods for group account-ing? Which method do you prefer?

Answer Controversy in accounting standards generally seems to arise between management and the standard-setters. Only in extreme cases do the government, the press or user groups become seriously involved. Academics can usually be relied upon to provide arguments, but generally on at least two sides. Controversy from management relates to extra disclosures, extra costs or a change to values or profit measures. In this case, most of the argument seems to relate to profit measurement. It is particularly in the United States where the controversy has been greatest. This is because most other countries fall into two categories: those where con-solidation of overseas subsidiaries has traditionally been unimportant and where taxation is an important influence in accounting so that group accounts are of little interest (e.g. Japan, Germany); and those who generally follow US practice (e.g. Canada, and many other countries to a lesser extent). In the United States, the problem seems to be that standard-setters have tried to establish theoretically coherent practice. By contrast, the United Kingdom standard-setters steered clear of the subject until the 1980s and then allowed current practice to continue, with a variety of options.

The history of US statements on currency translation is lengthy and is examined in the text. SFAS 8 of 1975 established the theoretically neat model of the temporal principle, which can be called the temporal method when applied to historical cost accounting. This method relates the choice of translation rate for any item or balance to the timing of its valuation basis. This results in assets being valued at historical cost both before and after translation (i.e. in both the subsidiary's and the parent's currency). By contrast, the closing rate method caused translated assets of subsidiaries with depreciating currencies to disappear gradually.

The problem with the temporal method is that it generates losses (in the group income statement) when the parent's currency is weak. Consequently, the temporal method led to greater volatility of profits, and in particular to losses when the dollar was weak in the late 1970s. These losses occur even if the subsidiary has matched overseas loans with overseas assets. This difficulty led to massive complaints from management, followed by a move to the closing rate method in SFAS 52. Because it is particularly obvious that the closing rate method gives ridiculous results when there are large exchange rate movements, the temporal method is still to be used for subsidiaries in highly inflationary countries (100 per cent or more, cumu-latively, in three years).

The fundamental problem is that exchange rate movements are linked to price changes. While accounting ignores the latter, any recognition of the former creates insuperable measurement difficulties.

There are several further arguments in favour of the closing rate method to be found in various UK or US exposure drafts and standards. These are dealt with in the chapter, and most of them seem to be 'excuses'.

In terms of quality of information for users of financial statements, the temporal method without gains and losses going to income might be the best. This was used by some German multinationals. Otherwise, it is a question of which faults are least worrying. Of course, if cur-rent value accounting were used, most of the problems of currency translation would go away.

Incidentally, this answer has been written on the assumption that the question concerns the translation of the financial statements of foreign subsidiaries. The other issue would be the translation of transactions or balances in foreign currency in an individual company's financial statements, which are carried through to group accounts. There is some controversy here, particularly concerning whether unsettled gains can be taken in income.

18.2

Question Why has it been difficult, particularly in the United States, to create a satisfactory accounting standard on foreign currency translation?

Answer Some elements of the answer to this question can be extracted from the answer to Question 18.1 above.

The United States seems to have looked for theoretical coherence, but this is a hopeless task in the context of historical cost accounting. If one ignores price changes but tries to adjust for exchange rate changes, the arithmetic will just not work because the former help to cause the latter.

The United Kingdom seems to have adopted simple and pragmatic approaches.

France and Germany have been relaxed about the issue because relatively few companies are concerned and there are no tax effects. The Seventh Directive steered clear of this issue because it was controversial (for example, the UK liked the closing rate method and the Germans liked the temporal method) and because several countries were happy with silence on the subject (including the United Kingdom).

CHAPTER 19

19.1

Question Explain why standard-setters have difficulty in drafting segment reporting standards.

Answer Standard-setters in the United Kingdom had difficulty with the arguments concerning the invasion of privacy and damage from competitors (see the answer to Question 19.2). In other words, there are questions relating to exemptions. For example, if 'small' companies are to be exempted, how does one define small. In the United States, this was not a problem, because FASB rules are only enforced on SEC-registered companies.

More generally, there are difficulties in defining what is meant by a segment. Too many segments would make the data unwieldy. Too few would risk losing valuable data. Also, how does one force companies to provide useful segments rather than superficially plausible ones? For example, on grounds of risk and growth, it might be useful to include Germany and Japan together, but it is very tempting for companies to include Germany with Albania (Europe) and Japan with Cambodia (Asia).

Further difficulties relate to whether sales should be segmented by producer or customer; whether profit should be net of extraordinary items and whether assets should be shown net of liabilities.

19.2

Question How could one demonstrate that the benefits of segment reporting outweigh the costs?

Answer The headings of benefits and costs are fairly easy to establish, but to measure some of the items is difficult.

The benefits are discussed in Section 19.2. Of course, although the initial impact is to assist analysts, the benefits should flow to the companies that provide good segmental data because this will improve the market's confidence in such companies. Researchers on the benefits of segment reporting have looked at whether: users want it; users use it; forecasts improve predictions; and share prices react to it.

The costs might accrue under two main headings:

(a) *Preparation, audit and publication.* However, most standards allow companies to use their own structures to determine segments. In this case, preparation costs seem unlikely to be large for data that management should already be using. There would be some audit and publication expenses but not more than attached to other notes of similar length. It might be possible to measure these costs.

(b) *Invasion of privacy, damage from competitors*. This seems a weak argument. Small companies may have only one segment. Large companies should perhaps not be allowed to gain privacy by pooling segments. Anyway, segments can be so large that segment reporting is unlikely to give surprising information to alert competitors. In the case of the UK rules, these points are taken into account by exempting small companies from segment reporting and by allowing directors to claim a 'seriously prejudicial' exemption. The US and IASB rules apply to companies with publicly traded securities.

CHAPTER 20

20.1

Question In an unharmonized world, how do preparers and users of annual financial statements of listed companies cope with international differences?

Answer It is in the interest of those preparers that operate overseas, and especially those that raise finance overseas, to make their financial statements more user-friendly to those to whom they wish to communicate, including those from whom they wish to raise money. They can do this in a number of ways, e.g. by translating them into English and/or other appropriate languages; by explaining how the accounting policies used differ from other accounting rules, e.g. US GAAP or IFRS; or by adopting internationally accepted accounting policies (where this is legally possible).

Users have the choices of: avoiding certain countries or companies; learning the foreign accounting policies; or insisting, if they can, on their replacement or supplementation by policies familiar to the user. In the longer term, users may push for harmonization.

All of these ways of coping have costs and benefits that vary with the starting position of the preparer or user, e.g. US companies may seldom need to produce anything other than English language US GAAP statements; British companies may need to quantify for US investors how IFRS differs from US GAAP; most German companies may see no need to adapt their financial statements to, say, US GAAP (although they may translate them into English) since they do not need to attract investors from other countries; and many Japanese companies prefer to be listed on relatively undemanding overseas stock exchanges.

In practice, many users do not make substantial adjustments because this is so complex and time consuming.

20.2

Question What are the major difficulties met by analysts when trying to compare companies' annual reports internationally? Which areas of financial reporting could be most usefully improved to aid such analysis?

Answer The major difficulties met by analysts when trying to compare companies internationally are:

(a) different levels of required disclosure;

(b) different measurement practices;

(c) lack of knowledge of the local context.

The first of these is sometimes tempered by voluntary disclosure by companies that need to raise capital on international markets. The second is more difficult, since not all measurement practices are legally acceptable in a company's home country, and the provision of two sets of figures is expensive. The third can only be overcome by the education of the analyst.

The sort of major accounting differences that are likely to affect analysis are:

- income smoothing with the aid of provisions;
- different measurement of pension expenses;
- the treatment of goodwill;
- the capitalization (or not) of leased assets;
- the use of LIFO in some countries.

The most fruitful area of improvement would seem to be publication by more companies of the extent to which their financial statements differ from US GAAP or IFRS. Another way of answering the 'improvement' part of the question is to say that analysts of large groups are always interested in bigger and better segmental disclosures.

CHAPTER 21

21.1

Question Why is it necessary to have international auditing standards?

Answer This question can be answered in two stages: (a) why has auditing become international? and (b) why are standards necessary?

As explained in the text, auditing has been internationalized because of the emergence of MNEs, and because of the demand for international auditing from international capital markets. International auditing standards have arisen because it is in the interest of MNEs and, especially, to international auditing firms to have no differences in auditing requirements between countries. It is also in the interests of those who interpret the financial reports of multinational groups.

21.2

Question Would it be better if international auditing standards were set by the United Nations rather than under the existing system?

Answer Under the present system, international auditing standards (ISAs) are issued by the International Auditing and Assurance Standards Board (IAASB), a private-sector body composed of professional accountants. This ensures the technical quality of the ISAs since they are drawn up by experts. On the other hand, the IAASB may be working in the self-interest of international accounting firms, which is not necessarily the general interest, and it has no means of ensuring compliance with its standards. The case for the UN to set ISAs rests on the argument that it would better represent the public interest. It is not clear, however, who the public is. It may be composed partly of the host countries of MNEs, but the primary stakeholders are the shareholders of the MNEs, who may prefer the existing IAASB. The UN probably does not possess sufficient international auditing experts but could buy them in. Unlike national governments, the UN possesses no power to enforce auditing standards. However, many UN member states, especially within the EU, have set up audit supervisory bodies which seek, *inter alia*, to enforce national auditing standards which closely follow ISAs.

CHAPTER 22

22.1

Question 'Corporate tax systems differ internationally more than accounting systems differ, so it is impossible to classify them into groups.' Discuss.

Answer It is perhaps not very useful to compare degrees of international difference of two quite different items (i.e. corporate taxes and accounting systems). Further, a large size of difference or large number of facets of difference should not make classification impossible. The dimensions of difference of corporate taxes are certainly substantial, including:

(a) tax basis (e.g. payroll, income, capital);

(b) national or local (e.g. US, German or Italian local corporation taxes as well as federal taxes);

(c) definition of taxable income compared to accounting income;

(d) tax rates;

(e) 'system' with respect to dividends (e.g. classical or imputation).

Despite this variation, the main features of a corporate tax are easier to define and measure than those of accounting systems, so classification may be an easier task than for accounting systems. Since any country can have more than one corporate tax, one should probably classify taxes rather than countries.

An example of a classification is shown in Figure A.1.

In two dimensions, it is difficult to include other features, such as high/low rates or the degree of connection between tax and accounting calculations. These could be the subject of other classifications.

22.2

Question 'There is no point in harmonizing tax systems and tax rates without harmonizing the calculation of taxable incomes.' Discuss.

Answer The EU harmonization programme for direct taxes has a history dating back to the 1960s, discussed in the main text. In the case of corporation taxes, the initial proposals related to tax systems and tax rates. There would be some point in this. For example, if all EU countries had imputation systems with similar tax credits and if the tax credits were available to all EU shareholders, this would remove one barrier to the movement of capital.

Nevertheless, the amount of tax that a company pays is directly connected to the way in which taxable income is calculated. A country could avoid the consequences of harmonized tax systems by manipulating the definition of taxable income. An obvious example of this would be the size of tax depreciation expenses (capital allowances in the United Kingdom).

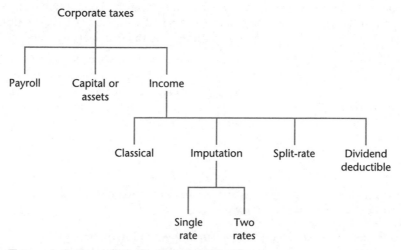

Figure A.1 **Example of a tax classification**

Many countries have large numbers of non-deductible expenses or non-taxable revenues. This makes harmonization of systems and rates of doubtful value except as part of a more general process. The initial EU proposals have foundered on this difficulty.

CHAPTER 23

23.1

Question Explain how and why the objectives of multinational enterprises vary depending on their home countries.

Answer Business objectives vary internationally in various ways, including the time horizon used, the degree of stress on quantitative targets, and the nature of the target (e.g. sales as opposed to profit).

Studies seem to find that Anglo-Saxon companies have shorter-term targets than Japanese or German companies. This may be because Anglo-Saxon companies and managers are subject to much more frequent and detailed scrutiny by stock market investors. Perhaps for the same reason, Anglo-Saxon targets tend to be highly quantitative. Anglo-Saxon companies tend to be more interested in profit measures, whereas Japanese companies stress sales or market share. This, too, may tie in with the longer-term nature of Japanese strategy.

When it comes to business units within a multinational enterprise, the targets naturally vary from unit to unit. For example, a sales branch may have a sales target, whereas an autonomous foreign subsidiary may have a profit target. However, even this varies by country of the parent, in ways noted above.

23.2

Question What various models of control could be used to describe the organization of multinational companies? Which ones are found in practice?

Answer One way of categorizing models of control is based on the work of Ouchi who suggested three models: behaviour, outcome and clan (see main text). The first involves setting up structures and rules; the second measures output; and the third involves careful selection of appropriately trained and motivated staff. For tasks of high uncertainty, clan control may be best.

In practice, research shows that multinationals tend to use outcome controls. This may be partly because most multinationals (and most researchers) are Anglo-American, and such multinationals also see objectives in terms of standardized quantitative targets (see answer to Question 23.1). Of course, this makes it especially important that the quantitative targets relate to issues that can actually be controlled by the managers who are being controlled.

Author index

Subject index